Search through the entire CCNP: Support Study Guide!

- Access the entire *CCNP: Support Study Guide*, complete with figures and tables, in electronic format.

- Search the *CCNP: Support Study Guide* chapters to find information on any topic in seconds.

- Use Adobe Acrobat Reader (included on the CD-ROM) to view the electronic book.

Test yourself on Cisco's new simulation question format.

- Apply your skills with sample simulations questions.

- Reinforce your knowledge and approach the exam with confidence.

D1379137

SYBEX

CCNP:
Support
Study Guide

CCNP™:
Support
Study Guide

Todd Lammle
Arthur Pfund, CCIE #7249

San Francisco • London

Associate Publisher: Neil Edde
Acquisitions and Developmental Editor: Heather O'Connor
Editor: Suzanne Goraj
Production Editor: Elizabeth Campbell
Technical Editors: Kevin Burgess, Andy Barkl
Graphic Illustrator: Jeff Wilson, Happenstance Type-O-Rama
Electronic Publishing Specialist: Interactive Composition Corporation
Book Designer: Bill Gibson
Proofreaders: Nancy Riddiough, Emily Hsuan, Suzanne Stein
Indexer: Ann Rogers
CD Coordinator: Dan Mummert
CD Technician: Kevin Ly
Cover Designer: Archer Design
Cover Illustrator: Natural Selection

Copyright © 2002 SYBEX Inc., 1151 Marina Village Parkway, Alameda, CA 94501. World rights reserved. No part of this publication may be stored in a retrieval system, transmitted, or reproduced in any way, including but not limited to photocopy, photograph, magnetic, or other record, without the prior agreement and written permission of the publisher.

First edition copyright © 2000 SYBEX Inc.

Library of Congress Card Number: 2002108070

ISBN: 0-7821-4152-8

SYBEX and the SYBEX logo are either registered trademarks or trademarks of SYBEX Inc. in the United States and/or other countries.

Screen reproductions produced with FullShot 99. FullShot 99 © 1991–1999 Inbit Incorporated. All rights reserved. FullShot is a trademark of Inbit Incorporated.

This study guide and/or material is not sponsored by, endorsed by or affiliated with Cisco Systems, Inc. Cisco®, Cisco Systems®, CCDA™, CCNA™, CCDP™, CCNP™, CCIE™, CCSI™, the Cisco Systems logo and the CCIE logo are trademarks or registered trademarks of Cisco Systems, Inc. in the United States and certain other countries. All other trademarks are trademarks of their respective owners.

TRADEMARKS: SYBEX has attempted throughout this book to distinguish proprietary trademarks from descriptive terms by following the capitalization style used by the manufacturer.

The author and publisher have made their best efforts to prepare this book, and the content is based upon final release software whenever possible. Portions of the manuscript may be based upon pre-release versions supplied by software manufacturer(s). The author and the publisher make no representation or warranties of any kind with regard to the completeness or accuracy of the contents herein and accept no liability of any kind including but not limited to performance, merchantability, fitness for any particular purpose, or any losses or damages of any kind caused or alleged to be caused directly or indirectly from this book.

Manufactured in the United States of America

10 9 8 7 6 5 4 3 2

SYBEX

To Our Valued Readers:

The Cisco Certified Network Professional program well deserves its position as the leading high-level certification in the internetworking arena. Sybex is proud to have helped hundreds of thousands of CCNP candidates prepare for their exams over the years, and we are excited about the opportunity to continue to provide individuals with the knowledge and skills they'll need to succeed in the highly competitive IT industry.

With the recent revision of the four exams required for the CCNP—BSCI, Switching, Remote Access, and Support—Cisco raised the bar considerably, adding simulation questions to two of the and refreshing the question pools of all exams to better reflect current technologies. Sybex welcomes these changes as we strongly advocate a comprehensive and practical instructional approach to certification exam preparation. It has always been Sybex's mission to teach exam candidates how new technologies work in the real world, not to simply feed them answers to test questions. Sybex was founded on the premise of providing technical skills to IT professionals, and we have continued to build on that foundation. Over the years, we have made significant improvements to our study guides based on feedback from readers, suggestions from instructors, and comments from industry leaders.

Cisco's new CCNP exams are indeed challenging. The authors have worked hard to ensure that this Study Guide is comprehensive, in-depth, and pedagogically sound. We're confident that this book, along with the collection of cutting-edge software study tools included on the CD, will meet and exceed the demanding standards of the certification marketplace and help you, the CCNP exam candidate, succeed in your endeavors.

Good luck in pursuit of your CCNP certification!

Neil Edde
Associate Publisher—Certification
Sybex, Inc.

To my wife Michele. Everything is better with you by my side.

—Art Pfund

Acknowledgments

First and foremost I would like to thank Heather, Elizabeth and Suzanne at Sybex. They were all great to work with and always were available to answer questions and provide suggestions when I needed them. Thanks to Bard Lowry for his years of mentoring helped get me to where I am today. I would also like to thank Rob Padjen and Todd Lammle whose support and encouragement helped me start down the right path. Finally, I would like to thank Brett Schaefer for his help assembling research information.

Thanks to my family for their support during the process. Especially, thanks to my wife Michele for putting up with the late nights and early mornings and my sister Kelly for understanding when I missed her birthday. I would also like to thank Mike Benjamin for encouraging me and helping me make sure I had time to get the work done. And finally, I would like to thank my cats Nermal and Picasso for helping me with the process by sleeping on the monitor and making sure it didn't fly away!

—Art Pfund

Contents at a Glance

Contents

Introduction

Welcome to the exciting world of Cisco certification! You have picked up this book because you want something better; namely, a better job with more satisfaction. Rest assured that you have made a good decision. Cisco certification can help you get your first networking job, or more money and a promotion if you are already in the field.

Cisco certification can also improve your understanding of the internetworking of more than just Cisco products: You will develop a complete understanding of networking and how different network topologies work together to form a network. This is beneficial to every networking job and is the reason Cisco certification is in such high demand, even at companies with few Cisco devices.

Cisco is the king of routing and switching, the Microsoft of the internetworking world. The Cisco certifications reach beyond the popular certifications, such as the MCSE and CNE, to provide you with an indispensable factor in understanding today's network—insight into the Cisco world of internetworking. By deciding that you want to become Cisco certified, you are saying that you want to be the best—the best at routing and the best at switching. This book will lead you in that direction.

How to Use This Book

If you want a solid foundation for the serious effort of preparing for the Cisco Certified Network Professional (CCNP) Support exam, then look no further. We have spent hundreds of hours putting together this book with the sole intention of helping you to pass the CCNP Support exam.

This book is loaded with lots of valuable information, and you will get the most out of your studying time if you understand how we put this book together.

To best benefit from this book, we recommend the following study method:

1. Take the assessment test immediately following this introduction. (The answers are at the end of the test.) It's OK if you don't know any of the answers; that is why you bought this book! Carefully read over the explanations for any question you get wrong and note which chapters the material comes from. This information should help you plan your study strategy.

2. Study each chapter thoroughly, making sure that you fully understand the information and the test objectives listed at the beginning of each chapter. Pay extra-close attention to any chapter where you missed questions in the assessment test.

3. If you do not have Cisco equipment available, be sure to study the examples carefully. Also, check www.routersim.com for router simulator software that provides drag-and-drop networking configurations.

4. Answer all of the review questions related to each chapter. (The answers appear at the end of the chapter.) Note the questions that confuse you and study those sections of the book again. Do not just skim these questions! Make sure you understand completely the reason for each answer.

5. Try your hand at the practice exams that are included on the companion CD. The questions in these exams appear only on the CD. This will give you a complete overview of what you can expect to see on the real CCNP Support exam.

6. Test yourself using all the flashcards on the CD. There are brand new and updated flashcard programs on the CD to help you prepare completely for the CCNP Support exam. These are a great study tool!

The electronic flashcards can be used on your Windows computer, Pocket PC, or Palm device.

7. Make sure you read the "Key Terms" and "Exam Essentials" lists at the end of the chapters. These study aids will help you finish each chapter with the main points fresh in the your mind; they're also helpful as a quick refresher before heading into the testing center.

To learn every bit of the material covered in this book, you'll have to apply yourself regularly, and with discipline. Try to set aside the same time period every day to study, and select a comfortable and quiet place to do so. If you work hard, you will be surprised at how quickly you learn this material.

If you follow the steps listed above, and really study and practice the review questions, CD exams, and electronic flashcards, it would be hard to fail the CCNP Support exam.

What Does This Book Cover?

This book covers everything you need to know in order to take the CCNP Support exam. However, taking the time to study and practice with actual routers and switches or a router simulator is the real key to success. In addition, be sure to understand the concepts behind the topics covered in this book. Though this book has everything you need in order to successfully pass the test, many of the topics are non-trivial. Therefore, if you only know how to answer a particular question without really understanding the concept, this could cause problems when taking the test.

The information you will learn in this book, and need to know for the CCNP Support exam, is listed in the following bullet points:

- Chapter 1 discusses the complexity of today's internetworks as well as introduces you to the Cisco Troubleshooting Methodology. This chapter also goes through what a network baseline is and why it is important to have a current baseline of your network. Be sure to go through the review questions at the end of the chapter.

- Chapter 2 reviews the OSI reference model, and then discusses connection-oriented and connectionless protocols. Following this, the IP, ICMP, TCP, and UDP protocols are examined. This leads into an overview of IP routing protocols, including RIP, IGRP, EIGRP, OSPF, and BGP. Finally, Novell, AppleTalk, and Layer 2 protocols are covered. As always, the review questions at the end of the chapter will help you retain the concepts in the chapter.

- Chapter 3 details the troubleshooting tools that are available for use in the internetwork. These tools include physical media testing equipment such as multimeters, cable testers, TDRs, and breakout boxes. This chapter also includes a discussion of software tools such as network monitors and analyzers. Following this, NMS stations will be detailed, including the Cisco-specific stations such as CiscoWorks 2000, Netsys, and CiscoSecure. You don't want to miss the review questions at the end of this chapter.

- Chapter 4 provides a detailed look at the Cisco router architecture. It looks at the routing and switching processes and how the buffers are used. This chapter also goes through the IOS commands that are needed to verify the correct functioning of the buffers and queues. The review questions at the end will assist you in understanding the terminology and functions each component plays in a Cisco router.

- Chapter 5 focuses on the skills and knowledge needed to use Cisco's built-in diagnostic tools in a TCP/IP environment. These tools include show, debug, and logging commands as well as how to execute a router core dump. This chapter also goes into the appropriate use of the ping and traceroute utilities. Following this, LAN and WAN problems, including those associated with Windows workstations, are examined. The last new topic covered in this chapter is access lists.

- Chapter 6 is dedicated to covering IP routing protocols. Specifically, RIP, IGRP, EIGRP, OSPF, and BGP are examined. The benefits and drawbacks of each of the protocols as well as the commands used to verify correct functionality are included in this chapter. We discuss the individual routing protocols as well as the issues around redistributing these protocols into each other. The review questions at the end of this chapter will reinforce the IP routing protocol material.

- Chapter 7 examines serial, Frame Relay, and X.25 connectivity. This chapter goes through the show and debug IOS commands that are needed to successfully troubleshoot problems in these environments. In addition, the functionality of each is explained, detailing some common problem areas. Be sure to do the review questions at the end of the chapter.

- Chapter 8 discusses ISDN and related protocols, specifically looking at what is necessary to set up an ISDN dial solution. In addition, time is spent looking at the debug output from the call setup to better show how an ISDN call is established. The review questions at the end of the chapter will help you prepare for the ISDN-related questions you will see on the exam.

- Chapter 9 introduces you to the wonderful world of Novell IPX. Since IPX is still around, Cisco thinks it is important to understand IPX routing. Many of the same troubleshooting tools that were looked at for TCP/IP in Chapter 4 are also available in IPX. In addition, we also look at the IPX-specific routing protocols and some of the unique issues in IPX, such as SAP updates. Use the review questions at the end of the chapter to ensure that you understand the concepts presented.

- Chapter 10 does for AppleTalk what Chapter 9 did for IPX. It provides an overview of the AppleTalk protocol, and discusses common problems as well as the routing options. In addition, time is spent detailing the show and debug commands that are available for troubleshooting AppleTalk. The review questions at the end of the chapter will help you ensure that you have the AppleTalk knowledge to pass the CCNP Support exam.

- Chapter 11 details the functioning of the Catalyst 5000 series switches. This chapter includes information on the architecture of the switch as well as the command syntax that is used to configure the switch. It also discusses the use of VLANs and trunking switch ports together.

- Chapter 12 goes over the support tools that are available on the Cisco website. These include the Software Center, Bug Toolkit, Troubleshooting Assistant, Open Forum, and TAC Case Management tools. In addition, the chapter also covers how to open a case with TAC.

- Chapter 13 is a summary chapter. It takes the information that was provided in the previous chapters and applies this to real-world examples. These examples demonstrate how to combine the troubleshooting methodology with the technical skills learned in this book. The Glossary is a handy resource for Cisco terms. This is a great tool for understanding some of the more obscure terms used in this book.

What's on the CD?

We worked hard to provide some really great tools to help you with your certification process. All of the following tools should be loaded on your workstation when studying for the test.

The EdgeTest Test Preparation Software

The test preparation software, provided by EdgeTek Learning Systems, prepares you to pass the CCNP Support exam. In this test engine, you will find all the review and assessment questions from the book, plus two additional bonus exams that appear exclusively on the CD. You can take the assessment test, test yourself by chapter or by topic, take the practice exams, or take a randomly generated exam comprising all the questions.

To find more test-simulation software for all Cisco and Microsoft exams, look for the exam link on www.lammleprep.com.

Electronic Flashcards for PC, Pocket PC, and Palm Devices

To prepare for the exam, you can read this book, study the review questions at the end of each chapter, and work through the practice exams included in the book and on the companion CD. But wait, there's more! You can also test yourself with the flashcards included on the CD. If you can get through these difficult questions and understand the answers, you'll know you're ready for the CCNP Support exam.

The flashcards include 190 questions specifically written to hit you hard and make sure you are ready for the exam. Between the review questions, practice exams, and flashcards, you'll be more than prepared for the exam.

CCNP Support Study Guide in PDF

Sybex offers the *CCNP Support Study Guide* in PDF format on the CD so you can read the book on your PC or laptop. This will be helpful to readers who travel and don't want to carry a book, as well as to readers who prefer to read from their computer. (Acrobat Reader 5 is also included on the CD.)

Commands Used in this Study Guide

We've compiled a list of all the Cisco commands used in each chapter. This list is in PDF format on the companion CD-ROM so you can easily search the list for the commands you need.

Simulation Questions

In addition to multiple-choice and drag-and-drop questions, Cisco has included some questions on their exams that simulate working on routers and switches in a network environment. In response, we have included a simulation question program on our test engine. We designed our program to help further your hands-on networking skills and to fully prepare you for taking the Support (640-606) exam. At the time of this printing, Cisco is only including simulation questions on the BSCI (640-901) and Remote Access (640-605) exams. Please visit the Cisco training and certification website (http://www.cisco.com/public/training_cert.shtml) for the latest exam information.

Cisco—A Brief History

Many readers may already be familiar with Cisco and what they do. However, those of you who are new to the field, just coming in fresh from your

MCSE, and those of you who maybe have 10 or more years in the field but wish to brush up on the new technology may appreciate a little background on Cisco.

In the early 1980s, Len and Sandy Bosack, a married couple who worked in different computer departments at Stanford University, were having trouble getting their individual systems to communicate (like many married people). So in their living room they created a gateway server that made it easier for their disparate computers in two different departments to communicate using the IP protocol. In 1984, they founded cisco Systems (notice the small *c*) with a small commercial gateway server product that changed networking forever. Some people think the name was intended to be San Francisco Systems but the paper got ripped on the way to the incorporation lawyers—who knows? In 1992, the company name was changed to Cisco Systems, Inc.

The first product the company marketed was called the Advanced Gateway Server (AGS). Then came the Mid-Range Gateway Server (MGS), the Compact Gateway Server (CGS), the Integrated Gateway Server (IGS), and the AGS+. Cisco calls these "the old alphabet soup products."

In 1993, Cisco came out with the amazing 4000 router and then created the even more amazing 7000, 2000, and 3000 series routers. These are still around and evolving (almost daily, it seems).

Cisco has since become an unrivaled worldwide leader in networking for the Internet. Its networking solutions can easily connect users who work from diverse devices on disparate networks. Cisco products make it simple for people to access and transfer information without regard to differences in time, place, or platform.

In the big picture, Cisco provides end-to-end networking solutions that customers can use to build an efficient, unified information infrastructure of their own or to connect to someone else's. This is an important piece in the Internet/networking–industry puzzle because a common architecture that delivers consistent network services to all users is now a functional imperative. Because Cisco Systems offers such a broad range of networking and Internet services and capabilities, users who need to regularly access their local network or the Internet can do so unhindered, making Cisco's wares indispensable.

Cisco answers this need with a wide range of hardware products that form information networks using the Cisco Internetwork Operating System (IOS) software. This software provides network services, paving the way for networked technical support and professional services to maintain and optimize all network operations.

Along with the Cisco IOS, one of the services Cisco created to help support the vast amount of hardware it has engineered is the Cisco Certified Internetwork Expert (CCIE) program, which was designed specifically to equip people to effectively manage the vast quantity of installed Cisco networks. The business plan is simple: If you want to sell more Cisco equipment and have more Cisco networks installed, ensure that the networks you install run properly.

Clearly, having a fabulous product line isn't all it takes to guarantee the huge success that Cisco enjoys—lots of companies with great products are now defunct. If you have complicated products designed to solve complicated problems, you need knowledgeable people who are fully capable of installing, managing, and troubleshooting them. That part isn't easy, so Cisco began the CCIE program to equip people to support these complicated networks. This program, known colloquially as the Doctorate of Networking, has also been very successful, primarily due to its extreme difficulty. Cisco continuously monitors the program, changing it as it sees fit, to make sure that it remains pertinent and accurately reflects the demands of today's internetworking business environments.

Building upon the highly successful CCIE program, Cisco Career Certifications permit you to become certified at various levels of technical proficiency, spanning the disciplines of network design and support. So, whether you're beginning a career, changing careers, securing your present position, or seeking to refine and promote your position, this is the book for you!

Cisco's Network Support Certifications

Initially, to secure the coveted CCIE, you took only one test and then you were faced with the (extremely difficult) lab, an all-or-nothing approach that made it tough to succeed. In response, Cisco created a series of new certifications to help you get the coveted CCIE, as well as aid prospective employers in measuring skill levels. With these new certifications, which added a better approach to preparing for that almighty lab, Cisco opened doors that few were allowed through before. So, what are these certifications and how do they help you get your CCIE?

Cisco Certified Network Associate (CCNA)

The CCNA certification was the first in the new line of Cisco certifications, and was the precursor to all current Cisco certifications. With the new certification programs, Cisco has created a type of stepping-stone approach to CCIE certification. Now, you can become a Cisco Certified Network Associate with the help of the *CCNA: Cisco Certified Network Associate Study Guide* (Sybex), and $125 for the test. And you don't have to stop there—you can choose to continue with your studies and achieve a higher certification, called the Cisco Certified Network Professional (CCNP). Someone with a CCNP has all the skills and knowledge he or she needs to attempt the CCIE lab. However, because no textbook can take the place of practical experience, we'll discuss what else you need to be ready for the CCIE lab shortly.

Cisco Certified Network Professional (CCNP)

So you're thinking, "Great, what do I do after passing the CCNA exam?" Well, if you want to become a CCIE in Routing and Switching (the most popular certification), understand that there's more than one path to that much-coveted CCIE certification. The first way is to continue studying and become a Cisco Certified Network Professional (CCNP), which means four more tests, in addition to the CCNA certification.

The CCNP program will prepare you to understand and comprehensively tackle the internetworking issues of today and beyond—and it is not limited to the Cisco world. You will undergo a metamorphosis, vastly increasing your knowledge and skills through the process of obtaining these certifications.

While you don't need to be a CCNP or even a CCNA to take the CCIE lab, it's extremely helpful if you already have these certifications.

What Skills Do You Need to Become a CCNP?

Cisco demands a certain level of proficiency for its CCNP certification. In addition to mastering the skills required for the CCNA, you should be able to do the following:

- Install, configure, operate, and troubleshoot complex routed LAN, routed WAN, and switched LAN networks, along with dial-access services.

- Understand complex networks, such as IP, IGRP, IPX, async routing, AppleTalk, extended access lists, IP RIP, route redistribution, IPX RIP, route summarization, OSPF, VLSM, BGP, serial, IGRP, Frame Relay, ISDN, ISL, X.25, DDR, PSTN, PPP, VLANs, Ethernet, ATM LAN emulation, access lists, 802.10, and transparent and translational bridging.

- Install and/or configure a network to increase bandwidth, quicker network response times, and improve reliability and quality of service.

- Maximize performance through campus LANs, routed WANs, and remote access.

- Improve network security.

- Create a global intranet.

- Provide access security to campus switches and routers.

- Provide increased switching and routing bandwidth—end-to-end resiliency services.

- Provide custom queuing and routed priority services.

How Do You Become a CCNP?

After becoming a CCNA, the four exams you must take to get your CCNP are as follows:

Exam 640-901: Building Scalable Cisco Internetworks (BSCI)   Cisco recently retired the Routing (640-603) exam and now uses this exam to build on the fundamentals of the CCNA exam. BSCI focuses on large multiprotocol internetworks and how to manage them. Among other topics, you'll be tested on IS-IS, OSFP, and BGP. The *CCNP/CCIP: BSCI Study Guide* (Sybex) covers all the objectives you need to understand to pass the BSCI exam.

Exam 640-604: Switching   This exam tests your knowledge of the 1900 and 5000 series of Catalyst switches. The *CCNP: Switching Study Guide* (Sybex) covers all the objectives you need to understand to pass the Switching exam.

Exam 640-605: Remote Access   This exam tests your knowledge of installing, configuring, monitoring, and troubleshooting Cisco ISDN and dial-up access products. You must understand PPP, ISDN, Frame Relay, and authentication. The *CCNP: Remote Access Study Guide* (Sybex) covers all the exam objectives.

Exam 640-606: Support   This tests you on the Cisco troubleshooting skills needed for Ethernet and Token Ring LANs, IP, IPX, and AppleTalk networks, as well as ISDN, PPP, and Frame Relay networks. This book covers all the objectives you need to understand to pass the Support exam.

www.routersim.com has a complete Cisco router simulator for all CCNP exams.

If you hate tests, you can take fewer of them by signing up for the Support exam and then taking just one more long exam called the Foundation R/S exam (640-509). Doing this also gives you your CCNP—but beware; it's a really long test that fuses all the material from the Routing, Switching, and Remote Access exams into one exam. Good luck! However, by taking this exam, you get three tests for the price of two, which saves you $125 (if you pass). Some people think it's easier to take the Foundation R/S exam because you can leverage the areas that you would score higher in against the areas in which you wouldn't.

Remember that test objectives and tests can change at any time without notice. Always check the Cisco website for the most up-to-date information (www.cisco.com).

Cisco Certified Internetwork Expert (CCIE)

You've become a CCNP, and now you fix your sights on getting your Cisco Certified Internetwork Expert (CCIE) in Routing and Switching—what do you do next? Cisco recommends that before you take the lab, you take the Cisco Internetwork Design (CID) exam (640-025) and the Cisco-authorized course called Installing and Maintaining Cisco Routers (IMCR). By the way, no Sylvan Prometric test for IMCR exists at the time of this writing, and Cisco recommends a *minimum* of two years of on-the-job experience before taking the CCIE lab. After jumping those hurdles, you then have to pass the CCIE-R/S Exam Qualification (350-001) before taking the actual lab.

How Do You Become a CCIE?

To become a CCIE, Cisco recommends you do the following:

1. Attend all the recommended courses at an authorized Cisco training center and pony up around $15,000–$20,000, depending on your corporate discount.

2. Pass the written qualification exam ($300 per exam—so hopefully, you'll pass it the first time).

3. Pass the one-day, hands-on lab at Cisco. This costs $1,250 per lab, and many people fail two or more times. (Some never make it through!) Also, there are a limited number of places to take the lab: San Jose, California; Research Triangle Park, North Carolina; Sydney, Australia;

Tokyo, Japan; Sao Paulo, Brazil; Bangalore, India; Johannesburg, South Africa; Beijing, China; and Brussels, Belgium. This means that you might just need to add travel costs to that $1,250. Cisco has added new sites lately for the CCIE lab; it is best to check the Cisco website for the most current information.

Cisco has changed the CCIE lab from a two-day to a one-day lab. Please see www.cisco.com for the latest information.

What Skills Do You Need to Become a CCIE?

The CCIE Routing and Switching exam includes the advanced technical skills that are required to maintain optimum network performance and reliability, as well as advanced skills in supporting diverse networks that use disparate technologies. CCIEs just don't have problems getting jobs; these experts are inundated with offers to work for six-figure salaries. But that's because it isn't easy to attain the level of capability that is mandatory for Cisco's CCIE. For example, a CCIE can easily do the following:

- Install, configure, operate, and troubleshoot complex routed LAN, routed WAN, switched LAN, and ATM LANE networks, and dial-access services.

- Diagnose and resolve network faults.

- Use packet/frame analysis and Cisco debugging tools.

- Document and report the problem-solving processes used.

- Understand general LAN/WAN characteristics, including data encapsulation and layering; windowing and flow control, and their relation to delay; error detection and recovery; link-state, distance vector, and switching algorithms; management, monitoring, and fault isolation.

- Understand a variety of corporate technologies—including major services provided by Desktop, WAN, and Internet groups—as well as the functions; addressing structures; and routing, switching, and bridging implications of each of their protocols.

- Understand Cisco-specific technologies, including router/switch platforms, architectures, and applications; communication servers; protocol translation and applications; configuration commands and system/network impact; and LAN/WAN interfaces, capabilities, and applications.

- Design, configure, install, and verify voice-over-IP and voice-over-ATM networks.

Cisco's Network Design Certifications

In addition to the network support certifications, Cisco has created another certification track for network designers. The two certifications within this track are the Cisco Certified Design Associate and Cisco Certified Design Professional certifications. If you're reaching for the CCIE stars, we highly recommend the CCNP and CCDP certifications before attempting the lab (or attempting to advance your career).

This certification will give you the knowledge you need to design routed LAN, routed WAN, and switched LAN and ATM LANE networks.

Cisco Certified Design Associate (CCDA)

To become a CCDA, you must pass the Designing Cisco Networks (DCN) exam (640-441). To pass this test, you must understand how to do the following:

- Design simple routed LAN, routed WAN, and switched LAN and ATM LANE networks.
- Use Network-layer addressing.
- Filter with access lists.
- Use and propagate VLAN.
- Size networks.

 The Sybex *CCDA: Cisco Certified Design Associate Study Guide* (1999) is the most cost-effective way to study for and pass your CCDA exam.

Cisco Certified Design Professional (CCDP)

If you're already a CCNP and want to get your CCDP, you can simply take the CID 640-025 test. If you're not yet a CCNP, however, you must take the CCDA, CCNA, BSCI, Switching, Remote Access, and CID exams.

CCDP certification skills include the following:

- Designing complex routed LAN, routed WAN, and switched LAN and ATM LANE networks
- Building upon the base level of the CCDA technical knowledge

CCDPs must also demonstrate proficiency in the following:

- Network-layer addressing in a hierarchical environment
- Traffic management with access lists
- Hierarchical network design
- VLAN use and propagation
- Performance considerations: required hardware and software; switching engines; memory, cost, and minimization

Where Do You Take the Exams?

You may take the exams at any of the more than 800 Sylvan Prometric Authorized Testing Centers around the world (www.2test.com), or call 800-204-EXAM (3926). You can also register and take the exams at a VUE authorized center (www.vue.com) or call (877) 404-EXAM (3926).

To register for a Cisco Certified Network Professional exam:

1. Determine the number of the exam you want to take. (The CCNP Support exam number is 640-606.)

2. Register with the nearest Sylvan Prometric Registration Center or VUE testing center. At this point, you will be asked to pay in advance for the exam. At the time of this writing, the exams are $125 each and must be taken within one year of payment. You can schedule exams up to six weeks in advance or as late as the same day you want to take it—but if you fail a Cisco exam, you must wait 72 hours before you will be allowed to retake the exam. If something comes up and you need to cancel or reschedule your exam appointment, contact Sylvan Prometric or VUE at least 24 hours in advance.

3. When you schedule the exam, you'll get instructions regarding all appointment and cancellation procedures, the ID requirements, and information about the testing-center location.

Tips for Taking Your CCNP Support Exam

The CCNP Support test contains 50 to 60 questions to be completed in 75 minutes. Cisco does not publish specific exam passing scores; however, in general you must get a score of about 80% to pass this exam. As was stated before, check the Cisco website for more information on the specifics before you take your exam.

Many questions on the exam have answer choices that at first glance look identical—especially the syntax questions! Remember to read through the choices carefully, because close doesn't cut it. If you get commands in the wrong order or forget one measly character, you'll get the question wrong. So, to practice, do the hands-on exercises at the end of the chapters over and over again until they feel natural to you.

Also, never forget that the right answer is the Cisco answer. In many cases, more than one appropriate answer is presented, but the *correct* answer is the one that Cisco recommends.

The CCNP Support 640-606 exam can include the following test formats:

- Multiple-choice single answer
- Multiple-choice multiple answer
- Drag-and-drop
- Fill-in-the-blank
- Router simulations

In addition to multiple choice and fill-in response questions, Cisco Career Certifications exams may include performance simulation exam items.

Here are some general tips for exam success:

- Arrive early at the exam center, so you can relax and review your study materials.

- Read the questions *carefully*. Don't jump to conclusions. Make sure you're clear about *exactly* what each question asks.

- When answering multiple-choice questions that you're not sure about, use the process of elimination to get rid of the obviously incorrect answers first. Doing this greatly improves your odds if you need to make an educated guess.

- You can no longer move forward and backward through the Cisco exams, so double-check your answer before clicking "Next" since you can't change your mind.

After you complete an exam, you'll get immediate, online notification of your pass or fail status, a printed Examination Score Report that indicates your pass or fail status, and your exam results by section. (The test administrator will give you the printed score report.) Test scores are automatically forwarded to Cisco within five working days after you take the test, so you don't need to send your score to them. If you pass the exam, you'll receive confirmation from Cisco, typically within two to four weeks.

How to Contact the Author

You can reach Todd Lammle through GlobalNet Training Solutions, Inc. (www.globalnettraining.com), his training and systems integration company in Dallas, Texas—or through his software company (www.routersim.com) in Denver, Colorado, which creates both Cisco and Microsoft software simulation programs.

To contact Arthur Pfund, you can e-mail him at arthur.pfund@cox.net.

Assessment Test

1. Which are reasons for using a troubleshooting method? (Choose all that apply.)

   A. Problem isolation and resolution will occur more quickly.

   B. No documentation needs to be done when following a method.

   C. Due to complex topologies and technologies, a systematic method is the most efficient way to resolve network problems.

   D. All of the above.

2. What is/are the benefit(s) of gathering additional facts for troubleshooting? (Choose all that apply.)

   A. Possible causes may be identified.

   B. A specific problem definition may be created.

   C. Information is provided for a baseline.

   D. All of the above.

3. Which of the following are key components of creating an action plan? (Choose all that apply.)

   A. Multiple changes as long as they are documented

   B. Changes that do not compromise security

   C. Changes that have only brief network impact

   D. Back-out plans

4. How many methods of problem isolation exist?

   A. 2

   B. 3

   C. 4

   D. 6

5. Which of the following steps are part of the troubleshooting method? (Choose all that apply.)

   A. Observation of results

   B. Observation of changes

   C. Iteration

   D. Documentation

   E. Problem definition

   F. Problem resolution

   G. Troubleshooting

6. Which protocol attributes are associated with the Internet Protocol (IP)? (Choose all that apply.)

   A. Connection-oriented

   B. Connectionless

   C. Layer 2

   D. Layer 3

7. Select the potential attributes of a connectionless protocol.

   A. Broadcast control

   B. Sequenced PDUs

   C. Broadcast transmissions

   D. Wireless connectivity

8. Choose all protocols that operate only at Layer 3 from the following list.

   A. PPP

   B. IP

   C. EIGRP

   D. SDLC

   E. NetWare

   F. X.25

   G. BGP

9. Choose all Layer 2 protocols listed below.

    A. TCP

    B. Ethernet

    C. UDP

    D. IP

    E. Token Ring

    F. FDDI

    G. EIGRP

10. Choose two attributes that a connection-oriented protocol possesses.

    A. Flow control

    B. Error control

    C. Broadcast control

    D. Collision detection

11. Which devices may be considered physical media test equipment? (Choose all that apply.)

    A. Time Domain Reflector

    B. Multimeter

    C. Optical Time Domain Reflector

    D. Breakout box

12. What are the five attributes of network management software?

    A. Connectivity

    B. Network Availability Monitoring

    C. Reachability

    D. Graphical User Interface

    E. Network Modeling and Simulation

    F. Security

    G. Quality of Service

    H. Traffic Monitoring and Analysis

13. What is SNMP used for?

    A. Creating network maps

    B. Traffic Analysis

    C. Statistical/Environmental data collection

    D. All of the above

14. Which Cisco NMS packages are included in CiscoWorks 2000? (Choose all that apply.)

    A. CiscoWorks 4.0

    B. Cisco Works for Switched Internetworks

    C. Threshold Manager

    D. NetSys

    E. Netflow Collector and Analyzer

    F. Resource Manager Essentials

    G. CiscoView

    H. ATM Director

15. Which is the primary function of a protocol analyzer?

    A. Collect and analyze frames or packets from the network.

    B. Analyze protocol distributions only.

    C. Monitor the network for security holes.

    D. Provide a real-time baseline.

16. Which of the following are valid switching types for Cisco routers? (Choose all that apply.)

A. Cisco Express Forwarding

B. Buffer switching

C. Netflow switching

D. Process switching

E. Silicon switching

F. Fast switching

G. Optimum switching

H. VIP switching

17. Choose the best definition of packet flow as it relates to a Cisco router.

A. The flow of packets from the source to a destination

B. The flow of packets from one router to another

C. The path a packet takes inside the router's architecture

D. The path that packets take to get from one place to another

18. Which commands should be used in conjunction for thorough problem isolation? (Choose two.)

A. `ping`

B. `show ip interface`

C. `traceroute`

D. `ar`

19. What command(s) may be issued on a Windows 98 system to provide interface IP information? (Choose all that apply.)

A. `show ip interface`

B. `ipconfig /all`

C. `winipcfg`

D. `ipcfg`

20. Which protocols are used for dynamic IP address assignment? (Choose two.)

   A. AutoIP

   B. AutoARP/IP

   C. BootP

   D. DHCP

21. Choose the troubleshooting tool that is used to test for reachability and connectivity.

   A. Traceroute

   B. Debug

   C. Show interface

   D. Ping

22. How many levels of `ping` and `traceroute` are there on Cisco routers?

   A. One

   B. Two

   C. Three

   D. Four

23. Choose the troubleshooting tool that is used for testing the path from a source host to a destination host.

   A. Traceroute

   B. Debug

   C. Show interface

   D. Ping

24. When is a "default gateway" used on the router?

   A. When a packet leaves the router

   B. When no route exists in the route table

   C. When a static route has been set

   D. Only when the router is in boot mode

25. Why is a default metric setting necessary for route redistribution?

    A. It isn't necessary.

    B. The routes being injected need to be assigned metrics that the parent protocol understands.

    C. It provides better metrics when performing route redistribution.

    D. It converts the parent protocol's metric to match the protocol being redistributed.

26. Which LMI (Local Management Interface) type is on by default on a Cisco router?

    A. LMI

    B. Cisco

    C. ANSI

    D. ITU-T

    E. IETF

27. What are the valid LMI types? (Choose all that apply.)

    A. LMI

    B. Cisco

    C. ITU-T

    D. ANSI

28. What are the valid Frame Relay encapsulation types? (Choose all that apply.)

    A. IETF

    B. ITU-T

    C. Cisco

    D. ANSI

29. Which encapsulation is used by default on Cisco Serial interfaces?

   A. SDLC

   B. PPP

   C. HDLC

   D. X.25

30. What type of tests are useful in testing for end-to-end serial link integrity?

   A. Ping

   B. Traceroute

   C. Loopback

   D. Loopup

31. Which channel do q.931 and q.921 use for communication?

   A. A channel

   B. B channel

   C. D channel

   D. Both B and D

32. Which ISDN protocol is used for Layer 3 connection setup?

   A. CHAP

   B. PPP

   C. q.921

   D. q.931

33. Which command should be used to display the connection setup for Layer 3?

   A. `show interface bri n`

   B. `debug isdn q931`

   C. `debug interface bri`

   D. `debug isdn q92`

34. Which ISDN protocol is used for Layer 2 connection setup?

    A. CHAP

    B. PPP

    C. q.921

    D. q.931

35. Which channel does PPP use when negotiating the connection?

    A. A channel

    B. B channel

    C. D channel

    D. Both B and D

36. Which of the following are characteristic of extended IPX access lists? (Choose all that apply.)

    A. Numbered between 100 and 199

    B. Numbered between 800 and 899

    C. Numbered between 900 and 999

    D. Filters on Novell Service

37. Which of the following protocols can be used with IPX? (Choose all that apply.)

    A. IGRP

    B. BGP

    C. EIGRP

    D. NLSP

    E. RIP

38. Which of the following are valid troubleshooting targets when troubleshooting Novell NetWare (IPX) networks? (Choose all that apply.)

    A. ARP

    B. GNS

    C. Encapsulation type

    D. SAP

39. Which of the following are main categories of troubleshooting targets for Novell NetWare networks? (Choose all that apply.)

    A. Novell client configuration

    B. Novell server configuration

    C. Cisco router configuration

    D. IP connectivity

40. Which of the following commands are troubleshooting commands specific to IPX troubleshooting? (Choose all that apply.)

    A. `show ipx servers`

    B. `ping <network.node>`

    C. `ping ipx <network.node>`

    D. `debug ipx servers`

41. Which of the following are possible causes for zones not appearing in a user's Chooser? (Choose all that apply.)

    A. Phase 1/Phase 2 addressing mismatch

    B. Duplicate network numbers

    C. ZIP storm

    D. Local configuration set to LocalTalk instead of EtherTalk

42. Which of the following are possible actions for resolving Phase 1/Phase 2 incompatibility? (Choose all that apply.)

    A. Use only one cable number

    B. Use one zone per network

    C. Use `show appletalk neighbors`

    D. Use `show appletalk global`

43. In the following line, what is the zone name?

```
(43199n,145a,244s)[0]:   'clientzone:AFPServer@Piper'
```

   A. clientzone

   B. piper

   C. AFPServer@Piper

   D. Piper

   E. 43199

44. Which of the following is a troubleshooting target for AppleTalk? (Choose all that apply.)

   A. Local host configuration

   B. Routers connected to AppleTalk networks

   C. Remote host configuration

   D. ARP protocol

45. Which of the following are possible actions for resolving a configuration mismatch? (Choose all that apply.)

   A. `debug NBP events`

   B. `show running-configuration`

   C. `show appletalk interface`

   D. `debug appletalk gns`

46. What are the three major roles of a router when configured with VLANs?

   A. Define the collision domain.

   B. Provide Layer 2 VLAN switching.

   C. Provide Layer 2 VLAN translation.

   D. Provide Layer 3 VLAN routing.

47. Which of the following VLAN encapsulation types do Cisco routers support? (Choose all that apply.)

    A. Inter-Switch Link (ISL)

    B. IEEE Ethernet 802.3

    C. IEEE 802.1Q

    D. IEEE 802.1Z

48. When using a router, which of the following scenarios will not work?

    A. VLAN 10 uses ISL while VLAN 20 uses 802.1q.

    B. The switch is configured to use ISL and the router uses 802.1q.

    C. VLAN 10 uses 802.1q, then tries to communicate with a remote host, not on a VLAN.

    D. Both VLAN 10 and VLAN 20 use 802.1q.

49. Which of the following are valid hardware components of the Catalyst switch? (Choose all that apply.)

    A. EARL

    B. DUKE

    C. SAINT

    D. SAGE

50. What does the term "blocking" mean with regard to a Catalyst 5000 port?

    A. An access list has been applied to the port.

    B. Packets are not allowed out of the port.

    C. Spanning tree has blocked the port to prevent a loop.

    D. The port has been shut down.

51. Which functions can be performed via the CCO Case Management Toolkit? (Choose all that apply.)

    A. Case priority escalation

    B. Opening a case

    C. Closing a case

    D. Updating a case

52. Which of the following Cisco resources was established to aid in preventing problems? (Choose all that apply.)

   A. Software Center

   B. Cisco Connection Documentation CD-ROM

   C. Cisco TAC

   D. Bug Navigator

53. Which of the following are information items that will be requested upon opening a TAC case? (Choose all that apply.)

   A. Output from a `show tech-support`

   B. Support contract number

   C. Mailing address

   D. Specify priority

54. Which of the following were established to correct problems? (Choose all that apply.)

   A. Software Center

   B. Bug Navigator

   C. Networking Professionals Connection or Open Q&A Forum

   D. Troubleshooting Assistant

55. How does the Troubleshooting Assistant work?

   A. Access is given to Cisco Systems; they in turn evaluate the router and suggest any necessary changes.

   B. An interactive dialog intended to resolve common networking/configuration problems is used.

   C. Questions can be posted, and CCIEs will respond.

   D. It is a Voice Response Unit that guides you through troubleshooting steps.

56. What do the following lines of router output indicate? (Choose all that apply.)

```
Router_C#show int ethernet 0/1
Ethernet0/1 is up, line protocol is up
```

```
Hardware is Lance, address is 0000.0c47.abea (bia
   0000.0c47.abea)
Internet address is 172.16.60.1/24
MTU 1500 bytes, BW 10000 Kbit, DLY 1000 usec, rely
   255/255,    load 46/255
Encapsulation ARPA, loopback not set, keepalive set
   (10 sec)
ARP type: ARPA, ARP Timeout 04:00:00
```

A. The interface is up and appears to be functioning properly.

B. This interface is in loopback.

C. The encapsulation type for this interface is ARPA.

D. The bandwidth metric for this interface is 100Mbps.

57. Which configuration register setting will cause the router to boot the IOS image from the boot ROM?

A. 0x2000

B. 0x2101

C. 0x1002

D. 0x2102

58. What do the following lines of router output indicate? (Choose all that apply.)

```
Router_A#show interface to0
... some output deleted ...
  MTU 4464 bytes, BW 16000 Kbit, DLY 630 usec, rely
     255/255,    load 1/255
  Encapsulation SNAP, loopback not set, keepalive set
     (10 sec)
  ARP type: SNAP, ARP Timeout 04:00:00
  Ring speed: 16 Mbps
... output removed ...
  Last clearing of "show interface" counters never
```

A. The ring speed is 4Mbps.

B. The ring speed is 16Mbps.

C. The interface counters have never been cleared.

D. Encapsulation is SNMP.

59. Look at the outputs from two different interfaces connected to each other. Why aren't the interfaces functioning properly?

```
Router_A#show interface to0
TokenRing0 is up, line protocol is down
  Hardware is TMS380, address is 0007.787c.e14b (bia
    0007.787c.e14b)
  Internet address is 172.16.30.1, subnet mask is
    255.255.255.0
  MTU 4464 bytes, BW 16000 Kbit, DLY 630 usec, rely
    255/255,    load 1/255
  Encapsulation SNAP, loopback not set, keepalive set
    (10 sec)
  ARP type: SNAP, ARP Timeout 04:00:00
  Ring speed: 16 Mbps
  Single ring node, Source Route Transparent Bridge
    capable
  Ethernet Transit OUI: 0x000000
  Last input never, output never, output hang never
  Last clearing of "show interface" counters never
  Queueing strategy: fifo
  Output queue 0/40, 0 drops; input queue 0/75, 0 drops
  5 minute input rate 0 bits/sec, 0 packets/sec
  5 minute output rate 0 bits/sec, 0 packets/sec
    0 packets input, 0 bytes, 0 no buffer
    Received 0 broadcasts, 0 runts, 0 giants
    0 input errors, 0 CRC, 0 frame, 0 overrun,
      0 ignored,       0 abort
    0 packets output, 0 bytes, 0 underruns
    0 output errors, 0 collisions, 0 interface resets
    0 output buffer failures, 0 output buffers swapped
      out
    5 transitions
Router_B#show interface to1
TokenRing0 is up, line protocol is down
  Hardware is TMS380, address is 0007.787c.e14b (bia
    0007.787c.e14b)
  Internet address is 172.16.30.2, subnet mask is
    255.255.255.0
  MTU 4464 bytes, BW 4000 Kbit, DLY 630 usec, rely
    255/255,    load 1/255
```

```
Encapsulation SNAP, loopback not set, keepalive set
   (10 sec)
ARP type: SNAP, ARP Timeout 04:00:00
Ring speed: 4 Mbps
Single ring node, Source Route Transparent Bridge
   capable
Ethernet Transit OUI: 0x000000
Last input never, output never, output hang never
Last clearing of "show interface" counters never
Queueing strategy: fifo
Output queue 0/40, 0 drops; input queue 0/75, 0 drops
5 minute input rate 0 bits/sec, 0 packets/sec
5 minute output rate 0 bits/sec, 0 packets/sec
   0 packets input, 0 bytes, 0 no buffer
   Received 0 broadcasts, 0 runts, 0 giants
   0 input errors, 0 CRC, 0 frame, 0 overrun,
      0 ignored,         0 abort
   0 packets output, 0 bytes, 0 underruns
   0 output errors, 0 collisions, 0 interface resets
   0 output buffer failures, 0 output buffers swapped
   out
   5 transitions
```

A. Duplicate IP addresses

B. Lobe wire fault

C. Ring speed mismatch

D. Five carrier transitions

60. Which of the following factors may contribute to excessive collisions on an Ethernet interface? (Choose all that apply.)

A. Ethernet interface

B. Transceiver

C. Cable

D. Encapsulation

Answers to Assessment Test

1. C.   Quick problem resolution is not guaranteed by using a model, and documentation should always be performed. For further explanation of the reasons for using a troubleshooting method, see Chapter 1.

2. A, B.   Option C is incorrect because a baseline contains information taken from a normally functioning network. For further explanation of gathering facts for troubleshooting, see Chapter 1.

3. B, D.   Making multiple changes creates more difficulty when trying to back out of changes, as well as not allowing for good observation results. Changes should not create any adverse network impact. For further explanation of creating an action plan, see Chapter 1.

4. B.   There are three methods for isolating the source of a network problem: outside-in, inside-out, and divide-by-half. For further explanation of methods of problem isolation, see Chapter 1.

5. A, C, E.   There are additional steps in the method, but they are not included here. Though not an official step in the process, documenting changes after they are complete is an important part of the overall process. For further explanation of Cisco's troubleshooting method, see Chapter 1.

6. B, D.   IP is a connectionless protocol and a Layer 3 protocol. For further information about IP, see Chapter 2.

7. C.   Connectionless protocols do not use any type of control. B is a type of control. Physical connectivity does not determine the protocol properties. For further information about connectionless protocols, see Chapter 2.

8. B, C, G.   NetWare covers the top five layers of the OSI model and is not isolated to Layer 3. The remaining protocols are all Layer 2. See Chapter 2 for further information.

9. B, E, F.   These are all Layer 2 technologies with their accompanying protocols. For further information, see Chapter 2.

10. A, B.   These two attributes allow for complete connection and data transfer control. For further information about connection-oriented protocols, see Chapter 2.

11. A, B, C, and D.   All of these devices are used to test physical media. For additional information on physical media test equipment, see Chapter 3.

12. B, E, F, G, H.   Connectivity and Reachability belong to the Network Availability Monitoring attribute. For additional information on Network Management Software, see Chapter 3.

13. C.   Simple Network Management Protocol is used to collect statistical/environmental data from network devices. For additional information on SNMP, see Chapter 3.

14. B, C, F, G, H.   These are all individual components of CiscoWorks 2000. NetSys is an analysis package that is a stand-alone from Cisco-Works 2000; Netflow Collector is also a stand-alone. For additional information about Cisco's NMS packages, see Chapter 3.

15. A.   Several different analyses may be executed once the frames or packets have been captured to a buffer. A protocol distribution can be performed, but it is a report or a specific type of analysis. An analyzer cannot monitor your network efficiently. It can be used to get an idea of real-time activity, but that is not its primary function. For additional information on protocol analyzers, see Chapter 3.

16. A, C, D, E, F, G.   Buffer switching is not a valid term and VIP switching is known as Distributed switching. See Chapter 4 for more details about switching types.

17. C.   The packet flow as it relates to the router is the path that it takes inside the router to get from one interface to another, otherwise through the router's architecture. See Chapter 4 for more information about packet flow.

18. A, C.   Using both of these tools in conjunction greatly aids problem isolation. See Chapter 5 for more information.

19. B, C.   Both commands are recognized in Windows 98. A is for use on a router, and D is incorrect syntax. See Chapter 5 for more information.

20. C, D.   These two protocols are used for IP address assignment. (The other two don't exist.) See Chapter 5 for more information.

21. D.   Ping uses ICMP to test for connectivity of remote hosts. See Chapter 5 for more details.

22. B. There are two levels, user and privileged. See Chapter 5 for more details.

23. A. Traceroute tests the route or path from a source to a destination. See Chapter 5 for more details.

24. B. The term "default" indicates that no other route has been specified. So instead of dropping the packet, the router forwards it out the default gateway. See Chapter 6 for more information.

25. B. Routes from the incoming protocol must be assigned new metrics so they can be redistributed. See Chapter 6 for more information.

26. B. Cisco LMI is on by default. See Chapter 7 for more information.

27. B, C, D. LMI is the Local Management Interface. See Chapter 7 for more information.

28. A, C. There are only two valid encapsulation types for Frame Relay. See Chapter 7 for more information.

29. C. HDLC is an enhancement over SDLC, and PPP is a protocol, not an encapsulation. X.25 is not configured by default. See Chapter 7 for more information.

30. C. Loopback tests can test for link integrity without any additional protocols such as PPP, IP, or others. See Chapter 7 for more details.

31. C. These protocols use the D channel for information signaling. See Chapter 8 for more information.

32. D. CHAP and PPP are not specific to ISDN and q.921 is used for Layer 2 setup. See Chapter 8 for more information.

33. B. This debug command displays all steps of the connection sequence. See Chapter 8 for more information.

34. C. CHAP and PPP are not specific to ISDN and q.931 is used for Layer 3 setup. See Chapter 8 for more information.

35. B. Since data (payload) is going to be from point to point, the PPP link must be set up between the local and remote TE on the B channel. See Chapter 8 for more information.

36. C. Novell services are filtered using SAP filters, which are different from IPX filters. See Chapter 9 for more details about IPX access lists.

37. C, D, E.   These protocols are known as IPX-EIGRP, NLSP, and IPX-RIP. These protocols can all be used in conjunction with IPX. See Chapter 9 for more information about IPX settings.

38. B, C, D.   ARP is associated with IP lookup; it is not related to the IPX protocol. See Chapter 9 for more detail about troubleshooting NetWare networks.

39. A, B, C, D.   All of these are main troubleshooting targets when working on Novell networks. The reason IP connectivity is a target is to provide isolation. If IP connectivity is malfunctioning, you can determine that it may not be solely an IPX issue. See Chapter 9 for more information about troubleshooting NetWare networks.

40. A, C.   In order to use the `<network.node>` address, you must specify the IPX ping. See Chapter 9 for more information about IPX troubleshooting.

41. C, D.   Both ZIP (Zone Information Protocol) storms and incorrect local configuration can cause this symptom. See Chapter 10 for more information.

42. A, B, C, D.   All of these are valid actions that will lead to the resolution of phase one/phase two incompatibility. See Chapter 10 for more information.

43. D.   Note that resource names are case-insensitive, but zone names are not. See Chapter 10 for more information.

44. A, B, C.   All of these items are major troubleshooting targets for AppleTalk. Of course, each major target will have subsequent targets. See Chapter 10 for more information.

45. B, C.   Both of these commands will allow you to see how the interface and router are configured for AppleTalk. See Chapter 10 for more information.

46. B, C, D.   A router provides other roles in a switched network as well, but the collision domain is defined by the switch port, not the router. See Chapter 11 for more information on this subject.

47. A, C.   Cisco routers support both ISL and 802.1Q. See Chapter 11 for more information.

48. B.   The router and switch must use the same encapsulation across the connection. Other interfaces do not matter. See Chapter 11 for more information.

49. A, C, D.   These are all valid components of the Catalyst 5000 series switches. You should be familiar with the role of each. See Chapter 11 for more information.

50. C.   Blocking is a step or state in the Spanning Tree Protocol that prevents loops. See Chapter 11 for more information.

51. B, C, D.   Users are not allowed to escalate a case priority via the Web; TAC must be contacted via phone or e-mail. See Chapter 12 for more information.

52. A, B.   The TAC is primarily for problem support and to provide information that a user may not have access to. See Chapter 12 for more information.

53. A, B, D.   In addition, you may be asked to provide the serial number of the device you are calling about. See Chapter 12 for more information.

54. B, C, D.   These services all provide solutions to known problems. See Chapter 12 for more information.

55. B.   Initial questions are posed and a response received; based on the response, additional questions are posed, and this process continues until the problem is resolved. See Chapter 12 for additional information.

56. A, C.   The interface is not in loopback and the bandwidth metric is only 10Mbps. See Chapter 13 for more information.

57. B.   0x2101 is the correct configuration register setting for a router to enter boot mode. See Chapter 13 for more details about configuration register settings.

58. B, C.   The ring speed is indicated by the `Ring speed: 16 Mbps` output and the clearing of the counters is indicated by the `Last clearing of "show interface" counters never` output. The encapsulation is SNAP, as indicated by the `Encapsulation SNAP` output. See Chapter 13 for more information.

59. C.   The carrier transitions could be caused by the ring speed mismatch. See Chapter 13 for more information.

60. A, B, C.   Collisions can be caused by any piece of hardware involved in an Ethernet connection. See Chapter 13 for more information about collisions.

Chapter

1

Troubleshooting Methodology

TOPICS COVERED IN THIS CHAPTER INCLUDE:

✓ Describe an efficient problem-solving method when troubleshooting and documenting internetwork problems.

roubleshooting is a skill that takes time and experience to fully develop. To be successful when trying to diagnose and repair network failures, a good set of troubleshooting tools and skills is essential.

While there's no specific exam objective that maps to this chapter, the information presented here is nevertheless important to the exam. This chapter emphasizes the importance of following a specific set of troubleshooting steps when you try to diagnose and solve network problems. An effective troubleshooting methodology is needed because of the complexity of today's network environments. As a Cisco Certified Network Professional, you need to understand and be able to apply an efficient and systematic troubleshooting methodology. Otherwise, you would be required to have a very intimate understanding of the network you are troubleshooting. The ability to learn troubleshooting skills and understand the information available to you while solving network problems is imperative.

The Complexity of Internetworks

When a network failure occurs, time is of the essence. When a production network goes down, several things are affected. The most important of these is the bottom line—network failures cost money. A good example is a call-center network. The company relies on the network to be available for its employees so that they may take phone orders, answer inquiries, or perform other business transactions that generate income. A failure in this environment needs to be diagnosed and repaired in a timely manner. The longer the network is down, the more money the company loses.

To minimize monetary and productivity losses, network failures must be resolved quickly. Troubleshooting is an integral part of getting the problem solved quickly. Intimate knowledge of a network also facilitates rapid resolution. However, armed with a few troubleshooting skills and intimate knowledge of the network, you can solve most problems rather quickly, thus saving money.

Hold on a minute. What if you're new on the job and you don't have an intimate knowledge of the network? You can probably get up to speed quickly enough, right? Although that may have been the case in the past, getting up to speed becomes overwhelming with today's complex networks. These networks consist of routing, dial-up, switching, video, WAN (ISDN, Frame Relay, ATM, and others), LAN, and VLAN technologies. Refer to Figure 1.1 to get an idea of how these technologies intertwine. Notice that ATM, Frame Relay, Token Ring, Ethernet, and FDDI all are present. Each technology has different properties and different commands to allow for troubleshooting. Different protocols are used for each of these technologies. In addition, different applications require specific network resources. (At least the seven-layer OSI model, which you will review in Chapter 2, is used to maintain a common template when designing new technologies and protocols.) It would take you a long time to master all of the technologies implemented in the network and to be able to solve network problems, based on your knowledge of the network alone. All of these factors contribute to today's complex network environments.

There must be an easier, more logical way to efficiently and successfully troubleshoot without having to become intimately familiar with every network environment. Well, you'll be happy to know that there is an easier option—following a troubleshooting model—and it is discussed in detail in this chapter. By following a troubleshooting model, the need for intimate knowledge of the network is minimized.

A troubleshooting model should be adopted to help resolve network malfunctions and reduce downtime. Now, let's move on to discuss Cisco's model in detail.

FIGURE 1.1 Today's complex enterprise network

The Problem-Solving Model

Imagine trying to solve a network failure by using a different approach every time. With such complex networks, the possible scenarios would be innumerable. Because so many different things can go wrong within a network, it would be possible to start from many different points. Not only is this an ineffective method of troubleshooting, but it is also time-consuming, and time is very valuable in a "network-down" situation.

Cisco has designed an effective *troubleshooting model* that contains seven steps. A troubleshooting model is a list of troubleshooting steps or processes that can be followed to provide an efficient manner of resolving network problems. The headings below contain information specific to each step of the troubleshooting model. (Two of the steps are combined into one section of the chapter—creating and implementing the action plan.) After the seven steps are completed and the problem is resolved, a few more steps follow, such as documentation.

To be effective when troubleshooting and to achieve faster resolution times, follow the model outlined in Figure 1.2. This flow chart shows the seven steps.

FIGURE 1.2   Cisco's troubleshooting model

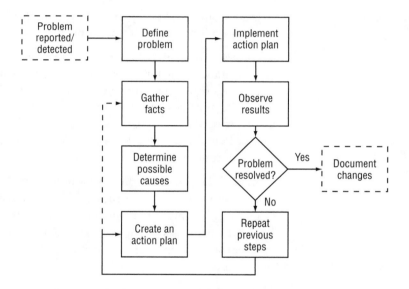

The process begins when a network failure is reported to you. The steps to take along with brief descriptions of the steps are as follows:

1. Define the problem.   At this point in the process it is important to make a determination of the issue in terms of sets of symptoms and potential problems.

2. Gather detailed information.   These facts about the problem can be obtained from a number of sources, including key users, network management systems, output from router and switch diagnostic commands, and protocol analyzer traces.

3. Consider possible scenarios. Brainstorm and come up with several possible or probable causes of the failure. Also, when developing this list, eliminate items that are definitely not the cause of the problem.

4. Create an action plan. Begin with the most likely problem and devise a plan to correct this issue changing only one variable at a time. If multiple items are changed simultaneously, it is possible that the problem will be resolved without identifying the root cause. This then leaves the potential for the problem to repeat itself in the future.

5. Implement the action plan. As you implement each step of the action plan, carefully check to see if the problem is resolved.

6. Observe the results of the implementation of the action plan. In many instances it will be clear when the problem is resolved; however, in those cases where the problem is subtler, a more structured observation technique must be used. This technique involves many of the same tools that were used in the fact-gathering portion of the process, such as talking to users, checking network management tools, and checking router and switch output.

7. Repeat the process if the action plan doesn't fix the problem.
Revise your action plan to address the next most likely problem. Be sure to undo the changes that were attempted in the previous attempt. Then repeat the process starting with step 4. If there are no more potential problems for which to create an action plan, start with step 2 and repeat the process.

The best way to understand how Cisco's model works and how you should use it is by looking at an example. For this example, assume you are in charge of operational support of the network pictured in Figure 1.3. There are two campus networks, connected via a Frame Relay cloud. Within each network, VLANs are connected to a Catalyst 5500 switch and then to a core router that has a connection to the Frame Relay cloud in one way or another.

The fun begins when you get a call from a user who "Can't get to Host Z." Based on this information, let's apply Cisco's troubleshooting model to solve the user's problem and fix the problem in the network.

FIGURE 1.3   Example campus network

Step 1: Define the Problem

As you can see, the user's problem is vague; you need more information if you are to solve the problem any time soon. This is where *problem definition* comes in. Problem definition is the step in the troubleshooting model when details are used to define what the most likely cause of a problem is. Now, while you still have the user on the line, the first step is to ask him what he means when he says he can't "get" to Host Z. The user then defines the situation by telling you that he can't FTP to Host Z. Ask the user if he experiences any other problems or if this is the only one. Verify where the user is currently located. After these preliminary questions, you have a basic idea of what is and isn't working. Unfortunately, you can't simply assume that the FTP is broken because there are many other pieces of the network that can contribute to the problem.

It is also important to realize that you may want or need to gather facts before you actually form your problem statement. By gathering facts to help define the problem, the diagnosis of the problem or problems will be more accurate and will help you solve the problem more quickly in the end. Problem definition and fact gathering should be used in tandem for a quick and accurate resolution.

Once you have enough information to define the problem, you should create a problem statement that is specific, concise, and an accurate description of the problem that needs to be solved. In this case, you can have a statement that says: *User A from Campus A cannot FTP to Host Z on Campus B*. With a good problem statement, it is easier to focus on the problem and not try to troubleshoot problems that do not fall within the problem definition.

Step back for a moment before you actually form your final problem statement. You need to gather more information before you can form an accurate problem statement. Now, you move on to the fact-gathering step. Keep in mind, however, that after you gather all the information, you have to come back and create your problem statement.

Step 2: Gather Facts

At this point, the problem is still pretty vague and needs more definition. This is where the fact-gathering step of the troubleshooting model is employed. *Fact gathering* is the process of using diagnostic tools to collect information specific to the network and network devices that are involved in a problem. Additional information should include data that excludes other possibilities and helps pinpoint the actual problem. An example is to verify that you can ping, Traceroute, or Telnet to Host Z, thus reducing the number of possible causes.

Depending on the user and situation, you may or may not be able to get more detailed information. It is up to you as a network engineer or administrator to solve the problem, which means that you may have to get the information yourself.

It is important that you gain as much information as possible to actually define the problem while in the problem-definition phase of the troubleshooting model. Without a proper and specific definition of what the problem is, it will be much harder to isolate and resolve. Information that is useful for defining a problem is listed in Table 1.1.

TABLE 1.1 Useful Information for Defining a Problem

Information	Example
Symptoms	Can't Telnet, FTP, or get to the WWW.
Reproducibility	Is this a one-time occurrence, or does it always happen?
Timeline	When did it start? How long did it last? How often does it occur? Has the current configuration ever worked properly?
Scope	What are you able to Telnet or FTP to? Which WWW sites can you reach, if any? Who else does this affect?
Baseline Info	Were any recent changes made to the network configurations?

All of this information can be used to guide you to the actual problem and to create the problem statement. Use your network diagram and go through the checklist.

Identify Symptoms

First, you need to define what is working and what isn't. You can do this by identifying the symptom and defining the scope. Figure 1.4 is a picture of your network. Although the large X on the Frame Relay cloud represents that there is an FTP connectivity issue, it does not indicate the location of the failure. Right now, all you know is that a single user could not FTP to Host Z.

Reproduce the Problem

Before spending time and effort trying to solve this problem, verify that it is still a problem. Troubleshooting is a waste of time and resources if the problem can't be reproduced. It's just like a dog chasing his tail. If it is an intermittent issue, further steps should be taken to capture as much information as possible about the event the next time it does occur. This will help narrow down the scope of items you will look at.

FIGURE 1.4 Host A can't FTP to Host Z

Understand the Timeline

In addition to verifying whether the problem is reproducible, it is important to investigate the frequency of the problem. For instance, maybe it happens only once or twice a day. By establishing a timeframe you can more readily identify any possible causes. In addition, you need to know whether this is the first time the user has attempted this function. There is a different set of variables involved with an item that worked yesterday but not today than there is with something that fails during first-time use. Obviously, if it worked yesterday, you can look at what changed overnight as well as looking for something that is broken. If the user has never used this feature before, there may be an access list or other security device that has been installed for months and is just now causing a problem due to the user's need to use this application.

Determine the Scope of a Problem

Next, you need to find out whether anyone else is unable to FTP to Host Z. If others can FTP to Host Z (for the sake of this example, assume that they can), you can be pretty sure that the problem is specific to the user, either on their station or on the destination host. This step is determining the scope of the problem and helps to differentiate between a user-specific problem and a more widely spread problem. Figure 1.5 shows that other hosts can FTP to Host Z without any problems.

FIGURE 1.5   Other hosts can FTP to Host Z

Now that you have the problem narrowed down to a single user, you need to define the *boundary of dysfunctionality*. The boundary of dysfunctionality is the limit or scope of the network problem. A distinction can be made between where nodes are functioning properly and where they are not. To define this boundary in this example, you need to know whether the user can successfully FTP anywhere.

There are three methods of establishing the boundary of dysfunctionality: outside-in troubleshooting, inside-out troubleshooting, and divide-by-half troubleshooting. Each of these techniques has its own advantages and disadvantages based on the situation. Each of these methods is explained in more detail below.

Outside-in Troubleshooting

The first method, *outside-in troubleshooting*, consists of starting the troubleshooting process at the opposite end of the connection. In this case, you would start at Campus B, VLAN 3, and work back toward the user's system. This method is depicted in Figure 1.6. The corresponding test would be for the user to try to FTP to another host on the same VLAN as Host Z, indicated by the X (2) on the diagram. If the result of that test is negative, then you need to come back one step. By coming back one step, you would try to FTP to a host on a different VLAN, indicated by the X (3) on the diagram. If that test failed, the only thing left to try would be to FTP to another host on the user's segment. In the example, assume that the user can FTP to other hosts that are directly connected to the same Ethernet segment. In general, outside-in troubleshooting is a good method to use when there are many hosts that cannot connect to a server or subset of servers.

Inside-out Troubleshooting

The second method is to start near the user and work your way toward Host Z, otherwise known as the *inside-out troubleshooting* method. Figure 1.7 contains a diagram that describes this testing method. You see that the user can FTP to hosts within the same network, but can't FTP to any host on the Campus B network. The steps are marked by the Xs, with the step number in parentheses.

FIGURE 1.6   Starting from the outside and working in

1. No FTP between Host A and Host Z

2. No FTP between Host A and any host on VLAN 3

3. No FTP between Host A and any host on Campus B

4. FTP works on local network.

Using the second method saved you one step—three instead of four. Statistically, however, you isolate the boundary with fewer steps by using the first method. The important thing is that the boundary be established.

FIGURE 1.7 Starting from the inside and working out

Divide-by-Half Troubleshooting

The third and final method is the *divide-by-half troubleshooting* method, which is depicted in Figure 1.8. Divide-by-half indicates that a point between two ends of a network problem is used as a troubleshooting reference point. Either half may be investigated first. In this example, you start by trying to FTP to any host within Campus B. Depending on the results, you can divide in half again and test. If the test results in a successful FTP to any host on the Campus B network, then the new point to test is another host on VLAN 3. If the test fails, the new testing point is to try to FTP to a local host. In this case, the divide-by-half method takes three steps, just as the inside-out method does.

FIGURE 1.8   Divide-by-half method

You now have isolated the problem to something outside the immediate network. Upon further inspection and fact gathering, you find that the user can't ping external hosts, either. With all of this information, you can now start to contemplate possible causes of this failure and move on to the following Consider Possibilities section.

Step 3: Consider Possibilities

This step within the troubleshooting model is used to contemplate the possible causes of the failure. Obviously, it is quite easy to create a very long list of possible causes. That is why it is so important to gather as much relevant information as you can and to create an accurate problem statement. By defining the problem and assigning the corresponding boundaries, the resulting list of possible causes diminishes because the entries in the list will be focused on the actual problem and not on "possible" problems.

First, review what you know about your sample problem:

- Host A can't FTP to Host Z.

- Host A can't FTP to any host on Campus B.

- Host A can't ping to anywhere outside its own network.

- Host A can FTP to any host on its own network.

- All other hosts on Host A's network can FTP to Host Z, as well as to other hosts.

Based on what you know, you now need to list possible causes. These possible causes are:

- No default gateway is configured on Host A.

- There is a duplicate IP address.

- The wrong subnet mask is configured.

- There is a misconfigured access list on the router connected to the switch on Campus A.

If you had not gathered such specific information, the list could have included all of the possible problems with any piece of equipment between Host A and Host Z. That would have been a long list, and it would take a lot of time to eliminate all of the possible causes.

Remember that because these are only possible causes, you still have to create an action plan, implement it, and observe to see whether the changes made were effective. When the list of possible problems is long, it may require more iterations to actually solve the problem. In this example, you have only four possible causes, so this is a much more manageable list. Although there may be other possible causes that you can think of (that's great), for this example and in the interest of simplicity, only these four are listed.

Here's where the fun starts. You now have to check each of these possibilities and fix them if they are the cause of the problem. To do this, move on to the next step, which is to create an action plan.

Steps 4 and 5: Create and Implement the Action Plan

Creating an *action plan* is actually very easy. It entails the documentation of steps that will be taken to remedy the cause of the network problem. Most of the hard work was done while gathering information about the problem. The investigation gave you four leads about the source of the problem. Now it is simply a matter of checking out each possibility and determining which one is most likely the source of the issue.

The majority of the possibilities point directly at the host machine, so start there first. The first three causes are configuration issues of the host. Now, assume that after checking the TCP/IP configuration on the host, everything is configured properly, and you can eliminate the host machine as the culprit.

You then move on to the last possible cause, which is an access list on the router. While looking at the configuration on the router, you see that an access list is applied to the Ethernet interface directly connected to the host segment. After reviewing the syntax of the access list, you determine that it is the cause of the failure.

Great—you've found the problem. Now what? Once you find the problem, you must decide what is needed to fix it. In this case, it is an access-list problem, so there are some special considerations about how to restore functionality. You must be careful because that list may have other entries that provide security or other network administrative functionality. You can't just remove it—you could cause new problems as you fix the original one.

The best thing to do in this situation is to make a copy of the access list in a text editor, and then make changes that are specific to your problem. When editing the access list, change the number of the access list. After all of the changes are made in your text editor, ensure that you have a current backup of the configuration on the router in case you need to restore the original configuration. Then paste the modified access list back into the router. Finally, go to the interface and apply the new access list. By following this procedure, the access list is never removed from the interface.

Obviously, you have now changed the access-list number that is applied to the interface, so any documentation that refers to the original number will need to be updated. If the access list that was causing the problem was applied only to Ethernet 0, you can now safely remove the old list, update this list with the corrections to address your problem, and put it back on the router. Then reapply this list to Ethernet 0. As was the case before, the access list is never removed from the interface.

When you create and implement action plans, it is important that you don't fix one problem and cause another. Before implementing an action plan, think it through or discuss it with coworkers to pick it apart, and make sure that your solution will fix the problem without doing anything to create adverse side effects.

Another good practice, when creating and implementing action plans, is to change only one thing at a time, if possible. If multiple changes must be made, it is best to make the changes in small sets. This way it is easier to keep track of what was done, what worked, and what didn't. The observation step becomes much more effective if only a few changes are made at one time; ideally, make only one change at a time.

To summarize, follow these practices and guidelines to create a good action plan:

- Make one change or a set of related changes at a time, and then observe the results.

- Make nonimpacting changes. This means trying not to cause other problems while implementing the changes. The more transparent the change, the better.

- Do not create security holes when changing access lists, TACACS+, RADIUS, or other security-oriented configurations.

- Most important, be able to revert to the original configuration if unforeseen problems occur as a result of the change. Always have a backup or copy of the configuration.

Now that you have reviewed creating and implementing changes, you need to be able to monitor the network and interpret the information to verify whether the changes implemented were effective.

Step 6: Observe Results

Observing results consists of using the exact same methods and commands that were used to obtain information to define the problem—to see whether the changes implemented were effective. By making a change and then testing it to see whether the change was effective, you move toward the correct solution.

It may take one or more changes to fix the problem, but you should observe each change separately to monitor progress and to make sure that the change doesn't create any adverse effects. After the first change is made, you should be able to gather enough information to learn whether or not the change was effective, even if it doesn't entirely solve the problem.

🌐 Real World Scenario

Looks Can Be Deceiving

One common mistake when observing the results is seeing symptoms go away and interpreting this as solving the problem. For example, assume that users are complaining about slow response time to the Internet. In the course of troubleshooting, you find and correct some nonoptimally configured interface settings on the router on the users' segment. You then go back to the user who originally reported the problem and she reports that everything is running fine now; however, she neglects to mention the fact that there was a shift change and now there are only two people connecting to the Internet where there used to be 50. The next day when all of the users are back online, the problem repeats itself. If an analysis of the observations had been done, it would have demonstrated that the traffic flow to the Internet had dropped off and that this could be a contributing factor to the improvement in response times.

As is demonstrated in this example, failure to analyze your observations creates the risk that important information can be overlooked and the problem will repeat itself in the future. To avoid this possibility, ensure that you look at the entire scope of the problem and use your network management tools to assist you in determining whether the problem is really resolved. You can also look at your network baseline information to determine what the "normal" traffic pattern looks like. It should show a sharp drop-off in utilization when the shift changes. This would tell you that the improvement in connection speed may not be due to the interface changes but just due to a lower volume of traffic and that more verification is needed.

Not until all of the changes from the action plan are implemented and the results are observed and analyzed can you verify whether the action plan solved the problem. If the problem is solved, move on and document the changes made to the network.

If the changes did not work, you need to go back and either gather more information or create a new action plan. These options are explained in more detail in the next section.

Step 7: Iterate as Needed

Iterations, or repetitions of certain steps within the troubleshooting model, are simply ways of whittling away at a larger problem. By implementing action plans and monitoring the results, you can move toward solving the overall problem.

Iterations of the troubleshooting process allow you to focus, with more and more detail, on the possible causes of the failure. The result of focusing on the problem is the ability to identify specific possible causes for the failure.

The iteration process has its own set of steps: While working through the action-plan process, you might get more ideas of possible causes. Write them down; if the current action plan doesn't work, you have notes about some other possibilities. If you feel that you exhausted all of the possible causes, you should probably go back and gather more information. You will probably find additional clues that can give you insights into more possible causes.

This is also the time to undo any changes that had adverse effects or that did not fix the problem. Make sure to document what was done, so it will be easier to undo the changes made to any configurations.

Document the Changes

The problem is resolved after you implement a change, observe that the symptoms of the problem have disappeared, and can successfully execute the tests that were used to aid in gathering information about the problem.

In this example, the way to verify that the problem is solved is for Host A to try to FTP to Host Z. If this test is successful, then the problem is resolved.

As was alluded to in the previous sections, documentation is an integral part of troubleshooting. When you keep track of the changes that were made; which routers, switches, or hosts were changed; and when the changes occurred, you have valuable information for future reference. There is always the possibility that something you changed affected something else, and you didn't notice it. If this happens, you have documentation to refer to, so you can undo the changes. If a similar problem occurs in the future, you can refer to these documents to resolve the current problem, based on what was done the last time.

Historical information is very useful in the case of a network failure. It provides a reference for the network engineer to use to see what changes were most recently made to the network.

The Network Baseline

The easiest way to solve network problems is to be able to compare current configurations against previous configurations. This sounds easy, but it requires a lot of effort to get a system established to keep a historical baseline of your network. A historical *baseline* is simply a collection of network settings and configurations kept over time. This baseline makes it easy to locate changes or differences between a current configuration and a previous one.

Baselines provide the following types of information:

- Network topology
- Router configurations
- Network and routing protocols
- Traffic levels and network events
- Router and switch CPU and memory loads
- Applications
- Changes made to network configurations
- Historical information that documents previous troubleshooting sessions

There are a number of tools that can greatly assist you in establishing and maintaining your baseline information. Some of these—CiscoWorks 2000, HP Openview, and CiscoSecure—will be discussed in greater detail in Chapter 3. The use of baseline information can not only assist you in your troubleshooting efforts, it can also alert you to trends in rising utilization that if left unchecked will cause a problem in the future.

In addition to having all of this data available to you, it is helpful to have a checklist that you can refer to when you troubleshoot. A list may be created from baseline information if desired. Each individual knows their network and the types of changes that are made on it; each network's checklist would look different. For me to create a model checklist here and say that this is the checklist that everyone should use when resolving network problems would be pointless.

Summary

With the complexity of today's networks it is important to adhere to a troubleshooting model to aid in efficiently and effectively isolating and resolving network problems.

Different methods of problem isolation and the troubleshooting method itself help administrators pinpoint problem areas and foresee future problems. Troubleshooting skills are gained through experience. It is unreasonable to expect that you can jump in on your first network failure and be able to solve it quickly. Experience is the best teacher. Following a problem-solving model helps you to reach a timely solution to network failures. Knowing your network helps, but the "shooting-from-the-hip" style of troubleshooting is nowhere near as effective as a methodical and logical process.

Using the seven steps of the Cisco troubleshooting model in order is a clear, calculated, and logical way to make a network run more smoothly. The three methods of problem isolation (outside-in, inside-out, and divide-by-half) are more subjective and it is up to each individual to use the method they are comfortable with. It is important to document changes so you have a "trail" of what was done on the network. It also aids in reversing any changes that were made that adversely affected the network. Finally, having a network baseline is an invaluable troubleshooting tool. The information contained in a network baseline can be used for reference and comparison to aid in quick problem resolution.

Exam Essentials

Know the seven steps to the Cisco troubleshooting model as well as the function that each performs.   The seven steps to the Cisco troubleshooting model are: define the problem, gather facts, determine possible causes, develop an action plan, implement the action plan, observe results, and repeat if necessary. These steps define an effective step-by-step methodology for troubleshooting any problem.

Be able to apply the Cisco troubleshooting methodology to example situations.   You should know how to apply each step of the model in real-life scenarios. You should be able to determine what step in a troubleshooting scenario is next in the series or to correlate a task with the correct step in the process.

Know the reasons for maintaining a network baseline.   Maintaining a network baseline allows you to compare the normal operating characteristics of your network to the characteristics the network exhibits in a problem situation. It also allows for comparison of old configurations and reduces overall downtime.

Know the items that make up a network baseline.   The items that go into a network baseline are as follows: network topology, router configurations, network and routing protocols, traffic levels, router and switch CPU and memory levels, application changes, and historical information.

Key Terms

Before you take the exam, be certain you are familiar with the following terms:

action plan	iterations
baseline	observing results
boundary of dysfunctionality	outside-in troubleshooting
divide-by-half troubleshooting	problem definition
fact gathering	troubleshooting model
inside-out troubleshooting	

Review Questions

1. What are valid reasons for using a troubleshooting model? (Choose all that apply.)

   A. Networks are complex and require thorough troubleshooting.

   B. Difficult problems require a systematic and logical method.

   C. Problems are always resolved more quickly by using a systematic model.

   D. Cisco equipment requires diagnostic commands to be entered in a systematic manner.

2. What are the seven steps of the Cisco troubleshooting model? (Choose all that apply.)

   A. Document the changes.

   B. Create a baseline.

   C. Create an action plan.

   D. Undo the wrong changes.

   E. Define the problem.

   F. Observe changes.

   G. Observe results.

   H. Implement an action plan.

   I. Gather facts.

   J. Consider solutions.

   K. Consider possibilities.

   L. Define the problem boundary.

   M. Iterate the process.

3. Place the seven steps of the troubleshooting model in the correct order.

    A. Define Problem, Gather Facts, Consider Possibilities, Create and Implement Action Plan, Observe Results, Iterate Process

    B. Define Problem, Gather Facts, Create and Implement Action Plan, Observe Results, Iterate Process, Consider Possibilities

    C. Consider Possibilities, Gather Facts, Define Problem, Create and Implement Action Plan, Observe Results, Iterate Process

    D. Define Problem, Create and Implement Action Plan, Gather Facts, Consider Possibilities, Observe Results, Iterate Process

4. What is the main purpose of the Define Problem step in the problem-solving model?

    A. To consider the possible causes of the problem

    B. To establish the correct troubleshooting method to be used

    C. To form a specific and concise problem statement that directs the focus of the troubleshooting effort

    D. To exactly diagnose the problem

5. What are the two major reasons for gathering facts when troubleshooting? (Choose two answers.)

    A. To isolate the possible causes of the failure.

    B. To isolate the boundary of the problem.

    C. To use as a substitute for the `debug` command.

    D. It is required as part of the troubleshooting model.

6. Which of the following types of information are relevant while gathering facts for troubleshooting? (Choose all that apply.)

    A. Network baseline info

    B. The scope of the failure

    C. Whether the trouble is reproducible

    D. The timeline of the failure

    E. Symptoms of the failure

7. Why is it important to keep network baseline information for use in troubleshooting? (Choose all that apply.)

    A. It helps identify normal versus abnormal network activity.

    B. It allows you to identify new bugs in IOS.

    C. It is not that important, as all required information can be collected at the start of troubleshooting.

    D. It helps to minimize downtime by giving you a reference point of normal network behavior.

8. Why is establishing the failure boundary important? (Choose all that apply.)

    A. It focuses on the portion of the network or application that is failing.

    B. You know whether you can assign the task to someone else.

    C. It focuses on the relevant information.

    D. It narrows the possibilities for causes of the failure.

9. Why should you gather specific information before considering the possible causes of the failure?

    A. It is part of the process.

    B. It shortens the list of possible causes of failure.

    C. It provides sufficient documentation.

    D. All of the above.

10. A good action plan should follow which of the following guidelines? (Choose all that apply.)

    A. Make one change at a time.

    B. Make any changes necessary to fix the problem.

    C. Make non-service-impacting changes.

    D. Do not create security holes while implementing changes.

    E. Leave an avenue available, in case you need to back out of the changes you made.

11. During the implementation of an action plan, which of the following is true?

    A. Steps should be taken to ensure that additional problems are not caused.

    B. Network diagrams should be drawn.

    C. Traffic should be isolated to the problem area.

    D. You should gather additional facts to see if the current action plan needs to be altered.

12. What are the benefits of the iteration process? (Choose all that apply.)

    A. It allows small steps to be made to resolve a larger network failure.

    B. It takes longer to solve the problem, but it is effective.

    C. It allows the troubleshooting process to focus on a problem with more and more detail.

    D. It allows for ineffective changes to be removed.

13. What important information can be found in a network baseline? (Choose all that apply.)

    A. Router configurations

    B. Software versions

    C. Applications that run on the network

    D. Recent changes made to the network

    E. Network topology

    F. Inventory of network equipment

14. What should you do after implementing the action plan? (Choose all that apply.)

    A. Call the user and tell them the problem is solved.

    B. Document the changes.

    C. Verify that the changes worked without causing additional problems.

    D. Iterate the process.

15. SNMP access to a router is no longer working. After this problem has been defined, what would be the next step in troubleshooting according to the Cisco troubleshooting model?

    A. Check the copy of the backed-up configuration.

    B. Go through the access-list changes that were implemented last night.

    C. Ping the router.

    D. Search Cisco web site for SNMP bugs.

16. Which of the following is the correct method of isolating the boundary of dysfunctionality? (Choose all that apply.)

    A. Divide-by-half

    B. Outside-in

    C. Inside-out

    D. Step-by-step

17. Why should you make only one change at a time? (Choose all that apply.)

    A. It further isolates the problem.

    B. It makes it easier to back out if the change was ineffective.

    C. It eliminates one possible cause at a time.

    D. All of the above.

18. What is an important part of the iteration process? (Choose all that apply.)

    A. Creating more possible causes

    B. Gathering more information

    C. Homing in on the cause of the failure

    D. Creating a new action plan

19. You have implemented an action plan and observed the results, but the original problem still exists. What should your next step be?

   A. Repeat the problem-solving process, continuing to change more items until the problem is resolved.

   B. Determine whether there are other possibilities for the cause of the problem.

   C. Document the changes that have been made and check for bugs on CCO.

   D. Repeat the problem-solving process, undoing the changes that were made in the previous attempt.

20. Over the weekend, changes were made in your network to prepare it for an upcoming migration. On Monday, users complain of slow response time to a server. What steps should be followed to correct this problem?

   A. Back out the changes one at a time.

   B. Verify utilization on the user segment.

   C. Start working from the beginning of the troubleshooting model.

   D. Verify utilization on the server segment.

Answers to Review Questions

1. **A, B.** Problems may not always be resolved more quickly with a troubleshooting model, but the models are still very efficient. Cisco equipment has no such requirement for troubleshooting.

2. **C, E, G, H, I, K, M.** Creating a baseline is a good method for identifying problems when they occur, but this is not part of the troubleshooting method. Undoing wrong changes is part of the iteration process—reversing changes is done when a new action plan is created. You can't observe changes, just the results of changes. Solutions also belong to the action plan step of the troubleshooting method. Defining the problem boundary is part of the fact-gathering process. In addition, documentation should be updated once the changes are complete, but this is not considered part of the model.

3. **A.** You must create an action plan before its implementation. You cannot consider possibilities if you do not know what the problem is. You cannot create an action plan without knowing the details of the problem.

4. **C.** Without forming a specific problem statement, it is more difficult to identify possible solutions.

5. **A, B.** By isolating the possible causes and the boundary of the problem, the possible solutions can be more accurately drawn.

6. **A, B, C, D, E.** All of these items are very helpful when gathering information about network problems.

7. **A, D.** Baseline information is gathered while the network is functioning normally, not once a problem occurs. It will let you see what is normal in your network, as well as provide information that will help you find problems more quickly, thus minimizing downtime.

8. **A, C, D.** In the case of B, instead of assigning the task to someone else if the failure is outside of your jurisdiction, you should coordinate efforts to solve the problem.

9. **B.** To consider possible causes of failure without having specific information regarding the problem would lead to a very long list.

10. **A, C, D, E.** Any changes made should be included in the action plan and documentation. By doing that, you can make sure you hold to the requirements listed in the other answers.

11. A.   One of the important considerations in implementing the action plan is to make sure that other users are not impacted by the changes you are making. You should already have your network diagrams, and observing and analyzing the results of the action plan will tell you whether or not your action plan needs modification.

12. A, C, D.   The iteration process actually allows you to shorten the time it would normally take to fix a problem if you were "shooting from the hip."

13. A, B, C, D, E, F.   All answers depict valuable information that can or should be found in a network baseline.

14. B, C.   The customer should not be told that a solution has been implemented until it has been verified. Iteration is useless as well without observing the results of the changes first.

15. C.   After the problem is defined, the next step in troubleshooting is to gather facts. Determining whether or not the router responds to ping, telnet, etc., is part of the fact-gathering process. The other three options are not part of the fact-gathering stage, but rather they determine possible causes or are part of creating an action plan.

16. A, B, C.   All three of these methods require step-by-step execution.

17. D.   These are all correct answers. When multiple changes are made, you can't be sure whether you caused any observed results or which of the changes solved the problem.

18. B, C, D.   If you use A as part of the iteration process, you are doing something wrong and you need to go back to the very beginning and gather facts regarding the problem.

19. D.   If an action plan does not solve the problem, the changes that were made in order to implement this plan should be backed out before proceeding. This ensures that unnecessary changes are not made to the network.

20. C.   Though it is tempting to start backing out changes, the correct answer is to start the Cisco troubleshooting model. The changes from the weekend will indeed need to be looked at as the possible cause of the slowness; however, the cause could be something totally unrelated.

Protocol Attributes

TOPICS COVERED IN THIS CHAPTER INCLUDE:

- ✓ Demonstrate knowledge of troubleshooting targets for connection-oriented and connectionless protocols.

- ✓ Demonstrate knowledge of common data-link layer characteristics and key troubleshooting targets likely to be found in a campus network.

- ✓ Demonstrate knowledge of connection sequences and key troubleshooting targets within TCP/IP, Novell IPX, and AppleTalk.

- ✓ Use proven problem-isolation techniques to list the symptoms of common TCP/IP problems.

As you know, to successfully troubleshoot network problems, it is important to have a good understanding of how network components, including PCs and servers, communicate with each other. Without this basic knowledge, troubleshooting a network problem is like trying to read a book in a foreign language. The information is there, but it just isn't comprehensible. Although the model discussed in Chapter 1 provides the method of retrieving all of the necessary information, the data is useless without an understanding of the information presented.

This chapter is a review of the protocols that are used by Layers 2, 3, and 4 of the OSI model. We briefly review the seven layers of the OSI model, and then discuss how they communicate with one another. We then discuss Layer 2 and Layer 3 protocols. More-specific information on some of the material covered here can be found in later chapters, cross-referenced here where appropriate.

The OSI Reference Model

This section is a review of the OSI model, which was originally discussed in *CCNA: Cisco Certified Network Associate Study Guide, 3rd ed.*, by Todd Lammle (ISBN 0-7821-4167-6, Sybex, 2002). The OSI model (or the Open Systems Interconnection reference model) is the template used to design applications or protocols that allow nonhomogenous computers or networks to communicate with one another. The ISO (International Organization for Standardization) developed the OSI model.

The OSI model consists of seven layers. Each layer communicates directly with its adjacent layers, as well as with the corresponding layer of the destination system (depicted in Figure 2.1). Communication between layers facilitates the transfer of data up and down the OSI model. Communication between the corresponding layers of the source system and the destination system enables two heterogeneous networks or computers to understand each other.

FIGURE 2.1   OSI layer communication scheme

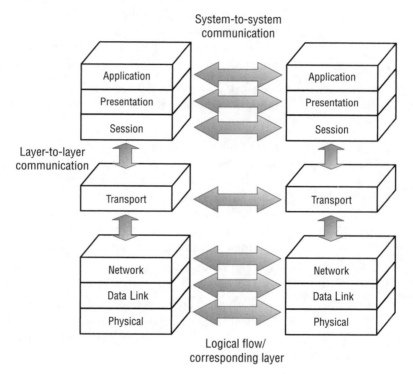

The OSI template defines the services and roles that each layer is to provide. Because each layer provides different services and functions, the layers need to communicate so that the data can be transmitted up and down the seven layers and onto the destination system. The following list summarizes the responsibility of each of the seven layers, starting from the Application layer and working down to the Physical layer:

Application   This is the user and application interface. The Application layer is responsible for data exchange and job management. It also handles file, print, message, database, and application services.

Presentation   This layer negotiates syntax, so it is responsible for the proper method of presenting the data to the Application layer. Some of the functions are compression and decompression, and encryption and decryption of data.

Session   This layer is responsible for coordinating communication between applications, which it does through dialogue-control methods.

Transport   This layer takes care of end-to-end communications. It is responsible for connection to the destination system, as well as packet segmentation and assembly. The Transport layer includes both connection-oriented and connectionless protocols (for example, TCP and UDP).

Network   This layer defines the topology of the network through the use of logical addressing. Routing protocols use this information to route packets.

Data-Link   This layer takes all of the data that is accumulated as packets are handed from one layer to the next, and then packages it into frames. This layer equates the Network layer address (IP address) to a data-link address, or MAC address, of the next hop. Once the physical address is known, the frame is sent to that address. The receiving interface uses the Data-Link layer to extract the packet from the frame, discards the frame, and then sends the packet up to the Network layer.

Physical   This layer sends and receives bits with values of ones or zeros. The Physical layer is in charge of determining how it sends these values. If the physical connection between two machines is fiber optic, then the Physical layer has to use light to transmit the ones and zeros. If the connection is electrical, then electrical signals are sent to represent the ones and zeros.

You saw how the logical data flow of the OSI model works, but look at Figure 2.2, in which you can see the actual data flow. The figure depicts data that is handed from the Application layer all the way down to the Physical layer. At that point, the data is transmitted across any variety of physical media to the next hop, or destination system. Once the ones and zeros arrive at the Physical layer of the destination system, the information is sent to Layer 2. This layer discards the frame, and then the extracted packet is handed up to the Network layer. The network packet header is stripped off, and the resulting packet is handed up to the Transport layer. This process is repeated for each layer until it arrives at the Application layer.

FIGURE 2.2 Data flow through the OSI model

System-to-system communication

Data flow

Application

Presentation

Session

Transport

Network

Data Link

Physical

Actual data flow

Application

Presentation

Session

Transport

Network

Data Link

Physical

Data flow

Binary 1's and 0's

Now that each layer of the OSI reference model has been explained briefly, you need to focus on the functions of each layer in detail. This detail provides the necessary background and information to effectively troubleshoot network problems that occur within specific layers of the OSI model.

Global Protocol Classifications

As mentioned before, each layer of the OSI model utilizes specific protocols that enable the layer to perform the necessary functions and communicate with each adjacent layer. Each protocol has different properties, based on the functions that it needs to accomplish. Throughout all seven layers, there are two major protocol classifications: connection-oriented and connectionless.

Connection-Oriented Protocols

Connection-oriented protocols are protocols that contain inherent functions that control the connection as well as data transfer. These functions are very detailed in the procedures that are followed to enable reliable and error-free data transfer. When a source open system needs to transfer data to a destination open system, the connection-oriented protocols actually establish a communication pipe. The *pipe*, as it is called here, is nothing more than a logical connection between two open systems. A great deal of information is used to establish this communication pipe, however.

In order to establish a connection, the two open systems must share certain information that allows them to negotiate terms and finally establish a link. The information includes the common protocol that will be used, required resources, and available resources. Look at Figure 2.3. This figure shows the steps taken as communication is established between two open systems when using TCP, a connection-oriented protocol.

FIGURE 2.3 Link establishment and data transfer using a connection-oriented protocol

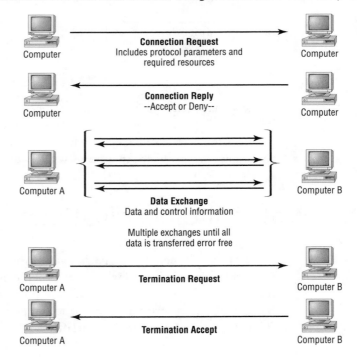

The originating system first sends a connection request to the destination system. This request contains information that the two systems need to agree upon before the connection can be established. Some of the information includes the common protocol, protocol parameters, and required resources. *Protocol parameters* are the window sizes and other possible parameters. The *window size* is the amount of data that a station can transmit before needing an acknowledgment from the destination system that all the data was received without error, or that errors existed and part of the data will need to be retransmitted. *Required resources* can include necessary bandwidth, specific port numbers, or other network resources.

The destination system receives this request; if it can accommodate the common protocol, protocol attributes, and required resources, it replies with a connection accept. If, for some reason, the destination system cannot accommodate any of the requirements sent by the originating system, it responds with a connection deny. A denied connection may result from a blocked port on the destination system, insufficient bandwidth between the systems, or other unavailable requested resources.

Assuming that a connection is established between the two systems, data and control information is exchanged during the life of the connection. This data exchange can be considered a dialogue. First, the originating system sends data until the window size is reached. It then waits for a response from the destination system. The destination system sends control information that informs the originating system what needs to happen next. The transmission can be an acknowledgment that all data in the transmission was received without error and that the originating system can send the next batch of data. In addition, the destination system can also send a message informing the originating system that some of the data was missing, corrupted, or had other errors that require the data to be retransmitted.

This procedure can be summarized with the description of three processes:

Sequenced data transfer   Each packet of a session is assigned a sequence number.

Flow control   Acknowledgments are required after a specified amount of data has been sent.

Error control   Verification of contiguous and non-erroneous packets.

You will learn more about each of these three processes in the following sections.

Sequenced Data Transfer

Systems send protocol data units (PDUs) to one another, and each level of the OSI model has its own type of PDU. Figure 2.4 shows the PDU names for all seven OSI layers. For example, the Application layer's PDU name is a Layer 7 PDU. Although this convention can be used for all layers, some layers use other names as well. For instance, a Layer 3 PDU can be called a *packet* and a Layer 2 PDU is called a *frame*. When a system sends data to another system, the data has to be segmented so that it fits the MTU (maximum transmission unit). Therefore, several frames may be needed to transfer the original data. Connection-oriented protocols assign a sequence number to each outgoing and incoming PDU.

FIGURE 2.4 OSI layer PDU names

Figure 2.5 shows you how sequencing works. There is a possibility that the destination system will receive the PDUs out of order. If this happens, the

protocol on the destination system uses the sequence numbers to put the PDUs back into the correct order so the original data is obtained.

FIGURE 2.5   Connection-oriented PDU sequencing

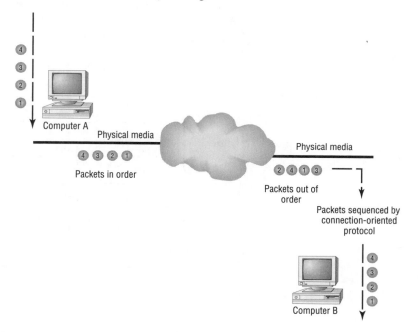

Flow Control

Although flow control was briefly described previously, this section contains more detail. Flow control is responsible for ensuring that the transmitting station does not send data faster than the receiving station can process it. This is done by establishing a window size for the transportation.

Look at Figure 2.6 to see how windowing works. Notice that the originating system sends out a specified number of PDUs. Once that number is reached, the originating system waits for a response from the destination system. After the response is received, the system continues to transmit data.

FIGURE 2.6 Flow and error control

Error Control

Error control is responsible for checking each transmission and verifying that all of the PDUs are contiguous and not erroneous. If there are missing or damaged PDUs, the destination will not send an ACK packet for the previous transmission. (Refer to Figure 2.6.)

Once all of the data is transferred without errors, the originating system sends a termination request, which tells the destination system that no more data needs to be transmitted. The destination system then responds with a termination acknowledgment.

As you can see, both systems do a lot of communicating, aside from the exchange of data. From the connection request to the termination acknowledgment, every exchange is accompanied with control information that keeps the data transfer reliable and error-free. Table 2.1 gives examples of several connection-oriented protocols.

TABLE 2.1 Connection-Oriented Protocols

Protocol Name	Protocol Description
ATM	ATM (Asynchronous Transfer Mode) uses virtual circuits from one node to another. The permanent virtual circuits, or PVCs, are established by using connection-oriented procedures.
TCP	TCP (Transmission Control Protocol) was developed to overcome reliability problems. It uses flow and error control extensively.
Novell SPX	Novell SPX (Sequenced Packet Exchange) is Novell's implementation of a network protocol that provides error-free and reliable data transport.
AppleTalk ATP	Apple uses ATP (AppleTalk Transaction Protocol) to provide connectivity between two socket clients. It is based on the request/response interaction of the two clients.

Connectionless Protocols

Now that connection-oriented protocols have been discussed, we'll move on to connectionless protocols. *Connectionless protocols* differ from connection-oriented protocols because they do not provide for flow control.

Figure 2.7 shows you how connectionless protocols work. This figure looks somewhat like Figure 2.3, except that there are no steps that involve a connection setup or termination. It is also missing the flow and error control information sent by the receiving system.

FIGURE 2.7 Connectionless data transfer

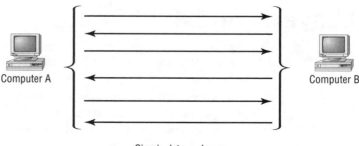

Computer A   Computer B

Simple data exchange
No flow or error control is used.

Connectionless protocols do not send data relative to any other data units. The data included in the PDU must contain enough information for the PDU to get to its destination and for the receiving system to properly process it. Because there is no established connection, flow and error control cannot be implemented. Without flow and error control, the originating system has no way of knowing whether all of the transmitted data was received by the destination system without errors. Table 2.2 shows examples of connectionless protocols.

TABLE 2.2 Connectionless Protocols

Protocol Name	Protocol Description
UDP	UDP (User Datagram Protocol) is a connectionless protocol used by IP.
AppleTalk DDP	DDP (Datagram Delivery Protocol) is a connectionless network protocol used for service between two network sockets.
Novell IPX	Novell IPX (Internetwork Packet Exchange) is Novell's Layer 3 protocol.

In this section, you learned the difference between connection-oriented and connectionless protocols. These protocol characteristics may be found at any level of the OSI model. The Transport layer, or Layer 4, of the OSI model is most notably known for the functions it provides by using connection-oriented or connectionless protocols. Some of the Transport layer's responsibilities are session establishment, flow and error control, and session teardown. The following sections begin discussions of protocols that are specific to the Network and Data-Link layers, respectively.

OSI Layer 3 and 4: IP Routed Protocols

The Network layer is used by the Transport layer to provide the best end-to-end services and path for PDU delivery. This means that the Network layer also uses protocols to accomplish this task. This section discusses seven different protocols that are used within Layer 3 of the OSI model. Some of these protocols use protocols within them for finer granularity of certain functions.

There are also some other differences between these seven protocols. Some are routing protocols and others are protocols that are routed by the routing protocols. Routing protocols are used to exchange route information and to create a network topology, thus enabling routing decisions to be made. The routed protocols are protocols that contain information regarding the end systems, how communication is established, and other information relevant to the transfer of data.

Internet Protocol (IP)

It is important to distinguish between the Internet Protocol suite and the actual Internet Protocol that is used in the Network layer of the OSI model. The IP suite consists of several different protocols that are implemented at different levels of the OSI model.

The *Internet Protocol (IP)* is a Network-layer protocol of the Internet Protocol suite. It is used to allow routing among internetworks and heterogeneous systems. IP is a connectionless protocol, even though it can provide error reporting, and performs the segmentation and reassembly of PDUs.

IP Packet Structure

Now that you know what IP is, look at the actual packet structure in more detail. Following is an IP packet that was broken down by EtherPeek. The entire header has six layers, and each layer consists of 32 bits. Look at each section of the header and get an explanation for each.

```
IP Header - Internet Protocol Datagram
   Version:                4
   Header Length:          5
   Precedence:             0
   Type of Service:        %000
   Unused:                 %00
   Total Length:           60
   Identifier:             0
   Fragmentation Flags:    %000
   Fragment Offset:        0
   Time To Live:           2
   IP Type:                0x58  IGRP
   Header Checksum:        0x10dc
   Source IP Address:      205.124.250.7
   Dest. IP Address:       224.0.0.10
No Internet Datagram Options
```

At this point, we will define each of the key fields that appear above. As you can see, the packet IP header starts out with the `Version` field. Right now, the standard is IPv4. The version parameter uses four bits of the 32 bits available.

The next field is the `IP Header Length`, or IHL. This field also uses another four bits and it specifies the datagram header length in 32-bit words.

The `Type of Service` (`TOS`) follows the IHL. This field uses eight bits and indicates datagram priority and how other OSI layers are to handle the datagram once they receive it.

Following the `TOS` is the `Total Length` parameter. This field indicates how long the packet is, including header and payload or data. The length is in units of bytes. The field itself uses 16 bits, which brings the total for the first layer to 32 bits. Because 32 bits have been used, move on to the next layer.

The second layer begins with the `Identifier` or `identification` field. The `Identifier` is a 16-bit field that contains an integer value that identifies the packet. It is like a sequencing number that is used when reassembling datagram fragments.

The `Flags` field follows, using only three bits. This field is used to control fragmentation of a datagram. If the datagram may be fragmented, the first bit has a value of 0. A value of 1 is assigned to the first bit if the datagram is not to be fragmented. The second bit is used to indicate the last fragment of a fragmented datagram. The third bit is an undefined bit and is set to 0.

`Fragment Offset` follows the `Flags` field. This value uses 13 bits and specifies the fragment's position in the original datagram. The position is measured from the beginning of the datagram and marked off in 64-bit increments. This again brings you to 32 bits, so you must move down to the next layer in the IP packet.

The third layer begins with the `Time-to-Live` (`TTL`) field. This field is a counter whose units are measured in hops. A starting value is given and it counts decrements by one as it passes through each hop or router. Once the value of this field is 0, the packet is discarded. This field uses eight bits.

The `protocol` field (`IP Type`) follows the TTL parameter. This field tells Layer 3 which upper-layer protocol is supposed to receive the packet. It uses a decimal value to specify the protocol. This field uses eight bits.

The `Header Checksum` field finishes the third layer. The checksum is used to help verify the integrity of the IP header. This field uses 16 bits.

Layers 4 and 5 are 32 bits long, Because IP addresses use four octets—eight bits each—the IP address occupies the entire level. Layer 4 is reserved for the source address, and the fifth layer is reserved for the destination address.

An `Options` field occupies the sixth and final layer of the header. The field needs to be 32 bits long, so any additional empty bits are padded.

Figure 2.8 gives a good visual representation of the IP packet structure.

FIGURE 2.8 The IP packet structure

0	4	8	16	19	31

Version	IHL	Type of service	Total length	
Identification			Flags	Fragment offset
TTL		Protocol	Header checksum	
Source IP address				
Destination IP address				
Options				Padding

IP Addressing Review

No review of TCP/IP networking would be complete without a review of IP addressing. In this section we will not go over the basics of IP addressing; rather, we will focus more on the application of *Variable Length Subnet Masking (VLSM)* and the calculation of networks as it pertains to troubleshooting in an IP environment. If you need a more detailed explanation, see *CCNA: Cisco Certified Network Associate Study Guide, 3rd ed.*, by Todd Lammle (ISBN 0-7821-4167-6, Sybex, 2002).

As internetworks grew and address space became scarcer, several methodologies were devised to make the address space go farther. One of these methodologies was VLSM. In older routing protocols, if you wanted to subnet a major network, you had to make all of the subnets the same size. This was because the routing protocols passed only network information and did not include subnet mask information. Newer routing protocols pass subnet information along with the individual routes, allowing for the use of VLSM. This enables better use of address space by allowing network administrators to size the subnets based on the need. For example, a point-to-point connection has only two nodes on it, and as such only needs two host addresses. Without VLSM, if your standard subnet mask was 255.255.255.0, a /24 subnet, 256 "addresses" would be used on this point-to-point connection (though 256 addresses are used, only 254 are usable by hosts). With VLSM, this same connection could use a 255.255.255.252 mask, /30, using only four addresses—two for the hosts, one for the subnet, and one for the broadcast address.

One drawback to VLSM is the complexity that it adds to the network. When there was only one mask used in an environment, the network administrators could easily memorize the subnet information; with VLSM, however, subnet information needs to be calculated based on the individual situation. Miscalculation of the subnets can lead to communication problems if machines are assigned outside a subnet boundary or on a subnet or broadcast address.

Internet Control Message Protocol (ICMP)

The *Internet Control Message Protocol (ICMP)* is used throughout IP networks. ICMP was designed to provide routing failure information to the source system. This protocol provides four different types of feedback that are used to make the IP routing environment more efficient. These feedback types are as follows:

Reachability   This is determined by using ICMP echo and reply messages.

Redirects   These messages tell hosts to redirect traffic or choose alternative routes.

Timeouts   These messages indicate that a packet's designated TTL is expired.

Router Discovery   These messages discover directly connected routers' IP addresses. Router discovery actually uses ICMP Router Discovery Protocol to do this. This passive method gathers directly connected IP addresses without having to understand specific routing protocols.

Here is a look at a couple of ICMP packets (echo request and reply):

```
ICMP - Internet Control Messages Protocol
   ICMP Type:              8  Echo Request
   Code:                   0
   Checksum:               0x495c
   Identifier:             0x0200
   Sequence Number:        512
   ICMP Data Area:
   abcdefghijklmnop    61 62 63 64 65 66 67 68 69 6a 6b 6c
      6d 6e 6f 70
   qrstuvwabcdefghi    71 72 73 74 75 76 77 61 62 63 64 65
      66 67 68 69
Frame Check Sequence:  0x342e3235
ICMP - Internet Control Messages Protocol
```

ICMP Type:	0 *Echo Reply*	
Code:	0	
Checksum:	0x515c	
Identifier:	0x0200	
Sequence Number:	512	
ICMP Data Area:		
abcdefghijklmnop 6d 6e 6f 70	61 62 63 64 65 66 67 68 69 6a 6b 6c	
qrstuvwabcdefghi 66 67 68 69	71 72 73 74 75 76 77 61 62 63 64 65	
Frame Check Sequence:	0x342e3235	

As with the IP packet structure, the ICMP structure is similar in that it has a type, checksum, identifier, and sequence number. The names differ a little, but have the same functionality.

Transmission Control Protocol (TCP)

The *Transmission Control Protocol (TCP)*, a connection-oriented protocol on the Transport layer that provides a reliable delivery of data, is an integral part of the IP suite. Look at the structure of the TCP packet. The following EtherPeek frame was taken during a POP3 transaction:

```
TCP - Transmission Control Protocol
```

Source Port:	110 *POP3*
Destination Port:	1097
Sequence Number:	997270908
Ack Number:	7149472
Offset:	5
Reserved:	%000000
Code:	%010000
	Ack is valid
Window:	8760
Checksum:	0x8064
Urgent Pointer:	0
No TCP Options	
No More POP Command or Reply Data	
Extra bytes (Padding):	
UUUUUU	55 55 55 55 55 55
Frame Check Sequence:	0x04020000

This structure is similar to the IP packet structure. The TCP header is 32 bits long and has a minimum length of five layers, but can be six layers deep when options are specified. The first layer starts with `Source` and `Destination Port` fields. Each of these fields is 16 bits long.

A `Sequence Number` field occupies all of the second layer, meaning that it is 32 bits long. TCP is a connection-oriented protocol and this field is used to keep track of the different requests that have been sent.

The third layer is a 32-bit length field that contains the acknowledgment sequence number that is used to track responses.

The fourth layer begins with the `Offset` field, which is four bits and specifies the number of 32-bit words present in the header. Six bits are reserved for future use (this is called the `Reserved` field). This field follows the `Offset` field.

The next field, called the `Flag` or `Code` field, is also a six-bit field, and it contains control information. Look at Table 2.3 for an explanation of the six bits within the `Flag` field.

The `Window` field specifies the buffer size for incoming data. Once the buffer is filled, the sending system must wait for a response from the receiving system. This field is 16 bits long.

Layer 5 of the TCP header begins with the `Checksum` Parameter, which also occupies 16 bits. It is used to verify the integrity of the transmitted data.

The `Urgent Pointer` field references the last byte of data, so the receiver knows how much urgent data it will receive. This is also a 16-bit field.

Finally, there is the `Option` field, which must also be 32 bits long. If the options do not occupy 32 bits, padding is added to reach the correct length.

TABLE 2.3 Flag Bit Assignments

Bit number (right to left)	Control Information	Definition
1	URG	Urgent pointer is significant.
2	ACK	Acknowledgment pointer is significant.
3	PSH	Push function.
4	RST	Reset connection.

TABLE 2.3 Flag Bit Assignments *(continued)*

Bit number (right to left)	Control Information	Definition
5	SYN	Synchronize sequence numbers.
6	FIN	No more data to transfer.

User Datagram Protocol (UDP)

The *User Datagram Protocol (UDP)* is a connectionless protocol on the Transport layer of the OSI model. The overall structure of UDP is simpler than TCP, as UDP is connectionless and therefore does not have overhead to maintain connection information. UDP is commonly used for real-time applications such as video and voice. In these time-sensitive applications, when a packet is lost or corrupted there is not enough time for the applications to recognize that there is a missing packet and request the packet be resent, and for this retransmitted packet to arrive. Therefore, the overhead that comes with TCP is not warranted for this type of data transfer. The following frame snippet was taken using EtherPeek and is of a DNS request:

```
UDP - User Datagram Protocol
    Source Port:      1213
    Destination Port: 53 domain
    Length:           38
    Checksum:         0xBFBA
```

As can be seen by the above, all of the overhead that is associated with the connection-oriented nature of the TCP frame, such as sequence and acknowledgment number, has been removed in UDP. As a result, the UDP packet is condensed down to four fields.

The first two of these fields, `Source` and `Destination Port`, are both 16 bits long. The `Destination Port` field must be filled in with the destination port of the service that is being requested; however, the `Source Port` field only needs a value when the sending station needs a reply from the receiver. If the conversation is unidirectional in nature and the source port is not used, it should be set to 0. If a reply is needed, the receiving station will reply to the sender on the port indicated in the original packet's source field.

The last two fields in a UDP header are Length and Checksum. Like the source and destination port information, the Length and Checksum fields are both 16 bits long. The Length field shows the total number of bytes in the UDP packet, including the UDP header and user data. The Checksum, though optional, allows the receiving station to verify the integrity of the UDP header as well as the data that is contained in the packet. If not used, it should be set to a value of 0.

OSI Layer 3: IP Routing Protocols

Now that we have discussed the routed protocols associated with IP, we will look at the routing protocols. The major routing protocols being examined are RIP, IGRP, EIGRP, OSPF, and BGP. Each has its own advantages and disadvantages that will be discussed in this section. Specific troubleshooting methodologies for these routing protocols will be covered in Chapter 6.

Routing Information Protocol (RIP)

The Routing Information Protocol (RIP) is a distance-vector routing protocol. The metric used by RIP is the *hop count*, which specifies the number of steps or nodes that a packet must transit in order to reach the destination host.

The major problem with RIP is that it has a hop-count limit. The maximum hop limit that the packet can travel is 15 hops. If the destination exceeds 15 hops, the destination is tagged as unreachable. This is good for small networks because it also helps prevent the count-to-infinity in a routing loop, but it is inefficient for today's Internet.

Now that you know a little about how RIP works, look at the packet structure in Figure 2.9. The packet is 24 bytes long. RIP uses five parameters to define packet information. The packet is divided into nine fields, and zeros are used to pad the packet to the full 24 bytes.

FIGURE 2.9 RIP packet structure

23	20	16	12	8	6	4	2 1 0
F	0	0	E	0	D	0	B A

Table 2.4 shows a legend of the five different parameters used within the RIP packet. As you can see from the figure, some of the fields are empty. They are just padded with zeros.

TABLE 2.4 RIP Parameters

Parameter Key	Description
A	Command: Identifies the packet as a request (value = 1) or a response (value = 2). Requests tell the receiving router to send its route table information. Response packets include the route table information.
B	Version number: Specifies the version of RIP being used.
D	Address family identifier: Address family type. This means which protocol is carrying the RIP packet.
E	Address: The 32-bit IP address.
F	Metric: The hop count to the destination system.

RIP version 1 is a classful protocol, which means it doesn't include any subnet information about the network with route information. However, RIP version 2 is classless, allowing it to function in environments using VLSM. More information on troubleshooting RIP will be covered in Chapter 6.

Interior Gateway Routing Protocol (IGRP)

The *Interior Gateway Routing Protocol (IGRP)* is a Cisco proprietary routing protocol that uses a distance-vector algorithm because it uses a vector (a one-dimensional array) of information to calculate the best path. This vector or metric can consist of five elements:

- Bandwidth
- Delay
- Load
- Reliability
- MTU

By default, only two of the elements are used in the calculation of the metric: bandwidth and delay. Bandwidth is the minimum bandwidth over the path, and delay is the cumulative delay over the path. IGRP is intended to replace RIP and create a stable, quickly converging protocol that will scale with increased network growth.

IGRP Features and Operation

IGRP has several features included in the algorithm—these features and brief descriptions can be found in Table 2.5. The features were added to make IGRP more stable, and a few were created to deal with routing updates and make network convergence happen faster. It also should be noted that IGRP is a classful routing protocol.

TABLE 2.5   IGRP Features

Feature	Description
Configurable metrics	Metrics involved in the algorithm responsible for calculating route information. They may be configured by the user.
Flash update	Updates are sent out prior to the default time setting. This occurs when the metrics for a route change.
Poison reverse updates	Implemented to prevent routing loops. These updates place a route in *holddown.* Holddown means that the router won't accept any new route information on a given route for a certain period.
Unequal-cost load balancing	Allows packets to be shared/distributed across multiple paths.

More information on IGRP and troubleshooting IGRP issues is covered in Chapter 6.

Enhanced IGRP (EIGRP)

Enhanced IGRP (EIGRP) is a hybrid link-state and distance-vector routing protocol that was created to resolve some of the problems with IGRP. These problems include the fact that the entire route table is sent when changes are made in the network and that there is a lack of formal neighbor relationships with connected routers. Like IGRP, EIGRP is also a proprietary Cisco routing protocol. EIGRP is a hybrid of both link-state and distance-vector routing algorithms, which brings the best of both worlds together. In addition to IP routing, EIGRP also has the ability to route IPX and AppleTalk. This will be discussed in more detail in the IPX and AppleTalk chapters, Chapters 9 and 10 respectively.

EIGRP's specific features are detailed in Table 2.6. The features offered by EIGRP make it a stable and scalable protocol.

TABLE 2.6 EIGRP Features

Feature	Description
Route tagging	Distinguishes routes learned via different EIGRP sessions.
Formal neighbor relationships	Uses the Hello protocol to establish peering.
Incremental routing updates	Only changes are advertised, instead of the entire route table.
Classless routing	EIGRP supports subnet and VLSM information.
Configurable metrics	Metric information can be set through configuration commands.
Equal-cost load balancing	Allows traffic to be sent equally across multiple connections.

To aid in calculating the best route and load sharing, EIGRP utilizes several databases of information. These databases are as follows:

- The route database, where the best routes are stored

- The topology database, where all route information resides

- A neighbor table, which is used to house information concerning other EIGRP neighbors

Each of these databases exists for IP-EIGRP, IPX-EIGRP, and AT-EIGRP or AppleTalk-EIGRP. Therefore, it is possible for EIGRP to have nine active databases when all three protocols are configured on the router.

Route Tagging

EIGRP functions within defined autonomous systems on a router. It is possible for multiple sessions of EIGRP to run on a single router. Each session is distinguished by the AS number assigned to it. Routers that have EIGRP sessions running under the same AS number speak to and share their routing information with the other routers in the same AS. Routes learned via other routers within the AS are considered to be internal EIGRP routes. It is also possible for one AS session to learn routes from a different EIGRP AS session through redistribution (redistribution is covered later in this section). When this occurs, the routes are tagged as being learned from an external EIGRP session. Each type of route is assigned its own administrative distance value.

Neighbor Relationships

The manner in which EIGRP establishes and maintains neighbor relationships is derived through its link-state properties. EIGRP uses the Hello protocol (similar to OSPF) to establish and maintain peering relationships with directly connected routers. Hello packets are sent between EIGRP routers to determine the state of the connection between them. Once the neighbor relation is established via the Hello protocol, the routers can exchange route information.

Each router establishes a neighbor table, in which it stores important information regarding the neighbors that are directly connected to it. The information consists of the neighbor's IP address, hold time interval, smooth round trip timer (SRTT), and queue information. These data are used to help determine when the link state changes.

When two routers initialize communication, their entire route tables are shared. Thereafter, only changes to the route table are propagated. These changes are shared with all directly connected EIGRP-speaking routers. The steps are summarized as follows:

1. Hello packets are multicast out of all the router's interfaces that are participating in the routing process.

2. Replies to the Hello packets include all routes in the neighbor router's topology database, including the metrics. Routes that are learned from the originating router are not included in the reply.

3. The originating router acknowledges the update to each neighbor via an ACK packet.

4. The topology database is then updated with the newly received information.

5. Once the topology database is updated, the originating router then advertises its entire table to all the new neighbors.

6. Neighbor routers acknowledge the receipt of the route information from the originating router by sending back an ACK packet.

These steps are used in the initialization of EIGRP neighbors; they change somewhat when only updates are sent to existing neighbors.

Route Calculation and Updates

Because EIGRP uses distance-vector and link-state information when calculating routes by using the DUAL algorithm, convergence is much faster than with IGRP. The trick behind the convergence speed is that EIGRP calculates new routes only when a change in the network directly affects the routes contained in its route table.

Like IGRP, EIGRP's metric can be based off of bandwidth, delay, load, reliability, and MTU. By default, only bandwidth and delay are used; however, the user has the option to use the remaining items if they wish. To make that a little clearer, look at Figure 2.10, in which you see three routers meshed, and each has an Ethernet segment connected as well.

It is important to understand the difference between accepting a routing update and calculating a new route. If a change occurs to a network that is directly connected to a router, all of the relevant information is used to *calculate* a new metric and route entry for it. After the router calculates the new route, it is advertised to the neighbors.

Using Figure 2.10 as the example, assume that Ethernet 0 on Router C is very congested because of high traffic volumes. Also assume that load has been added to the metric calculation for all routers in this mesh. Router C then uses the distance and link information to calculate a new metric for network 172.16.30.0. With the new metric in place, the change is propagated to Routers A and B. To understand completely, you need to recognize that the other routers don't do any calculation—they just receive the update. Routers A and B don't need to calculate a new route for network 172.16.30.0 because they learn it from Router C.

FIGURE 2.10 Route updates vs. calculation

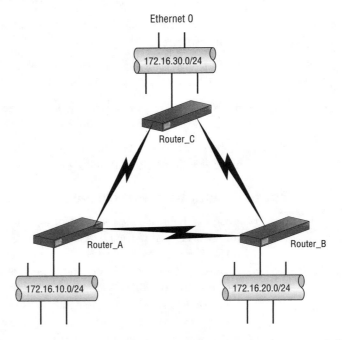

On the other hand, if the link between Router A and Router C becomes congested, both routers have to calculate a new route metric. The change is then advertised to Router B by both Routers A and C.

Topology and Route State Information

The topology database stores all routes and metrics known via adjacent routers. By default, six routes can be stored for each destination network. If there are multiple routes to the destination, the router chooses the route with the best (lowest) metric and installs this into the routing table. It is possible for multiple routes to a destination to have the same metric. In these cases, assuming these routes have the best metric, they all will be installed in the routing table, and traffic destined to this network will be load-shared across them. The remaining routes will then serve as backups for the primary route if they meet the feasibility condition. While the best route is being chosen for a destination, the route is considered to be in an *active* state. After the route is chosen, the route status changes to *passive*.

Information given in Table 2.7 closely, though not exactly, represents what is contained in an actual topology table. The `Status` field shows whether a new route is being calculated or whether a primary route has been selected. In our example, the route is in passive state because it has already selected the primary route.

TABLE 2.7   Topology Table Information

Status	Route—Adjacent Router's Address (Metrics)	Number of Successors	Feasible Distance
P	10.10.10.0/24 via 10.1.2.6 (*3611648*/3609600) via 10.5.6.6 (4121600/3609600) via 10.6.7.6 (5031234/3609600)	1 (Router C)	3611648

Updates and Changes

EIGRP also has link-state properties. One of these properties is that it propagates only changes in the route table instead of sending an entire new route table to its neighbors. When changes occur in the network, a regular distance-vector protocol sends the entire route table to neighbors. By avoiding sending the entire route table, less bandwidth is consumed. Neighboring routers don't have to reinitialize the entire route table, which would cause convergence issues. They just have to insert the new route changes. This is one of the big enhancements over IGRP.

Updates can follow two paths. If a route update contains a better metric or a new route, the routers simply exchange the information. If the update contains information that a network is unavailable or the metric is worse than before, an alternate path must be found. The flow chart in Figure 2.11 describes the steps that must be taken to choose a new route.

FIGURE 2.11 Handling route changes

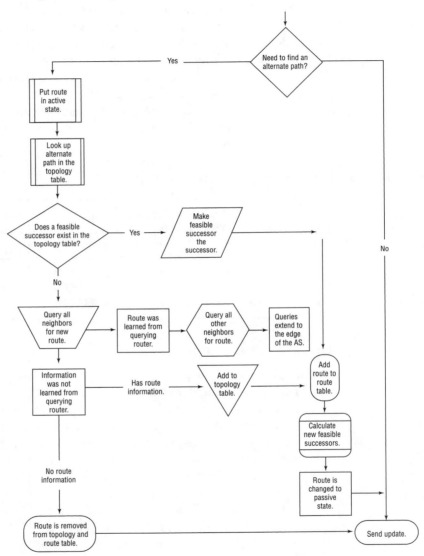

The router first searches the topology database for feasible successors. If no feasible successors are found, a multicast request is sent to all adjacent routers. Each router then responds to the query. Depending on how the router answers, different paths are taken. After the intermediate steps are taken, two final actions can occur. If route information is eventually found, the route is added to the route table and an update is sent. If the responses from the adjacent routers do not contain any route information, the route is removed from the topology and route tables. After the route table is updated, the new information is sent to all adjacent routers via a multicast.

 Real World Scenario

To Redistribute or Not to Redistribute

All major routing protocols that are in use today, through one method or another, ensure a loop-free topology as part of their basic operation. This methodology is fine for environments that are running only a single routing protocol; however, in today's more complex networks it is becoming more common to find multiple routing protocols in use in the same environment. This may be due to the need for special features available only in one protocol, or the need to connect to another company or ISP that is running a protocol different than the one you are running internally.

No matter the reason, when multiple protocols are running and there is a need to share routing information between the systems, some manner of route redistribution is needed. And when redistribution between the two protocols is occurring, there is a potential for routing loops to be introduced. In order to ensure that routing loops do not occur, several approaches can be taken. The first approach is to use a default route. This is a common method used for connections to the Internet. As you are not accepting any routes from the other routing protocol, there is no chance that your own routes will be sent back to you.

The next approach is to redistribute only in one direction. As was the case with the default route, there is no chance that you will accept your own routes from the neighboring router, as the redistribution is occurring in only one direction. One minor issue that must be taken into account in both of these scenarios is how the return traffic is going to come back. In most cases this is done through the use of a static route or routes.

The final potential solution to this issue is the use of a single bidirectional redistribution point or redundant bidirectional redistribution points. In the single redistribution point solution, the probability of your own routes being sent back to you is very low. However, this can occur if the network you are connecting to has a routing loop in it. Though it is simpler to implement than the redundant solution, the single bidirectional redistribution does have the drawback that if this single redistribution point fails, there is no backup, and any user attempting to use this path would not be able to connect.

With a redundant bidirectional redistribution solution, you gain the most flexibility but also expose yourself to the most risk. The probability of a route being advertised by one entry point and learned by the other is higher than in the other solutions examined. To mitigate this risk, redistribution filters, distribute lists, and/or prefix lists can be used to limit the routes that are sent and received between the neighboring routers that are participating in the redistribution. Though this solution will ensure a loop-free environment, in large installations it can become an administrative burden as networks are added, deleted, or moved.

Open Shortest Path First (OSPF)

Open Shortest Path First (OSPF) is a link-state routing protocol. OSPF differs from IGRP and EIGRP because it is a pure link-state routing technology. It is an open standard routing protocol, which means that it was not developed solely by Cisco. OSPF was designed and developed by the Internet Engineering Task Force (IETF) to provide a scalable, quickly converging, and efficient routing protocol that could be used by all routing equipment. Complete details for OSPF are found in RFC2328.

OSPF is an enhancement over RIP that provides a scalable routing solution. It supports several features that RIP version 1 does not—for example, VLSM and route summarization are supported.

The hop count was eliminated with OSPF, thus giving it limitless reachability. Because of the algorithm used to calculate and advertise routes, network convergence is fast with OSPF. OSPF is like EIGRP because it sends route updates only when changes occur in the network. A formal neighbor relationship is established with all adjacent OSPF routers.

Areas are used within OSPF to define a group of routers and networks belonging to the same OSPF session. Links connect routers, and the information about each link is defined by its link state. On each broadcast or multi-access network segment, two routers must be assigned the responsibilities of designated router (DR) and backup designated router (BDR).

Like EIGRP, OSPF maintains three databases: adjacency, topology, and route. The adjacency database is similar to the neighbor database used by EIGRP. It contains all information about OSPF neighbors and the links connecting them. The topology database maintains all route information. The best routes from the topology database are placed in the route database or route table.

Initializing OSPF

The Hello protocol is used to establish peering sessions between routers. Hello packets are multicast out of every interface that is participating in the routing process. The information that is multicast includes the router ID, timing intervals, existing neighbors, area identification, router priority, designated and backup router information, password authentication, and stub area information. All this information is used when establishing new peers. Descriptions of each element can be found in Table 2.8.

TABLE 2.8 OSPF Multicast Information

Information	Description
Router ID	This is the highest active IP address on the router.
Time intervals	Contains intervals between Hello packets and the dead time interval.
Existing neighbors	Contains addresses for any existing OSPF neighbors.
Area identification	OSPF area number and link information must be the same for a peering session to be established.

TABLE 2.8 OSPF Multicast Information *(continued)*

Information	Description
Router priority	This value is used when choosing the DR and BDR.
DR and BDR	If they have already been chosen, their information is contained in the Hello packet.
Authentication password	All peers within the same area must have the same authentication password if authentication is enabled.
Stub area flag	This is a special area—two routers must share the same stub information. This is not necessary to initiate a regular peering session with another OSPF router.

Figure 2.12 displays a flowchart that depicts each step of the initialization process. The process starts by sending out Hello packets. Every listening router then adds the originating router to the adjacency database. The responding routers reply with all of their Hello information so that the originating router can add them to its adjacency table.

Once adjacencies are established, the DR and BDR need to be chosen before route information and link-state information can be exchanged. After the DR and BDR are chosen, route information is exchanged, and the OSPF peers continue to multicast Hello packets every 10 seconds to determine whether neighbors are still reachable.

Before we go any further with peer initialization, we need to discuss several terms that are specific to OSPF. These terms are key to understanding OSPF and how it functions.

The easiest way to understand OSPF is to build from what you already know about EIGRP. You learned that EIGRP uses autonomous system numbers to specify routing processes and the routing process that individual routers belong to. OSPF uses areas in place of an autonomous system. An OSPF area consists of a group of routers or interfaces on a router that is assigned to a common area.

FIGURE 2.12   OSPF peer initialization

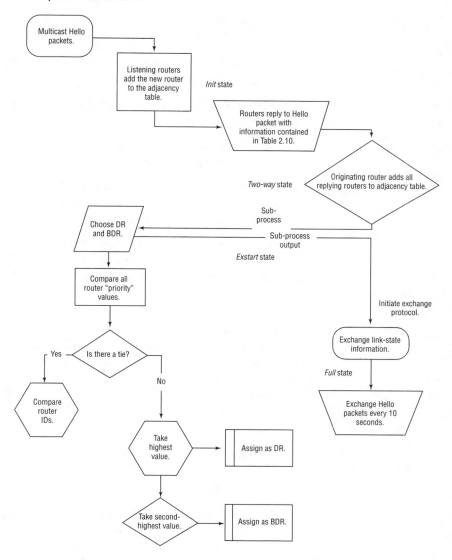

OSPF also allows and uses different area types. When deploying OSPF, there must be a backbone area. Standard and stub areas connect to the backbone area. Following is a list of each area type, followed by a short description of that area type:

Backbone   This area accepts all link-state advertisements (LSAs) and is used to connect multiple areas.

Stub   This area does not accept any external routing update, but it will accept summary LSAs.

Totally Stub   These areas are closed off from accepting external or summary advertisements.

Standard   This is the normal area that accepts internal and external LSAs, and summary information.

Not So Stubby   This type of area is similar to Stub areas except that Type 5 LSAs are not flooded into the area from the core. It can import external AS routes into the area.

Move on now to learn the different types of link-state advertisements. LSAs are the heart of OSPF's information exchange. Different types of LSAs represent different types of route information. All of the defined and used LSA types are summarized in Table 2.9.

TABLE 2.9   OSPF LSA Types

LSA Type	Description of LSA
(1) Router link entry	This LSA is broadcast only within its defined area. The LSA contains all of the default link-state information.
(2) Network entry	This LSA is multicast to all area routers by the DR. This update contains network-specific information.
(3/4) Summary entry	Type 3 LSAs contain route information for internal networks and are sent to backbone routers. Type 4 LSAs contain information about Autonomous System Border Routers (ASBRs). Summary information is multicast by the Area Border Router (ABR) and the information reaches all backbone routers.

TABLE 2.9 OSPF LSA Types *(continued)*

LSA Type	Description of LSA
(5) Autonomous System entry	As the name indicates, these advertisements originate from the ASBR. These packets contain information about external networks.
(7) Not So Stubby Area	Not So Stubby Area (NSSA) permits Type 7 AS external routes to be imported inside the NSSA area by redistribution.

Different LSA types represent the type of route that is being advertised, and assist in restricting the number and type of routes that are accepted by a given area. As is shown in the table, an LSA of Type 5 is sent only by the Autonomous System Border Router. This brings you to the point where you need to define the different router types that belong to OSPF areas.

Multiple router types can exist within an OSPF area. Table 2.10 lists all of the OSPF router types and the role that each plays within the area.

TABLE 2.10 OSPF Router Types

Router Type	Description of Responsibility
Internal	All interfaces are defined on the same area. All internal routers have an identical link-state database.
Backbone	This type of router has at least one interface assigned to area 0.
Area Border Router (ABR)	Interfaces are connected to multiple OSPF areas. Information specific to each area is stored on this type of router.
Autonomous System Border Router (ASBR)	This type of router has an interface connected to an external network or a different AS.

In addition to the above-listed responsibilities, a router can also be assigned additional responsibilities. These additions are assumed when a router is assigned the role of DR or BDR.

OSPF Packet Structure

Finally, look at the packet structure. It is important to realize that all OSPF packets begin with the same 24-byte header. Different information can be appended, depending on the type of OSPF packet, but all share the same first 24 bytes. Figure 2.13 gives a visual of the OSPF packet header.

FIGURE 2.13 OSPF packet header structure

23	16 14	12	8	4	2	1	0
Authentication	Authenti-cation type	Check-sum	Area ID	Router ID	Length	Type	Ver

As you can see, the 24-byte header was divided into eight segments. Each field contains specific information. Starting from the right and working left, you see that the first field is for the version number. This field is one byte long and contains the OSPF version number.

Moving on, you see that the second field is also one byte long and contains the packet Type. There are five values that can be used in this field: hello, database description, link-state request, link-state update (LSU), and link-state advertisement (LSA).

The next field is the packet Length. This field is two bytes long and includes the packet length in bytes.

The next two fields, Router ID and Area ID, are a little longer. Each field is four bytes long. The router ID is the source ID for the packet. Each router in an OSPF area has a unique ID. Each AS also has an ID that is included in the packet, so not only the packet's source router is identified, but the AS is as well.

The remaining fields consist of the remaining space of the 24 bytes. The fields are Checksum, Authentication type, and Authentication, respectively. The Checksum field, two bytes long, is used to calculate CRC information. The Authentication type field, two bytes, contains OSPF password information or other authentication types. Finally, the Authentication field contains authentication information.

BGP (Border Gateway Protocol)

The Internet consists of a number of commercial networks that connect to each other via tier-one providers such as Sprint, WorldCom/MCI/UUNet, and others. Each enterprise network or ISP must be identified by an autonomous system number. This number allows a hierarchy to be maintained when sharing route information.

We are now familiar with several IGPs (Interior Gateway Protocols), such as IGRP, EIGRP, and OSPF. For enterprise networks to communicate with other autonomous systems or ISPs, the IGP information has to be injected into BGP, which is used by all network entities that compose the Internet.

BGP (Border Gateway Protocol) is an open standard protocol that was developed and defined in several RFCs: 1163, 1267, 1654, and 1655. The two types of BGP are iBGP and eBGP. There are several differences between the two. Primarily, iBGP (internal BGP) is used to share BGP information with routers within the same AS, whereas eBGP (external BGP) is used to share route information between two different autonomous systems. More details will be given as we discuss each type separately.

iBGP (Internal Border Gateway Protocol)

Internal BGP is used by routers that belong to the same autonomous system. iBGP may use loopback interfaces to provide greater reachability. This is possible because the IGP can provide multiple routes to any given destination address if the network has redundant or multiple links to each router. If one interface on a router goes down, the TCP connection to the loopback address can be maintained by using redundant interfaces.

An important feature of iBGP is that route information from one peer is not advertised to another iBGP peer. This avoids inconsistent route information and routing loops. To share route information between all iBGP routers, establish a logical mesh. (Figure 2.14 shows a picture of what is meant by this.) Route information is exchanged only between routers. Router B can learn BGP networks only from Router A. When Router C sends its BGP information, only its information is sent. Routes learned from Router A are not included.

FIGURE 2.14   iBGP information exchange

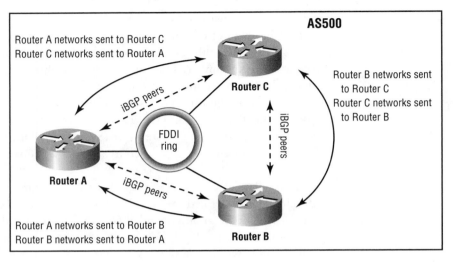

eBGP (External Border Gateway Protocol)

External BGP is used to exchange route information between two different autonomous systems. When only one link connects two autonomous systems, the IP address of the connected interface is used to establish the BGP session. It is also possible to use other IP addresses, but the address must be reachable without learning it through BGP. This can be accomplished by using static routes or additional BGP commands when configuring eBGP. If multiple links are used to connect to the other AS, using loopback addresses is the best option.

The purpose of eBGP is to inject routes owned by the enterprise network into another AS. Two prerequisites need to be met for internal routes to be propagated via BGP:

- The route to be advertised must be present in the router's IGP route table.

- BGP must learn the route.

You can fulfill the first condition by using one of three methods: inject the routes into a router's route table via an IGP, a static route, or directly connected networks. BGP has a synchronization option that requires BGP and the IGP routes to synchronize before BGP will advertise IGP learned networks. The no synchronization command indicates that BGP and the IGP do not have to synchronize before BGP advertises the routes.

You can also accomplish the second prerequisite in one of three ways: BGP learns of networks that it needs to advertise through other BGP advertisements, network statements, and redistribution of an IGP into BGP.

BGP Packet Structure

The BGP header is only 20 bytes long and contains three fields. The first field is 16 bytes long and is called the `Marker` field. This field contains a value that can be predicted by the receiving system. It is used for authentication purposes.

The next field is the `Length` field and it is two bytes long. The `Length` field contains the size of the entire message, in bytes. Finally, the `Type` field is the last field, and it is two bytes in length. It is used to indicate the message type. Figure 2.15 gives a graphical representation of a BGP packet header.

FIGURE 2.15   BGP packet header

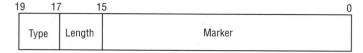

Now that we have mentioned message types, we need to explain them. BGP uses four different message types: open, update, notification, and keepalives.

Open messages are sent to each other after the TCP connection is established. The open messages must be accepted by the peer; otherwise, the remaining messages, update, notification, and keepalives are not sent.

Update messages are the actual routing updates exchanged among BGP peers. Other BGP-specific information is also included in these messages: origin, AS path, next hop, unreachable, and Inter-AS-metric.

Notification messages are used when errors are detected. Information includes an explanation about why the connection was closed. Each reason has a code. Notification updates use the following codes: message-header error, open-message error, update-message error, and hold time expired.

Keepalive messages are sent to make peers aware that the connection can be kept active. This is accomplished by updating the holddown timers.

Novell NetWare Routed and Routing Protocols

NetWare differs from the previous protocols because it is a network operating system and not a routing protocol. The basis of a network operating system is a hierarchy of clients and servers: clients request services and information from servers.

NetWare uses the top five layers of the OSI model to run the network operating system. It uses proprietary protocols that fulfill the respective OSI layer requirements. Figure 2.16 shows the relationship between the OSI layers and Novell NetWare's use of the upper five layers.

FIGURE 2.16 OSI to NetWare comparison

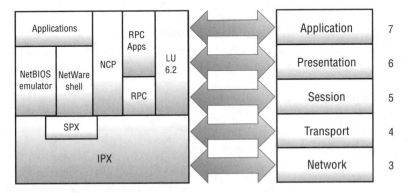

Because the upper five layers are proprietary to Novell, they must use special mappings to use the lower layers of the OSI model. To gain access to Layer 2, NetWare uses Ethernet/IEEE 802.3 or Token Ring/IEEE 802.5, FDDI, ARCnet, and PPP over WAN links.

IPX Packet Structure

Internetwork Packet Exchange (IPX) is Novell's equivalent for Layers 3 and 4 of the OSI model. Look at Figure 2.17 to get a picture of the IPX packet structure. Following is an EtherPeek analysis of an IPX packet, which gives you the information you need to define the packet structure:

```
IPX - NetWare Protocol
  Checksum:             0xffff
  Length:               73
  Transport Control:
    Reserved:           %0000
    Hop Count:          %0000
  Packet Type:          0   Novell
```

```
Destination Network:   0x00000000
Destination Node:      ff:ff:ff:ff:ff:ff Ethernet Brdcast
Destination Socket:    0x9001  IPX Static
Source Network:        0x00000010
Source Node:           00:00:0c:3e:82:2a
Source Socket:         0x9001  IPX Static
IPX Data Area:
...........>.*.     83 1b 02 00 0f 01 00 00 11 00 00 0c
                    3e 82 2a 00
..+@...>.*. ....    01 00 2b 40 00 00 0c 3e 82 2a 01 c0
                    08 00 00 00
..... ...           00 00 00 00 00 c5 04 00 00
Extra bytes (Padding):
. .                 05 dc 06
Frame Check Sequence:  0x00000000
```

FIGURE 2.17   IPX packet structure

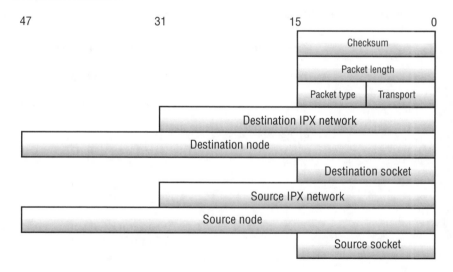

We start out with the 16-bit Checksum field with a default setting of 0xFFFF. This field is followed by the 16-bit Packet length field. The length field indi-cates the complete length, in bytes, of the IPX packet, header, and payload.

The next two fields (Transport control and Packet type) are eight bits each. Transport control is a counter that counts the number of routers a packet has transited. `Packet type` indicates which of the upper-layer protocols are to receive the PDU after Layer 4 is through processing it.

The fourth layer contains the `Destination IPX network` field, a 32-bit field that contains the IPX network for the destination host. The fifth layer is the `Destination node`. This field is 48 bits long and contains the MAC address of the destination host. The `Destination socket` is a 16-bit field on the sixth layer of the IPX header. This identifies the socket number for the upper layers.

Following the destination information, three more layers contain the same type of information for the source host. The seventh layer is the `Source IPX Network`, another 32-bit field containing the source network. This is followed by the `Source node`, a 48-bit field containing the MAC address of the source host. Finally, the last field of the header contains source host socket information, the `Source socket` field, which is 16 bits in length.

Certain codes are used to specify which socket numbers are assigned to which protocols. The codes used are shown in Table 2.11.

TABLE 2.11 IPX Socket Number Assignments

Socket Number	Upper-Layer Protocol
0451	NetWare Core Protocol
0452	SAP (Service Advertising Protocol)
0453	RIP
0455	NetBIOS
0456	Diagnostics
4000-6000	Temporary file server and network communications

NetWare has to use special formats to connect to the Data-Link layer. It uses encapsulation to do this. This encapsulation takes all of the upper-layer data and frames it in preparation for transport. NetWare originally used

802.3 raw. Now, NetWare uses several encapsulation types for Ethernet/ IEEE 802.3.

When you talk about frame types, you need to be careful to understand whose definition or name you are using. Table 2.12 summarizes the names and equivalencies for the Layer 2 frame types. Figure 2.18 gives a graphical description of the following encapsulations.

TABLE 2.12 Names for Layer 2 Ethernet Frame Types

Standard Name	Novell Equivalent	Cisco Equivalent	Characteristics
Ethernet V. 2	Ethernet_II	ARPA	Ethertype
IEEE 802.3	Ethernet_802.2	SAP	Length and SAPs
Novell 802.3 raw	Ethernet_802.3	Novell-Ether	Length but no SAPs
SNAP	Ethernet_SNAP	SNAP	SAP and SNAP headers

FIGURE 2.18 Encapsulation types

There are three main routing protocols used with IPX, RIP, EIGRP, and NLSP. The RIP and EIGRP versions that are used for IPX are similar in structure to their IP counterparts. As such, they will not be covered in further detail here; however, they are covered in Chapter 9.

NLSP

NetWare Link Services Protocol (NLSP) is based on ISO's IS-IS routing protocol. It is a link-state routing protocol, not a distance-vector protocol such as RIP. Most of the problems with RIP that were listed previously are common to all distance-vector routing protocols. NLSP is not subject to these problems.

The current version of NLSP, version 1.1, supports a multitude of advanced routing features:

- Multiple areas
- Route aggregation
- Hierarchical addressing
- Network summarization

NLSP is similar to IS-IS because it defines areas. It offers solutions to many of the problems that are common when using RIP and SAP, and can actually work as a replacement for all RIP and SAP communication between servers (or routers).

Every NLSP router (remember that NLSP-enabled NetWare servers are NLSP routers) builds and maintains three databases:

- Adjacency
- Link state
- Forwarding

These three databases are listed in the order in which they are built. The adjacency database can be unique on every router. On each of its NLSP-enabled interfaces, each router meets every other NLSP router on that network segment. On an Ethernet interface, for example, there can be several other NLSP-enabled devices (other routers, servers, and so on). On a point-to-point WAN interface, there is only one other device. All of this information goes into the adjacency database; once it is built, each router knows all of its NLSP neighbors on all connected networks.

AppleTalk Routed and Routing Protocols

Just as IP and IPX had their own rules, AppleTalk has its own way of doing things. Addressing, location of services, and communication are a bit different than with other protocols. There are also several concepts that just don't have parallels elsewhere.

AppleTalk is similar to NetWare because it is a client/server-based technology. Mac users launch an application called Chooser to locate resources on the internetwork. Once users launch the Chooser application, they select an AppleTalk zone and type of resource (file server, printer, and so on). Chooser then builds a dynamic list of workstation names that offers the requested service in the selected zone. The user selects one of the names and then proceeds with their work. The following steps give a more detailed explanation of the procedure:

1. The user launches the Chooser application.

2. The Chooser queries the router for available zones and presents the list of available zones to the user.

3. The user selects a zone and the type of resource requested.

4. The user's Mac issues an NBP (Name Binding Protocol) request, identifying the requested type of resource and zone.

5. The routers ensure that the NBP broadcast is forwarded to all specified network segments for that zone.

6. All nodes in the requested zone receive the NBP broadcast, and the nodes that provide the requested service reply to the requesting workstation.

7. Routers forward the responses to the requesting workstation's segment.

8. The Chooser builds a list of available services.

9. The user selects a service and proceeds with their work.

With this arrangement, it's obvious that the proper forwarding of broadcasts is crucial to locating resources on the internetwork. From the users' perspective, they can just use the dynamic Chooser to find out which resources are available on the internetwork. If you get a new laser printer, you simply plug it in and tell it which zone it's in, and Chooser automatically lets users looking for that type of printer know that it's available. Figure 2.19 depicts the location of AppleTalk services in relation to the OSI model.

FIGURE 2.19 AppleTalk's relation to the OSI model

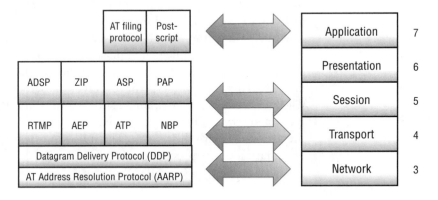

AppleTalk Addressing

AppleTalk uses a 24-bit address written in dotted decimal format—*network.node*. The network portion is always 16 bits long; the node portion is always eight bits long. Therefore, as with IPX, there's no subnetting and no classes. There are two versions of AppleTalk—Phase 1 and Phase 2. In Phase 1, there were certain limitations in addressing. Table 2.13 shows these limitations.

TABLE 2.13 AppleTalk Phase 1 Addressing

Item	Amount
Network addresses per segment	1
Host addresses per network	127
Server addresses per network	127
Zones per network	1

Because you can have only one network address per segment, the number of nodes per segment is also limited. If that isn't enough, there's also an imposed limitation of one zone per network, which obliterates an administrator's ability to create multiple logical networks within the same segment. There must be a better way! Thankfully, Apple thought so, too. Look at some changes made for AppleTalk Phase 2 (see Table 2.14).

TABLE 2.14   AppleTalk Phase 2 Addressing

Item	Amount
Network addresses per segment	Unlimited
Host addresses per network	Unlimited
Server addresses per network	Unlimited
Zones per network	255

With Phase 2, there can be an unlimited number of network addresses per segment. In addition, there are ample node addresses available, despite the fact that network addresses are still only eight bits long.

There really isn't an unlimited number of networks available per segment—you're still limited by the 16-bit network portion of the address, giving you approximately 65,000 potential networks. It's highly unlikely that you'd ever need anywhere near 65,000 network addresses for a single network.

In addition, you can now have multiple zones per network, allowing you to create multiple logical networks (zones) within a single network segment.

As is the case with IP, there are a few reserved network and node addresses. Network address 0 (zero) is reserved for use by nodes that haven't yet learned their segment's address, so it can't be assigned. Node addresses 254 and 255 are also reserved and can't be assigned to nodes.

The technique used by AppleTalk Phase 2 to assign multiple network addresses to a single segment is called *extended addressing*. Instead of having a single network address on a segment, you can assign a range—an extension—of addresses to a segment. Here's an example: A nonextended address for a segment can be network 100, and an extended address for the same segment can be network 100–110—a range of 11 network addresses. What if you need even more node addresses? Well, how about network 100–1000 (901 network addresses)? Need fewer node addresses? Try network 100–100 (one network address). All you have to do is specify a range of network addresses that you want included on the segment in the extended address.

AppleTalk nodes dynamically obtain node addresses upon startup. When a new machine starts up, it sends out a ZIP (Zone Information Protocol) to find the network address or the address range, if extended addressing is being used. The machine then selects a random node address and issues an AARP (AppleTalk Address Resolution Protocol) to see if anyone is using that particular network node address. If there's no response, the machine continues using that address. Node addressing is completely dynamic and requires no administration.

When an AppleTalk node starts up, it sets up a provisional address. If the node is being started for the very first time, it chooses a network number between 65,280 and 65,534 at random. This range is referred to as the *startup range*. The node number is also chosen at random. If the node was started before, it uses its previous address as a *hint*. In either case, the node uses AARP to check whether the selected provisional address is in use. If the address is in use, it selects another node number and checks again. If the node is using a hint and subsequently exhausts all available node numbers without finding an unused address, it chooses a new network address from the startup range and a new node number, and then repeats the check for an unused address.

Once the node has selected an unused provisional address, it can send a ZIP `GetNetInfo` request to a router to determine the actual segment's cable range. If the network number for the provisional address falls within the segment's cable range, the address is kept. Otherwise, a new network number is chosen from this cable range, and the resulting node address is checked by using AARP. If the address is in use, the node selects another node number. If it runs out of node numbers, it chooses another network number from within the segment's cable range and repeats the node-address check process. Once the node finds an unused network number and node number combination, it becomes its final node address. The address is saved and used as a future hint.

Datagram Delivery Protocol (DDP)

Datagram Delivery Protocol (DDP), in conjunction with *AppleTalk Address Resolution Protocol (AARP)*, makes up the OSI Layer 3 equivalent. DDP is responsible for connectivity to the upper-layer protocols, whereas AARP is charged with connectivity to the lower layers.

Look at a DDP packet. The following EtherPeek trace analysis gives you what you need to know about the packet. It is important to realize that there is a Layer 2 heading that is prepended to the DDP header. We start from the beginning of the DDP header in this discussion.

```
Long DDP Header - Datagram Delivery Protocol
    Unused:           %00
    Hop Count:        %0000
    Datagram Length:  21
    DDP Checksum:     0x0000
    Dest. Network:    107
    Source Network:   101
    Dest Node:        1
    Source Node:      217
    Dest. Socket:     6  Zone Information
    Source Socket:    245
    DDP Type:         3  ATP
```

As you can see, the DDP header starts with an unused field. The next field is four bits and is used for the hop count. The count is incremented as the packet transits additional routers.

Following the hop count, you see the Datagram Length field. This field is 10 bits long and it measures the length of the datagram in bytes. After the Datagram Length field, we move onto the DDP Checksum field. The DDP Checksum field is a full 16 bits, and is used to aid in CRC calculation.

The next four fields are used only in the long (extended) DDP header. They represent destination and source information, each according to the description. Following the extended information, you see the DSN and SSN. These fields are used to define destination and source socket numbers. The allowable socket numbers are RTMP (value = 1), names information (value = 2), echoer (value = 4), and zone information (value = 6).

There are seven different DDP types that can be specified by the DDP Type field using eight bits. These types include: RTMP response or data (value = 1), NBP (value = 2), ATP (value = 3), AEP (value = 4), RTMP requests (value = 5), ZIP (value = 6), and ADSP (value = 7). The actual DDP datagram follows the DDP type.

Routing Table Maintenance Protocol

Routing Table Maintenance Protocol (RTMP) is responsible for Apple-Talk routing tables and their information. This is AppleTalk's proprietary method of maintaining route tables on AppleTalk–enabled machines. RTMP packets are different from other packet structures. They contain x number of fields called *routing tuples*. Depending on the type of network, nonextended or extended, the tuple structure changes.

The example below is a sample from an extended network. The packet structure is 16 bits long. The packet starts with the router's network number, which occupies the full 16 bits. Following the network number, the ID Length field occupies eight bits. This field specifies the length of the sender's node address. The next field is used for specifying the actual router's node address.

After 16 bits of padding, the routing tuples 1 through x follow. Each tuple contains the same field, as long as it is of the same tuple type. Nonextended tuples actually follow 16 bits of padding with eight bits of version number identification. They begin with the network number field, followed by some padding and a distance field. Extended tuples follow 16 bits of padding, and then begin with a 16-bit start range. After the start range, there are three more fields: Distance, Range End, and Version. The version number becomes part of an extended tuple. It has a default value of 0x82.

```
RTMP - Routing Table Maintenance Protocol
   Router's Net:      106
   ID Length:         8
   Router's Node ID:  74
RTMP Tuple # 1
   Range Start:       100
   Range Flag:        %100    Extended
   Distance:          0
   Range End:         110
   Version:           0x82
RTMP Tuple # 2
   Range Start:       300
   Range Flag:        %100    Extended
   Distance:          1
   Range End:         210
   Version:           0x82
```

```
RTMP Tuple # 3
   Range Start:        500
   Range Flag:         %100   Extended
   Distance:           2
   Range End:          310
   Version:            0x82
RTMP Tuple # 4
   Range Start:        200
   Range Flag:         %100   Extended
   Distance:           0
   Range End:          1000
   Version:            0x82
RTMP Tuple # 5
   Range Start:        400
   Range Flag:         %100   Extended
   Distance:           1
   Range End:          1001
   Version:            0x82
   Frame Check Sequence:   0x00000000
```

OSI Layer 2: Data-Link Layer Protocols and Applications

This section is dedicated to Layer 2 protocols and applications. It is a very important section because it provides specific information on how the Layer 2 protocols work. What better way to be able to troubleshoot a problem than by understanding the intricacies of the protocol in question?

This section covers the following Layer 2 protocols:

- Ethernet/IEEE 802.3
- Token Ring/IEEE 802.5
- PPP
- SDLC

- X.25

- Frame Relay

- ISDN

As you can see, there are quite a few technologies to understand, and this is where we will start.

Ethernet/IEEE 802.3

These two terms actually refer to different things. *Ethernet* is a communication technology and *IEEE 802.3* is a variety of Ethernet. Ethernet, in the more specific sense, is a *carrier sense, multiple access/collision detection (CSMA/CD)* local area network. This means that the network uses these attributes—carrier sense, multiple access, and collision detection—to enhance communication. This definitely does *not* mean that Ethernet is the only technology that uses these attributes. In today's technical jargon, however, Ethernet is getting closer to meaning all CSMA/CD technologies.

Both Ethernet and IEEE 802.3 are broadcast networks. All frames that cross a given segment can be heard by all machines populating that segment. Because all machines on the segment have equal access to the physical media, each station tries to wait for a quiet spot before it transmits its data. If two machines talk at the same time, a collision occurs.

Ethernet services both the Physical and Data-Link layers, whereas IEEE 802.3 is more concerned with the Physical layer and how it talks to the Data-Link layer. Several IEEE 802.3 protocols exist; each one has a distinct name that describes how it is different from other IEEE 802.3 protocols. Table 2.15 summarizes the differences between the different IEEE 802.3 versions.

TABLE 2.15 IEEE 802.3 Characteristics

	802.3 Values 10Base5	10Base2	1Base5	10BaseT	100BaseT	10Broad36
Data rate (Mbps)	10	10	1	10	100	10
Signaling Method	Baseband	Baseband	Baseband	Baseband	Baseband	Broadband

TABLE 2.15 IEEE 802.3 Characteristics *(continued)*

802.3 Values	10Base5	10Base2	1Base5	10BaseT	100BaseT	10Broad36
Maximum Segment Length (m)	500	185	185	100	100	1800
Media	50 Ohm coax	50 Ohm coax	Unshielded twisted pair	Unshielded twisted pair	Unshielded twisted pair	75 Ohm coax
Topology	Bus	Bus	Star	Star	Star	Bus

This is an excerpt from Cisco; for the full document, please see http://www.cisco.com/univercd/cc/td/doc/cisintwk/ito_doc/ ethernet.htm.

Frame Structures

Frame formats are similar between Ethernet and IEEE 802.3. Figure 2.20 depicts the similarities and differences between the two frames. The frame structures are read right to left. Starting at the right, you see that both frames begin with a preamble. The Preamble is a seven-byte field. Notice that you have moved from bits to bytes to specify field lengths. This value consists of alternating 1s and 0s.

FIGURE 2.20 Ethernet vs. IEEE 802.3 frames

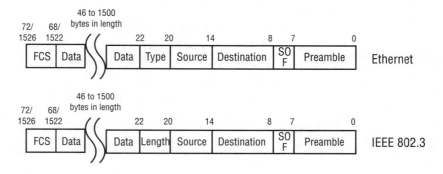

The next field is the SOF, or start-of-frame delimiter. It is used to synchronize the frame reception portions of all of the machines on the segment. This field is only one byte long.

The two fields following the SOF are six bytes each; they are the Destination and Source MAC addresses of the receiving and sending stations. Each MAC address is unique.

Up to this point, the frames were exactly the same. Now, the differences start. The following field is a two-byte field in both frame structures. Ethernet defines the field as a Type field, whereas IEEE 802.3 defines it as a Length field. Ethernet uses the field to specify which upper-layer protocol will receive the packet. IEEE 802.3 uses the field to define how many bytes the payload (802.2 header and data) field is.

The following field in both formats is the Data field. The only difference is that Ethernet uses a variable byte size between 46 and 1500 for data. This data is what will be handed to the upper-layer protocols. IEEE 802.3 uses a variable byte size between 46 and 1500 as well, but the information here contains the 802.2 header and the encapsulated data that will eventually be passed to an upper-layer protocol that is defined within the Data field.

Finally, you have the last field, which is the Frame Check Sequence (FCS) field. It is a four-byte-long field that is used to store information that will be used for calculating the CRC after the data has been sent or received.

Token Ring/IEEE 802.5

Token Ring and IEEE 802.5 have the same relationship as Ethernet and IEEE 802.3. However, in this case, the IEEE 802.5 specification follows IBM's Token Ring much more closely. Both implementations specify baseband signaling, token passing, and data rates. Token Ring is IBM's token-passing LAN technology. It has bandwidth capabilities of either 4Mbps or 16Mbps in a ring topology.

Token Ring/IEEE 802.5 differs greatly from Ethernet/IEEE 802.3. Ethernet/IEEE 802.3 is CSMA/CD LANs, whereas Token Ring/IEEE 802.5 is apportioned networks. *Apportioned* means that equal time is allotted to every station on a ring. This is achieved by passing a token around the ring. The next section explains in a little more detail.

Tokens

The physical design of Token Ring/IEEE 802.5 is just as the name indicates—a ring. Multiple stations connect to the same ring, just as Ethernet/IEEE 802.3 stations connect to the same segment.

The main idea behind Token Ring/IEEE 802.5 was that a station may not transmit data onto the ring without first possessing the *token*. The token is just a small frame containing control information. Use Figure 2.21 as a visual reference for the following example. The frame or token is sent around the ring. Each station on the ring waits its turn to receive the token. If a station receives the token but doesn't have anything to transmit, it simply passes the token on to the next station in line. However, if the station does have information to send, it alters the frame, changing it into a start-of-frame identifier, and then appends the data to the frame. While the token frame has been changed into a start-of-frame identifier, no other station on the ring can use the token to transmit data, thus eliminating collisions.

The altered frame leaves the source station and circles the ring in search of the destination station. Each station looks at the frame and determines whether it is the destination host. If a station is the destination, it copies the frame and then processes it, as necessary. The frame continues to travel around the ring until it reaches the source host. Once reaching the source, the frame is removed and a new token is generated and sent out onto the ring. This way, each station has an equal opportunity to transmit data.

FIGURE 2.21 Token passing

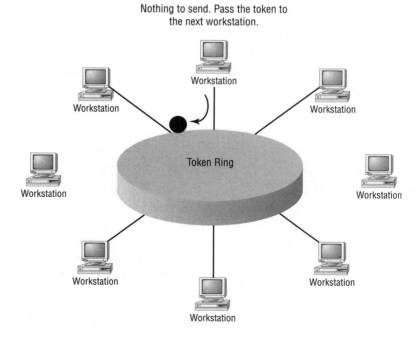

Fault Recovery

Token Ring/IEEE 802.5 uses several methods to help prevent and heal network failures quickly and efficiently. An *Active Monitor* is designated by the workstations on the ring. The Active Monitor is responsible for token monitoring, token generation when the token seems to have disappeared, purging recycling frames, and other ring maintenance.

The physical connectivity of Token Ring/IEEE 802.5 is also fault-tolerant. If a machine on a ring becomes unreachable, the machine is electrically disconnected from the ring. The multistation access unit (MAU) in which the Token Ring/IEEE 802.5 cabling is located shuts down the port that is unreachable, thus healing the ring. Physical connectivity is tested by using *beaconing*, which locates the fault and reports back with the nearest active upstream neighbor, or NAUN. This information helps to isolate network failures and shortens troubleshooting time.

Token Frame Format

We now look at the two frame types used by Token Ring/IEEE 802.5. Remember that while referencing, we will move from right to left. The two principal frame types used in Token Ring and IEEE 802.5, shown in Figure 2.22, are the token frame and the data, or command, frame formats.

FIGURE 2.22 Token and data/command frames

Figure 2.22 shows that both frames start with a Start delimiter and Access control. These two fields are each only one byte long. Start delimiter alerts each station on the ring that the frame is a data or command frame, not a simple token frame. The Access control field is used to assign priority to the frame and to help distinguish what frame type it is. Possible frame types are token, data/command, and monitor.

Here is where the difference starts. The data frame contains additional fields that the token frame does not have. All of the station's data is inserted into the frame following the `Access control` field. The data segment commences with a one-byte field that holds information regarding frame control. This is an indicator of whether the frame contains data or command information.

The next two fields are six bytes long and contain the packet's destination and source addresses. The `Data` field, of variable length, carries all of the data that is to be encapsulated. The length is determined by how long the sending station can hold a token.

Error-checking information follows the header and data fields. It is used in CRC calculation.

Now you are at the end of the frame and it is again the same as a token frame. Both data/command and token frames have end delimiters. The only difference is that end delimiters end a token frame, but a data/command frame has one more field.

The `End delimiter` field is only one byte long. It is used to indicate the end of a data/command frame. The last field, the `Frame status`, or FS, has two values that it can relay: frame-copied or address-recognized.

Point-to-Point Protocol (PPP)

Point-to-point Protocol (PPP) is used to transfer data over serial point-to-point links. It accomplishes this by using a Layer 2 serial encapsulation called *High-level Data Link Control (HDLC)*. HDLC is used for frame encapsulation on synchronous serial lines. It uses a Link Control Protocol (LCP) to manage the serial connection. Network Control Protocols (NCPs) are used to allow PPP to use other protocols from Layer 3, thus enabling PPP to assign IP addresses dynamically.

PPP uses the same frame structure as HDLC. Figure 2.23 gives you a picture of what the frame looks like. As always, we move from right to left.

FIGURE 2.23 PPP packet structure

2 or 4 bytes	Variable	5	3	2	1	0
FCS	Data	Protocol	Control	Address	Flag	

First, we have the `Flag` field, which uses one byte to specify the beginning or ending of a frame. Then there is another byte that is used in the `Address` field to hold a broadcast address of 11111111.

The `Address` field is followed by the one-byte `Control` field. The `Control` field requests a transmission of user data. The two-byte `Protocol` field follows the `Control` field. This field indicates the encapsulated data's protocol.

The `Data` field contains the information that will be handed to the upper-layer protocols. It is a variable-length field. Following the data field is the FCS. Like the other protocols, it is used for CRC calculation.

Synchronous Data Link Control (SDLC)

Synchronous Data Link Control (SDLC) is based on a synchronous, more efficient, faster, and flexible bit-oriented format. SDLC has several derivatives that perform similar functions with some enhancements: HDLC, LAPB (Link Access Procedure, Balanced), and IEEE 802.2, just to name a few. HDLC is the default encapsulation type on most Cisco router serial interfaces.

SDLC is used for many link types. Two node types exist within SDLC: *primary nodes* and *secondary nodes*. Primary nodes are responsible for the control of secondary stations and for link management, such as link setup and teardown. Secondary nodes talk only to the primary node when they fulfill two requirements. First, they have permission from the primary node; second, they have data to transmit. Even if a secondary node has data to send, it cannot send the data if it does not have permission from the primary node.

Both stations can be configured together in four different topologies:

Point-to-point This topology requires only two nodes—a primary and a secondary.

Multipoint This configuration uses one primary station and multiple secondary stations.

Loop This configuration uses one primary and multiple secondary stations. The difference between loop and multipoint setups is that here the primary station is connected between two secondary stations, which makes two directly connected secondary stations. When more secondary stations are added, they must connect to the other secondary stations that are currently in the loop. When one of these stations wants to send information to the primary node, it must transit the other secondary stations before it reaches the primary.

Hub go-ahead   This configuration also uses one primary and multiple secondary stations, but it uses a different communication topology. The primary station has an outbound channel. This channel is used to communicate with each of the secondary stations. An inbound channel is shared among the secondary stations and has a single connection into the primary station.

Frame Structure

SDLC uses three different frame structures: information, supervisory, and unnumbered. The overall structure of the frames is similar, except for the control frame. The control frame is varied to distinguish the type of SDLC frame that is being used. Figure 2.24 gives the structure for the different SDLC frames. Pay close attention to the bit values next to the send sequence number within the control frame.

FIGURE 2.24   SDLC frame structures

First, let's talk about the frame fields that are common among all three frame types. As you can see, all three frames depicted in Figure 2.24 start with a `Flag` field that is followed by an `Address` field. The `Address` field of SDLC frames is different from other frame structures because only the address of the secondary node is used instead of a destination and source address. The secondary address is used because all communication is either originated or received by the primary node; thus, it is not necessary to specify its address within the frame.

The control frame follows the `Address` field. Information contained within the control frame defines the SDLC frame type. The control frame begins with a receive sequence number. This sequence number is used to tell the protocol the number of the next frame to be received.

The P/F or Poll Final number, following the receive sequence number, is used differently by primary and secondary nodes. Primary nodes use the information to communicate to the secondary node that it requires an immediate response. The secondary node uses the information to tell the primary node that the frame is the last one in the current dialogue.

After the P/F bit, the send sequence number is used to identify the current frame's sequence number. Following the send sequence number, one or two bits are used to define the frame type. Table 2.16 specifies the bit values and the corresponding frame type.

TABLE 2.16   SDLC Frame Types

Bit Value	Frame Type
0	Information
0 1	Supervisory
1 1	Unnumbered

The `Data` field follows the control frame. As with other frame types, the FCS field follows and is used to calculate the CRC. SDLC frames differ again with the last field. As with the beginning of the frame, the frame ends with another `Flag` field.

Now that we have discussed the frame structure, we need to discuss the three different frame types. We will begin with Information frames. Information frames carry exactly that—information destined for the upper-layer protocols. Supervisory frames control SDLC communications; they are responsible for flow and error control for I-frame (information). Unnumbered frames provide the initialization of secondary nodes, as well as other managerial functions.

X.25

Layers 1, 2, and 3 of the OSI model coincide with the *X.25* protocol. Layer 3 X.25 is responsible for upper-layer protocol agreement and data exchange. Layer 2 X.25 uses LAPB as its protocol. Layer 1 X.25 maps to Layer 1 of the OSI model, which is in charge of data transmission across the physical medium.

X.25 uses virtual circuits to communicate with end systems. These circuits can be permanent (PVC) or switched (SVC) once they are inside of the carrier's switching network. The upper layers of X.25 are concerned only that communication is established with the destination system. Once a virtual circuit is created, it has unique numerical identifiers assigned to it, which distinguish it from other connections.

Figure 2.25 shows how PVCs or SVCs are used to connect two end systems. You can see four routers sitting outside of a switching cloud. Router A has a virtual circuit to Router B, and Router C has a virtual circuit to Router D. Within the switching cloud, it is possible that the center switch could have two circuits running on it. In order for this switch, or any of the switches, to keep data flowing to the right destinations, it assigns circuit identifiers to each virtual circuit. When a packet is sent, it is told which virtual circuit it belongs to.

FIGURE 2.25 Example of virtual circuits

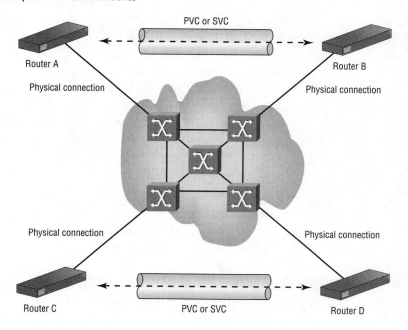

Frame Structure

Now that you understand how the two end systems communicate, move a little deeper into X.25 by looking at the frame structure. Refer to Figure 2.26 for the graphical representation of the X.25 frame. X.25 frames are very similar to SDLC frames. Each end is bounded with a `Flag` field. Starting from the right and moving to the left, we start with a `Flag` segment. After the `Flag` field, the frame contains the `Frame control and address` field.

FIGURE 2.26 X.25 frame structure

Flag	FCS	Data	Frame control and address	Flag

Next is the `Data` field that contains the Layer 3 X.25 packet, which in turn holds the Layer 3 packet header and upper-layer data. Finally, the frame ends with the `FCS` and `Flag` fields. The Layer 2 frame is simply an LAPB frame.

Frame Relay

The *Frame Relay* technology is more advanced than X.25. Frame Relay was developed as a digital packet-switching technology, whereas X.25 was an analog technology. The technology used in Frame Relay allows it to multiplex several different data flows over the same physical media.

Frame Relay also uses permanent and switched virtual circuits between data terminal equipment (DTE). These virtual circuits have unique identifiers that allow the Frame Relay to keep track of each logical data flow. The identifier is known as a DLCI (data link connection identifier). The DLCI number is used to create a logical circuit within a physical circuit. Multiple logical circuits can be created within one physical circuit. Look at the following router-configuration excerpt:

```
interface Serial1/5
 description Physical Circuit
 no ip address
 no ip directed-broadcast
 encapsulation frame-relay
!
interface Serial1/5.1 point-to-point
 description To Building A
 ip address 172.16.1.17 255.255.255.252
```

```
  no ip directed-broadcast
  frame-relay interface-dlci 17 IETF
  !
interface Serial1/5.2 point-to-point
  description To Building B
  ip address 172.16.1.25 255.255.255.252
  no ip directed-broadcast
  frame-relay interface-dlci 22 IETF
```

From this configuration, you can see that two logical circuits have been defined to communicate over one physical circuit. Notice that each subinterface or logical circuit has a unique DLCI. Each DLCI maps to another DLCI within the Frame Relay cloud. This mapping continues throughout the Frame Relay cloud until it maps to another DTE on the destination side of the virtual circuit.

Frame Structure

The frame used in Frame Relay is similar to the frame used in X.25, except for two major differences. The first difference is that Frame Relay leaves flow and error control to the upper-layer protocols. Frame Relay does provide congestion detection and can notify the upper layers of possible problems, but it is only concerned primarily with the transmission and reception of data. Because Frame Relay does not worry about flow and error control, it does not reserve any space within the frame for this information.

The second difference is the DLCI number. Ten bits of the two-byte `Address` field are used to define the DLCI. To a Frame Relay frame, the DLCI is the most significant address in the header. Figure 2.27 depicts a Frame Relay frame. As you can see, it is very similar to the X.25 frame, except for the flow/error control field.

FIGURE 2.27 Frame Relay frame structure

Flag	FCS	Data	Address	Flag

Integrated Services Digital Network (ISDN)

Integrated Services Digital Network (ISDN) is a service that allows telephone networks to carry data, voice, and other digital traffic. There are two types of ISDN interfaces: *Basic Rate Interface (BRI)* and *Primary Rate Interface (PRI)*. BRI uses two B channels and one D channel. Each of the two B channels operates at 64Kbps bidirectionally; the D channel operates at 16Kbps. The B channels are used for transmitting and receiving data. The D channel is used for protocol communications and signaling.

In contrast, PRI uses 23 B channels and one D channel. All 23 B channels are added to a rotary group as well. The D channel runs at the same line speed as the B channels—64Kbps. Because of the D channel's additional line speed, PRI has the equivalent line speed of a T1 circuit (1.5Mbps). In Europe, PRI offers 30 B channels and 1 D channel, making it the equivalent of an E1 circuit.

Just as there are two types of ISDN interfaces, there are two terminal equipment types. Type 1 (TE1) is equipment that was built specifically for use on ISDN. Type 2 (TE2) is equipment that was made before the ISDN specifications, and it requires a terminal adapter to actually interface with ISDN. Terminal equipment is comparable to DTE, mentioned in the Frame Relay section. It is equipment such as computers or routers.

In order for terminal equipment to work, there must be a network termination to connect to. Three types of ISDN network terminations exist. These devices are known as NT devices. Type 1 (NT1) devices are treated as customer premises equipment. Type 2 (NT2) devices perform Layer 2 and Layer 3 functions. The last type is a combination of the previous two types. It is known as a Type 1/2 or NT1/2.

Frame Structure

Look at Figure 2.28 to get a picture of the ISDN frame. As you can see, this frame is similar to the HDLC frame that you saw earlier. ISDN uses LAP on the D channel for Layer 2 functions. Just like X.25, the ISDN frame is bounded by Flag fields.

FIGURE 2.28 ISDN frame format

Starting from the right and working to the left, we see the Address field. The Address field contains several bits of key information:

SAPI   This field is the service access point identifier. It defines which services are provided to Layer 3.

C/R   This field designates the frame as a command or a response.

EA   This is the last bit of the first byte of the Address field. This bit defines the Address field as one or two bytes. If it is set to one byte, this is the last field within the Address field. If it is set to two, then one more field follows ending with another EA bit.

TEI   Terminal endpoint identifier. This is used to define a single terminal or multiple terminals.

Summary

A great deal of information was covered in this chapter. The focus of the chapter has been on Network and Data-Link layer protocols. It is important to understand this information to facilitate troubleshooting. If you do not sufficiently understand the protocols present in Layers 2 and 3 of the OSI model, you should study them in depth. The majority of networking problems occur in these two layers.

There are two major protocol classifications: connection-oriented and connectionless. Connection-oriented protocols allow for sequenced data transfer, flow control, and error control. Some examples of connection-oriented protocols include: ATM, TCP, Novell SPX, and AppleTalk ATP. Connectionless protocols require less overhead; however, they do so at the expense of the sequenced data transfer, and error and flow control that is offered by connection-oriented protocols. Some connectionless protocols include: UDP, Novell IPX, and AppleTalk DDP.

IP routing protocols come in two basic classifications, distance-vector and link-state. Distance-vector protocols are in general first-generation routing protocols that function well in smaller settings but have difficulty in large internetworks. Link-state protocols allow for incremental updates as well as faster convergence times over distance-vector protocols, but do so at the cost of CPU and memory utilization. RIP and IGRP are distance-vector protocols, OSPF is a link-state protocol, and EIGRP is a hybrid combination of a link-state and distance-vector protocol. Much like EIGRP, BGP does not fit into a single classification. It is sometimes referred to as a contract vector protocol, as it determines the best path based on the "contract" that has been established with its neighbors.

IPX and AppleTalk have many of the same general characteristics as IP. They all have connectionless and connection-oriented protocols as well as multiple different routing protocols. On Cisco routers EIGRP can be used for IP, IPX, and AppleTalk. In addition to EIGRP, IPX RIP and NLSP are routing protocols that can be used for IPX, and RTMP can be used for AppleTalk.

There are numerous different encapsulation types available at the second layer of the OSI model. The ones discussed in this chapter were Ethernet, Token Ring, PPP, SDLC, Frame Relay, ISDN, and X.25. Each has its own strengths and weaknesses that make it better suited for a particular installation.

Exam Essentials

Know the differences between connectionless and connection-oriented protocols.   Connection-oriented protocols have flow and error checking methodologies that are not present in connectionless protocols. Connectionless protocols offer better performance characteristics for real-time voice and video applications.

Know the functioning of the major IP routing protocols.   The routing protocols discussed were RIP, IGRP, EIGRP, OSPF, and BGP. Review the characteristics for each protocol given in the text.

Understand the functioning of IPX in an internetwork.   Much like IP, IPX has both connectionless and connection-oriented protocols associated with it. In addition, the routing protocols that can be used by IPX include RIP, EIGRP, and NLSP.

Understand the functioning of AppleTalk in an internetwork.   Be sure to know the different AppleTalk routed and routing protocols and how they function.

Know the Data Link protocols and technologies.   The major technologies covered in this section include Ethernet, Token Ring, PPP, SDLC (HDLC), Frame Relay, ISDN, and X.25.

Key Terms

Before you take the exam, be certain you are familiar with the following terms:

Active Monitor

AppleTalk Address Resolution Protocol (AARP)

Basic Rate Interface (BRI)

Border Gateway Protocol

carrier sense, multiple access/ collision detection (CSMA/CD)

connectionless protocols

connection-oriented protocols

Datagram Delivery Protocol (DDP)

Enhanced IGRP (EIGRP)

error control

Ethernet

extended addressing

flow control

Frame Relay

High-level Data Link Control (HDLC)

IEEE 802.3

Integrated Services Digital Network (ISDN)

Interior Gateway Routing Protocol (IGRP)

Internet Control Message Protocol (ICMP)

Internet Protocol (IP)

Internetwork Packet Exchange (IPX)

NetWare Link Services Protocol (NLSP)

Open Shortest Path First (OSPF)

Point-to-Point Protocol (PPP)

primary nodes

Primary Rate Interface (PRI)

protocol parameters

required resources

Routing Information Protocol (RIP)

Routing Table Maintenance Protocol (RTMP)

secondary nodes

sequenced data transfer

Synchronous Data Link Control (SDLC)

token

Token Ring

Transmission Control Protocol (TCP)

User Datagram Protocol (UDP)

Variable Length Subnet Masking (VLSM)

window size

X.25

Review Questions

1. Which global protocol type provides error and flow control?

   A. Connectionless

   B. Connection-oriented

   C. IP

   D. UDP

2. Which of the following protocols are considered connection-oriented protocols? (Choose all that apply.)

   A. ATM

   B. UDP

   C. TCP

   D. IP

   E. Novell SPX

   F. AppleTalk ATP

3. Which of the following protocols are considered connectionless protocols? (Choose all that apply.)

   A. Frame Relay

   B. UDP

   C. PPP

   D. Novell IPX

   E. SDLC

   F. AppleTalk DDP

   G. IP

4. Which protocol of the IP protocol suite provides environmental information regarding IP networks, such as congestion and reachability?

  A. ICMP

  B. UDP

  C. TCP

  D. SMTP

5. What are window sizes used for in TCP data transfers?

  A. They define the size of the packet, otherwise known as MTU.

  B. They define how long the TCP transfer can last.

  C. They define how many bytes are sent before an ACK is received.

  D. They define the port the transfer will use.

6. What advantage do connectionless data transfers have over connection-oriented transfers?

  A. Flow-and-error control

  B. Guarantee of data integrity

  C. A more secure transfer

  D. Less overhead and network traffic

7. What is RIP's major weakness?

  A. Hop count

  B. Distance-vector protocol

  C. Link-state protocol

  D. Inaccurate metric values

8. Which hosts are assigned legal IP addresses and would be able to communicate with each other without using a router, assuming the following IP addresses:

Host 1 IP address 10.2.25.47 /28

Host 2 IP address 10.2.25.48 /28

Host 3 IP address 10.2.25.46 /28

Host 4 IP address 10.2.25.33 /28

    A. Hosts 1 and 4

    B. Hosts 1, 2, and 3

    C. Hosts 3 and 4

    D. Hosts 1 and 2

    E. Hosts 1, 2, 3, and 4

9. What are the two elements used by default by IGRP and EIGRP to calculate routing metrics? (Choose two.)

    A. Bandwidth

    B. Delay

    C. Load

    D. Reliability

    E. MTU

    F. Hop count

10. What four attributes were added to IGRP to create Enhanced IGRP? (Choose four.)

    A. Poison reverse updates

    B. Incremental updates

    C. Classless routing

    D. Distance-vector metric calculation

    E. Formal peer relationships

    F. Configurable metric values

    G. Equal-cost load balancing

11. How does OSPF differ from EIGRP? (Choose two.)

    A. It is a pure link-state routing protocol.

    B. All OSPF areas should be connected to Area 0.

    C. It has incremental updates.

    D. It maintains a topology database.

12. What exchange must first occur before a BGP peering session can be established?

    A. There is a multicast request.

    B. The router must broadcast for all other BGP speakers.

    C. A SYN-ACK-SYN TCP handshake establishes a TCP connection.

    D. All of the above.

13. To which OSI layers does Novell NetWare specifically map?

    A. All layers

    B. Layers 3 through 7

    C. Layers 2 through 7

    D. Layers 4 through 7

14. What is the term that Cisco uses to refer to the special Ethernet frame format that Novell uses?

    A. ARPA

    B. SAP

    C. Novell-Ether

    D. SNAP

15. Which Ethernet IP encapsulation is the default for Cisco routers? Use Cisco terminology.

    A. ARPA

    B. SAP

    C. Novell-Ether

    D. SNAP

16. What features does Token Ring possess that Ethernet does not? (Choose two.)

    A. Faster speeds

    B. Token passing

    C. Fault isolation

    D. MAC addresses

17. What is CSMA/CD used for on an Ethernet segment? (Choose two.)

    A. Speed negotiation

    B. Collision detection

    C. Duplex negotiation

    D. Carrier sense

    E. Setting trunk type

18. Which interface type was PPP designed to use?

    A. Ethernet

    B. Token Ring

    C. Serial

    D. None of the above

19. Which node types exist within SDLC and its derivatives? (Choose two.)

    A. Master

    B. Slave

    C. Server

    D. Client

    E. Primary

    F. Secondary

20. Which layer(s) of the OSI model coincide with the X.25 protocol?

    A. All layers

    B. Layer 2

    C. Layers 1 and 2

    D. Layers 1 through 3

Answers to Review Questions

1. **B.**   Connection-oriented is a protocol type. In addition, it provides error and flow control. Connectionless protocols, such as IP and UDP, do not.

2. **A, C, E, F.**   UDP and IP are both connectionless protocols.

3. **B, D, F, G.**   Frame Relay, PPP, and SDLC are all connection-oriented protocols.

4. **A.**   ICMP provides environmental statistics for IP networks. The other protocols do not.

5. **C.**   Window sizes are transmission sizes. Once the window size is reached, the sending computer awaits an ACK packet, informing the sending computer that the receiving computer received the entire transmission.

6. **D.**   Due to the simplicity of connectionless protocols, they create less overhead and also use less bandwidth.

7. **A.**   The hop count indicates limitations on how far a packet could go.

8. **C.**   Since it is a /28 mask, the subnet boundaries are at 10.2.25.32 and 10.2.25.48. Therefore, 3 and 4 are on the same subnet. Host 1 is assigned the broadcast address for the 10.2.25.32 /28 subnet and 2 is assigned the network address for the 10.2.25.48 /28 subnet.

9. **A, B.**   Though bandwidth, delay, load, reliability, and MTU all can be part of the metric calculation for IGRP and EIGRP, only bandwidth and delay are used by default.

10. **B, C, E, G.**   These items were added to EIGRP to allow it to scale better as well as respond more quickly.

11. **A, B.**   EIGRP is a hybrid protocol that does not use areas. Both OSPF and EIGRP maintain topology databases and use incremental updates.

12. **C.**   A peer cannot connect if there is not a TCP connection first.

13. **B.**   NetWare protocols map to these layers and a special frame format is used to "access" the Data-Link layer.

14. **C.**   Novell uses the term Ethernet_802.3, Cisco uses Novell-Ether. See Table 2.12.

15. A.   Cisco uses ARPA as its default Ethernet encapsulation. The other encapsulation types can be set via the command line, but are not on by default.

16. B, C.   Ethernet does not use a token, nor does it provide fault isolation. It is possible that Ethernet can be faster than Token Ring, and Ethernet also uses MAC addresses.

17. B, D.   CSMA/CD stands for carrier sense, multiple access/collision detection. It allows multiple Ethernet stations to verify that there is a carrier signal on the line and access it if it is quiet. It also allows for the detection of and recovery from a collision.

18. C.   PPP uses serial connections.

19. E, F.   Primary and secondary are the correct terms for the node types within SDLC.

20. D.   X.25 covers layers 1 through 3 of the OSI model.

Chapter 3

Generic Troubleshooting Tools

TOPICS COVERED IN THIS CHAPTER INCLUDE:

✓ Describe the types and purposes of tools commonly used for network troubleshooting processes.

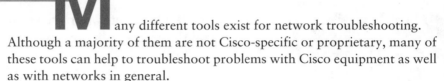

Many different tools exist for network troubleshooting. Although a majority of them are not Cisco-specific or proprietary, many of these tools can help to troubleshoot problems with Cisco equipment as well as with networks in general.

Troubleshooting tools can be used to analyze several aspects of a network, such as the physical connectivity and the protocols, as well as the applications running on the network. Each area requires a different set of tools and procedures. Often, troubleshooting tools and test equipment are used only when there is a network failure or problem. It is important to recognize that many tools can be used in a proactive method, such as monitoring. Certainly, some tools are not able or not designed to provide monitoring functions. Many are capable of this task, however.

We begin this chapter by discussing the tools designed for physical media troubleshooting, and then move on to network monitors and analyzers. After this, we will discuss using some of these tools in monitoring applications. Cisco has several software packages that provide excellent network monitoring using SNMP (Simple Network Management Protocol) and TCP/IP protocol debugging tools.

Some tools are part of the TCP/IP protocol stack, others are systems that capture frames and decode them using software, and yet others are used to test physical media. The use of all these types of tools provides coverage for many of the seven layers of the OSI model.

Physical Media Test Equipment

Starting at the bottom and working up, we begin with Layer 1 connectivity testing. It is amazing how many network problems can actually be solved by testing and then resolving wiring problems.

In this section, you will learn about several different types of *physical media test equipment*. These include:

- Volt-ohm meter
- Multimeters
- Cable testers
- Time domain reflectors (TDR) and optical TDRs (OTDR)
- Digital interface testing tools

Multimeters and Cable Testers

There is a large variety of physical media testing equipment. The most basic tools are multimeters and cable testers.

Both *volt-ohm meters* and *multimeters* measure voltage (AC and DC), resistance, and current. In addition, these devices can also be used to verify the continuity of a cable run from end to end. As is alluded to above, these devices deal with electrical signals. Therefore, they can only be used to test copper (or other electrically based) wiring, and cannot be used to test any fiber optic wiring.

Cable testers can be very general or they can be made for a specific type of cable. Some cable testers have adapters that allow them to test a wide range of cables such as unshielded twisted pair (UTP), shielded twisted pair (STP), or coaxial (coax) cable. Cable testers are made for electrical and optical cable.

Different from multimeters, cable testers can give the user much more information regarding the cable being tested. Cable testers come in varieties that can test both electrical and optical cables. Below are some examples of the attributes that are reported by an electrical cable tester:

- Electrical connectivity
- Open pairs
- Crossed pairs
- Out of distance specification
- Cross talk
- Attenuation

- Noise/interference
- Wiring maps
- MAC information
- Line utilization

Optical cable testers verify the same sort of information as electrical; however, they obviously use optical signals in place of electrical. In general, there are three different wavelengths that are predominantly used by optical cable testers: 850 nm, 1300 nm, and 1550 nm. Through the use of these wavelengths and by transmitting at a known power level, optical cable testers are able to measure attenuation and return loss on the fiber.

It is important to realize that not all cable testers provide all of this information. A given tester may provide only some of these attributes.

Time Domain Reflectors (TDRs) and Optical TDRs (OTDRs)

Time domain reflectors (TDRs) are complex cable testers. They are used to locate physical problems in a cable. They can detect where an open circuit, short circuit, crimped wire, or other abnormality is located in a cable.

TDRs and optical TDRs (OTDRs) work on the same principle: a signal is sent down the cable and the unit waits for the reflected signal to come back. Different abnormalities in cabling cause this signal to be reflected at different signal strengths, or amplitudes. Based on the amplitude, the meter distinguishes between opens, shorts, crimps, or other failures in the cable. These meters measure the time between the sending of the signal and the arrival of the reflected signal at the unit. This time interval is used to calculate where the failure is occurring in the cable. Optical TDRs can also provide information on conditions such as signal attenuation, fiber breaks, and losses through connectors.

Digital Interface Testing Tools

Digital interface testing tools consist of several different tools, such as *breakout boxes*, used to verify pin-outs (e.g., TD—transmit data, RD—receive data, CTS—clear to send) for all types of serial and parallel interfaces, and *bit/block error rate testers*, used for testing the quality of a communication link based on deviance from a known bit pattern. These tools are used to measure signals sent from computer and communication equipment. They are also able to test connections and communication between data terminal equipment and data communications equipment.

Although monitoring line conditions is an option with these types of tools, they are not capable of analyzing protocol information on a line. Their primary use is to verify that digital communication is sent and received by the two devices that are connected to the ends of the cable. A few examples: testing between a PC and a printer, a router and CSU/DSU, or even a modem and a PC.

For example, if you were troubleshooting a connection between a CSU and router and you wanted to verify that the router was indeed transmitting data appropriately, you could connect a breakout box in between the router and the CSU/DSU. Then while the communication takes place you can verify whether, when the router sets DTR high, the CSU/DSU sets CTS high before the transmission of data from the router occurs.

Software Test Equipment

There are many different types of *software test equipment* available that help to troubleshoot network problems. We begin by talking about generic programs that can provide troubleshooting capabilities, and then we will move on to Cisco-specific solutions. There are basically two types of software used for aiding network troubleshooting: network monitoring and network analyzing.

Network Monitors

As the word *monitor* describes, this software-based tool simply monitors the network. It can do this in several ways, including the Simple Network Management Protocol and the Internet Control Message Protocol.

The *Simple Network Management Protocol (SNMP)* is the most widely used method of gathering network statistics. Once a system has sufficient information about a network, it continually monitors the availability and connectivity of each device that is specified in its configuration.

No packet analysis is performed by network monitors. It is simply used to gather and keep statistical information about the network. The historical data that monitoring provides can be used to create a network *baseline*.

As was discussed in Chapter 1, a baseline is a very important tool. How can you effectively troubleshoot a new problem on a network if you don't know what the network used to be like or how it was configured? By keeping a baseline, you can compare previous performance and traffic levels to what you are currently seeing. Perhaps your problem is a new application that was introduced into your network.

SNMP is not the only method of monitoring a network, however. There are tools that use protocol tools to isolate network problems. For instance, the *Internet Control Message Protocol (ICMP)* can be used to ping a list of hosts. If a host does not respond, the program adds the host to a list and displays it to a monitor.

Network Analyzers

Network analyzers are also known as *protocol analyzers*. Examples of protocol analyzers are EtherPeek (used in the *CCNA: Cisco Certified Network Associate Study Guide* and in this book), Network Associate's Sniffer, and RADCOM's PrismLite.

These tools have the capability to passively examine the traffic that traverses a network without interrupting the traffic. This gives you the capability to take a detailed look, packet by packet, at what is occurring on your network. Network analyzers are made by numerous vendors and can be used to analyze many different network types. For example, there are analyzers for Ethernet, Token Ring, ATM, Frame Relay, HDLC, and many more.

Regardless of the analyzer you are using, to work effectively it must be connected to the network or broadcast domain that you are interested in troubleshooting. For example, Figure 3.1 depicts an Ethernet subnetwork. If there is a fault within the 172.16.1.0 subnetwork, the protocol analyzer must be placed on that segment of the subnetwork. Otherwise, you will not see the packets transiting the subnetwork. As you can see in Figure 3.1, the protocol analyzer is connected to the 172.16.1.0 subnetwork.

FIGURE 3.1   Placement of a protocol analyzer

172.16.1.0

Network
analyzer

To better handle the data that is captured by an analyzer, different filters
may be used. Most programs allow filters to be placed before or after the
packet is copied. After a full capture, display filters may be used to help narrow the field of troubleshooting. You can filter on many different types of
criteria. For example, you can look at all packets going to or coming from a
particular station (whether that be on a Layer 2 or Layer 3 level). You can
also filter on the protocol used or the port that is being accessed. By applying
the filters before the packet is captured into memory, the analyzer looks at
each packet and compares it to user-defined filters. If the necessary criteria
are met, the packet is then copied to memory; otherwise, it is dropped, thus
allowing you to save memory on the analyzer.

Protocol Analyzers and Switches

As we have already discussed, in order to be effective, a protocol analyzer
must be in the same broadcast domain as the workstation or workstations
that it is meant to monitor. On a switch, this can create a problem. Even if
the analyzer is put in the same VLAN as the workstation, in most cases it will
see only the broadcast traffic on the VLAN, as the unicast traffic is sent only
to the port on which its destination resides. To rectify this issue, Cisco switches
use a feature call *Switched Port Analyzer* or SPAN. This feature allows you to
set up a monitor port on a switch and to monitor all traffic coming to or from
a particular port or on a particular VLAN.

For example, assume you are having problems with a workstation attached
to port 2/1 of a switch, Switch_A, and wanted to analyze the packets it was
sending. Also assume that this workstation is in VLAN 200. You then plug
your network analyzer into port 2/12 and set up a span port to look at both

the incoming and outgoing packets on port 2/1. The commands to do this as well as verify the setup are shown below:

```
Switch_A> (enable) set span 2/1 2/12 both
Enabled monitoring of Port 2/1 transmit/receive traffic by
    Port 2/12
Switch_A> (enable) show span
Status           : enabled
Admin Source     : Port 2/1
Oper Source      : Port 2/1
Destination      : Port 2/12
Direction        : transmit/receive
Incoming Packets: disabled
```

It should be noted that when the span is enabled, the destination port will show a status of Monitor instead of the normal status of Connected. Also, the "both" at the end of the command indicates that transmitted and received packets are to be looked at. If you only wanted to look at packets being either transmitted or received, instead of both, you would use either tx or rx, respectively.

If, in our example, you were interested in seeing all traffic in VLAN 200, you could use a variation of the set span command as shown below:

```
Switch_A> (enable) set span 200 2/12 both
Enabled monitoring of VLAN 200 transmit/receive traffic by
    Port 2/12
Switch_A> (enable) show span
Status           : enabled
Admin Source     : VLAN 200
Oper Source      : Port 2/1-3,2/5-6,2/8-11,2/13-24,3/1-12
Destination      : Port 2/12
Direction        : transmit/receive
Incoming Packets: disabled
```

If you are going to span a VLAN, be aware that it is possible for the monitor port to become overwhelmed if the traffic flowing on the VLAN is more than can be handled by the port.

When you are done looking at traffic using the network analyzer, you can turn off the span port by using the set span disable command as shown below:

```
Switch_A> (enable) set span disable
```

```
Disabled monitoring of VLAN 200 transmit/receive traffic
   by Port 2/12
Switch_A> (enable) show span
Status          : disabled
Admin Source    : VLAN 200
Oper Source     : None
Destination     : Port 2/12
Direction       : transmit/receive
Incoming Packets: disabled
```

As you can see by the last show span command, though the monitoring port is no longer in use, the switch remembers the last port or VLAN that was analyzed and the port that was used for monitoring.

Sample Packet Captures: Multicast Packet

The sample multicast packet shown below was captured using EtherPeek. However, any protocol analyzer will give you the same information using the same, or a slightly different, format. As you see, the packet is broken down by protocol. The first section is the Ethernet header, which contains Layer 2 address information.

Layer 3 follows Layer 2, so you see the IP header. The IP header contains all pertinent information for IP, including the IP source and destination addresses. It also defines the protocol riding above IP, Internet Group Management Protocol (IGMP), which is used for multicast communications. Farther down the packet decode, you see the actual IGMP header.

```
Flags:          0x00
  Status:         0x00
  Packet Length:64
  Timestamp:      12:12:58.349000 03/22/1999
Ethernet Header
  Destination:  01:00:5f:00:00:04
  Source:       08:00:20:7e:55:5f
  Protocol Type:08-00   IP
IP Header - Internet Protocol Datagram
  Version:                4
  Header Length:          5
  Precedence:             0
```

```
    Type of Service:        %000
    Unused:                 %00
    Total Length:           32
    Identifier:             10603
    Fragmentation Flags:    %000
    Fragment Offset:        0
    Time To Live:           1
    IP Type:                0x02    IGMP
    Header Checksum:        0xe6e5
    Source IP Address:      172.16.10.10
    Dest. IP Address:       224.0.0.4
    No Internet Datagram Options
IGMP - Internet Group Management Protocol
    Version:        1
    Type:           3    STR# IP Protocols
    Unused:         1
    Checksum:       56080
    Group Address:1.14.8.3
Extra bytes (Padding):
    6... F..P_.  %m.    36 ee d1 ee ae 46 08 00 50 9e e4 e8
       20 25 6d 00
    ..                      00 00
Frame Check Sequence:   0x00000000
```

Sample Packet Captures: Cisco Proprietary Packet

Now look at a Cisco proprietary packet. The following is a decode for a Cisco Discovery Protocol (CDP) packet. As you can see, this is a Layer 2 packet. You can tell it is a Layer 2 packet because there is no IP or other Layer 3 header decode. The first header section is the Ethernet 802.3 header, followed by the Logical Link Control (LLC) header. This header contains the Cisco Discovery Protocol data.

```
    Flags:          0x80    802.3
      Status:       0x00
      Packet Length:200
      Timestamp:    14:49:03.211000 03/22/1999
    802.3 Header
      Destination:  01:00:0c:dd:cc:6f   [0-5]
```

Source: 00:10:7c:75:8d:cf [6-13]
LLC Length: 182
802.2 Logical Link Control (LLC) Header
Dest. SAP: 0xaa SNAP [14]
Source SAP: 0xaa SNAP Null LSAP [15]
Command: 0x03 Unnumbered Information [16]
Protocol: 00-00-0c-20-00 Cisco DP [17-21]
Packet Data:
. 06902459   01 b4 d7 af 00 01 00 19 30 36 39 30
  32 34 35 39   [22-37]
9(hostname)...   39 28 73 77 2d 75 65 6e 2e 6f 72 67
  29 00 02 00   [38-53]
.... |....   11 00 00 00 01 01 01 cc 00 04 cd 7c
  fa f8 00 03   [54-69]
..5/19..........   00 08 35 2f 31 39 00 04 00 08 00 00
  00 0e 00 05   [70-85]
.dWS-C5500 Softw   00 00 00 00 00 00 00 00 00 30 20 53
  6f 66 74 77   [86-101]
are, Version Mcp   61 72 65 2c 20 56 2d 00 00 00 00 00
  20 4d 63 70   [102-117]
SW: 4.4(1) NmpSW   53 57 3a 20 34 2e 34 28 31 29 20 4e
  6d 70 53 57   [118-133]
: 4.4(1).Copyrig   3a 20 34 00 00 00 00 00 00 00 00 00
  00 72 69 67   [134-149]
ht (c) 1995-1999   68 74 20 28 63 29 20 31 39 39 35 2d
  31 39 39 39   [150-165]
by Cisco System   20 62 79 20 43 69 73 63 6f 20 53 79 73
  74 65 6d   [166-181]
s.....WS-C5500   73 0a 00 06 00 0c 57 53 2d 43 35 35
  30 30   [182-195]
Frame Check Sequence: 0xffff00cd

Sample Packet Captures: POP3 Packet

The following example is of a POP3 packet. POP3 is the Post Office Protocol that is used to transfer e-mail from a server to a remote client. The packet decode gives you a great amount of information. It starts out with a Layer 2 header and then moves on to Layer 3 with the IP header. After Layer 3, you see TCP, which is a Layer 4 protocol. You can see all of the flow control information as part of the TCP packet. POP3 is part of the TCP suite, and is the final decode portion of this packet. The POP3 header shows the mail server as well as other POP3 data.

```
Flags:          0x00
  Status:         0x00
  Packet Length:99
  Timestamp:      14:48:51.539000 03/22/1999
Ethernet Header
  Destination:   01:a1:32:5a:a6:f1   [0-5]
  Source:        08:00:02:32:1f:f2   [6-11]
  Protocol Type:08-00  IP  [12-13]
IP Header - Internet Protocol Datagram
  Version:             4   [14 Mask 0xf0]
  Header Length:       5   [14 Mask 0xf]
  Precedence:          0   [15 Mask 0xe0]
  Type of Service:     %000  [15 Mask 0x1c]
  Unused:              %00  [15 Mask 0x3]
  Total Length:        81   [16-17]
  Identifier:          6039   [18-19]
  Fragmentation Flags: %010  Do Not Fragment   [20 Mask
    0xe0]
  Fragment Offset:     0   [20-22 Mask 0x1fffff]
  Time To Live:        255
  IP Type:             0x06  TCP  [23]
  Header Checksum:     0xd488  [24-25]
  Source IP Address:   172.16.12.10   [26-29]
  Dest. IP Address:    172.16.12.130   [30-33]
  No Internet Datagram Options
TCP - Transport Control Protocol
  Source Port:       110  POP3  [34-35]
  Destination Port: 1324  [36-37]
  Sequence Number:   3712383331  [38-41]
  Ack Number:        31151113  [42-45]
  Offset:            5   [46 Mask 0xf0]
  Reserved:          %000000  [46 Mask 0xfc0]
```

```
      Code:                %011000   [47 Mask 0x3f]
                  Ack is valid
                  Push Request
      Window:              8760  [48-49]
      Checksum:            0x2d24  [50-51]
      Urgent Pointer:      0  [52-53]
      No TCP Options
   POP - Post Office Protocol
      POP Reply:           +OK  Positive Reply  [54-56]
      Comment:                         [57]
      POP3 mail.somewhere.com  50 45 50 33 21 68 61 6d 2f 75
        65 6e 2d 6e 72 67   [58-73]
        v6.50 server re   21 76 36 2a 35 30 21 73 65 72 77 65
        78 20 72 65  [74-89]
      ady                  61 46 80   [90-92]
      Newline Sequence: 0x0d0a  [93-94]
   Frame Check Sequence:  0xffff00cd
```

Sample Packet Captures: IPX Packet

This last example shows an IPX packet. This is an IPX broadcast packet, as indicated by the destination MAC address within the 802.3 header. The LLC header has the source and destination SAP information. The IPX NetWare packet is a NetWare Core Protocol packet. The destination socket for every host on a broadcast domain is the same. The IPX broadcast is done by using the Service Advertising Protocol. The decode for that header is located at the bottom of the example. The packet tells you that a machine is using NSQ to find the nearest file server.

```
   Flags:         0x80  802.3
      Status:        0x00
      Packet Length:64
      Timestamp:     14:47:09.831000 03/22/1999
   802.3 Header
      Destination:  ff:ff:ff:ff:ff:ff Ethernet Brdcast  [0-5]
      Source:       00:00:1d:04:51:43  [6-13]
      LLC Length:   37
   802.2 Logical Link Control (LLC) Header
      Dest. SAP:    0xe0  NetWare  [14]
```

```
     Source SAP:    0xe0  NetWare  Null LSAP  [15]
     Command:       0x03  Unnumbered Information  [16]
IPX - NetWare Protocol
     Checksum:              0xffff  [17-18]
     Length:                34  [19-20]
     Transport Control:
       Reserved:            %0000  [21 Mask 0xf0]
       Hop Count:           %0000  [21-22 Mask 0xfff]
     Packet Type:           17  NCP - Netware Core Protocol
     Destination Network:  0x00000000  [23-26]
     Destination Node:      ff:ff:ff:ff:ff:ff Ethernet
       Brdcast     [27-32]
     Destination Socket:   0x0452  Service Advertising
       Protocol    [33-34]
     Source Network:       0x00000010  [35-38]
     Source Node:          00:00:1e:04:52:43  [39-44]
     Source Socket:        0x4010  IPX Ephemeral  [45-46]
SAP - Service Advertising Protocol
     Operation:            3  NetWare Nearest Service Query
       [47-48]
     Service Type:         4  File Server  [49-50]
Extra bytes (Padding):
     . ....NBU          03 c1 00 00 00 00 4e 42 55   [51-59]
     Frame Check Sequence:  0x01000000
```

As you see from the previous packet decodes, there is a lot of information that can be found out about a given network. The key is to know what you are searching for when looking through the results of a protocol analyzer. By looking at decodes and seeing where problems might be occurring, you can resolve network failures more quickly.

Network Management Systems (NMSs)

*N*etwork management systems (NMSs) are somewhat more complex than simple network monitoring systems. NMSs are more robust because they not only provide monitoring functions for network devices, they also allow for user interaction. Some examples of third-party NMSs are HP OpenView and Sun Net Manager management packages.

The basics behind these systems are that, with some configuration and guidance, they use different methods of *discovering* a network. This is done by starting out with a specified device—a *seed device*. The seed device polls all of its interfaces and comes back with the necessary information that enables the program to move on to the directly connected neighbors. The polling goes on until an edge is reached and there are no more neighbors to discover. Both of these systems draw logical topological network maps.

In addition to network discovery, the NMS monitors for device availability and reachability. If something does affect the connectivity, an alarm is tripped within the software, and it logs the event and displays an alarm.

Monitoring can also be done on a more detailed level (such as threshold monitoring). Thresholds can be defined within the software. They tell the program to trigger an alarm if a specified variable for a given host exceeds a maximum or descends below a minimal value. These alarms can be dealt with in various ways (for example, e-mail or pages may be sent).

The previous examples are just a few examples of what NMS packages can do. Here is a list of what most management systems try to do:

Availability management   This was described previously as network monitoring.

Network performance management   This is done by measuring traffic loads and other bandwidth-oriented data that can be used to calculate the network's overall performance.

Network security management   This is done by making the NMS the means by which changes are made to network devices. Because the software requires the user to log in, it can also track changes made by the user. Security management can also be done via having a user database within the NMS. When a network device is accessed or a change is attempted, the user is authenticated from the user profiles located within the NMS.

Network service simulation   In today's networks, it becomes very risky to test out configuration changes on a live production network. Simulation software that enables changes to be made offline and tested before being implemented is a big part of network management. It gives the administrator the ability to see whether the changes will cause any side effects, without endangering the applications on the production network.

Policy-based management This has to do with QoS, or quality of service. When an administrator knows that certain applications require more network resources, he or she can allocate resources accordingly. With policy-based management, the administrator can see where the most resources are needed and make it a higher priority that those resources are available when needed.

As was mentioned before, NMSs are third-party systems. Due to the complexity and diversity of network hardware, most vendors have their own management information base, or MIB, in addition to the standard ones. It doesn't stop there—Cisco has also created its own line of NMSs, which you will learn about in the next section.

Cisco Network Management Software

In order to achieve the five previously mentioned purposes of network management software, Cisco uses three software packages: CiscoWorks 2000, NetSys, and CiscoSecure. By using a combination of these packages, all five NMS purposes are fulfilled.

CiscoWorks 2000

CiscoWorks 2000 is the latest release of CiscoWorks. Cisco united several different network management packages into one centralized package. The primary components of CiscoWorks 2000 are Resource Manager Essentials and CiscoWorks for Switched Internetworks (CWSI). Within CWSI, you find further subcomponents: CWSI Campus, CiscoView, Threshold Manager, Traffic Director, VLAN Director, ATM Director, and UserTracking.

Each of these components fulfills an important role in the overall effectiveness of CiscoWorks 2000. We will now cover the role and basic functionality of each component.

Resource Manager Essentials

This component has taken the place of the original CiscoWorks. This portion of CiscoWorks 2000 is responsible for device inventory, configuration storage and changes, IOS upgrades and inventory, and some low-level security. It also provides monitoring functions, such as syslog monitoring.

This application, along with the other elements of CiscoWorks 2000, uses SNMP to manage the network. SNMP provides a way to retrieve device information and system information. Each device contains several *management information base* objects, otherwise known as *MIB* objects. These objects are simply variables that are assigned values. When an SNMP agent queries a device, it asks for specified MIB object values. The device then responds with the corresponding values. Look at the following example to see what we mean.

The first line of the debug shows an SNMP request from an SNMP agent (server). In this request, you see the MIB objects that the SNMP agent wants to get values for. The following lines show all MIB objects and their corresponding values. In this case, some of the MIB objects are the System Uptime and IP Address Entries. You can see that each MIB has a value assigned to it. We finish by looking at the line that confirms that the MIB object values were sent to the requesting machine.

Here is the debug:

```
debug snmp packets
SNMP packet debugging is on
Router_A#
Mar 23 22:05:49.751: SNMP: Packet received via UDP from
    172.16.2.2 on ATM1/0.2
Mar 23 22:05:49.755: SNMP: Get request, reqid 271128,
    errstat 0, erridx 0
sysUpTime.0 = 27315180
 lsystem.57.0 = 11
 lsystem.58.0 = 10
 ipAddrEntry.2.172.16.10.254 = 28
 ipAddrEntry.2.172.16.10.10 = 1
 ipAddrEntry.2.172.16.10.18 = 1
 ipAddrEntry.2.172.16.33.1 = 14
 ipAddrEntry.2.172.16.10.1 = 25
 ipAddrEntry.2.172.16.10.1 = 10
 ipAddrEntry.2.172.16.10.1 = 15
 ipAddrEntry.2.172.16.231.1 = 10
 ipAddrEntry.2.172.16.235.65 = 29
 ipAddrEntry.2.172.16.236.17 = 10
 ipAddrEntry.2.172.16.238.1 = 27
```

```
ipAddrEntry.2.172.16.10.5 = 45
ipAddrEntry.2.172.16.240.1 = 13
ipAddrEntry.2.172.16.246.1 = 12
ipAddrEntry.2.172.16.10.9 = 75
ipAddrEntry.2.172.16.10.21 = 58
ipAddrEntry.2.172.16.10.25 = 65
ipAddrEntry.2.172.16.10.29 = 60
ipAddrEntry.2.172.16.10.33 = 61
ipAddrEntry.2.172.16.10.37 = 76
ipAddrEntry.2.172.16.10.45 = 59
ipAddrEntry.2.172.16.10.49 = 67
ipAddrEntry.2.172.16.10.53 = 72
ipAddrEntry.2.172.16.10.57 = 73
ipAddrEntry.2.172.16.10.61 = 74
ipAddrEntry.2.172.16.10.65 = 56
ipAddrEntry.2.172.16.10.69 = 57
ipAddrEntry.2.172.16.10.81 = 55
ipAddrEntry.2.172.16.10.85 = 66
ipAddrEntry.2.172.16.10.89 = 68
ipAddrEntry.2.172.16.10.101 = 69
ipAddrEntry.2.172.16.10.105 = 70
ipAddrEntry.2.172.16.10.109 = 71
ipAddrEntry.2.172.16.10.121 = 62
ipAddrEntry.2.172.16.10.249 = 43
ipAddrEntry.2.172.16.10.9 = 47
Mar 23 22:05:49.815: SNMP: Packet sent via UDP to
    172.16.2.2
Router_A#un all
All possible debugging has been turned off
```

SNMP is a very rich protocol, and it is capable of providing detailed information. Because SNMP is not the focus of this book, we don't spend much time explaining its intricacies.

In summary, Resource Manager Essentials provides the following functions. It does all of this via SNMP, with some help from other protocols, such as TFTP for file transfer, even though the command is issued via SNMP.

- Availability/reachability monitoring
- Change reports
- Configuration management
- Device inventory
- IOS management
- Syslog analysis
- System administration
- CCO access and related tools
- Connection management
- Troubleshooting information

 Real World Scenario

SNMP and Security

The use of SNMP management and monitoring tools in a network can provide huge benefits to network administrators for such things as baselining and problem resolution. However, using these tools inappropriately can cause a serious security risk. The same items that enhance your ability to manage and monitor your network can also be used by a hacker to gain access to sensitive information. Therefore, when I implement SNMP monitoring and management in a company, I take certain precautions to ensure that the potential impact from a hacker is minimized.

The first of these precautions is rather obvious. I change the SNMP community strings from their default values of public, private, and secret. In addition, while choosing a string, I make sure I do not choose one that is easily guessed or in some way relates to the company for which I am installing the SNMP management. In this manner, I am able to deter the "casual" hacker looking for an easy target.

Next, I look for areas that are susceptible to attack from the outside. Examples of these areas are the border routers and the routers that are used by the web servers servicing external customers. In these areas, I use sets of SNMP community strings that are different from the ones used in the rest of the network. In this manner, if someone was able to get the strings for these at-risk devices, they do not have the strings for the entire network. Along with the different set of strings, I also make sure that SNMP, UDP port 161, is included in all access lists that filter traffic in these areas. This ensures that SNMP requests can come only from the internal network.

Next, I use access lists on all the routers and permit lists on our switches to allow SNMP access to only a small subset of devices in the network. On routers, I apply these access lists at the end of the `snmp-server community` command. This limits SNMP access to the router to networks or devices listed in the access list. On newer versions of switch CatOS, similar functionality is achieved through the use of the `set ip permit ip_address [mask] snmp` command.

Finally, as is the case with any feature that you are running on a switch or router, I examine the open bugs listed on the Cisco website on a regular basis to ensure that there are no security holes in the IOS or CatOS that I am using. In addition to going to the Cisco website and looking at the bugs, I also set up my Cisco account to e-mail me any time a security or performance bug is opened against the hardware and software versions I use. By taking security into account at the design phase of an SNMP implementation, you are able to better secure the network, while still gaining the benefits that SNMP management and monitoring have to offer.

CWSI

CiscoWorks for Switched Internetworks (CWSI) is a composite of several applications. The majority of the applications in CiscoWorks 2000 are applications of the CWSI element. The following lists a brief description of what each application is and what it is used for:

CWSI Campus This application is responsible for network discovery. It creates a logical topology map of the network and also provides views for VLANs.

VLAN Director This tool is used to configure, manage, and create reports for VLANs. It provides detailed information regarding physical devices, spanning tree configurations, and ATM-VLANs. It can also be used to provide quality of service (QoS) by providing different resources, based on VLAN assignment.

CiscoView   This application is used to display an image that physically represents the device. Within this program, you can monitor individual ports, the chassis, and interfaces. Some hardware platforms allow environmental information such as temperature and CPU utilization to be monitored.

Threshold Manager   This tool is actually part of CiscoView. It is used to configure the RMON (Remote Monitoring) threshold on network devices. Users can select default or custom MIB objects that are to be monitored. For a given MIB object, the user can then define thresholds that trigger alarms if the values of the MIB object do not fall within the specified criteria.

Traffic Director   This application complements the Threshold Manager. Because Threshold Manager is only a GUI to configure a device with thresholds, the Traffic Director uses RMON to gather the threshold information from the device. In addition to RMON information, Traffic Director provides protocol analysis, traffic monitoring and analysis, and application utilization.

ATM Director   This tool is used to discover ATM devices. It can provide information based on VPI/VCI pairs; it interfaces with switches to provide ATM-VLAN information; and it provides statistical information for PVCs and SVCs, as well as other ATM information.

UserTracking   Because VLANs are simply logical associations, User-Tracking is used to aid in moving user information from one VLAN to another or to provide consistent VLAN assignment if the physical cable is moved from one port to another on the switch.

Cisco provides a very thorough set of network management applications. These programs were developed specifically for Cisco equipment. For example, CWSI uses Cisco Discovery Protocol (CDP) to discover the network. Only Cisco devices respond to CDP packets. Because these tools were developed for Cisco devices, the MIB objects that are needed to manage the devices are preprogrammed into the software. With the CiscoWorks 2000 package, three of the five goals for NMS are fulfilled.

NetSys

NetSys is an offline tool. It is a complex program that inputs and parses Cisco device configurations, and then creates a model based on the configurations. The program is used to model changes to a network before they are actually implemented. The original configurations can be used to establish a baseline.

The engine used within NetSys can decipher the configurations and pinpoint any problems that might occur with the implementation of the configuration. NetSys creates topological maps, and then enables the user to make changes on the map, thus affecting configurations. There is a connectivity tool that allows the user to test connectivity between any two specified devices.

NetSys also has a performance tool. It can be configured to poll information from the network, download it, and then analyze it. The information copied from the network is used to show protocol distribution, link distribution, and application utilization. Using this tool, the user can create models that enable the network to scale and grow, according to the demands placed on it.

NetSys fulfills the role of an NMS because it allows changes to be modeled offline, tested, and then implemented into the production network. NetSys is a very powerful tool, and has been called a "CCIE in a can."

CiscoSecure

The CiscoSecure access control server (ACS) application is used to define access levels to individual users. CiscoSecure maintains a user profile for each user. This profile contains authorization and authentication information that is unique to each user. The information can either be stored on the server itself or reside in an external database. This allows Cisco Secure to function with secure token authentication devices and even interact with NT domain authentication. In this manner, a user can use their NT account for network authentication, eliminating the administrative need for multiple separate accounts.

CiscoSecure provides AAA (Authentication, Authorization, and Accounting) functionality for network devices and can be used with Terminal Access Controller Access Control System Plus (TACACS+), or Remote Authentication Dial-In User Service (RADIUS) configured devices. TACACS+ is an authentication methodology originally created by Cisco and is supported on most Cisco routers and switches. Its predecessors, XTACACS and TACACS, were the predominant authentication protocols used in older versions of IOS. In the newer versions of IOS and CatOS, support for RADIUS was added. As RADIUS is a standards-based protocol, the ability of CiscoSecure to understand RADIUS allows it to authenticate non-Cisco devices if they are using RADIUS.

CiscoSecure is flexible and scalable because it is capable of providing services to several devices simultaneously. Multiple servers can be deployed to allow for scalability. In addition, its web-based user interface makes administration of the CiscoSecure application possible from anywhere in the network. This management software completes the five requirements for a network management system by fulfilling the role of security.

Summary

This chapter was concerned with different types and applications of network testing equipment. We discussed physical media testers, as well as software methods for troubleshooting network problems.

We first looked at the use and functioning of volt-ohm meters and multimeters. These devices allow for simple testing of electrical continuity and the current and resistance on a section of cable. Cable testers give much more information about the condition of the cable than a multimeter or volt-ohm meter. Specifically, cable testers can also test for crossed pairs, crosstalk, attenuation, wiring maps, and many other items. Cable testers come in varieties that can test both electrically based cabling and optical fiber. TDRs and OTDRs can be used to detect where an open circuit, short circuit, crimped wire, or other abnormality is located in a cable. Finally, breakout boxes and bit/block error rate testers can be used to determine whether the digital communication between two devices, such as a router and CSU/DSU, is functioning as it should.

The protocol analyzer is a powerful tool that allows you to examine packet by packet what is happening on your network. Because of the amount of data that is captured by a protocol analyzer, it is a good idea to use filters to limit the data that is captured and/or displayed. In a switched environment, setting the span port on a switch will allow you to effectively use this tool.

Finally, though there are third-party Network Management Systems available, Cisco has a line of management tools specifically designed for use with Cisco products. When used together, these tools—CiscoWorks 2000, NetSys, and CiscoSecure—provide a complete network management package.

Exam Essentials

Know the physical test equipment and what it is used for. Physical test equipment includes volt-ohm meters, multimeters, cable testers, TDRs, OTDRs, and breakout boxes. Each device has a specific use. You should know the uses and the differences between each.

Know what protocol analyzers are used for. Protocol analyzers actually copy and analyze packets on a network. The information provided by protocol analyzers can be invaluable when troubleshooting network problems.

Know how to look at and analyze a packet as displayed by a protocol analyzer. When looking at a decoded packet, you should be able to determine the protocol and general function of the packet.

Know the purpose of Network Management Systems (NMSs). NMSs are very robust programs that provide great manageability for small and large networks. An NMS should have five attributes: network availability monitoring, network modeling and simulation, network security, quality of service management, and traffic monitoring and analysis.

Know the names and functions of the components of the Cisco network management suite. CiscoWorks 2000 provides the network availability monitoring, quality of service management, and traffic monitoring and analysis components of the systems. Network modeling and simulation is provided by NetSys, and CiscoSecure provides the network security component.

Commands Used in This Chapter

The following list contains a summary of all the commands used in this chapter.

Commands	Descriptions
debug snmp packets	Provides detail for SNMP packets destined for the router.
set span	Sets the port or VLAN to monitor, the port on which to monitor this information, and enables or disables these functions.
show span	Shows the status of the span port on a switch.

Key Terms

Before you take the exam, be certain you are familiar with the following terms:

baseline	network management systems (NMSs)
bit/block error rate testers	physical media test equipment
breakout boxes	protocol analyzers
cable testers	seed device
management information base	Simple Network Management Protocol (SNMP)
MIB	software test equipment
monitor	Switched Port Analyzer
multimeters	time domain reflectors (TDRs)
network analyzers	volt-ohm meters

Review Questions

1. Of the physical media testing tools below, which one is most appropriate to use when testing signals between a PC and its modem?

    A. TDR

    B. OTDR

    C. Multimeter

    D. Breakout box

2. Which tool do you use if you have to test a cabling infrastructure and functionality of your LAN?

    A. TDR

    B. Cable tester

    C. Network analyzer

    D. Breakout box

3. What tools can be used to verify fiber optic cable length, cable attenuation, or the approximate location of a fault with the cable?

    A. Optical time domain reflector (OTDR)

    B. Cable tester

    C. Multimeter

    D. Time domain reflector (TDR)

4. Which device do you use to test for physical (electrical) connectivity?

    A. OTDR

    B. Cable tester

    C. Multimeter

    D. TDR

5. Which tool do you use if you want to test fiber optic cable for attenuation at three wavelengths—850 nm, 1300 nm, and 1550 nm?

A. OTDR

B. TDR

C. A flashlight

D. A cable tester

6. Which protocol is used to collect device and statistical information?

   A. SNA

   B. SAP

   C. SMTP

   D. SNMP

7. On what basis do protocol or network analyzers work?

   A. All packets are analyzed as they pass through the analyzer.

   B. All packets are copied into a buffer if they meet specified criteria.

   C. Random packets are selected, based on the line speed of the media.

   D. Random packets are selected if they meet the specified criteria.

8. What types of filters do most network analyzers use? (Choose all that apply.)

   A. Access lists

   B. Capture

   C. Display

   D. Size

9. What are four functions of a cable tester? (Choose four.)

   A. Tests attenuation

   B. Shows runt packets

   C. Shows packet properties

   D. Shows crossed pairs

   E. Shows cross talk

   F. Shows noise/interference

10. Use the following decode information to determine what type of packet you are looking at. (Choose all that apply.)

```
Flags:                  0x80       802.3
    Status:             0x00
    Packet Length:64
    Timestamp:              10:19:42.712000 12/04/1998
802.3 Header
    Destination:     09:00:07:ff:ff:ff          [0-5]
    Source:          00:10:7b:a4:4a:a1          [6-13]
    LLC Length:         37
802.2 Logical Link Control (LLC) Header
    Dest. SAP:               0xaa      SNAP      [14]
    Source SAP:     0xaa     SNAP      Null LSAP [15]
    Command:                           0x03
      Unnumbered Information [16]
    Protocol:       08-00-07-80-9b       ETalkPh2  [17-21]
Long DDP Header - Datagram Delivery Protocol
    Unused:                        %00    [22 Mask 0xc0]
    Hop Count:                     %0000  [22 Mask 0x3c]
    Datagram Length:      29      [22-23 Mask 0x3ff]
    DDP Checksum:                  0x8a38        [24-25]
    Dest. Network:                 0             [26-27]
    Source Network:    1105      [28-29]
    Dest Node:         255       [30]
    Source Node:               179        [31-32]
    Dest. Socket:      1       RTMP       [33]
    Source Socket:     1       RTMP       [34]
    DDP Type:          1       RTMP Response or Data
RTMP - Routing Table Maintenance Protocol
    Router's Net:                  1105    [35-37]
ID Length:                          8      [38]
Router's Node ID: 179
```

```
RTMP Tuple # 1
     Range Start:              1100      [39-40]
     Range Flag:               %100      Extended
        [47 Mask 0xe0]
     Distance:                 0         [41 Mask 0x1f]
     Range End:                1109      [42-43]
     Version:                  0x82      [44]
RTMP Tuple # 2
     Range Start:              1000      [45-46]
     Range Flag:               %100      Extended
        [47 Mask 0xe0]
     Distance:                 0         [47 Mask 0x1f]
     Range End:                1005      [48-49]
     Version:                  0x82      [50]
Extra bytes (Padding):
     ........                     00 00 00 00 00 00 00
        00 00                  [51-59]
Frame Check Sequence:             0xfff0000a
```

   A. AppleTalk

   B. IPX

   C. RTMP

   D. Tuple

11. You look at a protocol distribution report from a network analyzer, and it says that there is a large amount of SNMP traffic. What does it mean?

   A. SNMP is using a high percentage of the total available bandwidth.

   B. SNMP is the most important protocol listed, which is why it has the highest percentage.

   C. SNMP needs to be turned off because the link can't handle that much SNMP traffic.

   D. SNMP uses the largest packet size relative to other protocols.

12. What *simple* software tools are used to test for device availability/reachability?

    A. Cable testers

    B. Network monitors

    C. Network analyzers

    D. NMSs

13. Name the five attributes needed by network management systems.

    A. Network availability monitoring, network modeling and simulation, network security, quality of service management, and traffic monitoring and analysis

    B. SNMP collection, change auditing, configuration inventory, IOS inventory, quality of service

    C. SNA, SNMP, PING, TRACEROUTE, DNS

    D. Configurable, manageable, effective, robust, detailed

14. Choose two third-party NMSs.

    A. Solaris

    B. Windows NT

    C. HP OpenView

    D. Sun Net Manager

15. Which attribute or type of NMS do you use if you need to test a new configuration?

    A. NetSys

    B. Simulation/modeling tools

    C. VLAN Director

    D. Performance monitoring

16. Which Cisco product provides the security NMS attribute?

    A. TACACS+

    B. RADIUS

    C. CiscoWorks

    D. CiscoSecure

17. How does CiscoWorks (CWSI, specifically) discover the network? (Choose all that apply.)

   A. CDP

   B. ping

   C. Telnet

   D. SNMP

18. Which Cisco product uses RMON to manage threshold events once they occur?

   A. Threshold Manager

   B. CiscoView

   C. Traffic Director

   D. VLAN Director

19. Which NMS attributes does CiscoWorks 2000 possess? (Choose all that apply.)

   A. Availability monitoring

   B. Modeling and simulation

   C. Network security

   D. Quality of service management

   E. Traffic monitoring and analysis

20. What two devices commonly perform the same functions, such as measuring resistance, AC/DC current, and verifying continuity in electrically based cabling? (Choose two.)

   A. Breakout box

   B. Multimeter

   C. TDR

   D. OTDR

   E. Cable tester

   F. Bit/block error rate testers

   G. Volt-ohm meter

Answers to Review Questions

1. **D.** A breakout box is the best choice for this application. A multi-meter could be used to check for electrical signaling, but you would have to manually test for the proper pin-out.

2. **B.** A TDR could be used, but a quick test can be accomplished with a cable tester.

3. **A.** Since the question specifically called out fiber optic cable, you need to use an OTDR. A TDR provides the same information for an electrically based cable.

4. **C.** A multimeter is the best tool for this job because it provides information regarding electrical properties such as resistance, voltage, and current.

5. **D.** An optical cable tester will test attenuation and predominantly uses these three wavelengths for testing.

6. **D.** Simple Network Management Protocol collects several types of statistical and environmental information from routers, switches, and computers.

7. **B.** B is the best answer because it allows for the possibility of filters. If no filter were applied, all packets would be copied into the buffer.

8. **B, C.** Capture filters define what will be captured, and display filters allow frames matching the criteria to be displayed.

9. **A, D, E, F.** Protocol analyzers, not cable testers, show runt frames and display packet properties.

10. **A, C.** RTMP is an AppleTalk protocol, thus the packet is both an RTMP and an AppleTalk packet.

11. **A.** Protocol distributions analyze all protocol types on a segment and supply a percentage distribution.

12. **B.** Monitors are simple because they are not intrusive and don't require much configuration or interaction.

13. **A.** These attributes make a complete network management system.

14. **C, D.** In addition to the built-in functions of HPOV and SNM, CiscoWorks is integrated into these applications.

15. B.   The question asks for the NMS attribute, not the software package.

16. D.   This question asks for the NMS software that corresponds to the attribute. TACACS+ and RADIUS provide security, but they are not NMS packages.

17. A, D.   CDP is used for Cisco proprietary neighbors and then SNMP is used to gather further information about the connected devices.

18. C.   Traffic Director uses the information provided by RMON and RMON probes to retrieve threshold information.

19. A, D, E.   CiscoWorks 2000 is a combined product of several different NMS programs that allow it to cover a wide range of NMS attributes.

20. B, G.   Though some of the other items listed may have the capabilities to perform these tasks, the multimeter and volt-ohm meter were specifically designed for this purpose.

Chapter

4

Cisco Router Architecture

TOPICS COVERED IN THIS CHAPTER INCLUDE:

- ✓ Use troubleshooting tools and minimize their impact on a Cisco router's switching type and data flow.
- ✓ Identify and use Cisco IOS software commands and debug utilities to filter, capture, and display protocol traffic flows.

Cisco equipment functions in accordance with the OSI model. Routers are known as Layer 3—Network devices. Cisco has developed many ways to efficiently and effectively move incoming data to the correct outbound interface. These methods are described in detail in this chapter.

Because different applications use different packet sizes, it is important to gain an understanding of the buffers implemented by Cisco and how they can be configured to provide more efficient use of memory buffers. Buffer configuration is also addressed in this chapter.

Armed with the general information regarding protocols and troubleshooting tools, you're ready to cover Cisco-specific material. This chapter discusses the output of Cisco diagnostic commands, and Cisco-specific routing and switching procedures.

Understanding the Output from Diagnostic Commands

Before an engineer can effectively and successfully troubleshoot network problems, he or she needs to understand the processes being analyzed. If this understanding is not present, information provided by troubleshooting tools is useless. Troubleshooting is like learning another language—if you don't have a basic vocabulary and knowledge of the jargon, you can't pick up a book written in a foreign language and understand it. Troubleshooting is similar—if you don't understand the technology and processes present in the problems you troubleshoot, diagnostic information is of little use. This section is dedicated to a discussion of the processes that occur on Cisco routers.

Several processes exist simultaneously on a router, and it is important to single out which processes are of interest. Sometimes diagnostic tools can affect available resources on the router. Not only can resources be used, but the efficiency with which routers handle packets may also be affected.

We begin by discussing the routing process that occurs on a router, then we move on to switching paths that routers implement to facilitate and accelerate packet forwarding. Don't confuse switching paths with Layer 2 switching, which does not occur on a router. As we discuss these processes and tools, we will also emphasize proper utilization to avoid excessive intrusion while troubleshooting.

The Routing Process

Routers are Layer 3 devices that are used to forward incoming packets to their destination by using logical addressing. IP addresses are logical addresses. Routers share information about these logical addresses with each other, and this information is stored in route tables. The router uses the route table to map the path through the router to the destination IP address.

Two *processes* must be present for routing to work properly. The first is *path determination*, which means that the router is aware of a route that leads to the desired destination address. The second is the actual moving of the packet from the inbound interface to the proper outbound interface. Look at Figure 4.1 to get a visual idea of this process.

FIGURE 4.1 Routing components

As you can see, a packet is forwarded to Router B via the routing process. Router B told Router A that it knew a route to the destination address. Once Router B has the packet, it must find the outgoing port associated with the destination address of `172.16.1.10`. In this case, there is a route in the routing table of Router B that matches the destination of 172.16.1.10, specifically 172.16.1.0/24. Once the route has been found, the router must move the packet to the outgoing interface Serial 1. After the packet reaches interface Serial 1, it is routed toward the destination network of `172.16.1.10`.

This is the basic routing process. For routes to be shared among adjacent routers, a *routing protocol* must be used. Routing protocols are used so that routers can calculate, learn, and advertise route table information.

Metrics are associated with each route that is present in the route table. Metrics are calculated by the routing protocol to define a cost of getting to the destination address. Some algorithms use hop count (the number of routers between it and the destination address), whereas others use a vector of values.

Once a metric is assigned to a route, a router advertises this information to all adjacent routers. Thus, each router maintains a topology and map of how to get to connected networks. By *connected*, we do not mean directly connected, but simply that there exists some type of network connection between the destination network and the router.

The Switching Process

We now have an overview of how routing works. It is also important to understand the intricate flow of a packet through routers in general. This packet flow is considered to be switching. The description that follows is meant to associate the routing process with the OSI model.

A router leads a pretty boring life (see Figure 4.2 for an example). When a router receives a frame on any of its interfaces, it asks the question "Is this packet for me?" After looking at the Layer 3 header, it sees the destination network and answers its own question. At this point, there are only two possibilities: the packet is intended for the router, or it is not.

We'll back up a little here. You just read that the router receives a frame. Right now we are going to be very specific with our nomenclature. As you learned in Chapter 2, a frame is a Layer 2 PDU and a packet is a Layer 3 PDU. The router receives a frame because the Layer 3 PDU from the adjacent router had to be encapsulated in order to be sent.

Start with Step 1, pictured in Figure 4.2. Step 1 consists of Layer 2 receiving an incoming frame. Because these are routers, the packet (Layer 3 PDU) must be extracted from the frame, the frame discarded, and the packet passed up to Layer 3.

FIGURE 4.2   Packet flow through a router

Layer 3 then performs Step 2. It looks at the packet and says, "Is this for me?" The router then identifies the destination address within the Layer 3 header. If the packet is destined for the router, Layer 3 strips off the Layer 3 header and passes the PDU up to the higher layers. If the packet is not destined for the router, it follows the remaining steps outlined in Figure 4.2.

Assuming that the packet is not intended for the router, it is sent back down to Layer 2 to be encapsulated (Step 3). At this point, the router has done a route table look-up and knows which interface it must send the packet to, but it needs to know the Layer 2 address (MAC address if Ethernet, FDDI, or Token Ring—LAN Media) of the adjacent interface. In the case of Ethernet, if the MAC address does not exist in the ARP table, the router will issue an ARP request for the MAC address for the interface on Router B. Once the MAC address is known, the frame header can be created. With the frame header created, the packet is encapsulated and sent to the next hop (Step 4).

The process is repeated at Router B. The router receives a frame, and then gets the packet and asks, "Is this for me?" Depending on the answer, the packet is forwarded to the upper layers or to an exiting interface. This same procedure is followed along every hop en route to the destination router. Remember that the logical address specified in the packet does not change— only the MAC address changes. The logical address allows the packet to be routed to its destination, whereas the MAC address allows the frame to be forwarded to each next-hop. It seems monotonous, but it is necessary.

We have now discussed generalities concerning packet flow through a router. You may notice that no reference was made about which paths were taken inside the router. The switching path taken by a PDU depends implicitly on the type of router on which it is implemented. Because Cisco makes such a wide variety of routers, we will look at each type individually. By covering the different architectures, you can then better understand the switching types that are described later in this section.

Cisco 7000/7500 Series Router Architecture

The architecture of the 7000 and 7500 series routers are very similar. Both are high-end routers designed for the core portion of the network, and both can use the same basic set of interface cards. However, the 7000 is older, and therefore does not have all of the features or throughput capabilities that are available in the 7500 series. One of the major differences between the two is that in most cases, the 7000 has separate route processor and switch processor cards, whereas these functions are combined into one card in the 7500 series. As you will see in Table 4.1, the exception to this is the RSP7000 card, which has these functions combined. In many cases, to get the newer cards and functions on a 7000 platform, the RSP7000 must be used.

T A B L E   4 . 1   Comparison of 7000 Series and 7500 Series Routers

Feature	7000	7500
Backplane type	CxBus	CyBus
Backplane speed	533 Mbps	1.067 Gbps
Number of backplanes	1	1 for 7505 2 for 7507 & 7513
Route/switch processor card options	RSP7000	RSP1, RSP2, RSP4 & RSP8
Individual route processor card options	RP (route processor)	--
Individual switch processor card options	SP (switch processor) SSP (silicon switched processor)	--

The 7500 series supports four different Route Switch Processors: RSP1, RSP2, RSP4, and RSP8 (the difference is additional processing power). Figure 4.3 depicts the relation between the RSP and IP slots on a dual CyBus. It is important to realize that though the 7500 series can support redundant RSPs, only one RSP is active at a time. One RSP can control both CyBuses; however, traffic generated on one CyBus does not affect the other. This means that the 7507 and 7513 series routers have a combined backplane speed of 2.134Gbps.

FIGURE 4.3   Dual CyBus architecture

Cisco 2500/4000 Series Architecture

The 2500/4000 series routers are an older style of router. In most new implementations, 2600/3600 series routers would be used in their place. However, because there is a large install base of the older routers, they are relevant for this discussion.

These routers are not nearly as robust as the 7000/7500 series, nor were they intended to be. The 2500 series routers offer many interface configurations, but these configurations are not modular, except the 2524 and 2525. The model used depends on the network interfaces needed. The Cisco 4000 series is a modular system, thus providing for more flexibility with network interfaces.

The key to these routers is that the interfaces do not have independent processors like those in the 7000/7500 series routers. This greatly restricts the possible switching paths. The router's CPU must handle all of the interfaces for the router.

Fast switching is possible on these routers due to the shared memory on the processor board. The specifics of the different switching paths will be discussed next; for now, we'll just say that fast switching is used on the 2500/4000 series routers. Now that we have discussed the switching types supported by various router platforms, we will explain the different switching methods in detail.

🌐 Real World Scenario

Phasing Out Old Equipment

I have found that in many ways designing for a new installation is easier than living with older equipment. Not only does older equipment have a smaller feature set than its new counterparts, when it does support these features, in many instances hardware upgrades are needed. However, as most companies I have worked for do not have the luxury of replacing the existing equipment with new any time a new product line comes out, there are a few things that can be done to make it easier to deal with this situation.

First, wherever possible I try to run the same IOS or CatOS code on all like devices in the environment. For example, all 7500s should run the same code, all 2500s should run the same code, and all 5500s should run the same code. Since I need to focus on only one particular code level, I am better able to track hardware requirements such as memory and flash. In addition, when I do need to upgrade I already know what code level each of my devices is starting from. This allows me to focus my research on the release notes for the two code levels, the code I am starting from and the code I am upgrading to, as well as the caveats for these codes.

Another step I take to better manage mixed environments is keeping an inventory of devices and cards that are in use. This inventory can be easily compared to the minimum requirements for running a new code level as well as compared to the End of Life announcements Cisco issues. Along with the card or component part number, also track the memory and flash that each device has. In many cases, a support for existing equipment is carried to the next code level only if a card has enough memory. By tracking this in my inventory I am able to gauge how large an undertaking upgrading will be.

Finally, when an older piece of equipment is retired from the production environment, in many cases I find it still can have benefit in a testing or learning lab environment. Though it cannot run the latest feature set or have the throughput needed to handle production traffic loads, it still can handle the traffic in a lab environment. This then provides an environment where network engineers can safely test new ideas and concepts before putting them into production.

Cisco 2600/3600 Series Architecture

Unlike the 2500 series, the 2600/3600 series routers are modular. Most come with a fixed interface, such as Fast Ethernet or Token Ring, and a varying number of slots that can be used for any other interface type. In addition, because of their similar design many of the interfaces are interchangeable between the 2600 and 3600 series routers.

As was stated before, these routers were designed as replacements for the 2500 series and the 4000 series product lines. As such, they do not have the throughput capabilities of a 7500-class router, but do have better throughput than the 2500/4000 routers. In addition, with the correct IOS, the 2600 and 3600 series routers can use the more advanced switching options such as Netflow and CEF.

 Real World Scenario

Hardware Interchangeability

It is not necessarily surprising that the 2600 and 3600 routers can both use some of the same interface types. However, what about using the same hardware on a switch and a router? This is exactly what Cisco has accomplished with the port adapter, or PA. A PA is primarily used in a VIP processor that is used with the higher end routers such as the 7000 or 7500. PAs come in models supporting both LAN and WAN interfaces. Some of the different interfaces supported include Fast Ethernet, Token Ring, HSSI, Fast Serial, and ATM. The unique part about the PAs is that many can also be used in 5500 series and 6500 series switches.

In order to use the PAs in these switches, special cards resembling the VIP cards need to be added for the PAs to be inserted into. For the 5500, this card comes attached to an RSM. Taking up two slots in the chassis, the bottom portion functions as a normal RSM, and up to two different PAs can be installed in the upper portion. The 6500 solution uses the FlexWAN card. This card takes up only a single slot in the chassis. Though not attached to the MSFC (or supervisor), an MSFC with PFC is required in order to use the FlexWAN. In both switch types, configuration of the interfaces on the PAs is done through the router (i.e., the RSM in the 5500 and the MSFC in the 6500).

As not all of the PAs are supported on all platforms, before purchasing a PA, be sure to verify that the particular PA you are buying will work in the chassis type you plan to use. By being able to use interface cards in different network devices, you can reduce the overall cost of keeping onsite spares as well as make migrations to newer technologies more cheaply.

Switching Methods

The *switching path* is the logical path that a packet follows when it's switched through a router. As we have discussed, there are many types of switching and it is important not to confuse them. This section explains methods used by routers to move a packet from an incoming interface to the correct outgoing interface. By using switching paths, extra lookups in route tables are eliminated, and processing overhead is reduced.

The router's physical design and its interfaces allow for a variety of switching processes on the router. This frees up the processor to focus on other tasks, instead of looking up the source and destination information for every packet that enters the router.

We have already discussed router architecture, so we will focus directly on the details of each switching type. The most processor-intensive method is discussed first; we end with the most efficient method of switching.

Process Switching

Process switching is the action of the processor having to determine the exiting interface for every packet. As a packet arrives on an interface to be forwarded, eventually it is copied to the router's process buffer, and the router performs a lookup on the Layer 3 address (*eventually* means that there are a few steps before the packet is copied to the route processor buffer). Using the route table, an exit interface is associated with the destination network. The processor encapsulates and forwards the packet with the added new information to the exit interface while the router initializes the fast-switching cache. Subsequent packets that require process switching and are bound for the same destination network follow the same path as the first packet.

Overhead ensues because the processor is occupied with Layer 3 lookups—determining which interface the packet should exit from and calculating the CRC for the packets. If every packet required all of that to be routed, the processor could get really bogged down. The answer is to use other types of switching whenever and wherever possible.

Fast Switching

Fast switching is an enhancement from process switching because it uses a fast switching cache that resides on the route processor board. The first packet of a new session is copied to the interface processor buffer. The packet is then copied to the CxBus and sent to the switch processor. A check is made against other switching caches (for example, silicon or autonomous) for an existing entry. Fast switching is then used because no entries exist within the more efficient caches. The packet header is copied and sent to the route processor, where the fast switching cache resides. Assuming that an entry exists in the cache, the packet is encapsulated for fast switching and sent back to the switch processor. Finally, the packet is copied to the buffer on the outgoing interface processor. From there, it is sent out the interface.

Fast switching is on by default for lower-end routers like the 2500/4000 series. Sometimes it's necessary to turn fast switching off when troubleshooting network problems. Because packets don't move across the route processor after the first packet is process-switched, you can't see them with packet-level tracing. It's also helpful to turn off fast switching if the interface card's memory is limited or consumed, or to alleviate congestion when low-speed interfaces become flooded with information from high-speed interfaces.

Autonomous Switching

Autonomous switching works by comparing packets against the autonomous switching cache. You probably recognize a pattern by now. When a packet arrives on the interface processor, it checks the switching cache closest to it. So far, all of these caches reside on other processor boards. The same is found with autonomous switching. The silicon-switching cache is checked first; the autonomous cache is then checked. The packet is encapsulated for autonomous switching and sent back to the interface processor. Notice that this time, the packet header was not sent to the route processor.

Autonomous switching is available only on AGS+ and Cisco 7000 series routers that have high-speed controller interface cards.

Silicon Switching

Silicon switching is available only on the Cisco 7000 with an SSP (Silicon Switch Processor). Silicon-switched packets are compared to the silicon-switching cache on the SSE (silicon switching engine). The SSP is a dedicated switch processor that offloads the switching process from the route processor, which provides a fast-switching solution. Packets must still traverse the backplane of the router to get to the SSP and then back to the exit interface, however.

Optimum Switching

Optimum switching follows the same procedure as the other switching algorithms. When a new packet enters the interface, it is compared to the optimum switching cache, rewritten, and sent to the chosen exit interface. Other packets associated with the same session then follow the same path. All processing is carried out on the interface processor, including the CRC. Optimum switching is faster than both fast switching and Netflow switching, unless you have implemented several access lists.

Optimum switching replaces fast switching on the high-end routers. As with fast switching, optimum switching also needs to be turned off to view packets while troubleshooting a network problem.

Distributed Switching

Distributed switching happens on the VIP (Versatile Interface Processor) cards (which have a switching processor onboard), so it's very efficient. All required processing is done right on the VIP processor, which maintains a copy of the router's routing cache. With this arrangement, even the first packet doesn't need to be sent to the route processor to initialize the switching path, as it does with the other switching algorithms. Router efficiency increases as more VIP cards are added.

Netflow Switching

Netflow switching is really more of an administrative tool than a performance-enhancement tool. It collects detailed data for use with circuit accounting and application-utilization information. Because of all the additional data that Netflow collects (and may export), expect an increase in router overhead—possibly as much as a five-percent increase in CPU utilization.

Netflow switching can be configured on most interface types and can be used in a switched environment. ATM, LAN, and VLAN technologies all support Netflow switching, and the Cisco 3600, 7200, and 7500 series routers provide its implementation.

As we discussed, Netflow switching does much more than just switching—it also gathers statistical data, including protocol, port, and user information. All of this is stored in the Netflow switching cache, according to the individual flow that's defined by the packet information (destination address, source address, protocol, source and destination port, and the incoming interface). The data can be sent to a network management station to be stored and processed there.

The Netflow switching process is very efficient: an incoming packet is processed by the fast or optimum switching process, and then all path and packet information is copied to the Netflow cache. The remaining packets that belong to the flow are compared to the Netflow cache and forwarded accordingly.

The first packet that is copied to the Netflow cache contains all security and routing information, and if an access list is applied to an interface, the first packet is matched against it. If it matches the access-list criteria, the cache is flagged so that the remaining packets in the flow can be switched without being compared to the list (this is very effective when a large amount of access-list processing is required).

Do you remember reading that distributed switching on VIP cards is really efficient because it lessens the load to the RSP? Well, Netflow switching can also be configured on VIP interfaces.

Netflow gives you amenities, such as the security flag in the cache that allows subsequent packets of an established flow to avoid access-list processing. It's comparable to optimum and distributed switching, and it is actually superior to them if access lists (especially long ones) are placed in the switching path. The detailed information Netflow gathers and exports does load down the system, however, so plan carefully before implementing Netflow switching on a router.

Cisco Express Forwarding

Cisco Express Forwarding (CEF) is a switching function, designed for high-end backbone routers. It functions on Layer 3 of the OSI model, and its biggest asset is the capability to remain stable in a large network. However, it's also more efficient than both the fast and optimum default switching paths.

CEF is wonderfully stable in large environments because it doesn't rely on cached information. Instead of using a CEF cache, it refers to two alternate resources. The *Forwarding Information Base (FIB)* consists of information duplicated from the IP route table. Every time the routing information changes, the changes are propagated to the FIB. Thus, instead of comparing old cache information, a packet looks to the FIB for its forwarding information. CEF stores the Layer 2 MAC addresses of connected routers (or next-hop) in the *adjacency table*.

Even though CEF features advanced capabilities, you should consider several restrictions before implementing CEF on a router. According to the document "Cisco Express Forwarding," available from the Cisco web page Cisco Connection Online (CCO) at www.cisco.com, system requirements are quite high. The processor should have at least 128MB of RAM, and the line cards should have 32MB each. dCEF, distributed CEF, takes the place of VIP distributed switching on VIP interfaces. The following features aren't supported by CEF:

- ATM DXI (data exchange interface)
- Token Ring
- Multipoint PPP
- access lists on the GSR
- policy routing
- NAT
- SMDS

Nevertheless, CEF does many things—even load balancing is possible through FIB. If there are multiple paths to the same destination, the IP route table knows about them all. This information is also copied to the FIB, which CEF consults for its switching decisions.

Load balancing can be configured in two different modes. The first mode is load balancing based on the destination (called *per-destination load balancing*); the second mode is based on the packet (called *per-packet load balancing*). Per-destination load balancing is on by default, and must be turned off to enable per-packet load balancing.

Accounting may also be configured for CEF, thus furnishing you with detailed statistics about CEF traffic. Two specifications can be made when collecting CEF statistics:

- Collect information on traffic that's forwarded to a specific destination.
- Collect statistics for traffic that's forwarded through a specific destination.

CEF was designed for large networks—if reliable and redundant switching paths are necessary, CEF is the way to go. Keep in mind that its hardware requirements are significant, however, and it lacks support for many Cisco IOS features.

Packet Flow—High-End Routers

You now have all of the pieces of the puzzle, and you understand the router architectures and the switching methods. With this knowledge, you can easily follow a packet as it transits a router. Don't confuse this packet flow with the OSI comparison given earlier in the chapter.

To emphasize, the switching type depends on two factors: which encapsulation is configured on the interface and whether a cache entry exists for the configured method. Look at Figure 4.4 to see a flow chart that describes the process for each packet entering a router.

FIGURE 4.4   Switching method and packet flow

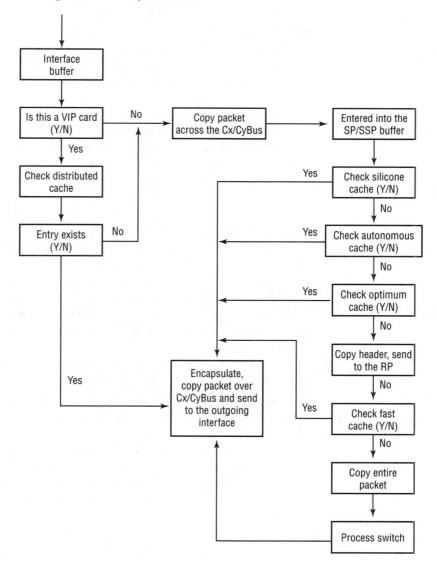

Let's work through the flow chart in Figure 4.4. You can see that the incoming packet is immediately copied to the interface processor buffer. If the card is a VIP/VIP2 card, then the packet will use distributed switching if there is an entry; if not, it is processed like other packets.

The next step in the process is to copy the packet to the SP/SSP/RSP across the CxBus/CyBus. Once the packet reaches the buffers on the SP/SSP/RSP, it is compared to the silicon-switching cache. Two paths can be followed from here. If an entry exists in the silicon-switching cache, the packet is encapsulated and copied to the outgoing interface processor across the CxBus/CyBus. The interface processor then sends out the packet. If an entry is not found in the silicon-switching cache, the autonomous cache is checked.

If an entry exists in the autonomous cache, the packet is encapsulated by the switch processor, copied across the CxBus/CyBus to the outgoing interface processor, and sent. Again, if an entry does not exist, the next step is taken and the optimum cache is compared.

Optimum switching follows the same exit route as autonomous switching: the packet is encapsulated by the switch processor, copied to the outgoing interface, and sent. With each additional step, the packet gets closer and closer to being process-switched.

At this point, if there is no entry in the optimum cache, the Layer 3 header is copied, sent to the RP, and then compared against the fast cache. A fast cache can reside in two different places, depending on the router's hardware configuration. If an RSP is used, the fast cache is on the same board as the optimum cache. If an SP/SSP and an RP are used, the silicon and autonomous caches reside on the switch processor and the fast cache resides on the RP.

If the Layer 3 header does not match any entry in the fast cache, the entire packet is copied and sent to the processor, where the processor does a lookup in the route table. If a route exists, the packet is encapsulated and copied back to the exiting interface. If no route exists, the packet is dropped.

The first packet of each data flow requires process switching. Once the route lookup and proper encapsulation are made, the header is copied into the corresponding switch-type cache. Subsequent packets find the entry in the correct cache and are forwarded along the same outgoing path as the first packet.

The Route Processor

Although you don't like sending packets to the route processor, sometimes it is unavoidable. Packets that are destined or intended for the router require processing. Broadcasts, SNMP requests, access-list processing (in some cases), debugging, protocol updates, error logging, and queuing all require processor time.

This is just another reason why switching is such a good practice. Why burden the route processor with every packet if it's not necessary? By using switching methods, the route processor is free to use valuable CPU time on more important things than doing route lookups for every packet that comes into the router.

There are times when a packet must be processed or process-switched, however. For this reason, the router is engineered so that it can handle the processing and process switching of numerous packets. A system of buffers and queues exists on the route processor, switch processor, and interface processor that allows packets to be held, processed, and forwarded with few packet drops. Different router types have different buffer architecture, so we'll discuss each type in detail.

Buffers and Queues

The system buffers reside on the RP, with the memory being allocated from the system memory. The buffers on the RP are used to store packets that are waiting to be processed by the CPU.

The buffers come configured with default settings. They can be modified, if necessary, but it is usually a good idea to have a Cisco TAC engineer look at the memory allocation and suggest the new buffer settings. Following is an example of the buffer settings:

```
Buffer elements:
     499 in free list (500 max allowed)
     32642751 hits, 0 misses, 0 created
Public buffer pools:
Small buffers, 104 bytes (total 120, permanent 120):
     110 in free list (20 min, 250 max allowed)
     15486216 hits, 322 misses, 364 trims, 364 created
     26 failures (0 no memory)
```

```
Middle buffers, 600 bytes (total 90, permanent 90):
    87 in free list (10 min, 200 max allowed)
    3984956 hits, 113 misses, 105 trims, 105 created
    36 failures (0 no memory)
Big buffers, 1524 bytes (total 90, permanent 90):
    88 in free list (5 min, 300 max allowed)
    471484 hits, 24 misses, 6 trims, 6 created
    20 failures (0 no memory)
VeryBig buffers, 4520 bytes (total 10, permanent 10):
    10 in free list (0 min, 300 max allowed)
    177588 hits, 10 misses, 1 trims, 1 created
    10 failures (0 no memory)
Large buffers, 5024 bytes (total 10, permanent 10):
    10 in free list (0 min, 30 max allowed)
    10 hits, 0 misses, 0 trims, 0 created
    0 failures (0 no memory)
Huge buffers, 18024 bytes (total 0, permanent 0):
    0 in free list (0 min, 13 max allowed)
    0 hits, 0 misses, 0 trims, 0 created
    0 failures (0 no memory)
Header pools:
```

You can view six buffer distinctions in this output: small, middle, big, very big, large, and huge; and each division is allocated a different amount of buffer space. The output details the buffer name and size, with the buffer size following immediately after its name. The (total 120, permanent 120) for the small pool specifies that there are a total of 120 spaces allocated to the small pool. The permanent means that the 120 buffer spaces are permanently assigned to the small buffer pool. When a buffer's space is permanent, it cannot be de-allocated and given back to the system memory for other uses.

In the next field, you can see the number of free buffer spaces that are open to accepting a packet. Each pool maintains a minimum and maximum threshold, which it uses to decide whether more buffer space needs to be allocated to the pool. This is seen in the min and max allowed.

The last two lines of information given for each pool describe the activity happening there. This information, which includes all hits, misses, trims, created, and failures, is described in the following list:

Hits   Represents how many times the pool was used successfully.

Misses   Represents the number of times a packet tried to find a space within a pool, but found no available spaces.

Trims   Represents the number of spaces removed from the pool because the amount exceeded the number of *allowed* buffer spaces.

Created   Represents the number of spaces created to accommodate requests for space when there wasn't enough at the time the request was made.

Failures   Represents how many times a buffer pool tried to create space, but was unsuccessful. When a failure occurs, the requesting packet is dropped.

The last field is the `no memory` field, which records the number of failures that occurred due to the lack of sufficient system memory required to create additional buffer space.

If you observe a significant increase in the number of misses while monitoring buffers with the `show buffers` command, the pool can be tuned by assigning different values to the `max-free`, `min-free`, and `permanent` parameters. Increasing the values for these parameters overrides the system defaults—instead of having to create additional spaces on demand within a pool, the spaces can be statically allocated and assigned. This helps you avoid racking up missed and failed packet statuses.

You can adjust these parameters with the following command:

```
buffers {small | middle | big | verybig | large | huge |
   type number} {permanent | max-free | min-free |
   initial} number
```

The `type` represents interface type, and `number` is the number to be assigned to the specified parameter.

Table 4.2 depicts the sizes of the buffer space within a pool. When a packet needs to be stored in a buffer, it requests space from the pool in proportion to its size requirement. For example, a full-size Ethernet packet at a 1500MTU requires one buffer space from the Big buffer pool.

TABLE 4.2 Sizes of the Buffer within a Pool

Pool Name	Buffer Size (in Bytes)
Small	104
Middle	600
Big	1524
Very Big	4520
Large	5024
Huge	18,024

Buffer and Queue Architecture

Now that you understand the buffer's global setup, let's discuss the buffer architecture and queuing process using a 7000 series router as an example. The architecture is similar to the cache buffers that were explained with the switching methods, and the concepts are basically the same for the other router types.

Hardware Buffers

Each interface (not interface processor) has a hardware buffer, which is used as a first line of defense for bursty traffic. If the hardware buffer on certain interfaces fills up, the Layer 2 protocol will signal the sending interface to slow down. This behavior is dependent on the Layer 2 protocol and whether or not it supports congestion control.

Three conditions can exist at the interface level: *ignore*, *overrun*, and *underrun*. An *ignore* can be caused in three ways. We already discussed the first—the hardware buffer fills up and it signals to the transmitting interface to throttle down. The second occurs when the interface is receiving frames faster than the SP can pull them off. The third occurs when the CxBus is so busy that the interface processor is unable to copy the packet from the hardware buffer to the SP buffers. Figure 4.5 depicts all three of these scenarios.

Overruns occur on the physical interface. Think of the physical interface as consisting of three parts: the buffer, the receiver, and the transmitter. An *overrun* occurs when the receiver receives packets faster than it can transfer them to the hardware buffer. Figure 4.6 gives a graphical description of the process.

FIGURE 4.5   Ignore scenarios for hardware buffers

Hardware buffer
(Full)

Slow down!

SP buffer

Busy condition

CxBus

Interface
processor

Unable to copy from
Hardware buffer to the
SP buffer due to the
busy CxBus

Hardware
buffer

SP buffer
(Can't get them
here fast enough.)

Hardware buffer
(Full)

FIGURE 4.6   Overruns

Overrun condition

Hardware buffer

Receiver

An *underrun* is just the opposite of an overrun. When the transmitter runs at a higher rate than the packets sent from the hardware buffer, an underrun occurs. Look at Figure 4.7.

FIGURE 4.7 Underruns

Interface Buffers

Interface buffers are intermediate storage. Packets from all of the hardware buffers are copied to the interface buffers. The switch processor houses the intermediate buffers by using 512KB for the SP board memory. This memory is also shared with the autonomous switching cache. Other boards can have up to 2MB of memory.

Let's get a better understanding of the interface buffers. To see what the router is doing, issue the show controllers cbus command. Here is the output from a 7507 router with one EIP board in it:

```
Router_A# show controllers cbus
MEMD at 40000000, 2097152 bytes (unused 128, recarves 1,
   lost 0)
  RawQ 48000100, ReturnQ 48000108, EventQ 48000110
  BufhdrQ 48000120 (2353 items)
  IpcbufQ_classic 48000140 (8 items, 4096 bytes)
  3570 buffer headers (48002000 - 4800FF10)
  pool0: 9 buffers, 256 bytes, queue 48000128
  pool1: 1196 buffers, 1536 bytes, queue 48000130
  pool2: 4 buffers, 1568 bytes, queue 48000138
  slot5: EIP, hw 1.5, sw 20.06, ccb 5800FF70, cmdq
  480000A8,    vps 4096
```

```
software loaded from system
Ethernet5/0, addr 0010.29d1.68a0 (bia 0010.29d1.68a0)
   gfreeq 48000130, lfreeq 48000148 (1536 bytes),
   throttled 0
   rxlo 4, rxhi 598, rxcurr 1, maxrxcurr 1
   txq 48000150, txacc 48000082 (value 341), txlimit
   341
Ethernet5/1, addr 0010.29d1.68a1 (bia 0010.29d1.68a1)
   gfreeq 48000130, lfreeq 48000158 (1536 bytes),
      throttled 0
   rxlo 4, rxhi 598, rxcurr 0, maxrxcurr 0
   txq 48000160, txacc 4800008A (value 0), txlimit 341
Ethernet5/2, addr 0010.29d1.68a2 (bia 0010.29d1.68a2)
   gfreeq 48000130, lfreeq 48000168 (1536 bytes),
      throttled 0
   rxlo 4, rxhi 598, rxcurr 0, maxrxcurr 0
   txq 48000170, txacc 48000092 (value 0), txlimit 341
Ethernet5/3, addr 0010.29d1.68a3 (bia 0010.29d1.68a3)
   gfreeq 48000130, lfreeq 48000178 (1536 bytes),
      throttled 0
   rxlo 4, rxhi 598, rxcurr 0, maxrxcurr 0
   txq 48000180, txacc 4800009A (value 0), txlimit 341
Ethernet5/4, addr 0010.29d1.68a4 (bia 0010.29d1.68a4)
   gfreeq 48000130, lfreeq 48000188 (1536 bytes),
      throttled 0
   rxlo 4, rxhi 598, rxcurr 0, maxrxcurr 0
   txq 48000190, txacc 480000A2 (value 0), txlimit 341
Ethernet5/5, addr 0010.29d1.68a5 (bia 0010.29d1.68a5)
   gfreeq 48000130, lfreeq 48000198 (1536 bytes),
      throttled 0
   rxlo 4, rxhi 598, rxcurr 0, maxrxcurr 0
   txq 480001A0, txacc 480000AA (value 0), txlimit 341
```

At the top of the output, you can see three pools allocated: pool0, pool1, and pool2. Each interface processor is allocated a certain share of the buffer pool. By default, EIPs are allocated 1524 bytes of the 512KB. Other default settings are listed in Table 4.3.

TABLE 4.3 Interface Processor Buffer Size Allocation

Board Type	Buffer Size (bytes)
FIP	4470
FSIP	4470
AIP	4470
HSSI	4470
TRIP	4470
EIP	1524

Input and Output Queues

Input queues reside on the RP, and they are used to link the SP buffers to the RP buffers. The queue reserves RP buffer space for a packet that was forwarded from the SP/SSP. If the route processor doesn't process the queued packets at the same rate, the queue fills up and the incoming packets are dropped.

The *output queue* works in the same manner. Output queues reside on the RP as well, and once a packet is processed, it must be sent to the exiting interface. The *output queue* is used to hold the packet until the packet can be copied to the buffers on the SP/SSP; from there, it is forwarded to the specified interface processor. The interface processor then sends the packet to the interface queue/buffer from which the packet will be sent to the destination.

Packets can be dropped from the output queue, as well. If the other processes on the router are so busy that they can't accept the outgoing packet, they are dropped. These drops are considered normal because the Layer 3 protocol is in the process of slowing down to avoid any further drops.

Buffers and Queues in Low-End Routers

As with switching caches, all buffers are located in shared memory (with the exception of the hardware buffer). The hardware buffer resides on the physical interface.

The difference between the 2500/4000 series routers and the 7000/7500 series routers is that there are no intermediate buffers. A packet is copied directly from the hardware buffer to the system buffers in shared memory.

show Commands

There are numerous show commands that are specifically designed to give you insight into the health of the buffers and queues on a router as well as to look at the packet flow. These commands are broken down into three separate categories: global, interface, and process. Examples of each type of these commands are detailed in the following sections. In addition to the commands listed here, more show commands, primarily for TCP/IP, will be detailed in the next two chapters.

Global Commands

Global commands deal with global router settings. This means that information that does not relate to interfaces or protocols, yet has overall router information, is considered a global show command. The global show commands dealing with buffers and queue information are detailed below.

show buffers

The show buffers command was described in detail in the earlier "Buffer and Queue Architecture" section. Please refer to that section if you need to review the output of the show buffers command.

show memory

This command is helpful for diagnosing memory problems such as allocation failures, low amounts of free memory, and so on. From the following output, you can see that the first field has the memory divided between processor memory and fast memory. The fields are self-explanatory because they describe the total, used, and free amounts of memory.

```
Router_C>show memory
        Head       Total(b)    Used(b)    Free(b)    Lowest(b)   Largest(b)
Proc  60DC38E0    52676384    34896328   17780056   15823612    14764584
Fast  60DA38E0    131072      128344     2728       27282684
Processor memory
Address   Bytes Prev.       Next     Ref PrevF NextF Alloc PC   What
60DC38E0  1056  0           60DC3D2C  1                601342A4   List Elements
60DC3D2C  2656  60DC38E0    60DC47B8  1                601342A4   List Headers
60DC47B8  9000  60DC3D2C    60DC6B0C  1                60135498   Interrupt Stack
60DC6B0C  9000  60DC47B8    60DC8E60  1                60135498   Interrupt Stack
```

Interface Commands

Interface commands deal with detailed interface settings and configurations. Because each type of interface uses different protocols and technologies, the show interface command is capable of displaying all data related to the specified interface.

show queueing and *show queue*

To verify the configuration and operation of the queuing system, you can issue the following two commands:

```
show queueing [fair | priority | custom]
show queue [interface-type interface-number]
```

Results from these commands on Router C can be seen as follows. Because weighted fair queuing is the only type of queuing that has been enabled on this router, it wasn't necessary to issue the optional command of fair, custom, or priority.

```
Router_C#show queueing
Current fair queue configuration:
Interface  Discard       Dynamic      Reserved
           threshold     queue count  queue count
  Serial0    96            256           0
  Serial1    64            256           0
Current priority queue configuration:
Current custom queue configuration:
Current RED queue configuration:
Router_C#
```

This command shows that weighted fair queuing is enabled on both serial interfaces, and that the discard threshold for Serial 0 was changed from 64 to 96. There's a maximum of 256 dynamic queues for both interfaces—the default value. The lines following the interface information are empty because their corresponding queuing algorithms aren't configured yet.

The next command displays more detailed information pertaining to the specified interface:

```
Router_C#show queue serial0
 Input queue: 0/75/0 (size/max/drops); Total output drops: 0
 Queueing strategy: weighted fair
 Output queue: 0/1000/96/0 (size/max total/threshold/ drops)
```

```
    Conversations 0/1/256 (active/max active/max total)
    Reserved Conversations 0/0 (allocated/max allocated)
Router_C#
```

show interface

The show interface command has many derivatives. A simple show
interface command can be issued, and you will get the detailed status and
configuration of every interface on the router. That can be overwhelming—
so many options exist for the command. These options allow you, the engineer, to focus the area of your troubleshooting. If you know that you need to
solve a problem on the network that is connected to interface Ethernet 5/0,
you don't want to waste your time looking at the status of every interface
on the router. More information on the show interface command will
be covered in Chapter 5; for now, we will just focus on the information
this command can provide in regard to buffers and queues. Let us look at a
sample output from an Ethernet interface.

```
Router_A#show interface Ethernet 5/4
Ethernet5/4 is up, line protocol is up
   Hardware is cxBus Ethernet, address is 009a.822e.51b6
      (bia 90.323f.acdb)
   Description: Connection to Router_B
   Internet address is 172.16.1.1/24
   MTU 1500 bytes, BW 10000 Kbit, DLY 1000 usec, rely 255/
      255, load 33/255
   Encapsulation ARPA, loopback not set, keepalive set (10
      sec)
   ARP type: ARPA, ARP Timeout 04:00:00
   Last input 00:00:00, output 00:00:00, output hang never
   Last clearing of "show interface" counters never
   Queueing strategy: fifo
   Output queue 0/40, 101553 drops; input queue 0/75, 1327
      drops
   5 minute input rate 247000 bits/sec, 196 packets/sec
   5 minute output rate 1329000 bits/sec, 333 packets/sec
      421895792 packets input, 2524672293 bytes, 1 no
      buffer
      Received 453382 broadcasts, 0 runts, 0 giants
      6 input errors, 1 CRC, 5 frame, 0 overrun, 494
```

```
      ignored,          0 abort
      0 input packets with dribble condition detected
      618578101 packets output, 977287695 bytes, 0
      underruns
      0 output errors, 30979588 collisions, 1 interface
    resets
      0 babbles, 0 late collision, 0 deferred
      0 lost carrier, 0 no carrier
      0 output buffers copied, 0 interrupts, 0 failures
  Router_A#
```

As can be easily seen by looking at the output, the show interface command not only shows information about runts, giants, and other Physical layer errors, it also shows the number of overruns, underruns, and ignored packets. A runt is a frame that is smaller than the minimum frame size of the encapsulation used on an interface and a giant is a frame that is larger than the MTU on the interface. This information can be helpful in diagnosing issues resulting from buffer or queue problems.

Process Commands

There are two very important process commands that can be executed. Process commands deal directly with the process running on the router. If the standard show processes command is issued, you get a result similar to a ps −ef executed on a Unix box. The output details each process, process ID number (PID), time running, and stack information. The output is too general to be used effectively while troubleshooting.

The two options available with the show processes command are cpu and memory. Each of these options refines the processes output, and makes it more useful and user-friendly.

Start with the cpu command. The output from this command is shown below. This output relates the router's processes and CPU utilization. The first line of the output displays the router's CPU utilization over three periods. In addition, you will notice that the CPU utilization for the five-second interval has two percentages, 15% and 6%. The first number is the average CPU utilization for all processes on the router over the last five seconds. The second number is the percentage of the CPU spent on interrupt-driven processes. In general, interrupt-driven tasks are ones that are core to the router's ability to route packets. Examples of these tasks include fast- or process-switched packets, input from the console or auxiliary ports, or correcting memory-alignment issues. Items such as maintaining VTY sessions and responding to SNMP queries are non-interrupt-driven processes that would only show up in the first percentage.

Underneath the CPU utilization line, you can see the processes running on the router. Starting from the left, you can see the PID, followed by the runtime and other data. The three columns that deal with CPU utilization detail the percentage of CPU cycles that the specified process uses. The process description is found in the far-right column.

```
Router_C>show processes cpu
CPU utilization for five seconds: 15%/6%; one minute: 7%;    five minutes: 7%
 PID   Runtime(ms)   Invoked   uSecs    5Sec    1Min    5Min   TTY  Process
   1            76   1564143       0   0.00%   0.00%   0.00%     0  Load Meter
   2             0         1       0   0.00%   0.00%   0.00%     0  LAPF Input
   3       3638844    872510    4170   0.00%   0.04%   0.00%     0  Check heaps
   4             4        28     142   0.00%   0.00%   0.00%     0  Pool Manager
   5             0         2       0   0.00%   0.00%   0.00%     0  Timers


. . . [output removed] . . .
```

When the overall CPU utilization gets high, you can identify which process is using the most CPU cycles, and then focus your attention on that process. For example, if the IP-EIGRP CPU utilization runs high, you can determine that there is a problem within EIGRP, perhaps a routing loop or some other instability.

The second option, show processes memory, is used to associate memory utilization with the router's processes. Here is a sample output:

```
Router_D>show processes memory
Total: 52503792, Used: 45141524, Free: 7362268
 PID  TTY   Allocated       Freed     Holding    Getbufs   Retbufs  Process
   0    0       54400         304     8898364          0         0  *Init*
   0    0         632  3906083084         632          0         0  *Sched*
   0    0   700723436   729437084      472484    1091352         0  *Dead*
   1    0          96           0        6876          0         0  SSCOP Input
   2    0           0           0        6780          0         0  Check heaps
   3    0    17262036      152680        6916   12351248    260336  Pool Manager


. . . [output removed] . . .
```

The first line details the total, used, and free amounts of system memory. Following that, you see the PID, allocated, freed, and holding memory. This means that the processor has allocated a given amount of memory to the process; if the process does not need all of that memory, it frees some of it and retains the rest.

Summary

Understanding how a packet flows through a router to the destination is an important part of troubleshooting. This knowledge helps you better understand and utilize the commands on the Cisco router to determine the cause of a problem. While a packet is flowing through a router, it must pass through a series of buffers and queues. Though the specific implementation of queues and buffers differs slightly between router types, the concept behind them remains the same: give the packet a location to be stored while a switching decision is made. You can tune queues and buffers to allow for better router performance under specific circumstances, but this should be done only with the assistance and/or direction of TAC.

One of the core features of a router is the forwarding of packets from the ingress interface to the egress interface (switching). The faster this can be done, the greater the throughput of the router. Over the years, Cisco has been continually improving on their switching techniques and the hardware that is needed to support the techniques. Many of the new switching methods can now be applied and used at the interface level. This allows the router to make a determination of where a packet should be sent as the packet arrives, thus saving time and bandwidth on the backplane.

As with any features or hardware on the router, there needs to be a way to view what is occurring in the buffers and queues as well as the different switching methods. This information can be obtained through the use of show commands on the router. The show commands provide real-time as well as, in some cases, historical information about the performance of these items. There are three categories of show commands that can provide this type of information: global, interface, and process.

Exam Essentials

Know the different switching types and when they are used.   The switching types are: process switching, fast switching, autonomous switching, silicon switching, optimum switching, distributed switching, Netflow switching, and CEF.

Understand how buffers work.   Buffers are used by the router to store packets and other information in while waiting for this information to be processed. Also, understand the difference between the terms *hit*, *miss*, *trim*, *created*, and *failure*. Understand the different size buffer pools: small, middle, big, very big, large, and huge.

Know the congestion control conditions that can occur at the interface level.   Congestion control conditions include: ignore, overrun, and underrun. An ignore can be caused in three ways: the hardware buffer fills up, the interface is receiving packets faster than the SP can pull them off, or the bus on the switch is too busy for the hardware buffer to copy the frame off. An overrun is when the receiver receives packets faster than they can be transferred to the hardware buffer, and an underrun is when the transmitter runs at a higher rate than it receives packets from the hardware buffer.

Know the show commands that are available and how to interpret the output.   The commands specifically highlighted in this chapter include: `show buffers`, `show memory`, `show interface`, `show process CPU`, `show processes memory`, `show queue`, and `show queueing`.

Commands Used in This Chapter

The following list contains a summary of all the commands used in this chapter.

Commands	Descriptions
`show buffers`	Displays buffer statistics for the router.
`show controllers cbus`	Displays the buffer information on line cards connected to the cbus.

Commands	Descriptions
show interface	Displays interface-specific settings and statistics.
show memory	Displays the statistics and status of the router's memory.
show processes cpu	Displays the router's processes and the percentage of CPU utilization over 5 seconds, 1 minute, and 5 minutes.
show processes memory	Displays the router's processes and the amount of memory allocated to each.
show queue	Displays interface-specific queuing information.
show queueing	Displays queuing information for the router.

Key Terms

Before you take the exam, be certain you are familiar with the following terms:

adjacency table

autonomous switching

Cisco Express Forwarding (CEF)

distributed switching

fast switching

Forwarding Information Base (FIB)

ignore

input queues

interface buffers

metrics

Netflow switching

optimum switching

output queue

overrun

path determination

process switching

processes

routing protocol

silicon switching

switching path

underrun

Review Questions

1. Which of the following are valid switching methods? (Choose all that apply.)

   A. Process switching

   B. Path switching

   C. Fast switching

   D. Cut-over switching

   E. Distributed switching

   F. Optimum switching

   G. Netflow switching

   H. Cisco Express Forwarding

2. You are troubleshooting an issue on a router. What command displays information regarding an interface on this router?

   A. `show ethernet 1/0 interface`

   B. `show controller cbus ethernet 1/0`

   C. `show interface ethernet 1/0`

   D. `show interface 1/0`

   E. `show logging ethernet 1/0`

3. You execute a `show processes cpu` command on the router and receive the following output:

   `CPU utilization for five seconds: 75%/25%; one minute: 50%; five minutes: 45%`

   What does the 75% mean?

   A. The peak CPU utilization over the past five seconds was 75%.

   B. The average CPU utilization for non-interrupt processes over the last five seconds was 75%.

   C. The average CPU utilization for interrupt processes over the last five seconds was 75%.

   D. The average CPU utilization over the last five seconds for all processes was 75%.

4. What device processes items such as VTY sessions, SNMP queries, and debug information?

   A. Silicon Switch Processor

   B. SAINT

   C. Switch Processor

   D. Route Switch Processor

   E. Forwarding Information Base

5. What important information is provided by the `show buffers` command? (Choose all that apply.)

   A. Hits

   B. Misses

   C. Trims

   D. Created

   E. Failures

   F. Overruns

   G. Underruns

   H. Memory-allocation errors

6. What does `show interface <interface-type> <interface-number>` do? (Choose all that apply.)

   A. Interface description

   B. Interface status

   C. Statistical information

   D. Error statistics

   E. Layer 4 encapsulation type

   F. All of the above

7. What information is provided by issuing the `show processes cpu` command? (Choose all that apply.)

   A. Memory utilization

   B. Processes

   C. CPU utilization percentages

   D. PID

   E. Free memory

8. What information is provided by issuing the `show processes memory` command? (Choose all that apply.)

   A. Free memory

   B. Used memory

   C. Total memory

   D. PID

   E. Memory allocated to the router's individual processes

9. You execute a `show processes cpu` command on the router and receive the following output:

   ```
   CPU utilization for five seconds: 75%/25%; one minute:
   50%; five minutes: 45%
   ```

   What does the 25% mean?

   A. The peak CPU utilization over the past five seconds was 25%.

   B. The average CPU utilization for non-interrupt processes over the last five seconds was 25%.

   C. The average CPU utilization for interrupt processes over the last five seconds was 25%.

   D. The average CPU utilization over the last five seconds for all processes was 25%.

10. The output from a `show interface` command shows overruns. Where is congestion occurring?

    A. The interface hardware buffer

    B. The route processor (RP)

    C. Router bus

    D. ROM

    E. NVRAM

11. You execute a `show interface` command and see that there have been some input queue drops. What could this be an indication of?

    A. ARP cache problems.

    B. Routing instability.

    C. Switched packet drops.

    D. The interface is resetting, causing packets to be dropped.

12. You execute a `show buffers` command and see that there are misses indicated. What does a miss represent?

    A. It represents the number of time the buffer pool tried to create space but was unable to do so.

    B. It represents the number of times the router removed a space from the buffer pool because the max-allowed spaces was exceeded.

    C. It represents the number of times a packet tried to find space in a pool but no space was available.

    D. It represents the number of times a packet was put in the next larger pool because no space was available in the first pool tried.

13. A packet comes in with a size of 1500 bytes. What buffer size would this correspond to?

    A. Huge

    B. Big

    C. Middle

    D. Very big

14. A packet comes in with a size of 6000 bytes. What buffer size would this correspond to?

   A. Huge

   B. Large

   C. Middle

   D. Very big

15. In a `show buffers` command, what does "permanent" refer to?

   A. It represents the number of buffers that exist in ROM.

   B. It represents the number of buffers of a given type that are always in existence.

   C. It represents the number of buffers of a given type that contain information that will be used repeatedly and thus should not be deleted.

   D. It represents the total number buffers that are always in existence.

16. This switching methodology is the one used if none of the other methodologies can determine how to route a packet. It can become very processor intensive if a large number of packets need to use it. What is this switching methodology?

   A. Autonomous switching

   B. Silicon switching

   C. Distributed switching

   D. CEF

   E. Process switching

17. What are the two tables used by CEF to make forwarding decisions? (Choose two.)

   A. Routing Table

   B. FIB

   C. MIB

   D. ARP

   E. FID

   F. HSRP

   G. Adjacency table

   H. Neighbor table

18. What information is in the output of a `show memory` command that is not in the `show process memory` command?

   A. Largest

   B. Free

   C. Lowest

   D. Used

   E. PID information

   F. Total

19. You execute a `show interface` command on a particular Ethernet interface and see that there are some runt frames. What does this mean?

   A. There have been carrier losses on the interface.

   B. There have been packets seen on the interface that were the minimum allowable size for Ethernet, indicating they had no data.

   C. It is an indication that someone is trying to hack into that interface.

   D. Packets smaller than 64 bytes were seen on the interface.

20. What is the default queuing strategy on most Cisco router interfaces?

    A. Priority

    B. FIFO

    C. FILO

    D. Weighted fair

    E. Custom

    F. RED

Answers to Review Questions

1. A, C, E, F, G, H.   Path switching is a general term for the manner in which packets get from the incoming interface to the outgoing interface. Cut-over switching is not a valid term.

2. C.   The show interface command shows information regarding an interface.

3. D.   The first percentage is the average CPU utilization for all processes on the router and the second number is the average CPU utilization for interrupt-driven events.

4. D.   The route processor (RP) handles all of the items listed, and is a component in the Route Switch Processor. You will learn more about the SAINT in Chapter 11.

5. A, B, C, D, E.   Overruns and underruns deal with errors on interfaces. Memory allocation errors are seen using the show memory command.

6. A, B, C, D.   Layer 4 encapsulation is not included in the output of the above command.

7. B, C, D.   Memory information is not displayed via this command.

8. A, B, C, D, E.   All of the above information is provided by the specified command.

9. C.   The first percentage is the average CPU utilization for all processes on the router and the second number is the average CPU utilization for interrupt-driven events.

10. A.   An overrun occurs when the receiver receives packets faster than it can transfer them to the hardware buffer.

11. C.   Input queue drops are dropped packets that are a result of the input queue of the buffer being full when a packet arrives and are usually caused by traffic bursts.

12. C.   Answer A is a failure, B is a trim, and D is not a function that the router will perform.

13. B.   Any packet between the size of 600 and 1524 bytes will use the big buffer pool.

14. A.   Any packet between the size of 5024 and 18,024 bytes will use the huge buffer pool.

15. B.   Permanent buffers are not de-allocated by the system when not in use. In the `show buffers` command, permanent buffers are shown by buffer type, not as a single total value for all buffer pools.

16. E.   As the processor has responsibilities other than switching packets, it is beneficial if one of the other switching methods is used for switching packets to reduce the overall load on the processor.

17. B, G.   The two components used by CEF are the Forwarding Information Base (FIB) and the adjacency table. It is true the FIB is derived from components of the routing table, but the routing table is not directly used by CEF.

18. A, C.   The `show memory` command contains a field for Largest and Lowest, which is not in the `show process memory` command. On the other side, the `show process memory` command has PID information, which is not included in the `show memory` command.

19. D.   A runt is a frame that is smaller than the minimum frame size of in this case Ethernet, which is 64 bytes. Runts are usually caused by collisions. Therefore, if you have more runts then collisions there is most likely a problem on the segment.

20. D.   By default, weighted fair queuing is used on most Cisco router interfaces. The other queuing strategies, except First In Last Out (FILO), can be applied if needs dictate.

Cisco Diagnostic Commands and TCP/IP Connectivity Troubleshooting

---

TOPICS COVERED IN THIS CHAPTER INCLUDE:

✓ Use troubleshooting tools and minimize their impact on a Cisco router's switching type and data flow.

✓ Identify and use Cisco IOS software commands and debug utilities to filter, capture, and display protocol traffic flows.

✓ Use proven problem isolation techniques to list the symptoms of common TCP/IP problems.

✓ Apply diagnostic tools to solve network problems that include systems running TCP/IP with Windows NT/95 clients and servers.

The next two chapters are primarily focused on covering essential TCP/IP troubleshooting skills and tools. In this chapter, we will explain show and debug commands. In addition, generic commands such as ping and traceroute will be applied to network problems. Problem isolation techniques that are used in troubleshooting LAN and WAN will be outlined and implemented. We will also cover troubleshooting common problems with Windows 95/98/NT stations. Finally, the use and kinds of access lists will be examined.

In the next chapter, Chapter 6, IP routing protocols are the primary focus. The protocols that are covered include RIP, IGRP, EIGRP, OSPF, and BGP. In addition to an explanation of these routing protocols, the show and debug commands used for these protocols will be examined. The final part of this chapter deals with redistribution issues and solutions.

Many of the show and debug commands are not protocol specific. Though these commands do not deal exclusively with the TCP/IP protocol, they are used in troubleshooting many TCP/IP problems and therefore are included in this chapter for completeness. As is the case with the show and debug commands, logging and core dumps are not limited to the TCP/IP but can be used to assist in the troubleshooting of TCP/IP problems. Therefore, they are also being included in this chapter for completeness.

In addition to detailed problem-solving techniques, quick reference summary charts are located at the end of Chapter 6. These tables help to quickly associate a cause to many TCP/IP symptoms.

Troubleshooting Commands

We will cover several troubleshooting tools in this chapter, each of which is part of the Cisco IOS. There are many show commands that are supported by the router. In addition to show commands, there is a tool, called *debug*, that is used to see specific information regarding packet transfer and exchange.

Part of effectively using these tools is to learn how to use them without adversely affecting the router or its other processes. You will learn the specifics of several troubleshooting commands, along with the information needed in order to use them without causing additional problems on your network.

We start with nonintrusive, Cisco-specific show commands. After discussing the show commands, we move on to the debug tool. To finalize this section, we discuss some non-Cisco-specific troubleshooting tools: ping and traceroute.

show Commands

A large number of show commands are supported by Cisco IOS. It is unrealistic to explain every one of them in this book. The most effective and useful show commands are described in the following sections. To get an idea of all of the show commands, execute the show ? command from the router prompt. Some useful show commands are listed in Table 5.1.

T A B L E 5 . 1 Frequently Used show Commands

show Command	Description
access-lists	List access lists
accounting	Accounting data for active sessions
adjacency	Adjacent nodes
buffers	Buffer pool statistics
cdp	Cisco Discovery Protocol (CDP) information
cef	Cisco Express Forwarding
configuration	Contents of the NVRAM
controllers	Interface controller status
debugging	State of each debugging option

TABLE 5.1 Frequently Used show Commands *(continued)*

show Command	Description
environment	Environmental monitor statistics
extended	Extended interface information
frame-relay	Frame Relay information
interfaces	Interface status and configuration
ip	IP information
line	TTY line information
logging	Show the contents of logging buffers
memory	Memory statistics
ppp	PPP parameters and statistics
processes	Active process statistics
protocols	Active network routing protocols
queue	Show queue contents
queueing	Show queuing configuration
running-config	Current operating configuration
stacks	Process stack utilization
startup-config	Contents of startup configuration
tcp	Status of TCP connections
tech-support	Show system information for Tech Support
version	System hardware and software version and status

From the information provided in Table 5.1, you can categorize the show commands into four types: global, interface, process, and protocol-related. The main process show commands, show process memory and show process CPU, were detailed in Chapter 4 and therefore will not be covered in this chapter.

Depending on the problem you are troubleshooting, you can focus on the problem by using appropriate commands. For example, if you are troubleshooting a protocol-related problem, then you will probably use the protocol family of show commands. If you notice problems on a circuit, you can use the interface family of show commands to give you detailed information about the interface.

Global Commands

Global commands deal with global router settings. This means that information that does not relate to interfaces or protocols, yet has overall router information, is considered to be a global show command. Table 5.2 shows useful global show commands. A detailed description of the commands as well as sample output is included after the table.

TABLE 5.2 Global show Commands

Global show Command	Description
version	System hardware and software status
running-config	Current operating configuration
startup-config	Contents of start-up configuration
logging	Show the contents of logging buffers
buffers	Buffer pool statistics
stacks	Process stack utilization
tech-support	Show system information for Tech Support
access-lists	List access lists
memory	Memory statistics

show version

This command is used to display the system hardware and software versions. It also includes information about how long the router was running and the reason it was last restarted. Review the output of the show version command.

```
Router_B>show version
Cisco Internetwork Operating System Software
IOS (tm) GS Software (RSP-JV-M), Version 11.1(25)CC, EARLY
    DEPLOYMENT RELEASE SOFTWARE (fc1)
V111_25_CC_THROTTLE_BRANCH Synced to mainline version:
    11.1(25)CA
Copyright (c) 1986-1998 by cisco Systems, Inc.
Compiled Mon 11-May-98 19:42 by richardd
Image text-base: 0x60010910, data-base: 0x60A64000


ROM: System Bootstrap, Version 11.1(8)CA1, EARLY
    DEPLOYMENT RELEASE SOFTWARE (fc1)
ROM: GS Software (RSP-BOOT-M), Version 11.1(8)CA1, EARLY
    DEPLOYMENT RELEASE SOFTWARE (fc1)


Router_B uptime is 14 hours, 43 minutes
System restarted by reload at 05:13:16 MST Wed April 10
    2002
System image file is "slot0:rsp-jv-mz.111-25.CC.bin",
    booted via slot0


cisco RSP4 (R5000) processor with 65536K/2072K bytes of
    memory.
R5000 processor, Implementation 35, Revision 2.1 (512KB
    Level 2 Cache)
Last reset from power-on
G.703/E1 software, Version 1.0.
G.703/JT2 software, Version 1.0.
SuperLAT software copyright 1990 by Meridian Technology
    Corp).
Bridging software.
X.25 software, Version 2.0, NET2, BFE and GOSIP compliant.
TN3270 Emulation software (copyright 1994 by TGV Inc).
```

```
Chassis Interface.
2 EIP controllers (12 Ethernet).
3 FSIP controllers (24 Serial).
2 AIP controllers (2 ATM).
12 Ethernet/IEEE 802.3 interfaces.
24 Serial network interfaces.
2 ATM network interfaces.
123K bytes of non-volatile configuration memory.
20480K bytes of Flash PCMCIA card at slot 0 (Sector size
    128K).
8192K bytes of Flash internal SIMM (Sector size 256K).
Slave in slot 7 is running Cisco Internetwork Operating
    System Software
IOS (tm) GS Software (RSP-DW-M), Version 11.1(25)CC, EARLY
    DEPLOYMENT RELEASE SOFTWARE (fc1)
V111_25_CC_THROTTLE_BRANCH Synced to mainline version:
    11.1(25)CA
Copyright (c) 1986-1998 by cisco Systems, Inc.
Compiled Mon 11-May-98 19:44 by richardd
Slave: Loaded from system
Slave: cisco RSP4 (R5000) processor with 65536K bytes of
    memory.
Configuration register is 0x102
Router_B>
```

As you can see, the output contains a great deal of information. We'll move through it field by field. The first field indicates the revision of software that is actively running on the router. In this case, it is Cisco IOS11.1(25)CC.

The next field is the bootstrap version, which indicates the Cisco IOS that is used in case the IOS isn't found. This IOS is stored on the PROMS or FLASH memory of the router. The router boots by using 11.1(8)CA. This allows the router to actually boot so that you may fix software problems.

Current router status information is located in the field following the bootstrap information. This output tells you the length of time the router has been up and the last date it was reloaded. If an error caused the router to reload, the error message is included in this field. Finally, the file that was used while booting is listed.

The final field describes the route processor and amount of RAM. At the end of the field, all interface processors are listed, followed by the number of interfaces. The last three lines indicate the different amounts and types of memory.

Because this output is from a Cisco 7513 that contains two RSP4 processor boards, the `show version` command also lists information about the slave board. (In routers with two RSP boards, one board takes the role of the master and the other becomes the slave.)

show startup-config and running-config

These two commands are used to view the syntax of the router's configuration. The `show startup-config` command displays the contents of the configuration that was written to NVRAM. The `show running-config`, `show config`, and `write term` commands are all equivalent commands. The results of these commands display the configuration that was loaded into memory and is running on the router.

Although you should already be familiar with these commands, it is a very good troubleshooting tip to compare the two configurations when working on network problems. It is always possible that configuration changes were made to the running configuration and were not copied to the start-up configuration. There may be extra or missing commands in the different configuration versions. You may be able to solve the problem of missing commands in the running configuration quickly by copying the `startup-config` to the `running-config`.

These commands provide you with global, protocol, and interface information. You can analyze them for proper configuration and make changes, if needed. Many problems can be isolated by viewing the configuration. Most of the time you will see something that wasn't there before, see something that shouldn't be there, or notice that something is missing that needs to be there. For this technique to work, you must be familiar with the router and its configuration. If backups are made of the configurations, you may compare them to the `running-config` to look for differences.

show stacks

The `show stacks` command is not very useful to you, but it is invaluable information for the Cisco TAC. The output from the command appears below. As you can see, it doesn't make a lot of sense to the user. The information is sent to Cisco; Cisco runs it through a stack decode that provides the information relevant to system problems.

Stacks are used to provide information on the router's processes and processor utilization. The output displayed is from a healthy router. If the router were to crash, the latest stack information is saved so it can be captured once the router comes back up. The data contains information regarding the reason for the reload and any errors that are attributed to the crash.

```
Router_A#show stack
Minimum process stacks:
  Free/Size   Name
10288/12000  Init
 5196/6000   Router Init
 9672/12000  Virtual Exec

Interrupt level stacks:
  Level    Called Unused/Size  Name
    1       49917  8200/9000   Network Interrupt
    2           2  8372/9000   Network Status Interrupt
    3           0  9000/9000   OIR interrupt
    4           0  9000/9000   PCMCIA Interrupt
    5        2561  8652/9000   Console Uart
    6           0  9000/9000   Error Interrupt
    7    27140712  8608/9000   NMI Interrupt Handler
Router_A#
```

show tech-support

The tech-support command is a compilation of several show commands (version, running-config, controllers, stacks, interfaces, diagbus, buffers, process memory, process cpu, context, boot, flash bootflash, ip traffic, and controllers cbus). You can get most of the information you need by issuing the show tech-support command, instead of issuing all of the commands separately.

The tech-support command does not allow you to scroll through it on the router because of the enormous amount of information that is displayed. To capture the output, you need a terminal with a large line buffer setting, or you can log the output directly to a terminal.

show access-lists

The show access-lists command is useful to view the access list configuration without sorting through the running or start-up configuration. In addition to displaying the line entries of the access list, the command uses the access list number to define what type of access list is being displayed. The output from the show access-lists command follows:

```
Router_B#show access-lists
Extended IP access-list 105
    permit ip 172.16.0.0 0.0.255.255 any (97160 matches)
    permit ip 10.0.0.0 0.255.255.255 any
    deny   ip any any (102463 matches)
Novell access-list 801
    permit 606E3000 (3245 matches)
    permit 506E3074
    permit B06F2E00 (655 matches)
    permit D06F2EFE
    permit 717B012C
    permit E06F2E67
    permit F9BE0714 (5038 matches)
    permit A054AB00
    permit 617B07C4
    permit 017B1900
```

This information gives you a summary of each access list on the router. The access list type is defined and the number assigned to it is shown. Each line of the list is displayed individually. The list also specifies which network is matched by using which wildcard mask.

Interface Commands

Interface commands deal with detailed interface settings and configurations. Because each type of interface uses different protocols and technologies, the show interface command is capable of displaying all data related to the specified interface. Table 5.3 shows useful interface-related show commands. The show queueing and show queue were detailed in the previous chapter. Therefore, in this section we will focus on the show interface and show ip interface commands.

TABLE 5.3   show interface Commands

show interface Command	Description
queuing/queue	Show queuing configuration and contents
interface <interface-type> <interface-number>	Interface status and configuration
controllers	Interface controller status
ip interface	Shows information specifically related to IP interfaces

show interface

As was mentioned before, the show interface command has many derivatives. Table 5.4 lists many of the options that are available with the show interface command. It is important to recognize that the interface processors listed are there because they are present on the router. For example, you won't see a Token Ring interface listed unless there is a Token Ring interface on the router.

TABLE 5.4   show interface Command Options

show interface Command Option	Description
atm (interface type)	ATM interface
ethernet (interface type)	IEEE 802.3
serial (interface type)	Serial
hssi (interface type)	HSSI interface
accounting	Show interface accounting
fair-queue	Show interface Weighted Fair Queueing (WFQ) info

TABLE 5.4 show interface Command Options *(continued)*

show interface **Command Option**	**Description**
rate-limit	Show interface rate-limit info
mac-accounting	Show interface MAC accounting info

Now look at sample outputs from an Ethernet and a Serial interface. After each sample, we will go through a detailed explanation.

```
Router_A#show interface Ethernet 5/4
Ethernet5/4 is up, line protocol is up
  Hardware is cxBus Ethernet, address is 009a.822e.51b6
    (bia 90.323f.acdb)
  Description: Connection to Router_B
  Internet address is 172.16.1.1/24
  MTU 1500 bytes, BW 10000 Kbit, DLY 1000 usec, rely 255/
    255, load 33/255
  Encapsulation ARPA, loopback not set, keepalive set (10
    sec)
  ARP type: ARPA, ARP Timeout 04:00:00
  Last input 00:00:00, output 00:00:00, output hang never
  Last clearing of "show interface" counters never
  Queueing strategy: fifo
  Output queue 0/40, 101553 drops; input queue 0/75, 1327
    drops
  5 minute input rate 247000 bits/sec, 196 packets/sec
  5 minute output rate 1329000 bits/sec, 333 packets/sec
    421895792 packets input, 2524672293 bytes, 1 no
    buffer
    Received 453382 broadcasts, 0 runts, 0 giants
    6 input errors, 1 CRC, 5 frame, 0 overrun, 494
    ignored,        0 abort
    0 input packets with dribble condition detected
```

```
     618578101 packets output, 977287695 bytes, 0
     underruns
     0 output errors, 30979588 collisions, 1 interface
     resets
     0 babbles, 0 late collision, 0 deferred
     0 lost carrier, 0 no carrier
     0 output buffers copied, 0 interrupts, 0 failures
Router_A#
```

The output starts with the most pertinent information—the physical interface and line protocol status. In this case, both are up. There is much argument as to what constitutes an "up" interface. It is very simple—the controller sends a signal that there are electrons flowing through the physical interface. So, just doing a "no shut" on an interface brings it into an "up" status, even if nothing is plugged into the interface. Line protocol "up" means that the interface is able to send itself a frame and receive it back.

The next fields contain the Layer 2 MAC address, the interface description, and the Layer 3 IP address. Below the interface address information, you'll find the line settings for the interface. An MTU, bandwidth, delay, reliability, and load are listed. These values are used to calculate a distance-vector protocol route metric.

Default Ethernet encapsulation for Cisco is ARPA. You can see that this is true and that the keepalive is the default at 10 seconds. This line is a very important line when troubleshooting Ethernet problems. If the encapsulation type is not compatible with other machines on the network, you will have communication problems. In order to better demonstrate this, review the example given in the following paragraph.

When the router broadcasts from an interface, it uses the encapsulation that is configured. Look at Figure 5.1. In this case, an ARPA frame (#1) is sent. If the hosts on the network do not understand ARPA, they do not respond to the broadcast. On the other hand, if a host broadcast uses a SNAP frame (#2), the router is designed to understand any incoming frame encapsulation and can respond to the broadcast. Another bit of useful information that the router adds to the ARP table is the encapsulation type of that host. Then, the next time that the router wants to speak with the given host, it uses the documented frame type instead of the type configured on the interface. Here's a look at the ARP table (notice that the

Type field is SNAP):

```
Router_C>show arp
Protocol  Address       Age (min)  Hardware Addr    Type  Interface
Internet  172.16.1.1    -          0010.296a.a820   ARPA  Ethernet5/0
Internet  172.16.1.22   62         0010.29d1.68a0   SNAP  Ethernet5/0
Router_C>
```

FIGURE 5.1 Ethernet frame encapsulation compatibility

Continuing on: From the output from the show interface command, you can see a great deal of statistical information. You can see that the counters for the interface have not been cleared since the router booted. Queuing type for the interface is first-in-first-out (FIFO). You should be familiar with the next few fields. The input and output queue were discussed in detail previously. Here, you have statistical information that displays the number of drops. The interface traffic statistics follow.

Statistical information includes the number of packets that travel across the interface and the bandwidth utilization. The following fields are dedicated to Ethernet troubleshooting. The cyclic redundancy check field counts the number of frames that were received that do not pass the CRC test. Next are frame errors and overruns. We discussed overruns previously (they occur when the receiver on the interface receives frames faster than it can move them to the hardware buffer on the interface). The ignore signal is sent if there are buffer problems.

Output errors consist of underruns and collisions. The other fields are counters for the physical interface: resets, lost carrier, and no carrier. These are followed by more buffer error counters.

Now we'll review the output from a Serial interface:

```
Router_D#sho int s1/0
Serial1/0 is up, line protocol is up
  Hardware is cxBus Serial
  Description: Connection to frame-relay cloud
  MTU 1500 bytes, BW 1544 Kbit, DLY 20000 usec, rely 255/
  255, load 1/255
  Encapsulation FRAME-RELAY, loopback not set, keepalive
  set     (10 sec)
  LMI enq sent  195167, LMI stat recvd 195165, LMI upd
  recvd     10, DTE LMI up
  LMI enq recvd 0, LMI stat sent  0, LMI upd sent  0
  LMI DLCI 1023  LMI type is CISCO  frame relay DTE
  Broadcast queue 0/64, broadcasts sent/dropped 0/0,
  interface broadcasts 908350
  Last input 00:00:00, output 00:00:00, output hang never
  Last clearing of "show interface" counters never
  Input queue: 0/75/4 (size/max/drops); Total output
  drops:     22795
  Queueing strategy: weighted fair
  Output queue: 0/64/22795 (size/threshold/drops)
     Conversations  0/59 (active/max active)
     Reserved Conversations 0/0 (allocated/max allocated)
  5 minute input rate 7000 bits/sec, 9 packets/sec
  5 minute output rate 9000 bits/sec, 8 packets/sec
     55695166 packets input, 3680326698 bytes, 1 no buffer
     Received 0 broadcasts, 0 runts, 0 giants
     1 input errors, 0 CRC, 0 frame, 0 overrun, 0 ignored,
     1 abort
     56424159 packets output, 569801054 bytes, 0 underruns
     0 output errors, 0 collisions, 2 interface resets
```

```
    8656902 output buffers copied, 0 interrupts, 0
    failures
    3 carrier transitions
    RTS up, CTS up, DTR up, DCD up, DSR up
Router_D#
```

This output has a lot of Frame Relay information that we will discuss in a later chapter. For now, we'll just review the fields of information that are available by using this command.

You can see that the first line is the interface status line. The metric values are also listed. Following the Frame Relay information, you see the interface traffic statistics. At the bottom of the output are the buffer error fields, as well as the physical interface counters. A carrier transition is counted any time the carrier status change occurs. (We will cover this output in detail in Chapter 7.)

show ip interface

This command provides information specific to the TCP/IP configuration of the specified interface. Information regarding the interface status, IP address, subnet mask, broadcast address, and applied access lists is all contained in the show ip interface command. In addition, the command also provides information on proxy ARP, which will be explained in further detail later in this chapter; helper addresses, which are used for DHCP configurations; Network Address translation (NAT); and many other items. Next to the show interface command, the output of the show ip interface command has the most information about a particular interface. A sample output follows:

```
Router_B#show ip interface serial 0
Serial0 is up, line protocol is up
  Internet address is 172.16.30.6/30
  Broadcast address is 255.255.255.255
  Address determined by non-volatile memory
  MTU is 1500 bytes
  Helper address is not set
  Directed broadcast forwarding is enabled
  Multicast reserved groups joined: 224.0.0.10
  Outgoing access list is not set
  Inbound  access list is not set
  Proxy ARP is enabled
```

```
                  Security level is default
                  Split horizon is enabled
                  ICMP redirects are always sent
                  ICMP unreachables are always sent
                  ICMP mask replies are never sent
                  IP fast switching is enabled
                  IP fast switching on the same interface is enabled
                  IP multicast fast switching is enabled
                  Router Discovery is disabled
                  IP output packet accounting is disabled
                  IP access violation accounting is disabled
                  TCP/IP header compression is disabled
                  Probe proxy name replies are disabled
                  Gateway Discovery is disabled
                  Policy routing is disabled
                  Network address translation is disabled
             Router_B#
```

TCP/IP Protocol Commands

We will discuss the major TCP/IP protocol commands in this section. In addition to the TCP/IP commands listed here, we will also discuss other protocol-related commands later in the book. The other principal types of protocols that are discussed in this book are HDLC, Frame Relay, X.25, ISDN, IPX, and AppleTalk. Table 5.5 lists the frequently used IP options.

TABLE 5.5 Frequently Used show IP Command Options

show ip Command Option	Option Description
access-lists	Lists IP access lists.
accounting	The active IP accounting database.
arp	Shows information regarding the IP ARP entries in the ARP cache.
interface	IP interface status and configuration.

TABLE 5.5 Frequently Used show IP Command Options *(continued)*

show ip Command Option	Option Description
protocols	Gives information regarding the IP routing protocols running on a router.
route	IP routing table.
traffic	IP protocol statistics.

show ip access-list

This command provides information regarding a specified access list, or all access lists that fall within the 1–199 range. When different access lists are configured on the router, the show ip access-list command shows NAMED IP access lists only. From the following sample output, you can see that it lists both standard and extended lists:

```
Standard IP access list 5
    permit 172.16.14.2
    permit 172.16.91.140
    permit 172.16.10.51
    permit 172.16.1.7
    permit 172.16.155.0, wildcard bits 0.0.0.255
Extended IP access list 152
    deny ip any 172.16.91.0 0.0.0.63 log (268436 matches)
    deny ip any host 172.16.91.66 log (81058 matches)
    permit tcp any any established (8809 matches)
    permit ip host 172.16.2.55 any
    permit ip host 172.60.22.10 any (2194226 matches)
    permit ip host 172.140.64.8 any (7930443 matches)
    permit ip 172.16.10.0 0.0.255.255 any (9076 matches)
```

show ip arp

This command provides information contained in the router's ARP cache. Information includes the IP address, MAC address, encapsulation type, and interface that it learned the MAC from. Here is a sample:

```
Router_C#show ip arp
Protocol  Address         Age (min)  Hardware Addr    Type  Interface
Internet  172.16.60.1          -     0010.7bd9.2881   ARPA  Ethernet0/1
Internet  172.16.50.2          -     0010.7bd9.2880   ARPA  Ethernet0/0
Internet  172.16.50.1          6     0000.0c09.99cc   ARPA  Ethernet0/0
Router_C#
```

show ip protocols

This command provides information about the IP routing protocols that run on the router. The sample output includes only EIGRP information because that is all that is being run on the router. As you can see, global filters are not applied. Metric values are displayed for each individual routing protocol. Route redistribution information is also provided.

```
Router_B#show ip protocols
Routing Protocol is "eigrp 100"
  Outgoing update filter list for all interfaces is not
  set
  Incoming update filter list for all interfaces is not
  set
  Default networks flagged in outgoing updates
  Default networks accepted from incoming updates
  EIGRP metric weight K1=1, K2=0, K3=1, K4=0, K5=0
  EIGRP maximum hopcount 100
  EIGRP maximum metric variance 1
  Redistributing: eigrp 100
  Automatic network summarization is not in effect
  Routing for Networks:
    172.16.0.0
  Routing Information Sources:
    Gateway          Distance       Last Update
  Distance: internal 90 external 170
Router_B#
```

show ip route

This command returns information stored in the IP route table. The command can be issued as a general command, and all IP routes and corresponding information will be displayed. Additionally, a given network may be specified, and the command will return information regarding that network only. Here are two samples. Notice that the two outputs are different. The general command provides summary information for every IP route in the route table. However, when a network is specified, the results are much more detailed. Information such as the exact routing protocol responsible for learning the route, the source interface, and the next-hop router's IP address is all included.

```
Router_A>show ip route
Codes: C - connected, S - static, I - IGRP, R - RIP, M -
    mobile, B - BGP
    D - EIGRP, EX - EIGRP external, O - OSPF, IA - OSPF
    inter area
    N1 - OSPF NSSA external type 1, N2 - OSPF NSSA
    external type 2
    E1 - OSPF external type 1, E2 - OSPF external type 2,
    E - EGP
    i - IS-IS, L1 - IS-IS level-1, L2 - IS-IS level-2, *
    - candidate default
U - per-user static route, o - ODR

Gateway of last resort is not set

    172.16.0.0/16 is variably subnetted, 2 subnets, 2
    masks
D       172.16.50.0/24 [90/2195456] via 172.16.30.6,
    00:00:19, Serial1
C       172.16.30.4/30 is directly connected, Serial1
Router_A>

Router_A>show ip route 172.16.50.0
Routing entry for 172.16.50.0/24
  Known via "eigrp 100", distance 90, metric 2195456, type
    internal
  Redistributing via eigrp 100
  Last update from 172.16.30.6 on Serial1, 00:02:03 ago
  Routing Descriptor Blocks:
  * 172.16.30.6, from 172.16.30.6, 00:02:03 ago, via
  Serial1
```

```
        Route metric is 2195456, traffic share count is 1
        Total delay is 21000 microseconds, minimum bandwidth
        is 1544 Kbit
        Reliability 128/255, minimum MTU 1500 bytes
        Loading 1/255, Hops 1


Router_A>
```

show ip traffic

This command returns information pertaining to IP traffic statistics. When the command is issued, the output is organized according to the IP protocol. Here is a sample:

```
Router_B#show ip traffic
IP statistics:
  Rcvd:  400 total, 400 local destination
         0 format errors, 0 checksum errors,
         0 bad hop count
         0 unknown protocol, 0 not a gateway
         0 security failures, 0 bad options,
         0 with options
  Opts:  0 end, 0 nop, 0 basic security,
         0 loose source  route
         0 timestamp, 0 extended security, 0 record route
         0 stream ID, 0 strict source route, 0 alert,
         0 cipso
         0 other
  Frags: 0 reassembled, 0 timeouts, 0 couldn't reassemble
         0 fragmented, 0 couldn't fragment
  Bcast: 0 received, 0 sent
  Mcast: 398 received, 401 sent
  Sent:  404 generated, 0 forwarded
         0 encapsulation failed, 0 no route

ICMP statistics:
  Rcvd: 0 format errors, 0 checksum errors, 0 redirects, 0
  unreachable
```

```
                         0 echo, 0 echo reply, 0 mask requests, 0 mask
                         replies, 0 quench
                         0 parameter, 0 timestamp, 0 info request, 0 other
                         0 irdp solicitations, 0 irdp advertisements
                   Sent: 0 redirects, 0 unreachable, 0 echo, 0 echo reply
                         0 mask requests, 0 mask replies, 0 quench, 0
                         timestamp
                         0 info reply, 0 time exceeded, 0 parameter problem
                         0 irdp solicitations, 0 irdp advertisements

            UDP statistics:
              Rcvd: 0 total, 0 checksum errors, 0 no port
              Sent: 0 total, 0 forwarded broadcasts

            TCP statistics:
              Rcvd: 0 total, 0 checksum errors, 0 no port
              Sent: 0 total

            Probe statistics:
              Rcvd: 0 address requests, 0 address replies
                    0 proxy name requests, 0 where-is requests, 0
                    other
              Sent: 0 address requests, 0 address replies (0 proxy)
                    0 proxy name replies, 0 where-is replies

            EGP statistics:
              Rcvd: 0 total, 0 format errors, 0 checksum errors, 0 no
              listener
              Sent: 0 total

            IGRP statistics:
              Rcvd: 0 total, 0 checksum errors
              Sent: 0 total

            OSPF statistics:
              Rcvd: 0 total, 0 checksum errors
```

```
                     0 Hello, 0 database desc, 0 link state req
                     0 link state updates, 0 link state acks

             Sent: 0 total

      IP-IGRP2 statistics:
        Rcvd: 402 total
        Sent: 406 total

      PIMv2 statistics: Sent/Received
        Total: 0/0, 0 checksum errors, 0 format errors
        Registers: 0/0, Register Stops: 0/0

      IGMP statistics: Sent/Received
        Total: 0/0, Format errors: 0/0, Checksum errors: 0/0
        Host Queries: 0/0, Host Reports: 0/0, Host Leaves: 00
        DVMRP: 0/0, PIM: 0/0

      ARP statistics:
        Rcvd: 0 requests, 0 replies, 0 reverse, 0 other
        Sent: 1 requests, 5 replies (0 proxy), 0 reverse
      Router_B#
```

debug Commands

The debug commands and options are very powerful tools. The messages produced by the debugging process give detailed information and provide insight into what is happening on a very low level.

This power does not come free of charge. In most cases, debugging requires every packet to be process-switched, meaning that the route processor has to look at every packet entering the router, if valid information is to be obtained. In addition, there are many other processes the router must run and manage. Debugging can cause a great deal of additional overhead on a router. Therefore, it is important to use the tool with discretion. It should be used to provide additional information on an existing problem, not used to monitor a router. As a rule of thumb, debug commands should not be run on a router that already has a CPU utilization greater than 50%.

Because the majority of problems are reported while the network is in production, the last thing you want to do is crash a router or cause unnecessary overhead by using the debug tool. By focusing the application of the debug command by using various options and access lists, you can effectively troubleshoot problems without causing any additional ones. Always remember to turn the debugging function off after you obtain the necessary data. If left on, it can cause another network problem.

There are two "tricks" to successfully using the debug tool. First, make sure that your router is configured to apply timestamps to all messages. This is done with the following commands:

```
Router_A(config)#service timestamps debug datetime msec
    localtime
Router_A(config)#service timestamps log datetime msec
    localtime
```

Next, make sure that you see these messages. By default, error and debug messages are sent only to the console. If you are telneted to the router, you do not see the debug or log messages unless you issue the following command:

```
Router_A#terminal monitor
```

You can turn messages off by issuing the "no" form of the command. An example follows:

```
Router_A#terminal no monitor
```

If the output messages from the debug become excessive, it becomes difficult, if not impossible, to enter commands. If this happens, there are two commands that you can issue to stop the messages. The first one was already mentioned (the terminal no monitor—term no mon for short—command). You type, but you don't see anything echo back. It can get confusing. Remember that the text messages that echo to the screen are not entered on the command line of the router. You can safely type **term no mon** and hit Enter, even with hundreds of messages scrolling past you on the screen. The router eventually recognizes and processes the command. That stops the messages from scrolling down the screen, but it does not stop the processor from looking at every packet.

To stop the debug process, the easiest way is to type the shorthand form of undebug all, as demonstrated below:

```
Router_A#un all
```

It is short and sweet, yet effective. It works especially well when the router seems to be having a runaway. This command stops all debug processes and all associated messages. This command can be entered safely while messages are scrolling wildly down the screen. It may take the router a few CPU cycles to accept the command and actually stop the debug process, so don't panic.

As an alternative to this, you can also have the command ready to go if you allow multiple telnet sessions to the same router. In this instance you would telnet to the router twice. In one of the telnet session you would set up the `terminal monitor` command so that you would receive the debug output. In the other window you would type in the `undebug all` command but not hit Enter. You then return to your first telnet session and execute the `debug` command you need. If the output is overwhelming, go back to your other telnet session and hit Enter. As was the case before, it may take several seconds for the router to process the command and the messages to stop appearing on the screen.

Limiting Debug Output

Because of the potential impact to the router, precautions should be taken any time `debug` commands are used. You should be as specific as possible when entering the `debug` commands so that you look at only information relevant to your issue. In addition to the commands themselves, access lists can be applied to the `debug` commands to further limit the information that you are looking at.

For example, if you wanted to see ping (ICMP) packets going between stations with IP addresses of 10.20.20.20 and 10.30.30.30, you could create an access list that looked like the following:

```
access-list 100 permit icmp host 10.20.20.20 host
   10.30.30.30
```

Then apply this access list to the `debug` command as shown below:

```
Router_C#debug ip packet detail 100
IP packet debugging is on (detailed) for access list 100
Router_C#
IP: s=10.20.20.20 (Serial0), d=10.30.30.30 (Serial1),
   g=10.5.30.30, len 100, forward ICMP type=8, code=0
```

In this manner, only ICMP packets going from 10.20.20.20 to 10.30.30.30 are shown in the debug output, not all of the packets going through the router.

As with the `show` commands, there are global-, interface-, and protocol-debugging options. Because these tools and commands are used in detail in upcoming chapters, they are only summarized here according to usage.

Real World Scenario

Verify the Packet Flow without Using Debug

One question that frequently arises during troubleshooting is whether a particular packet is making it through or even to a particular router. One way to verify this is through the use of debugging commands. However, as mentioned before, using debugging commands can have a severe impact on the overall functionality of the router. Therefore, alternate solutions should be examined. In this case, one alternate solution is to use the log feature of an access list.

The best way to explain this is through the use of an example. In this case, we will use the same example that was used in the "Limiting Debug Output" section. Assume that you want to verify that pings from 10.20.20.20 and destined to 10.30.30.30 are getting to the router. To do this, we first create an access list with two lines as is shown below:

```
access-list 100 permit icmp host 10.20.20.20 host 10.30.30.30 log
access-list 100 permit ip any any
```

Notice the log at the end of the first line of the access list. This will put an entry in the log any time a packet meeting the criteria specified in the line is met. Also note the permit ip any any at the end. This line ensures that other traffic on the interface will not be affected.

At this point, make sure you are on the console or have your telnet session set up as a terminal monitor, and apply the access list inbound on the interface the packets will use to enter the router. This is shown below:

```
Router_A(config)#interface serial0
Router_A(config-if)#ip access-group 100 in
%SEC-6-IPACCESSLOGDP: list 100 permitted icmp 10.20.20.20 ->
    10.30.30.30 (0/0), 1 packet
```

By using access lists in this manner, you are able to verify that particular traffic is flowing over this router. Though potentially safer than using debug, the log option on access lists can also create a large amount of data if there is a large amount of traffic that meets the selection criteria specified in the access list. In addition, if an access list is already in place on a particular interface, modifications to accommodate this list will need to be part of the implementation. Even with these caveats, this "trick" can save you time and aggravation over using the debug commands.

Global Debugging

Some global **debug** commands are listed in Table 5.6. The table is not comprehensive; it is just a list of commonly used global **debug** commands. To obtain a comprehensive list of **debug** commands, issue the following command:

```
Router_A#debug ?
```

TABLE 5.6 Global debug Command

Global debug Command	Description
aaa	AAA Authentication, Authorization, and Accounting
adjacency	Adjacency
all	Enable all debugging
cbus	ciscoBus events
cdp	CDP information
chat	Chat scripts activity
dhcp	DHCP client activity
dialer	Dial on Demand
domain	Domain Name System
entry	Incoming queue entries
snmp	SNMP information
tacacs	TACACS authentication and authorization
tbridge	Transparent bridging

Interface Debugging

Interface debugging is used to obtain information that is specific to interfaces, interface signaling, and interface processes. The same caution should be used with interface-related **debug** commands as with the global commands.

The more focused the debug through the use of options, the easier it is to isolate the problem.

Interface-oriented commands are provided in Table 5.7. Again, each of these commands has additional options available. To see the related options, use the commands listed, followed by a question mark. Most of these commands will be described and applied in later chapters.

TABLE 5.7   Interface-Related debug Commands

debug Command	Description
atm	ATM interface information
channel	Channel interface information
ethernet-interface	Ethernet network interface events
fastethernet	Fast Ethernet interface information
serial	Serial interface information
token	Token Ring information
tunnel	Generic tunnel interface

Protocol Debugging

There are two protocol classes that may be debugged: desktop, or routed, protocols and routing protocols. There are several debug options for protocol information, and each protocol has its own associated debug options. These options can be obtained by using the command line help on the router.

Table 5.8 shows a list of the protocol-related debug commands available.

TABLE 5.8   Protocol-Related debug Commands

debug Command	Description
apple	AppleTalk information
arp	IP ARP and HP probe transactions
atm	ATM signaling

TABLE 5.8 Protocol-Related debug Commands *(continued)*

debug Command	Description
broadcast	MAC broadcast packets
decent	DECnet information
dlsw	Data Link Switching (DLSw) events
eigrp	EIGRP protocol information
frame-relay	Frame Relay
ip	IP information
ipx	Novell/IPX information
isis	IS-IS information
ppp	PPP (Point to Point Protocol) information
qllc	qllc debug information
sna	SNA information
spanning	Spanning-tree information
sscop	SSCOP
telnet	Incoming telnet connections
translate	Protocol translation events
vlan	VLAN information
x25	X.25 information

IP Debugging

Just as with the show commands, there are numerous debug commands and options specifically for IP. The problem being analyzed will dictate which IP debug commands need to be used. Table 5.9 lists many of the available debug commands and options within IP. The first command, arp, is not an IP-specific command, yet it provides valuable IP information.

TABLE 5.9 IP debug Commands and Options

Command	Description
arp	IP ARP and HP Probe transactions
bgp	BGP information
cache	IP cache operations
cef	IP CEF operations
cgmp	CGMP protocol activity
egp	EGP information
eigrp	IP EIGRP information
error	IP error debugging
ftp	FTP dialogue
http	HTTP connections
icmp	ICMP transactions
igmp	IGMP protocol activity
igrp	IGRP information
mbgp	MBGP information
mcache	IP multicast cache operations
mds	IP distributed multicast information
mobile	Mobility protocols
mpacket	IP multicast packet debugging
mrouting	IP multicast routing table activity
msdp	Multicast Source Discovery Protocol (MSDP)

T A B L E 5 . 9 IP debug Commands and Options *(continued)*

Command	Description
mtag	IP multicast tagswitching activity
nat	NAT events
ospf	OSPF information
packet	General IP debugging and IPSO security transactions
peer	IP peer address activity
pim	PIM protocol activity
policy	Policy routing
rip	RIP protocol transactions
routing	Routing table events
rsvp	RSVP protocol activity
security	IP security options
socket	Socket event
tcp	TCP information
trigger-authentication	Trigger authentication
udp	UDP-based transactions

You can use any of these commands. The **debug ip packets** command contains an option to provide an access list, which narrows the scope of the debug even more. There are some prerequisites, though. In order to properly use **debug ip packets**, the packets must be process-switched, which means that all switching types must be turned off. Fast, optimum, and other switching types do not provide the necessary information regarding the IP transactions.

logging Commands

The last set of commands being examined are the logging commands. Logging commands allow you to save errors and other messages for later review. This information can be sent to the console, to a terminal, to an internal buffer on the router, and/or to a syslog server. You can view the logging information on a router by executing the show logging command that was referenced in the "show Commands" section. A sample output of this command is shown below:

```
Router_B>show logging
Syslog logging: enabled (6519 messages dropped, 0 flushes,
    0 overruns)
    Console logging: level debugging, 9047 messages logged
    Monitor logging: level debugging, 1256 messages logged
    Buffer logging: level debugging, 9047 messages logged
    Trap logging: level notifications, 3276 message lines
        logged
        Logging to 10.20.20.20, 3276 message lines logged


Log Buffer (65536 bytes):

Feb 11 01:00:45: %CLEAR-5-COUNTERS: Clear counter on all
    interfaces by user1 on vty0 (10.20.20.20)
Feb 11 19:40:26: %SYS-4-SNMP_WRITENET: SNMP WriteNet
    request. Writing current configuration to 10.30.30.30
Feb 12 07:40:39: %DUAL-5-NBRCHANGE: IP-EIGRP 64700:
    Neighbor 10.40.40.40 (Serial1/1/1.30) is down: holding
    time expired
```

As can be seen by the above command, the four different logging locations available—console, monitor, buffer, and trap (syslog server)—are referenced in the output. In addition to the locations, there are some logging "levels" indicated as well. We already talked about the locations; we'll now take a look at the logging levels.

There are eight possible logging levels on a Cisco router. These values or levels range from 0 to 7 and are detailed in Table 5.10. The logging level, indicated after each of the locations in the show logging command, represents the level of severity that is required for a message to be logged. Any message with a severity equal to or less than the logging level will be recorded. For example, the trap logging level in the example above was set to notifications, or 5. This means that all messages with a level of 5 or less (i.e., notifications, warnings, errors, critical, alerts, and emergencies) will be sent to the syslog server. Alternatively, the console has its level set to debugging. Since debugging is the highest level, all messages, no matter what level, will be sent to the console.

T A B L E   5 . 1 0   Logging Levels

Logging Level	Name	Description
0	Emergencies	System unusable messages
1	Alerts	Take immediate action
2	Critical	Critical condition
3	Errors	Error message
4	Warnings	Warning messages
5	Notifications	Normal but significant condition
6	Informational	Information messages
7	Debugging	Debug messages

The next logical question is "How do I know what level of debugging I need?" By default, the console, monitor, and buffer logging are set to the debugging level and the trap logging level is set to informational. If you want to modify these values, you can gauge the value you want to use by looking at the messages that already have been logged. Most messages include the logging level as part of the entry. For instance, in the example above, -5- in the middle of `clear counters` and -4- between `sys` and SNMP indicate that the first message was a level 5 notification and the second a level 4 warning. Also, if you go back to the "Verify the Packet Flow Without Using Debug" sidebar, you will note the -6- in the log output from the access list. This message would be treated as a level 6 informational message.

Finally, it should be noted that logging messages does require router CPU cycles to complete. As was the case with the debug, care must be taken with logging. If too many messages are being logged and the router is already busy, performance issues can result. In most cases, the messages that are being logged are being generated by a **debug** command. Therefore, if you know you are going to run a **debug** command that will have a large amount of output, you can turn off some of the logging to help minimize the performance impact of this debug. However, not all of the logging types are created equal when it comes to load on the router. Specifically, in order of most load to least load, the logging options are as follows: console, monitor, trap, and buffer. Therefore, if you are doing a debug that is going to cause a large number of messages, in order to minimize the load on the router, ensure that only the buffer logging is enabled.

The commands that are used with the logging options are shown in Table 5.11.

TABLE 5.11   Logging-Related Commands

`logging` Command	Description
buffered	Sets buffer size, as well as the logging level for the buffer. The no form of the command disables the logging buffer.
clear logging	Clears the logging buffer.
console	Sets the logging level for the console. The no form of the command disables logging to the console.
monitor	Sets the logging level for the monitor. The no form of the command disables logging to the monitor.
trap	Sets the logging level for the syslog server. The no form of the command disables logging to the syslog server.

Executing a Router Core Dump

The information contained in a core dump can be useful for diagnosing router problems. A core dump contains an exact copy of the information that currently resides in system memory. Depending on the amount of RAM and the memory utilization, the core dump file can be very large. The information provided is normally used only by Cisco engineers.

There are two general methods for capturing the information contained in memory. In the first method, a router is configured to execute a core dump when the router crashes. The second method is to use a user-privileged `exec` command from the command line.

exception Command

The `exception` command allows you to configure a router to execute a core dump if the router crashes. An integral part of the `exception` command is the TFTP, FTP, or RCP server. Here is a sample configuration:

```
Router_A#conf t
Enter configuration commands, one per line. End with CNTL/Z.
Router_A(config)#exception dump 172.16.10.10
Router_A(config)#^Z
Router_A#
```

The IP address in the command is the IP address of the TFTP, FTP, or RCP server. The router needs this address so it knows where to download the core dump. It uses any of the three protocols mentioned before.

Configuration varies, depending on which type of server is used. TFTP does not require any additional configuration than the example previously shown.

FTP and RCP require additional commands in order to support the file transfer. Here is an example:

```
Router_A#conf t
Enter configuration commands, one per line. End with CNTL/Z.
Router_A(config)#exception dump 172.16.10.11
Router_A(config)#ip ftp username kevin
Router_A(config)#ip ftp password aloha
Router_A(config)#ip ftp source-interface e0
Router_A(config)#exception protocol ftp
Router_A(config)#^Z
Router_A#
```

Because FTP servers require some type of username and password combination to allow access to the file system, they must be specified on the router. You can map the FTP server to the exiting interface on the router by using the `source-interface` command. This is just like a static route. If the route table did not have the route in its table, it would still know how to get to the FTP server. You must also specify which protocol is going to be used.

RCP requires configuration on the RCP server by editing the .rhosts files, as well as the router configuration. Here is a sample:

```
Router_A#conf t
Enter configuration commands, one per line. End with CNTL/Z.
Router_A(config)#exception protocol rcp
Router_A(config)#exception dump 172.16.10.12
Router_A(config)#ip rcmd remote-username kevin
Router_A(config)#ip rcmd rcp-enable
Router_A(config)#ip rcmd rsh-enable
Router_A(config)#ip rcmd remote-host kevin 172.16.10.12
   kevin
Router_A(config)#^Z
Router_A#
```

The commands are mostly the same for the RCP server, as well. The remote-host command is configured by providing the local username, followed by the IP address for the RCP server and the remote username for the RCP server. This allows the router to log in on the RCP server and commence transferring the core dump.

write core Command

The write core command allows the user to execute a core dump without crashing the router. It is not advisable to use this command unless it is requested by Cisco TAC. Because it is copying the contents of memory via TFTP, it could have an adverse effect on the router. Here is a sample of the write core command:

```
Router_A#write core
Remote host? 172.16.10.10
Name of core file to write [Router_A-core]?
Write file Router_A-core on host 172.16.10.10? [confirm]
Writing Router_A-core !!!!! [OK]
Router_A#
```

The router output has been truncated in this example. You will see exclamation marks until the file is completely transferred. The more memory that needs to be copied, the longer it will take.

Again, this information will only be useful to Cisco engineers for diagnosing and resolving router problems.

ping Commands

The previous tools are in-depth tools used for problems that require a high level of granularity. This means that these tools are used to provide very detailed and specific information at a very low-level view. The ping command is a high-level simple tool. It is used to test for reachability and connectivity throughout a network.

This tool can be used to effectively isolate network problems. If certain hosts on a network respond to the pings when others do not, this directs your efforts to focus more on the individual hosts that are not responding.

Cisco provides two implementations of the ping command: the user and privileged levels. ping works for the following protocols on both levels:

- IP
- IPX
- AppleTalk
- CLNS
- Apollo
- VINES
- DECnet
- XNS

We will specifically focus on the IP ping command for this chapter. The IPX and AppleTalk ping commands will be covered in Chapters 9 and 10 respectively.

User EXEC Mode

The user mode for ping is restricted. Only the non-verbose method is allowed for the user level. IP ping uses ICMP as the protocol to provide connectivity and reachability messages. It works on a simple principle: an ICMP echo message is sent to the specified IP address. If the address is reachable, the receiving station sends an ICMP echo-reply message back to the sending station.

It is important to be able to decipher the symbols that are echoed to the screen while a ping is taking place. By default and for user mode, five ICMP echo messages are sent. Here are a few samples:

```
Router_A>ping 172.16.1.10
Type escape sequence to abort.
```

```
Sending 5, 100-byte ICMP Echoes to 172.16.1.10, timeout is
    2 seconds:
!!!!!
Success rate is 100 percent (5/5), round-trip min/avg/max
    = 1/2/4 ms
Router_A>
Router_A>ping 172.16.2.130
Type escape sequence to abort.
Sending 5, 100-byte ICMP Echoes to 172.16.2.130, timeout is
    2 seconds:
.....
Success rate is 0 percent (0/5)
Router_A>
```

It looks good so far, but what do the different characters mean? Table 5.12 defines them.

TABLE 5.12   ping Character Map

Character	Explanation
!	Received an echo-reply message
.	Timeout
U / H	Destination unreachable
N	Network unreachable
P	Protocol unreachable
Q	Source quench
M	Unable to fragment
A	Administratively denied
?	Unknown packet-type

Now that the characters are defined, you can analyze the sample outputs. In the first ping, all five packets received echo-reply messages, which indicates that the host is reachable. Notice that the output gives a success percentage based on the five requests that were sent. It also gives the minimum, average, and maximum response times.

The second ping doesn't look so good. All five requests timed out. This means that each request waited two seconds for a response. When no response was received, a "." was echoed to the screen. It is possible that a request was received, but it was after the two-second waiting period. Either way, the host cannot be considered reachable.

Privileged EXEC Mode

The privileged mode for ping is known as an *extended ping*. This mode allows many options to aid in providing additional detailed information. The functionality of the ping command is based on the same technology as with user mode. The extended ping offers options to change some of the ping settings.

The best way to understand it is to see it:

```
Router_B #ping
Protocol [ip]:
Target IP address: 172.16.12.93
Repeat count [5]:
Datagram size [100]:
Timeout in seconds [2]:
Extended commands [n]: y
Source address or interface: 172.16.1.2
Type of service [0]:
Set DF bit in IP header? [no]:
Validate reply data? [no]:
Data pattern [0xABCD]:
Loose, Strict, Record, Timestamp, Verbose[none]: r
Number of hops [ 9 ]:
Loose, Strict, Record, Timestamp, Verbose[RV]:
Sweep range of sizes [n]:
Type escape sequence to abort.
Sending 5, 100-byte ICMP Echoes to 172.16.12.93, timeout is
    2 seconds:
Packet has IP options:  Total option bytes= 39, padded
    length=40
  Record route: <*> 0.0.0.0 0.0.0.0 0.0.0.0 0.0.0.0
            0.0.0.0 0.0.0.0 0.0.0.0 0.0.0.0 0.0.0.0
```

```
Reply to request 0 (1 ms). Received packet has options
 Total option bytes= 40, padded length=40
 Record route: 172.16.1.2 172.16.0.13 172.16.12.1
    172.16.12.93 172.16.0.14 172.16.0.21 172.16.1.2 <*>
    0.0.0.0 0.0.0.0
 End of list
Reply to request 1 (4 ms). Received packet has options
 Total option bytes= 40, padded length=40
 Record route: 172.16.1.2 172.16.0.13 172.16.12.1
    172.16.12.93 172.16.0.14 172.16.0.21 172.16.1.2 <*>
    0.0.0.0 0.0.0.0
 End of list
Reply to request 2 (4 ms). Received packet has options
 Total option bytes= 40, padded length=40
 Record route: 172.16.1.2 172.16.0.13 172.16.12.1
    172.16.12.93 172.16.0.14 172.16.0.21 172.16.1.2 <*>
    0.0.0.0 0.0.0.0
 End of list
Reply to request 3 (1 ms). Received packet has options
 Total option bytes= 40, padded length=40
 Record route: 172.16.1.2 172.16.0.13 172.16.12.1
    172.16.12.93 172.16.0.14 172.16.0.21 172.16.1.2 <*>
    0.0.0.0 0.0.0.0
 End of list
Reply to request 4 (1 ms). Received packet has options
 Total option bytes= 40, padded length=40
 Record route: 172.16.1.2 172.16.0.13 172.16.12.1
    172.16.12.93 172.16.0.14 172.16.0.21 172.16.1.2 <*>
    0.0.0.0 0.0.0.0
 End of list
Success rate is 100 percent (5/5), round-trip min/avg/max
    = 1/2/4 ms
Router_B#
```

The character echoes have the same meaning as with the user mode of the ping command. In addition, the summary information provided at the end of the extended ping is the same as that of the user mode ping. However, the dialog used in the extended ping is slightly different than that of the user ping. The extended ping mode is accessed by just typing the word **ping**. The default protocol is IP. The next field is the target IP address. The default values are located within the brackets of each dialog question. The repeat count is five ICMP requests. The next field is the datagram size, followed by the timeout.

Additional commands are available by answering **yes** to the extended commands prompt. Extended options include the source IP address (it must be an IP address that is present on the router), type of service, don't fragment bit, data pattern, and header options.

Header options enable the route processor to analyze the packet header. There are five header options:

- Loose

- Strict

- Record

- Timestamp

- Verbose

The record option records the ICMP packet's route to the destination address. It records up to nine hops. You can see the results of using the record packet header option in the previous output. The IP addresses are the addresses of the exiting interface. If you follow the route, you can see the packet leave the router and finally get to the destination on the fourth hop. But wait a minute—there are still more addresses. Yes, they are the addresses of the path back to the router. The path is recorded for both directions, not just to the destination.

There is a final option that allows the router to increment the packet size between 76 bytes and 18,024 bytes. Because it is an Ethernet interface, it does not exceed 1500 bytes.

traceroute Command

The `traceroute` command is used for displaying the packet's path toward its destination. The functionality of the traceroute utility works on error messages that are generated by expired TTL values in the IP packet header. When the TTL value in an IP header reaches zero, the entire packet is discarded. At the same time, the IP host responsible for discarding the packet sends an error message to the source IP address in the header, informing the source that the packet was dropped. The TTL value is decremented by one every time the packet transits a router or IP host.

Traceroute capitalizes on this message exchange. When the traceroute function is used, the TTL in the IP header is set to a value of one. It then sends the packet to the specified destination. Because the next-hop decrements the TTL counter to zero, the packet is discarded and a message is sent back to the source address. The traceroute utility records the IP address from the error message and echoes it to the screen. An `nslookup` is performed on the IP address; if a result is received, the DNS name is displayed in addition to the IP address.

The TTL is then incremented to two and sent out. The packet transverses the first hop, the TTL is decremented to one, and it is forwarded on to the next hop. When the second hop receives the packet, the TTL is decremented to zero and the error message is sent to the source address.

This process is followed until the destination host responds or until the TTL is exceeded. By default, the maximum TTL is 30. This means that if the destination host does not respond, the traceroute utility will attempt 30 times. Multiple requests are sent each attempt, which results in three RTT responses. In addition to the TTL error messages, port unreachable messages provide sufficient information for a path to the destination.

Table 5.13 lists the explanation for the response characters available within the traceroute utility.

TABLE 5.13 traceroute Response Meanings

Character	Explanation
xx msec	The RTT for each packet
*	Timeout
H	Host unreachable
U	Port unreachable
N	Network unreachable
P	Protocol unreachable
A	Administratively denied
Q	Source quench
?	Unknown packet type

Successful functionality of the `traceroute` command depends on the IP configuration on each host along the path to the destination. It is possible that the IP configuration does not send error messages when the TTL expires, TTL is not decremented, or no port unreachable messages are sent. If any of these problems exist, you'll probably get timeout responses.

In addition, it is important to note that not all trace utilities use the same protocol. Cisco Routers and some Linux stations use a UDP packet as the probe packet, whereas many Unix and Windows stations use an ICMP packet to probe. Therefore, if you are blocking UDP in a firewall but allowing ICMP, it is possible that a trace from a Cisco device will be blocked while one from an NT station will get through without difficulty.

User EXEC Mode

The user mode of the `traceroute` command allows only the default options when using the command. Here is a sample output:

```
Router_B>traceroute www.netscape.com
Translating "www.netscape.com"...domain server (172.16.4.2)
   [OK]
Type escape sequence to abort.
Tracing the route to www-ld1.netscape.com (207.200.75.200)
1 172.16.2.1 0 msec 0 msec 0 msec
2 172.16.4.53 [AS 209] 12 msec 8 msec 8 msec
  3 den-core-02.inet.qwest.net (205.171.16.137) [AS 209]
     12 msec 12 msec 8 msec
   4 sfo-core-02.inet.qwest.net (205.171.4.1) [AS 209]
     32 msec 36 msec 36 msec
   5 sjo-core-01.inet.qwest.net (205.171.4.101) [AS 209]
     36 msec 36 msec 40 msec
   6 sjo-core-03.inet.qwest.net (205.171.22.6) [AS 209]
     36 msec 36 msec 36 msec
   7 sjo-edge-05.inet.qwest.net (205.171.22.50) [AS 209]
     36 msec 40 msec 36 msec
   8 205.171.48.154 [AS 209] 36 msec 36 msec 36 msec
   9 h-207-200-69-241.netscape.com (207.200.69.241)
     [AS 6992] 40 msec 40 msec 36 msec
10 www-ld1.netscape.com (207.200.75.200) [AS 6992] 36 msec
     36 msec 36 msec
Router_B>
```

As you can see, the `nslookup` for the first two hops failed. The RTTs for the three probes follow. The times increment as the packet moves closer to the destination address. In addition to the DNS entry, IP address, and RTT, the AS number is also listed.

Here is another sample that includes timeouts and administratively denied probes:

```
Router_B>traceroute www.novell.com
Translating "www.novell.com"...domain server (172.16.4.2)
  [OK]
Type escape sequence to abort.
Tracing the route to www.novell.com (137.65.2.5)
1 172.16.1.13 0 msec 0 msec 0 msec
  2 205.171.48.53 [AS 209] 8 msec 8 msec 12 msec
  3 den-core-01.inet.qwest.net (205.171.16.109) [AS 209]
12 msec 8 msec 12 msec
  4 den-brdr-01.inet.qwest.net (205.171.16.114) [AS 209]
8 msec 12 msec 12 msec
5 s2-0-0.den-bb1.cerf.net (134.24.112.77) [AS 1740] 8
msec    16 msec 12 msec
  6 s10-0-0.slc-bb1.cerf.net (134.24.46.98) [AS 1740]
88 msec 84 msec 84 msec
  7 novell-gw.slc-bb1.cerf.net (134.24.116.54) [AS 1740]
84 msec 84 msec 84 msec
  8 134.24.116.58 [AS 1740] 84 msec 84 msec 84 msec
  9  *   *   !A
Router_B>
```

Here, the probe made it to the destination address, but instead of receiving a TTL expired or port unreachable message, we get an administratively denied message.

Privileged EXEC Mode

The privileged mode has options that are similar to the ping privileged mode. The dialog contains several prompts that change the traceroute settings. The default settings are listed in the brackets. They can be selected by hitting Enter or changed by substituting a new value. We'll now look at the privileged dialog, and then we can explain each of the prompts:

```
Router_B#traceroute
Protocol [ip]:
Target IP address: 137.65.2.11
Source address: 172.16.2.9
```

```
Numeric display [n]:
Timeout in seconds [3]:
Probe count [3]:
Minimum Time to Live [1]:
Maximum Time to Live [30]:
Port Number [33434]:
Loose, Strict, Record, Timestamp, Verbose[none]:
Type escape sequence to abort.
Tracing the route to www.novell.com (137.65.2.11)
1 172.16.0.1 0 msec 0 msec 0 msec
   2 205.171.48.53 [AS 209] 8 msec 8 msec 12 msec
   3 den-core-02.inet.qwest.net (205.171.16.137) [AS 209]
12 msec 8 msec 12 msec
   4 den-brdr-01.inet.qwest.net (205.171.16.142) [AS 209]
8 msec 12 msec 12 msec
   5 s2-0-0.den-bb1.cerf.net (134.24.112.77) [AS 1740]
12 msec 12 msec 12 msec
   6 s10-0-0.slc-bb1.cerf.net (134.24.46.98) [AS 1740]
84 msec 84 msec 88 msec
   7 novell-gw.slc-bb1.cerf.net (134.24.116.54) [AS 1740]
84 msec 84 msec 84 msec
   8 134.24.116.58 [AS 1740] 84 msec 88 msec 84 msec
   9 134.24.116.58 [AS 1740] !A  *   *
Router_B#
```

Target IP address   The IP address of the destination host.

Source address   The IP address present on the router. This is used to select an address that is not directly connected to the next hop.

Numeric display   Disables nslookup on the IP address. Consequently, if this option is chosen, only the IP address is displayed.

Timeout   The threshold for response times for the returning error message.

Probe count   The number of probes sent at each TTL level.

Minimum TTL   The numerical value for the first TTL level.

Maximum TTL   The maximum TTL value; an equivalent of 30 hops is the default, and is the highest value possible.

Port Number   The port number used by UDP that creates a port unreachable error message.

Loose Source Routing   Specifies nodes that must be included in the path to the destination.

Strict Source Routing   Specifies the only nodes allowed in the path to the destination.

Record   Specifies the number of hops for the verbose path to display.

Timestamp   Specifies the number of timestamps to display.

Verbose   Automatically selected if any of the previous options are selected.

Problem Isolation in TCP/IP Networks

Chapter 1 described three methods of attack for isolating network problems. Here is a quick review:

Outside-In   This approach entails starting troubleshooting at the remote system and working back to the local host, one hop at a time.

Divide-by-Half   This approach works by starting the troubleshooting in the middle. From there, divide the isolated area in half again, and continue the troubleshooting until the problem is isolated.

Inside-Out   This approach entails starting with the local host and then working your way to the remote host, one hop at a time.

All of these methods are effective because they are all systematic approaches. When troubleshooting, it is very important to be systematic. By following systematic procedures while troubleshooting, you can better manage the situation. If the correct process is followed, you will have documentation that records all attempts made to fix the problem. This can stop you from chasing your tail.

The outside-in method will be used in this section. Certain steps should be followed when trying to isolate the problem. The easiest step is to use built-in tools such as `ping` and `traceroute`. These commands are designed specifically to test reachability and path connectivity. Many problems can be isolated by analyzing the output of these two commands.

As shown in Figure 5.2, a good first step for isolating a problem between Host A and Host C would be to ping Host C. This test indicates whether Host C is reachable. If the ping fails, the next step would be to traceroute to Host C. The results of the traceroute indicate where the problem is most likely occurring.

FIGURE 5.2   TCP/IP network failure isolation

We'll use a simple example: Host A cannot ping Host C. The traceroute stops at Router C, indicating that the problem can be said to be on or behind Router C. With the problem thus isolated, troubleshooting can be concentrated in that area.

Although further isolation can be done via the `show` commands previously mentioned, no matter where the problem lies, the next step is the same—fix it.

Many times, the problem you have isolated is on a system to which you do not have access. A perfect example is a WAN link. You were notified that a remote site is unreachable. Upon further investigation, you isolate the problem to the local carrier. You do not have access to run any diagnostics on their equipment, so your hands are tied. The only thing you can do in this case is to notify the carrier that a problem exists in their network.

Figure 5.3 depicts a flowchart with simple TCP/IP fault isolation steps. It is important to remember that you need to deal with host configurations, as well as router configurations, when troubleshooting TCP/IP failures.

FIGURE 5.3 TCP/IP isolation flowchart

Problem Isolation for Windows 95/98/NT

Different traffic types may exist when sending Windows 95/98/NT client/server information through a Cisco router or switch. Router configurations change, depending on what traffic types need to be supported. Some examples of the traffic types are NetBEUI, transparent or source route bridging (SRB), Novell type 20 NetBIOS, Microsoft TCP/IP stack, and UDP NetBIOS broadcasts.

Proper troubleshooting requires diagnostic information from the host, router, and server. The Cisco troubleshooting tools can be used to gather information concerning the router. Windows provides diagnostic tools to enable you to obtain the information necessary to isolate and diagnose Windows 95/98/NT problems. Table 5.14 contains some of the diagnostic tools available in Windows 95/98/NT.

TABLE 5.14 Windows 95/98/NT TCP/IP Diagnostic Tools

Tool	Description
ipconfig	IP information for all interfaces, including IP address, subnet mask, DNS server, DHCP information, and some NetBIOS (available only in Windows 98/NT)

TABLE 5.14   Windows 95/98/NT TCP/IP Diagnostic Tools *(continued)*

Tool	Description
winipcfg	IP information for Windows 95 interfaces
event viewer	System log containing TCP/IP or DHCP events, among others (available only in Windows NT)
ping	TCP/IP ICMP utility
tracert	ICMP utility, same as traceroute
telnet	Allows for IP testing
nbtstat	NetBIOS statistics

Here is a sample output of the ipconfig /all command issued in an MS-DOS window:

```
C:\WINDOWS>ipconfig /all

Windows 98 IP Configuration

        Host Name . . . . . . . . . : loco.somewhere.com
        DNS Servers . . . . . . . . : 172.16.1.2
        Node Type . . . . . . . . . : Broadcast
        NetBIOS Scope ID. . . . . . :
        IP Routing Enabled. . . . . : No
        WINS Proxy Enabled. . . . . : No
        NetBIOS Resolution Uses DNS : Yes

0 Ethernet adapter :

        Description . . . . . . . . : PPP Adapter.
        Physical Address. . . . . . : 45-44-35-45-00-00
        DHCP Enabled. . . . . . . . : Yes
        IP Address. . . . . . . . . : 172.16.50.101
```

```
        Subnet Mask . . . . . . . . : 255.255.255.0
        Default Gateway . . . . . . : 172.16.50.101
        DHCP Server . . . . . . . . : 255.255.255.255
        Primary WINS Server . . . . :
        Secondary WINS Server . . . :
        Lease Obtained. . . . . . . : 01 01 80 12:00:00 AM
        Lease Expires . . . . . . . : 01 01 80 12:00:00 AM

1 Ethernet adapter :


        Description . . . . . . . . : ELPC3R Ethernet
    Adapter
        Physical Address. . . . . . : 00-A0-24-A5-06-57
        DHCP Enabled. . . . . . . . : No
        IP Address. . . . . . . . . : 172.16.40.130
        Subnet Mask . . . . . . . . : 255.255.255.0
        Default Gateway . . . . . . : 172.16.40.1
        Primary WINS Server . . . . :
        Secondary WINS Server . . . :
        Lease Obtained. . . . . . . :
        Lease Expires . . . . . . . :

C:\WINDOWS>
```

You can review similar information on Windows 95/NT clients and servers. Verify that the host is configured properly, and then you can eliminate it as a suspect.

Depending on the traffic type transiting the router, you can check several different configuration settings. If NetBEUI traffic is running across the router, make sure that the router is properly configured for transparent or source-route bridging. If Novell type 20 NetBIOS is being used, make sure that the router has the command ipx type-20-propagation. If clients reside on a network different from the server's network, IP helper addresses and protocol forwarding must be enabled on the router.

Name Resolution

Name to IP resolution on 95/98/NT systems can be performed in multiple ways. The resolution methods that are available are as follows:

- Internal cache of recently used entries
- Broadcast message to the local network
- Local LMHOSTS file
- Local HOSTS file
- WINS server
- DNS server

The internal cache and broadcast message are the first items used to try to resolve a name into an IP address. Following this, the LMHOSTS and HOSTS files are used. Both files are usually located in the %SystemRoot% \System32\Drivers\Etc directory of each Windows NT host. These files are text-based files that can be edited to provided static name-to-IP-address translation.

A Windows Internet Name Service (WINS) server is Microsoft's version of a NetBIOS name server. This server dynamically updates the names of other Windows clients that are on the network. The server can then be queried in much the same manner as a DNS server for name-to-IP-address resolution. The final item used by a 95/98/NT station is a DNS server. As is the case with any station using DNS, the 95/98/NT station sends a query to the DNS server and the server responds with the IP address or a notification saying it does not know the address.

Browsing

In a 95/98/NT environment, connecting to network resources is most often done by using the Network Neighborhood. This function graphically displays the other 95/98/NT stations that are on the network, with the information broken down into workgroups and/or domains. In this manner, a user can simply double-click on a workgroup or domain to see the stations that are currently in that area and connect to any shared resources on these stations.

The Network Neighborhood feature is enabled by a Microsoft feature called *browsing*. Depending on network size and the number of 95/98/NT stations involved, the browsing configuration can become very complex. Though designed to be self-updating and not to require administrative support, there can be problems with browsing. The two main problems that can arise are incomplete or inaccurate resolution of the names and shares into the associated IP addresses. This could be due to problems in configuration, or a problem in the functioning of any of the above-mentioned name-resolution methods.

Another relatively common problem that can arise is a rogue master browser. One of the conditions needed for browsing to work correctly is, for every workgroup or domain on a segment, one of the machines assuming the role of a master browser. It is the master browser's responsibility to collect browser information and to respond to browser queries for that subnet. And, if a domain master browser is configured, the master browser for a subnet forwards its browse list to the domain master browser as well. If there are two machines on a subnet that believe they are the master browser for the subnet, all machines on the subnet can be affected. The easiest way to find a rogue master browser is to use the Microsoft Resource Kit utility BROWSTAT. BROWSTAT can be run on any NT machine in the affected subnet.

NT Workstation as a Router

By enabling Microsoft's Multi-Protocol Router (MPR), it is possible to turn on a RIP process for an NT host. If this NT station has two or more NICs installed, it will route between them. In addition, it can be configured to send and receive RIP broadcasts, for both IP and IPX. If only one NIC is installed, the NT device will only listen to any broadcast on the subnet and update its routing table. It will not send any RIP broadcasts until a second NIC is added.

LAN Connectivity Problems

Troubleshooting LAN connectivity was covered in part through the discussion of troubleshooting Ethernet and Token Ring problems. Those are LAN technologies. This section deals with host connectivity in relation to Cisco routers.

Obtaining an IP Address

Hosts can obtain an IP address in one of two ways: statically or dynamically. Once an IP address is configured on a host, it is assigned to that host until the administrator removes it. If the address, mask, and gateway were configured correctly, and it is not a duplicate IP address, the host will not have any problems connecting to the LAN that could be attributed to its IP address and configuration.

There are two protocols used to allow hosts to obtain their IP address dynamically: *Bootstrap Protocol (BootP)* and *Dynamic Host Configuration Protocol (DHCP)*.

DHCP

DHCP is a superset of the Bootstrap Protocol (BootP). This means that it uses the same protocol structure as BootP, but it has enhancements added. Both of these protocols use servers that dynamically configure clients when requested. The two major enhancements are address pools and lease times.

The process for each differs somewhat. DHCP clients broadcast a Discover message that contains the MAC address, hostname, and other options. The broadcast is sent from UDP port 67 to UDP port 68. Servers respond by sending from UDP port 68 destined to UDP port 67. When the server sends the response, it is called an Offer. The Offer includes the information sent in the client's Discover request, IP configuration information, and lease information. If the client chooses to accept the offer, it sends a Request that includes the Offer information as well as the original Discover information. If the DHCP server is still able to grant the Offer configuration, it will send an acknowledgment to the client. If it cannot grant the Offer, it sends a Decline message to the client. Figure 5.4 gives a clearer picture of these transactions.

Lease information is one of the enhancements of DHCP. It allows an IP address to be assigned for a preconfigured amount of time. When the lease expires, the IP address is added back to the available address pool. Each host tries to renew the lease when the time is half-expired.

FIGURE 5.4 DHCP client/server sequence

BootP

The BootP process is much simpler. When a host tries to obtain an IP address, it sends a bootrequest, which contains the client's MAC address. When the BootP server receives the request, it checks its database for the MAC address. If it finds an entry, then a bootreply, which contains the IP address and other configuration settings, is sent. If the BootP server does not find the client's MAC address in its database, it does not respond.

Helper Addresses

As was mentioned above, DHCP and BOOTP messages are broadcast messages. Therefore, by default the router will not forward them. In small environments, the solution to this is the have a DHCP or BOOTP server on each segment. However, this solution does not scale well as the size of a network grows. In these situations, you can use the `ip helper-address <address>` command on the router. The IP address referenced in the command is the address of the centralized DHCP or BOOTP server.

By adding this command to each interface on which you have DHCP or BOOTP clients, all DHCP and BOOTP broadcasts will be forwarded via unicast to the DHCP or BOOTP server. This server then responds to the requesting station via the router in the form of a unicast packet. In addition, if there are redundant DHCP or BOOTP servers, the command could be put on the interface multiple times, once for each server. In this manner, if one of the servers were to go down, the others would still be available to handle requests.

One downside to this command is that after it is enabled, by default it not only forwards DHCP/BOOTP UDP broadcasts, it also forwards UDP broadcasts destined for the following ports:

- Time service (port 37)

- IEN-116 Name Service (port 42)

- TACACS service (port 49)

- Domain Naming System (port 53)

- Trivial File Transfer Protocol (TFTP) (port 69)

- NetBIOS Name Server (port 137)
- NetBIOS Datagram Server (port 138)

In order to only forward DHCP/BOOTP broadcasts you can use the global configuration command no ip forward-protocol udp *<port>* for each of the services in the above list.

DHCP Services on a Router

Beginning with IOS 12.0(1) T, you can also configure a router as a DHCP server. In contrast to the helper address, which forwards requests to an external DHCP server, this allows the router to service DHCP requests locally. This option allows the router to become a full-featured DHCP server and provide DHCP addresses, from separate IP address pools to any device on a connected interface.

Troubleshooting DHCP and BootP

Because these protocols are dynamic, there may be times when they fail or when an end user is unable to connect to the network. If you have a protocol analyzer, you could capture the DHCP and BootP sequences to make sure that the clients and servers are talking.

You can also use the show commands available to aid in troubleshooting DHCP on Cisco routers.

```
Router_C#show dhcp server
DHCP Proxy Client Status:
    DHCP server: ANY (255.255.255.255)
      Leases:   0
      Offers:   0       Requests: 0      Acks: 0       Naks: 0
      Declines: 0       Releases: 0      Bad:  0
Router_C#
```

If the router is configured to use DHCP, you can also get information regarding the lease by issuing the show dhcp lease command.

ARP

Address Resolution Protocol maps Layer 2 MAC addresses to Layer 3 IP addresses. An ARP table is built on the router through the exchange of ARP requests and replies. Here is a sample ARP table:

```
Router_C>show arp
Protocol  Address        Age (min)  Hardware Addr   Type   Interface
Internet  172.16.60.1    -          0010.7bd9.2881  ARPA   Ethernet0/1
Internet  172.16.50.2    -          0010.7bd9.2880  ARPA   Ethernet0/0
Internet  172.16.50.1    108        0000.0c09.99cc  ARPA   Ethernet0/0
Router_C>
```

Notice the Age field in the ARP table. ARP entries are stored or cached for future use. This allows a router to look up the MAC address, instead of having to send a broadcast to learn it again. However, the ARP entry does not stay in the table indefinitely.

Several problems could occur if a MAC address were permanently mapped to an IP address. You learned that DHCP can assign a given IP address to any requesting host, if it is available. In this scenario, the IP address could be assigned to different MAC addresses. If this were to happen, any existing entry in an ARP table would be invalidated. If a NIC is replaced on a host, the MAC address is changed as well. If the ARP cache was not cleared and updated, the IP address would still be mapped to the old MAC address. You get the picture. These mappings are not permanent, so the cache entries cannot be permanent either.

Sometimes problems occur within a network because of ARP problems. The best way to troubleshoot these issues is by looking at the ARP table on the router with the show arp command and (if necessary) using the debug arp tool. Problems may be fixed by simply clearing the ARP cache and allowing the router to rebuild the table.

Proxy ARP

By default, Cisco router interfaces have *proxy ARP* enabled. Proxy ARP, defined in RFC 1027, aids in routing packets from workstations that have no default gateway set or that have misconfigured subnet information. Specifically, a Cisco router will reply to an ARP request with its own MAC address if the following conditions are met:

- Proxy ARP is enabled on the interface on which the ARP was seen.

- The ARP request is for an address not on the local subnet.

- The router has a route for that subnet in its routing table.

- All routes in the routing table for the requested address are out an interface other than the interface on which the ARP was seen.

The host that originated the ARP request will then send packets destined for this address to the router, which will then forward them on to their destination. If you want to disable proxy ARP on an interface, you can use the no ip proxy-arp command.

Sample TCP Connection

In order to properly troubleshoot a connection issue, it is important to clearly understand how this connection is set up from the start. As was discussed in Chapter 2, TCP is a connection-oriented protocol. As such, before data can be exchanged, a connection needs to be established. This connection is established by the TCP three-way handshake. To better explain exactly how this works, we'll give you an example. Figure 5.5 has a graphical representation of this example.

Assume that two computers on the same segment, Computer A and B, have just been powered on. A user on Computer A wants to initiate a telnet session to Computer B. Computer A has an IP address of 192.168.1.100 and B has an address of 192.168.1.101. To keep things simple for this example, assume that the user is telnetting to computer B by its IP address, not the name.

When the user hits Enter on her telnet request, the first thing that Computer A does is look at its ARP cache and see if it has a MAC address associated with the IP address of B, 192.168.1.101. Since this computer was just powered on, it does not. Computer A now checks to verify that Computer B is on the subnet. Since it is, Computer A sends out an ARP request for the MAC address of 192.168.1.101. If Computer B were on a different subnet, Computer A would have sent out an ARP request for the default gateway instead.

As ARP requests are Layer 2 broadcasts, all computers connected to the subnet, including Computer B, receive this ARP request. Computer B sees that the ARP is for its IP address and responds directly to Computer A with its MAC address. Computer B also gleaned Computer A's IP address and MAC information from the ARP request and added this information to its own ARP cache.

Now that Computer A has the IP and MAC information, the TCP three-way handshake can begin. The start of this process is Computer A sending a SYN (synchronize) packet to Computer B on TCP port 23, letting it know that it wants to set up a connection. Computer B then responds with a SYN ACK (synchronize and acknowledgment) packet. Computer A responds to the SYN ACK message from B with an ACK (acknowledgment) packet.

FIGURE 5.5   Sample Connection Scenario

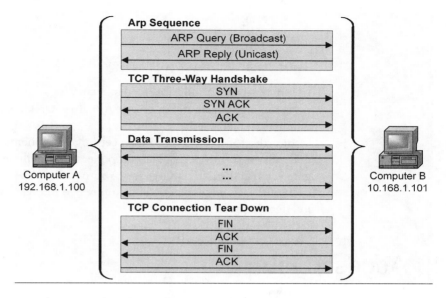

At this point the TCP session is set up and the telnet session data can flow normally between A and B. Once the user is done with the telnet session, the connection needs to be torn down. In order to do this, Computer A sends a FIN (Finished or Finalize) packet to Computer B. B then responds with an ACK packet. At this point communication from A to B has been torn down; however, B also needs to indicate that it has finished with the connection as well. Computer B sends a FIN packet to Computer A to do this. Computer A responds with an ACK packet and the connection is terminated.

WAN Access Problems

The function of a *wide area network (WAN)* is to connect multiple local area networks (LANs). There are several technologies and topologies for connecting LANs. Here are a few examples:

- Serial lines
- HSSI (High-Speed Serial Interface)
- ATM

- ISDN

- Frame Relay

- DDR

- POSIP (Packet over Sonet IP)

No matter what physical media, technology, or topology is used, one thing remains constant: For information to get from one LAN to another, the data has to be routed.

In order for data to be routed, certain components must be configured and must work properly. The components that will be discussed are default gateways, and static and dynamic routing. Troubleshooting methods for each of these components will be addressed in their corresponding sections in later chapters.

IP Access Lists

Troubleshooting access lists is a very simple task if you understand how they are written and if you are familiar with the different protocols that can be managed by using extended access lists.

Standard Access Lists

A *standard access list* is a sequential list of permit or deny statements that are based on the source IP address of a packet. When a packet reaches a router, the packet has to follow a different procedure, based on whether it's trying to enter or leave an interface. If there is an access list on the interface, the packet must go through every line in it until the packet matches the specified criteria. If the packet goes through the entire list without a match, it is dropped. For the packet to be forwarded, there has to be a permit statement at the end of the list allowing that, or else the packet will simply be dropped.

In Cisco IOS, there's an implied deny statement at the end of the access list, so if the purpose of your access list is to deny a few criteria but forward everything else, you must include a permit statement as the final line of the access list. However, you do not have to end the access list with a deny statement if the list's purpose is to permit only certain criteria and drop the rest—this is automatically understood.

Figure 5.6 shows a flowchart that describes the steps taken when a packet enters or leaves an interface.

FIGURE 5.6   Flowchart process of a standard access list

Stepping through the flowchart, you can see that the packet arrives at the specific interface through which it must enter or leave. The router's first step is to check whether there is an access list applied to the interface. If so, it passes through each line of the access list until the packet's source address matches one of the source addresses listed. If a packet's information matches multiple lines in the access list, the first match will be the one used, whether that line is a permit or a deny. If the packet fails to match any of the source addresses, it is denied. However, if the packet's source address does find a match in the list, the packet is then subjected to any condition applied on that line of the access list. The two conditional possibilities are to deny the packet or permit it. When a packet is denied, it is dropped; when it is permitted, it is forwarded to the next hop.

Exiting packets are first routed to the exiting interface and then verified by the access list, which determines whether the packet will be dropped or forwarded through the interface. Incoming packets arrive from the forwarding machine or router, and are then checked against the access list. If the packet is permitted by the list, the packet is accepted through the interface and forwarded to the exit interface.

This is important information to understand when troubleshooting any access list. It does depend on whether the packet is incoming or outgoing, so you can tell which interfaces to look at and analyze access lists for.

Troubleshooting standard access lists is very simple because they are based on only one criterion, the source IP address. The basic method of troubleshooting an access list is to read it line by line and analyze it to determine whether any lines are out of order or typed incorrectly.

If, after analyzing the access list, you cannot see any problems but the problem is still occurring, you can temporarily remove the access list from the interface to see what effect this has on the problem. If the problem disappears after the access list is removed, something is wrong with the access list and it needs to be fixed. If the problem does not go away with the removal of the access list from the interface, you can eliminate it as a possible cause.

The commands used to view IP access lists are simply **show running-config**, **show startup-config**, or **show ip access-list <access-list number>**. These commands provide the information regarding each line of the access list. In addition to these commands, you can issue the **show ip interface** command, which provides you with information regarding which access lists are applied to the interface. Here is a sample output from the **show ip interface** command:

```
Router_B>show ip interface
Ethernet0 is up, line protocol is up
  Internet address is 172.16.50.1/24
  Broadcast address is 255.255.255.255
  Address determined by non-volatile memory
  MTU is 1500 bytes
  Helper address is not set
  Directed broadcast forwarding is disabled
  Multicast reserved groups joined: 224.0.0.10
  Outgoing access list is not set
  Inbound  access list is not set
  Proxy ARP is enabled
  Security level is default
  Split horizon is enabled
  ICMP redirects are always sent
  ICMP unreachables are always sent
  ICMP mask replies are never sent
  IP fast switching is enabled
  IP fast switching on the same interface is disabled
  IP multicast fast switching is disabled
  Router Discovery is disabled
  IP output packet accounting is disabled
  IP access violation accounting is disabled
  TCP/IP header compression is disabled
```

```
Probe proxy name replies are disabled
Gateway Discovery is disabled
Policy routing is disabled
```

As you can see from this output, interface Ethernet0 does not have any access lists applied to it.

Extended Access Lists

Extended access lists offer filtering on port numbers, session-layer protocols, and destination addresses, in addition to filtering by source address. Although these extended filtering features make this kind of access list much more powerful, they can also make the list more difficult to troubleshoot because of the potential complexity.

A packet must follow the same basic process when arriving at an interface with an extended access list applied to it as it does when confronting an interface with an applied standard list. Figure 5.7 illustrates the procedure that a packet follows when being compared against an extended list—the only difference is the much greater scope of criteria that are specifiable.

FIGURE 5.7 Packet processing through an extended access list

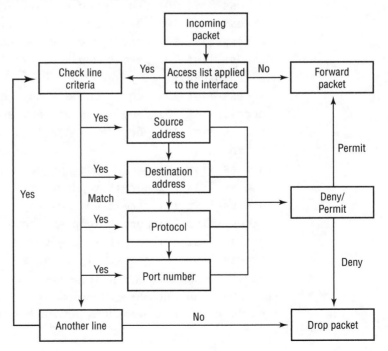

In addition to correctly analyzing the lines of the access list, you must know which way the list is applied to the interface. By conceptualizing the packet flow through an interface and the subsequent access list, you will be successful in troubleshooting access list–related problems. Here is a sample extended access list:

```
access-list 101 deny    tcp any any eq chargen
access-list 101 deny    tcp any any eq daytime
access-list 101 deny    tcp any any eq discard
access-list 101 deny    tcp any any eq echo
access-list 101 deny    tcp any any eq finger
access-list 101 deny    tcp any any eq kshell
access-list 101 deny    tcp any any eq klogin
access-list 101 deny    tcp any any eq 37
access-list 101 deny    tcp any any eq uucp
access-list 101 deny    udp any any eq biff
access-list 101 deny    udp any any eq bootpc
access-list 101 deny    udp any any eq bootps
access-list 101 deny    udp any any eq discard
access-list 101 deny    udp any any eq netbios-dgm
access-list 101 deny    udp any any eq netbios-ns
access-list 101 permit udp host 172.16.10.2 any eq snmp
access-list 101 deny    udp any any eq snmp
access-list 101 permit udp host 172.16.10.2 any eq
   snmptrap
access-list 101 deny    udp any any eq snmptrap
access-list 101 deny    udp any any eq who
access-list 101 permit udp 172.16.50.0 0.0.0.255 any eq
   xdmcp
access-list 101 deny    udp any any eq xdmcp
access-list 101 permit tcp any any
access-list 101 permit udp any any
access-list 101 permit icmp any any
access-list 101 permit igmp any any
access-list 101 permit eigrp any any
```

As you can see, there are many line options that need to be understood when troubleshooting extended access lists. Not only do you have to understand the significance of the line, but you have to be familiar with the protocol you are troubleshooting. If necessary, debug options can be used in conjunction with access lists to isolate and diagnose network failures.

Named Access Lists

Beginning with IOS 11.2, in addition to the numbered standard and extended access lists, you can also use named access lists. Named access lists can be either standard or extended. Though the concepts of named and numbered access lists are the same, there are a couple major differences between the two. The first is that a named access list has a logical name, not an arbitrary number like their numbered counterpart. In addition, if you want to remove a single line from a named access list you can. To accomplish this same function with a numbered access list, you most remove and reapply the entire list. Finally, a named access list does not have the access list name at the beginning of each line, thus making it slightly easier to read. Instead, the name is shown at the top of the access list, and then the individual permit/deny statements follow. For example, if the access list from the "Extended Access List" section were converted to a named list, it would look like the following:

```
ip access-list extended ENGINEERING-DEPT-IN
  deny    tcp any any eq chargen
  deny    tcp any any eq daytime
  deny    tcp any any eq discard
  deny    tcp any any eq echo
  deny    tcp any any eq finger
  deny    tcp any any eq kshell
  deny    tcp any any eq klogin
  deny    tcp any any eq 37
  deny    tcp any any eq uucp
  deny    udp any any eq biff
  deny    udp any any eq bootpc
  deny    udp any any eq bootps
  deny    udp any any eq discard
  deny    udp any any eq netbios-dgm
  deny    udp any any eq netbios-ns
  permit udp host 172.16.10.2 any eq snmp
  deny    udp any any eq snmp
  permit udp host 172.16.10.2 any eq snmptrap
  deny    udp any any eq snmptrap
```

```
deny    udp any any eq who
permit  udp 172.16.50.0 0.0.0.255 any eq xdmcp
deny    udp any any eq xdmcp
permit  tcp any any
permit  udp any any
permit  icmp any any
permit  igmp any any
permit  eigrp any any
```

Note the keyword extended in the first line of the access list. This denotes the list as an extended access list. If it were a standard access list, this keyword would have been standard.

Though there are some differences between named and numbered access lists, the overall functionality remains the same. If a named list is a standard access list, the flowchart pictured in Figure 5.6 applies to the logical flow of data. If it is an extended access list, refer to Figure 5.7. As such, the restriction on standard access lists only filtering on source address still applies to a named list.

Summary

When used properly, the show and debug commands can be powerful tools in troubleshooting a problem or just finding out information about the performance of a router. However, these commands, especially the debug commands, should be used with care, as they can cause an increase in the load on the router. Therefore, when debugging, it is advisable to use access lists to limit the information that is being debugged.

In addition to the show and debug commands, logging is another method to determine whether there is a problem on the router. Logging information can be sent to the console, the terminal monitor, an internal buffer on the router, and/or an external syslog server. In addition to the different locations that can be used to view logging information, the logging messages can also be viewed based on the severity of the problem.

Other troubleshooting commands, such as core dump, ping, and traceroute, can be used to further define an issue. The exception dump command causes the router to write to a file the information that is in the memory at the time of a crash. This file can later be used by TAC to help isolate the cause of the problem. The ping and traceroute commands can be used to verify the reachability of hosts as well as the path taken to get to the hosts.

In order to effectively troubleshoot network problems, an engineer needs to understand how the protocols in the network work. This includes the ARP protocol, the TCP connection and teardown sequence, as well as how DHCP and BootP function.

In addition to the network protocols, an engineer also needs to understand the basic network functions performed by the computers in the network. As the major platform type in use today is Windows based, it is important that the engineer has an understanding of how Windows performs networking functions. Some of these functions include determining the IP address of a machine, name resolution, and browsing.

IP access lists come in multiple varieties—named, numbered, standard, and extended—and all use the same basic structure and have the same basic function. Primarily used for protecting networks from unwanted traffic, the access list is read from the top down. If at any point the packet matches a line in the list, whether this line is a permit or a deny, the list is exited and the associated function is performed on the packet. In addition to looking at packet flow, access lists are also used for many other tasks, such as restricting routing updates, limiting access to telnet sessions to the router, and limiting SNMP access to the router.

Exam Essentials

Know the show and debug commands that are available and how to interpret the output.   There are several show and debug commands used in the CCNP Support exam. In addition to knowing the commands, you should also know how to limit the output of the debug command using access lists.

Know and understand the logging levels on a router.   The logging levels are: debugging, informational, notifications, warnings, errors, critical, alerts, and emergencies. You should be able to determine the logging levels for each logging destination on a router.

Know how to use the ping and traceroute commands.   The ping command is used to test for reachability and connectivity throughout a network and the traceroute command is used for displaying the packet's path toward its destination. Knowing how to use the commands includes knowing the extended ping and traceroute options available under privileged mode.

Understand the basics of 95/98/NT networking. You should have a general understanding of Windows 95/98/NT networking. This includes but is not limited to browsing, routing, and use of the `ipconfig` command.

Understand how DHCP and BOOTP function. DHCP and BOOTP are broadcast messages; DHCP is a superset of BOOTP. You should know the specific functions of each and understand the similarities and differences between the two. Also, understand how a helper address on a router works.

Understand what an ARP broadcast is and how it is used in networking. ARP stands for Address Resolution Protocol. ARP provides a table of information that the router can look up, instead of having to broadcast for information. Be sure you also understand the proxy ARP protocol.

Understand the TCP three-way handshake. TCP uses the three-way handshake—SYN, SYN ACK, ACK—to establish a connection. To tear down a connection, the packet sequence is FIN, ACK, FIN ACK.

Know the different types of access lists and their functions. The two types of IP access lists are standard and extended. Both types can be used as either named or numbered lists.

Commands Used in This Chapter

The following list contains a summary of all the commands used in this chapter.

Commands	Descriptions
`access-list`	Can be used to limit debug output, traffic flow, or other access on a router.
`clear logging`	Clears the logging buffer.
`debug`	Used to show more-detailed information about the router performance.
`exception dump`	Configures the router to perform a core dump via RCP, TFTP, or FTP if and when the router crashes.

Commands	Descriptions
`logging buffered`	Sets buffer size, as well as the logging level for the buffer. The no form of the command disables the logging buffer.
`logging console`	Sets the logging level for the console. The no form of the command disables logging to the console.
`logging monitor`	Sets the logging level for the monitor. The no form of the command disables logging to the monitor.
`logging trap`	Sets the logging level for the syslog server. The no form of the command disables logging to the syslog server.
`ping`	Initiates an ICMP echo request. There are two levels, User and Privileged. The IP protocol is used.
`show access-lists`	Displays the specified access list from the configuration.
`show arp`	Displays the contents of the ARP table as well as status.
`show interface`	Displays interface-specific settings and statistics.
`show logging`	Displays logs for the router, including traps and system errors. Can also provide logs when logging access lists.
`show running-config`	Displays the current configuration that is loaded into memory.
`show stacks`	Displays the router's stack information.
`show startup-config`	Displays the configuration version that is saved in NVRAM.

Commands	Descriptions
show tech-support	A comprehensive command that includes show running-config, show version, show stacks, show processes cpu, and show processes memory, along with many others.
show version	Displays the version of IOS, the reason for last reload, and the router's hardware configuration.
terminal monitor	Enables the router to echo console message to the active TTY port. This facilitates the debug tool.
terminal no monitor	Disables the echo.
traceroute	A hop-by-hop ICMP traceroute. This command has two levels, User and Privileged.
un all	Turns off all possible debugging.
write core	Initiates a core dump to the specified host.
show queueing	Displays queuing information for the router.

Key Terms

Before you take the exam, be certain you are familiar with the following terms:

Bootstrap Protocol (BootP)

browsing

debug

Dynamic Host Configuration Protocol (DHCP)

extended access lists

extended ping

proxy ARP

standard access list

wide area network (WAN)

Review Questions

1. What information is provided by the `show logging` command? (Choose all that apply.)

    A. Access list logs

    B. Debug messages

    C. Syslog messages

    D. Console messages

    E. None of the above

2. What information is provided by issuing the `show version` command? (Choose all that apply.)

    A. Hardware and software version

    B. Reason for last upgrade

    C. Reason for last reload

    D. Up time

    E. Configuration version

3. What information is provided by issuing the `show startup-config` command?

    A. The current configuration

    B. The configuration held in FLASH

    C. The configuration held in NVRAM

    D. The configuration held in RAM

4. What information is provided by issuing the `show running-config` command?

    A. The current configuration

    B. The configuration held in FLASH

    C. The configuration held in NVRAM

    D. The configuration held in RAM

5. Which Cisco IOS `show` command provides comprehensive information that is sent to the Cisco TAC?

   A. show all

   B. show processes

   C. show tech-support

   D. show stacks

6. What is the default Ethernet IP encapsulation on a Cisco router?

   A. SNAP

   B. ARPA

   C. Ethernet II

   D. Novell-Ether

7. What information is provided by the `show arp` command? (Choose all that apply.)

   A. Layer 3 address

   B. Layer 2 address

   C. Encapsulation

   D. Interface MAC address

   E. TTL timer

8. What configuration changes should be added to a router to provide accurate debug information? (Choose all that apply.)

   A. debug all

   B. service timestamps debug datetime msec localtime

   C. service timestamps log datetime msec localtime

   D. service udp-small-servers

   E. service tcp-small-servers

9. What command do you issue to view messages being sent to the console?

   A. `monitor terminal`

   B. `terminal monitor`

   C. `show console`

   D. `echo terminal`

10. What command turns off all debugging?

    A. `no debug all`

    B. `no debug`

    C. `un all`

    D. `undebug all`

    E. All of the above

11. In general, what is the maximum percentage utilization a router's CPU should be at to run `debug` commands?

    A. 25%

    B. 50%

    C. 66%

    D. 75%

12. What is the purpose of the `ping` command?

    A. Step-by-step connectivity

    B. Reachability and connectivity

    C. Test the ICMP protocol

    D. Test routing protocols

13. What is the purpose of the `traceroute` command?

    A. Step-by-step path connectivity

    B. Reachability and connectivity

    C. Test the ICMP protocol

    D. Test routing protocols

14. What are the default logging settings and levels for a Cisco router? (Choose all that apply.)

    A. Buffer, console, and trap are enabled and set to Debugging.

    B. Trap is enabled and set to Informational.

    C. Monitor is enabled and set to Informational.

    D. Buffer, console, and monitor are enabled and set to Debugging.

    E. Trap is disabled and set to Informational.

    F. Monitor is disabled and set to Informational.

15. How can you limit the amount of debug information that is displayed?

    A. Use the keyword brief in the **debug** command.

    B. Enable Netflow Switching.

    C. Use an access list with the **debug** command.

    D. Run the **debug** command from a telnet session.

16. What logging feature causes the most load on the router?

    A. Buffer

    B. Console

    C. Monitor

    D. Trap

17. You notice intermittent packet loss in your network and it seems to have some correlation to packet size. What option(s) in extended ping can help you diagnose this problem further? (Choose all that apply.)

    A. Datagram size

    B. Timeout

    C. Type of service

    D. DF bit

    E. Validate reply data

    F. Data pattern

    G. Sweep range of sizes

18. A host wants to set up a new TCP connection. What type of packet is sent?

  A. SYN

  B. ACK

  C. SYN ACK

  D. ARP broadcast

19. Which debug command can be used to provide important IP information, yet is not part of the IP debug commands?

  A. debug ospf

  B. debug eigrp

  C. debug arp

  D. debug ip arp

20. What does the output of the command ipconfig /all display?

  A. IP information for all interfaces, including IP address, subnet mask, DNS server, DHCP information, and some NetBIOS

  B. All Layer 3 information

  C. IP address and subnet mask only

  D. None of the above

Answers to Review Questions

1. A, B, C, D.   All of these messages are displayed by the command.

2. A, C, D.   The command will not provide you with information regarding the reason for the last upgrade nor the version of configuration that resides on the router.

3. C.   The start-up configuration is held in the NVRAM memory.

4. A.   The running configuration is the configuration currently being run by the router.

5. C.   show tech-support is the command that contains the information requested by TAC.

6. B.   ARPA is the default encapsulation used by Cisco. The other three are valid encapsulation types, but are not turned on by default.

7. A, B, C, D.   The TTL timer is not shown in the show arp command.

8. B, C.   Timestamps are important to debugging so correlations can be made when events occur. Debug all is a command that implements debugging—it has nothing to do with how accurate the information is. D and E are commands that enable certain UDP and TCP services to the router. They have nothing to do with debug.

9. B.   terminal monitor is the correct command. Term mon can be used as a shorthand version of B.

10. A, C, D.   un all is a shortcut to turn off debug. The full command is undebug all. In addition, you can use no debug all to accomplish the same thing. The no debug command is incomplete.

11. B.   Though some debug commands require less overhead than others, to be on the safe side if a router is over 50% utilized, try to get the information without using debug.

12. B.   The ping packets are used to test for connectivity to a remote IP address.

13. A.   Traceroute is used to map the hop-path connectivity.

14. B, D.   By default, buffer, console, monitor, and trap logging are enabled. The buffer, console, and monitor logs are set to a level of debugging and the trap log is set to Informational. It is true that you must use the terminal monitor command to see the log information for the monitor, but it is on. Likewise, before the trap log can be used, a syslog server must be defined.

15. C.   You can limit the information that the debug command applies to by applying an access list to the command.

16. B.   The console logging takes the most overhead, followed by monitor, trap, and buffer.

17. A, D, G.   Since you believe it is a problem related to packet size, setting the datagram size and sweeping a range of sizes will be of value. In addition, setting the DF (Don't Fragment) bit will also assist in this endeavor.

18. A.   It is true that if a station does not have an ARP entry for the destination station, it must send an ARP. However, since the question specifically asked about a TCP connection, A is the correct answer.

19. C.   The debug arp command provides important IP information even though it is not part of the IP debug set.

20. A.   The command is issued on a Windows 98/NT host and provides the information specified in A.

Chapter 6

TCP/IP Routing Protocol Troubleshooting

TOPICS COVERED IN THIS CHAPTER INCLUDE:

- ✓ Identify and use Cisco IOS software commands and debug utilities to filter, capture, and display protocol traffic flows.

- ✓ Use proven problem isolation techniques to list the symptoms of common TCP/IP problems.

- ✓ Apply diagnostic tools to solve network problems that include systems running TCP/IP with Windows NT/95 clients and servers.

This chapter is dedicated to covering essential TCP/IP routing protocol troubleshooting skills and tools. Starting with a description of default gateways and the difference between static and dynamic routing, specifics on troubleshooting the different routing protocols will be discussed. Specifically, the routing protocols that will be covered are RIP, IGRP, EIGRP, OSPF, and BGP. In addition to going over the routing protocols themselves, redistribution and how to filter information being passed from one protocol to another will be reviewed.

In addition to covering detailed problem-solving techniques, we have included quick-reference summary charts at the end of the chapter that summarize information provided in both this chapter and Chapter 5. These tables help to quickly associate a cause with many TCP/IP symptoms.

Default Gateways

The capability of a router to route or forward data depends on its knowledge of the world around it. This knowledge comes in the form of a route table. The route table is populated by the router's own networks, as well as by advertisements received from neighboring routers. This will be covered in detail when static and dynamic routing are discussed.

What happens if a router doesn't have a route to a destination? There are two possibilities. If the router is configured to do so, it will send the packet to a neighboring router that is considered the default gateway, with the hope that the default gateway will know where to send the packet. If the router is not configured to do that, it will simply drop the packet.

How do you configure a router to send packets to a neighbor without a route? That is where the gateway of last resort comes in. A gateway of last resort tells the router that if it doesn't have a route to a given network, it should send the packet out the specified interface, or default gateway.

The purpose of a default gateway is somewhat of a last-ditch effort to forward a packet. Look at Figure 6.1. In this example, Router A receives a packet from Host A that is destined for network 10.1.2.0. The problem is that Router A does not have a route for 10.1.2.0. The only chance of getting the packet forwarded to network 10.1.2.0 is to send it to Router B and hope that Router B has a route to network 10.1.2.0. Router A considers Router B as its default gateway, so it sends the packet to Router B. For this example, assume that Router B does have the route and sends the packet on its way.

FIGURE 6.1 Default gateways

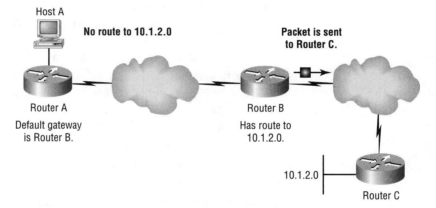

TCP/IP hosts also have default gateways set. If the default gateway for a router or a host is configured improperly, data will not be routed. Default gateways are used on TCP/IP hosts so that they don't have to keep individual route tables. All hosts need to point to a router on the same network to be used as the default gateway.

When the default gateway is not working properly, whether it is on a host or on a router, the problem is probably caused by incorrect configuration. To check for proper configuration on Windows, issue the ipconfig /all command from a DOS prompt. Here is a sample:

```
1 Ethernet adapter :

        Description . . . . . . . . : ELPC3R Ethernet
    Adapter
        Physical Address. . . . . . : 00-A0-24-A5-06-57
        DHCP Enabled. . . . . . . . : No
```

```
                    IP Address. . . . . . . . : 172.16.50.130
                    Subnet Mask . . . . . . . : 255.255.255.0
                    Default Gateway . . . . . : 172.16.50.1
                    Primary WINS Server . . . . :
                    Secondary WINS Server . . . :
                    Lease Obtained. . . . . . . :
                    Lease Expires . . . . . . . :
```

C:\WINDOWS>

The way to check for a default gateway on a Cisco router is to use the show ip route command. The output follows:

```
Router_C#show ip route
Codes: C - connected, S - static, I - IGRP, R - RIP, M -
   mobile, B - BGP
    D - EIGRP, EX - EIGRP external, O - OSPF, IA - OSPF
    inter area
    E1 - OSPF external type 1, E2 - OSPF external type 2,
    E - EGP
    i - IS-IS, L1 - IS-IS level-1, L2 - IS-IS level-2, *
    - candidate default
       U - per-user static route

Gateway of last resort is 172.16.50.2 to network 10.1.2.0

     172.16.0.0/16 is variably subnetted, 2 subnets, 2
     masks
C       172.16.50.0/24 is directly connected, Ethernet0/0
D       172.16.30.4/30 [90/2195456] via 172.16.50.1,
   00:00:18, Ethernet0/0
Router_C#

Router_B#sho ip route
Codes: C - connected, S - static, I - IGRP, R - RIP, M -
   mobile, B - BGP
    D - EIGRP, EX - EIGRP external, O - OSPF, IA - OSPF
       inter area
```

```
N1 - OSPF NSSA external type 1, N2 - OSPF NSSA
external type 2
 E1 - OSPF external type 1, E2 - OSPF external type 2,
E - EGP
 i - IS-IS, L1 - IS-IS level-1, L2 - IS-IS level-2, *
- candidate default
    U - per-user static route, o - ODR

Gateway of last resort is 172.16.50.2 to network 0.0.0.0

    172.16.0.0/16 is variably subnetted, 2 subnets, 2
      masks
C      172.16.50.0/24 is directly connected, Ethernet0
C      172.16.30.4/30 is directly connected, Serial0
S*   0.0.0.0/0 [1/0] via 172.16.50.2
Router_B#
```

The difference between the two examples is that one is dynamically set by using the ip default-network command and the other is set by using a static route. Both methods end with the same results. If Router B does not have a route for a requested destination, it forwards the packet to the next hop of 172.16.50.2.

An example was given previously that demonstrated the importance of having a default gateway configured. The ping and traceroute commands can be used to isolate default gateway problems. When the router uses a dynamic method of selecting a default gateway, there is a greater possibility that it may fail.

Static and Dynamic Routing

  • **S**tatic routing depends solely on a manual input of routes. If you do not want to enable a routing protocol on the router, you can manually enter all the routes that you believe will be necessary; for everything else, the default gateway is used. This is a very cumbersome and poor way to configure a router. Static routes are only used locally and are not advertised to neighboring routers unless they are redistributed into a routing protocol session.

Dynamic routing is based on active routing protocols that share route information with one another. When a destination is no longer reachable, the route is removed from the routing table and the change is propagated throughout the network. If a new destination becomes available, the router adds the information into the route table and propagates the change throughout the network.

This approach is much better than static routes. If a host that is entered in the route table via a static route fails, the route can remain in the route table. If this static route is redistributed, other routers would still learn the route and send traffic there. Once the packets reach the router with the static address, the packet will be dropped.

By issuing the show ip route command, you can tell which routes are learned dynamically and which are learned statically. Here is an example:

```
Router_B>show ip route
Codes: C- connected, S- static, I- IGRP, R - RIP, M -
   mobile, B - BGP
    D - EIGRP, EX - EIGRP external, O - OSPF, IA - OSPF
    inter area
    N1 - OSPF NSSA external type 1, N2 - OSPF NSSA
    external type 2
      E1 - OSPF external type 1, E2 - OSPF external type
      2, E - EGP
      i - IS-IS, L1 - IS-IS level-1, L2 - IS-IS level-2,
      *   - candidate default
      U - per-user static route, o - ODR

Gateway of last resort is 172.16.50.2 to network 0.0.0.0

      172.16.0.0/16 is variably subnetted, 3 subnets, 2
      masks
C       172.16.50.0/24 is directly connected, Ethernet0
D       172.16.60.0/24 [90/2195456] via 172.16.50.2,
   00:31:39, Ethernet0
C       172.16.30.4/30 is directly connected, Serial0
S*  0.0.0.0/0 [1/0] via 172.16.50.2
Router_B>
```

The "S" indicates that the route is a static route. The other routes are either directly connected or learned via a routing protocol—in this case, EIGRP.

Troubleshooting RIP

*R*outing Information Protocol (RIP) was first designed for Xerox. The protocol, known as routed, was later used in Unix. Thereafter, RIP was implemented as a TCP/IP routing protocol. RIP is used by most versions of Novell NetWare for routing. Other protocols have been derived from RIP.

RIP1 and RIP2

The original version of RIP (RIP1) had several limitations that restricted its use and scalability. Problems such as the frequent routing updates and limited hop-count needed to be overcome.

RIP uses UDP broadcasts to flood route updates. Every router floods the network with its update. RIP also features split horizon and poison reverse updates to prevent routing loops. RIP updates every 30 seconds and has a hop-count limit of 16 hops.

RIP2 functions in much the same way as RIP1, but with a few enhancements. RIP2 supports classless routing (CIDR), route summarization, and variable length subnet masks (VLSM).

show Commands

The show commands that are useful for troubleshooting RIP1 and RIP2 are listed in Table 6.1.

T A B L E   6 . 1   RIP-Related show Commands

Command	Description
show ip route rip	Displays the RIP route table
show ip route	Displays the IP route table
show ip interface	Displays IP interface configuration
show running-config	Displays the running configuration

debug Commands

As was mentioned before, the `debug` command should always be used with caution and, in many circumstances, as a last resort. If the previous `show` commands do not provide you with enough information to isolate and resolve the RIP problem, you can enable the debug tool.

The syntax for the debug mode in RIP is `debug ip rip events`. If you need even more general RIP information, use the global form of the command, `debug ip rip`. This command provides you with all possible RIP protocol information.

Typical Problems

Because RIP uses UDP broadcasts by default, it can cause network congestion or broadcast storms if not configured correctly. The way to avoid this problem is to configure RIP to allow unicast updates. This is done with the `neighbor` statement from within the RIP protocol configuration mode. In addition to using the `neighbor` statement, specified interfaces can be made passive by using the `passive-interface` command. This command stops routing updates from being sent out to the specified interfaces. Even if neighbor statements are used, too-frequent routing updates can also cause network congestion. This can be controlled or remedied by adjusting the various RIP timers.

Problems can also occur due to RIP version mismatches. By default, Cisco routers can understand both versions, but they advertise and forward data using RIP1. It is possible to configure interfaces to send and receive only one version. The problem occurs when the RIP versions on the two connected interfaces do not match.

For example, if Router A's interfaces are configured to send and receive only RIP2, and Router B's interfaces are configured to listen to and speak RIP1, the two routers won't be able to share RIP information. This problem can be resolved by analyzing the interface configuration on both routers and changing them so they match.

Troubleshooting IGRP

The *Interior Gateway Routing Protocol (IGRP)* is a Cisco proprietary routing protocol that uses a distance-vector algorithm because it uses a vector (a one-dimensional array) of information to calculate the best path. This vector or metric can consist of five elements:

- Bandwidth
- Delay
- Load
- Reliability
- MTU

By default, only two of the elements are used in the calculation of the metric: bandwidth and delay. Bandwidth is the minimum bandwidth over the path, and delay is the cumulative delay over the path. IGRP is intended to replace RIP and create a stable, quickly converging protocol that will scale with increased network growth.

IGRP Features and Operation

IGRP has several features included in the algorithm—these features and brief descriptions can be found in Table 6.2. The features were added to make IGRP more stable, and a few were created to deal with routing updates and make network convergence happen faster. It also should be noted that IGRP is a classful routing protocol.

TABLE 6.2   IGRP Features

Feature	Description
Configurable metrics	Metrics involved in the algorithm responsible for calculating route information. They may be configured by the user.
Flash update	Updates are sent out before the default time setting. This occurs when the metrics for a route change.
Poison reverse updates	Implemented to prevent routing loops. These updates place a route in *holddown*. Holddown means that the router will not accept any new route information on a given route for a certain period.
Unequal-cost load balancing	Allows packets to be shared/distributed across multiple paths.

show Commands

The show commands that are useful for troubleshooting IGRP are listed in Table 6.3.

TABLE 6.3 IGRP show Commands

Command	Description
show running-config	Displays the current configuration
show ip route igrp	Displays IGRP routes only
show ip route	Displays the entire route table

debug Commands

IGRP events—as well as the protocol itself—can be analyzed by the debug tool. To watch IGRP events and protocol communications, you can enter the following debug commands:

- debug ip igrp events
- debug ip igrp transactions

Depending on the problem or the activity within IP, these commands can produce a great number of messages being logged to the console and the router's logging buffer.

Typical Problems

Because IGRP is a distance-vector protocol, you will not encounter problems with neighbor relationships or different databases that link-state protocols use.

For IGRP, the most typical problems are caused by access lists, improper configuration, or the line to an adjacent router being down. The easiest way to tell if the router is receiving and sending IGRP information is to use the two debugging tools.

The primary symptom of a problem with IGRP is the lack of IGRP learned routes. This can be verified through the use of the show commands listed in Table 6.3.

Troubleshooting EIGRP

*E*nhanced IGRP (EIGRP) is a hybrid link-state and distance-vector routing protocol that was created to resolve some of the problems with IGRP. For example, in IGRP the entire route table is sent when changes are made in the network, and there is a lack of formal neighbor relationships with connected routers. Like IGRP, EIGRP is also a proprietary Cisco routing protocol. EIGRP is a hybrid of both link-state and distance-vector routing algorithms, which brings the best of both worlds together.

EIGRP's specific features are detailed in Table 6.4. The features offered by EIGRP make it a stable and scalable protocol. Just as IGRP is a Cisco proprietary protocol, so is EIGRP.

TABLE 6.4 EIGRP Features

Feature	Description
Route tagging	Distinguishes routes learned via different EIGRP sessions.
Formal neighbor relationships	Uses the Hello protocol to establish peering.
Incremental routing updates	Only changes are advertised, instead of the entire route table.
Classless routing	EIGRP supports subnet and VLSM information.
Configurable metrics	Metric information can be set through configuration commands.
Equal-cost load balancing	Allows traffic to be sent equally across multiple connections.

To aid in calculating the best route and load sharing, EIGRP utilizes several databases of information. These databases are as follows:

- The route database, where the best routes are stored
- The topology database, where all route information resides

  - A neighbor table, which is used to house information concerning other EIGRP neighbors

Neighbor Formation

The manner in which EIGRP establishes and maintains neighbor relationships is derived through its link-state properties. EIGRP uses the Hello protocol (similar to OSPF) to establish and maintain peering relationships with directly connected routers. Hello packets are sent between EIGRP routers to determine the state of the connection between them. Once the neighbor relation is established via the Hello protocol, the routers can exchange route information.

Each router establishes a neighbor table, in which it stores important information regarding the neighbors that are directly connected. The information consists of the neighbor's IP address, hold time interval, smooth round-trip timer (SRTT), and queue information. These data are used to help determine when the link state changes.

When two routers initialize communication, their entire route tables are shared. Thereafter, only changes to the route table are propagated. These changes are shared with all directly connected EIGRP-speaking routers. Each of these steps is summarized below.

1. Hello packets are multicast out all of the router's interfaces.

2. Replies to the Hello packets include all routes in the neighbor router's topology database, including the metrics. Routes that are learned from the originating router are not included in the reply.

3. The originating router acknowledges the update to each neighbor via an ACK packet.

4. The topology database is then updated with the newly received information.

5. Once the topology database is updated, the originating router then advertises its entire table to all the new neighbors.

6. Neighbor routers acknowledge the receipt of the route information from the originating router by sending back an ACK packet.

These steps are used in the initialization of EIGRP neighbors and change only slightly when updates are sent to existing neighbors.

show Commands

Due to the complexity of EIGRP, there are several more show commands available to aid in troubleshooting EIGRP problems. The majority of the commands are listed in Table 6.5.

TABLE 6.5 EIGRP show Commands

Command	Description / Output
show running-config	Displays the current configuration.
show ip route	Displays the full IP route table.
show ip route eigrp	Displays the EIGRP routes.
show ip eigrp interfaces	Displays EIGRP peer information for that interface.
show ip eigrp neighbors	Displays all EIGRP neighbors, along with summary information about each neighbor.
show ip eigrp topology	Displays the contents of the EIGRP topology table.
show ip eigrp traffic	Displays a summary of EIGRP routing statistics, such as the number of Hellos and routing updates.
show ip eigrp events	Displays a log of the most recent EIGRP protocol events. This information includes the insertion and removal of routes from the route table, updates, and neighbor status.

debug Commands

There are also several debug commands within EIGRP that allow you to specify what processes you want to debug. Here is a list of commands:

- debug ip eigrp <AS number>
- debug ip eigrp neighbor
- debug ip eigrp notifications

- debug ip eigrp summary

- debug ip eigrp

Here is a sample of the information that can be obtained by using these commands:

```
Router_C#debug ip eigrp
IP-EIGRP Route Events debugging is on
IP-EIGRP: Processing incoming QUERY packet
IP-EIGRP: Int 172.16.30.4/30 M 4294967295 - 0 4294967295
   SM 4294967295 - 0 4294967295
IP-EIGRP: 172.16.30.4/30 routing table not updated
IP-EIGRP: 172.16.30.4/30, - do advertise out Ethernet0/0
IP-EIGRP: Int 172.16.30.4/30 metric 4294967295 - 1657856
   4294967295
IP-EIGRP: Processing incoming UPDATE packet
IP-EIGRP: Int 172.16.30.4/30 M 2195456 - 1657856 537600 SM
   2169856 - 1657856 512000
IP-EIGRP: Int 172.16.30.4/30 metric 2195456 - 1657856 537600
IP-EIGRP: Processing incoming QUERY packet
IP-EIGRP: Int 172.16.30.4/30 M 4294967295 - 0 4294967295
   SM 4294967295 - 0 4294967295
IP-EIGRP: 172.16.30.4/30 routing table not updated
IP-EIGRP: 172.16.30.4/30, - do advertise out Ethernet0/0
IP-EIGRP: Int 172.16.30.4/30 metric 4294967295 - 1657856
   4294967295
IP-EIGRP: Processing incoming UPDATE packet
IP-EIGRP: Int 172.16.30.4/30 M 2195456 - 1657856 537600 SM
   2169856 - 1657856 512000
IP-EIGRP: Int 172.16.30.4/30 metric 2195456 - 1657856 537600
```

You can see from this information when routes are removed from the route table and they are no longer advertised. Once the route is advertised to the router, it inserts the route back into the route table and commences advertisement.

Typical Problems

Some of the typical problems with EIGRP are the loss of neighbor adjacencies, lost routes in earlier versions of IOS, and lost default gateways.

Neighbor failures can be attributed to link failures just as much as they can be attributed to software problems. If a neighbor relation has problems establishing, use the proper **debug** command to see what is occurring between both routers.

When troubleshooting an EIGRP problem, it is always a good idea to get a picture of the network. The most relevant picture is provided by the **show ip eigrp neighbors** command. This command shows all adjacent routers that share route information within a given autonomous system. If neighbors are missing, check the configuration and link status on both routers to verify that the protocol has been configured correctly.

If all neighbors are present, verify the routes learned. By executing the **show ip route eigrp** command, you gain a quick picture of the routes in the route table. If the route does not appear in the route table, verify the source of the route. If the source is functioning properly, check the topology table.

The topology table is displayed by using the **show ip eigrp topology** command. If the route is in the topology table, it is safe to assume that there is a problem between the topology database and the route table. There must be a reason why the topology database is not injecting the route into the route table.

Other commands, such as **show ip eigrp traffic**, can be used to see whether updates are being sent. If the counters for EIGRP input and output packets don't increase, no EIGRP information is being sent between peers.

The **show ip eigrp events** command is an undocumented command. This command displays a log of every EIGRP event—when routes are injected and removed from the route table, and when EIGRP adjacencies reset or fail. This information can be used to see whether there are routing instabilities in the network.

Troubleshooting OSPF

*O*pen *Shortest Path First (OSPF)* differs from IGRP and Enhanced IGRP because it is a pure link-state routing technology. Also, it is an open standard routing protocol, which means that it was not developed solely by Cisco. OSPF was designed and developed by the IETF to provide a scalable, quickly converging, and efficient routing protocol that can be used by all routing equipment. Complete details for OSPF are found in RFC 2178.

Areas are used within OSPF to define a group of routers and networks belonging to the same OSPF session. Links connect routers, and the information about each link is defined by its link state. On each broadcast or multi-access network segment, two routers must be assigned the responsibilities of designated router (DR) and backup designated router (BDR).

Like EIGRP, OSPF maintains three databases: adjacency, topology, and route. The adjacency database is similar to the neighbor database used by EIGRP. It contains all information about OSPF neighbors and the links connecting them. The topology database maintains all route information. The best routes from the topology database are placed in the route database, or route table.

Neighbor and Adjacency Formation

The Hello protocol is used to establish peering sessions between routers. Hello packets are multicast out every interface. The information that is multicast includes the router ID, timing intervals, existing neighbors, area identification, router priority, designated and backup router information, authentication password, and stub area information. All this information is used when establishing new peers. Descriptions of each element can be found in Table 6.6.

TABLE 6.6 OSPF Multicast Information

Information	Description
Router ID	Highest active IP address on the router.
Time intervals	Intervals between Hello packets, and the allowed dead time interval.
Existing neighbors	Addresses for any existing OSPF neighbors.
Area identification	OSPF area number and link information, which must be the same for a peering session to be established.
Router priority	Value assigned to a router and used when choosing the DR and BDR.
DR and BDR	If they have already been chosen, their Router ID and address is contained in the Hello packet.

TABLE 6.6   OSPF Multicast Information *(continued)*

Information	Description
Authentication password	All peers must have the same authentication password if authentication is enabled.
Stub area flag	This is a special area—two routers must share the same stub information. This is not necessary to initiate a regular peering session with another OSPF router.

Figure 6.2 displays a flowchart that depicts each step of the initialization process. The process starts by sending out Hello packets. Every listening router then adds the originating router to the adjacency database. The responding routers reply with all of their Hello information so that the originating router can add them to its adjacency table.

FIGURE 6.2   OSPF peer initialization

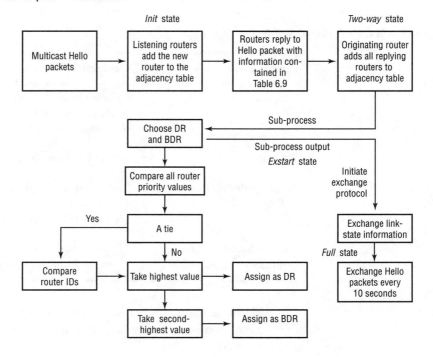

OSPF Area Types

OSPF uses areas in place of an autonomous system. An OSPF area consists of a group of routers or interfaces on a router that is assigned to a common area.

OSPF also allows and uses different area types. When deploying OSPF, there must be a backbone area. Standard and stub areas connect to the backbone area. Below is a list of each router type, followed by a short description of the area type.

Backbone   This area accepts all LSAs and is used to connect multiple areas.

Stub   This area does not accept any external routing update, but it accepts summary LSAs.

Totally Stub   These areas are closed off from accepting external or summary advertisements.

Standard   This is the normal area that accepts internal and external LSAs, and summary information.

Multiple router types can exist within an OSPF area. Table 6.7 lists all of the OSPF router types and the role that each plays within the area.

TABLE 6.7   OSPF Router Types

Router Type	Description of Responsibility
Internal	All interfaces are defined on the same area. All internal routers have an identical link-state database.
Backbone	Has at least one interface assigned to area 0.
Area border router (ABR)	Interfaces are connected to multiple OSPF areas. Information specific to each area is stored on this type of router.
Autonomous system boundary router (ASBR)	This type of router has an interface connected to an external network or a different AS.

In addition to the previous responsibilities, a router can also be assigned additional responsibilities. These additions are assumed when a router is assigned the role of DR or BDR.

show Commands

Because of the complexity of OSPF, several show commands are available to provide information regarding the configuration and functionality of OSPF on a router. Table 6.8 lists most of the available OSPF-related show commands.

TABLE 6.8   OSPF show Commands

Command	Description / Output
show running-config	Displays the current router configuration
show ip route	Displays the entire IP route table
show ip route ospf	Displays OSPF routes
show ip ospf	Displays information for OSPF
show ip ospf <process-id>	Displays information relevant to the specified process ID
show ip ospf border-routers	Displays the routers that join different areas, or border routers
show ip ospf database	Provides an OSPF database summary
show ip ospf interface	Displays OSPF information on a interface
show ip ospf neighbor	Displays OSPF neighbor information
show ip ospf request-list	Displays the link-state request list
show ip ospf retransmission list	Displays the link-state retransmission list
show ip ospf summary-address	Displays summary-address redistribution information
show ip ospf virtual-links	Displays virtual link information
show ip interface	Displays IP interface settings

These commands provide you with a great amount of information valuable for troubleshooting OSPF routing problems.

debug Commands

OSPF runs many processes to maintain all of its databases, routing updates, and peering connections. Most of these processes use link-state advertisements (LSAs) to share information.

We'll briefly explore the different types of link-state advertisements. LSAs are the heart of OSPF's information exchange. Different types of LSAs represent different types of route information. All of the LSA types are summarized in Table 6.9.

TABLE 6.9 OSPF LSA Types

LSA Type	Description of LSA
(1) Router link entry	This LSA is broadcast only within its defined area. The LSA contains all of the default link-state information.
(2) Network entry	This LSA is multicast to all area routers by the DR. This update contains network-specific information.
(3/4) Summary entry	Type 3 LSAs contain route information for internal networks and are sent to backbone routers. Type 4 LSAs contain information about ASBRs. Summary information is multicast by the ABR, and the information reaches all backbone routers.
(5) Autonomous system entry	As the name indicates, these advertisements originate from the ASBR. These packets contain information about external networks.
(7) NSSA autonomous system entry	Not So Stubby Area (NSSA) permits Type 7 AS external routers to be imported inside the NSSA area by redistribution.

Different LSA types represent the type of route that is being advertised, and they assist in restricting the number and types of routes that are accepted by a given area. As is shown in the table, an LSA of type 5 is sent only by the ASBR. Here are the available debug options for OSPF:

debug ip ospf adj   Provides debug information about events concerning adjacency relationships with other OSPF routers.

debug ip ospf events   Provides debug information for all OSPF events.

debug ip ospf flood   Provides information about OSPF flooding. (Flooding is the way that an OSPF router sends updates.) It broadcasts a change in its route table, and all other members of the OSPF area receive the update.

debug ip ospf lsa-generation   Gives detailed information regarding the generation of LSA messages.

debug ip ospf packet   Gives detailed information regarding OSPF packets.

debug ip ospf retransmission   If OSPF has to retransmit information, it triggers a retransmission event that **debug** captures and echoes to the console.

debug ip ospf spf   Provides debug information for all SPF transactions. By enabling SPF debugging, OSPF events debugging is also turned on.

debug ip ospf tree   Provides information for the OSPF database tree.

Following is a debug ip ospf trace. Notice that OSPF event debugging was turned on as well (lines 2 through 3 of the output). SPF is an algorithm used to select the best route to each destination.

```
Router_A#debug ip ospf spf
OSPF spf intra events debugging is on
OSPF spf inter events debugging is on
OSPF spf external events debugging is on
Router_A#
%LINEPROTO-5-UPDOWN: Line protocol on Interface Serial1,
    changed state to down
%LINK-3-UPDOWN: Interface Serial1, changed state to down
OSPF: running SPF for area 0
OSPF: Initializing to run spf
  It is a router LSA 172.16.40.1. Link Count 1
```

Processing link 0, id 172.16.30.4, link data
255.255.255.252, type 3

Add better path to LSA ID 172.16.30.7, gateway
172.16.30.4, dist 64

Add path fails: no output interface to 172.16.30.4,
next hop 0.0.0.0

OSPF: Adding Stub nets

OSPF: Path left undeleted to 172.16.30.4

OSPF: Entered old delete routine

OSPF: No ndb for STUB NET old route 172.16.60.0, mask /24,
next hop 172.16.30.6

OSPF: No ndb for STUB NET old route 172.16.30.4, mask /30,
next hop 172.16.30.5

OSPF: No ndb for NET old route 172.16.50.0, mask /24, next
hop 172.16.30.6

OSPF: delete lsa id 172.16.60.255, type 0, adv rtr
172.16.60.1 from delete list

OSPF: delete lsa id 172.16.30.7, type 0, adv rtr
172.16.40.1 from delete list

OSPF: delete lsa id 172.16.50.1, type 2, adv rtr
172.16.50.1 from delete list

OSPF: running spf for summaries area 0

OSPF: sum_delete_old_routes area 0

OSPF: Started Building Type 5 External Routes

OSPF: ex_delete_old_routes

OSPF: Started Building Type 7 External Routes

OSPF: ex_delete_old_routes

%LINK-3-UPDOWN: Interface Serial1, changed state to up

%LINEPROTO-5-UPDOWN: Line protocol on Interface Serial1,
changed state to up

OSPF: running SPF for area 0

OSPF: Initializing to run spf

It is a router LSA 172.16.40.1. Link Count 1

Processing link 0, id 172.16.30.4, link data
255.255.255.252, type 3

Add better path to LSA ID 172.16.30.7, gateway
172.16.30.4, dist 64

Add path: next-hop 172.16.30.5, interface Serial1

OSPF: Adding Stub nets

```
OSPF: insert route list LS ID 172.16.30.7, type 0, adv rtr
    172.16.40.1
OSPF: Entered old delete routine
OSPF: running spf for summaries area 0
OSPF: sum_delete_old_routes area 0
OSPF: Started Building Type 5 External Routes
OSPF: ex_delete_old_routes
OSPF: Started Building Type 7 External Routes
OSPF: ex_delete_old_routes
```

This is a lot of information over a very short period. You can get an idea of what the CPU goes through when there is a link-state change in a OSPF network.

Typical Problems

Because of the great number of processes and calculations that must be made by the CPU when changes occur in an OSPF network, the router can become overwhelmed with all the processing that has to be done. The bigger the OSPF network, the more calculations must be made, not to mention the greater probability of changes that need to be propagated throughout the network.

A general rule of thumb is to not add more than 100 routers per area, and to not have more than 700 routers throughout the network. It is possible to have smaller or larger networks, but the numbers here are given simply as a guideline. As links are added to a network, the likelihood of instability also increases. When a large network experiences instability, the routers have to spend a great deal of time and CPU cycles processing link and route updates.

Another problem common to OSPF is wrongly configured wildcard masks in the OSPF network statements. OSPF uses wildcard bits to specify the networks that should be advertised instead of using multiple network statements. Either approach works, but be aware of potential wildcard mask problems.

Troubleshooting BGP

You are now familiar with several IGPs (Interior Gateway Protocols), such as IGRP, EIGRP, and OSPF. For enterprise networks to communicate with other autonomous systems or ISPs, the IGP information has to be injected into BGP, which is used by all network entities that compose the Internet.

BGP (Border Gateway Protocol) is an open standard protocol that was developed and defined in several RFCs: 1163, 1267, 1654, and 1655. The two types of BGP are iBGP and eBGP. There are several differences between the two. Primarily, iBGP (internal BGP) is used to share BGP information with routers within the same AS, whereas eBGP (external BGP) is used to share route information between two different autonomous systems. More details will be given as we discuss each type separately.

Neighbor Relationship

The key to BGP configuration is the neighbor relationship. Unlike many of the previous protocols, BGP uses TCP to establish neighbor relationships. Specifically, a TCP connection, on port 179, is set up when the neighbor relationship is formed, and remains up during the entire time that the relationship exists. This connection is used to send routing updates, notifications, and keepalives between the routers.

BGP is an EGP, and as such, its design assumes it will be used to connect many different companies with varying configurations and levels of trust. Because of this design assumption, there are numerous configuration options for each neighbor relationship. You can set up BGP to prefer one neighbor's routes over another (all the time or only some of the time), update the next-hop information to one neighbor but not another, advertise a route only if another route is in the routing table, update the path information for some but not all routes from a neighbor, and perform many other different manipulations on the routes that are entered into the routing table. In addition, most of these attributes can be assigned based on groups of neighbors as well as on an individual neighbor-by-neighbor basis.

The cost of this flexibility is complexity. A simple BGP configuration, with a couple of neighbors and little or no manipulation of the routes, is no harder to manage and maintain than any IGP, such as OSPF or EIGRP. However, if significant route manipulation and neighbor relationship management is needed in your implementation, troubleshooting any issue can become a major undertaking. Therefore, where possible create groups for neighbors and simplify any route manipulation to adjust a minimum number of terms.

eBGP vs. iBGP

The distinguishing characteristic between an iBGP neighbor and an eBGP neighbor is that an iBGP neighbor is in the same autonomous system and eBGP neighbor is in a different autonomous system. The way that iBGP and eBGP peers are treated differs greatly. In general, eBGP neighbors share a common subnet while iBGP neighbors can be anywhere within the same AS. In addition, by default an eBGP route has an administrative distance of 20, compared to 200 for an iBGP route.

It is not a requirement for eBGP neighbors to share a common subnet. If they do not—for example, if you are using loopbacks—the path to the neighbor's loopback needs to be known by a means other than BGP, such as a static route. Once this is complete, add a `neighbor <ip address>` ebgp-multihop command for that neighbor in the BGP configuration.

In iBGP, route information learned from one iBGP peer is not advertised to another iBGP peer. This avoids inconsistent route information and routing loops. To share route information between all iBGP routers, establish a logical mesh. By default, when routes are exchanged between iBGP peers, the "next hop" attribute is not updated. This goes back to the assumption that there is a logical mesh of all iBGP peers. With this mesh, it is assumed that every device in the mesh knows how to get to all of the same networks, and therefore the next hop does not need to be updated because the iBGP peers should know about it. As is the case with most things in BGP, this behavior can be changed if your needs dictate.

The purpose of eBGP is to inject routes owned by the enterprise network into another AS. Two prerequisites need to be met for internal routes to be propagated via BGP:

- The route to be advertised must be present in the router's IGP route table.

- BGP must learn the route.

You can fulfill the first condition by using one of three methods: inject the routes into a router's route table via an IGP, a static route, or directly connected networks. BGP has a synchronization option that requires BGP and the IGP routes to synchronize before BGP will advertise IGP learned networks. The `no synchronization` command indicates that BGP and the IGP do not have to synchronize before BGP advertises the routes.

You can also accomplish the second prerequisite in one of three ways: BGP learns of networks that it needs to advertise through other BGP advertisements, network statements, and redistribution of an IGP into BGP.

show Commands

There are numerous show commands available for BGP. Many are similar to ones that were issued for other routing protocols. The major show commands that are available are shown in Table 6.10.

TABLE 6.10 BGP-Related show Commands

Command	Description
show ip bgp	Shows information about BGP learned routes, including indicating which ones will be in the routing table
show ip bgp <network>	Shows BGP information on a specific network
show ip bgp neighbors	Shows information on BGP neighbors
show ip bgp neighbors <ipaddress> advertised-routes	Shows all routes being advertised to a particular neighbor
show ip bgp neighbors <ipaddress> received-routes	Shows all routes being received from a particular neighbor
show ip bgp peer-group	Shows information about BGP peer groups
show ip bgp summary	Shows a summary of all BGP connections
show ip route bgp	Displays the BGP route table
show ip route	Displays the IP route table
show ip interface	Displays IP interface configuration
show running-config	Displays the running configuration

debug Commands

Compared to the overall complexity of BGP, there are relatively few debug commands. Those that do exist are very focused as to the information that they show. This does require you to know specifically what you are looking for, but also makes the debug commands less of a burden on the router to run. Therefore, the debug commands that are available are usable in most real life installations. As with all debug commands, care needs to be taken when using the BGP debug options. Even though they are focused, if there are a large number of routes in the routing table, significant load can be placed on the processor. Some of the more frequently used commands are as follows:

- debug ip bgp <*ipaddress*> updates

- debug ip bgp dampening

- debug ip bgp events

- debug ip bgp keepalives

- debug ip bgp updates

An example of the output from debug ip bgp <*ipaddress*> updates is shown below:

```
Router_B#debug ip bgp 172.16.20.6 updates
BGP updates debugging is on for neighbor 172.16.20.6
BGP: 172.16.20.6 computing updates, neighbor version 0,
    table version 2, starting at 0.0.0.0
BGP: 172.16.20.6 send UPDATE 10.0.0.0/8, next 172.16.20.5,
    metric 0, path 100
BGP: 172.16.20.6 1 updates enqueued (average=50,
    maximum=50)
BGP: 172.16.20.6 update run completed, ran for 0ms,
    neighbor version 0, start version 2, throttled to 2,
    check point net 0.0.0.0
BGP: 172.16.20.6 rcv UPDATE w/ attr: nexthop 172.16.20.6,
    origin ?, metric 0, path 200
BGP: 172.16.20.6 rcv UPDATE about 19.0.0.0/8
BGP: 172.16.20.6 rcv UPDATE about 100.100.0.0/16
BGP: 172.16.20.6 rcv UPDATE about 100.200.0.0/14
BGP: 172.16.20.6 rcv UPDATE about 199.199.0.0/16
BGP: 172.16.20.6 rcv UPDATE about 200.200.1.0/24
BGP: 172.16.20.6 rcv UPDATE about 200.200.64.0/18
BGP: 172.16.20.6 computing updates, neighbor version 2,
    table version 8, starting at 0.0.0.0
```

```
BGP: 172.16.20.6 update run completed, ran for 0ms,
   neighbor version 2, start version 8, throttled to 8,
   check point net 0.0.0.0
Router_B#
```

Typical Problems

Most problems with BGP are a result of the complexity of the implementation. These problems will most likely occur during the implementation itself. Once set up and running, BGP is a very stable protocol that can effectively manage the routing table for the entire Internet.

Many of the typical problems that occur in BGP affect the areas in which BGP differs from other routing protocols. For example, in other routing protocols when a route is learned from a neighbor and there is no other route in the routing table for this network, the route is installed in the network. In BGP, certain other conditions may need to be met before this occurs. In addition, BGP's network statements work differently than other routing protocols'. For example, in EIGRP a network 10.0.0.0 command would tell EIGRP to route out any network between 10.0.0.0 and 10.255.255.255. In BGP, this same statement means to send the 10.0.0.0 /8 network if it is in the routing table. If the 10.2.2.0 /24 network is in the table, in BGP this will not be sent (assuming auto-summary is off).

Redistribution of Routing Protocols

When multiple routing protocols are used within a network and they need to be redistributed into one another, it is important that it be done correctly by assigning the proper metrics through the redistribution. If protocols are redistributed without metric adjustment, many networking problems can occur.

Although redistribution allows multiple protocols to share routing information, it can result in routing loops, slow convergence, and inconsistent route information. This is caused by the different algorithms and methods used by each protocol. It is not a good practice to redistribute bidirectionally (if, for example, you have both IGRP 100 and RIP routing sessions running on your router). Bidirectional redistribution occurs if you enter redistribution commands under each protocol session. Here is an example:

```
Router_A#config t
Enter configuration commands, one per line. End with CNTL/Z.
Router_A(config)#router igrp 100
Router_A(config-router)#redistribute RIP
Router_A(config-router)#router RIP
Router_A(config-router)#redistribute igrp 100
Router_A(config-router)#^Z
Router_A#
```

When a route from RIP, IGRP, or OSPF is injected into another routing protocol, the route loses its identity and its metrics are converted from the original format to the other protocol's format. This can cause confusion within the router. The method of ensuring that the metric is converted properly is done through metric commands. In most cases, the specific command used is `default-metric`.

Dealing with Routing Metrics

The router in which multiple protocols or sessions meet is called the *autonomous system boundary router (ASBR)*. When routes from one protocol or session are injected or redistributed into another protocol or session, the routes are tagged as external routes. Following is a simple example of a route table that has external routes:

```
Router_X#show ip route eigrp
     172.16.0.0/16 is variably subnetted, 301 subnets, 10
     masks
D EX     172.16.27.230/32
             [170/24827392] via 172.16.131.82, 02:33:32,
             ATM6/0/0.3114
D EX     172.16.237.16/29
             [170/40542208] via 172.16.131.82, 23:40:32,
             ATM6/0/0.3114
             [170/40542208] via 172.16.131.74, 23:40:32,
             ATM6/0/0.3113
```

```
D EX    172.16.237.24/29
           [170/40542208] via 172.16.131.82, 23:40:32,
           ATM6/0/0.3114
           [170/40542208] via 172.16.131.74, 23:40:32,
           ATM6/0/0.3113
D EX    172.16.52.192/26
           [170/2202112] via 172.16.131.82, 23:40:27,
           ATM6/0/0.3114
D EX    172.16.41.216/29
           [170/46232832] via 172.16.131.82, 23:40:28,
           ATM6/0/0.3114
D EX    172.16.38.200/30
           [170/2176512] via 172.16.131.82, 23:40:27,
           ATM6/0/0.3114
D EX    172.16.237.0/29
           [170/40542208] via 172.16.131.82, 23:40:32,
           ATM6/0/0.3114
           [170/40542208] via 172.16.131.74, 23:40:32,
           ATM6/0/0.3113
D       172.16.236.0/24
           [90/311808] via 172.16.131.82, 23:40:32,
           ATM6/0/0.3114
           [90/311808] via 172.16.131.74, 23:40:32,
           ATM6/0/0.3113
D       172.16.235.0/24
           [90/311808] via 172.16.131.82, 23:40:32,
           ATM6/0/0.3114
```

IGRP and EIGRP

Each protocol has its own method of route redistribution. You must be familiar with each protocol's implementation of route redistribution and default-metric settings.

IGRP and EIGRP use the same command to adjust metrics. It is done through the `default-metric` command. Here is an example:

`default-metric` *bandwidth delay reliability load MTU*

This command takes the metrics for the protocol being injected into IGRP or EIGRP, and converts them directly to values that IGRP or EIGRP can use.

The *bandwidth* is the capacity of the link; *delay* is the time in microseconds; *reliability* and *load* are values from 1 to 255; and *MTU* is the maximum transmission unit in bytes.

Finally, you can also change the distance values that are assigned to EIGRP (90 internal; 170 external). The distance value tells the router which protocol to believe. The lower the distance value, the more believable the protocol. The administrative distance values for EIGRP are changed with the following command from within the EIGRP session:

```
distance eigrp internal-distance external-distance
```

Internal distance and external distance have a range of values from 1 to 255.

Remember that a value of 255 tells the router to ignore the route. So, unless you want the routes from the protocol to be ignored, never use the value of 255.

This can be a source of problems when troubleshooting routing problems. If multiple protocols advertise the same routes, it is possible that differences in the administrative distance may cause the route to be learned by the wrong protocol, and thus it is not propagated correctly throughout the network.

Metrics used by EIGRP are essentially equal to 256 times the IGRP metrics. As with IGRP, metrics decide how the routes are selected. The higher the metric associated with a route, the less desirable the route is.

OSPF

The metrics associated with OSPF are different from those associated with IGRP and EIGRP. OSPF uses bandwidth as the main metric in selecting a route. The cost is calculated by using the bandwidth for the link. The equation is 100,000 divided by the bandwidth. You may change bandwidth on the individual interface.

The cost is manipulated by changing the value to a number within the range of 1 to 65,535. Because the cost is assigned to each link, the value must be changed on each interface. The command to do this follows:

```
ip ospf cost
```

Cisco bases link cost on bandwidth. Other vendors may use other metrics to calculate the link's cost. When connecting links between routers from different vendors, you may have to adjust the cost to match the other router. Both routers must assign the same cost to the link for OSPF to work.

You can configure the OSPF distance with the following command:

```
distance ospf [external | Intra-area | Inter-area] distance
```

This command allows the distance metric to be defined for external OSPF, and intra-area and inter-area routes. (Intra-area and inter-area routes are discussed in the "Configuring OSPF" subsection.) Distance values range from 1 to 255—and the lower the distance, the better.

Other values important to OSPF's operation are not actually metrics, but can be configured as well. Values such as the router ID and router priority are important in router initialization and for DR and BDR selection. You can change these values with some minor configuration changes.

To change the router priority, use the following command on the desired interface:

```
ip ospf priority number
```

The *number* can range from 0 to 255—the higher value indicates a higher priority when choosing the DR and BDR for the area.

Just as with EIGRP, new metrics must be assigned to route information that is injected into the OSPF session. The command is much simpler than the command used when assigning metrics for EIGRP or IGRP—it is almost the same, but only one metric is assigned. The value of the metric is the cost for the route.

```
default-metric cost
```

Distribute Lists

Distribute lists are access lists applied to an interface from within a routing protocol. The purpose of a distribute list is to control which routes are advertised to adjacent routers. As of IOS 12.0(3)T, you can also use a *prefix list* in place of the access list. A prefix list, specified by the `ip prefix-list` command, allows greater flexibility in specifying the networks that should be allowed. For example, with a prefix list you can tell the routing protocol to accept all routes as long as the mask length for the route is between /8 and /24. This particular command is shown below:

```
ip prefix-list MASK-SIZE permit 0.0.0.0/0 ge 8 le 24
```

Problems can occur if distribute lists are missing or improperly configured. Figure 6.3 shows a picture of three meshed routers. Undesired routing can occur if the advertised routes are not controlled through the use of distribute lists.

FIGURE 6.3   Distribute lists to prevent routing loops

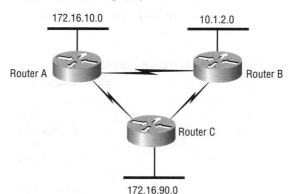

Router A and Router B are core-level routers. Router C is a small access router. The potential problem is that Router A could learn about network 10.1.2.0 via Router C instead of Router B, if no distribute lists are used to control what routes are advertised from Router C.

If all of Router A's traffic destined for 10.1.2.0 were routed through Router C, it could easily overwhelm the small router. In this scenario, you'd only want Router C to have redundant links to the core, and not let the core transit an access router to reach another core router.

The problem can be solved or avoided by configuring an access list that permits only networks connected to Router C. The access list would be applied outbound to the interfaces connecting Routers A and B with the `distribute-list` command. The command is issued from within the routing protocol configuration mode.

Distribute lists can solve problems as well as cause problems. If the downstream routers are configured to learn their default gateway dynamically, the router must have the default network in the route table. If the route is not present, the router will lose the gateway of last resort. When a distribute list is applied, you must verify that it allows route advertisement of the default network, as well as any other crucial routes.

Route Maps

Route maps are used to manipulate routing. They are small scripts that can contain multiple instances and multiple conditions for each instance. Route maps are somewhat like access lists if you specify that the packet must match an access list. In addition to the capability of permitting or denying the packet, you can define what is done before the packet is forwarded.

Route maps can be used to set metrics for route updates, set a command to its default value, and so on. Table 6.11 gives a list of what a route map can do.

TABLE 6.11 Route Map Configuration Commands

Command	Description
default	Sets a command to its defaults.
exit	Exits from route-map configuration mode.
help	Describes the interactive help system.
match	Matches values from routing table.
no	Negates a command or sets its defaults.
set	Sets values in destination routing protocol.

Here is a sample route map:

```
route-map test permit 10
 match ip address 1
 set metric-type type-2
!
route-map test permit 20
 match ip address 2
 set metric-type type-1
!
route-map test permit 30
 set metric 100
```

The router runs through this route map, just as it runs through an access list. The only difference is that there are commands that the router performs instead of simply forwarding or dropping the packet. In this example, any packet matching the addresses listed in the IP access list 1 has its metric set as an OSPF type-2 metric. Any packet matching the addresses specified in access list 2 has its OSPF metric set to type-1. The final instance of the route map "test" is to set the metric of the route update to 100.

Real World Scenario

Managing Access Lists and Route Maps

In the previous few sections, access lists and route maps were used to assist in route control. As is the case with many items, managing these items in a smaller environment is not a problem. However, as the environment gets larger and more components are added, an effective management plan can save administrative overhead and potentially eliminate some problems before they occur. The first item that needs attention in this plan is naming.

Whenever possible, use named access lists. Some commands, such as `snmp-server community` and `access-class`, accept only numbered lists; however, in most instances you can use the named lists. By using named lists, you will be able to easily tell the use of the access list as well as, potentially, the direction it is applied.

When naming your access lists and route maps, be sure to use descriptive names. Also, if the access list will be used to filter traffic on an interface, indicate whether the list will be applied inbound or outbound on the interface in the name of the list. If they are to be used in a route map, name the route map and access list similarly. All of the above naming suggestions will allow for easier correlation during troubleshooting. As the named access list and route map are case sensitive, it is a good practice to use either all capital or all lowercase letters. In this manner, it is easier to spot whether a letter is out of place.

For example, if your naming standard was to use all capital letters for named access lists, the access list that would be applied inbound on the interface connecting to the engineering department could be ENGINEERING-DEPT-IN.

If you are running a code level above 12.0(2)T, you can also use remarks to assist in documenting what a particular access list line is used for. Examples of the remark command for both named and numbered lists are given below:

Numbered List:

```
access-list 100 remark Do not allow Sales Dept subnet to telnet out
access-list 100 deny tcp 10.30.30.0 0.0.0.255 any eq telnet
```

Named List:

```
ip access-list extended SALES-DEPT-IN
  remark Do not allow Sales Dept subnet to telnet out
  deny tcp 10.30.30.0 0.0.0.255 any eq telnet
```

Finally, if the same access list or route map is used on multiple routers, be sure to name them the same. This will avoid confusion and allow for easier documentation and updating. For example, if you have a standard numbered access list that is used to limit SNMP read-only traffic on the router, always use the same number on every router. By using these simple procedures, life with access lists and route maps will be that much more bearable.

TCP/IP Symptoms and Problems: Summary Sheet

Table 6.12 lists several common TCP/IP symptoms and their probable causes.

TABLE 6.12 TCP/IP Symptoms and Causes

Symptom	Problems
Local host cannot communicate with a remote host	(a) DNS not working properly (b) no route to remote host (c) missing default gateway (d) administrative denial (access lists)
Certain applications won't work properly	(a) administrative denial (access lists) (b) network not configured to handle the application
Booting failures	(a) BootP server did not have an entry for the MAC address (b) missing IP helper-address (c) access lists (d) change in the NIC or MAC address (e) duplicate IP address (f) improper IP configuration

TABLE 6.12   TCP/IP Symptoms and Causes *(continued)*

Symptom	Problems
Can't ping a remote station	(a) access lists (b) no route to host (c) no default gateway set (d) remote host down
Missing routes	(a) improper routing protocol configuration (b) distribute lists (c) passive interface (doesn't receive updates) (d) neighbor not advertising routes (e) protocol version mismatch (f) neighbor relation not established
Adjacencies not forming	(a) improper routing protocol configuration (b) improper IP configuration (c) misconfigured network or neighbor statements (d) mismatched Hello timers (e) mismatched area ID
High CPU utilization	(a) several routing updates due to instabilities (b) debug wasn't turned off (c) a process gone amok
Route stuck in active mode	(a) misconfigured timers (b) hardware problems (c) unstable link

TCP/IP Symptoms and Action Plans: Summary Sheet

Table 6.13 contains action plans for each of the problems outlined in Table 6.12.

T A B L E   6 . 1 3   Action Plans for Common TCP/IP Problems

Problem	Action Plan
DNS not working properly	Check the DNS configuration on host and DNS server. May use the nslookup utility to verify functionality of the DNS server.
No route to remote host	This can be caused by several different things: 1. Check the default gateway using the `ipconfig /all` or `winipcfg` command if you are on a Windows machine. 2. Using the `show ip route` command, check to see whether the router has a route. 3. If the router doesn't have a route, use the `show ip route` command to see whether a gateway of last resort is set. 4. If there is a gateway, check the next hop in the path toward the destination. If there is not a gateway, fix the problem or investigate why the router does not have a route.
Access lists	If you isolate the problem to an access list, you need to analyze the list, rewrite it correctly, and then apply the new access list.
Network not configured to handle the application	When applications use NetBIOS, NetBEUI, IPX, or other non-IP applications, verify that the routers involved are configured to properly handle them by using transparent bridging, SRB, tunneling, and so on.
Booting failures	1. Check the DHCP or BootP server, and verify that it has an entry for the MAC address of the problem station. 2. Use `debug ip udp` to verify that packets are being received from the host.

TABLE 6.13 Action Plans for Common TCP/IP Problems *(continued)*

Problem	Action Plan
	3. Verify that the helper addresses are correctly configured.
	4. Check for access lists that might be denying the packets.
	5. Make the necessary changes.
Missing routes	1. Look on the first router to see what routes are being learned. Issue the show ip route command.
	2. Depending on the routing protocol, verify that adjacencies have been formed with neighboring routers.
	3. Using the show running-config command, look at the router's configuration and verify that the routing protocol has the proper network or neighbor statements.
	4. When troubleshooting OSPF, verify that the wildcard mask permits the correct routes.
	5. Check the distribute lists that are applied to the interfaces. Analyze the inbound filters.
	6. Verify that both neighbors have the correct IP configuration.
	7. Verify the metric if routes are being redistributed.
	8. Verify that the routes are being redistributed properly.

TABLE 6.13 Action Plans for Common TCP/IP Problems *(continued)*

Problem	Action Plan
Adjacencies not forming	1. Perform a show ip <protocol> neighbors command to list the adjacencies that have formed.
	2. Look at the protocol configuration to confirm which adjacencies have not formed.
	3. Check the network statements in the protocol configuration.
	4. Show the ip <protocol> interface to obtain interface-specific information such as Hello timers.
	5. Once you have isolated the problem, make the necessary changes.

Summary

Before the advent of the routing protocol, the only way available to get packets from point A to point B was to use static routes. As the size of internetworks grew, it became impractical to keep adding new routes manually. Therefore, engineers began creating and using dynamic routing protocols. One of the first of these, RIP, provided dynamic updates as well as automatic failover in the event of a failure. However, it did not have many of the other features common in routing protocols today. As new routing protocols were created, more features and capabilities were added. With each generation, engineers gained more flexibility in determining how packets were routed through the network.

Today, there are a number of protocols that can be used to route TCP/IP traffic. These include the ones looked at in this chapter—RIP, IGRP, EIGRP, OSPF, and BGP. Each of these protocols has its own strengths and weaknesses and is best suited for particular environments. However, problems can arise when one routing domain must redistribute its routes into another. This redistribution can cause suboptimal routing or routing loops.

To prevent these issues, special steps should be taken at the redistribution points. Specifically, distribution lists, prefix lists, and/or route maps should be used. These tools allow for the filtering of the routes that are being redistributed as well as the filtering of the routes that are sent to or received from a neighbor. In addition to the distribution lists, prefix lists and/or route maps, engineers also have the ability to use a wide array of show and debug commands to determine exactly what a routing protocol is doing. These commands vary in granularity. Some show information about the general routing characteristics on a router, while others show detailed information about a singular route learned from a particular protocol. By using these commands together, any size or type of routing problem can be effectively troubleshot.

Exam Essentials

Know the concept of the default gateway and how it is used. The default gateway can be either dynamically learned or statically defined. In either case, the default gateway is used as the destination path for any packet for which there is no specific route in the routing table.

Know the difference between static and dynamic routing. Static routing allows the administrator to define routes on a router-by-router basis. However, the cost of this flexibility is a high amount of overhead any time there is a change in the network. Dynamic routing, using one of the routing protocols mentioned in this chapter, automatically distributes routing tables to all participating routers. Dynamic routing also allows automatic updates to all routers when there is a change in the network.

Know the routing protocols and the show and debug commands that they can use. The routing protocols covered in this chapter are RIP, IGRP, EIGRP, OSPF, and BGP. Be sure to review the tables showing the show and debug commands available for each protocol.

Know the issues surrounding the redistribution of one routing protocol into another. Redistribution if not done properly can cause routing loops. Special care needs to be taken when bidirectional redistribution takes place. In addition to routing loops, using multiple routing protocols with different administrative distances can cause suboptimal routing.

Know how to use distribution lists, prefix lists, and route maps to filter routing information.   Distribute lists, prefix lists, and route maps can be used to filter and manipulate routing updates in different ways. Though all three are similar in function, distribute lists are really nothing more than access lists that are applied to routing updates. Prefix lists add the ability to filter based on the address as well as the subnet mask of the route. Finally, route maps allow for the manipulation as well as the filtering of routing updates.

Commands Used in This Chapter

The following list contains a summary of all the commands used in this chapter.

Commands	Descriptions
debug ip bgp *<ipaddress>* updates	Debugs BGP update packets from the neighbor specified in the command.
debug ip bgp dampening	Debugs neighbor-dampening activities for BGP.
debug ip bgp events	Debugs major BGP events.
debug ip bgp keepalives	Debugs BGP keepalive packets.
debug ip bgp updates	Debugs BGP update packets from all neighbors.
debug ip eigrp	Causes a general debug to be performed on all EIGRP.
debug ip eigrp *<AS number>*	Debugs EIGRP for the specified AS.
debug ip eigrp neighbor	Debugs the transactions and exchanges among EIGRP neighbors.
debug ip eigrp notifications	Provides detailed information about neighbor notifications.
debug ip eigrp summary	Provides summarized information during a debug.
debug ip igrp events	Provides information regarding IGRP events (protocol-related).

Commands	Descriptions
`debug ip igrp transactions`	Provides more detailed information regarding IGRP events (protocol-related).
`debug ip ospf adj`	Provides debug information about events concerning adjacency relationships with other OSPF routers.
`debug ip ospf events`	Provides debug information for all OSPF events.
`debug ip ospf flood`	Provides information about OSPF flooding. (Flooding is the way that OSPF router sends updates.) It broadcasts a change in its route table and all other members of the OSPF area receive the update.
`debug ip ospf lsa-generation`	Gives detailed information regarding the generation of LSA messages.
`debug ip ospf packet`	Gives detailed information regarding OSPF packets.
`debug ip ospf retransmission`	When OSPF has to retransmit information, this command triggers a retransmission event that debug captures and echoes to the console.
`debug ip ospf spf`	Provides debug information for all SPF transactions. By enabling SPF debugging, OSPF events debugging is also turned on.
`debug ip ospf tree`	Provides information for the OSPF database tree.
`debug ip rip`	Provides you with all possible RIP protocol information.
`debug ip rip events`	Provides output regarding RIP protocol events.
`default-metric`	Sets the metric value used when redistributing one routing protocol into another.
`show ip bgp`	Shows information about BGP learned routes, including indicating which ones will be in the routing table.

Commands	Descriptions
`show ip bgp neighbors`	Shows information on BGP neighbors.
`show ip bgp neighbors <ipaddress> advertised-routes`	Shows all routes being advertised to a particular neighbor.
`show ip bgp neighbors <ipaddress> received-routes`	Shows all routes being received from a particular neighbor.
`show ip bgp peer-group`	Shows information about BGP peer groups.
`show ip bgp summary`	Shows a summary of all BGP connections.
`show ip eigrp events`	Displays a log of the most recent EIGRP protocol events. This information includes the insertion and removal of routes from the route table, updates, and neighbor status.
`show ip eigrp interfaces`	Displays EIGRP peer information for that interface.
`show ip eigrp neighbors`	Displays all EIGRP neighbors, along with summary information about each neighbor.
`show ip eigrp topology`	Displays the contents of the EIGRP topology table.
`show ip eigrp traffic`	Displays a summary of EIGRP routing statistics, such as the number of Hellos and routing updates.
`show ip interface`	Displays the interface's status as well as the IP configuration and settings for the interface.
`show ip ospf`	Displays information for OSPF.
`show ip ospf <process-id>`	Displays information relevant to the specified process ID.
`show ip ospf border-routers`	Displays the routers that join different areas, or border routers.
`show ip ospf database`	Provides an OSPF database summary.
`show ip ospf interface`	Displays OSPF information on a interface.

Commands	Descriptions
`show ip ospf neighbor`	Displays OSPF neighbor information.
`show ip ospf request-list`	Displays link-state request list.
`show ip ospf retransmission list`	Displays link-state retransmission list.
`show ip ospf summary-address`	Displays summary-address redistribution information.
`show ip ospf virtual-links`	Displays virtual link information.
`show ip protocols`	Provides information about the IP routing protocols that run on the router.
`show ip route`	Displays the contents of the IP route table as well as the default gateway for the router.
`show ip route bgp`	Displays the BGP route table.
`show ip route eigrp`	Displays the EIGRP routes.
`show ip route igrp`	Displays IGRP routes only.
`show ip route ospf`	Displays OSPF routes.
`show ip route rip`	Displays the RIP route table.

Key Terms

Before you take the exam, be certain you are familiar with the following terms:

autonomous system boundary router (ASBR)

Open Shortest Path First (OSPF)

Border Gateway Protocol (BGP)

prefix list

distribute lists

route maps

Enhanced IGRP (EIGRP)

Routing Information Protocol (RIP)

Interior Gateway Routing Protocol (IGRP)

Review Questions

1. Choose four common IP show commands.

   A. `show ip route`

   B. `show ip interface`

   C. `show running-config`

   D. `show ip access-lists`

   E. `show ip default-gateway`

   F. `show ip mrm`

2. What is the function of a default gateway?

   A. It is a default next hop if the router or host does not know a route to the destination.

   B. It is used to provide the default network.

   C. It provides the method of returning network management information to a router.

   D. None of the above.

3. What are the methods of setting the gateway of last resort on a Cisco router? (Choose two.)

   A. Configure `ip default-route`

   B. Configure `ip default neighbor`

   C. Configure a static route

   D. Configure an IP default-network

4. Match each command with its corresponding output. The output choices are as follows: (1) Displays IP; (2) Displays the running configuration; (3) Displays the RIP route table; (4) Displays the IP route table.

   A. `show ip route rip`

   B. `show ip route`

   C. `show ip interface`

   D. `show running-config`

5. Match each command with its corresponding output. The output choices are as follows: (1) Displays IGRP routes only; (2) Displays the entire route table; (3) Displays the current configuration.

   A. `show running-config`

   B. `show ip route igrp`

   C. `show ip route`

6. Match each command with its corresponding output. The output choices are as follows: (1) Displays EIGRP peer information for that interface; (2) Displays a summary of EIGRP routing statistics, such as the number of Hellos and routing updates; (3) Displays the contents of the EIGRP topology table; (4) Displays the EIGRP routes; (5) Displays a log of most recent EIGRP protocol events (including the insertion and removal of routes from the route table, updates, and neighbor status); (6) Displays all EIGRP neighbors, along with summary information about each neighbor.

   A. `show ip route eigrp`

   B. `show ip eigrp interfaces`

   C. `show ip eigrp neighbors`

   D. `show ip eigrp topology`

   E. `show ip eigrp traffic`

   F. `show ip eigrp events`

7. Match each command with its corresponding output. The output choices are as follows: (1) Displays OSPF routes; (2) Displays the routers that join different areas or border routers; (3) Displays OSPF neighbor information; (4) Displays summary-address redistribution information; (5) Displays information for OSPF; (6) Displays process ID number that displays information relevant to the specified process ID; (7) Displays link-state request list; (8) Displays link-state retransmission list; (9) Provides an OSPF database summary; (10) Displays virtual link information; (11) Displays OSPF information on an interface.

A. `show ip route ospf`

B. `show ip ospf`

C. `show ip ospf <process-id>`

D. `show ip ospf border-routers`

E. `show ip ospf database`

F. `show ip ospf interface`

G. `show ip ospf neighbor`

H. `show ip ospf request-list`

I. `show ip ospf retransmission list`

J. `show ip ospf summary-address`

K. `show ip ospf virtual-links`

8. Where are distribute lists applied?

A. Directly to the interface

B. To the interface via the routing protocol

C. To the routing protocol

D. None of the above

9. What command(s) is/are used to see the contents of a route map? (Choose all that apply.)

A. `show running-config`

B. `show ip route-map`

C. `show route-map`

D. `show ip interface`

10. What is the difference between a route map and an access list?

A. There is no difference.

B. Access lists have greater impact on the router's CPU.

C. The route map allows actions other than forwarding or dropping the packet.

D. None of the above.

11. Why should metrics be set properly when redistributing routing protocols?

   A. To avoid confusion.

   B. So the protocol receiving the injected routes can propagate the correct information.

   C. Routing will not work without them.

   D. None of the above.

12. You are doing bidirectional redistribution of routes between EIGRP and OSPF. All of the EIGRP routes are showing up in OSPF; however, none of the OSPF routes are showing up in EIGRP. What are the possible problems? (Choose all that apply.)

   A. Distribute lists configured incorrectly.

   B. Route-maps set up incorrectly.

   C. Physical connectivity issue.

   D. Router IOS levels do not match.

   E. Default metric not configured for EIGRP.

   F. OSPF and EIGRP have different AS numbers.

13. What are the administrative distances for an eBGP and iBGP route by default?

   A. 90 for eBGP and 170 for iBGP

   B. 200 for eBGP and 20 for iBGP

   C. 20 for both

   D. 20 for eBGP and 200 for iBGP

   E. 170 for eBGP and 90 for iBGP

   F. 90 for both

14. What are the administrative distances for an internal and external EIGRP route default?

    A. 90 for internal and 170 for external

    B. 90 for both

    C. 170 for internal 90 for external

    D. 70 for internal 190 for external

    E. 190 for internal 70 for external

    F. 70 for both

15. What are the administrative distances for RIP1 and a RIP2 route by default?

    A. 120 for RIP1 110 for RIP2

    B. 110 for RIP1 120 for RIP2

    C. 120 for both

    D. 110 for both

    E. 15 for both

    F. 16 for both

16. Match each command with its corresponding output. The output choices are as follows: (1) Displays BGP routes; (2) Shows information on BGP neighbors; (3) Shows all routes being received from a particular neighbor; (4) Shows all routes being advertised to a particular neighbor; (5) Shows information about BGP learned routes including indicating which ones will be in the routing table; (6) Shows a summary of all BGP connections; (7) Shows information about BGP peer groups.

    A. `show ip bgp`

    B. `show ip bgp neighbors`

    C. `show ip BGP neighbors <ipaddress> advertised-routes`

    D. `show ip BGP neighbors <ipaddress> received-routes`

    E. `show ip bgp peer-group`

    F. `show ip bgp summary`

    G. `show ip route bgp`

17. You want to change the AS path information of a BGP route you learn from an eBGP neighbor. What command type will be used in the BGP configuration to accomplish this?

   A. Route map

   B. Prefix list

   C. Distribute list

   D. BGP AS list

   E. Access list

18. You issue a show IP route command and receive the following output:

   B 10.20.20.0/24 [20/0] via 10.30.30.1, 3w0d

   What does the 20 in [20/0] mean?

   A. The next hello will be sent in 20 seconds.

   B. The metric of this route is 20.

   C. There are 20 hops to the destination network.

   D. The administrative distance of this route is 20.

19. You issue a show IP route command and receive the following output:

   D EX 172.16.38.200/30
        [170/2176512] via 172.16.131.82, 23:40:27,
        ATM6/0/0.3114

   What does the EX mean?

   A. The route is a candidate default route.

   B. This is an external route.

   C. The route is in holddown.

   D. The route is being redistributed into BGP.

20. You issue a show IP route command and receive the following output:

   S*   0.0.0.0/0 [1/0] via 172.16.50.2

   What does the * mean?

   A. The route is a candidate default route.

   B. This is an external route.

   C. The static route is pointed to a destination that does not exist.

   D. The route redistributed.

Answers to Review Questions

1. A, B, C, D. `show ip default-gateway` is not a valid command, and `show ip mrm` is only used when working with multicast issues.

2. A. The default gateway indicates the next hop for packets with no route to the destination address.

3. C, D. These are the valid methods, though not stated here in the exact syntax. The first two answers are invalid as to both method and syntax.

4. A (3), B (4), C (1), D (2). IP-related information for an interface is given by the `show ip interface` command.

5. A (3), B (1), C (2). The current configuration is also known as the running configuration.

6. A (4), B (1), C (6), D (3), E (2), F (5). These are all EIGRP-related commands. They can be verified by logging onto the router and experimenting with the output of each of these commands.

7. A (1), B (5), C (6), D (2), E (9), F (11), G (3), H (7), I (8), J (4), K (10). These are all OSPF-related commands and can be verified by logging onto a router and experimenting with the output of each of these commands.

8. B. The list must be applied to an interface from within the routing protocol.

9. A, C. Route maps are not IP specific.

10. C. Route maps use access lists to match a packet. After a match is made, many different actions may be taken.

11. B. Different protocols do not share the same metric values. A translation has to occur for the injected routes to be understood by the new protocol. This is done via setting default metrics.

12. A, B, E. A and B should be obvious, but E is not as obvious. If a default metric is not configured, the redistribution will not occur.

13. D. Because BGP is an EGP, it gives a better administrative distance for external routes.

14. A. As an IGP, EIGRP prefers internal routes of those learned from another protocol.

15. C.   Though there are differences between RIP version 1 and 2, administrative distance is not one of them.

16. A (5), B (2), C (4), D (3), E (7), F (6), G (1).   These are all BGP-related commands and can be verified by logging onto a router and experimenting with the output of each of these commands.

17. A.   In the BGP configuration, a route map will be specified. The route map will most likely use an access list or prefix list to define the traffic that will be affected, but these will not show up in the BGP configuration.

18. D.   The first number in the bracket is the administrative distance the second is the metric.

19. B.   The EX indicates that it is an external route in EIGRP. You can also tell this by looking at the metric of the route, which is 170.

20. A.   In addition, notice that the administrative distance of a static route is 1.

Chapter

7

Troubleshooting Serial Line and Frame Relay Connectivity

TOPICS COVERED IN THIS CHAPTER INCLUDE:

✓ Use Cisco IOS commands and problem isolation techniques to identify the symptoms of common WAN and Frame Relay problems.

Many of the commands that are available to troubleshoot serial and Frame Relay problems are similar. This chapter will first discuss topics relating to troubleshooting serial lines as well as X.25 lines. After those topics have been covered in detail, the show and debug commands relating to Frame Relay will be discussed.

Troubleshooting summaries will be provided at the end of each section. These summaries will be valuable as quick-reference guides when isolating and diagnosing serial line and Frame Relay problems.

Troubleshooting Serial Lines

There are numerous commands available to aid in troubleshooting serial lines. Some of them are show commands; others are debug commands. Here is a list of the commands that will be covered in this section:

- `clear counters serial`
- `show interface serial`
- `show controllers serial`
- `show buffers`
- `debug serial interface`
- `debug serial packet`

An integral part of serial connections is the hardware involved. Look at Figure 7.1. In this graphic, you see Router A connected to a channel service unit/digital service unit (CSU/DSU), through a serial cable that is connected to another CSU/DSU, and then connected to Router B.

FIGURE 7.1 Serial line setup

HDLC Encapsulation

High-level Data Link Control (HDLC) is an encapsulation method used by serial links. HDLC provides a 32-bit checksum and three different transfer modes: normal, asynchronous response, and asynchronous balanced.

HDLC is used by default on Cisco serial interfaces. The first important point of troubleshooting serial line problems is to verify that both sides of the link are using the same encapsulation types. Here is a look at a serial interface from a Cisco 2501. Notice that the encapsulation type is HDLC:

```
Router_A>show interface serial0
Serial0 is administratively down, line protocol is down
  Hardware is HD64570
  Internet address is 172.16.20.6/30
  MTU 1500 bytes, BW 1544 Kbit, DLY 20000 usec, rely 255/
  255, load 1/255
  Encapsulation HDLC, loopback not set, keepalive set (10
  sec)
  Last input never, output never, output hang never
  Last clearing of "show interface" counters never
  Input queue: 0/75/0 (size/max/drops); Total output
  drops: 0
  Queueing strategy: weighted fair
  Output queue: 0/1000/64/0 (size/max total/threshold/
drops)
     Conversations  0/0/256 (active/max active/max total)
     Reserved Conversations 0/0 (allocated/max allocated)
```

```
5 minute input rate 0 bits/sec, 0 packets/sec
5 minute output rate 0 bits/sec, 0 packets/sec
   0 packets input, 0 bytes, 0 no buffer
   Received 0 broadcasts, 0 runts, 0 giants, 0 throttles
   0 input errors, 0 CRC, 0 frame, 0 overrun, 0 ignored,
   0 abort
   0 packets output, 0 bytes, 0 underruns
   0 output errors, 0 collisions, 1 interface resets
   0 output buffer failures, 0 output buffers swapped
   out
   0 carrier transitions
   DCD=down  DSR=down  DTR=down  RTS=down  CTS=down
Router_A>
```

Other encapsulations may be used on serial interfaces, but HDLC is used for synchronous data link control.

show interface serial Command

The show interface serial commands provide you with a great deal of information to help you when you troubleshoot serial line and other serial interface–related problems, such as Frame Relay. However, in order to get correct information, you should first clear the counters for the interface of interest.

Before you do so, look at the output of the show interface serial 1 command:

```
Router_A>show interface serial 1
Serial1 is up, line protocol is up
  Hardware is HD64570
  Internet address is 172.16.30.5/30
  MTU 1500 bytes, BW 1544 Kbit, DLY 20000 usec, rely 255/
    255, load 1/255
  Encapsulation HDLC, loopback not set, keepalive set (10
    sec)
  Last input 00:00:08, output 00:00:07, output hang never
  Last clearing of "show interface" counters never
  Input queue: 0/75/0 (size/max/drops);
Total output drops: 0
```

```
Queueing strategy: weighted fair
Output queue: 0/1000/64/0 (size/max total/threshold/
  drops)
    Conversations  0/1/256 (active/max active/max total)
    Reserved Conversations 0/0 (allocated/max allocated)
5 minute input rate 0 bits/sec, 0 packets/sec
5 minute output rate 0 bits/sec, 0 packets/sec
    1307 packets input, 85380 bytes, 0 no buffer
    Received 695 broadcasts, 0 runts, 0 giants, 0
        throttles
    0 input errors, 0 CRC, 0 frame, 0 overrun, 0 ignored,
    0 abort
    1308 packets output, 85652 bytes, 0 underruns
    0 output errors, 0 collisions, 116 interface resets
    0 output buffer failures, 0 output buffers swapped
    out
    238 carrier transitions
    DCD=up  DSR=up  DTR=up  RTS=up  CTS=up
Router_A>
```

The output tells you that the interface is up and the line protocol is also up. The information contained in the show interface serial command will be discussed in more detail in just a moment. For now, it is important to recognize that many of the counters have elevated numbers. Also, notice that the seventh line of the output declares that the counters were never cleared.

You cannot effectively troubleshoot if you do not have accurate data returned through the many diagnostic commands. One way to ensure that the data you are analyzing is accurate and directly applies to the problem at hand is to perform the clear counters serial <*number*> command, which resets the interface counters to zero. This ensures that the data retrieved from the interface command is representative of what is happening at that moment on the network.

Here is how it is done and what the interface looks like after the command has been issued:

```
Router_A#clear counters serial 1
Clear "show interface" counters on this interface
    [confirm]
%CLEAR-5-COUNTERS: Clear counter on interface Serial1 by
    console
```

```
Router_A#show interface serial 1
Serial1 is up, line protocol is up
  Hardware is HD64570
  Internet address is 172.16.30.5/30
  MTU 1500 bytes, BW 1544 Kbit, DLY 20000 usec, rely 255/
    255, load 51/255
  Encapsulation HDLC, loopback not set,
  keepalive set (10  sec)
  Last input 00:00:00, output 00:00:00, output hang never
  Last clearing of "show interface" counters 00:28:48
  Input queue: 1/75/0 (size/max/drops);
Total output drops: 0
  Queueing strategy: weighted fair
  Output queue: 0/1000/64/0 (size/max total/threshold/
    drops)
     Conversations  0/2/256 (active/max active/max total)
     Reserved Conversations 0/0 (allocated/max allocated)
  5 minute input rate 321000 bits/sec, 48 packets/sec
  5 minute output rate 320000 bits/sec, 48 packets/sec
     12439 packets input, 13257786 bytes, 0 no buffer
     Received 202 broadcasts, 0 runts, 0 giants, 0
            throttles
     0 input errors, 0 CRC, 0 frame, 0 overrun, 0 ignored,
     0 abort
     12438 packets output, 13256434 bytes, 0 underruns
     0 output errors, 0 collisions, 0 interface resets
     0 output buffer failures, 0 output buffers swapped
     out
     0 carrier transitions
        DCD=up  DSR=up  DTR=up  RTS=up  CTS=up
Router_A#
```

Notice the seventh line of the output. It says that the counters were cleared 28 minutes before. After the counters are cleared, you can associate any new data with current network events. If you try to associate current network events with inaccurate data, you will never find the problem. In addition to the individual interface, executing the clear counters command without specifying an interface will clear all of the counters on the router.

Now we'll go through the available data provided by the `show interface serial` command. Refer to the output previously listed.

The first line provides information regarding the status of the interface and the line protocol:

`Serial1 is up, line protocol is up`

In this case, both are up and functional. If the interface is down, the line protocol must also be down.

Cabling problems, carrier problems, or hardware problems can all be reasons for a serial interface to report as down. These problems can be addressed by verifying proper cable connectivity, replacing hardware (including cables), and checking the CSU/DSU for carrier signal. If you cannot resolve the problem by using these techniques, you can and should contact the local carrier, who can verify the carrier service.

Another possibility for the interface status is that the interface is up but the line protocol is down. When this happens, it can be one or more of a variety of problems, as follows:

- Failed CSU/DSU

- Router interface problems

- Mismatched timing on CSU/DSU or carrier network

- Misconfigured interface

- Keepalive signals not received from remote router

- Carrier problem

You should verify that the local interface and the remote interface are properly configured. Loopback tests can be performed. These tests will be discussed in the CSU/DSU section of the chapter.

Continuing with the description of the output of the `show interface serial` command, you see that the second line of the output displays the hardware type of the interface:

`Hardware is HD64570`

The third line shows the Layer 3 IP address with the associated subnet mask:

`Internet address is 172.16.30.5/30`

Line 4 contains all of the information needed to create a route metric for the interface. The data includes MTU, bandwidth, delay, reliability, and load.

```
MTU 1500 bytes, BW 1544 Kbit, DLY 20000 usec, rely 255/
    255, load 51/255
```

Line 5 indicates the type of encapsulation that is being used on the line, as well as loopback and keepalive information:

```
Encapsulation HDLC, loopback not set, keepalive set (10
    sec)
```

The sixth line displays the last time the interface saw any traffic:

```
Last input 00:00:00, output 00:00:00, output hang never
```

Again, the seventh line shows the time that transpired since the last time the interface counters were cleared:

```
Last clearing of "show interface" counters 00:28:48
```

Lines 8 through 12 contain information regarding the buffers on the interface:

```
Input queue: 1/75/0 (size/max/drops);
Total output drops: 0
  Queueing strategy: weighted fair
  Output queue: 0/1000/64/0 (size/max total/threshold/
  drops)
     Conversations  0/2/256 (active/max active/max total)
     Reserved Conversations 0/0 (allocated/max allocated)
```

Lines 13 and 14 display the five-minute average for input and output bits per second, and packets per second on the interface:

```
5 minute input rate 321000 bits/sec, 48 packets/sec
5 minute output rate 320000 bits/sec, 48 packets/sec
```

Beginning with line 15 and until line 17, the output displays interface input information. The first line is a counter that keeps track of the number of incoming packets on the interface. Because it is a counter, it will reach a maximum value and then reset. The next line displays information for broadcast, runt, giant, and throttled packets. The last line (line 17) displays any input, CRC, frame, overrun, ignored, or abort errors:

```
12439 packets input, 13257786 bytes, 0 no buffer
     Received 202 broadcasts, 0 runts, 0 giants,
     0 throttles
     0 input errors, 0 CRC, 0 frame, 0 overrun, 0 ignored,
     0 abort
```

The output interface statistics begin with line 18 and end on line 21. This data reflects the number of output packets, underruns, output errors, collisions, interface resets, output buffer failures, swapped output buffers, and carrier transitions:

```
12438 packets output, 13256434 bytes, 0 underruns
     0 output errors, 0 collisions, 0 interface resets
     0 output buffer failures,
     0 output buffers swapped out
     0 carrier transitions
```

Interface resets should be warning flags. If you see a large number of interface resets after clearing the counter, you should be concerned. Interface resets are caused by the following:

- Queued packets not sent for several seconds
- Hardware problems (for example, router interface, cable, or CSU/DSU)
- Mismatched clocking signals
- Looped interface
- Interface shut down
- Line protocol down and the interface resetting periodically

The next warning flag should be carrier transitions. This counter counts the number of times that the DCD (data carrier detect) signal changes state. If the carrier keeps fluctuating, you do not have a stable circuit. This is often a carrier problem, and the local carrier must be contacted.

The final line of the show interface serial command displays carrier-specific information:

```
DCD=up   DSR=up   DTR=up   RTS=up   CTS=up
```

show controllers Command

The show controllers command is used to display interface status and whether a cable is connected to the interface. Following are a couple of different outputs from the show controllers command.

The first output is from interface serial 0. There is no cable attached to the interface:

```
Router_A#show controllers serial 0
HD unit 0, idb = 0x94AEC, driver structure at 0x99870
buffer size 1524  HD unit 0, No cable, clockrate 4000000
```

```
cpb = 0x41, eda = 0x4940, cda = 0x4800
RX ring with 16 entries at 0x414800
.
.   {some output omitted}
.
TX ring with 2 entries at 0x415000
.
.   {some output omitted}
.
0 missed datagrams, 0 overruns
0 bad datagram encapsulations, 0 memory errors
0 transmitter underruns
0 residual bit errors

Router_A#
```

The second output is from interface serial 1, which does have a cable connected and is functioning properly:

```
Router_A#show controllers serial 1
HD unit 1, idb = 0x9D4E0, driver structure at 0xA2260
buffer size 1524  HD unit 1, V.35 DCE cable, clockrate
    4000000
cpb = 0x42, eda = 0x3104, cda = 0x3118
RX ring with 16 entries at 0x423000
.
.   {some output omitted}
.
TX ring with 2 entries at 0x423800
.
.   {some output omitted}
.
0 missed datagrams, 0 overruns
0 bad datagram encapsulations, 0 memory errors
0 transmitter underruns
0 residual bit errors

Router_A#
```

The basic information provided by this command is the interface status regarding missed datagrams, overruns, bad encapsulation, memory errors, underruns, and bit errors. In addition, it indicates the interface clock rate, as well as the cable type that is connected to the interface.

If you don't see a cable connected to the interface, verifying that a cable is properly connected is a good item to include in a troubleshooting action plan. If there are excessive errors on the interface, it can be faulty hardware.

show buffers Command

The show buffers command can be used to look at system buffer pools, but it also provides information regarding interface buffers. Look at the sample output from a 2514 router:

```
Router_B>show buffers
Buffer elements:
      500 in free list (500 max allowed)
      52587626 hits, 0 misses, 0 created

Public buffer pools:
Small buffers, 104 bytes (total 50, permanent 50):
      50 in free list (20 min, 150 max allowed)
      7709985 hits, 0 misses, 0 trims, 0 created
      0 failures (0 no memory)
Middle buffers, 600 bytes (total 25, permanent 25):
      24 in free list (10 min, 150 max allowed)
      2045756 hits, 0 misses, 0 trims, 0 created
      0 failures (0 no memory)
Big buffers, 1524 bytes (total 50, permanent 50):
      50 in free list (5 min, 150 max allowed)
      2541768 hits, 774 misses, 217 trims, 217 created
      24 failures (0 no memory)
VeryBig buffers, 4520 bytes (total 10, permanent 10):
      10 in free list (0 min, 100 max allowed)
      52464 hits, 0 misses, 0 trims, 0 created
      0 failures (0 no memory)
Large buffers, 5024 bytes (total 0, permanent 0):
      0 in free list (0 min, 10 max allowed)
```

```
        0 hits, 0 misses, 0 trims, 0 created
        0 failures (0 no memory)
Huge buffers, 18024 bytes (total 0, permanent 0):
        0 in free list (0 min, 4 max allowed)
        0 hits, 0 misses, 0 trims, 0 created
        0 failures (0 no memory)

Interface buffer pools:
Ethernet0 buffers, 1524 bytes (total 32, permanent 32):
        5 in free list (0 min, 32 max allowed)
        255684 hits, 64696 fallbacks
        8 max cache size, 5 in cache
Ethernet1 buffers, 1524 bytes (total 32, permanent 32):
        0 in free list (0 min, 32 max allowed)
        300993 hits, 1024384 fallbacks
        8 max cache size, 6 in cache
Serial0 buffers, 1524 bytes (total 32, permanent 32):
        7 in free list (0 min, 32 max allowed)
        25 hits, 0 fallbacks
        8 max cache size, 8 in cache
Serial1 buffers, 1524 bytes (total 32, permanent 32):
        7 in free list (0 min, 32 max allowed)
        25 hits, 0 fallbacks
        8 max cache size, 8 in cache
```

Notice that the interface buffers are listed at the end of the output. This information can be useful to troubleshoot serial interface problems. It is important to look at the number of free buffers. These numbers indicate the memory that is available on the interface for buffering incoming and outgoing packets.

debug serial interface Command

As always with debug tools, you must exercise caution. When executing a serial debug or Frame Relay debug, the router can generate large amounts of data that can encumber the router. Make sure that the specific command is used when possible. debug can be used in conjunction with access lists to focus the application of the debug tool.

The debug of a serial interface displays HDLC or Frame Relay communication messages. A sample follows that includes Frame Relay information. It is important to understand that the output of this command varies with the encapsulation type used on the interface:

```
Router_A#debug serial interface
Serial network interface debugging is on
Serial0(out): StEnq, myseq 135, yourseen 134, DTE up
Serial0(in): Status, myseq 135
Serial1(out): StEnq, myseq 2, yourseen 8, DTE up
Serial1(in): Status, myseq 2
Serial2(out): StEnq, myseq 247, yourseen 247, DTE up
Serial2(in): Status, myseq 247
Serial3(out): StEnq, myseq 30, yourseen 28, DTE up
Serial3(in): Status, myseq 30
Serial0(out): StEnq, myseq 136, yourseen 135, DTE up
Serial0(in): Status, myseq 136
Serial1(out): StEnq, myseq 3, yourseen 9, DTE up
Serial1(in): Status, myseq 3
Serial2(out): StEnq, myseq 248, yourseen 248, DTE up
Serial2(in): Status, myseq 248
Serial3(out): StEnq, myseq 31, yourseen 29, DTE up
Serial3(in): Status, myseq 31
Serial0(out): StEnq, myseq 137, yourseen 136, DTE up
Serial0(in): Status, myseq 137
Serial1(out): StEnq, myseq 4, yourseen 10, DTE up
Serial1(in): Status, myseq 4
Serial2(out): StEnq, myseq 249, yourseen 249, DTE up
Serial2(in): Status, myseq 249
Serial3(out): StEnq, myseq 32, yourseen 30, DTE up
Serial3(in): Status, myseq 32
```

This sample includes output from many interfaces. The boldface type is used to highlight interface serial 0. Here is the definition of what you see:

StEnq   An LMI (Local Management Interface) status inquiry sent from the router to the Frame Relay switch.

Status   Reply sent to the router from the Frame Relay switch.

myseq   The local keepalive number. The value is the sequence identifier.

yourseen   The keepalive sent by the other side of the serial connection.

DTE   The data-termination equipment status. In this example, it is up.

The in and out specify the directions that the packets are sent. The outbound packets are keepalives sent by the local side, whereas the inbound packets are the keepalives sent from the other end.

If the sequence numbers for a given interface don't increment, then there is probably a timing or line problem at one end or the other of the connection. The line will reset if two out of six consecutive keepalive packets fail to increment. Although the Layer 3 protocol considers the line protocol to be down, the Layer 2 protocol continues to send keepalive messages. Once the Layer 2 protocol achieves three consecutive sequences, the line protocol is brought back up.

Here is a sample of HDLC communication:

```
Router_A#debug serial interface
Serial network interface debugging is on
Serial0: HDLC myseq 172188, mineseen 172188*, yourseen
    172326, line up
Serial0: HDLC myseq 172189, mineseen 172189*, yourseen
    172327, line up
Serial0: HDLC myseq 172190, mineseen 172190*, yourseen
    172328, line up
Serial0: HDLC myseq 172191, mineseen 172191*, yourseen
    172329, line up
Router_A#
```

The field values are very similar to the field values in the Frame Relay output. Here are the field definitions:

myseq   The local keepalive number. The value is the sequence identifier.

yourseen   The keepalive sent by the other side of the serial connection.

mineseen   The value of the keepalive sent by the local interface seen by the remote side.

debug serial packet Command

The debug serial packet command is used to provide additional information regarding serial interfaces. According to information contained in CCO UniverCD, the debug serial packet only provides information for interfaces that use SMDS encapsulation.

A sample output is not shown here because the information included in the output is useful only when you have an understanding of the SMDS protocol, which has not been discussed in this book.

CSU/DSU Loopback Tests

Loopback tests aid in physically isolating serial line and Frame Relay problems. Four different loopback tests can be performed to troubleshoot the circuit. You can perform two of them, and the local provider has access to perform the other two. Here is a list of four loopback tests:

- Local loopback on the local CSU/DSU

- Local loopback on the remote CSU/DSU

- Remote loopback from the local NIU to the remote CSU/DSU

- Remote loopback from the remote NIU to the local CSU/DSU

Though it is possible to perform a subset of these loopback commands on certain interface types on a router, they are more commonly performed on the CSU/DSU. Therefore, it is the CSU/DSU variation of the loopbacks that is focused on in this chapter.

Look at Figure 7.2 to see how the tests are performed.

FIGURE 7.2 CSU/DSU loopback tests

The tests that you can perform are the two local loopback tests. You can perform these tests because you have access to the equipment. The local provider has to perform the remote loopback tests because it has access to the equipment within the cloud.

When using loopback tests for troubleshooting, you should follow these steps:

1. Perform the local loopback test for the local router (Router A in this example).

2. Verify the line status. This means to check for LMI status when using Frame Relay on the interface.

3. Perform the local loopback test for the remote router, Router B.

4. Verify the line status. This means to check for LMI status when using Frame Relay on the interface.

5. If you see LMI but cannot get remote connectivity, contact your local service provider, who can run the remote loopback tests.

Remember that LMI stands for Local Management Interface. When you see LMI up on a router interface during a loopback test, it means that the protocol is working locally but not necessarily working remotely. By putting a CSU/DSU into loopback, the signal is sent back to the interface, so the line protocol shows up. For end-to-end connectivity, both end sites must have LMI up status. In addition, all of the Frame Relay switches that participate in the permanent virtual circuit (PVC) must be working properly. Remote loopback tests confirm the functionality of the circuit.

 Real World Scenario

Troubleshooting Red, Yellow, and Blue

When troubleshooting a serial connection, many times you need the assistance of your local telephone company or carrier in order to resolve the problem. Though it is tempting to call and open a ticket with them at the first sign of trouble, I have found that in many cases you can assist them in finding the problem, or solve it yourself, with some testing of your own.

The first thing that I do when a circuit is down is to perform the loopback tests described above to ensure that my router, in-house wiring, and CSU/DSU are working correctly. Assuming that these items test correctly, I put a DS-1/DS-3 test on the circuit and look at the signal coming to and from the carrier. In most cases I will get either a red, yellow, or blue alarm coming from them.

If I get a red alarm on the signal from the carrier, this means that I am not receiving any signal on the link. I may or may not be transmitting information correctly. If I see a yellow alarm, this means the far end device is not receiving any information. However, since I am receiving the yellow alarm signal it is sending, I know that my receive path is fine, therefore the problem lies on my transmitting path somewhere between my current location and the destination device. Finally, a blue alarm is an all-ones signal. This usually is generated by one of the carrier's systems that needs to be reset or reconfigured.

With this information in hand, I then can open a trouble ticket with the carrier and help them isolate where to start looking for the problem, thus decreasing the time it takes to correct the problem.

Serial Line Summary

Several encapsulations and protocols may be used over serial lines. Because of this variety, many different problems can occur. It is also important to realize that the output of many show commands may differ, depending on the interface configuration.

To aid you in diagnosing and resolving serial line problems, this section includes two quick reference tables for your convenience.

Symptoms and Problems

Table 7.1 lists several common serial line conditions and their related possible problems.

TABLE 7.1   Serial Line Symptoms and Problems

Symptom or Condition	Associated Problem(s)
Interface is administratively down; line protocol is down	(a) The interface has been placed in shutdown via a configuration command. (b) Duplicate IP addresses are not allowed and one of the two interfaces with the same IP address will be shut down.

TABLE 7.1 Serial Line Symptoms and Problems *(continued)*

Symptom or Condition	Associated Problem(s)
Interface is down; line protocol is down	(a) Improper cabling. (b) No carrier signal from local provider. (c) Hardware failure (interface or CSU/DSU, cabling).
Interface is up; line protocol is down	(a) Misconfigured interface, local or remote. (b) Local provider problem. (c) Keepalive sequencing not incrementing. (d) Hardware failures (local or remote interfaces and CSU/DSU). (e) Noisy line. (f) Timing mismatches.
Interface is up; line protocol is up (looped)	(a) The circuit is in loopback.
Incrementing carrier transition counter	(a) Unstable signaling coming from the local provider. (b) Faulty cabling. (c) Failing hardware (for example, interface or CSU/DSU).
Incrementing inter-face resets	(a) Faulty cabling, causing the loss of the CD signal. (b) Hardware failure. (c) Line congestion.
Input drops, errors, CRC, and framing errors	(a) Line speed oversubscribes the router interface capacity. (b) Local provider problem. (c) Noisy line. (d) Faulty cabling. (e) Improper cabling. (f) Failing hardware.
Output drops	(a) The interface is capable of transmitting at higher than line speed.

Problems and Action Plans

Now that you have seen the list of symptoms with their problems, you need a quick reference for resolving the problems. Table 7.2 provides summary action plans for resolving the listed serial line problems.

TABLE 7.2 Action Plans for Common Serial Line Problems

Problem	Resolution Action Plan
Local provider problems	1. Check the CSU/DSU for a CD signal. Check for other signals, such as RX and TX, to see if the circuit is transmitting and receiving information.
	2. If you do not get a CD signal or have other problems, contact the local service provider to troubleshoot and fix the problem.
Improper or faulty cabling	1. Make sure that you are using the proper cable for the equipment being used.
	2. Use a breakout box to check the control leads.
	3. Swap faulty cables.
Misconfigured interface	1. View the interface configuration using the show running-config command.
	2. Make sure that the same encapsulation type is used at both ends of the circuit by using the show interface command.
Keepalive problems	1. Verify that keepalives are being sent. You can check this via the router configuration or by using the show interface command.
	2. If the configuration says that keepalives are being sent, you may want to enable debug serial interface for the interface.
	3. Verify that the sequence numbers are incrementing.

TABLE 7.2 Action Plans for Common Serial Line Problems *(continued)*

Problem	Resolution Action Plan
	4. If they don't increment, run loopback tests on the local and remote sites.
	5. If the sequences don't increment, even when the CSU/DSU is in loopback, you have a hardware problem.
	6. Replace faulty hardware.
Hardware failure	1. Replace the hardware.
Interface is in loop-back mode	1. Check the interface configuration.
	2. If there is a loopback entry in the interface configuration, remove it with the no form of the command.
	3. If the interface configuration is clean, check the CSU/DSU to see if it is placed in loopback.
	4. If it is, remove the CSU/DSU from loop-back mode.
	5. If the CSU/DSU is not in loopback mode, contact the local provider; it may have placed the circuit in loopback.
Interface is adminis-tratively down	1. Check the configuration. Verify that the IP address is not a duplicate.
	2. Enter the configuration mode and issue the no shutdown command within the interface.
Line speed is larger than the interface capacity	1. Reduce input queue size by using the hold-queue in command.
	2. Increase output queues on exiting interfaces.

TABLE 7.2   Action Plans for Common Serial Line Problems *(continued)*

Problem	Resolution Action Plan
Interface speed is larger than the line speed	1. Reduce broadcast traffic. 2. Increase output queue. 3. Implement queuing algorithms, if necessary.

Troubleshooting X.25

Troubleshooting X.25 is accomplished the same way as serial line and Frame Relay troubleshooting. The following sections will discuss the commands used to troubleshoot X.25. In addition to the commands, the output of the respective command will also be discussed.

show interface serial Commands

When a serial interface is configured to use X.25, the show interface serial command provides information specific to the X.25 protocol. Here is a sample of an X.25 interface:

```
Router_A#show interface serial 1
Serial1 is up, line protocol is up
  Hardware is HD64570
  Internet address is 172.16.30.5/30
  MTU 1500 bytes, BW 1544 Kbit, DLY 20000 usec, rely 255/
    255, load 51/255
  Encapsulation X25, loopback not set
LAPB DTE, state CONNECT, modulo 8, k 7, N1 12043, N2 10
T1 3000, interface outage (partial T3) 0, T4 0
VS 1, VR 1, Remote VR 1, Retransmissions 0
  IFRAMEs 1/1 RNRs 0/0 REJs 0/0 SABM/Es 1/0 FRMRs 0/0
    DISCs 0/0
X25 DTE, address 190118, state R1, modulo 8, timer 0
```

```
Defaults: cisco encapsulation, idle 0, nvc 1
Input/output window sizes 2/2, packet sizes 128/128
Timers: T20 180, T21 200, T22 180, T23 180, TH 0
Channels: Incoming-only none, Two-way 5-1024, Outgoing-
    only none
RESTARTs 1/1 CALLs 0+0/0+0/0+0 DIAGs 0/0
  Last input 00:00:00, output 00:00:00, output hang never
  Last clearing of "show interface" counters 00:28:48
  Input queue: 1/75/0 (size/max/drops);
  Total output drops: 0
  Queueing strategy: weighted fair
  Output queue: 0/1000/64/0 (size/max total/threshold/
  drops)
     Conversations  0/2/256 (active/max active/max total)
     Reserved Conversations 0/0 (allocated/max allocated)
  5 minute input rate 321000 bits/sec, 48 packets/sec
  5 minute output rate 320000 bits/sec, 48 packets/sec
     12439 packets input, 13257786 bytes, 0 no buffer
     Received 202 broadcasts, 0 runts, 0 giants,
     0 throttles
     0 input errors, 0 CRC, 0 frame, 0 overrun, 0 ignored,
     0 abort
     12438 packets output, 13256434 bytes, 0 underruns
     0 output errors, 0 collisions, 0 interface resets
     0 output buffer failures, 0 output buffers swapped
     out
     0 carrier transitions
     DCD=up  DSR=up  DTR=up  RTS=up  CTS=up
Router_A#
```

The output contains all of the relevant serial data, as well as all of the LAPB and X.25 information. Following are explanations of these new fields:

RNRs   Number of Receiver Not Ready events (LAPB data)

REJs   Number of rejects (LAPB data)

SABMs   Number of Set Asynchronous Balance Mode requests (LAPB data)

FRMRs   Number of protocol frame errors (LAPB data)

DISCs   Number of disconnects (LAPB data)

RESTARTs   Number of restarts (X.25 data)

For more detailed information about LAPB or X.25, the debug command must be used.

debug Commands

There are several debug commands associated with X.25. A few of them are debug x25 all, debug x25 events, debug x25 vc, debug x25 interface, and debug lapb. The two that will be discussed in this section are the debug x25 events and debug lapb.

debug x25 events

When the events option is used, the output does not contain any information regarding data or Receive Ready (RR) flow control packets. Calls and other data flow packets are not recorded because of the large amount of output they generate.

debug lapb

This tool can be used when X.25 interfaces experience frequent restarts and instability. X.25 relies on LAPB Layer 2 protocol for stable data links. If there are problems with the LAPB protocol, it propagates to the X.25 protocol and interface. The output from LAPB debugging contains information regarding all packets and traffic that use LAPB encapsulation.

Complete documentation regarding the output from the LAPB debug trace can be found within the documentation included in the UniverCD.

X.25 Link Summary

This section includes the quick reference guide for recognizing, diagnosing, isolating, and resolving X.25 problems.

Symptoms and Problems

Table 7.3 contains common X.25 symptoms and their corresponding problems.

TABLE 7.3 X.25 Symptoms and Problems

Symptom or Condition	Associated Problem(s)
X.25 connection failures	(a) Link is down
	(b) Faulty hardware
	(c) Incorrect or faulty wiring
	(d) Improper interface configuration
Excessive errors	(a) Faulty hardware
	(b) Incorrect or faulty wiring

Problems and Action Plans

Table 7.4 summarizes the action plans that are necessary to resolve the problems listed in Table 7.3. The table is meant only as an overall guideline for resolving X.25 problems.

TABLE 7.4 Action Plans for Common X.25 Problems

Problem	Resolution Action Plan
Link down	Follow steps for troubleshooting serial lines.
Faulty hardware or cabling	1. Check the interface status. Verify that the LAPB is in CONNECT state.
	2. If it is not in CONNECT state, use the debug LAPB command.
	3. If there is a definite problem, check the cabling and hardware. Replace equipment as needed.

TABLE 7.4 Action Plans for Common X.25 Problems *(continued)*

Problem	Resolution Action Plan
Misconfigured interfaces or protocol	1. Verify the current configuration by using the show running-config command.
	2. If needed, use debug LAPB to look for SABMs. If no SABMs are sent, change the debugging to debug x25 events.
	3. Watch for RESTART messages and also check the LAPB parameters on the interface.

Troubleshooting Frame Relay

Frame Relay is a popular WAN solution in many networks. Frame Relay supports PVCs and switched virtual circuits (SVCs). These virtual circuits are built by using DLCI numbers. A *Data-Link Connection Identifier (DLCI)* is used to identify the virtual circuits in a Frame Relay cloud. Figure 7.3 depicts a Frame Relay network. Notice the DLCI numbers assigned to the different interfaces throughout the network.

It is important to remember that the DLCI is only locally significant. The DLCI maps to Layer 3 IP addresses, as shown in Figure 7.3. The IP addresses given on the diagram suggest the PVCs that exist through the Frame Relay cloud.

When Frame Relay problems occur, you follow this troubleshooting checklist:

1. Check Layer 1, the Physical layer, for any cabling or interface problems.

2. Check the interface encapsulation.

3. Check the LMI type.

4. Verify the DLCI-to-IP address mapping.

5. Verify the Frame Relay PVCs.

6. Verify the Frame Relay LMI.

7. Verify the Frame Relay map.

8. Verify the loopback tests, as described in the "CSU/DSU Loopback Tests" section.

FIGURE 7.3 Frame Relay network

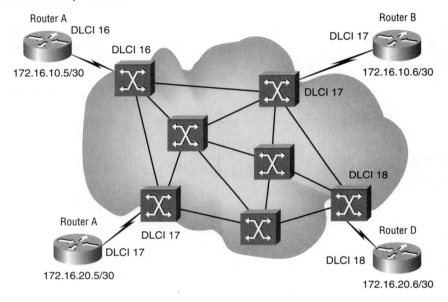

The following commands describe how to execute each of these steps.

Frame Relay *show* Commands

Here is a list of the show commands that will be covered in this section:

- show interface
- show frame-relay lmi
- show frame-relay pvc
- show frame-relay map

You probably noticed a term you didn't recognize. *LMI (Local Management Interface)* provides support for keepalive devices to verify data flow. You will see this term a great deal when dealing with Frame Relay troubleshooting.

show interface

The show interface command is used to provide information on serial lines. In addition to normal serial line information, Frame Relay information is included in the output if the interface is configured for Frame Relay.

Line-by-line detail has already been given for a normal serial interface. Therefore, only the fields relating to Frame Relay are listed. Here is a sample of a Frame Relay interface output:

```
Router_A#show interface serial0
Serial0 is up, line protocol is up
  Hardware is HD64570
  MTU 1500 bytes, BW 1544 Kbit, DLY 20000 usec, rely
    255/255, load 1/255
  Encapsulation FRAME-RELAY, loopback not set, keepalive
    set (10 sec)
  LMI enq sent  823406, LMI stat recvd 823403, LMI upd
    recvd 507, DTE LMI up
  LMI enq recvd 0, LMI stat sent  0, LMI upd sent  0
  LMI DLCI 1023  LMI type is CISCO  frame relay DTE
  Broadcast queue 0/64, broadcasts sent/dropped 0/0,
    interface broadcasts 36752578
  Last input 00:00:00, output 00:00:00, output hang never
  Last clearing of "show interface" counters never
  Input queue: 0/75/0 (size/max/drops); Total output
   drops: 0
  Queueing strategy: weighted fair
  Output queue: 0/64/0 (size/threshold/drops)
    Conversations  0/20 (active/max active)
    Reserved Conversations 0/0 (allocated/max allocated)
  5 minute input rate 5000 bits/sec, 6 packets/sec
  5 minute output rate 5000 bits/sec, 6 packets/sec
    134880248 packets input, 102288228 bytes, 0 no buffer
    Received 823910 broadcasts, 0 runts, 0 giants
    1 input errors, 1 CRC, 0 frame, 0 overrun, 0 ignored,
    1 abort
    136835759 packets output, 3397101778 bytes, 0
      underruns
    0 output errors, 0 collisions, 14 interface resets
```

```
        0 output buffer failures, 0 output buffers swapped
        out
        2 carrier transitions
        DCD=up  DSR=up  DTR=up  RTS=up  CTS=up
Router_A#show interface serial 0.2
Serial0.2 is up, line protocol is up
  Hardware is HD64570
  Internet address is 172.16.30.6/30
  MTU 1500 bytes, BW 1544 Kbit, DLY 20000 usec, rely 255/
    255, load 1/255
  Encapsulation FRAME-RELAY
Router_A#
```

Here are the relevant Frame Relay terms:

Encapsulation   Frame Relay encapsulation type used; either Cisco (default) or IETF.

LMI enq sent   Number of LMI enquiries sent.

LMI stat recvd   Number of LMI status packets received.

LMI upd recvd   Number of LMI updates received.

DTE LMI   Status of the DTE Local Management Interface.

LMI enq recvd   Number of LMI enquiries received.

LMI stat sent   Number of LMI status packets sent.

LMI upd sent   Number of LMI updates sent.

LMI DLCI   The DLCI number used for LMI. Cisco LMI type uses DLCI 1023. When ANSI is used, the LMI DLCI is 0.

LMI type   The LMI type used by the interface. Default is Cisco. The other two types are ANSI and ITU-T. The LMI type must match on the router and the Frame Relay switch. Simply put, LMI type must match on the DTE and DCE equipment.

show frame-relay lmi

The show frame-relay lmi command displays LMI-relevant information. The output contains the LMI type, inquiry, update, and status information:

```
Router_B#show frame-relay lmi
LMI Statistics for interface Serial0 (Frame Relay DTE) LMI
    TYPE = CISCO
```

```
Invalid Unnumbered info 0    Invalid Prot Disc 0
Invalid dummy Call Ref 0     Invalid Msg Type 0
Invalid Status Message 0     Invalid Lock Shift 0
Invalid Information ID 0      Invalid Report IE Len 0
Invalid Report Request 0     Invalid Keep IE Len 0
Num Status Enq. Sent 823406     Num Status msgs Rcvd 823403
Num Update Status Rcvd 507     Num Status Timeouts 3
```

show frame-relay pvc

When you issue the show frame-relay pvc command, you get output that contains the LMI status of every DLCI on the router, or you may be more specific and check only certain PVCs.

There are two types of DLCI usage: local DTE and switched. Things to check for in the output of the command include dropped frames, congestion notifications, and discard-eligible packets.

Here is a sample output. The data provided includes PVC information. It has the input and output packets for the interface, as well as FECN and BECN packet information. These statistics are available for every DLCI PVC on the router. Here, only two PVCs are shown:

```
Router_A#show frame-relay pvc

PVC Statistics for interface Serial0 (Frame Relay DTE)

DLCI = 18, DLCI USAGE = LOCAL, PVC STATUS = ACTIVE,
    INTERFACE = Serial0.4

input pkts 37515875 output pkts 38589330 in bytes
    4113557032
out bytes 2755391175 dropped pkts 16 in FECN pkts 0
in BECN pkts 0 out FECN pkts 0 out BECN pkts 0
in DE pkts 315420 out DE pkts 0
pvc create time 13w4d, last time pvc status changed
    06:40:12

DLCI = 19, DLCI USAGE = UNUSED, PVC STATUS = ACTIVE,
    INTERFACE = Serial0

input pkts 38 output pkts 0 in bytes 8372
out bytes 0 dropped pkts 0 in FECN pkts 0
```

```
in BECN pkts 0 out FECN pkts 0 out BECN pkts 0
in DE pkts 0 out DE pkts 0
pvc create time 13w4d, last time pvc status changed 7w4d
Num Pkts Switched 0
```

Problems can be detected by watching the number of FECN or BECN packets increase, which indicates line congestion. Forward explicit congestion notification, FECN, notifies the receiving station (DTE) that congestion was experienced en route to the destination. Backward explicit congestion notification, BECN, notifies the sending station that congestion was experienced. FECN messages are sent in the direction of the congestion, and BECN messages are sent in the opposite direction of the congestion.

show frame-relay map

The show frame-relay map command contains information about the DLCI numbers and the encapsulation of all Frame Relay interfaces. The status of the interface is indicated with the up or down state found within the parentheses. The next field indicates the type of interface: point-to-point or multipoint. The DLCI for the interface and the encapsulation type are also included in the output. Here is a sample:

```
Router_B#show frame-relay map
Serial0.10 (down): point-to-point dlci, dlci
    24(0x18,0x480), broadcast, IETF, BW = 1024000 status
    defined, inactive
Serial0.7 (down): point-to-point dlci, dlci
    21(0x15,0x450), broadcast, IETF, BW = 1024000 status
    defined, inactive
Serial0.5 (up): point-to-point dlci, dlci 20(0x14,0x440),
    broadcast, IETF, BW = 1024000 status defined, active
Serial0.6 (up): point-to-point dlci, dlci 30(0x1E,0x4E0),
    broadcast, IETF, BW = 48000 status defined, active
Serial0.4 (up): point-to-point dlci, dlci 18(0x12,0x420),
    broadcast, IETF, BW = 1024000 status defined, active
Serial0.2 (up): point-to-point dlci, dlci 27(0x1B,0x4B0),
    broadcast, IETF, BW = 48000 status defined, active
Serial0.11 (up): point-to-point dlci, dlci 31(0x1F,0x4F0),
    broadcast, IETF, BW = 48000 status defined, active
Serial0.9 (up): point-to-point dlci, dlci 29(0x1D,0x4D0),
    broadcast, IETF, BW = 48000 status defined, active
```

```
Serial0.12 (up): point-to-point dlci, dlci 32(0x20,0x800),
     broadcast, IETF, BW = 48000 status defined, active
Serial0.8 (up): point-to-point dlci, dlci 28(0x1C,0x4C0),
     broadcast, IETF, BW = 48000 status defined, active
Serial1.1 (up): point-to-point dlci, dlci 16(0x10,0x400),
     broadcast, IETF, BW = 1024000 status defined, active
```

Frame Relay *debug* Commands

As always, you must exercise caution when using **debug** commands, due to the amount of output they can generate. The more traffic that exists on an interface, the more output that will be generated on the router. The commands that will be discussed in this section are:

- debug frame-relay lmi

- debug frame-relay events

debug frame-relay lmi

An LMI Frame Relay debug displays LMI exchange information. The exchange consists of LMI status enquiries and responses, including sequencing numbers. Here is a sample:

```
Router_B#debug frame-relay lmi
Frame Relay LMI debugging is on
Displaying all Frame Relay LMI data
Serial0(out): StEnq, myseq 142, yourseen 141, DTE up
datagramstart = 0x40081DA0, datagramsize = 13
FR encap = 0xFCF10309
00 75 01 01 01 03 02 8E 8D
Serial0(in): Status, myseq 142
RT IE 1, length 1, type 1
KA IE 3, length 2, yourseq 142, myseq 142
Serial1(out): StEnq, myseq 9, yourseen 15, DTE up
datagramstart = 0x40000528, datagramsize = 13
FR encap = 0xFCF10309
00 75 01 01 01 03 02 09 0F

Serial1(in): Status, myseq 9
```

```
RT IE 1, length 1, type 1
KA IE 3, length 2, yourseq 16, myseq 9
Serial2(out): StEnq, myseq 254, yourseen 254, DTE up
datagramstart = 0x40000528, datagramsize = 13
FR encap = 0xFCF10309
00 75 01 01 01 03 02 FE FE
```

The StEnq, myseq, and yourseen are similar to the data provided by the serial debug command. The newly introduced fields are as follows:

RT IE   Report Type Information Element

KA IE   Keepalive Information Element

This debug command does not generate a great deal of output, as you can see. Therefore, it can be used even during high traffic times. Some outputs will include more information than the sample displayed previously. Additional information includes clocking, PVC, and Committed Information Rate detail.

debug frame-relay events

Data provided by this command is useful because it gives details about protocols and applications using the DLCI. A sample follows. The (i) and (o) specify inbound and outbound traffic:

```
Router_A#debug frame-relay events
Serial3(i): dlci 1023(0xFCF1), pkt type 0x309,
    datagramsize 13
Serial3.6(o): dlci 1023(0xFCF1), pkt type 0x309,
    datagramsize 13
Serial3(i): dlci 1023(0xFCF1), pkt type 0x309,
    datagramsize 13
Serial3.6(o): dlci 1023(0xFCF1), pkt type 0x309,
    datagramsize 13
Serial0.2(o): dlci 1023(0xFCF1), pkt type 0x309,
    datagramsize 13
Serial3(i): dlci 1023(0xFCF1), pkt type 0x309,
    datagramsize 13
```

The pkt type is used to distinguish the packet type that transits the DLCI. Several different packet types may appear in the pkt type field. The packet type tells you which applications are on the circuit.

Frame Relay Summary

This summary includes tables that can be used for quick reference when diagnosing, isolating, and resolving Frame Relay problems.

Symptoms and Problems

Table 7.5 includes Frame Relay symptoms and their related problems.

TABLE 7.5 Frame Relay Symptoms and Problems

Symptom or Condition	Associated Problem(s)
Frame Relay link is down	(a) Faulty cabling
	(b) Faulty hardware
	(c) Local service provider problem
	(d) LMI type mismatch
	(e) Keepalives not being sent
	(f) Encapsulation type
	(g) DLCI mismatch
Cannot ping remote host across a Frame Relay network	(a) DLCI assigned to wrong subinterface
	(b) Encapsulation mismatch
	(c) Access list problem
	(d) Interface misconfiguration

Problems and Action Plans

Table 7.6 includes the resolution action plans for the problems listed in Table 7.5.

TABLE 7.6 Action Plans for Common Frame Relay Problems

Problem	Resolution Action Plan
Faulty cabling	1. Check the cabling and use a breakout box to test the control leads.
	2. Replace cabling as needed.
Faulty hardware	1. Isolate hardware problems by performing loopback tests.
	2. Change the cable to a new interface on the router, and configure the new interface to match the configuration of the old interface. If the link comes up, you know that you must replace the hardware.
Local service provider problem	1. If loopback tests bring the LMI state up, but you cannot connect to the remote site, contact the local carrier.
	2. Problems can include carrier problems as well as Frame Relay misconfiguration, such as DLCI mismatch or encapsulation mismatch.
LMI type mismatch	1. Verify that the LMI type on the router matches the LMI type for every device in the PVC.
	2. You won't have access to see the LMI information inside a public provider network; you need to contact the carrier.
Keepalive problems	1. Use the show interface command to see whether keepalives are disabled or are configured properly.
	2. If the keepalive is not set, enter the configuration mode and enter the keepalive interval on the proper interface.
Encapsulation type	1. Verify that the encapsulation type is the same on both routers. If non-Cisco equipment is used, the encapsulation must be set for IETF. You can display this information by using the show frame-relay map command.

TABLE 7.6 Action Plans for Common Frame Relay Problems *(continued)*

Problem	Resolution Action Plan
	2. The encapsulation can be changed by using the encapsulation `frame-relay ietf` command.
DLCI mismatch	1. Use the `show running-config` command to display the DLCI number assigned to the proper interface. The `show frame-relay pvc` command can also display the DLCI assigned to the interface.
	2. If the correct DLCI number is configured on the proper interface, contact the local carrier to verify that it has the same DLCI configured on the Frame Relay switch.
Access list problem	1. Use the `show ip interface` command to display the access list applied to the interface.
	2. Analyze the access list, and then remove and modify it, if necessary.

Summary

Though the protocols involved are different, troubleshooting WAN connectivity uses the same basic troubleshooting techniques that were used to troubleshoot LAN connectivity issues earlier in the book. These techniques will continue to be applied through the rest of the book as well.

While there are several different types of interfaces, some form of a serial interface will most often be used to create the WAN connection. This serial interface may or may not have a built-in CSU/DSU. In either case, there are numerous **show** and **debug** commands that can be used to see the health of this interface as well as the connection or connections it supports. Many of these same commands, such as **show interface** and **show controllers**, are used to examine LAN interfaces as well. In addition to the **show** and **debug** commands, loopbacks can also be set up on the Cisco routers or, more commonly, on the CSU/DSU that are used in the circuit path.

There are different encapsulation types that can be used on a WAN circuit. By default, a Cisco serial interface uses High-level Data Link Control (HDLC) as the encapsulation type. This encapsulation type is used for synchronous data link control. Another common encapsulation type is Frame Relay. Frame Relay allows for multiple locations to be connected to each other on a single physical interface. This is done through the use of virtual circuits, either permanent or switched, and Data-Link Connection Identifiers or DLCIs. X.25 is an older encapsulation methodology that is still in use today for many legacy applications. X.25's structure allows for reliable data delivery even over networks that are prone to errors. As was the case with the serial interfaces, there are show and debug commands that are specifically designed to assist in the diagnosis of problems involving these encapsulation types.

Exam Essentials

Know how to determine the encapsulation type of an interface.   By looking at the output of a show interface command, you can determine the encapsulation type of an interface. You should also know the major characteristics of the encapsulation used and how to identify these characteristics.

Know the show and debug commands that are used to troubleshoot serial line problems.   Among the show and debug commands that can be used to troubleshoot serial line problems are: show interface serial, debug serial interface, and debug serial packet. You should know the show and debug commands for the interfaces as well as the protocol being used. Also, you need to understand the buffer information that is displayed as part of the output from some of these commands.

Know how HDLC functions and how to troubleshoot issues.   HDLC is a point-to-point protocol that is based on SDLC. It is also the default protocol used on Cisco router serial interfaces. The show interface command as well as the serial debug command provides detailed information about the functioning of HDLC.

Know how X.25 functions and how to troubleshoot issues.   X.25 is an older encapsulation type primarily used for legacy applications. X.25

relies on LAPB to maintain a stable data link. Commands such as `show interface`, `debug lapb`, and `debug x25` events can be used to troubleshoot X.25 issues.

Know how Frame Relay functions and how to troubleshoot issues. Frame Relay can be used as a point-to-point, point-to-multipoint, or multipoint-to-multipoint protocol. It provides this functionality through the use of one or multiple Virtual Circuits (VC) per physical circuit. `Show frame-relay pvc`, `show frame-relay map`, `show frame-relay lmi`, `show interface`, `debug frame-relay lmi`, and `debug frame-relay events` are commands that can be used to diagnose Frame Relay issues.

Understand DLCI and LMI information and how they are used in Frame Relay. DLCIs are only locally significant and represent the VC, either switched or permanent. LMI is used for management of the Frame Relay link.

Know the purposes of loopbacks and how they can be applied. Loopbacks are used to help isolate a problem to a specific section of the circuit. They are most often applied on the local or remote CSU/DSU.

Commands Used in This Chapter

The following list contains a summary of all the commands used in this chapter.

Commands	Descriptions
`clear counters serial`	Clears the statistical counters on the interface.
`debug frame-relay events`	Gives details about protocols and applications using the DLCI.
`debug frame-relay lmi`	Displays LMI exchange information. The exchange consists of LMI status inquiries and responses, including sequencing numbers.
`debug lapb`	Contains information regarding all packets and traffic that use LAPB encapsulation.

Commands	Descriptions
`debug serial interface`	Displays signaling information for the interface.
`debug serial packet`	Displays information regarding serial packets.
`debug x25 events`	Displays X.25 events in detail.
`show buffers`	Displays buffer statistics for the router.
`show controllers serial`	Shows specific hardware information regarding the serial controller.
`show frame-relay lmi`	Displays LMI-relevant information. The output contains the LMI type, inquiry, update, and status information.
`show frame-relay map`	Contains information about the DLCI numbers and the encapsulation of all Frame Relay interfaces. The status of the interface is indicated with the up or down state found within the parentheses.
`show frame-relay pvc`	Contains the LMI status of every DLCI on the router, or you may be more specific and check only certain PVCs.
`show interface serial`	The `show interface` command executed on a serial interface. Provides important information regarding serial interfaces, including IP, encapsulation, and line statistics.

Key Terms

Before you take the exam, be certain you are familiar with the following terms:

Data-Link Connection Identifier (DLCI)

loopback tests

Local Management Interface (LMI)

Review Questions

1. What is the output of the `clear counters` command?

   A. It displays all counters for the specified interface, and then resets the counters.

   B. It displays the value of the counters before the last time the interface was reset.

   C. There is no output.

   D. It clears the statistical counter on the specified interface.

2. Which of the following elements are displayed by using the `show interface serial` command? (Choose all that apply.)

   A. Frame Relay information

   B. Encapsulation type

   C. Interface error information

   D. IOS version number

3. Which of the following elements are displayed by using the `show controller serial` command? (Choose all that apply.)

   A. Encapsulation type

   B. LMI type

   C. Clock rate

   D. Cable type

   E. Cable connection status

   F. Error information

4. Which of the following elements are displayed by using the `show buffers` command? (Choose all that apply.)

   A. Interface buffers (on low-level routers)

   B. Very huge buffers

   C. Huge buffers

   D. Tiny buffers

5. Which of the following information fields are displayed by using the debug serial interface command? (Choose all that apply.)

A. myseq

B. yourseen

C. mineseen

D. StEnq

6. What are two of the four CSU/DSU loopback tests? (Choose two.)

A. Local loopback at local site

B. Remote loopback from remote site

C. Local remote loopback from local site

D. Remote local loopback from remote site

7. Which of the following fields is X.25-related from the show interface serial command?

A. RNRs

B. REJs

C. LMI type

D. SABMs

E. FRMRs

F. DLCI

G. DISCs

H. RESTARTs

8. Which of the following fields are LAPB-related from the show interface serial command? (Choose all that apply.)

A. RNRs

B. REJs

C. LMI type

D. SABMs

9. Which of the following fields are Frame Relay/LMI-related from the show interface serial command? (Choose all that apply.)

A. LMI enq sent

B. LMI stat recvd

C. RESTARTs

D. LMI encapsulation

10. Which of the following fields are Frame Relay/LMI-related from the show interface serial command? (Choose all that apply.)

A. LMI upd recvd

B. DTE LMI

C. LMI enq recvd

D. Frame Relay enq sent

11. Which of the following fields are Frame Relay/LMI-related from the show interface serial command? (Choose all that apply.)

A. LMI stat sent

B. LMI upd sent

C. LMI DLCI

D. LMI type

12. Which command(s) display the LMI type? (Choose all that apply.)

A. show interface serial

B. show frame-relay map

C. show frame-relay pvc

D. show frame-relay lmi

13. Which of the following information fields are displayed by the show frame-relay pvc command? (Choose all that apply.)

 A. BECN statistics

 B. FECN statistics

 C. Configuration register setting

 D. VPI number

14. Which of the following commands provide the DLCI number of the serial interface? (Choose all that apply.)

 A. show running-config

 B. show frame-relay map

 C. show serial dlci

 D. show frame-relay lmi

15. What property must the DLCI number have?

 A. It must match the DLCI on the other end of the PVC.

 B. It must be between 0 and 16.

 C. It has only local significance.

 D. All of the above.

16. Which of the following statements is true of the LMI type on the router? (Choose all that apply.)

 A. It must match the remote end.

 B. It must have the same DLCI.

 C. It can be set to Cisco.

 D. It can be set to ANSI.

17. Which statements are true regarding the encapsulation used when connecting a Cisco router to a non-Cisco router?

A. It must be Cisco.

B. It must be ANSI.

C. It must be IETF.

D. It must be ITU.

18. Which statements are true regarding the encapsulation on the router's interface? (Choose all that apply.)

A. Both sides of the PVC must be using the same type.

B. Encapsulation is local to the router.

C. ITU-T is a valid encapsulation type.

D. IETF is a valid encapsulation type.

19. Which of the following `debug` commands can be detrimental to a router?

A. `frame-relay packets`

B. `frame-relay events`

C. `frame-relay lmi`

D. None of the above

20. The `debug frame-relay lmi` command does not generate a large amount of output. Why?

A. Infrequent LMI exchanges between the router and switch

B. Small amounts of data in each LMI packet

C. Non-detailed information provided

D. None of the above

Answers to Review Questions

1. C.   Other than the dialog of the command, there is no output.

2. A, B, C.   All three of these elements are displayed using the `show interface serial` command. You can determine the IOS version number with the `show version` command.

3. C, D, E, F.   A and B are displayed using the `show interface serial` command.

4. A, C.   B and D are not valid names for the buffer pools. There are others, but they are not listed here.

5. A, B, C, D.   All of these fields are available via the output from the `debug serial interface` command.

6. A, B.   A loopback test is either local or remote.

7. H.   RESTARTs can be seen on an X.25 `show interface serial` command.

8. A, B, D.   All of these fields can be seen from the command. There are more, but they are not listed here.

9. A, B.   These are the Frame Relay/LMI-related fields. There are more, but they are not listed here.

10. A, B, C.   These are also valid Frame Relay/LMI fields.

11. A, B, C, D.   As you can see, a great number of fields are related to Frame Relay/LMI via the `show interface serial` command.

12. A, D.   These are the two commands that can provide information regarding the LMI type.

13. A, B.   These, along with other statistics, can be found via the `show frame-relay pvc` command.

14. A, B.   These are two commands that provide DLCI number information. There are additional commands, but they are not shown here.

15. C.   The DLCI does have a limit in values, but it is of local significance only. It does not need to match.

16. A, C, D.   It doesn't matter what type is set, as long as both ends of the PVC are configured to use the same type.

17. C.   It must be IETF, because non-Cisco equipment will not understand Cisco-specific encapsulation.

18. A, D.   IETF and Cisco are valid encapsulations. They must be the same on both sides of the connection.

19. A.   The `frame-relay packets debug` can be very detrimental due to the fact that every packet would be analyzed by the debug process.

20. A.   The data provided by the `debug` command is summarized and exchanges are not as frequent as Frame Relay packets are.

Chapter 8

Troubleshooting ISDN

TOPICS COVERED IN THIS CHAPTER INCLUDE:

- ✓ Use Cisco IOS commands and problem isolation techniques to identify the symptoms of common ISDN BRI problems.

- ✓ Apply diagnostic tools to trouble tickets and solve ISDN BRI problems that simulate real-life WAN malfunctions.

"It Still Does Nothing."

"Yes, this is the phone company. May I please speak with Mr. Isdn?"

The jokes and stories regarding Integrated Services Digital Networks (ISDN) have been merciless and, in some cases, more prevalent than the service itself.

Although it is true that ISDN is difficult to order and configure, ISDN is an important option for administrators to consider when designing networks. Frame Relay and xDSL are strong contenders, but ISDN's availability and cost advantages in certain situations are difficult to ignore. In addition, the difficulties in configuration have been removed to a large degree as the service becomes better known.

Some of the commands listed in this chapter are unavailable on certain Cisco routers because of hardware and software considerations. The Cisco 804 router with internal ISDN BRI was used to provide the screen output for this chapter.

ISDN Fundamentals

ISDN was developed in large part from the phone company's conversion to digital networks from analog switches. This conversion, which started in the 1960s, resulted in the following features:

- Clearer, cleaner signals

- Compressible voice, resulting in better trunking utilization
- Longer distances between switching devices
- Value-added features, including caller ID and three-way calling
- Greater bandwidth—a single connection to the phone company can service more than one phone number
- Elimination of load coils and amplifiers in the network

The concept of ISDN was originally conceived as a means to move the digital network into the home, where a single ISDN connection would provide two standard phone lines and digital services for data. This migration from the analog phone would continue to use the existing copper wire plant, while adding services that would ultimately increase revenues.

Unfortunately, users failed to accept ISDN in the numbers desired. This was especially true in the United States, where installation problems, service availability, and pricing all conspired to hinder acceptance.

In the late 1990s, ISDN was finding a new marketplace. Always On ISDN uses the D channel to replace legacy X.25 networks, especially in point-of-sale transactions. (A description of the B and D channels is included later in this chapter.) Standard ISDN service is popular for videoconferencing and as a residential connection to the Internet. However, cable modems and DSL technologies have replaced much of this market in the current environment.

Common ISDN Problems

As with problems affecting other protocols and networking devices, ISDN problems appear in certain common areas. Some frequently encountered problems are presented in this section for administrators to consider when evaluating real-world issues. Later in this chapter, the commands that are appropriate for troubleshooting these problems with Cisco routers will be presented.

ISDN problems may be divided into three general categories: misconfigured routers, physical wiring and ISDN protocol issues, and misconfigured switches. You will learn about each type of problem in this section.

Misconfigured Routers

The router configuration is one of many areas that can require attention when researching ISDN problems. Misconfiguration issues can happen due to a variety of reasons, including typographical errors, erroneous information from service providers, and failure to correctly configure the router itself.

Service Profile Identifiers (SPIDs)

The *Service Profile Identifiers*, or SPIDs, are analogous to phone numbers in the analog phone environment. The numbers usually include the telephone number with area code and, occasionally, extra digits used by the switch. This results in a SPID of 41555512340101, for example, which corresponds to number 415-555-1234, with additional parameters of 0101. The local service provider should document these numbers for the administrator.

ISDN is unique in that the local device must learn its identifying number. This is contrasted with analog phones, which remain unaware of their actual phone number—relying on a switch to trigger the ringer.

SPIDs are used only in North America, and the integration of the phone number into the SPID is most applicable for public ISDN installations. Private ISDN networks usually use SPIDs without a phone number.

It is surprisingly common for administrators to assign IP addresses within two different subnets on ISDN interfaces that connect to each other. It is important to consider each end of an ISDN DDR connection to be part of a single subnet. From a Layer 3 perspective, they are the same as any other point-to-point WAN connection.

Challenge Handshake Authentication Protocol (CHAP)

ISDN provides the capability to control access by requiring authentication, which helps to make use of the public network acceptable from a business/security perspective.

The inner workings of the *Challenge Handshake Authentication Protocol (CHAP)* are beyond the scope of this chapter; basically, CHAP is used to provide a layer of security on inbound connections. When troubleshooting, it is important to confirm that the CHAP configuration on both routers matches. As noted in the output that follows, Cisco also supports the Microsoft CHAP and PAP protocols. MS-CHAP was added in IOS 12.

CHAP authentication requires the point-to-point protocol (PPP). This is enabled on the interface with the command encapsulation ppp.

```
Top(config-if)#ppp auth ?
  chap      Challenge Handshake Authentication Protocol
  (CHAP)
  ms-chap  Microsoft Challenge Handshake Authentication
  Protocol (MS-CHAP)
  pap       Password Authentication Protocol (PAP)
```

When troubleshooting, remember that it is quite common for the username parameters that define the passwords to be set incorrectly, including a typo in the password itself or an omitted username. With encrypted passwords, this is made more difficult to research. If a password problem is suspected, an administrator should enable the debug ppp authentication function. As shown in the output that follows (italics added), the authentication failed, due to an incorrect password.

```
Bottom#debug ppp authentication
PPP authentication debugging is on
Bottom#ping 10.1.1.1
Type escape sequence to abort.
Sending 5, 100-byte ICMP Echos to 10.1.1.1, timeout is 2
  seconds:
01:54:14: %LINK-3-UPDOWN: Interface BRIO:1, changed state
  to up.
01:54:14: BRO:1 PPP: Treating connection as a callout
01:54:14: BRO:1 PPP: Phase is AUTHENTICATING, by both
01:54:14: BRO:1 CHAP: O CHALLENGE id 7 len 27 from
  "Bottom"
01:54:14: BRO:1 CHAP: I CHALLENGE id 7 len 24 from "Top"
01:54:14: BRO:1 CHAP: O RESPONSE id 7 len 27 from "Bottom"
01:54:14: BRO:1 CHAP: I FAILURE id 7 len 25 msg is "MD/DES
  compare failed"
```

```
01:54:15: %ISDN-6-DISCONNECT: Interface BRIO:1
    disconnected from 18008358661 , call lasted 1 seconds
01:54:15: %LINK-3-UPDOWN: Interface BRIO:1, changed state
    to down.
01:54:18: %LINK-3-UPDOWN: Interface BRIO:1, changed state
    to up.
01:54:18: BRO:1 PPP: Treating connection as a callout
01:54:18: BRO:1 PPP: Phase is AUTHENTICATING, by both
01:54:18: BRO:1 CHAP: O CHALLENGE id 8 len 27 from
    "Bottom"
01:54:18: BRO:1 CHAP: I CHALLENGE id 8 len 24 from "Top"
01:54:18: BRO:1 CHAP: O RESPONSE id 8 len 27 from "Bottom"
01:54:18: BRO:1 CHAP: I FAILURE id 8 len 25 msg is "MD/DES
    compare failed"
01:54:19: %ISDN-6-DISCONNECT: Interface BRIO:1
    disconnected from 18008358661 , call lasted
    1 seconds
01:54:19: %LINK-3-UPDOWN: Interface BRIO:1, changed state
    to down.
01:54:22: %LINK-3-UPDOWN: Interface BRIO:1, changed state
    to up.
```

 Real World Scenario

One-Way Chap Authentication

In many businesses today, ISDN lines are no longer being used for one specific function. They are being used to connect remote locations back to the corporate network; they are being used for dial-backup, for connecting to the Internet, and in many more scenarios. I have also seen the same line being used for multiple different purposes simultaneously.

If all of these connections are made within like company devices, bidirectional CHAP does not create a problem, as all of the configurations can be set up to use this authentication methodology. However, when connecting to an ISP or an ISDN device made by a company other than Cisco, this can become an issue. In many of these instances, CHAP is not configured on the device. In other cases, the far-end device does not support CHAP challenges from the calling device.

In these problematic situations, the simplest solution that I have found is to use the Cisco IOS command ppp authentication chap callin to enable one-way CHAP authentication. This command is used at the interface level and will send a CHAP challenge only when it is called, not when the router calls out. This allows you to connect to devices that don't support bidirectional CHAP authentication or are not configured for CHAP without giving up the security that CHAP provides when you receive an incoming call. It also should be noted that a similar command also exists for PAP if you are running PAP in your environment.

Dialer Map Entries

Dialer map statements relate upper-layer addresses to their associated phone numbers. Therefore, it is critical that these entries contain valid IP addresses and numbers. Note that individual dialer map statements are needed for each protocol, as follows:

```
dialer map ip 10.11.3.20 name Top broadcast 18005551212
dialer map appletalk 310.10 name Top broadcast 18005551212
```

Some ISDN switches require the area code and escape character, even when the phone numbers are in the same area code. Thus, it is recommended that dialer-map entries always include the full 11-digit number (North American Dialing Plan).

Access Lists

Access lists are commonly used in ISDN connections to prevent certain types of traffic from triggering a connection. Most frequently, this is done to save money, because ISDN is often tariffed on a per-minute, per-B-channel basis. As of this writing, some providers offered Centrix ISDN and other options that circumvented this issue, but it is common for Frame Relay and other technologies to provide the same or greater bandwidth at lower cost. This is usually true after approximately 40 hours per month or utilization on the B channels. The xDSL technologies are quickly gaining market share at an unlimited usage tariff, as well.

To control usage, administrators frequently configure an access list based on permitted functions only, and all other services are denied. This causes problems when a new service is added that is not explicitly added to the list.

Troubleshooting any ISDN configuration that worked in the past should include a thorough review of all access lists, including the dialer lists.

```
Bottom(config)#dialer-list 1 protocol ip ?
  deny    Deny specified protocol
  list    Add access list to dialer list
  permit  Permit specified protocol
```

A dialer list to provide IP, IPX, and AppleTalk services is shown as follows:

```
dialer-list 1 protocol ip permit
dialer-list 1 protocol appletalk permit
dialer-list 1 protocol ipx permit
```

Point-to-Point Protocol

Although the point-to-point protocol (PPP) is recommended for ISDN connectivity, there are other options available, including the default HDLC. PPP is recommended in large part to provide security via CHAP, described previously in this chapter.

In troubleshooting, PPP provides additional information regarding the connection, including the protocol type. This rarely presents itself in a manner that is usable to administrators, however. Rather, an understanding of the protocol and its capability to provide useful functions, including CHAP, is often more helpful to administrators. Note that the PPP protocol is the same for analog or ISDN connections, so the configuration of PPP on a workstation using an analog modem requires PPP encapsulation on an ISDN host router. PPP also supports compression.

PPP contains protocol field values that document the upper layer information included in the datagram. A list of some protocol field values is given in Table 8.1.

TABLE 8.1 Point-to-Point Protocol Field Values

Hex Value of Field	Protocol
0021	IP
0029	AppleTalk
002B	IPX

TABLE 8.1 Point-to-Point Protocol Field Values *(continued)*

Hex Value of Field	Protocol
003D	Multilink
0201	802.1d Hellos
0203	Source Route Bridging Bridge Protocol Data Units
8021	IPCP
8029	ATCP
802B	IPXCP
C223	CHAP
C023	PAP

The debug ppp output later in this chapter provides additional magic number information.

Physical Layer Connections

It is important to consider the Physical layer when troubleshooting, especially in new installations. Wiring is particularly important when connecting ISDN videoconferencing equipment to internal PBX equipment. Some administrators use Category 5 wiring for internal ISDN connections, although Category 3 is acceptable. This chapter focuses on the Basic Rate Interface, which operates over standard copper pairs.

The Basic Rate Interface

Most installations of ISDN in the field are Basic Rate Interface (BRI). This differs from the available primary rate interface (PRI), which uses a T1 as the conduit. The primary rate of telecommunications connections is usually measured in DS-1 increments. A DS-1, or T1, is equivalent to 24 T1 voice channels. The basic rate for a voice connection is referred to as a DS-0, or a single 64Kbit channel of the T1. In ISDN, this refers to the single B-channel capacity of the circuit. The formal description of BRI is specified in I.430, whereas the I.431 specification addresses PRI ISDN.

ISDN BRI was designed to provide digital services over existing pairs of copper. The service is used for videoconferencing, voice services, data, and out-of-band management. In addition, the D-channel function of BRI is used for replacement of legacy X.25 networks.

The ISDN BRI Channels

ISDN BRI is a 192Kbps circuit that is divided into three distinct channels. The two primary data channels are the B channels. Each B channel provides 64Kbps. The third channel provides 16Kbps of bandwidth for commands and signaling, and is referred to as the D channel. The remaining bandwidth of 48Kbps is overhead.

The physical frame in ISDN BRI is 48 bits, and the circuit sends 4000 frames per second.

Services are available to send data over the D channel. These services are often referred to as *always on*, reflecting the non-demand nature of this channel. Always on services are often used to replace X.25 point-of-sale circuits and are provisioned to offer 9.6Kbit bandwidth to the application.

The Local Loop

Although the majority of administrators troubleshoot only the local side of the ISDN circuit, there is a remote side that is critical to the successful operation of ISDN.

The local loop refers to the circuit between the customer premises and the central office (CO). This may include an access layer, referred to as an RT, which permits digital connections to be greater distances from the central office. The local loop interconnects the ISDN device to an ISDN switch—a DMS-100, for example. Note that all digital services are sensitive to the distance between the switch and end device.

The Physical Layer

In order to properly troubleshoot ISDN, it is very important that you have a good understanding of its technology, terminology, architecture, and functionality. Figure 8.1 shows the ISDN components and where these components' points fit into the ISDN installation. In addition to the components, the figure also shows the reference points that are commonly used in troubleshooting ISDN issues. Following this figure are descriptions of the components and reference points.

FIGURE 8.1 ISDN components and reference points

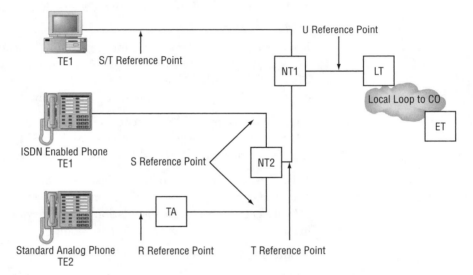

LT/ET   The line termination and exchange termination points are called LT and ET, respectively. They handle the termination of the local loop and switching functions.

NT1   The NT1 is the network termination point. It is often the demarc. It connects the four-wire subscriber line to the two-wire local loop. In North America, the NT1 is provided by the customer and is considered Customer Premise Equipment. However, in most other parts of the world this device is provided and managed by the carrier.

NT2   The NT2 is primarily seen only in larger companies that are using PBXs. The NT2 is used to perform Layer 2 and 3 protocol functions and as a concentration point.

TA   The TA is the Terminal Adapter. This device is used to connect non-ISDN enable devices, TE2, to the ISDN network. A TA may be added to the device itself or may be a stand-alone unit.

TE1   A device with a four-wire, twisted-pair digital interface is referred to as terminal equipment type one. Most modern ISDN devices are of this type.

TE2   Terminal equipment type two devices do not contain ISDN interfaces. A TA is required.

R reference point   Devices without internal ISDN functions are called TE2s, and require a connection to a TA for operation in ISDN networks. There is no standard connection between these devices, however—the connection is referred to as the R reference point.

S reference point   The S reference point is the interface between the ISDN router (or other user equipment) and the NT2 or NT1. Note that the user equipment is referred to as the TE1 or TA.

S/T reference point   If no NT2 is installed, the connection between the NT1 and either the TA or the TE1, depending on which is installed, is the S/T reference point. As the installation of NT2 devices is rare, most ISDN installations will have an S/T reference point.

T reference point   The interface between the NT1, or the local loop termination point, and the NT2, or customer site switching equipment, is referred to as the T reference point. This point, along with the S reference point, is within the customer premises, and faulty wiring may be the cause of a problem within this context.

U reference point   The U reference point is between the NT1 and the LE. It is normally serviced on a single pair to reduce costs and simplify installations.

Layer 1 S/T Interface   This connection uses a physical connector of RJ-45, as defined in ISO 8877. A straight-through pin configuration connects the TE to the network termination (NT). Table 8.2 reflects the specific pinning.

TABLE 8.2   The RJ-45 ISDN S/T Interface

Pin	Terminal End-Point (TE)	Network Termination (NT)
1	Power +	Power +
2	Power –	Power –
3	Transmit +	Receive +
4	Receive +	Transmit +
5	Receive –	Transmit –
6	Transmit –	Receive –
7	Power –	Power –
8	Power +	Power +

Some installers use RJ-11 or RJ-14 connections for ISDN terminations. Although these connections work, it is recommended that RJ-45 be used in all circumstances. Wires 1, 2, 7, and 8 may be used for alternate mark inversion (AMI) encoding, and RJ-45 connections provide a visual variance from standard phone jacks.

Misconfigured Phone Switches

Administrators must consider the possibility that the service provider failed to properly configure the ISDN switch. Although this is a very rare occurrence, the possibility exists and should be considered, especially in new installations.

An understanding of ISDN as it relates to the OSI model can greatly assist the network troubleshooter in locating problem causes. In addition, administrators must be aware of the ISDN switch types and their impact on connectivity.

Troubleshooting Layer 2

There are two Layer 2 troubleshooting targets that should be identified and analyzed when working on ISDN networks: the q.921 protocol and PPP.

q.921

ISDN maps well with the OSI reference model. Layer 2 is defined in *q.921*.

The q.921 signaling is carried over the D channel by using *Link Access Procedure protocol*, or LAPD. This connection between the central office switch (or the Teltone ILS-2000 in this test network) and the router must occur and complete before Layer 3 connections are possible.

Troubleshooting q.921 problems is most frequently handled with the `debug isdn q921` command. Often, problems relate to the terminal end point identifier, or TEI. This value uniquely identifies each terminal in the network, and a TEI of 127 represents a broadcast. TEIs 64 through 126 are reserved for assignment during the activation of a Layer 2 ISDN connection. This assignment is dynamic.

TEI has different message types that allow the engineer to identify what type of information is being exchanged, thus identifying any failures in the TEI process. Refer to Table 8.3 for descriptions of these types.

TABLE 8.3 TEI Message Types

Type Number	Type Description
1	ID Request
2	ID Assigned
3	ID Denied
4	ID Check Request
5	ID Check Response
6	ID Remove
7	ID Verify

By using these references, you will be able to understand the exchanges during the TEI process.

Administrators may also need to review the SAPI, or service access point identifier. This field may include a SAPI of 0, which represents that Layer 3 signaling is present. Such signaling is provided by q.931. Other values may include 63, which is a management SAPI for the assignment of the TEI_values, or 64, which is used for call control.

One last target to check while troubleshooting the q.921 with the `debug isdn q.921` command is the SABME messages. The SABME is exchanged along with the ID verify messages. If the SABME fails and sends a disconnect response, no further link establishment will occur, and you should investigate the reason for the SABME failure. If the SABME succeeds, an acknowledgment is sent and the Layer 2 connection is complete, and the TE will begin to send INFO frames.

Sample outputs for the `show interface` and `debug isdn q921` commands are displayed later in the chapter. The outputs are long and cover multiple pages. However, you should look through the output carefully and try to follow what is happening using the information you have learned thus far.

PPP

Troubleshooting targets within the PPP protocol are also important when trying to isolate and resolve ISDN BRI problems. LCP, or Link Control Protocol, is the protocol used by PPP to set up and maintain links. It also assists in setting the PPP options. Before getting into the sequence used to set up PPP, let's look at some of the LCP options. The major options are detailed in Table 8.4 below.

TABLE 8.4 LCP Type Options

Type Number	Type	Description
0	Reserved	Not used.
1	Maximum Receive Unit (MRU)	Sets the maximum packet size. Default is 1500 bytes.
3	Authentication Protocol	Sets the Authentication protocol to be used (CHAP or PAP).
4	Quality Protocol	Sets the protocol to use for link quality monitoring. By default Link Quality Monitoring is disabled.

TABLE 8.4 LCP Type Options *(continued)*

Type Number	Type	Description
5	Magic Number	Used to detect loopback links and other Layer 2 issues.
7	Protocol Field Compression	Used to negotiate compression of the PPP protocol field.
8	Address and Control Field Compression	Used to negotiate compression of the Data-Link layer address and control fields.

In addition to LCP for link control, PPP also uses Network Control Protocol (NCP) for configuring and establishing different network layer protocols. Administrators also need to review the steps in PPP and CHAP negotiation. Let's look at the steps taken by PPP to establish a link.

1. LCP at the router (TE) sends a configuration request known as a CONFREQ. Options are specified by the requesting router.

2. The request is either accepted or denied. If it is accepted, an acknowledgment, known as a CONFACK, is returned to the TE. If the request is denied, a negative CONFACK is returned. The difference between a normal and a negative CONFACK is the acceptance or denial of the request. If the CONFREQ was not recognized by the remote TE, a configuration reject message, known as a CONFREJ, is sent to the requesting TE.

3. If the CONFREQ was recognized and accepted and CHAP is being used for authentication, the process continues with the three-way handshake.

   A. Challenge is sent to the remote TE.

   B. The remote TE responds.

   C. If the values match, authentication is given.

The troubleshooting targets in this process are the request/response sequence between the peers as well as all of the CHAP targets.

Troubleshooting Layer 3

The third layer of ISDN is addressed in the ITU-T I.451 specification, also called *q.931*. An easy way to remember the difference between q.921 and q.931 is to look at the tens digit of the number. q.921 corresponds to Layer 2 and q.931 corresponds to Layer 3. The q.931 protocol includes several message commands, which are viewed with the debug isdn q931 command. These commands include call setup, connect, release, cancel, status, disconnect, and user information.

The output of the show and debug commands will be covered later in the chapter. It is important to identify the troubleshooting targets that exist in Layer 3 for ISDN BRI. It is important to recognize that the Layer 3 connection is between the local router (TE) and the remote ISDN switch (ET).

Just as the q.931 operates on the D channel, so does all debugging. Troubleshooting targets include the call reference flag, message types, and information elements. Tables 8.5, 8.6, and 8.7 provide summaries for the messages and their meaning.

TABLE 8.5 Call Reference Flag Definitions

Field Value	Definition
0	From call originator
1	To call originator

TABLE 8.6 q.931 Message Types

Field Value	Definition
0x05	Setup
0x45	Disconnect
0x7d	Status

TABLE 8.7 q.931 Information Elements

Field Value	Definition
0x04	Bearer capability
0x2c	Keypad facility

TABLE 8.7   q.931 Information Elements *(continued)*

Field Value	Definition
0x6c	Calling party number
0x70	Called party number
0x3a	SPID

Again, all of this information is provided by the debug isdn q931 command. A sample output is provided later in the chapter. The easiest way to keep track of the different calls is with the call reference number indicated in the output of the debug command. This way you will be able to follow the same call all the way through the process.

Note that these messages are carried on the D channel and are not end-to-end. Rather, they are for connections and setup between the central office switch and the router. The B channel is then available for data transfer.

ISDN calls are established between the router and the local switch over the D channel. The local switch establishes a separate connection to the remote switch, which is responsible for the call setup to the remote router or other ISDN device.

Now let's discuss the call setup on Layer 3 via q.931. It will aid you in troubleshooting and isolating ISDN BRI network problems. This information is provided by the debug isdn q931 command.

1. SETUP: The SETUP process sends information elements; this occurs between the local TE and the remote TE.

2. CALL_PROC: The call proceeding signal is given; this occurs between the ET and the TE.

3. ALERT: The remote TE alerts the local TE via a ring back.

4. CONNECT: The remote TE answers, thus stopping the local ring back.

5. CONNECT_ACK: A message from the remote ET to the remote TE is sent, acknowledging that the setup is complete.

This is the process that must be followed. You can use the output of the debug isdn q931 to verify that the process is happening correctly.

Switch Types

Recall that ISDN is a connection between the ISDN router and the phone company's central office switch. Therefore, it is important to define the type of switch in use to the router. This is configured with the isdn switch-type command. The isdn switch ? command reports the available switch types and their usual country or continent for the Cisco router.

```
Top(config)#isdn switch-type ?
  basic-1tr6      1TR6 switch type for Germany
  basic-5ess      AT&T 5ESS switch type for the U.S.
  basic-dms100    Northern DMS-100 switch type
  basic-net3      NET3 switch type for UK and Europe
  basic-ni        National ISDN switch type
  basic-ts013     TS013 switch type for Australia
  ntt             NTT switch type for Japan
  vn3             VN3 and VN4 switch types for France
```

If the switch type is unknown (North America), an administrator may wish to use the auto-configuration command. The command is isdn autodetect. If the SPID is unknown, the command isdn spidn 0 may be used. Some administrators prefer to specify this information manually. Please be advised that this option is not available on many routers; however, it is available on the Cisco 804 router, and it may be helpful in new installations. It is likely that Cisco will add this function to new products.

It is important to note that the switch type is specific to the local loop switch, and not the remote connection or entire connection. For example, when connecting a router in North America to use for connections to Europe, the North American router is likely to be set to basic-dms100, for example. The European router is set to basic-net3.

Different switch types and configurations may set each B channel at 56Kbps, instead of the potentially available 64Kbps. Failure to match speeds causes connectivity problems.

ISDN Troubleshooting Commands

T he Cisco IOS provides a broad range of troubleshooting commands to assist administrators in the deployment and configuration of ISDN, including the common problems noted previously. Although many of these commands are common to other typologies and protocols (ping, for example), other commands are specific to ISDN, including debug isdn q931.

Figure 8.2 diagrams the network used for this chapter.

FIGURE 8.2 ISDN Troubleshooting network design

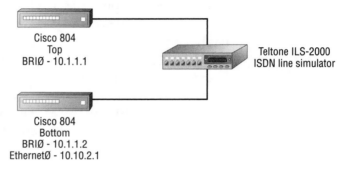

Cisco 804
Top
BRI0 - 10.1.1.1

Teltone ILS-2000
ISDN line simulator

Cisco 804
Bottom
BRI0 - 10.1.1.2
Ethernet0 - 10.10.2.1

ping

As with non-dial-on-demand (DDR) connections, the ping command is one of the most useful troubleshooting tools. ping verifies routes and other connections; in DDR, the command triggers a call.

```
Bottom#ping 10.1.1.1
Type escape sequence to abort.
Sending 5, 100-byte ICMP Echos to 10.1.1.1, timeout is
    2 seconds:
.
00:37:12: %LINK-3-UPDOWN: Interface BRI0:1, changed state
    to up
00:37:13: %LINEPROTO-5-UPDOWN: Line protocol on Interface
    BRI0:1, changed state to up.!!!
Success rate is 60 percent (3/5), round-trip min/avg/max =
    32/38/48 ms
```

```
Bottom#
00:37:14: %LINK-3-UPDOWN: Interface BRIO:2, changed state
    to up
00:37:15: %LINEPROTO-5-UPDOWN: Line protocol on Interface
    BRIO:2, changed state to up
```

Note that the five pings generated by the router completed before the second B channel came up. The ping command is perhaps the most common troubleshooting tool in TCP/IP networks.

It is quite common for the first three pings to fail in DDR ISDN connections. This is due to the two- to three-second delay in establishing the connection. It is usually not an indication of a problem.

clear interface bri n

The clear interface bri n command resets the various counters that are available on the interface and terminates a connection on the interface. The n value should equal the port, or port and slot, of the interface. This command is most useful for clearing a call that was activated by a dialer-map or other catalyst, which may be desired when configuring and testing new access lists and other call triggers.

```
Bottom#clear int bri0
Bottom#
00:26:158913789951: %ISDN-6-DISCONNECT: Interface BRIO:2
    disconnected from 8358663 , call lasted 104 seconds
00:26:154624128828: %LINK-3-UPDOWN: Interface BRIO:2,
    changed state to down
00:26:36: %ISDN-6-LAYER2UP: Layer 2 for Interface BR0, TEI
    92 changed to up
00:26:36: %ISDN-6-LAYER2UP: Layer 2 for Interface BR0, TEI
    93 changed to up
00:26:37: %LINEPROTO-5-UPDOWN: Line protocol on Interface
    BRIO:2, changed state to down
```

show interface bri n

Information regarding the ISDN BRI D channel is available with the show interface bri n command. Note that the command reports the B channel's status, as well as spoofing on the interface. This is due to the dynamic nature of DDR connections—they are up only when necessary. In addition, note that the interface was not configured for point-to-point protocol (PPP), but is using the default encapsulation of HDLC.

It is important for administrators to review the output of the `show interface` command, especially when researching user reports of slow performance. For example, the `txload` and `rxload` parameters provide a strong indication of bandwidth loads. Observe the (spoofing) tag in the following output as well. This indicates that the router is maintaining the link as though it was always active, even though ISDN is dynamic.

```
Bottom#show int bri0
BRI0 is up, line protocol is up (spoofing)
  Hardware is BRI with U interface and POTS
  Internet address is 10.1.1.2/24
  MTU 1500 bytes, BW 64Kbit, DLY 20000 usec,
    reliability 255/255, txload 1/255, rxload 1/255
  Encapsulation HDLC, loopback not set
  Last input 00:00:05, output 00:00:05, output hang never
  Last clearing of "show interface" counters never
  Input queue: 0/75/0 (size/max/drops); Total output
   drops: 0
  Queueing strategy: weighted fair
  Output queue: 0/1000/64/0 (size/max total/threshold/
   drops)
     Conversations  0/1/256 (active/max active/max total)
     Reserved Conversations 0/0 (allocated/max allocated)
  5 minute input rate 0 bits/sec, 0 packets/sec
  5 minute output rate 0 bits/sec, 0 packets/sec
     85 packets input, 791 bytes, 0 no buffer
     Received 4 broadcasts, 0 runts, 0 giants, 0 throttles
     0 input errors, 0 CRC, 0 frame, 0 overrun, 0 ignored,
    0 abort
     92 packets output, 701 bytes, 0 underruns
     0 output errors, 0 collisions, 4 interface resets
     0 output buffer failures, 0 output buffers swapped
    out
     1 carrier transitions
```

show interface bri n 1 2

The show interface bri n 1 2 command is used to display a single B channel of the BRI interface. In this example, the circuit is down.

Although this command can be important when isolating an individual B channel problem, the show interface bri n command usually suffices for the majority of troubleshooting processes.

```
Bottom#show interface bri0 1
BRI0:1 is down, line protocol is down
  Hardware is BRI with U interface and POTS
  MTU 1500 bytes, BW 64Kbit, DLY 20000 usec,
      reliablility 255/255, txload 1/255, rxload 1/255
  Encapsulation PPP, loopback not set, keepalive set (10
  sec)
  LCP Closed, multilink Closed
  Closed: BACP, CDPCP, IPCP
  Last input 00:02:09, output 00:02:09, output hang never
  Last clearing of "show interface" counters never
  Queueing strategy: fifo
  Output queue 0/40, 0 drops; input queue 0/75, 0 drops
  5 minute input rate 0 bits/sec, 0 packets/sec
  5 minute output rate 0 bits/sec, 0 packets/sec
     219 packets input, 3320 bytes, 0 no buffer
     Received 219 broadcasts, 0 runts, 0 giants, 0
  throttles
     146 input errors, 9 CRC, 59 frame, 0 overrun, 0
  ignored, 78 abort
     279 packets output, 16195 bytes, 0 underruns
     0 output errors, 0 collisions, 0 interface resets
     0 output buffer failures, 0 output buffers swapped
  out
     15 carrier transitions
```

show controller bri

The interface hardware controller information is displayed with the show controller bri command. This command is most useful for troubleshooting with Cisco's TAC, but some information can assist the administrator.

Most important, the status of the interface, in this case a U type connection, and the superframe error counter are available in this **show** command.

```
Bottom#show controller bri
BRI unit 0:BRI unit 0 with U interface and POTS:
Layer 1 internal state is ACTIVATED
Layer 1 U interface is ACTIVATED.
ISDN Line Information:
    Current EOC commands:
        RTN - Return to normal
    Received overhead bits:
        AIB=1, UOA=1, SCO=1, DEA=1, ACT=1, M50=1,
    M51=1, M60=1, FEBE=1
    Errors:  [FEBE]=0, [NEBE]=0
    Errors:  [Superframe Sync Loss]=0, [IDL2 Data
        Transparency Loss]=0
                [M4 ACT 1 -> 0]=0
BRI U MLT Timers:  [TPULSE]=0, [T75S]=0
. . . some output omitted . . .
  0 missed datagrams, 0 overruns
  0 bad datagram encapsulations, 0 memory errors
  0 transmitter underruns
```

show isdn status

The **show** isdn status command is one of the more significant trouble-shooting commands because the output reports not only the status of the interface, but a breakdown of each layer. As shown in the first screen, the router has established a connection at Layer 1, but Layer 2 either remains in a negotiation mode or has failed to negotiate due to an improperly set switch or router.

```
Top#show isdn status
Global ISDN Switchtype = basic-ni
ISDN BRI0 interface
dsl 0, interface ISDN Switchtype = basic-ni
    Layer 1 Status:
ACTIVE
    Layer 2 Status:
```

```
TEI = 79, Ces = 1, SAPI = 0, State = MULTIPLE_FRAME_
   ESTABLISHED
   Spid Status:
TEI 79, ces = 1, state = 8(established)
   spid1 configured, no LDN, spid1 NOT sent, spid1 NOT
      valid
TEI Not Assigned, ces = 2, state = 1(terminal down)
   spid2 configured, no LDN, spid2 NOT sent, spid2 NOT
      valid
   Layer 3 Status:
0 Active Layer 3 Call(s)
   Activated dsl 0 CCBs = 1
CCB:callid=0x0, sapi=0x0, ces=0x1, B-chan=0 calltype =
   INTERNAL
Total Allocated ISDN CCBs = 1
```

The following display reports a correctly configured router and switch. Note that the SPIDs are confirmed and all layers are active on both B channels.

```
Top#show isdn status
Global ISDN Switchtype = basic-ni
ISDN BRI0 interface
dsl 0, interface ISDN Switchtype = basic-ni
   Layer 1 Status:
ACTIVE
   Layer 2 Status:
TEI = 83, Ces = 1, SAPI = 0, State = MULTIPLE_FRAME_
   ESTABLISHED
TEI = 84, Ces = 2, SAPI = 0, State = MULTIPLE_FRAME_
   ESTABLISHED
   Spid Status:
TEI 83, ces = 1, state = 5(init)
   spid1 configured, no LDN, spid1 sent, spid1 valid
   Endpoint ID Info: epsf = 0, usid = 1, tid = 1
TEI 84, ces = 2, state = 5(init)
   spid2 configured, no LDN, spid2 sent, spid2 valid
   Endpoint ID Info: epsf = 0, usid = 3, tid = 1
   Layer 3 Status:
```

```
    0 Active Layer 3 Call(s)
        Activated dsl 0 CCBs = 0
    Total Allocated ISDN CCBs = 0
```

Although this command is most frequently used for new installations, field installations and SOHO (small office, home office) installations frequently find the ISDN device turned off when not in use. This is usually caused by the router being plugged into a power strip attached to a PC.

When the router is disconnected from the ISDN circuit, the D channel (which is always "on") suddenly disconnects. Some phone companies view this as an error, and disconnect the circuit on the central office switch. When the user returns power to the circuit, this prevents connectivity because the switch no longer expects a connection. The show isdn status command provides an indication of problems that require contacting the phone company, and this should be considered if the user has disconnected the power or the ISDN phone cable. It is recommended that administrators instruct users to never disconnect the cable or power.

show dialer

The show dialer command reports information regarding the DDR connections, including the number dialed, the success of the connection, the idle timers that control the duration of a DDR connection without data packets, and the number of calls that were screened or rejected due to administrative policy.

This command is useful for verifying a previous connection or checking the number called. Note that dialer map statements, which link network addresses to ISDN numbers, can be implemented incorrectly—for example, IP address one is linked to number B instead of A. Although the router dials and the ISDN connection may succeed, it cannot pass packets due to Layer 3 mismatches. Note the Idle timer (120 secs) notation, which reflects the default Idle timer of two minutes for each B channel. The Idle timer shuts down the connection when no packets have traversed the link.

```
Bottom#show dialer
BRIO - dialer type = ISDN
Dial String      Successes    Failures    Last called   Last status
18008358661              2           0     00:02:49      successful
0 incoming call(s) have been screened.
```

```
0 incoming call(s) rejected for callback.
BRI0:1 - dialer type = ISDN
Idle timer (120 secs), Fast idle timer (20 secs)
Wait for carrier (30 secs), Re-enable (15 secs)
Dialer state is idle
BRI0:2 - dialer type = ISDN
Idle timer (120 secs), Fast idle timer (20 secs)
Wait for carrier (30 secs), Re-enable (15 secs)
Dialer state is idle
```

show ppp multilink

Multilink is an extended portion of the point-to-point protocol. As shown in the following, the service is configured with the ppp multilink bap and ppp bap commands (italicized below). PPP multilink allows for the combining of both B channels in a connection to allow 128Kbps of throughput.

```
interface BRI0
 ip address 10.1.1.2 255.255.255.0
 no ip directed-broadcast
 encapsulation ppp
 dialer map ip 10.1.1.1 name Top broadcast 18008358661
 dialer-group 1
 isdn switch-type basic-ni
 isdn spid1 0835866201
 isdn spid2 0835866401
 ppp multilink bap
 ppp bap call accept
 ppp bap timeout pending 20
 hold-queue 75 in
```

Debugging ISDN

The debug commands in ISDN are extremely helpful for researching problem causes and resolving them. This section addresses the commands and provides some useful methods for employing them, and attempts to provide scenarios where such commands may be needed.

The debug command is assigned a high CPU priority and can generate a high processor load. Always use caution when using a debug command. The resulting processor load and output can degrade router performance or render the system unusable.

It is recommended that routers be configured with timestamps for debug and log output. Use the service timestamps debug datetime msec and show-timezone localtime command to provide debug time information.

debug bri

The debug bri command provides information regarding the B channels of the BRI. An example of the command's output is provided below. Note that bandwidth information is also provided.

The B channels of the BRI are the data-carrying channels; therefore, an error in the activation of a B channel prevents data flow. It is also possible for the router to command one B channel to connect while the other B channel fails, which may be due to a misconfigured SPID or configuration problem. The command provides some insight into this potential problem.

```
Bottom#debug bri
Basic Rate network interface debugging is on
Bottom#ping 10.1.1.1
Type escape sequence to abort.
Sending 5, 100-byte ICMP Echos to 10.1.1.1, timeout is 2
    seconds:
00:29:48: BRI: enable channel B1
00:29:48: BRI0:MC145572 state handler current state 3
    actions 1 next state 3
00:29:48: BRI0:Starting activation
00:29:48: %LINK-3-UPDOWN: Interface BRI0:1, changed state
    to up.
00:29:49: BRI 0 B1: Set bandwidth to 64Kb
00:29:50: %LINEPROTO-5-UPDOWN: Line protocol on Interface
    BRI0:1, changed state to up
```

```
00:29:50: BRI 0 B2: Set bandwidth to 64Kb
00:29:50: BRI: enable channel B2
00:29:50: BRIO:MC145572 state handler current state 3
    actions 1 next state 3
00:29:50: BRIO:Starting activation
00:29:50: %LINK-3-UPDOWN: Interface BRIO:2, changed state
    to up.!!!
Success rate is 60 percent (3/5), round-trip min/avg/max =
    36/41/52 ms
00:29:50: BRI: enable channel B2
00:29:50: BRIO:MC145572 state handler current state 3
    actions 1 next state 3
00:29:50: BRIO:Starting activation
00:29:50: BRI 0 B2: Set bandwidth to 64Kb
00:29:51: %LINEPROTO-5-UPDOWN: Line protocol on Interface
    BRIO:2, changed state to up
```

debug isdn q921

The q.921 protocol addresses Layer 2 of the OSI model and its relationship to ISDN. Information regarding the D channel interface is available via the debug isdn q921 command.

The D channel is always connected in ISDN, and the channel is used for signaling between the switch and local ISDN device. Connections over the B channels cannot occur without signaling commands on the D channel. Administrators should use this command to monitor the proper flow of messages when calls do not connect. It is recommended that a baseline debug be performed and recorded to compare against suspected problem debug output.

```
Bottom#debug isdn q921
ISDN Q921 packets debugging is on
00:19:15: ISDN BRO: TX -> RRp sapi = 0  tei = 92 nr = 12
00:19:64424550400: ISDN BRO: RX <- RRf sapi = 0  tei = 92
    nr = 12
Bottom#ping 10.1.1.1
Type escape sequence to abort.
Sending 5, 100-byte ICMP Echos to 10.1.1.1, timeout is 2
    seconds:
```

```
.
00:19:23: ISDN BRO: TX -> INFOc sapi = 0  tei = 92
   ns = 12     nr = 12  i = 0x080
10305040288901801832C0B313838303038333538363631
00:19:98789554100: ISDN BRO: RX <- INFOc sapi = 0
   tei = 92     ns = 12  nr = 13
i =
   0x08018302180189952A1B809402603D8307383335383636318E0B2
      054454C544F4E45203120
00:19:23: ISDN BRO: TX -> RRr sapi = 0  tei = 92  nr = 13
00:19:103079256064: ISDN BRO: RX <- INFOc sapi = 0
   tei = 92  ns = 13  nr = 13
 i = 0x08018307
00:19:24: ISDN BRO: TX -> RRr sapi = 0  tei = 92  nr = 14
00:19:24: %LINK-3-UPDOWN: Interface BRIO:1, changed state
   to up
00:19:24: ISDN BRO: TX -> INFOc sapi = 0  tei = 92
   ns = 13     nr = 14  i = 0x080
1030F
00:19:103079215104: ISDN BRO: RX <- RRr sapi = 0
   tei = 92     nr = 14
00:19:25: %LINEPROTO-5-UPDOWN: Line protocol on Interface
   BRIO:1, changed state to up
00:19:107379488692: ISDN BRO: RX <- UI sapi = 0
   tei = 127    i = 0x08010A05040288
9018018A3401403B0282816C094181383335383636337008C138333538
   36   3632
00:19:25: %LINK-3-UPDOWN: Interface BRIO:2, changed state
   to up.!!!
Success rate is 60 percent (3/5), round-trip min/avg/max =
   32/38/48 ms
00:19:25: ISDN BRO: TX -> INFOc sapi = 0  tei = 92
   ns = 14     nr = 14  i = 0x080
18A0718018A
00:19:107374223360: ISDN BRO: RX <- INFOc sapi = 0
   tei = 92  ns = 14  nr = 15
 i = 0x08010A0F
00:19:25: ISDN BRO: TX -> RRr sapi = 0  tei = 92  nr = 15
```

```
00:19:27: %LINEPROTO-5-UPDOWN: Line protocol on Interface
    BRIO:2, changed state to up
00:19:36: ISDN BRO: TX ->  RRp sapi = 0  tei = 93 nr = 0
00:19:154618822656: ISDN BRO: RX <-  RRf sapi = 0
    tei = 93       nr = 0
```

debug isdn q931

The q.931 specification addresses Layer 3 of the OSI model for ISDN. Events occurring at Layer 3 may be monitored with the debug isdn q931 command. In the following output, the two B channels are disconnected.

The output from this command is best compared to a baseline debug captured on a working connection. However, administrators may use the output to verify acknowledgments and messages without a complete understanding of the protocol. There is a great deal of information provided by the following command. Among other valuable uses, this abundance of information can be used to verify the Layer 3 (q.931) setup.

```
Bottom#debug isdn q931
ISDN Q931 packets debugging is on
00:15:184683593728: ISDN BRO: RX <-  STATUS_ENQ pd = 8
    callref = 0x82
00:15:43: ISDN BRO: TX ->  STATUS pd = 8  callref = 0x02
00:15:43:         Cause i = 0x809E - Response to STATUS
    ENQUIRY or number unassigned
00:15:43:         Call State i = 0x0A
00:15:188978601984: ISDN BRO: RX <-  STATUS_ENQ pd = 8
    callref = 0x06
00:15:44: ISDN BRO: TX ->  STATUS pd = 8  callref = 0x86
00:15:44:         Cause i = 0x809E - Response to STATUS
    ENQUIRY or number unassigned
00:15:44:         Call State i = 0x0A
00:16:55834615808: ISDN BRO: RX <-  STATUS_ENQ pd = 8
    callref = 0x82
00:16:13: ISDN BRO: TX ->  STATUS pd = 8  callref = 0x02
00:16:13:         Cause i = 0x809E - Response to STATUS
    ENQUIRY or number unassigned
00:16:13:         Call State i = 0x0A
00:16:60129583104: ISDN BRO: RX <-  STATUS_ENQ pd = 8
    callref = 0x06
```

```
00:16:14: ISDN BR0: TX ->  STATUS pd = 8  callref = 0x86
00:16:14:          Cause i = 0x809E - Response to STATUS
    ENQUIRY or number unassigned
00:16:14:          Call State i = 0x0A
00:16:188978601984: ISDN BR0: RX <-  DISCONNECT pd = 8
    callref = 0x82
00:16:188978561024:          Cause i = 0x8290 - Normal call
    clearing
00:16:188978601984:          Signal i = 0x3F - Tones off
00:16:44: %ISDN-6-DISCONNECT: Interface BRI0:1
    disconnected    from 18008358661 To p, call lasted 120
    seconds
00:16:44: %LINK-3-UPDOWN: Interface BRI0:1, changed state
    to down
00:16:44: ISDN BR0: TX ->  RELEASE pd = 8  callref = 0x02
00:16:188978601984: ISDN BR0: RX <-  RELEASE_COMP pd = 8
    callref = 0x82
00:16:188978561024: %ISDN-6-DISCONNECT: Interface BRI0:2
    disconnected from 8358 663 , call lasted 120 seconds
00:16:44: ISDN BR0: TX ->  DISCONNECT pd = 8  callref =
    0x86
00:16:44:          Cause i = 0x8090 - Normal call clearing
00:16:188978561024: ISDN BR0: RX <-  RELEASE pd = 8
    callref = 0x06
00:16:44: %LINK-3-UPDOWN: Interface BRI0:2, changed state
    to down
00:16:44: ISDN BR0: TX ->  RELEASE_COMP pd = 8  callref =
    0x86
00:16:45: %LINEPROTO-5-UPDOWN: Line protocol on Interface
    BRI0:1, changed state to down
00:16:45: %LINEPROTO-5-UPDOWN: Line protocol on Interface
    BRI0:2, changed state to down
```

debug ppp negotiation

When the router is configured for point-to-point protocol, the debug ppp negotiation command provides real-time information about the establishment of a session. This is useful if connections are possible with the HDLC protocol and failures occur with the PPP protocol. There is a great deal of information provided by the following command. However, it can be used to verify the PPP negotiation described earlier in the chapter. You should use this output to verify the troubleshooting targets in PPP negotiation.

```
Bottom#debug ppp negotiation
PPP protocol negotiation debugging is on
Bottom#ping 10.1.1.1
Type escape sequence to abort.
Sending 5, 100-byte ICMP Echos to 10.1.1.1, timeout is 2
    seconds:
00:22:28: %LINK-3-UPDOWN: Interface BRI0:1, changed state
    to up
00:22:28: BR0:1 PPP: Treating connection as a callout
00:22:28: BR0:1 PPP: Phase is ESTABLISHING, Active Open
00:22:28: BR0:1 LCP: O CONFREQ [Closed] id 3 len 10
00:22:28: BR0:1 LCP:    MagicNumber 0x50239604
    (0x050650239604)
00:22:28: BR0:1 LCP: I CONFREQ [REQsent] id 13 len 10
00:22:28: BR0:1 LCP:    MagicNumber 0x5023961F
    (0x05065023961F)
00:22:28: BR0:1 LCP: O CONFACK [REQsent] id 13 len 10
00:22:28: BR0:1 LCP:    MagicNumber 0x5.023961F
    (0x05065023961F)
00:22:28: BR0:1 LCP: I CONFACK [ACKsent] id 3 len 10
00:22:28: BR0:1 LCP:    MagicNumber 0x50239604
    (0x050650239604)
00:22:28: BR0:1 LCP: State is Open
00:22:28: BR0:1 PPP: Phase is UP
00:22:28: BR0:1 CDPCP: O CONFREQ [Closed] id 3 len 4
00:22:28: BR0:1 IPCP: O CONFREQ [Closed] id 3 len 10
00:22:28: BR0:1 IPCP:    Address 10.1.1.2 (0x03060A010102)
00:22:28: BR0:1 CDPCP: I CONFREQ [REQsent] id 3 len 4
00:22:28: BR0:1 CDPCP: O CONFACK [REQsent] id 3 len 4
00:22:28: BR0:1 IPCP: I CONFREQ [REQsent] id 3 len 10
00:22:28: BR0:1 IPCP:    Address 10.1.1.1 (0x03060A010101)
00:22:28: BR0:1 IPCP: O CONFACK [REQsent] id 3 len 10
00:22:28: BR0:1 IPCP:    Address 10.1.1.1 (0x03060A010101)
00:22:28: BR0:1 CDPCP: I CONFACK [ACKsent] id 3 len 4
```

```
00:22:28: BR0:1 CDPCP: State is Open
00:22:28: BR0:1 IPCP: I CONFACK [ACKsent] id 3 len 10
00:22:28: BR0:1 IPCP:    Address 10.1.1.2 (0x03060A010102)
00:22:28: BR0:1 IPCP: State is Open
00:22:28: BR0 IPCP: Install route to 10.1.1.1
00:22:2.!!!
Success rate is 60 percent (3/5), round-trip min/avg/max =
   32/38/48 ms
Bottom#9: %LINEPROTO-5-UPDOWN: Line protocol on Interface
   BRI0:1, changed state to up
00:22:29: %LINK-3-UPDOWN: Interface BRI0:2, changed state
   to up
00:22:29: BR0:2 PPP: Treating connection as a callin
00:22:29: BR0:2 PPP: Phase is ESTABLISHING, Passive Open
00:22:29: BR0:2 LCP: State is Listen
00:22:30: BR0:2 LCP: I CONFREQ [Listen] id 3 len 10
00:22:30: BR0:2 LCP:    MagicNumber 0x50239CC8
   (0x050650239CC8)
00:22:30: BR0:2 LCP: O CONFREQ [Listen] id 3 len 10
00:22:30: BR0:2 LCP:    MagicNumber 0x50239CDA
   (0x050650239CDA)
00:22:30: BR0:2 LCP: O CONFACK [Listen] id 3 len 10
00:22:30: BR0:2 LCP:    MagicNumber 0x50239CC8
   (0x050650239CC8)
00:22:30: BR0:2 LCP: I CONFACK [ACKsent] id 3 len 10
00:22:30: BR0:2 LCP:    MagicNumber 0x50239CDA
   (0x050650239CDA)
00:22:30: BR0:2 LCP: State is Open
00:22:30: BR0:2 PPP: Phase is UP
00:22:30: BR0:2 CDPCP: O CONFREQ [Closed] id 3 len 4
00:22:30: BR0:2 IPCP: O CONFREQ [Closed] id 3 len 10
00:22:30: BR0:2 IPCP:    Address 10.1.1.2 (0x03060A010102)
00:22:30: BR0:2 CDPCP: I CONFREQ [REQsent] id 3 len 4
00:22:30: BR0:2 CDPCP: O CONFACK [REQsent] id 3 len 4
00:22:30: BR0:2 IPCP: I CONFREQ [REQsent] id 3 len 10
00:22:30: BR0:2 IPCP:    Address 10.1.1.1 (0x03060A010101)
00:22:30: BR0:2 IPCP: O CONFACK [REQsent] id 3 len 10
```

```
00:22:30: BR0:2 IPCP:    Address 10.1.1.1 (0x03060A010101)
00:22:30: BR0:2 CDPCP: I CONFACK [ACKsent] id 3 len 4
00:22:30: BR0:2 CDPCP: State is Open
00:22:30: BR0:2 IPCP: I CONFACK [ACKsent] id 3 len 10
00:22:30: BR0:2 IPCP:    Address 10.1.1.2 (0x03060A010102)
00:22:30: BR0:2 IPCP: State is Open
00:22:31: %LINEPROTO-5-UPDOWN: Line protocol on Interface
   BRI0:2, changed state to up
00:21:22: BR0:1 LCP: O ECHOREQ [Open] id 12 len 12 magic
   0x5020C645
00:21:22: BR0:1 LCP: echo_cnt 1, sent id 12, line up
00:21:22: BR0:1 PPP: I pkt type 0xC021, datagramsize 16
00:21:22: BR0:1 LCP: I ECHOREP [Open] id 12 len 12 magic
   0x5020C654
00:21:22: BR0:1 LCP: Received id 12, sent id 12, line up
00:21:22: BR0:2 LCP: O ECHOREQ [Open] id 12 len 12 magic
   0x5020CD1B
00:21:22: BR0:2 LCP: echo_cnt 1, sent id 12, line up
00:21:22: BR0:2 PPP: I pkt type 0xC021, datagramsize 16
00:21:22: BR0:2 LCP: I ECHOREP [Open] id 12 len 12 magic
   0x5020CD0D
00:21:22: BR0:2 LCP: Received id 12, sent id 12, line up
00:21:23: BR0:1 PPP: I pkt type 0xC021, datagramsize 16
00:21:23: BR0:1 LCP: I ECHOREQ [Open] id 12 len 12 magic
   0x5020C654
00:21:23: BR0:1 LCP: O ECHOREP [Open] id 12 len 12 magic
   0x5020C645
00:21:23: BR0:2 PPP: I pkt type 0xC021, datagramsize 16
00:21:23: BR0:2 LCP: I ECHOREQ [Open] id 12 len 12 magic
   0x5020CD0D
00:21:23: BR0:2 LCP: O ECHOREP [Open] id 12 len 12 magic
   0x5020CD1B
00:21:24: BR0:2 PPP: I pkt type 0x0207, datagramsize 15
00:21:25: BR0:2 PPP: I pkt type 0x0207, datagramsize 312
00:21:25: %ISDN-6-DISCONNECT: Interface BRI0:1
   disconnected from 18008358661 To p, call lasted 120
   seconds
00:21:25: %LINK-3-UPDOWN: Interface BRI0:1, changed state
   to down
```

```
00:21:107379488949: %ISDN-6-DISCONNECT: Interface BRIO:2
   disconnected from 8358 663 , call lasted 120 seconds
00:21:25: %LINK-3-UPDOWN: Interface BRIO:2, changed state
   to down
00:21:26: %LINEPROTO-5-UPDOWN: Line protocol on Interface
   BRIO:1, changed state to down
00:21:26: %LINEPROTO-5-UPDOWN: Line protocol on Interface
   BRIO:2, changed state to down
```

debug ppp packet

The debug ppp packet command reports real-time PPP packet flow, including the type of packet and the specific B channel used. Although this command generates a significant amount of output, it is quite useful for locating errors that involve upper-layer protocols.

As with other debug packet commands, the debug ppp packet command records each packet that moves through the router using PPP. The administrator can thus monitor traffic flows as if there was a protocol analyzer attached to the interface. This may be useful for troubleshooting Application layer problems, but a formal protocol analyzer is highly recommended.

```
Bottom#debug ppp packet
PPP packet display debugging is on
Bottom#ping 10.1.1.1
Type escape sequence to abort.
Sending 5, 100-byte ICMP Echos to 10.1.1.1, timeout is 2
   seconds:
00:24:49: %LINK-3-UPDOWN: Interface BRIO:1, changed state
   to up.
00:24:50: BRO:1 LCP: O CONFREQ [Closed] id 4 len 10
00:24:50: BRO:1 LCP:    MagicNumber 0x5025BF23
   (0x05065025BF23)
00:24:50: BRO:1 PPP: I pkt type 0xC021, datagramsize 14
00:24:50: BRO:1 PPP: I pkt type 0xC021, datagramsize 14
00:24:50: BRO:1 LCP: I CONFREQ [REQsent] id 14 len 10
00:24:50: BRO:1 LCP:    MagicNumber 0x5025BF46
   (0x05065025BF46)
00:24:50: BRO:1 LCP: O CONFACK [REQsent] id 14 len 10
00:24:50: BRO:1 LCP:    MagicNumber 0x5025BF46
   (0x05065025BF46)
00:24:50: BRO:1 LCP: I CONFACK [ACKsent] id 4 len 10
```

```
00:24:50: BR0:1 LCP:     MagicNumber 0x5025BF23
   (0x05065025BF23)
00:24:50: BR0:1 PPP: I pkt type 0x8207, datagramsize 8
00:24:50: BR0:1 PPP: I pkt type 0x8021, datagramsize 14
00:24:50: BR0:1 CDPCP: O CONFREQ [Closed] id 4 len 4
00:24:50: BR0:1 PPP: I pkt type 0x8207, datagramsize 8
00:24:50: BR0:1 IPCP: O CONFREQ [Closed] id 4 len 10
00:24:50: BR0:1 IPCP:     Address 10.1.1.2 (0x03060A010102)
00:24:50: BR0:1 CDPCP: I CONFREQ [REQsent] id 4 len 4
00:24:50: BR0:1 CDPCP: O CONFACK [REQ.!!!
Success rate is 60 percent (3/5), round-trip min/avg/max =
   36/41/52 ms
. . . some output omitted . . .
00:25:03: BR0:2 LCP: O ECHOREP [Open] id 2 len 12 magic
   0x5025C605undebug all
All possible debugging has been turned off
Bottom#
```

debug dialer

The debug dialer command provides information regarding the cause of a dialing connection and the status of the connection. Note in the following output that an IP packet caused the dial to occur. This information can provide assistance for tuning connections. Administrators frequently do this to limit the use of an ISDN circuit when charged on distance and per-minute tariffs.

```
Bottom#debug dialer
Dial on demand events debugging is on
Bottom#ping 10.1.1.1
Type escape sequence to abort.
Sending 5, 100-byte ICMP Echos to 10.1.1.1, timeout is 2
   seconds:
00:27:26: BRI0: Dialing cause ip (s=10.1.1.2, d=10.1.1.1)
00:27:26: BRI0: Attempting to dial 18008358661
00:27:27: %LINK-3-UPDOWN: Interface BRI0:1, changed state
   to up.
00:27:27: dialer Protocol up for BR0:1
```

```
00:27:28: %LINEPROTO-5-UPDOWN: Line protocol on Interface
    BRI0:1, changed state to up
00:27:29: %LINK-3-UPDOWN: Interface BRI0:2, changed state
    to up.!!!
Success rate is 60 percent (3/5), round-trip min/avg/max =
    32/37/48 ms
Bottom#
00:27:29: dialer Protocol up for BR0:2
00:27:30: %LINEPROTO-5-UPDOWN: Line protocol on Interface
    BRI0:2, changed state to up
```

Summary

Though originally designed to bring digital networking to the home environment, ISDN has evolved into a commonly used business tool. It allows small offices to connect to multiple different locations without the need for a dedicated circuit. This connectivity includes connecting back to the corporate office, to other businesses, to an ISP, and to many other locations. In addition, ISDN has also been used to provide backup services when a primary link fails.

Numerous component and connection types are used in ISDN. In order to better describe how each major component interacts with the other major ISDN components, one was given an acronym. In addition, commonly used connections between major components were given abbreviations called reference points. The specific component acronyms and reference points are detailed in Figure 8.1 and textually explained in the section that follows this figure.

An ISDN BRI channel is made up of two 64Kbps B channels used for carrying traffic and a single 16Kbps D channel used for signaling. The signaling that is used over the D channel for call setup is q.921 for Layer 2 and q.931 for Layer 3. In addition, the most common protocol used for encapsulation on an ISDN link is PPP. With negotiation occurring over the B channels, PPP supports multiple different Layer 3 protocols, such as IP, IPX, and Apple-Talk. PPP also supports CHAP and PAP security.

When troubleshooting ISDN, there are numerous different show and debug commands that can be used. These commands allow for detailed analysis of the interface, q.921, q.931, and PPP. Some of the more common

commands are show interface, show ISDN status, show dialer, debug
isdn q921, debug ISDN q931, and debug ppp authentication.

Exam Essentials

Know the basics of how ISDN operates.   Know that ISDN is a digital
service. Also know the number and size of B channels and D channels and
the use of SPIDs.

Know the ISDN components.   The components that are used in ISDN
are TE1, TE2, TA, NT2, NT1, LT, and ET. In North America, the NT1
is the last component that is considered CPE, whereas in most other places
the NT1 is carrier provided and maintained.

Know the ISDN reference points.   The reference points used in an ISDN
connection are R, S, T, and U. If no NT2 is used, the S and T reference
points combine to make an S/T reference point.

Know how ISDN calls are set up.   Access lists are used in conjunction
with dialer maps to define the traffic type that will bring up a link as well
as the number that is dialed. In addition, authentication can be set up to
ensure the validity of an incoming call.

Know the function of q.921.   q.921 in combination with LAPD is used
to set up the Layer 2 connection over the D channel. The debug ISDN q921
command allows for the debugging of specific q.921 information.

Know the function of q.931.   q.931 is used to set up the Layer 3 connection over the D channel. The debug ISDN q931 command allows for
the debugging of specific q.931 information.

Know how PPP is used and how it is set up.   LCP is used as the Layer 2
protocol for link establishment and maintenance. NCP performs similar
functions for Layer 3 protocols. PPP also has the capability to use
authentication. The debug ppp negotiation command can be used to
look specifically at the PPP setup.

Know how CHAP and PAP function.   CHAP and PAP are both authentication protocols used with PPP. These protocols allow for verification of
both calling and called device. The debug ppp authentication command
can be used to look at the CHAP or PAP authentication process.

Commands Used in This Chapter

The following list contains a summary of all the commands used in this chapter.

Commands	Descriptions
clear interface bri n	Resets the various counters that are available on the Basic Rate Interface (BRI) and terminates a connection on the interface.
debug bri	Provides information regarding the B channels of the interface.
debug dialer	Provides information regarding the cause of a dialing connection and the status of the connection.
debug isdn q921	Gives details regarding the Layer 2 connection sequence for ISDN.
debug isdn q931	Gives details regarding the Layer 3 connection sequence for ISDN.
debug ppp authentication	Gives details regarding the PPP / CHAP authentication connection sequence.
debug ppp negotiation	Provides real-time information about the establishment of a session.
debug ppp packet	Reports real-time PPP packet flow, including the type of packet and the specific B channel used.
ping	Initiates an ICMP echo request. There are two levels, User and Privileged. The IP protocol is used.
show controller bri	Displays the interface status and the superframe error counter.
show dialer	Reports information regarding the DDR connections, including the number dialed, the success of the connection, the idle timers that control the duration of a DDR connection without data packets, and the number of calls that were screened or rejected due to administrative policy.

Commands	Descriptions
`show interface bri n`	Reports the B channel's status, as well as spoofing on the interface.
`show interface bri n 1 2`	Displays a single B channel of the BRI interface.
`show isdn status`	Reports the status of the interface, as well as a breakdown of each layer.
`show ppp multilink`	Displays configuration settings for PPP multilink.

Key Terms

Before you take the exam, be certain you are familiar with the following terms:

access lists	q.931
Challenge Handshake Authentication Protocol (CHAP)	R reference point
dialer map statements	S reference point
ISDN BRI	Service Profile Identifiers (SPIDs)
Layer 1 S/T Interface	T reference point
Link Access Procedure protocol (LAPD)	TE1
LT/ET	TE2
NT1	U reference point
q.921	

Review Questions

1. Where does the q.931 signaling operate?

   A. At Layer 3 of the OSI model on the B channel

   B. At Layer 2 of the OSI model on the B channel

   C. At Layer 3 of the OSI model on the D channel

   D. At Layer 2 of the OSI model on the D channel

   E. On all channels of the BRI

2. What does the Basic Rate Interface (BRI) provide?

   A. 64Kbps of bandwidth in each direction

   B. 192Kbps of user bandwidth

   C. Two 64Kbps data channels and one management channel of 16Kbps

   D. Two 64Kbps data channels

   E. 128Kbps for user data

3. The remote router is connected to a DMS-100 switch using the basic-dms100 setting. The local router would be configured with what command?

   A. `isdn switch-type basic-dms100`

   B. `isdn switch-type basic-basic-ni1`

   C. `isdn switch basic dms100`

   D. The answer cannot be determined from the information given.

4. Challenge Handshake Authentication Protocol requires which of the following? (Choose all that apply.)

   A. ISDN

   B. PPP

   C. A defined username

   D. Encrypted passwords on the router

   E. An external server running TACACS+

5. Router_A is configured for ISDN BRI and PPP, with an IP address of 192.168.10.1 and a subnet mask of 255.255.255.252. Router_B would be configured with which of the following?

   A. 192.168.10.254

   B. 192.168.10.2

   C. 192.168.10.3

   D. `ip unnumbered`

   E. The answer cannot be determined from the information given.

6. An ISDN call initially succeeds, but pings and other packets fail. What is the likely cause? (Choose all that apply.)

   A. A faulty cable

   B. A misconfiguration of CHAP

   C. Incorrect speeds between the switch and router

   D. An incorrect route or missing route

7. An administrator finds that an ISDN router does not dial. What are the possible causes? (Choose all that apply.)

   A. A misconfigured dialer map

   B. A dialer list filter

   C. An incorrect switch type

   D. Incorrect SPIDs

8. What does the `clear interface bri n` command accomplish?

   A. Clears the interface counters for interface *n*

   B. Disconnects all calls on the router

   C. Disconnects the active calls on interface *n*

   D. None of the above

9. What are the advantages of CHAP? (Choose all that apply.)

    A. Password authentication

    B. Compression

    C. Encryption of data packets

    D. Encryption of the authentication process

10. The command(s) to restrict dialing on an ISDN router can include which of the following?

    A. `dialer-list 1 protocol ip list 101`

    B. `dialer list 1 protocol ip list 110`

    C. `access-list 200 permit ip any any`

    D. `dialer-map deny packet bri0`

11. Which of the following is required for CHAP services?

    A. TCP/IP

    B. PPP

    C. PAP

    D. TACACS+

    E. Radius

12. Which channels must be active in order for ISDN BRI to send packets?

    A. Both B channels

    B. One B channel and the D channel

    C. Both B channels and the D channel

    D. All 24 B channels

13. Which of the following commands provides information regarding superframe sync loss?

    A. `show interface bri`

    B. `show controller bri`

    C. `show isdn sync`

    D. `show isdn controller`

14. In North America, a SPID might appear as which of the following?

   A. 10.1.1.1

   B. e415.5551.2120

   C. 41555512120101

   D. 5551212

15. To verify all three layers of an ISDN circuit prior to dialing, an administrator should use which of the following commands?

   A. `show ppp multilink`

   B. `show dialer`

   C. `debug bri`

   D. `show isdn status`

16. How long is the default ISDN idle timer for each B channel?

   A. 30 seconds

   B. 60 seconds

   C. 90 seconds

   D. 120 seconds

   E. 300 seconds

17. Layer 3 of ISDN (q.931) is responsible for which of the following?

   A. Determining the switch type

   B. Call setup and disconnect

   C. Assignment of the TEI

   D. Encapsulation of packets on the B channel

18. What is the D channel used for? (Choose all that apply.)

   A. q.921 messages

   B. q.931 messages

   C. TCP/IP

   D. AppleTalk

19. If the switch type is unknown, which command may the administrator use?

   A. `isdn switch type 0`

   B. `isdn auto switch`

   C. `isdn autodetect`

   D. `isdn switch generic`

   E. None of the above

20. An administrator has a non-ISDN device (TE2). Which of the following is required to connect the device to the ISDN network?

   A. A terminal adapter (TA)

   B. Category 5 wiring

   C. Category 3 wiring

   D. A codec

   E. Device cannot be connected

Answers to Review Questions

1. C.   q.931 runs on the D channel and is located at Layer 3.

2. C.   While D and E are partially correct, the BRI includes both B channels and the D channel.

3. D.   Because ISDN switch type is only locally significant, the remote end of a connection could use a different switch. Therefore, more information is needed before the switch-type is configured.

4. B, C.   PPP is required for CHAP to work on ISDN. Usernames must be defined on the routers for authentication purposes. The other options are not required for proper CHAP operation.

5. B.   The subnet mask indicates only two hosts on the network. The only other host allowed is 192.168.10.2.

6. B, D.   A faulty cable can be eliminated because the call would not succeed if there were a cable fault. Speeds are default.

7. A, B, C, D.   Any of these can be the cause of the router not dialing.

8. C.   The interface must be specified to clear the call.

9. A, D.   CHAP was intended for password authentication and encryption.

10. A.   The correct syntax requires a hyphen.

11. B.   PPP is a required protocol for CHAP to function.

12. B.   One B channel may be used without the use of the other. The D channel must be active to handle the call.

13. B.   The controller command shows the superframe information.

14. C.   The SPID is appended to the 10-digit phone number.

15. D.   The status command provides the necessary information.

16. D.   The timer is set for 2 minutes idle time.

17. B. q.931 is responsible for the call setup and disconnect, since this occurs on Layer 3.

18. A, B. The D channel is used for administration and not data (payload) transfers.

19. C. Autodetect tells the router to listen for the switch type and set it accordingly.

20. A. A terminal adapter is required for a non-ISDN device.

Chapter

9

Troubleshooting Novell Connectivity

TOPICS COVERED IN THIS CHAPTER INCLUDE:

✓ Use proven problem isolation techniques to list the symptoms of common Novell IPX problems on router networks.

ovell NetWare remains one of the more popular network operating systems. Gaining particular favor with the release of NetWare 3.11, NetWare quickly earned market share and a reputation for easy installation and maintenance.

Part of this reputation is due to the simplicity of NetWare's network protocol—IPX (Internetwork Packet Exchange). IPX removed many of the client-configuration issues that were inherent in other protocols.

With the release of NetWare 5.0, Novell departed from the IPX/SPX (Sequenced Packet Exchange) protocol in favor of the more universal TCP/IP. This was due in large part to the growth of the Internet and the advantages of using a single network protocol. There are many legacy applications and networks that still make use of IPX, however, and there are still advantages to using it. There are also specific issues that arise in NetWare environments that require troubleshooting by the network administrator.

In this chapter, troubleshooting commands, connection sequences, and diagnostic tools will be presented as they relate to an IPX environment. This includes an overview of IPX networks and addressing. In this chapter, too, you will be provided the opportunity to work on a lab exercise that will allow you to troubleshoot general problems as well as IPX-specific symptoms.

IPX Networking Fundamentals

Although IPX operates at the Network layer of the OSI model and shares addressing concepts with IP, it is much easier to configure and administer. IPX addresses appear in the format *network.node*, where the network is an administrator-assigned address of four octets. This address is combined with the MAC layer address of the node, creating a ten-octet address. This system greatly reduces the administrative overhead at the network node—workstation, printer, or other device. In addition, the addressing scheme is independent of the IP subnet mask concept, and any number of nodes can belong to an IPX network within the constraints of the medium and the broadcast limitations of IPX itself.

As with TCP/IP addresses, IPX addresses can be written in several formats. Most often, they're written in hexadecimal—for example, 00007C80.0000 .8609.33E9. The first eight hex digits (00007C80) represent the network portion of the address; the remaining 12 hex digits (0000.8609.33E9) represent the node portion and are the MAC address of the workstation. When referring to the IPX network, it's a common IPX custom to drop leading 0s. Thus, the above network address is referred to as IPX network 7C80. The node portion is commonly divided into three sections of four hex digits that are divided by periods, as shown.

 Real World Scenario

IPX Addressing

As is the case with IP, an appropriate addressing methodology with IPX can make installing and maintaining IPX networks easier. In most IPX networks I have worked with, IPX was running concurrently with IP. In these cases it is helpful to have some correlation between the IP and IPX addresses. A common convention is to use the IP decimal or hex values to make up the IPX network number; thus, 10.11.10.0 becomes IPX network 10d11d10 or 10d0Bd10 (the "d" is for "dot"). In other cases, the IP address is converted to its hexadecimal equivalent. For instance, the 10.11.10.0 address in the previous example would become 0A0B0A00. If your IP address ranges are implemented in a logical manner that allows for summarization, this method also allows you to summarize the IPX address space along the same boundaries, assuming that you are running an IPX routing protocol that supports summarization, such as NLSP. By keeping a direct correlation between IP and IPX addresses, I have found that maintaining the overall network is easier.

However, some network administrators alter this convention in favor of a frame type–location-segment format. For example, F4150001 could refer to the first IPX network using the Ethernet II frame type in the San Francisco office (area code 415). This allows for easy identification of services located in a particular area as well as the framing that is used. Whichever method is chosen, keep in mind that IPX network numbers must be unique within the entire network.

IPX simplifies functions for the network and server administrators, in that the IP functions of DHCP, ARP, and DNS/WINS are included in the base functionality of the protocol. ARP packets are unnecessary because the MAC address is part of the overall network address. Address assignment (the DHCP function in IP) is also handled by IPX because all MAC addresses are unique, by design. The network number is presumed unique as a function of both the internetwork design and the administrator's policies. Finally, name resolution is a function of the SAP (service advertising protocol) process, which automatically updates all resources with the address and socket of all services. This simplification is not without its penalties, because IPX and its higher-level protocol SPX have a reputation for being chattier than TCP/IP.

Connecting to a Novell Network

Although a myriad of problems can confront network administrators in NetWare environments, a significant percentage of issues occurs during the initial connection between the client and server. This connection, by its very nature, may be the first indication of an erred configuration or other problem within the network.

Connecting to a NetWare server first requires an administrator to select an encapsulation method for the network. Once connectivity is established at this layer, service broadcasts begin. This section covers the following issues related to IPX:

- Encapsulation

- Get Nearest Server

- Service Advertising Protocol

Encapsulation

In NetWare, *encapsulation and framing* refer to the method used to take an IPX datagram, a Layer 3 element, and add it to an appropriate Layer 2 frame. In this section, the framing process is outlined as it relates to Ethernet. Framing is also relevant in Token Ring and FDDI topologies, however.

Encapsulation is one of the more common troubleshooting problems in NetWare networks. If the frame type does not match on all network resources, the various components cannot communicate. This is akin to speaking a different language from everyone else in the room—communication is impossible without a translator. If client A speaks SNAP and the server speaks 802.3, they do not understand each other. They must both speak either 802.3 or SNAP.

The four Ethernet IPX frame options are 802.3, 802.2, SNAP, and Ethernet II. Note that Cisco refers to these Novell names with different terminology, as shown in Table 9.1.

TABLE 9.1 Novell Ethernet Encapsulations

NetWare Frame Type	Features	Cisco Term
Ethernet_802.3	Default IPX frame type through Net-Ware 3.11. 802.3 supports only IPX and contains a length field after the source MAC address. It is available only on Ethernet.	novell-ether
Ethernet_802.2	Default IPX frame type since NetWare 3.12. This frame type is supported for Ethernet, FDDI, and Token Ring. It is recommended in environments that have a combination of physical media.	sap or iso1
Ethernet_II	Supports both TCP/IP and IPX. The ether type is placed after the source MAC address. IPX uses 8137 for the ether type; IP uses 0800.	arpa
Ethernet_SNAP	AppleTalk, IPX, and TCP/IP are supported on Token Ring, Ethernet, and FDDI. It includes a SNAP header.	snap

It was noted earlier that all resources need to use the same frame type on the network. There are times, however, when more than one frame type might be supported on a particular segment. This may be during a transition from one frame type to another, or to support a specific hardware or software platform. This usually involves configuring the server and/or router for all applicable frame types, and it adds a great deal of unnecessary overhead for both the server and the network. It is recommended that administrators select one frame type for new installations and remove as many frame types as possible in legacy installations.

Although the default protocol for NetWare 5.0 is IP, the IPX default (when used) is Ethernet 802.2, and 802.2 has been the default since NetWare 3.12. Prior to version 3.12, Novell used Ethernet 802.3, or raw Ethernet. This frame type supports only IPX, and places a length field after the source MAC address in an Ethernet frame. As noted in Table 9.1, the selection of frame type is dependent on existing network applications and configurations, as well as on the features needed.

IPX external network numbers must be unique for each frame type used, even if two frame types are bound to the same physical network.

Get Nearest Server

Before connecting to a Novell server, clients must locate an appropriate resource. This is accomplished with the *GNS (get nearest server)* request that is specified within the SAP. The next section addresses the SAP process specifically, whereas the focus of this section is the GNS process itself.

GNS is a broadcast datagram that is answered by any IPX server on the network. If there are multiple servers on a network segment, the client receives a response from each one and accepts the first one for the rest of the initialization process. Note that the first server may not be the preferred server listed in the client's configuration file.

When a client wishes to connect to a network resource, it uses the GNS broadcast, which is captured with an EtherPeek analyzer, as follows. In this example, the workstation's MAC address is `00:60:08:9e:2e:44` and the first packet is the client's GNS request.

```
Flags:   0x80 802.3
 Status:  0x00
 Packet Length:64
 Timestamp: 22:56:14.565643 05/07/2002
802.3 Header
```

Destination: ff:ff:ff:ff:ff:ff Ethernet Brdcast
Source: 00:60:08:9e:2e:44
LLC Length: 38
802.2 Logical Link Control (LLC) Header
Dest. SAP: 0xe0 NetWare
Source SAP: 0xe0 NetWare Individual LLC Sublayer
  Management Function
Command: 0x03 Unnumbered Information
IPX - NetWare Protocol
Checksum: 0xffff
Length: 34
Transport Control:
Reserved: %0000
Hop Count: %0000
Packet Type: 0 Novell
Destination Network: 0x00000000
Destination Node: ff:ff:ff:ff:ff:ff Ethernet Brdcast
Destination Socket: 0x0452 Service Advertising Protocol
Source Network: 0xf3df9b36
Source Node: 00:60:08:9e:2e:44
Source Socket: 0x4000 IPX Ephemeral
SAP - Service Advertising Protocol
Operation: 3 NetWare Nearest Service Query
Service Type: 4 File Server
Extra bytes (Padding):
.... 00 04 00 04 00 04 00 04 00
Frame Check Sequence: 0x00000000

Novell networking adheres to a client-server model in almost all cases. As such, servers are strictly servers and clients are resources that use the services provided by servers. This differs from AppleTalk and Microsoft networking, where clients can be servers as well.

Note that the GNS request is a broadcast and is not forwarded by a router. Although this might lead an administrator to believe that an IPX server needs to be installed on each network segment, this is not the case. IPX places a GNS listener on each IPX network. The router also contains a SAP table and responds as necessary to GNS requests.

Cisco routers do not respond to a GNS request if a NetWare server is on the segment.

In the next capture, the Ecorp server responded to the GNS broadcast sent previously, and is providing the client with its IPX network address and status as a file server:

```
Flags:   0x80 802.3
 Status:   0x00
 Packet Length:118
 Timestamp: 22:56:14.565643 05/07/2002
802.3 Header
 Destination: 00:60:08:9e:2e:44
 Source:   00:60:08:9d:2a:8e
 LLC Length: 99
802.2 Logical Link Control (LLC) Header
 Dest. SAP: 0xe0 NetWare
 Source SAP: 0xe0 NetWare Group LLC Sublayer Management
    Function
 Command:   0x03 Unnumbered Information
IPX - NetWare Protocol
 Checksum:     0xffff
 Length:    96
 Transport Control:
 Reserved:    %0000
 Hop Count:    %0000
 Packet Type:   4 PEP
 Destination Network: 0xf3df9b36
 Destination Node:   00:60:08:9e:2e:44
 Destination Socket: 0x4000 IPX Ephemeral
 Source Network:   0xf3df9b36
```

```
Source Node:    00:60:08:9d:2a:8e
Source Socket:  0x0452 Service Advertising Protocol
SAP - Service Advertising Protocol
Operation:  4 NetWare Nearest Service Response
Service Advertising Set #1
Service Type:  4 File Server
Service Name: ECORP......................................
Network Number: 0x34b62f24
Node Number:  00:00:00:00:00:01
Socket Number: 0x0451
Hops to Server: 1
Extra bytes (Padding):
   .    00
Frame Check Sequence: 0x00000000
```

The return packet from Ecorp is a unicast back to the requesting client. This is more efficient than a broadcast-based return, and the packet includes information about the services provided and the internal network number.

At this point in the connection, the client has no knowledge of the services available—the SAP table that contains the information about all servers was not sent to the client. Rather, the client has a single server from which to obtain this information. The GNS process presumes that the first server to respond to the GNS request is the closest (or least busy) of equally preferable servers.

Following the GNS response, the client requests routing information from the router. Once this information is provided, the client establishes a direct connection to the server.

Figure 9.1 provides a visual representation of the GNS process in an IPX network where the server is separated from the client by a router. The first two transmissions from the client are broadcasts, whereas the responses are unicasts. NCP (NetWare Control Protocol) is a connection-oriented protocol that is used for primary Novell functions. Once the client and server establish an NCP session, the client proceeds to the login phase.

FIGURE 9.1 The Novell connection sequence with a remote server

Service Advertising

NetWare servers advertise their services by sending *SAP (service advertising protocol)* broadcasts. These advertisements are sent every 60 seconds by default, and are heard by all servers and routers. In order for clients to find their desired resource initially, the nearest server needs to have an entry in its SAP table for that resource. The advantage to the SAP system is that all servers (barring access lists) are aware of all resources in the internetwork, and the client can obtain the information from any server. The disadvantage is that the SAP process doesn't scale well—the server's processor and the network itself must transmit and process all the information about all the resources. This can reduce overall network availability for user functions. These issues will be reviewed later in this chapter.

It is important to note that services are learned and incorporated into each individual IPX resource's SAP table. This summarized information is then re-sent out each interface on the router or server to populate all other resources. This is an important consideration in troubleshooting, because a problem in forwarding or storing the SAP table on any server or router can cause services to be unavailable.

Because SAP information is shared among all servers, the servers eventually become aware of all available services and are thereby equipped to respond to client GNS requests. As new services are introduced, they're automatically added to local SAP tables and added to new broadcasts to populate other servers.

Unless the configuration is modified, SAPs are sent from each IPX router interface at 60-second intervals—identical to NetWare servers. This is a significant point, especially with WAN links, where bandwidth may be limited. The router isolates SAP broadcasts to individual segments and passes along only the summarized information to each segment.

A SAP broadcast decodes with an EtherPeek analyzer, as follows:

```
Flags:      0x00
 Status:     0x00
 Packet Length:306
 Timestamp:  23:48:36.362000 06/28/2002
Ethernet Header
 Destination: ff:ff:ff:ff:ff:ff Ethernet Brdcast
 Source:      00:80:5f:ad:14:e4
 Protocol Type:81-37 NetWare
IPX - NetWare Protocol
 Checksum:        0xffff
 Length:          288
 Transport Control:
  Reserved:       %0000
  Hop Count:      %0000
 Packet Type:     4 PEP
 Destination Network: 0xcc715b00
 Destination Node:    ff:ff:ff:ff:ff:ff Ethernet Brdcast
 Destination Socket:  0x0452 Service Advertising Protocol
 Source Network:      0xcc715b00
 Source Node:     00:80:5f:ad:14:e4
 Source Socket:       0x0452 Service Advertising Protocol
SAP - Service Advertising Protocol
 Operation:       2 NetWare General Service Response
Service Advertising Set #1
 Service Type:    263 NetWare 386
```

```
Service Name:
        BORDER3...................................
Network Number:  0x12db8494
Node Number:  00:00:00:00:00:01
Socket Number:  0x8104
Hops to Server:  1
Service Advertising Set #2
 Service Type:   4 File Server
 Service Name:
        BORDER3...................................
Network Number:  0x12db8494
Node Number:  00:00:00:00:00:01
Socket Number:  0x0451
Hops to Server:  1
Service Advertising Set #3
 Service Type:   632
 Service Name:   BORDER_____R.S.I@@@@@D.PJ..
Network Number:  0x12db8494
• Node Number:  00:00:00:00:00:01
Socket Number:  0x4006
Hops to Server:  1
Service Advertising Set #4
 Service Type:   993
 Service Name:
        BORDER3...................................
Network Number:  0x12db8494
Node Number:  00:00:00:00:00:01
Socket Number:  0x9056
Hops to Server:  1
Frame Check Sequence: 0x00000000
```

This SAP is from a NetWare server named Border3. Four services were offered. Each service, as well as its address and socket information, is included in the SAP table of all IPX-enabled devices attached to this network (including routers) and rebroadcast.

When troubleshooting, especially in unfamiliar networks, remember that SAP announcements are occasionally filtered with access lists. This may be for traffic management or to establish a security policy. Researching a service-unavailable type of problem should include a review of the access lists on all intermediate routers.

Novell Router Diagnostic Tools

A wide variety of troubleshooting commands is available within the Cisco IOS for resolving IPX networking problems. Although it is important to use all available tools to resolve a network problem—including protocol analyzers and workstation and server applications—most troubleshooting steps are augmented by the IOS commands. As such, there is an emphasis on the following commands and their capabilities to assist as part of an overall problem-resolution strategy:

The most widely used commands include the following:

- `ping` commands
- `show` commands
- `debug` commands

ping Commands

Cisco routers provide a ping utility for troubleshooting IPX connectivity problems, much like the IP ping utility. This utility can be used to verify that the routing tables are being updated correctly, and that all interfaces and segments are available.

Novell IPX resources do not respond to the Cisco IPX ping without the config-uration command `ipx ping-default novell` or the Novell Standard Echo.

The following example demonstrates an IPX ping to a Cisco router's network 200 interface:

```
Router_A#ping ipx 200.0000.30c0.9690
Type escape sequence to abort.
Sending 5, 100-byte IPX cisco Echoes to 200.0000.30c0.9690,
  timeout is 2 seconds
:
```

```
!!!!!
Success rate is 100 percent (5/5), round-trip min/avg/max
   = 16/20/32 ms
```

In the following example, the Novell Standard Echo option and verbose were selected by using the extended commands:

```
Router_A#ping
Protocol [ip]: ipx
Target IPX address: 200.0000.30c0.9690
Repeat count [5]:
Datagram size [100]:
Timeout in seconds [2]:
Verbose [n]: y
Novell Standard Echo [n]: y
Type escape sequence to abort.
Sending 5, 100-byte IPX Novell Echoes to
   200.0000.30c0.9690, timeout is 2 seconds:
0 in 20 ms
1 in 20 ms
2 in 20 ms
3 in 16 ms
4 in 20 ms
Success rate is 100 percent (5/5), round-trip min/avg/max
   = 16/19/20 ms
```

show Commands

The Cisco router's show commands provide a great deal of information regarding IPX. This output is available from the show ipx ? command. As presented in Table 9.2, the show ipx command provides information regarding routing and routing protocols, in addition to NetWare servers.

TABLE 9.2 The IPX show Options

Show IPX Option	Brief Description
accounting	The active IPX accounting database
cache	IPX fast-switching cache

TABLE 9.2 The IPX show Options *(continued)*

Show IPX Option	Brief Description
compression	IPX compression information
eigrp	IPX EIGRP show commands
interface	IPX interface status and configuration
nasi	NetWare Asynchronous Services Interface status
nhrp	NHRP information
nlsp	Show NLSP information
route	IPX routing table
servers	SAP servers
spx-protocol	Sequenced Packet Exchange protocol status
spx-spoof	SPX spoofing table
traffic	IPX protocol statistics

Some commands have additional options. Because of changes in different versions of the IOS, it is recommended that administrators use the ? command to review the specific syntax of the command on their router.

show ipx interface

The show ipx interface command provides information on all IPX-configured interfaces. The output appears in the format shown below. In this example, the router has a high-speed serial interface (HSSI) that is configured for IPX. In addition to show running-config, this command is useful for locating IPX access lists that may block SAP traffic.

As indicated previously, out-of-date access lists are a frequent cause of network problems. Access lists serve as a powerful tool for network management and security, but misunderstood or forgotten lists can prevent connectivity when needed.

The output from this command also provides information about NetBIOS over IPX (type 20) packets, the number of packets sent and received for IPX RIP and SAP, and the status of watchdog and SPX spoof functions.

```
Router_A#show ipx interface
Hssi3/0 is up, line protocol is up
IPX address is F100.0010.0d28.6760 [up] line-up, RIPPQ: 0,
  SAPPQ: 0
Delay of this IPX network, in ticks is 1 throughput 0 link
  delay 0
IPXWAN processing not enabled on this interface.
IPX SAP update interval is 1 minute(s)
IPX type 20 propagation packet forwarding is disabled
Incoming access list is not set
Outgoing access list is not set
IPX helper access list is not set
SAP GNS processing enabled, delay 0 ms, output filter
  list is not set
SAP Input filter list is not set
SAP Output filter list is not set
SAP Router filter list is not set
Input filter list is not set
Output filter list is not set
Router filter list is not set
Netbios Input host access list is not set
Netbios Input bytes access list is not set
Netbios Output host access list is not set
Netbios Output bytes access list is not set
Updates each 60 seconds, aging multiples RIP: 3 SAP: 3
SAP interpacket delay is 55 ms, maximum size is 480 bytes
RIP interpacket delay is 55 ms, maximum size is 432 bytes
Watchdog spoofing is disabled, SPX spoofing is disabled,
  idle time 60
IPX accounting is disabled
IPX fast switching is configured (enabled)
RIP packets received 3228022, RIP packets sent 121313
SAP packets received 3507665, SAP packets sent 3003606
```

show ipx route

The show ipx route command is useful for reviewing the state of the Net-Ware network, and it should be used to confirm that a path exists to the desired resource. The output reports connected IPX RIP, NLSP, and IPX EIGRP routes, in addition to IPXWAN and static routes.

The following example includes routers for the connected IPX network 200 on the FDDI 8/0 interface; and three routes to networks 1, 101 and 201, reachable via 100.0060.833c.4d49 on Hs3/0. The interface is using the FDDI SNAP-frame type and the routes were learned via IPX RIP.

```
Router_A#show ipx route
Codes: C - Connected primary network
c - Connected secondary network, S - Static, F - Floating
   static, L - Local (internal), W - IPXWANR - RIP,
   E - EIGRP, N - NLSP, X - External,
A - Aggregate
s - seconds, u - uses
128 Total IPX routes. Up to 3 parallel paths and 16 hops
   allowed.
No default route known.
C    200 (SNAP),      Fd8/0
R      1 [03/02] via    100.0060.833c.4d49,   8s, Hs3/0
R    101 [04/03] via    100.0060.833c.4d49,   8s, Hs3/0
R    201 [04/03] via    100.0060.833c.4d49,   8s, Hs3/0
```

WARNING   Please do not confuse the IPX RIP protocol with the RIP routing protocol in TCP/IP. Both are routing protocols and there are similarities, but they are different protocols.

show ipx servers

The show ipx servers command displays all servers known to the router through SAP advertisements. Recall that, in the absence of filters, this list should include all resources in the internetwork. If elements are missing, there may be an issue with access lists, down interfaces, down networks, congestion, or frame types.

This command is also useful for locating duplicate network numbers:

```
Router_A#show ipx servers
Codes: S - Static, P - Periodic, E - EIGRP, N - NLSP,
 H - Holddown, + = detail
117 Total IPX Servers
Table ordering is based on routing and server info
Type Name      Net Address         Port  Route Hops Itf
P+ 4 SRV-00001  1.0000.0000.0001:0451  4/03   3    Hs3/0
P+ 4 SRV-00002  2.0000.0000.0001:0451  4/03   3    Hs3/0
```

Note that the MAC addresses in this display are 00:00:00:00:00:01. This is the internal IPX network address indicator; and the first server, SRV-00001, has an internal IPX network number of 1.

show ipx traffic

The show ipx traffic command reports information about the IPX packets transmitted and received. This breakdown includes information regarding IPX SAPs and watchdog packets, as well as IPX RIP, IPX EIGRP, and NLSP routing packets. A sample of this information is presented as follows:

```
Router_A#show ipx traffic
System Traffic for 0.0000.0000.0001 System-Name: Router_
  ARcvd:  92678244 total, 158 format errors, 0 checksum
  errors, 0 bad hop count,1677 packets pitched, 65955970
  local destination, 0 multicast
Bcast: 65957365 received, 63751306 sent
Sent:  75752069 generated, 26672221 forwarded
     50141 encapsulation failed, 1465 no route
SAP:  48 SAP requests, 0 SAP replies, 399 servers
     58523476 SAP advertisements received, 61481958 sent
     0 SAP flash updates sent, 6 SAP format errors, last
     seen from 500.0010.0b4f.2660
RIP:  48 RIP requests, 0 RIP replies, 128 routes
     7432398 RIP advertisements received, 2261621 sent
     8498 RIP flash updates sent, 0 RIP format errors
Echo:  Rcvd 0 requests, 0 replies
     Sent 0 requests, 0 replies
     0 unknown: 0 no socket, 0 filtered, 0 no helper
     0 SAPs throttled, freed NDB len 0
```

```
Watchdog:
    0 packets received, 0 replies spoofed
Queue lengths:
    IPX input: 0, SAP 0, RIP 0, GNS 0
    SAP throttling length: 0/(no limit), 0 nets pending
      lost route reply
    Delayed process creation: 0
EIGRP: Total received 0, sent 0
    Updates received 0, sent 0
    Queries received 0, sent 0
    Replies received 0, sent 0
    SAPs received 0, sent 0
NLSP:  Level-1 Hellos received 0, sent 0
    PTP Hello received 0, sent 0
    Level-1 LSPs received 0, sent 0
    LSP Retransmissions: 0
    LSP checksum errors received: 0
    LSP HT=0 checksum errors received: 0
    Level-1 CSNPs received 0, sent 0
    Level-1 PSNPs received 0, sent 0
    Level-1 DR Elections: 0
    Level-1 SPF Calculations: 0
    Level-1 Partial Route Calculations: 0
```

debug Commands

As with other network protocols, there is a wide variety of IPX debug commands available within the Cisco IOS. The debug IPX commands provide the administrator with a means to view Novell traffic in real time as it enters or leaves the router.

The debug command is assigned a high CPU priority and can generate a high processor load. Always use caution when using a debug command. The resulting processor load and output can degrade router performance or render the system unusable.

debug ipx routing

The debug ipx routing command reports all IPX routing processes at the router, including IPX RIP, IPX EIGRP, and NLSP. The first line reports the standard IPX RIP broadcast, whereas the remainder demonstrate the events related to the recovery of an interface configured for IPX. In this case, the TO0 interface cable was reinserted:

```
*Mar 1 00:34:26.515 UTC: IPXRIP: sending update to
  0.ffff.ffff.ffff via [all]
*Mar 1 00:38:43.455 UTC: IPX: Setting state of [itf]:[net]
  To0:D to [up]:[down]
*Mar 1 00:38:43.455 UTC: IPX: cache flush
*Mar 1 00:38:43.459 UTC: IPXRIP: Marking network D for
  Flash  Update
*Mar 1 00:38:43.459 UTC: IPXRIP: Deleting network D
*Mar 1 00:38:43.463 UTC: IPX: cache flush
*Mar 1 00:38:43.467 UTC: IPX: Setting state of [itf]:[net]
  To0:D to [up]:[up]
*Mar 1 00:38:43.467 UTC: IPX: cache flush
*Mar 1 00:38:43.467 UTC: IPXRIP: Marking network D for
  Flash  Update
```

debug ipx packet

The debug ipx packet command displays all IPX traffic that enters or leaves the router. Thus, this command can generate a great deal of output, and its use is recommended only with caution.

IPX packets that are fast-switched are not captured by the debug ipx packet command. In order to view all packets, add the no ipx route-cache command to each interface that you wish to include in the debug capture. If the initial problem is related to fast switching, this may lead to erroneous troubleshooting results.

The following example contains the entry of a packet destined for server 130—internal network number. The response was sent to the gateway on network 120:

```
IPX: src=100.0000.0c4c.42fa, dst=130.0000.0000.0001,
  packet    received
```

```
IPX: src=100.0000.0c4c.42fa,    dst=130.0000.0000.0001,
   gw=120.0000.0ca3.1bd0, sending packet
```

debug ipx sap activity

As previously reviewed, SAP traffic provides the foundation for all Novell functions. Incorrect functioning of the SAP process can prevent access to services and cause other connectivity problems. As such, the debug ipx sap activity command provides an administrator with additional information and possible indications of problem causes:

```
Router_A#debug ipx sap activity
IPX service debugging is on
Feb 1 10:08:38.424:  type 0x30C, "PTR_1",
   105.0006.0d86.5380(401C), 4 hops
Feb 1 10:08:38.424:  type 0x30C, "PTR_2",
   105.0006.0d6e.1a65(400C), 4 hops
Feb 1 10:08:38.648:  type 0x44C, "AR3",
   102.0000.0000.0001(8600), 3 hops
Feb 1 10:08:38.648:  type 0x23F, "SRL03",
   102.0000.0000.0001(907B), 3 hops
Feb 1 10:08:38.704: IPXSAP: at 690465B4:
I SAP Response type 0x2 len 480 src:100.0060.837b.4a19
   dest:100.ffff.ffff.ffff(452)
```

debug ipx sap events

The debug ipx sap events command appears to include the same information as the debug ipx sap activity command. However, the router defines events as interesting, and the events keyword limits the output of information. Although the information is limited, there are times when events may provide sufficient data for problem resolution. A sample of the output is provided below. (Note that there are two SAP broadcasts.)

```
Router_A#debug ipx sap event
IPX service events debugging is on
Feb 17 11:09:13.556: IPXSAP: at 608FD48C:
O SAP Update type 0x2 len 480 src:200.0006.c13e.b20c
   dest:200.ffff.ffff.ffff(452)
Feb 17 11:09:13.556:  type 0x4, "SRV-NDS",
   101.0000.0000.0001(451), 3 hops
```

```
Feb 17 11:09:13.556:  type 0x4, "SRV-NMS",
  701.0000.0000.0001(451), 3 hops
Feb 17 11:09:13.556:  type 0x4, "SRV-ORD",
  801.0000.0000.0001(451), 3 hops
Feb 17 11:09:13.556:  type 0x4, "SRV-SAA",
  501.0000.0000.0001(451), 3 hops
Feb 17 11:09:13.560: IPXSAP: at 608BD614:
O SAP Update type 0x2 len 480 src:500.0006.c13e.b20c
  dest:500.ffff.ffff.ffff(452)
Feb 17 11:09:13.560:  type 0x4, "SRV-NDS",
  101.0000.0000.0001(451), 3 hops
Feb 17 11:09:13.560:  type 0x4, "SRV-NMS",
  701.0000.0000.0001(451), 3 hops
Feb 17 11:09:13.560:  type 0x4, "SRV-ORD",
  801.0000.0000.0001(451), 3 hops
Feb 17 11:09:13.560:  type 0x4, "SRV-SAA",
  501.0000.0000.0001(451), 3 hops
```

WARNING Remember to use the undebug all or no debug commands to shut down debug sessions. Failure to shut down debug sessions can cause performance degradation.

Common Novell Troubleshooting Issues

Standard troubleshooting procedures can and should be used when approaching a NetWare-related issue, as they would be used for any other network problem. This includes identifying and defining the problem, fact gathering, assessing possible solutions, creating an action plan, and implementing that plan. Based on the results, the problem may be resolved, new information may be added to the assessment, or another action plan may be needed.

There are some common issues that present themselves in NetWare networks, however. For example, the router may not correctly propagate SAP updates, which are very important in NetWare. Causes for this may include access lists, duplicate network numbers, incorrect frame types, timing problems, or incorrectly set timers.

Although the `debug` and `show` commands can provide a great deal of information that is useful for resolving the problem, protocol analyzers and knowledge of the server and client platforms should also be used to provide rapid resolutions.

In NetWare, most problems can be isolated by doing the following:

- Check the client configuration. This includes the frame type, hardware (IRQ/DMA settings), and physical connectivity.

- Review the router and any local server configurations. Although this chapter focuses on Cisco routers, it is important to confirm the internal and external IPX network numbers on the server, in addition to the frame type. Novell documentation addresses other concerns, including network interface cards, overloaded processors, licenses, and drive space. All should be included in the troubleshooting process.

- Verify that non-IPX problems, such as overloaded segments or down links, are not the cause. Note that many IPX environments today are also using IP and AppleTalk.

Ethernet Encapsulation Mismatches and Network Settings

As noted previously, Novell networks and their clients can use any of four different frame types in Ethernet. A client, server, and router all must use the same frame type in order to communicate, however. The IOS commands `write terminal` or `show running-config` are useful for reviewing the encapsulation settings. Note that in this example there are no settings to reflect the frame type. The router is using the Cisco default of novell-ether or Ethernet 802.3 on all interfaces. It is important for the administrator to realize that, as with most of the default configuration settings in Cisco routers, if the default encapsulation type is used, it will not show up in the configuration. The encapsulation type only shows up in the configuration if it is changed from the default value. Therefore, encapsulation difference between Novell servers and Cisco routers may be difficult to detect if the default settings of the two are different.

```
Router_A#show running-config
Building configuration...
Current configuration:
!
version 11.1
```

```
service timestamps debug datetime localtime show-timezone
service timestamps log datetime localtime show-timezone
!
service password-encryption
service udp-small-servers
service tcp-small-servers
!
hostname Router_A
!
ipx routing 0010.0d28.6710
ipx maximum-paths 3
!
interface Ethernet0
 mtu 1500
 ip address 10.11.10.1 255.255.255.0
 ipx network 10
!
interface Ethernet1
 ip address 10.11.20.1 255.255.255.0
 no keepalive
 ipx network 2000
!
end
```

In this example, the router interface is displayed with the show ipx
interface command, and the interface is FDDI with the default SNAP
frame type in use:

```
Router_A#show ipx interface
Fddi0 is up, line protocol is up
  IPX address is 100000.0060.837c.4d31, SNAP [up] line-up,
    RIPPQ: 0, SAPPQ: 0
```

In addition to frame type, a common issue with interconnectivity is incorrectly configured network addresses. All servers and routers on an IPX
network must be manually configured with the same external IPX network
number. A typical problem scenario occurs as follows:

After realizing that at least one server on the network is unreachable, the
administrator notes the following error on the router console or in the router
log. A similar message may appear on the server console:

```
00:60:08:40:1F:1C claims network 100 should be 200
```

In addition to confirming that the frame type of all network resources is set to the same value, all servers and routers also need to have their external IPX network numbers set to the same value. In this case, the unreachable server is configured for IPX network 200, where the router has been configured for network 100. After the correct network number is determined, the incorrect setting should be modified.

Problems Attaching to Remote Servers

Frequently, IPX networks are designed without a locally attached server. The file server may be installed on another local segment or may be remotely connected via a serial connection.

Although this serial connection may be a T1, many sites still use 56Kbps DDS circuits or low CIR (committed information rate) Frame Relay connections.

As a NetWare network grows, the volume of RIP and SAP traffic also grows. Eventually, a 56Kbps connection (or Frame Relay connection) will be overwhelmed with RIP and SAP updates, to the point where user data can no longer be transferred. A saturated T1 may also have difficulty providing adequate bandwidth to support large RIP and SAP updates.

In addition, the connection to a file server from the client requires a response to the GNS broadcast described previously. Although the router responds in the absence of a server, the subsequent connections may fail due to timeouts or other issues. In addition, the server or client may be overloaded. A protocol analyzer is a good way to review this issue, although `debug` commands can be used with caution. If the issue involved is an overloaded server, a solution may involve use of the `ipx gns-round-robin` configuration command. If more than one NetWare server is listed in the SAP table as being an equal distance away, this command provides a limited form of load balancing.

Conversely, there may be times when the router responds to the client too quickly. Although this is a rare occurrence in modern networks, the default delay of 0ms can be changed with the `ipx gns-response-delay` configuration command.

There is also a scenario referred to as the *backdoor bridge*. In this example, a bridge connects two IPX networks and leaks routing information. The `show ipx traffic` command should be used to determine whether the bad hop counter is incrementing. If it is, a protocol analyzer should be used to find a source address that matches the remote node and not the router.

SAP Congestion Management in IPX RIP

Service advertisements can generate a significant amount of traffic in medium-scale networks. In large networks, they can cause high processor utilization and overall degradation of the network.

Without using NetWare's NLSP to control IPX RIP and SAP datagrams, an administrator may use access lists to block SAP traffic from crossing an interface. This solution does have shortcomings, however. Any resource that is restricted by an access list is unavailable to the opposing portion of the network.

In many large networks, this solution is quite appropriate—even considering the negatives. Users in Chicago rarely need to print files in San Francisco, and users in London may not need files in Tokyo. By reviewing the business needs of the users, a balance between filter restrictions and service can be obtained. In addition to traffic management, an administrator may also use the filtering of certain IPX packets for network security.

An IPX access list is not dissimilar to an IP access list. Both standard and extended access lists are available. Standard IPX access lists are numbered from 800 to 899, and extended lists are numbered from 900 to 999. As with IP, more options are available with extended access lists, and a list is applied with the `access-group` command on the interface.

Standard IPX Access Lists

The syntax of the standard IPX access list is presented for review:

```
access-list access-list-number [deny | permit] source-
    network[.source-node [source-node-mask]] [destination-
    network[.destination-node [destination-node-mask]]]
```

There are few parameters that can be used in standard access lists. Packets can be filtered based on the source and destination address information only. To filter on socket numbers, extended access lists must be used. It is recommended that standard lists be used only when configuring small networks—most administrators find that eventually they need the flexibility of extended access lists.

Extended IPX Access Lists

An extended IPX access list filters on source and destination address information as standard lists do. Extended lists may also be used to filter on:

- Source network/node

- Destination network/node

- IPX protocol (SAP, SPX, etc.)

- IPX socket

The syntax of the command provides a number of options, including the use of masks for both the network and node sections of the packet:

```
access-list access-list-number [deny|permit] protocol
    [source-network][[[.source-node] source-node-mask] |
    [.source-node source-network-mask.source-node-mask]]
    [source-socket]
    [destination.network][[[.destination-node] destination-
    node-mask] | [.destination-node destination-network-
    mask.destination-nodemask]] [destination-socket]
```

As an example, a simple extended access list is presented by using the format `access-list [number] [permit|deny] [protocol] [source] [socket][destination] [socket]`. As shown previously, this format can be expanded with additional masks.

```
RouterA#config t
Enter configuration commands, one per line. End with CNTL/Z.
RouterA(config)#access-list 910 deny -1 50 0 10 0
RouterA(config)#access-list 910 permit -1 -1 0 -1 0
RouterA(config)#int e0
RouterA(config-if)#ipx access-group 910 out
RouterA(config-if)#^Z
```

The any command word may be used in place of the –1 network parameter, depending on the IOS version in use. Also, some versions of the IOS may report an "unrecognized command" error from the command access-list 910 deny –1 ?. Administrators should use the online help and test configuration commands within the specific IOS installed.

Extended access list 910 is configured to deny all IPX protocols from network 50 that are destined for network 10. Using a -1 in the protocol section of the command serves as a wildcard for all protocols. Use of a -1 in the source or destination field serves as a wildcard for all networks. Recall that access lists include an implicit deny—access list 910 negates this deny by permitting all packets to pass that were not denied previously.

Online help is available by typing **?** and should be referenced when using any unfamiliar command.

SAP Access Lists

Although standard and extended access lists are useful for blocking traffic between IPX networks, Cisco provides a better solution for filtering the SAP traffic between networks. The 1000–1099 range of access lists may be used to permit or block SAP packets specifically, as compared to the general IPX traffic filtering that is available from the standard and extended lists.

Using the syntax `access-list [number] [permit/deny] [source] [service type]`, access list 1010 is configured to permit all SAP traffic from the server. Service type zero represents all service types. Service type four is used for file servers, and type seven represents print servers. This access list was configured on interface e0 as an input SAP filter—all SAP traffic from server 11 (internal IPX network number) is permitted, and all other SAPs are denied.

```
RouterA#config t
Enter configuration commands, one per line. End with CNTL/Z.
RouterA(config)#access-list 1010 permit 11.0000.0000.0001 0
RouterA(config)#int e0
RouterA(config-if)#ipx input-sap-filter 1010
RouterA(config-if)#^Z
```

When troubleshooting, remember to use the following commands to quickly disable IPX access lists. (They need to be reinstated when troubleshooting is complete.)

- `no ipx access-group access-group number`
- `no ipx input-sap-filter access-list number`
- `no ipx output-sap-filter access-list number`

It is possible to alter the default 60-second SAP timer with the `ipx sap-interval` command. The improper use of this command can cause significant problems with SAP updates, and can cause servers to appear and disappear in the SAP table.

Debugging Scalable NetWare Protocols

Although NetWare's RIP and SAP are fine for smaller networks, they do not scale well. As networks increase in size, the broadcast traffic generated by these processes can quickly overwhelm the network. In addition, RIP is slow to converge and is limited regarding redundant network paths. Because convergence and redundancy are important considerations as the network expands, it becomes important to consider the scalable IPX protocols: IPX EIGRP and NLSP. Note that Cisco routers automatically redistribute IPX EIGRP and NLSP to IPX RIP. The redistribution of NLSP routing information into IPX EIGRP requires manual configuration.

IPX EIGRP

Cisco's EIGRP is a good choice for building scalability into IPX networks. The protocol is proprietary, however, and administrators need to commit to an all-Cisco environment when choosing this solution. Table 9.3 contrasts IPX RIP with IPX EIGRP.

TABLE 9.3 IPX RIP and IPX EIGRP Compared

	IPX RIP	IPX EIGRP
Network diameter	15	224
Convergence	Slow	Fast
Bandwidth	High	Low
Updates	60 seconds	As needed

The Cisco IOS provides information regarding EIGRP with the show ipx eigrp commands, identified with the following output:

```
Router_A#show ipx eigrp ?
  interfaces IPX EIGRP Interfaces
  neighbors  IPX EIGRP Neighbors
  topology   IPX EIGRP Topology Table
  traffic    IPX EIGRP Traffic Statistics
```

show ipx eigrp neighbors

As can be seen in Figure 9.2, Router_A is running IPX EIGRP process 10, and is connected to IPX network B via its Ethernet1 interface and IPX network D via its Token Ring 0 interface. This command is most beneficial for verifying initial EIGRP configurations, and an example follows:

```
Router_A#show ipx eigrp neighbors
IPX EIGRP Neighbors for process 10
H  Address
1  B.0000.0c1b.367c
0  D.0000.30da.5842
```

FIGURE 9.2 Network configuration EIGRP show commands

show ipx eigrp topology

Router_C is connected to Router_A via a Token Ring connection, IPX network D. Networks B and A are available via Router_A—Router_B has a connection to IPX network A. Figure 9.2 shows this connectivity. Note the higher metric for network A.

```
Router_C#show ipx eigrp topology
IPX EIGRP Topology Table for process 10
Codes: P - Passive, A - Active, U - Update, Q - Query,
   R - Reply, r - Reply status
P A, 1 successors, FD is 323328
     via D.0000.30e8.6d0f (323328/307200), TokenRing0
P B, 1 successors, FD is 297728
     via D.0000.30e8.6d0f (297728/281600), TokenRing0
P D, 1 successors, FD is 176128
     via Connected, TokenRing0
```

show ipx route

The show ipx route command provides information on static, IPX RIP, NLSP, and IPX EIGRP routes in the network. Note that the following example contains a single connected route, in addition to an IPX EIGRP route. Also, note that only one parallel path is permitted, according to this example. Reviewing this output is recommended, following the use of the `ipx maximum-paths` command. The default behavior of a Cisco router is to consider only one IPX route. The `ipx maximum-paths` command changes this default.

```
Router_C#show ipx routes
Codes: C - Connected primary network, c - Connected
  secondary network, S - Static, F - Floating static,
  L - Local (internal), W - IPXWAN, R - RIP, E - EIGRP,
  N - NLSP, X - External, A - Aggregate
s - seconds, u - uses
2 Total IPX routes. Up to 1 parallel paths and 16 hops
  allowed.
No default route known.
C D (SAP), To0
E B [297728/0] via D.0000.30e8.6d0f, age 00:02:30, 1u, To0
```

In addition to network D, this routing table was populated via IPX EIGRP with network B. Network D is connected to Token Ring 0, and network B is accessible through router D.0000.30e8.6d0f. There is only one known route to network B.

NLSP and IPXWAN

NLSP, or NetWare Link Services Protocol, affords network designers and administrators some advantages over IPX RIP, in the same way that IP RIP networks benefit by changing to IGRP and EIGRP.

Like IP RIP, IPX RIP supports networks of no more than 15 hops. NLSP expands the routing diameter to 127 hops. In addition, NLSP's link-state packets, LSPs, are sent only when there are changes to the routing topology—unlike IPX RIP packets, which are sent every 60 seconds. This greatly reduces the impact of updates on slower WAN links. Cisco routers automatically redistribute information learned from NLSP to IPX RIP on non-NLSP segments. It is important to use care when using NLSP on a non-WAN point-to-point link, because NLSP-only segments do not contain the regular IPX RIP and SAP updates that are needed by non-NLSP resources.

NLSP provides the capability to remove IPX SAP from a network segment by handling updates via NLSP. The protocol reduces both IPX RIPs and SAPs by sending updates on changes to the database, rather than updating every 60 seconds. NLSP also requires use of the `ipx internal-network` command, unlike IPX RIP and IPX EIGRP.

To enable NLSP, type the `ipx nlsp enable` command. This is configured on each interface that will run NLSP. If there are routing problems and the network is supposed to use NLSP, manually verify this command on each interface and on each network resource.

Unlike IPX RIP, NLSP will send an update only if there is a change to the routing topology. If no modifications occur for two hours, NLSP sends an update to all neighbors. Also, NLSP is configured with an area address, which is defined in the command `area-address address mask`. Using an address and mask of zero defines that all IPX networks belong to the NLSP area. Typically, administrators disable IPX RIP when enabling NLSP.

Additional information about NLSP configuration is available in the *CCNP: Advanced Cisco Router Configuration Study Guide* by Todd Lammle, Kevin Hales, and Donald Porter (ISBN 0-7821-2403-8, Sybex, Inc., 1999).

An NLSP Hello packet is sent regularly to inform neighbor routers of its status. An Ethernet example appears, as follows:

```
Flags:       0x80 802.3
 Status:      0x00
 Packet Length:92
 Timestamp:   00:55:25.715452 05/21/2002
802.3 Header
 Destination: ff:ff:ff:ff:ff:ff Ethernet Brdcast
 Source:      00:00:0c:3e:82:2a
 Length:      74
IPX - NetWare Protocol
 Checksum:        0xffff
 Length:          73
 Transport Control:
  Reserved:       %0000
  Hop Count:      %0000
 Packet Type:     0 Novell
 Destination Network: 0x00000000
 Destination Node:    ff:ff:ff:ff:ff:ff Ethernet Brdcast
 Destination Socket:  0x9001 IPX Static
```

Source Network: 0x00000010
Source Node: 00:00:0c:3e:82:2a
Source Socket: 0x9001 IPX Static
IPX Data Area:

............>.*. 83 1b 02 00 0f 01 00 00 11 00 00 0c 3e
 82 2a 00

..+@...>.*. 01 00 2b 40 00 00 0c 3e 82 2a 01 c0 08
 00 00 00

....   00 00 00 00 00 c5 04 00 00

Extra bytes (Padding):

 . .   05 dc 06

Frame Check Sequence: 0x00000000

A functional NLSP network presents different routing table entries than a network using IPX RIP.

```
Router_C#show ipx route
Codes: C - Connected primary network,
       c - Connected secondary network
       S - Static, F - Floating static, L - Local
       (internal), W - IPXWAN
       R - RIP, E - EIGRP, N - NLSP, X - External,
       A - Aggregate
       s - seconds, u - uses
7 Total IPX routes. Up to 1 parallel paths and 16 hops
   allowed.
No default route known.
L C is the internal network
C 40 (HDLC), Se0
C 50 (NOVELL-ETHER), Et0
N A  [72][13/02] via B.0000.0000.0001,    1990s, Se0
N B  [27][02/01] via B.0000.0000.0001,    1991s, Se0
N 10 [72][12/02] via B.0000.0000.0001,    1991s, Se0
N 30 [27][01/01] via B.0000.0000.0001,    1991s, Se0
```

There are four NLSP routes displayed, in addition to two connected networks and the internal IPX network of the router. Also note that the list of servers is different under NLSP.

```
Router_C#show ipx servers
Codes: S - Static, P - Periodic, E - EIGRP, N - NLSP, H -
  Holddown, + = detail
3 Total IPX Servers
Table ordering is based on routing and server info
Type Name    Net Address        Port Route  Hops Itf
N    4 server1 10.0000.0000.0001:0000 12/02   3    Se0
N    4 server2 10.0000.0000.0002:0000 12/02   3    Se0
N    4 server3 10.0000.0000.0003:0000 12/02   3    Se0
```

show ipx nlsp neighbors

The show ipx nlsp neighbors command displays all NLSP neighbors. A *neighbor* is defined as an NLSP resource that is directly connected—NLSP packets traverse only the local segment because they are not forwarded by the router.

```
Router_A#show ipx nlsp neighbors
NLSP Level-1 Neighbors: Tag Identifier = notag
System Id Interface State Holdtime Priority  Circuit Id
Router_B  Se0       Up    55       0          04
```

Router_A has one NLSP neighbor, Router_B. By adding the detail command, the output includes the IPX internal network number and the uptime.

```
Router_A#show ipx nlsp neighbors detail
NLSP Level-1 Neighbors: Tag Identifier = notag
System Id Interface State Holdtime Priority Circuit Id
Router_B  Se0       Up    43       0         04
 IPX Address: B.0000.0000.0001
 IPX Areas: 00000000/00000000
 Uptime: 01:13:09
```

show ipx nlsp database

This command provides data regarding the local NLSP process. The LSPID (link-state protocol identifier) comprises the system identifier, the pseudo-node circuit identifier, and the fragment number. LSP (link-state protocol) is the foundation of NLSP, and the show ipx nlsp database command reports significant information, including the last sequence number, the checksum, and the LSP holdtime. The *hold timer* reflects the times in seconds before the information expires, assuming that Hello packets are received. ATT and OL refer to the L2 attached and overload bits; the P bit (partition) is not used.

```
Router_A#show ipx nlsp database
NLSP Level-1 Link State Database
LSPID              LSP Seq Num    LSP Checksum LSP Holdtime ATT/P/OL
Router_A.00-00  *  0x00000003       0xF99B        7443        0/0/0
Router_A.04-00  *  0x00000002       0x9F16        7441        0/0/0
Router_B.00-00     0x00000003       0x1C33        7423        0/0/0
Router_B.03-00     0x00000002       0x9DE9        7421        0/0/0
Router_C.00-00     0x00000002       0x459D        7440        0/0/0
```

debug ipx ipxwan

IPXWAN, as described in RFC 1634, is used to exchange necessary router-to-router information before exchanging standard IPX routing information and traffic. IPXWAN can be used with PPP or HDLC links. However, if it is used with HDLC links, both of the routers in the link need to be Cisco routers.

The `debug ipx ipxwan` command produces information during state changes and the start-up of serial interfaces configured for IPXWAN. Although it is seldom used in Cisco networks, IPXWAN is defined in RFC 1634, and may be required for connecting IPX resources on WAN links. This is especially true when connecting to non-Cisco devices.

Summary

IPX is still widely utilized in networks in today's business environment. Therefore, it is important for a network administrator to understand how IPX functions. IPX addresses are written in the format *network.node*, where the network is an administrator-assigned address of four octets. This address is combined with the MAC layer address of the node, creating a ten-octet address.

There are four Ethernet IPX frame options available. In the Novell classifications, these are referred to as 802.3, 802.2, SNAP, and Ethernet II. The Cisco terminology for these is slightly different. Cisco refers to 802.3 as novell-ether, 802.2 as sap, Ethernet SNAP as SNAP, and Ethernet II as arpa. Unlike IP, IPX also uses Service Advertising Protocol, or SAP, to advertise the availability of a particular service. By default, SAPs are sent out every 60 seconds. SAP traffic can therefore become an issue in medium to large-scale networks if steps are not taken to limit SAP propagation.

There are numerous `show` and `debug` commands that can be used to troubleshoot and view the status of IPX in the network. Some of the more common `show` commands are `show ipx interface`, `show ipx servers`, `show ipx traffic`, and `show ipx route`. The more common debug commands for IPX include `debug IPX packet`, `debug ipx sap events`, `debug ipx sap activity`, and `debug ipx routing`.

In addition to the above, IPX also has its own routing protocols. The three primary protocols used are RIP, EIGRP, and NLSP. By default, RIP is used. Because of the difficulty in scaling RIP, medium to large IPX networks usually use either EIGRP or NLSP. For troubleshooting and verification, there are numerous `show` and `debug` commands available for each of these routing protocols.

Exam Essentials

Know the format and makeup of the IPX address.   The IPX address is made up of a network portion and a node portion. The network portion is four octets or 32 bits long. The node portion of the address is 6 octets or 48 bits long and is the MAC address of the station.

Know the function of GNS and how it works.   The get nearest server (GNS) request is a broadcast sent out by a workstation on startup to locate the nearest Novell server. As this is a broadcast, it is restricted to the local subnet. However, a router can respond to a GNS request.

Understand the purpose of SAPs in an IPX network.   SAPs are used to advertise services that are available to IPX clients. By default, SAP advertisements are sent out every 60 seconds.

Know the `show` commands that are available to troubleshoot IPX. These include but are not limited to `show ipx interface`, `show ipx servers`, `show ipx traffic`, and `show ipx route`.

Know the `debug` commands that are available to troubleshoot IPX. These include but are not limited to `debug IPX packet`, `debug ipx sap events`, `debug ipx sap activity`, and `debug ipx routing`.

Know the differences between IPX access lists and SAP filter lists.   IPX access lists can be standard (800–899) or extended (900–999) and are used to filter IPX traffic. SAP filter lists numbers 1000–1099 are used to filter SAP updates. In both lists, a −1 for the address indicates "any."

Understand how IPX RIP, IPX EIGRP, and NLSP operate.   IPX RIP is the default routing protocol used by IPX; it sends broadcasts containing all of the routes in the routing table every 60 seconds. IPX EIGRP and NLSP are more advanced routing protocols for IPX. As such, they send updates only when there are changes in the environment.

Know how to interpret the output for the show and debug commands for the IPX routing protocols.   These commands include but are not limited to show ipx eigrp neighbors, show ipx eigrp topology, show ipx nlsp database, show ipx nlsp neighbors, and debug ipx ipxwan.

Key Terms

Before you take the exam, be certain you are familiar with the following terms:

encapsulation and framing   service advertising protocol (SAP)

get nearest server (GNS)

Commands Used in This Chapter

The following list contains a summary of all the commands used in this chapter.

Command	Description
debug ipx ipxwan	Produces information during state changes and the start-up of serial interfaces configured for IPXWAN.
debug ipx packet	Displays all IPX traffic that enters or leaves the router.

Command	Description
debug ipx routing	Reports all IPX routing processes at the router, including IPX RIP, IPX EIGRP, and NLSP.
debug ipx sap activity	Provides an administrator with additional information and possible indications of problem causes.
debug ipx sap events	Displays events as *interesting*, and the events keyword limits the output of information.
ping ipx	Initiates an IPX ping. Allows for User- and Privileged-level execution.
show ipx eigrp neighbors	Provides detailed IPX EIGRP neighbor information.
show ipx eigrp topology	Displays multiple paths to IPX EIGRP learned routes.
show ipx interface	Provides information on all IPX-configured interfaces.
show ipx nlsp database	Reports significant information, including the last sequence number, the checksum, and the LSP holdtime.
show ipx nlsp neighbors	Displays all NLSP neighbors.
show ipx route	Displays the state of the NetWare network, and it should be used to confirm that a path exists to the desired resource. The output reports connected IPX RIP, NLSP, and IPX EIGRP routes, in addition to IPXWAN and static routes.
show ipx servers	Displays all servers known to the router through SAP advertisements.
show ipx traffic	Reports information about the IPX packets transmitted and received. This breakdown includes information regarding IPX SAPs and watchdog packets, as well as IPX RIP, IPX EIGRP, and NLSP routing packets.

Laboratory Exercise

In this exercise, three routers will be connected via their Ethernet interfaces. Configure the routers with the following commands to set up NLSP. Figure 9.3 illustrates the connections.

FIGURE 9.3   Network configuration for the NLSP laboratory

```
Router_A#conf t
Enter configuration commands, one per line. End with CNTL/Z.
Router_A(config)#ipx routing
Router_A(config)#ipx internal-network A
Router_A(config)#int e0
Router_A(config-if)#ipx network 1
Router_A(config-if)#ipx nlsp enable
Router_A(config-if)#^Z
Router_A#wr t


Router_B#conf t
Enter configuration commands, one per line. End with CNTL/Z.
Router_B(config)#ipx routing
Router_B(config)#ipx internal-network B
Router_B(config)#int e0
Router_B(config-if)#ipx network 1
Router_B(config-if)#ipx nlsp enable
Router_B(config-if)#int e1
Router_B(config-if)#ipx network 2
Router_B(config-if)#ipx nlsp enable
Router_B(config-if)#^Z
Router_B#wr t
```

```
Router_C#conf t
Enter configuration commands, one per line. End with CNTL/Z.
Router_C(config)#ipx routing
Router_C(config)#ipx internal-network C
Router_C(config)#int e1
Router_A(config-if)#ipx network 2
Router_C(config-if)#ipx nlsp enable
Router_C(config-if)#^Z
Router_C#wr t
```

Does NLSP work? What commands were used to determine that NLSP was working? What changes to the configuration are needed, if any?

Review Questions

1. What command would provide the administrator with a list of Novell servers on the network?

   A. `show ipx route`

   B. `show ipx servers`

   C. `show ipx traffic`

   D. `debug ipx ipxwan`

2. When does a Cisco router respond to a GNS request?

   A. For every GNS unicast request.

   B. For every GNS broadcast request.

   C. For every GNS broadcast request when there is no local server on the network segment.

   D. A Cisco router does not respond to GNS requests.

3. A Novell client is configured for the Ethernet II frame type. The Cisco router needs which encapsulation type?

   A. `Ethernet II`

   B. `802.3`

   C. `arpa`

   D. `isol`

4. When IPX clients first attempt to locate services, how do they find them?

   A. SAP

   B. RIP

   C. NLSP

   D. GNS

5. Duplicate network numbers are suspected as a cause of problems in the network. What command is used to locate the problem?

   A. `show ipx servers`

   B. `debug ipx sap events`

   C. `debug ipx ipxwan`

   D. `show int e0`

6. The default interval between SAP packets is how long?

   A. 300 seconds.

   B. 10 seconds.

   C. 60 seconds.

   D. There is no interval—SAP packets are sent only when needed.

7. An IPX RIP network is limited to how many network hops?

   A. 3

   B. 15

   C. 127

   D. There is no limit.

8. Which of the following are problems with RIP and SAP? (Choose all that apply.)

   A. TCP/IP incompatibility

   B. AppleTalk incompatibility

   C. Convergence time

   D. Bandwidth utilization

   E. Scalability

9. All IPX networks need to be included in NLSP. Which of the following is the correct command?

   A. `area-address 0 FFFFFFFF`

   B. `area-address 0 0`

   C. `network FFFFFFFF`

   D. `ipx nlsp rip on`

10. IPX EIGRP is available on which of the following platforms?

    A. Novell servers

    B. Cisco routers

    C. Ascend routers

    D. Windows NT servers

    E. All of the above

11. To permit all SAP traffic from the Novell server, an access list with which command is needed?

    A. `access-list 1080 permit 1.0000.0000.0001 0`

    B. `access list 1080 permit 1.0000.0000.0001 0`

    C. `access-list 910 permit 1.FFFF.FFFF.FFFF 0`

    D. `access-list 910 deny neq 1.0000.0000.0001`

    E. `access-list 1080 permit 1.0000.0000.0001 FFFFFFFF`

12. To block all IPX traffic from network 50 destined for network 30 and permit all other IPX traffic, the access list needs to be which of the following?

    A. `access-list 940 deny 50 -1 0 30 -1 0,access-list 940 permit -1 -1`

    B. `access-list 940 deny FFFFFFFF 50 30`

    C. `access-list 940 deny -1 50 0 30 0`

    D. `access-list 940 permit -1 30 0 50 0`

    E. `access-list 940 deny -1 50 0 30 0, access-list 940 permit -1 -1 0 -1 0`

13. IPX extended access lists filter on what? (Choose all that apply.)

    A. IPX socket

    B. IPX protocol

    C. RTMP

    D. Source network/node

    E. Destination network/node

14. How are standard IPX access lists numbered?

    A. 1–99

    B. 1000–1099

    C. 800–899

    D. 900–999

    E. 500–599

15. On Ethernet, when do IPX devices send an ARP request?

    A. Locating the nearest server.

    B. Locating the local router.

    C. Locating a remote server.

    D. IPX does not use ARP.

    E. The ARP process in IPX is handled by NLSP.

16. Which of the following are valid IPX network addresses? (Choose all that apply.)

    A. 2.14

    B. 2.0000.0000.0001

    C. 2.1

    D. 2.0000.0C04.0311

    E. FACE.0000.0C04.0311

    F. Server_A.0000.0000.0001

17. There are two frame types on the same physical interface of the router, and the router is running NLSP and IPX RIP. In total, how many network numbers are needed?

    A. None

    B. One

    C. Two

    D. Three

    E. Four

18. When using the `debug ipx packet` command, the administrator should consider using which of the following?

    A. `no ipx route-cache`

    B. `no ipx sap`

    C. `debug all`

    D. `debug ipx sap-input-filter all`

    E. None of the above

19. The SAP interpacket delay is available from which of the following commands?

    A. `debug ipx sap`

    B. `debug ipx sap delay brief`

    C. `show ipx interface`

    D. `show sap interpacket delay`

20. To view the available options for IPX debugging, type which of the following?

    A. `ipx debug ?`

    B. `debug ipx ?`

    C. `debug all`

    D. `ipx debug help`

    E. `ipx debug options`

Answers to Review Questions

1. B. The correct command for server information is given by B.

2. C. If there is no local server, the router will respond as the server. If there is a local server, the router will not respond.

3. C. Ethernet II and arpa are synonymous. Novell calls it Ethernet II while Cisco calls it arpa.

4. D. Before a client can locate services, it needs to know where the servers are. This is done with the GNS request.

5. A. The `show ipx servers` output provides specific enough information that duplicate networks can be found.

6. C. The default setting is 60 seconds.

7. B. Somewhat similar to an IP RIP hop count, there is a 15-hop limit with IPX RIP. NLSP does expand this limit to 127.

8. C, D, E. TCP/IP and AppleTalk have nothing to do with SAP, and RIP is compatible with TCP/IP and AppleTalk.

9. B. This command provides the right network and mask.

10. B. Since EIGRP is Cisco proprietary, it can only be on Cisco routers.

11. A. This provides the correct syntax, network, and mask.

12. E. Recall that access lists have implicit deny statements; therefore, C would block all IPX traffic.

13. A, B, D, E. These are the valid criteria for extended access list filtering.

14. C. 800–899 is the defined range for standard IPX access lists.

15. D. IPX does not use ARP.

16. B, D, E. There must be four octets, in hex, that specify the network and six octets, in hex node. The leading zeros in the network portion can be omitted.

17. D. There must be two for the external networks and one for the internal network required by NLSP.

18. A. If the packets are route-cached (i.e., switched), they will not cross the processor—thus, debug will not be able to see them.

19. C. The configured value appears when using this command.

20. B. This answer provides the correct syntax.

Chapter

10

Troubleshooting AppleTalk Connectivity

TOPICS COVERED IN THIS CHAPTER INCLUDE:

✓ Use proven problem isolation techniques to list the symptoms of common AppleTalk problems on router networks.

In the 1980s, Apple Computer released the Macintosh—a platform that would later be regarded with almost religious reverence. The Mac has certainly established a niche for itself, and all but controls the education and desktop publishing environments. It is also frequently found in businesses, especially in smaller companies.

Although an all-Macintosh network traditionally used the AppleTalk network protocol, the explosive growth of the Internet has generated a need for TCP/IP, as well. With the latest releases of the Macintosh OS and AppleShare IP, many administrators, especially those in combined Mac and PC environments, have migrated away from AppleTalk in favor of IP only.

To its credit, AppleTalk does simplify administration, as compared to TCP/IP. Further, some applications will continue to need AppleTalk, and there are still good reasons to understand and use this protocol. This chapter addresses many of the troubleshooting issues commonly found in AppleTalk networks.

The AppleTalk Protocol

The AppleTalk protocol is designed primarily for ease of administration. In fact, small networks can be created with virtually no formal training and little administration. This is made possible by the following protocols that are part of AppleTalk:

AppleTalk Address Resolution Protocol   *AARP* performs two different functions in AppleTalk. First, it is responsible for mapping AppleTalk addresses to hardware addresses. This Layer 3 to Layer 2 mapping is similar to the ARP process in IP. Second, AARP handles the dynamic assignment of node addresses. (This will be covered in greater detail later in this chapter.)

Datagram Delivery Protocol   *DDP* provides unique addressing of all nodes on the AppleTalk internetwork, and is responsible for connection-less delivery of datagrams between nodes.

Name Binding Protocol   *NBP* provides name-to-address resolution that is similar to DNS in TCP/IP; it also handles additional functions.

Routing Table Maintenance Protocol   AppleTalk's default routing protocol is *RTMP*. Updates are sent every 10 seconds, and routes are aged out of the table after 20 seconds. This can result in route flapping on congested segments as the RTMP updates are dropped.

Zone Information Protocol   Zones are logical divisions of AppleTalk resources. *ZIP* maps zone names to network addresses. Although nodes belong to one zone, zones can span multiple physical networks.

AppleTalk Addressing

An AppleTalk address contains network and node information in the format *network.node*. This is similar to the IPX protocol—there is no subnet as with IP. The administrator defines the network portion of the address by defining a cable range. This range varies in size, depending on the phase (version) of AppleTalk and the needs of the network. The network portion of the address is composed of a 16-bit number, whereas the node is defined with eight bits.

AppleTalk Cable Range

AppleTalk networks define their network numbers by assigning a cable range. This range, in the more common AppleTalk *Phase 2*, can be very large in scope—accommodating a virtually unlimited number of nodes. AppleTalk *Phase 1* is capable only of addressing one cable number, and it is further restricted to 127 hosts. Table 10.1 presents the differences between AppleTalk Phase 1 and Phase 2.

T A B L E   1 0 . 1   Comparison of AppleTalk Phase 1 and AppleTalk Phase 2

	AppleTalk Phase 1	**AppleTalk Phase 2**
Number of network addresses per segment	1	65,279
Number of host addresses per network	254–127 servers, 127 hosts	253 per network address, virtually unlimited
Number of zones per network	1	255

Table 10.1 presents AppleTalk Phase 2 as being virtually unlimited in terms of host addresses. This is because of the theoretical capability of AppleTalk to consider cable range 1–65,279 as one network, with 253 hosts per single cable range (cable range 1–1, for example). Thus, the true number of maximum nodes in an AppleTalk network is approximately 16 million. Although possible, this is well beyond the broadcast and physical limitations of most networks, and most cable ranges do not span more than 10 digits (10–19, for example).

A cable range is defined at an AppleTalk router, and it provides the network portion of the address. In Phase 1, this range consists of a single number (five, for example). In Phase 2, this number can span any sequential set of numbers. For example, a valid network in Phase 2 AppleTalk is 10–17. This range provides for 2024 nodes. Note that there are no subnet masks or other IP-style parameters.

AppleTalk Routing

By default, AppleTalk uses RTMP and ZIP, which are protocols that contribute to AppleTalk's chatty reputation. RTMP updates are sent every 10 seconds; by default, routes are aged out after 20 seconds. This results in a high volume of traffic and an extreme sensitivity to congestion—a route announcement may not be sent due to other traffic.

Networks using Cisco routers can also use AT EIGRP, which provides significant advantages in terms of the bandwidth required. As with IP EIGRP and IPX EIGRP, the protocol is proprietary and can require a significant amount of processor and memory on the router. Because non-Cisco devices cannot use the EIGRP protocol, its use is usually limited to WAN and backbone links. This assumes that RTMP is disabled on the segment. This is accomplished with the `no appletalk protocol rtmp` command. Cisco routers automatically redistribute RTMP and AT EIGRP.

AppleTalk Update-Based Routing Protocol (AURP) is a method of encapsulating AppleTalk traffic. This occurs within the header of another protocol, usually TCP/IP. The resulting connection is referred to as an AURP tunnel. AURP maintains routing table information and permits AppleTalk networks to span WANs that do not service the AppleTalk protocol. While AURP is considered an AppleTalk routing protocol, this chapter will focus on RTMP and AT EIGRP.

Unlike IP and IPX EIGRP, which use an autonomous system number or process number, AT EIGRP uses a router number. This number must be unique for each router in the network.

AppleTalk *ping* Command

The AppleTalk `ping` command is used for troubleshooting, in much the same way as the TCP/IP `ping` command is used. This command is useful for verifying connectivity if the administrator knows the AppleTalk address or node name.

A command line `ping` is displayed as follows:

```
Router_C#ping apple 1.87
Type escape sequence to abort.
Sending 5, 100-byte AppleTalk Echos to 1.87, timeout is
    2 seconds:
!!!!!
Success rate is 100 percent (5/5), round-trip min/avg/max
    = 1/2/4 ms
```

The extended `ping` option with verbose mode selected is as follows:

```
Router_C#ping
Protocol [ip]: apple
```

```
Target AppleTalk address: 1.87
Repeat count [5]:
Datagram size [100]:
Timeout in seconds [2]:
Verbose [n]: y
Sweep range of sizes [n]:
Type escape sequence to abort.
Sending 5, 100-byte AppleTalk Echos to 1.87, timeout is
  2 seconds:
0 in 4 ms from 1.87 via 1 hop
1 in 4 ms from 1.87 via 1 hop
2 in 4 ms from 1.87 via 1 hop
3 in 4 ms from 1.87 via 1 hop
4 in 4 ms from 1.87 via 1 hop
Success rate is 100 percent (5/5), round-trip min/avg/max
  = 4/4/4 ms
```

AppleTalk *show* Commands

As with other protocols, the Cisco IOS show commands provide a wealth of information regarding AppleTalk, including routing, zone, and cache data. A list of options is displayed as follows with the show appletalk ? command. Many options have suboptions—use the ? command to review further.

```
Router_C#show appletalk ?
  access-lists      AppleTalk access lists
  adjacent-routes   AppleTalk adjacent routes
  arp               AppleTalk arp table
  aurp              AURP information
  cache             AppleTalk fast-switching cache
  domain            AppleTalk Domain(s) information
  eigrp             AppleTalk/EIGRP show commands
  globals           AppleTalk global parameters
  interface         AppleTalk interface status and
                    configuration
  macip-clients     Mac IP clients
  macip-servers     Mac IP servers
  macip-traffic     Mac IP traffic
```

name-cache	AppleTalk name cache
nbp	AppleTalk NBP name table
neighbors	AppleTalk Neighboring router status
remap	AppleTalk remap table
route	AppleTalk routing table
sockets	AppleTalk protocol processing information
static	AppleTalk static table
traffic	AppleTalk protocol statistics
zone	AppleTalk Zone table information

show appletalk interface

The show appletalk interface command displays the interface status, cable range, and network and node address, in addition to the zone name and route cache status. In this example, the zone name is "one" and the interface is 1.230. AppleTalk also verifies the configuration of the port—in this case, router 1.87 performed this function.

```
Router_C#show appletalk interface
TokenRing0 is up, line protocol is up
  AppleTalk cable range is 1-1
  AppleTalk address is 1.230, Valid
  AppleTalk zone is "one"
  AppleTalk port configuration verified by 1.87
  AppleTalk address gleaning is disabled
  AppleTalk route cache is enabled
```

Note that in troubleshooting, there may be cause to use the clear appletalk commands, which includes the clear appletalk interface option. A list of the clear appletalk options is included as follows.

WARNING
The clear appletalk interface command resets the specified interface(s), disrupting connectivity.

```
Router_C#clear appletalk ?
  arp          Reset AppleTalk information
  eigrp        Clear AppleTalk/EIGRP
  interface    Clear & restart AppleTalk interface
  nbp          Reset AppleTalk NBP cache information
```

```
neighbor       Reset AppleTalk down neighbor information
route          Reset AppleTalk routing table
route-cache    Reset AppleTalk fast-switching cache(s)
traffic        Reset AppleTalk traffic counters
```

show appletalk route

The show appletalk route command provides a summary of all known routes and the protocol that distributed them. In addition, the primary zone of each network is displayed. Recall that a network can contain up to 255 zones in AppleTalk Phase 2. Although the example here displays the zone names "one" and "Two," most administrators will name zones for the workgroup served—"Marketing Zone," for example. Note that zone names are also case-sensitive.

```
Router_C#show appletalk route
Codes: R - RTMP derived, E - EIGRP derived, C - connected,
    A - AURP, S - static  P - proxy
2 routes in internet
The first zone listed for each entry is its default
    (primary) zone.
C Net 1-1 directly connected, TokenRing0, zone one
R Net 2-2 [1/G] via 1.87, 9 sec, TokenRing0, zone Two
```

show appletalk zone

The show appletalk zone command displays the zone names and networks that are known to the router through ZIP updates. This command is most useful for troubleshooting reports of "missing" zones.

As noted previously, zones are the logical definitions of network resources. For example, a zone called "Marketing" can be used to define those resources (including file servers and printers) that are used by the marketing group. This is also a better name than "Zone1" because the name denotes the department or other business boundary. Naming zones for groups of users can greatly simplify troubleshooting and assist users because they will select resources based on the zone name first.

Zone names are useful in grouping geographically separated workgroups, as well. The Marketing zone may include cable range 5–10 when initially created, but a new marketing group in another building may be needed. This group can be placed on cable range 1000–1005, yet remain in the Marketing zone.

WARNING   AppleTalk does not provide a mechanism for updating zone names. For example, if an administrator changes the zone name from "Finance" to "Marketing," the local router zone name changes, but the remote routers continue to reference "Finance." This is referred to as a *ghost zone*. It is recommended that administrators disable all networks that are related to the zone name being changed. This ages out the routing table; upon reinstatement, the routers learn the route and new zone name information.

The output of the show appletalk zone command follows:

```
Router_C#show appletalk zone
Name                              Network(s)
one                               1-1
Two                               2-2
Dilbert                           14000-14005
Kenny                             22638-22639
Total of 4 zones
```

show appletalk access-lists

Access lists are usually configured to restrict access to various resources within the network. This may be for broadcast control, data security, or other considerations. Regarding AppleTalk, access lists are numbered from 600 to 699. In addition, the Cisco IOS filters zone and network information simultaneously. Because administrators may wish to write lists that block certain traffic and permit all other traffic, it is important to consider both the access-list permit other-access and access-list permit additional-zones statements. As with other access lists, implicit denies are automatically assumed at the end of an AppleTalk access list. In the example, access-list 605 demonstrates the more common AppleTalk access list, in which certain packets are permitted and all items not permitted are denied. This is a default behavior of AppleTalk access-lists, but is explicitly restated in this example.

```
Router_C#show appletalk access-lists
AppleTalk access list 605:
   permit zone Padjen
   permit zone Robert
```

```
permit zone Tyler
permit zone Kristie
permit zone Eddie
permit zone Dilbert
permit zone Cessna
deny additional-zones
deny other-access
```

show appletalk adjacent-routes

The show appletalk adjacent-routes command shows connected and one-hop-away routes that are known to the router. Two examples of the command are displayed:

```
Router_A#show appletalk adjacent-routes
Codes: R - RTMP derived, E - EIGRP derived, C - connected,
    A – AURP, S - static  P - proxy
796 routes in internet

The first zone listed for each entry is its default
    (primary) zone.

C Net 144-144 directly connected, FastEthernet0/0, zone
    This
C Net 147-147 directly connected, Ethernet1/2, zone That
C Net 148-148 directly connected, Ethernet4/5, zone The
    Other
R Net 151-151 [1/G] via Router_C.Ethernet5, 8 sec,
    Ethernet4/2, Zone: "Backbone"
Router_C#show appletalk adjacent-routes
Codes: R - RTMP derived, E - EIGRP derived, C - connected,
    A – AURP, S - static  P - proxy
2 routes in internet
The first zone listed for each entry is its default
    (primary) zone.
C Net 1-1 directly connected, TokenRing0, zone one
R Net 2-2 [1/G] via 1.87, 5 sec, TokenRing0, zone Two
```

show appletalk arp

The show appletalk arp command displays the ARP cache of the router for all AppleTalk addresses. This is populated by the AppleTalk Address

Resolution Protocol (AARP). Address resolution is needed to link the MAC layer address to the Layer 3 address.

```
Router_C#show appletalk arp
Address  Age (min) Type      Hardware Addr         Encap
   Interface
1.87     7         Dynamic   0000.30e8.6d0f.0000   SNAP
   TokenRing0
1.230    -         Hardware  0000.30da.5842.0000   SNAP
   TokenRing0
```

The ARP cache can be cleared with the `clear appletalk arp` command. This may be useful if a corrupt ARP cache is suspected when troubleshooting.

show appletalk globals

This command is one of the most valuable in AppleTalk troubleshooting. The `show appletalk globals` command provides information about Phase 1 compatibility, ZIP, RTMP, AARP, and DDP functions. In addition, routing information is displayed.

```
Router_C#show appletalk globals
AppleTalk global information:
    Internet is compatible with older, AT Phase1, routers.
    There are 2 routes in the internet.
    There are 2 zones defined.
    Logging of significant AppleTalk events is disabled.
    ZIP resends queries every 10 seconds.
    RTMP updates are sent every 10 seconds.
    RTMP entries are considered BAD after 20 seconds.
    RTMP entries are discarded after 60 seconds.
    AARP probe retransmit count: 10, interval: 200 msec.
    AARP request retransmit count: 5, interval: 1000 msec.
    DDP datagrams will be checksummed.
    RTMP datagrams will be strictly checked.
    RTMP routes may not be propagated without zones.
    Routes will be distributed between routing protocols.
    Routing between local devices on an interface will not
        be performed.
```

IPTalk uses the udp base port of 768 (Default).
AppleTalk EIGRP is not enabled.
Alternate node address format will not be displayed.
Access control of any networks of a zone hides the zone.

show appletalk name-cache

The show appletalk name-cache displays a list of NBP services from other AppleTalk routers and devices that support NBP. The output, as shown, includes the network, address, socket information, and NBP type.

```
Router_C#show appletalk name-cache
AppleTalk Name Cache:
Net Adr Skt Name                        Type         Zone
144  46 254 Router_C.FastEthernet0/0 ciscoRouter  Dilbert
147  96 254 Router_C.Ethernet1/2      ciscoRouter  Robert
148 252 254 Router_C.Ethernet4/5      ciscoRouter  Piper
157  93 254 Router_C.Ethernet4/2      ciscoRouter  Info
157 102 254 Router_A.Ethernet         ciscoRouter  Info
157 188 254 Router_B.Ethernet5        ciscoRouter  Info
```

show appletalk traffic

The show appletalk traffic command summarizes all AppleTalk traffic that enters or leaves the router—including erred packets, routing counters, and broadcast information. This information can be very useful for obtaining a quick overview of the state of the AppleTalk protocol. Although a baseline is valuable for comparison, the counters presented in this command usually present an indication of errors that need resolution.

The output of the command is shown as follows:

```
Router_C#show appletalk traffic
AppleTalk statistics:
  Rcvd:  167 total, 0 checksum errors, 0 bad hop count
    167 local destination, 0 access denied
      0 for MacIP, 0 bad MacIP, 0 no client
      0 port disabled, 109 no listener
      0 ignored, 0 martians
  Bcast: 0 received, 52 sent
  Sent:  53 generated, 0 forwarded, 0 fast forwarded, 0
    loopback
```

```
       0 forwarded from MacIP, 0 MacIP failures
       0 encapsulation failed, 0 no route, 0 no source
DDP:   167 long, 0 short, 0 macip, 0 bad size
NBP:   10 received, 0 invalid, 0 proxies
       0 replies sent, 10 forwards, 10 lookups, 0 failures
RTMP:  45 received, 0 requests, 0 invalid, 0 ignored
       45 sent, 0 replies
ATP:   0 received
ZIP:   7 received, 3 sent, 5 netinfo
Echo:  0 received, 0 discarded, 0 illegal
       0 generated, 0 replies sent
Responder:  0 received, 0 illegal, 0 unknown
       0 replies sent, 0 failures
AARP:  1 requests, 0 replies, 10 probes
       0 martians, 0 bad encapsulation, 0 unknown
AppleTalk statistics:
       11 sent, 0 failures, 0 delays, 0 drops
Lost: 0 no buffers
Unknown: 0 packets
Discarded: 0 wrong encapsulation, 0 bad SNAP discriminator
AURP: 0 Open Requests, 0 Router Downs
       0 Routing Information sent, 0 Routing Information
         received
       0 Zone Information sent, 0 Zone Information
         received
       0 Get Zone Nets sent, 0 Get Zone Nets received
       0 Get Domain Zone List sent, 0 Get Domain Zone
         List received
       0 bad sequence
```

show appletalk neighbors

To view information about directly connected AppleTalk routers, use the show appletalk neighbors command. This command provides information about the AppleTalk address, the routing protocol that connects the two routers, and the local interface.

```
Router_C#show appletalk neighbors
AppleTalk neighbors:
```

```
1.87          TokenRing0, uptime 00:07:31, 1 sec
Neighbor is reachable as a RTMP peer
```

show appletalk nbp

The output of the show appletalk nbp command is similar to the output from the show appletalk name-cache command because both are populated from the same function. In this example, the Type field includes ciscoRouter and SNMP Agent. The command displays the contents of the NBP registration table.

```
Router_C#show appletalk nbp
  Net Adr Skt  Name                        Type         Zone
  17   93 254 Router_C.Ethernet4/2      ciscoRouter  Dilbert
  186 181 254 Router_C.FastEthernet6/1  ciscoRouter    Kenny
  144  46 254 Router_C.FastEthernet0/0  ciscoRouter     Info
  144  46   8 Router_C                  SNMP Agent      Info
  186 181   8 Router_C                  SNMP Agent     Piper
```

AppleTalk *test* Commands

The test commands are not limited to AppleTalk. They include AppleTalk, EIGRP, Banyan Vines, and interfaces. As shown in the following output, the test apple command includes specific sequences for ARP, AT EIGRP, and NBP.

```
Router_C#test apple
Router_C(atalk test)#?
  arp    APPLETALK ARP test commands
  eigrp  APPLETALK EIGRP test commands
  end    Exit AppleTalk test mode
  nbp    AppleTalk NBP test commands
```

Please note that most of these commands include further options.

Use of the following commands requires entering test apple mode. The prompt will change to (atalk test).

The NBP tests are perhaps the most beneficial for testing. The options include confirm, lookup, parameters, and poll. The parameters command sets options for the other commands and is rarely necessary.

The `test appletalk nbp` suboptions are listed as follows:

```
Router_C(atalk test)#nbp ?
  confirm      Confirm NBP
  lookup       Send NBP Lookup
  parameters   Set NBP timeouts
  poll         Poll all devices in internet
```

nbp poll

Within the `test apple` syntax, it is possible to send an NBP poll. This command searches for all devices in all zones. A brief example is included as follows:

```
Router_C(atalk test)#nbp poll
poll:  sent 2 lookups
(1n,230a,254s)[1]:    'Router_C.TokenRing0:ciscoRouter@one'
(2n,111a,254s)[1]:    'Router_A.Ethernet1:ciscoRouter@Two'
NBP polling completed.
Processed 2 replies, 2 events
```

WARNING   Use the nbp poll command with caution. It generates a great deal of traffic on the entire network.

A more extensive example is included here. Note that non-Cisco router types were also discovered.

```
Router_C(atalk test)#nbp poll
poll:  sent 439 lookups
(449n,48a,136s)[4]:    'Server02:DceDspRpc Endpoint
  Mapper@Corp'
(449n,160a,2s)[1]:    'Server31@Server02:Microsoft:A8
  Windows NT:AA Prt 4.00@ Dilbert'
(595n,30a,254s)[1]:    'lear.Ethernet3/5:ciscoRouter@
  Kenny'
(43199n,145a,244s)[0]:    'what:AFPServer@Piper'
(455n,121a,254s)[1]:    'widget.Ethernet0:ciscoRouter@
  Kenny'
```

nbp lookup

The `nbp lookup` command can be used to provide the AppleTalk address of a known NBP service. The syntax is `nbp lookup object:type@zone`.

nbp confirm

The nbp confirm command is seldom used in production environments because the show and ping commands are more familiar to administrators. Since IOS release 11.1, however, the command has been available to verify the AppleTalk address against its name and zone information. The syntax is nbp confirm appletalk-address [:skt] object: type@zone. In the following example, the nbp confirm was responded to with the socket information included.

```
Router(atalk test)#nbp confirm 19.71
    server:AFPServer@Dilbert
confirmed server:AFPServer@Dilbert at 19n,71a,250s
```

nbp parameters

The NBP parameters permit control over retransmissions, replies, and intervals used by the other NBP test commands. Table 10.2 defines the values that are entered in the syntax nbp parameters [retransmissions] [replies] [interval].

TABLE 10.2 NBP Parameter Values

Option	Definition	Range of Values	Default
Retransmissions	Maximum number of lookup retransmissions	1 to 5	5
Replies	Maximum number of replies per lookup	1 to 500	1
Interval	Number of seconds between each retry	1 to 60	5

AppleTalk *debug* Commands

The AppleTalk debug commands are helpful for isolating and resolving network problems by providing the administrator with real-time data. Care must be exercised in using these commands, however, because they may disrupt network handling by the router. Also, there are instances when a protocol analyzer may be a better troubleshooting tool; and, as with all troubleshooting procedures, it is helpful to understand the client, server, and network components. A listing of the debug apple commands from the ? option is listed as follows:

```
Router_C#debug apple ?
  arp                     Appletalk address resolution
                            protocol
  aurp-connection         AURP connection
  aurp-packet             AURP packets
  aurp-update             AURP routing updates
  domain                  AppleTalk Domain function
  eigrp-all               All AT/EIGRP functions
  eigrp-external          AT/EIGRP external functions
  eigrp-hello             AT/EIGRP hello functions
  eigrp-packet            AT/EIGRP packet debugging
  eigrp-query             AT/EIGRP query functions
  eigrp-redistribution    AT/EIGRP route redistribution
  eigrp-request           AT/EIGRP external functions
  eigrp-target            Appletalk/EIGRP for targeting
                            address
  eigrp-update            AT/EIGRP update functions
  errors                  Information about errors
  events                  Appletalk special events
  fs                      Appletalk fast-switching
  iptalk                  IPTalk encapsulation and
                            functionality
  load-balancing          AppleTalk load-balancing
  macip                   MacIP functions
  nbp                     Name Binding Protocol (NBP)
                            functions
  packet                  Per-packet debugging
  redistribution          Route Redistribution
  remap                   AppleTalk Remap function
  responder               AppleTalk responder debugging
  routing                 (RTMP&EIGRP) functions
  rtmp                    (RTMP) functions
  zip                     Zone Information Protocol
                            functions
```

The debug command is assigned a high-CPU priority and can generate a high processor load. Always use caution when using a debug command. The resulting processor load and output can degrade router performance or render the system unusable.

debug apple arp

The ARP process is responsible for resolving Layer 3 addresses to their Layer 2 devices. The debug appletalk arp command reports all real-time events that are related to this process.

In the following example, the ARP table is displayed with the show appletalk arp command. There are two entries in the table: the remote router interface at 1.87 and the local AppleTalk interface at 1.230. The table is then cleared with the clear arp command.

```
Router_C#debug appletalk arp
AppleTalk ARP debugging is on
Router_C#show appletalk arp
Address     Age (min) Type      Hardware Addr      Encap Interface
1.87        10        Dynamic   0000.30e8.6d0f.0000  SNAP TokenRing0
1.230       -         Hardware  0000.30da.5842.0000  SNAP TokenRing0
Router_C#clear arp
Router_C#
TokenRing0: AARP: Removing entry for 1.87(0000.30e8.6d0f)
TokenRing0: AARP: Removing entry for 1.230(0000.30da.5842)
AARP: creating entry for TokenRing0, 1.230(0000.30da.5842)
TokenRing0: AARP aarp_insert, initial NULL entry
AARP: aarp_insert, entry 60C57FD8 for node 1.230(0000.30da.5842)
    added on TokenRing0
```

debug apple errors

AppleTalk errors, including incorrect encapsulation, invalid ping packets, NetInfoReply errors, configuration mismatch problems, and bad responder packet types, are all presented by the debug apple errors command.

Decoding of the debug apple errors command usually is helped with reference to CCO (Cisco Connections Online). This support tool is very helpful and provides the latest information available.

```
Router_C#debug apple errors
AppleTalk packet errors debugging is on
TokenRing0: input AT packet: enctype SNAP, size 65
C000040000000000030E86D0FAAAA03080007809B|00418B4700000001
  FF575858580205EDAC
0000000000000000000000000000000010001000C010001000000000F02
  04000C0001000100
TokenRing0: input AT packet: enctype SNAP, size 65
C000040000000000030E86D0FAAAA03080007809B|00418B4700000001F
  F575858580205EDAC
0000000000000000000000000000000010001000C010001000000000F02
  04000C0001000100
TokenRing0: input AT packet: enctype SNAP, size 65
C000040000000000030E86D0FAAAA03080007809B|00418B4700000001F
  F575858580205EDAC
0000000000000000000000000000000010001000C010001000000000F02
  04000C0001000100
TokenRing0: input AT packet: enctype SNAP, size 65
C000040000000000030E86D0FAAAA03080007809B|00418B4700000001F
  F575858580205EDAC
0000000000000000000000000000000010001000C010001000000000F02
  04000C0001000100
```

debug apple events

The debug apple events command reports AppleTalk special events, including interfaces going up or down, and neighbor unreachability. In a stable network, this command produces no output.

Although Cisco recommends that administrators enable this command prior to making configuration changes, few administrators heed this advice. Many sites do use the apple event-logging command, however, which reports special events to a syslog server.

Note that when the command is used during configuration changes (specifically, the enabling of a new router interface), the following sequence should be observed:

- Line down

- Restarting

- Probing—this is an AARP process to find its address

- Acquiring via GetNetInfo requests

- Sending ZIP requests for a list of zones on the cable

- Verification that the router's configuration matches the information received from the previous requests; note that an error at this point will result in a port configuration mismatch

- Zone verification to confirm that the router's zone list is valid

- Operational status and interface up

debug apple nbp

The debug apple nbp command should be used to confirm receipt of valid NBP updates. This is usually warranted after a problem viewed with the show appletalk nbp command.

```
Router_A# debug apple nbp
AT: NBP ctrl = LkUp, ntuples = 1, id = 77
AT: 410.19, skt 2, enum 0, name: =:ciscoRouter@Lab
AT: LkUp =:ciscoRouter@Lab
AT: NBP ctrl = LkUp-Reply, ntuples = 1, id = 77
AT: 4160.154, skt 254, enum 1, name:
    lestat.Ether0:ciscoRouter@Lab
AT: NBP ctrl = LkUp, ntuples = 1, id = 78
AT: 410.19, skt 2, enum 0, name: =:IPADDRESS@Lab
AT: NBP ctrl = LkUp, ntuples = 1, id = 79
AT: 410.19, skt 2, enum 0, name: =:IPGATEWAY@Lab
AT: NBP ctrl = LkUp, ntuples = 1, id = 83
AT: 410.19, skt 2, enum 0, name: =:ciscoRouter@Lab
AT: LkUp =:ciscoRouter@LabAT: NBP ctrl = LkUp, ntuples = 1,
    id = 84
AT: 410.19, skt 2, enum 0, name: =:IPADDRESS@Lab
AT: NBP ctrl = LkUp, ntuples = 1, id = 85
AT: 410.19, skt 2, enum 0, name: =:IPGATEWAY@Lab
AT: NBP ctrl = LkUp, ntuples = 1, id = 85
AT: 410.19, skt 2, enum 0, name: =:IPGATEWAY@Lab
```

debug apple packet

This command reports all inbound and outbound AppleTalk datagrams at the router. Although this command can be very useful when troubleshooting, it is recommended that care be used. A protocol analyzer may prove to be a more useful diagnostic tool.

As displayed in the following, the output includes RTMP and other Apple-Talk packets that can be displayed with more limiting **debug** commands.

```
Router_C#debug apple packet
AppleTalk packets debugging is on
TokenRing0: input AT packet: enctype SNAP, size 29
C00040000000000030E86D0FAAAA03080007809B|001DD8F900000001F
    F5701010100010857
0001800001820002800002820 1FF570101010001085700018000018200
    0280000282B73A6E
TokenRing0: input AT packet: enctype SNAP, size 29
C00040000000000030E86D0FAAAA03080007809B|001DD8F900000001F
    F5701010100010857
0001800001820002800002820 1FF570101010001085700018000018200
    0280000282B73A6E
TokenRing0: input AT packet: enctype SNAP, size 65
C00040000000000030E86D0FAAAA03080007809B|00418B4700000001F
    F575858580205EDAC
0000000000000000000000000000010001000C010001000000000F02
    04000C0001000100
TokenRing0: encap'ed output packet AT packet: enctype
    SNAP, size 45
000000000000000000000000000000000000000000|0040C000400000000
    00030DA5842AAAA03
080007809B$0017BEE200000001FFE6010101000108E6000180000182D
    10000000000000000
AT: src=TokenRing0:1.230, dst=1-1, size=10, 0 rtes, RTMP
    pkt sentg all
```

debug apple routing

The debug apple routing command displays transaction information on all RTMP and AppleTalk EIGRP packets. This example includes the report (italicized) that network 2-2 is no longer available. A disconnected wire caused this outage.

```
Router_C#debug apple routing
AppleTalk RTMP routing debugging is on
AppleTalk EIGRP routing debugging is on
```

```
Router_C#
AT: src=TokenRing0:1.230, dst=1-1, size=10, 0 rtes, RTMP
    pkt sent
AT: Route ager starting on Main AT RoutingTable (2 active
    nodes)
AT: Route ager finished on Main AT RoutingTable (2 active
    nodes)
AT: RTMP from 1.87 (new 0,old 1,bad 0,ign 0, dwn 0)
AT: src=TokenRing0:1.230, dst=1-1, size=10, 0 rtes, RTMP
    pkt sent
AT: Route ager starting on Main AT RoutingTable (2 active
    nodes)
AT: Route ager finished on Main AT RoutingTable (2 active
    nodes)
AT: RTMP from 1.87 (new 0,old 1,bad 0,ign 0, dwn 0)
AT: src=TokenRing0:1.230, dst=1-1, size=10, 0 rtes, RTMP
    pkt sent
AT: Route ager starting on Main AT RoutingTable (2 active
    nodes)
AT: Route ager finished on Main AT RoutingTable (2 active
    nodes)
%AT-6-PATHNOTIFY: TokenRing0: AppleTalk RTMP path to 2-2
    down; reported bad by 1.87
AT: RTMP from 1.87 (new 0,old 0,bad 0,ign 0, dwn 1)
AT: src=TokenRing0:1.230, dst=1-1, size=10, 0 rtes, RTMP
    pkt sent
```

debug apple zip

As presented previously, zone updates are critical to the proper functioning of AppleTalk networks. The debug apple zip command reports all ZIP packet information in real time for troubleshooting zone problems. The following output includes the response to a ZIP query on network 2-2. Note the "name Two" entry within the output.

```
Router_C#debug apple zip
AppleTalk ZIP Packets debugging is on
AT: NextNbrZipQuery: [2-2] zoneupdate 0 gw: 1.87 n: 1.87
AT: NextNbrZipQuery: r->rpath.gwptr: 60C60D20, n: 60C60D20
AT: maint_SendNeighborQueries, sending 1 queries to 1.87
AT: 1 query packet sent to neighbor 1.87
```

```
AT: Recvd ZIP cmd 2 from 1.87-6
AT: 1 zones in ZIPreply pkt, src 1.87
AT: net 2, zonelen 3, name Two
AT: in CancelZoneRequest, cancelling req on 2-2...succeeded
AT: atzip_GC() called
```

Common AppleTalk Troubleshooting Issues

As with most networks, AppleTalk nets are prone to common issues that prompt troubleshooting. This section addresses these common problems and outlines their resolutions in the context of the Cisco IOS show and debug commands.

Note that the following section should not take the place of a methodical troubleshooting procedure. In AppleTalk, this process should include verifying the local configuration and/or outlining the scope of the problem. This includes determining whether the problem affects more than one system or location.

Further generic troubleshooting should also include the verification of the local router and the impact of any access lists. In addition, the test commands that are referenced in this chapter will help isolate problems with AppleTalk ARP, AppleTalk EIGRP, and NBP. Non-AppleTalk issues should also be reviewed, including high utilization and error rates. In summary, the main troubleshooting targets for AppleTalk are as follows:

- Local host configuration

- Routers connected to AppleTalk networks

- Remote host configuration

It is important to realize that these are very general and high-level troubleshooting targets, and that each one has several more low-level targets.

ZIP Storms

A ZIP storm can occur when a zone name does not map to an AppleTalk route. Although storms are prevented by the Cisco IOS, other routers can permit this problem. Because AppleTalk has no mechanism for alerting stations to changes in the zone list, routers request ZIP updates upon learning about a new route.

When troubleshooting ZIP storms, use the `show appletalk traffic` command. Evidence of a storm can be found by reviewing the number of ZIP requests over a period of 30 seconds, and noting a higher than normal increment. Although `debug` commands can provide further troubleshooting information, it is recommended that a protocol analyzer be used. This is because of the high processor utilization that the `debug` command requires and other network issues that are usually associated with ZIP storms.

Higher than normal assumes that the administrator has established a baseline for the network. This is a troubleshooting step that occurs before an incident. By comparing the network when it is operating correctly to the degraded network metrics, a course of action should become clear.

AARP Broadcast Frames

When connecting to an AppleTalk network, the workstation (or other device) sends AARP probe frames to verify that its address is unique. On Ethernet and Token Ring, the station sends 10 broadcasts. If there is a response, the workstation must send another set of AARP broadcasts with a different address to find an available address. On networks with a low number of available addresses, this can result in a significant amount of traffic.

Prevention of this problem can be more beneficial than detection. When setting up networks, make certain that there is sufficient growth room for addresses. If troubleshooting, use the `show appletalk traffic` command to review the status of AARP broadcast frames. In addition, you can use the `arp` keyword option under the `test apple` command to further determine what is occurring with AARP.

Phase 1/Phase 2 Compatibility Problems

Although this problem is very unlikely in most modern networks, the differences between the versions of the AppleTalk protocol can create significant service disruptions.

The Cisco IOS has supported Phase 2 since version 8.2, and few administrators have any reason to not use Phase 2 throughout the network. However, it is possible that a legacy or misconfigured router can cause a

Phase 1/Phase 2 mismatch. The show appletalk globals command provides the administrator with a simple method of troubleshooting this potential cause. If the show appletalk globals command reports incompatibility with a Phase 1 device, the show appletalk neighbors and show appletalk route commands should provide sufficient information for resolution.

Duplicate or Crossed Network Numbers

It is very easy for an administrator to use the same cable range on two physical media or to cross address ranges on different media. For example, placing cable range 5–10 on the Ethernet interface of Router_A and 5–10 on the FDDI interface results in a duplicate network number. It is even more common for an administrator to accidentally use 5–10 for one network and 7–12 for another. Because of the overlap, the route table becomes unstable. In troubleshooting, it is helpful to disable the suspected duplicate interface, and then use the show appletalk route command to confirm that the network still exists.

 Real World Scenario

Using AppleTalk Discovery Mode

In many cases, there are numerous zones or an unknown cable range defined on a particular interface. In these instances, AppleTalk discovery mode can be used to automatically discover the cable ranges used as well as the zones. You can put an interface in discovery mode by using either the appletalk discovery interface command or appletalk cable-range 0-0 command. In either case, when the router comes up it will query another active router on the cable for the cable range and zone information. It is important to note that if there is not another active router on the segment that can provide this information, the interface will not come up.

Once the discovery process is complete, you can remove the appletalk discovery command from the interface with the no appletalk discovery statement. All information learned by the interface, both the cable range and the zone list, will then appear under the interface configuration. This information can then be saved to the start-up configuration with the copy running-config startup-config command. Following these steps can save you time and effort and ensure that all the cable range and zone information on an interface is correct. This can be especially important when there are a large number of zones in use.

Overloaded Network

As with all other protocols, it is possible for AppleTalk to be affected by an overloaded segment or router. This may be due to other traffic or traffic within the AppleTalk network itself. It is also possible for the overload to be a function of ZIP or RTMP traffic within AppleTalk.

Troubleshooting should begin with the `show interface` command. Note that this is without physical or protocol parameters because initially the overload itself is only being researched. At the initial troubleshooting point, it is not possible to specify a specific protocol or interface. If an interface (or interfaces) shows high loads, the administrator should use a protocol analyzer to further determine the cause. Although `debug` and `show` commands may be used as well, caution must be exercised with the `debug` command in this situation.

No Resources Listed in Chooser

The Chooser is the Macintosh application that users use to select file and print services. Frequently, the help desk will receive a report that there are no resources available—sometimes only reported as an unavailable service.

Although the resource becoming unavailable or a down network can cause this problem, it is also possible for the cause to be an access-list or workstation problem.

To troubleshoot an access-list issue or other restriction, the administrator should use the `show appletalk access-list` command to review any filters and the `no appletalk access-group` command to disable the list for testing. After locating the offending access list, the administrator will likely wish to reconfigure the list with appropriate permit and deny statements, as warranted by security policies.

However, it is also possible that the problem is isolated to the workstation. Ideally, help-desk staff will have performed a preliminary assessment of the problem, which should include asking the caller if other users are currently experiencing the problem. If the problem does not affect other users, it is possible that the workstation itself has a disconnected cable or that the internal network configuration has changed. Macintosh systems can use a network card for their network connections or the serial port, with the default being a serial port connection. This should be checked by using the AppleTalk control panel.

A specific type of access list is available to limit zone information. Applied to individual interfaces, the administrator may use the `appletalk` `getzonelist-filter 610` command. This command would apply access list 610 to any zone updates composed by the router. Such an access list would be a likely candidate for missing resources in the Chooser.

Summary

Though not as common as IP, there are still a number of AppleTalk networks in use today. AppleTalk was designed to provide the end user a seamless networking experience with little or no configuration required. This is accomplished through the protocols that are used by AppleTalk.

The first of these protocols is AARP, or AppleTalk Address Resolution Protocol. This protocol provides Layer 3 to Layer 2 address mapping as well as the dynamic assignment of the node addresses. The next protocol, Datagram Delivery Protocol (DDP), is responsible for connectionless delivery of packets. Among other things, Name Binding Protocol (NBP) performs a function similar to DNS in that it resolves logical names to their associate addresses. Zone Information Protocol (ZIP) provides the zone-to-address mapping that is needed for AppleTalk clients to get the resources they need. Finally, RTMP—Routing Table Maintenance Protocol—is the default AppleTalk routing protocol.

There have been two different "phases" in the evolution of AppleTalk, Phase 1 and Phase 2. In AppleTalk Phase 1, only one cable range is supported. With the introduction of AppleTalk Phase 2, up to 65,536 cable ranges are supported. In addition, with AppleTalk Phase 2, multiple zones are supported on a cable range whereas only one was supported in Phase 1. The address for AppleTalk is made up of a 16-bit network portion and an 8-bit node portion written as *network.node*.

As was the case with IP and IPX, there are numerous `show` commands that are used with AppleTalk. These commands can be used to check the current status of the AppleTalk configuration as well as verify that it is working correctly. Some of the more common commands are `show appletalk interface`, `show appletalk route`, `show appletalk zone`, `show appletalk arp`, `show appletalk globals`, `show appletalk traffic`, `debug apple arp`, `debug apple errors`, `debug apple events`, and `debug apple packet`. In addition, AppleTalk also has a test mode that will allow you to test ARP, EIGRP, and NBP functions.

Finally, some of the more common issues that are experienced in an AppleTalk network include ZIP storms, malfunctioning AARP broadcast frames, Phase 1/Phase 2 incompatibility, duplicate or crossed network numbers, overloaded networks, and Chooser problems. Each of these problems can usually be avoided with careful planning. However, if they do occur, they can be identified and solved by using the troubleshooting methodology detailed in Chapter 1.

Exam Essentials

Know the differences between AppleTalk Phase 1 and Phase 2. AppleTalk Phase 1 supports only up to 254 hosts per network, and only one zone. Phase 2 addresses support up to 65,279 hosts per segment and up to 255 different zones per segment. Both have an address that has a 16-bit network component and an 8-bit node component.

Know the AppleTalk Routing options. By default, RTMP is used for routing AppleTalk. In addition, AT EIGRP can be used to save bandwidth. Also, AURP can be used to route AppleTalk packets across areas that do not support AppleTalk. This is accomplished by encapsulating AppleTalk packets in another protocol such as TCP/IP.

Know how to use the AppleTalk `ping` command. The `ping apple` command can be used to verify simple connectivity, or the extended `ping` command can be used to see more detail on the connectivity.

Know the `show` commands that are available to troubleshoot AppleTalk. These include but are not limited to `show appletalk interface`, `show appletalk route`, `show appletalk zone`, `show appletalk arp`, `show appletalk globals`, and `show appletalk traffic`.

Know the `debug` commands that are available to troubleshoot AppleTalk. These include but are not limited to `debug apple arp`, `debug apple errors`, `debug apple events`, and `debug apple packet`.

Know how to use the AppleTalk test feature. By using the `test apple` command, you can enter into the `test apple` mode on the router. This will allow you to test such features as NBP, ARP, and EIGRP.

Know the causes and how to deal with common AppleTalk problems. Common AppleTalk problems include but are not limited to ZIP storms, Chooser issues, Phase 1 and Phase 2 compatibility problems, and duplicated or crossed networks.

Key Terms

Before you take the exam, be certain you are familiar with the following terms:

AppleTalk Address Resolution Protocol (AARP)

Routing Table Maintenance Protocol (RTMP)

Datagram Delivery Protocol (DDP)

Zone Information Protocol (ZIP)

Name Binding Protocol (NBP)

Commands Used in This Chapter

The following list contains a summary of all the commands used in this chapter.

Commands	Descriptions
`debug apple arp`	Reports all real-time events that are related to the process of resolving Layer 3 addresses to Layer 2 devices.
`debug apple errors`	Reports AppleTalk errors, including incorrect encapsulation, invalid ping packets, NetInfoReply errors, configuration mismatch problems, and bad responder packet types.
`debug apple events`	Reports AppleTalk special events, including interfaces going up or down, and neighbor unreachability.
`debug apple nbp`	Confirms receipt of valid NBP updates.
`debug apple packet`	Reports all inbound and outbound AppleTalk datagrams at the router.
`debug apple routing`	Displays transaction information on all RTMP and AppleTalk EIGRP packets.
`debug apple zip`	Reports all ZIP packet information in real time for troubleshooting zone problems.
`nbp confirm appletalk-address [:skt] object: type@zone`	Verifies the AppleTalk address against its name and zone information.

Commands	Descriptions
`nbp lookup object:type@zone`	Provides the AppleTalk address of a known NBP service.
`nbp parameters`	Permits control over retransmissions, replies, and intervals used by the other NBP `test` commands.
`nbp poll`	Searches for all devices in all zones.
`ping apple`	Pings Apple addresses.
`show appletalk access-lists`	Displays the AppleTalk access lists.
`show appletalk adjacent-routes`	Shows connected and one-hop-away routes that are known to the router.
`show appletalk arp`	Displays the ARP cache of the router for all AppleTalk addresses.
`show appletalk globals`	Provides information about Phase 1 compatibility, ZIP, RTMP, AARP, and DDP functions. In addition, displays routing information.
`show appletalk interface`	Shows the AppleTalk settings for the interface.
`show appletalk name-cache`	Cache displays a list of NBP services from other AppleTalk routers and devices that support NBP.
`show appletalk nbp`	Displays a list of NBP services from other AppleTalk routers and devices that support NBP.
`show appletalk neighbors`	Provides information about the AppleTalk address, the routing protocol that connects the two routers, and the local interface.
`show appletalk route`	Provides a summary of all known routes and the protocol that distributed them.
`show appletalk traffic`	Summarizes all AppleTalk traffic that enters or leaves the router, including erred packets, routing counters, and broadcast information.
`show appletalk zone`	Displays the zone names and networks that are known to the router through ZIP updates.
`test appletalk`	Enables the testing mode for AppleTalk.

Review Questions

1. AppleTalk addresses appear in what format?

   A. workstation@applezone

   B. 172.16.2.56

   C. 5.42

   D. 82.000C.3090.8730

   E. `http://www.aeroventure.com`

2. On a Cisco router, a Phase 1 cable range (or compatible cable range) is which of the following?

   A. 172.16.2.0/24

   B. 5–10

   C. 5–5

   D. ZoneOne

3. An AppleTalk node can do which of the following?

   A. It can belong to a single zone.

   B. It can belong to multiple zones.

   C. It can belong to multiple zones as long as it is a server.

   D. It cannot belong to a zone.

4. What protocol associates an AppleTalk address with a MAC layer address?

   A. NBP

   B. AARP

   C. RTMP

   D. ZIP

5. Which of the following steps occur during AppleTalk node address assignments? (Choose all that apply.)

    A. Conflicting address sends a conflict message indicating a problem.

    B. The node chooses a new address.

    C. The node chooses a network address.

    D. The node chooses its first network node address.

    E. The node checks to see whether a network address is in use.

6. AppleTalk can be routed with which of the following? (Choose all that apply.)

    A. Static

    B. AURP

    C. RIP

    D. RTMP

    E. EIGRP

    F. OSPF

    G. IGRP

7. Zone Widget can belong to which cable ranges?

    A. 1–1, 5–5, 6–6

    B. 1–1

    C. 1–6

    D. 1–6, 200–300

    E. All of the above

    F. None of the above

8. Which AppleTalk protocol is used to establish and maintain routing tables?

    A. ZIP

    B. NBP

    C. RTMP

    D. IGRP

9. Which protocol in AppleTalk is most similar to TCP/IP DNS?

   A. RTMP

   B. AT DNS

   C. NBP

   D. AURP

   E. AT EIGRP

10. Which of the following probably causes user inability to see zones or services outside of their own network?

   A. Clients not configured with a default gateway

   B. Phase 1, Phase 2 incompatibility

   C. Incorrect AppleTalk encapsulation

   D. Too many zones configured for a single network

11. The AppleTalk access lists are defined by which of the following?

   A. 500–599

   B. 600–699

   C. 900–999

   D. 100–199

12. Which of the following protocols is part of AppleTalk? (Choose all that apply.)

   A. AARP

   B. DDP

   C. ZIP

   D. RTMP

   E. RIP

   F. NBP

   G. All of the above

13. A Macintosh user uses which of the following application(s) to select resources?

    A. The Control Panel

    B. The Finder

    C. The Chooser

    D. The Selector

    E. Network Neighborhood

    F. NIS+

14. A Macintosh can bind AppleTalk to which of the following interfaces? (Choose all that apply.)

    A. The modem serial port

    B. The printer serial port

    C. An Ethernet card in the workstation

    D. Macintosh systems running MacTalk

    E. All of the above

15. Which command is used on an AppleTalk network to find problems when neighbors become reachable or unreachable, and interfaces come up or down?

    A. `show apple rtmp`

    B. `debug apple traffic`

    C. `protocol apple verbose`

    D. `debug apple events`

16. Why is AppleTalk easy to administer?

    A. All frames are 53 bytes long.

    B. The administrator controls addressing.

    C. Many functions are handled automatically by the protocol.

    D. DNS is easier than NBP.

17. Which command can be used to record significant changes to interfaces?

   A. debug apple routing

   B. apple event-logging

   C. debug apple significant event

   D. debug apple all

   E. debug apple nbp

18. Based on the debug apple zip command that follows, what is the network number for the zone named Dilbert?

```
AT: Sent GetNetInfo request broadcast on Ether1
AT: Recvd ZIP cmd 6 from 10.152-6
AT: 3 query packets sent to neighbor 10.251
AT: 1 zones for 700, ZIP XReply, src 10.251
AT: net 700, zonelen 7, name Dilbert
```

   A. 10

   B. 251

   C. 700

   D. Cannot be determined from the information given

19. Which protocol is responsible for establishing unique addressing?

   A. RTMP

   B. TACACS+

   C. ZIP

   D. DDP

   E. AT EIGRP

20. To review AppleTalk access lists on the router, type which of the following commands?

   A. show appletalk access lists

   B. show access-lists appletalk

   C. debug apple access-lists

   D. show appletalk access-lists

Answers to Review Questions

1. C. AppleTalk addresses have the form *network.node* with only one decimal point in the address. B is an IP address, D is an IPX address, and E is a URL.

2. C. Phase 1 allowed for only one cable range per segment or network. Answer A is an IP address, B is a valid Phase 2 cable range, and D is a zone name.

3. A. Nodes can only belong to a single zone.

4. B. Just as ARP works with IP to provide address resolution, AARP resolves the AppleTalk address to a MAC address. NBP is used similar to DNS, RTMP is a routing protocol, and ZIP controls zone information in AppleTalk.

5. A, B, C, D, E. Each one of the answers is part of the sequence of obtaining a node address.

6. A, B, D, E. These protocols route AppleTalk. RIP has an IP and IPX component, and OSPF and IGRP are limited to IP only.

7. E. A zone can belong to or have many cable ranges.

8. C. RTMP deals with AppleTalk routes and route tables. NBP is used similar to DNS, ZIP controls zone information in AppleTalk, and IGRP is only used with IP.

9. C. NBP is the protocol most similar to TCP/IP's DNS. RTMP, AURP, and AT EIGRP are routing protocols, and AT DNS is not a valid protocol.

10. B. If the addressing is incompatible, routing cannot take place. Therefore anything outside of a given cable range would not be reachable. A client in an AppleTalk network automatically discovers its default gateway; it does not need to be configured.

11. B. The range for AppleTalk access lists is from 600 to 699. 500–599 is Extended XNS, 900–999 is Extended IPX and 100–199 is Extended IP.

12. A, B, C, D, F. RIP is not part of AppleTalk.

13. C. The Chooser is the application that provides selection of the servers and print services. The Control Panel and Network Neighborhood are used in Windows, and NIS+ is used in Unix.

14. A, B, C. All of these connections are valid connection media for AppleTalk.

15. D. The `events debug` allows the administrator to view when interfaces change state. The other commands given are not valid.

16. C. AppleTalk was developed to not require much administrative overhead. ATM, not AppleTalk, has uniform 53 byte cells.

17. B. Logging records messages, and the correct syntax is indicated by the answer B. `debug apple routing` is used to troubleshoot routing issues, and `debug apple nbp` is used to debug NBP-related events.

18. C. The network is identified with the field `AT: net 700`. 10 is the network the neighbor is on that provided the information, and 251 is the node address of this neighbor.

19. D. DDP is used for establishing addressing. RTMP and AT EIGRP are routing protocols, TACACS+ is a Authentication, Authorization, and Accounting (AAA) protocol for IP, and ZIP controls zone information in AppleTalk.

20. D. The correct syntax is shown by D.

Chapter 11

Troubleshooting Switched Ethernet

TOPICS COVERED IN THIS CHAPTER INCLUDE:

✓ Apply diagnostic VLAN tools to switched and routed VLAN configuration problems.

✓ Use Cisco IOS router troubleshooting commands with Catalyst switch troubleshooting commands.

✓ Use proven problem isolation techniques to list the symptoms of Catalyst 5000 and VLAN problems on switched Ethernet Networks.

✓ Apply diagnostic tools to trouble tickets and solve classroom network Catalyst 5000 problems that simulate real-life networking malfunctions.

Switching and virtual networking became the Holy Grail of manufacturers and customers alike in the 1990s. High-speed, low-latency bridging at Layer 2 provided the first inducement for administrators to purchase and install switches. By the late 1990s, switches were no longer restricted to Layer 2, and route- and port-based switching at Layers 3 and 4 were becoming commonplace.

Switching provides many significant advantages, including greater aggregate bandwidth at lower cost and collision (full-duplex) control. The downside frequently includes a forklift upgrade in the wiring closet and slightly modified troubleshooting procedures. For example, it is not possible to simply plug a protocol analyzer into a port and see all traffic on the segment.

The Cisco Catalyst product line includes Ethernet, FDDI, Token Ring, and ATM switching. Although this section focuses primarily on the Catalyst 5000 product line, other Catalyst products are capable of additional functions, including voice switching and Layer 3 processing.

Switches, Bridges, and Hubs

An understanding of switches and their functions requires an understanding of the differences between broadcast and collision domains.

The *broadcast domain* defines the scope of broadcasts within the network. Usually this is equal to the diameter of the subnet, because most upper-layer protocols rely on broadcasts to function. As such, the broadcast domain is usually controlled by routers.

Collision domains are defined by the scope of impact that a collision may have. With hubs, this scope is equal to all stations connected to the shared media; as the number of nodes and traffic load increases, collisions become a more significant problem for administrators and designers. Switches reduce this scope to two: the switch port and the end node. By using full-duplex Ethernet, which is an option available on most switches and newer NICs, collisions are no longer a factor.

On an Ethernet hub, the collision domain and the broadcast domain are the same—all ports receive all frames and the receivers are required to analyze the destination address. If the frame is a broadcast or a unicast to the station (omitting multicasts), the frame will be processed further. The negative to this is unnecessary processing at all the workstations for which the frames were not intended. The collision domain on a hub is inclusive of all ports and stations on that hub. The broadcast domain on a hub is identical to the collision domain, although this assumes that a single hub represents the entire network or that a single hub is the only device connected to the router port. Technically, routers contain the broadcast domain. All other stations will hear any frame sent from a station on the hub.

The collision domain on a switch is limited to the individual port on the switch and its directly connected resource (workstation or other device). This greatly reduces workstation overhead because the frames received by the workstation should be intended for that station. In addition, the switch can provide a dedicated pipe to the workstation. Thus, a 10Mbit network interface card can provide 10Mbit, rather than sharing that bandwidth with all other stations. A small 12-port Ethernet switch provides a theoretical 120Mbit of bandwidth, compared to the 10Mbit provided by an Ethernet hub.

Table 11.1 compares the differences between switches and hubs.

TABLE 11.1 Comparison of Switches and Hubs

Type	Switch	Hub
Unicasts	Sent only to destination port.	Sent to all ports.
Broadcasts	Sent to all ports defined to the same VLAN.	Sent to all ports.

TABLE 11.1 Comparison of Switches and Hubs *(continued)*

Type	Switch	Hub
Aggregate Bandwidth	Equal to bandwidth of each port times number of ports. A 12-port Ethernet switch is capable of providing a total bandwidth of 120Mbit. (Note that backplane, processor, and other factors may change this simplification.)	Equal to speed of medium—an Ethernet hub would provide a total of 10Mbit.
Full/half duplex	Full duplex connections available.	Half duplex only.
Support for mixed media—Token Ring, Ethernet, FDDI, and so on	Depending on the switch, translations may occur between frame types or physical media.	Supports single media.

Table 11.2 contrasts the differences between switches and bridges.

TABLE 11.2 Switches and Bridges

Specification	Switches	Bridges
Support for mixed media	Usually	Depends on bridge configuration
Processing of frames	Hardware (ASIC)	Software or generic hardware
Number of ports	From 12 to over 100	Usually under 16; sometimes only two
Frame type translation	Usually	Depends on bridge configuration

Catalyst Troubleshooting Tools

The Catalyst system provides for significant diagnostic and administrative tools. These are included in the CLI (command line interface) and CWSI (CiscoWorks for Switched Internetworks). Troubleshooting switched networks frequently includes correlating Layer 2 addressing to Layer 3, and researching Physical layer problems. Although this section focuses primarily on the tools and commands themselves, a review of standards and typical problems will be presented later in the chapter.

Catalyst Command Line Interface

Many administrators prefer the command line interface (CLI), especially if they are already experienced with the Cisco IOS. Although the GUI applications can simplify many functions, and (in some cases) address functions not available from the CLI, they fail to provide the speed and simplicity of CLI.

The CLI provides a wealth of configuration and diagnostic tools for the administrator. Commands include the set and clear options that are used to configure the switch, and the show commands to monitor the current settings.

The show commands, displayed in enable mode with the show ? command, include the following:

```
show alias           Show aliases for commands
show arp             Show ARP table
show bridge          Show bridge information
show cam             Show CAM table
show cdp             Show Cisco Discovery Protocol
                     Information
show cgmp            Show CGMP info
show config          Show system configuration
show drip            Show DRiP Information
show fddi            Show FDDI module entries
show fddicam         Show FDDI module CAM table
show flash           Show system flash information
show help            Show this message
show interface       Show network interfaces
show ip              Show IP Information
```

```
show log                Show log information
show logging            Show system logging information
show mac                Show MAC information
show microcode          Show microcode versions
show module             Show module information
show multicast          Show multicast information
show netstat            Show network statistics
show ntp                Show ntp statistics
show port               Show port information
show rif                Show Routing Information Field
                          (RIF)Table
show rsmautostate       Show RSM derived interface state
                        enabled/disabled
show snmp               Show SNMP information
show span               Show switch port analyzer information
show spantree           Show spantree information
show station            Show Tokenring Station info
show summertime         Show state of summertime information
show system             Show system information
show tacacs             Show TACACS information
show test               Show results of diagnostic tests
show time               Show time of day
show timezone           Show the current timezone offset
show tokenring          Show tokenring information
show trunk              Show trunk ports
show users              Show active Admin sessions
show version            Show version information
show vlan               Show Virtual LAN information
show vmps               Show VMPS information
show vtp                Show VTP information
```

show system

The show system command provides high-level summary information regarding the switch, including the status of power supplies, uptime and administrative settings, and the percentage of traffic on the backplane.

```
Switch_A> (enable) show system
PS1-Status PS2-Status Fan-Status Temp-Alarm Sys-Status Uptime d,h:m:s Logout
---------- ---------- ---------- ---------- ---------- -------------- ------
ok         ok         ok         off        ok         153,19:29:57   none


PS1-Type   PS2-Type   Modem   Baud  Traffic Peak Peak-Time
---------- ---------- ------- ----- ------- ---- ------------------------
WS-C5008B  WS-C5008B  disable 9600  0%      0%   Fri Feb 22 2002, 12:14:38


System Name   System Location          System Contact
------------- ------------------------ --------------------
Switch_A      Maui, Hawaii             Robert Padjen
```

show port

The show port commands provide specific information about ports or all ports on a module. This includes commands that are available from other show commands, including show mac, for example.

```
Switch_A> (enable) show port ?
Usage: show port
       show port <mod_num>
       show port <mod_num/port_num>
Show port commands:
show port broadcast        Show port broadcast information
show port cdp              Show port CDP information
show port channel         Show port channel information
show port counters        Show port counters
show port fddi            Show port FDDI information
show port filter          Show Token Ring port filtering
                              information
show port help            Show this message
show port mac             Show port MAC counters
show port multicast       Show port multicast information
show port security        Show port security information
show port spantree        Show port spantree information
show port status          Show port status
```

```
show port trap        Show port trap information
show port trunk       Show port trunk information
```

The show port command output appears as follows. Note that VLAN membership, port speed and configuration, and error statistics are available.

```
Switch_A> (enable) show port 3/20
Port  Name      Status    Vlan Level Duplex Speed Type
----- --------- --------- ---- ------ ------ ------ -------
3/20 connected 1 normal half 10 10BaseT


Port Security Secure-Src-Addr Last-Src-Addr Shutdown Trap
---- -------- --------------- ------------- -------- --------
3/20 disabled No disabled


Port     Broadcast-Limit Broadcast-Drop
-------- --------------- --------------
3/20           -               0


Port  Align-Err  FCS-Err   Xmit-Err   Rcv-Err    UnderSize
----- ---------- ---------- ---------- ---------- ---------
3/20     0          0          0          0          0


Port  Single-Col Multi-Coll Late-Coll Excess-Col Carri-Sen Runts Giants
----- ---------- ---------- ---------- ---------- --------- ----- ------
3/20    3922        703        0          0          0       0     0
```

show log

The show log command does not report events the same way that a Cisco router does. The command reports significant events, including reboots of all modules, traps, and power supply failures. Note that the following output reports four power supply failures in the period that may be useful information for the administrator if users report intermittent connectivity problems.

```
Switch_A> (enable) show log
Network Management Processor (ACTIVE NMP) Log:
  Reset count:   4
```

```
Re-boot History:    Jan 22 2002 23:06:05 0, Jan 17 2002
                      11:28:27 0
                    Jan 16 2002 18:48:02 0, Jan 14 2002
                      12:18:05 0
Bootrom Checksum Failures:       0
UART Failures:                   0
Flash Checksum Failures:         0
Flash Program Failures:          0
Power Supply 1 Failures:         4
Power Supply 2 Failures:         0
Swapped to CLKA:                 0
Swapped to CLKB:                 0
Swapped to Processor 1:          0
Swapped to Processor 2:          0
DRAM Failures:                   0

Exceptions:                      4
  Last Exception occurred on  ...
  Software version = 3.2(1b)
  Error Msg:
  PID = 0 Kernel
  PC: 10000D0C, Status: 2704, Vector: 007C
  sp+00: 27041000 0D0C007C 2604101F 0D3A007C
  sp+10: 00000000 101785A2 00000030 102FB11C
  sp+20: 10FFFF9C 10179C06 10357A90 102FB11C
  sp+30: 10FFFFA8 101FB86E 00000000 10FFFFE8
  sp+40: 101FC0D4 00000000 10278814 00002000
  sp+50: 00000080 0000101F B9862078 01000001
  sp+60: 1CD80000 001E0000 00010000 00000000
  sp+70: 00000000 00000000 00000007 68000000
  sp+80: 00000000 00000000 00000000 00000000
  sp+90: 00000000 103FFFEC 10000420 100009C2
  sp+A0: 10000940 10000A4E 10001030 10001030
  sp+B0: 10001030 10001030 10000BD0 10000AD0
  sp+C0: 10000B28 10001030 10001030 10001030
  sp+D0: 10001030 10001030 10001030 10001030
```

```
            sp+E0: 10001030 10001030 10001030 10001030
            sp+F0: 10001030 10001030 10001030 493798E4
            D0: 00000000, D1: 00002604, D2: 00000030, D3: 00005C05
            D4: 11000000, D5: 11000000, D6: 10FF0008, D7: 11000000
            A0: 68000000, A1: 00000000, A2: 10357A90, A3: 103C182C
            A4: 103C182C, A5: 64000000, A6: 10FFFF8C, sp: 10FFFF6C

NVRAM log:


Module 2 Log:
   Reset Count:    4
   Reset History: Tue Jan 22 2002, 23:07:05
                  Thu Jan 17 2002, 11:29:27
                  Wed Jan 16 2002, 18:49:01
                  Mon Jan 14 2002, 12:19:05


Module 3 Log:
   Reset Count:    4
   Reset History: Tue Jan 22 2002, 23:07:05
                  Thu Jan 17 2002, 11:29:27
                  Wed Jan 16 2002, 18:49:01
                  Mon Jan 14 2002, 12:19:29

Module 4 Log:
   Reset Count:    4
   Reset History: Tue Jan 22 2002, 23:07:05
                  Thu Jan 17 2002, 11:29:27
                  Wed Jan 16 2002, 18:49:01
                  Mon Jan 14 2002, 12:19:30
```

show logging buffer

The equivalent to the show log command on a router is the show logging buffer command on a switch. Depending on the logging level, this command can report on port up, port down, or spanning tree issues as well as just about anything else that is happening on the switch. The output of this command is shown below.

```
Switch_A> show logging buffer
2002 May 04 13:42:55 EST -04:00 %MLS-5-ROUTERADD:Route Processor 10.4.0.254
  added
2002 May 04 13:44:32 EST -04:00 %SNMP-5-MODULETRAP:Module 2 [Down] Trap
2002 May 04 13:44:32 EST -04:00 %SPANTREE-5-PORTDEL_FAILNOTFOUND:2/1 in
  vlan 1 not found (RedundantTask)
2002 May 04 13:44:32 EST -04:00 %SPANTREE-5-PORTDEL_FAILNOTFOUND:2/2 in
  vlan 1 not found (RedundantTask)
2002 May 04 13:44:34 EST -04:00 %SYS-5-SUP_MODSBY:Module 2 is in standby
  mode
2002 May 04 13:44:34 EST -04:00 %SNMP-5-MODULETRAP:Module 2 [Up] Trap
2002 May 04 13:45:01 EST -04:00 %SYS-5-SUP_IMGSYNCSTART:Active supervisor
  is synchronizing the NMP image
2002 May 04 13:45:09 EST -04:00 %SYS-5-SUP_IMGSYNCFINISH:Active supervisor
  has synchronized the NMP image
```

show interface

The show interface command reports the IP configuration of the Supervisor module. Although SLIP (Serial Line Internet Protocol) connection is configured on sl0, most installations use the in-band sc0 connection. As shown, it belongs to VLAN 1, which always exists on the switch.

```
Switch_A> (enable) show interface
sl0: flags=51<UP,POINTOPOINT,RUNNING>
        slip 0.0.0.0 dest 0.0.0.0
sc0: flags=63<UP,BROADCAST,RUNNING>
        vlan 1 inet 10.11.10.1 netmask 255.255.255.0
          broadcast 10.11.10.255
```

show cdp

Cisco Discovery Protocol is an incredibly powerful troubleshooting tool. Available on all Cisco routers and switches, the protocol operates between Cisco devices on media that support SNAP. The protocol has been available since IOS 10.3.

CDP packets are sent as a multicast and are not forwarded by the router or switch.

Following is a sample of the CDP report on a Catalyst 5505 switch with three neighbors:

```
Switch_A> (enable) show cdp neighbor detail
Device-ID: Router_A.domain.com
Device Addresses:
  IP Address: 10.1.1.1
Holdtime: 142 sec
Capabilities: ROUTER
Version:
  Cisco Internetwork Operating System Software
  IOS (tm) 4500 Software (C4500-J-M), Version 11.2(15a)P, P RELEASE
    SOFTWARE (fc1)
  Copyright (c) 1986-1998 by cisco Systems, Inc.
Platform: cisco 4700
Port-ID (Port on Device): FastEthernet0
Port (Our Port): 2/1
```

```
Device-ID: Router_B.domain.com
Device Addresses:
  IP Address: 10.1.2.1
Holdtime: 130 sec
Capabilities: ROUTER
Version:
  Cisco Internetwork Operating System Software
  IOS (tm) 4500 Software (C4500-J-M), Version 11.2(15a)P, P
    RELEASE SOFTWARE (fc1)
  Copyright (c) 1986-1998 by cisco Systems, Inc.
Platform: cisco 4700
Port-ID (Port on Device): FastEthernet0
Port (Our Port): 2/2
```

```
Device-ID: Router_C.domain.com
Device Addresses:
  IP Address: 10.10.1.1
Holdtime: 177 sec
Capabilities: ROUTER SR_BRIDGE
Version:
  Cisco Internetwork Operating System Software
```

```
 IOS (tm) C2600 Software (C2600-JS-M), Version 12.0(2a), RELEASE
   SOFTWARE (fc1)
 Copyright (c) 1986-1999 by cisco Systems, Inc.
Platform: cisco 2612
Port-ID (Port on Device): Ethernet1/0
Port (Our Port): 2/17
```

A CDP datagram decodes with EtherPeek, as follows:

```
Packet 3 captured at 02/22/2002 09:08:57 AM; Packet size is
  302(0x12e)bytes
        Relative time: 000:00:01.473
        Delta time: 0.042.868
Ethernet Protocol
        Address: 00-00-0C-1B-63-97 --->01-00-0C-CC-CC-CC
        Length: 288
Logical Link Control
        SSAP Address: 0xAA, CR bit = 0 (Command)
        DSAP Address: 0xAA, IG bit = 0 (Individual address)
        Unnumbered frame: UI
SubNetwork Access Protocol
        Organization code: 0x00000c
        Type: Custom Defined
Flags:        0x80  802.3
  Status:        0x00
  Packet Length:339
  Timestamp:     16:40:23.689000 03/16/2002
802.3 Header
  Destination:  01:00:0c:cc:cc:cc
  Source:       00:00:0c:17:b6:f2
  LLC Length:   321
802.2 Logical Link Control (LLC) Header
  Dest. SAP:    0xaa  SNAP
  Source SAP:   0xaa  SNAP
  Command:      0x03  Unnumbered Information
  Protocol:     00-00-0c-20-00
  Packet Data:
  . _'....Router_A  01 b4 9e 27 00 01 00 0c 52 6f 75 74 65 72 5f 41
  ...6............  00 02 00 36 00 00 00 03 01 01 cc 00 04 0a 02 01
```

```
...  ...._7.....    01 02 08 aa aa 03 00 00 00 81 37 00 0a 00 00 00
..... ...  ...._    0b 00 00 0c 17 b6 f2 02 08 aa aa 03 00 00 00 80
....o....Ethern     9b 00 03 00 02 6f 00 03 00 0d 45 74 68 65 72 6e
et1........... C    65 74 31 00 04 00 08 00 00 00 01 00 05 00 d0 43
isco Internetwor    69 73 63 6f 20 49 6e 74 65 72 6e 65 74 77 6f 72
k Operating Syst    6b 20 4f 70 65 72 61 74 69 6e 67 20 53 79 73 74
em Software .IOS    65 6d 20 53 6f 66 74 77 61 72 65 20 0a 49 4f 53
 (tm) 4000 Softw    20 28 74 6d 29 20 34 30 30 30 20 53 6f 66 74 77
are (XX-J-M), Ve    61 72 65 20 28 58 58 2d 4a 2d 4d 29 2c 20 56 65
rsion 11.0(17),     72 73 69 6f 6e 20 31 31 2e 30 28 31 37 29 2c 20
RELEASE SOFTWARE    52 45 4c 45 41 53 45 20 53 4f 46 54 57 41 52 45
 (fc1).Copyright    20 28 66 63 31 29 0a 43 6f 70 79 72 69 67 68 74
 (c) 1986-1997 b    20 28 63 29 20 31 39 38 36 2d 31 39 39 37 20 62
y cisco Systems,    79 20 63 69 73 63 6f 20 53 79 73 74 65 6d 73 2c
 Inc..Compiled T    20 49 6e 63 2e 0a 43 6f 6d 70 69 6c 65 64 20 54
hu 04-Sep-97 14:    68 75 20 30 34 2d 53 65 70 2d 39 37 20 31 34 3a
44 by richv....c    34 34 20 62 79 20 72 69 63 68 76 00 06 00 0e 63
isco 4000           69 73 63 6f 20 34 30 30 30
Frame Check Sequence:   0x00000000
```

show config

The show config command is similar to the show running-config command on Cisco routers. The command provides all configuration settings on the switch for all modules, with a few exceptions for certain modules such as the RSM (Route Switch Module).

The output of the command appears as follows:

```
Switch_A> (enable) show config
.....
.........
.........
.........
.........
..

begin
set password $1$0o6Z$GChAFNM/MGi
```

```
set enablepass $1$CeBqb$zRTAOr.Cukh/
set prompt Switch_A>
set length 24 default
set logout 0
set banner motd ^C

This is Switch_A. For additional information contact an
    administrator.
^C
!
#system
set system baud   9600
set system modem disable
set system name   Switch_A
set system location Maui, Hawaii
set system contact  Robert Padjen
!
#snmp
set snmp community read-only      public
set snmp community read-write     private
set snmp community read-write-all all
set snmp rmon disable
set snmp trap enable   module
set snmp trap enable   chassis
set snmp trap enable   bridge
set snmp trap enable   repeater
set snmp trap enable   vtp
set snmp trap enable   auth
set snmp trap enable   ippermit
set snmp trap enable   vmps
!
#ip
set interface sc0 1 10.1.2.10 255.255.255.0 10.1.2.255
set interface sl0 0.0.0.0 0.0.0.0
set arp agingtime 1200
set ip redirect   enable
```

```
set ip unreachable    enable
set ip fragmentation enable
set ip route 0.0.0.0          10.1.2.1   0
set ip alias default          0.0.0.0
!
#Command alias
!
#vmps
set vmps server retry 3
set vmps server reconfirminterval 60
set vmps tftpserver 0.0.0.0 vmps-config-database.1
set vmps state disable


!
#dns
set ip dns disable
!
#tacacs+
set tacacs attempts 3
set tacacs directedrequest disable
set tacacs timeout 5
set authentication login tacacs disable
set authentication login local enable
set authentication enable tacacs disable
set authentication enable local enable
!
#bridge
set bridge ipx snaptoether    8023raw
set bridge ipx 8022toether    8023
set bridge ipx 8023rawtofddi snap
!
#vtp
set vtp domain Global
set vtp mode transparent
set vtp v2 disable
set vtp pruneeligible 2-1000
```

```
clear vtp pruneeligible 1001-1005
set vlan 1 name default type ethernet mtu 1500 said 100001
  state active
set vlan 1002 name fddi-default type fddi mtu 1500 said
  101002 state active
set vlan 1004 name fddinet-default type fddinet mtu 1500
  said 101004 state active bridge 0x0 stp ieee
set vlan 1005 name trnet-default type trbrf mtu 1500 said
  101005 state active bridge 0x0 stp ieee
set vlan 1003 name Token-Ring-default type trcrf mtu 1500
  said 101003 state active parent 0 ring 0x0 mode srb
  aremaxhop 7 stemaxhop 7
!
#spantree
#uplinkfast groups
set spantree uplinkfast disable
#vlan 1
set spantree enable      1
set spantree fwddelay 15     1
set spantree hello     2     1
set spantree maxage    20     1
set spantree priority 32768 1
#vlan 1003
set spantree enable      1003
set spantree fwddelay 4       1003
set spantree hello     2       1003
set spantree maxage    10       1003
set spantree priority 32768 1003
set spantree portstate 1003 auto 0
set spantree portcost 1003 80
set spantree portpri   1003 4
set spantree portfast 1003 disable
#vlan 1005
set spantree enable      1005
set spantree fwddelay 15     1005
set spantree hello     2       1005
set spantree maxage    20       1005
```

```
set spantree priority 32768 1005
set spantree multicast-address 1005 ieee
!
#cgmp
set cgmp disable
set cgmp leave disable
!
#syslog
set logging console enable
set logging server disable
set logging level cdp 2 default
set logging level cgmp 2 default
set logging level disl 5 default
set logging level dvlan 2 default
set logging level earl 2 default
set logging level fddi 2 default
set logging level ip 2 default
set logging level pruning 2 default
set logging level snmp 2 default
set logging level spantree 2 default
set logging level sys 5 default
set logging level tac 2 default
set logging level tcp 2 default
set logging level telnet 2 default
set logging level tftp 2 default
set logging level vtp 2 default
set logging level vmps 2 default
set logging level kernel 2 default
set logging level filesys 2 default
set logging level drip 2 default
set logging level pagp 5 default
!
#ntp
set ntp broadcastclient disable
set ntp broadcastdelay 3000
```

```
set ntp client disable
set timezone PST 0 0
set summertime disable
!
#permit list
set ip permit disable
!
#drip
set tokenring reduction enable
set tokenring distrib-crf disable
!
#module 1 : 2-port 100BaseFX MM Supervisor
set module name     1
set vlan 1      1/1-2
set port channel 1/1-2 off
set port channel 1/1-2 auto
set port enable     1/1-2
set port level      1/1-2  normal
set port duplex     1/1-2  half
set port trap       1/1-2  enable
set port name       1/1-2
set port security   1/1-2  disable
set port broadcast  1/1-2  100%
set port membership 1/1-2  static
set cdp enable    1/1-2
set cdp interval 1/1-2 60
set trunk 1/1   auto 1-1005
set trunk 1/2   auto 1-1005
set spantree portfast     1/1-2 disable
set spantree portcost     1/1-2 19
set spantree portpri      1/1-2 32
set spantree portvlanpri 1/1  0
set spantree portvlanpri 1/2  0
set spantree portvlancost 1/1  cost 18
set spantree portvlancost 1/2  cost 18
```

```
!
#module 2 : 24-port 10/100BaseTX Ethernet
set module name     2
set module enable   2
set vlan 1      2/1-24
set port enable     2/1-24
set port level      2/1-24   normal
set port speed      2/3-24   auto
set port speed      2/1-2  100
set port duplex     2/1-2   full
set port trap       2/1-24   enable
set port name       2/1-24
set port security   2/1-24   disable
set port broadcast  2/1-24   0
set port membership 2/1-24   static
set cdp enable      2/1-24
set cdp interval 2/1-24 60
set spantree portfast      2/1-24 disable
set spantree portcost      2/9   100
set spantree portcost      2/10 100
set spantree portcost      2/11 100
set spantree portcost      2/12 100
set spantree portcost      2/17 100
set spantree portcost      2/18 100
set spantree portcost      2/19 100
set spantree portcost      2/21 100
set spantree portcost      2/1-8,2/13-16,2/20,2/22-24 19
set spantree portpri       2/1-24 32
!
. . . some output omitted . . .

#switch port analyzer
set span disable
!
#cam
set cam agingtime 1,1003,1005 300
end
```

show test

The status of the switch, including interface cards, power supplies, and memory, is available by using the show test command.

Observe that the first show test output reports only the status of the supervisor module and no information specific to the other modules.

```
Switch_A> (enable) show test
Environmental Status (. = Pass, F = Fail, U = Unknown)
  PS (3.3V):   .  PS (12V): .  PS (24V):   .  PS1: .
  PS2: .
  Temperature: .  Fan:      .  Clock(A/B): A   Chassis-Ser-EEPROM: .


Module 1 : 2-port 100BaseFX MM Supervisor
Network Management Processor (NMP) Status: (. = Pass, F =  Fail,
   U = Unknown)
  ROM:  .  Flash-EEPROM: .  Ser-EEPROM: .  NVRAM: .  MCP  Comm: .


  EARL Status :
         NewLearnTest:           .
         IndexLearnTest:         .
         DontForwardTest:        .
         MonitorTest             .
         DontLearn:              .
         FlushPacket:            .
         ConditionalLearn:       .
         EarlLearnDiscard:       .
         EarlTrapTest:           .

LCP Diag Status for Module 1  (. = Pass, F = Fail, N = N/A)
  CPU        : .  Sprom    : .  Bootcsum : .    Archsum  : N
  RAM        : .  LTL : .  CBL    : .    DPRAM     :.SAMBA : .
  Saints     : .  Pkt Bufs : .  Repeater : N     FLASH    : N

  MII Status:
  Ports 1  2
  -----------
       N  N
```

```
SAINT/SAGE Status :
 Ports 1  2  3
 --------------
        .  .  .


Packet Buffer Status :
 Ports 1  2  3
 --------------
        .  .  .


Loopback Status [Reported by Module 1] :
 Ports  1  2  3
 --------------
        .  .  .


Channel Status :
 Ports  1  2
 -----------
        .  .
```

The following output provides the test results from module three of a Catalyst 5505. The module has 48 ports providing 10Mbit Ethernet. By using the show test 3 command, the switch reports the test results of the entire card, including the SAINT and EARL ASICs. These ASICs (Application Specific Integrated Circuits) will be reviewed later in this chapter.

```
Switch_A> (enable) show test 3

Module 3 : 48-port 10BaseT Ethernet

LCP Diag Status for Module 3  (. = Pass, F = Fail, N = N/A)
CPU       : .   Sprom    : .   Bootcsum : .   Archsum  : .
RAM       : .   LTL      : .   CBL      : N   DPRAM    : N  SAMBA : .
Saints    : .   Pkt Bufs : .   Repeater : N   FLASH    : .

 SAINT/SAGE Status :
  Ports 1  2  3  4  5  6  7  8  9  10 11 12 13 14 15 16 17 18 19 20 21 22 23 24
  -----------------------------------------------------------------------------
        .  .  .  .  .  .  .  .  .  .  .  .  .  .  .  .  .  .  .  .  .  .  .  .

  25 26 27 28 29 30 31 32 33 34 35 36 37 38 39 40 41 42 43 44 45 46 47 48
  -----------------------------------------------------------------------------
         .  .  .  .  .  .  .  .  .  .  .  .  .  .  .  .  .  .  .  .  .  .  .  .
```

```
Packet Buffer Status :
  Ports 1  2  3  4  5  6  7  8  9  10 11 12 13 14 15 16 17 18  19 20 21 22 23 24
------------------------------------------------------------------------------
        .  .  .  .  .  .  .  .  .  .  .  .  .  .  .  .  .  .   .  .  .  .  .  .

        25 26 27 28 29 30 31 32 33 34 35 36 37 38 39 40 41 42 43 44 45 46 47 48
------------------------------------------------------------------------------
        .  .  .  .  .  .  .  .  .  .  .  .  .  .  .  .  .  .  .  .  .  .  .  .


Loopback Status [Reported by Module 1] :
  Ports 1  2  3  4  5  6  7  8  9  10 11 12 13 14 15 16 17 18 19 20 21 22 23 24
        ----------------------------------------------------------------------
        .  .  .  .  .  .  .  .  .  .  .  .  .  .  .  .  .  .  .  .  .  .  .  .

  Ports 25 26 27 28 29 30 31 32 33 34 35 36 37 38 39 40 41 42 43 44 45 46 47 48
        ----------------------------------------------------------------------
        .  .  .  .  .  .  .  .  .  .  .  .  .  .  .  .  .  .  .  .  .
```

show mac

The following output is provided from the **show mac** command. Although it is quite long, it was truncated from the original capture. For highly populated switches, this command requires a capturing program for later analysis. Note that numerous counters are maintained in normal operation, including the frame traffic per port; the total number of incoming frames, including discards; and the total number of transmits and aborts due to excessive deferral or MTU violations. Broadcast counters are also maintained in addition to discards due to EARL page-full errors. (EARL is covered in greater detail later in this chapter.) In some cases, an administrator may find the **show port** command more helpful in troubleshooting.

The following output has been slightly modified for space considerations. RCV-M is representative of RCV-Multi. Xmit-M is used in place of Xmit-Multi, and Dcrd is used for Discard.

```
Switch_A> (enable) show mac
MAC  Rcv-Frms  Xmit-Frms  Rcv-M  Xmit-M  Rcv-Broad  Xmit-Broad
1/1      0          0        0       0         0           0
1/2      0          0        0       0         0           0
2/1    1840       1997       53     136         8          91
2/2     941       1026       56     133         4          95
2/3    6001       6489        0     187        26          73
2/4     776       1179        0     187         1          98
```

2/5	4951	6115	0	187	0	99
2/6	0	0	0	0	0	0
2/7	26	301	0	187	1	98
2/8	246	524	0	187	0	99
2/9	0	0	0	0	0	0

. . . some output omitted . . .

MAC	Dely-Exced	MTU-Exced	In-Dcrd	Lrn-Dcrd	In-Lost	OutLost
1/1	0	0	0	0	0	0
1/2	0	0	0	0	0	0
2/1	0	0	0	0	0	0
2/2	0	0	0	0	0	0
2/3	0	0	0	0	0	0
2/4	0	0	0	0	0	0
2/5	0	0	0	0	0	0
2/6	0	0	0	0	0	0
2/7	0	0	0	0	0	0
2/8	0	0	0	0	0	0
2/9	0	0	0	0	0	0

. . . some output omitted . . .

Port	Rcv-unicast	Rcv-Multicast	Rcv-Broadcast
1/1	0	0	0
1/2	0	0	0
2/1	1814	56	8
2/2	882	58	8
2/3	5996	0	26
2/4	793	0	2
2/5	5099	0	0
2/6	0	0	0
2/7	26	0	1
2/8	252	0	0
2/9	0	0	0

. . . some output omitted . . .

Port	Xmit-Unicast	Xmit-Multicast	Xmit-Broadcast
1/1	0	0	0
1/2	0	0	0
2/1	1819	141	97
2/2	798	140	101
2/3	6260	195	83
2/4	921	195	107

```
2/5              6104              195              109
2/6                 0                0                0
2/7                16              195               08
2/8               242              195              109
2/9                 0                0                0
. . . some output omitted . . .
Port                   Rcv-Octet              Xmit-Octet
1/1                            0                       0
1/2                            0                       0
2/1                       445231                  405059
2/2                       208680                  300413
2/3                      2935182                 2876636
2/4                        61427                  114408
2/5                       716265                  601719
2/6                            0                       0
2/7                         3125                   53564
2/8                        36993                   96826
2/9                            0                       0
. . . some output omitted . . .

Last-Time-Cleared
----------------------------
Fri Feb 22 2002, 12:14:38
```

show vtp domain

The VLAN Trunk Protocol (VTP) is designed to simplify the introduction of VLANs in multi-switch networks. Within the management domain, a new VLAN is only specified once, and the configuration is propagated throughout the network. The configuration information includes the parameters needed for differing topologies within the switched network.

The show vtp domain command provides the following status information. Note that VTP updates are sent over VLAN 1 when troubleshooting VTP issues.

```
Switch_A> (enable)  show vtp domain
Domain Name             Domain Index VTP Version Local Mode   Password
---------------------   ------------ ----------- ------------ --------
Global                       1            2       Transparent  -
```

```
Vlan-count Max-vlan-storage Config Revision Notifications
---------- ---------------- --------------- -------------
5          1023             0               enabled

Last Updater    V2 Mode  Pruning  PruneEligible on Vlans
--------------- -------- -------- ------------------------
10.1.2.20       disabled disabled 2-1000
```

show cam

Switches operate at Layer 2 of the OSI model, so MAC addresses are the basis for forwarding decisions. Although VLANs are typically assigned on Layer 3 boundaries, the switch directs unicast frames in the same manner as a bridge.

The show cam command reports the MAC address associated with the ports of the switch, as follows. Note the specifications that must be included with the command in the first output, followed by the actual MAC list in the second.

```
Switch_A> (enable) show cam
Usage: show cam [count] <dynamic|static|permanent|system> [vlan]
       show cam <dynamic|static|permanent> <mod_num/port_num>
       show cam <mac_addr> [vlan]
       show cam agingtime

Switch_A> (enable) show cam dynamic 1
VLAN   Dest MAC/Route Des   Destination Ports or VCs
1      00-80-2f-9f-54-5f    2/3
1      00-08-27-ca-c9-cd    3/18
1      00-08-27-ca-cd-da    3/23
1      00-08-27-ca-d1-20    3/27
1      00-08-27-29-89-80    3/44
1      00-08-27-29-88-a7    4/41
1      00-08-27-d2-ce-43    4/1
1      00-08-27-9a-0e-e9    3/13
1      00-08-27-ca-db-5e    4/38
1      00-08-27-ca-db-70    4/30
1      00-08-27-29-82-5d    2/22
1      00-08-27-8c-fd-e5    3/7
```

```
1        00-08-27-8c-fc-c0    3/32
1        00-08-27-d2-f8-10    4/43
1        00-08-27-ca-e0-47    4/29
1        00-08-27-ca-e0-6c    2/20
1        00-08-27-d2-fd-ab    3/2
1        00-08-27-d2-fe-4a    4/36
1        00-08-27-d2-fe-f5    2/24
1        00-08-27-d2-ff-c7    2/23
1        00-08-27-d2-ff-dd    4/45
1        00-08-27-d2-f1-87    2/8
Total Matching CAM Entries Displayed = 21
```

Duplicate MAC Addresses

Some network devices may be configured with the same MAC address on each interface, including certain dual-homed Unix workstations. This is a common event that can create substantial problems in the network. The show cam command is one of the best methods for finding this issue, although prevention via communication and change control can be more beneficial. If the administration of workstations and network services is divided in an administrator's organization, it is recommended that this issue be reviewed and that duplicate MAC addresses be used only when required. Documentation of the installation should accompany such a decision.

show spantree

Although the spanning tree process is covered later in this chapter, the use of spanning trees is crucial to the successful running of switched networks where loops may occur. The show spantree command reports the status of the spanning tree process for each VLAN, when enabled as follows:

```
Switch_A> (enable) show spantree
VLAN 1
Spanning tree enabled
Spanning tree type          ieee

Designated Root             00-90-86-fc-48-00
Designated Root Priority    32768
Designated Root Cost        0
Designated Root Port        1/0
```

```
Root Max Age    20 sec    Hello Time 2  sec    Forward Delay  15 sec

Bridge ID MAC ADDR          00-90-86-fc-48-00
Bridge ID Priority          32768
Bridge Max Age 20 sec    Hello Time 2  sec    Forward Delay  15 sec

Port    Vlan  Port-State      Cost  Priority  Fast-Start  Group-method
------- ----  -------------   ----- --------  ----------  -----------
1/1     1     not-connected    19      32      disabled
1/2     1     not-connected    19      32      disabled
2/1     1     forwarding       19      32      disabled
2/2     1     forwarding       19      32      disabled
2/3     1     forwarding       19      32      disabled
2/4     1     forwarding       19      32      disabled
2/5     1     forwarding       19      32      disabled
2/6     1     not-connected    19      32      disabled
2/7     1     forwarding       19      32      disabled
2/8     1     forwarding       19      32      disabled
2/9     1     not-connected   100      32      disabled
. . . some output omitted . . .
```

show flash

Cisco switches operate with software that is very similar to the Cisco IOS on routers. This software is stored and may be upgraded in flash stored on the Supervisor module. The show flash command reports the space required for the installed software and the version of code.

```
Switch_A> (enable) show flash
File          Version  Sector   Size Built
c5000 nmp     3.2(1b)  02-11  1571059 05/04/98 22:37:19
      epld    3.2      30      72920 05/04/98 22:37:23
      lcp atm  3.2(1)  12-15   23822 05/04/98 15:29:01
      lcp tr   3.2     12-15   29016 05/04/98 15:30:46
      lcp c5ip 3.2     12-15   23744 05/04/98 15:33:40
      lcp 64k  3.2     12-15   57046 05/04/98 15:32:12
      atm/fddi 3.2     12-15   24507 05/04/98 15:27:10
      lcp 360  3.2(1)  12-15  123108 05/04/98 15:37:04
```

```
            lcp       3.2      12-15     27561 05/04/98 15:25:48
            smcp      3.2      12-15     34155 05/04/98 15:22:38
            mcp       3.2      12-15     26378 05/04/98 15:24:20
```

show version

The show version command provides hardware and software version numbers, in addition to memory and system uptime statistics. The output of the command appears as follows:

```
Switch_A> (enable) show version
WS-C5505 Software, Version McpSW: 3.2(1) NmpSW: 3.2(1b)
Copyright (c) 1995-1998 by Cisco Systems
NMP S/W compiled on May  4 1998, 15:20:25
MCP S/W compiled on May 04 1998, 15:22:38

System Bootstrap Version: 3.1(2)

Hardware Version: 1.0  Model: WS-C5505  Serial #: 066911349

Module Ports Model     Serial #    Hw   Fw        Fw1       Sw
1      2     WS-X5506  009071826   2.3  3.1(2)    2.4(1)    3.2(1b)
2      24    WS-X5224  006711612   1.4  3.1(1)              3.2(1)
3      48    WS-X5012  010128192   2.3  2.3(2)              3.2(1)
4      48    WS-X5012  010127211   2.3  2.3(2)              3.2(1)

       DRAM                     FLASH                 NVRAM
Module Total  Used  Free   Total Used  Free   Total Used  Free
1      16384K 7846K 8538K  8192K 3840K 4352K  256K  107K  149K

Uptime is 171 days, 8 hours, 23 minutes
```

CiscoWorks for Switched Internetworks

CiscoWorks for Switched Internetworks (CWSI) can augment HP Open-View, SunNet Manager, or NetView/AIX, in addition to running as a stand-alone application on NT or Unix—including Solaris, HP-Unix, and AIX. The application includes a number of tools for installation, monitoring, and troubleshooting. Table 11.3 documents some of the more relevant functions within CWSI.

TABLE 11.3 CWSI Applications Matrix

Application	Function
CiscoView	A graphical application that provides virtual chassis viewing, configuration tools, performance monitoring, and minor troubleshooting functions.
VlanDirector	Switching is most useful when combined with virtual LANs. The VlanDirector application provides a graphical administration tool for adding users, assigning ports, and changing associations.
TrafficDirector	RMON, or Remote Monitoring, is one of the best baselining and troubleshooting tools in switched environments. TrafficDirector provides a united view of the switched network, including trunk links and switch ports.
AtmDirector	In Asynchronous Transfer Mode networks, this tool eases installation and administration.
User Tracking	Cisco switches permit VLAN assignments based on dynamic parameters, including the MAC layer address. User Tracking defines these dynamic VLANs and tracks stations within the network.

RMON

Modern network devices provide greater visibility into the functioning of the network. Simple Network Management Protocol (SNMP) and *Remote Monitoring (RMON)* provide much of this visibility. RMON is another method for obtaining environmental and statistical information from devices. Much of the RMON technology implementation is based on the deployment of RMON probes that gather the information from the circuit (physical media) because the router or switch may not support all levels of RMON information.

Catalyst 5000 series switches provide internal support for four of the nine RMON groups defined in RFC 1757. These groups include port utilization and error statistics, historical statistics, alarm notification, and event logging. Additional monitoring may use the Switched Port Analyzer (SPAN) function, which is also referred to as *port mirroring*. Cisco's SwitchProbe product line can provide access to the other five layers of RMON in addition to the RMON2 groups. Examples of the commands used to configure a SPAN port appear later in this chapter.

Indicator Lights

In addition to the command line interface and the functions of CWSI, the Catalyst provides diagnostic information via LEDs on the line modules and the Supervisor engine.

The Supervisor engine includes load LEDs that indicate the current utilization of the switch. A high load (over 80 percent) may indicate a network problem, including a broadcast storm or the need for review of the network design. This set of lights is useful when troubleshooting in the main equipment room or wiring closet.

Following start-up, during which the LEDs will flash, the LEDs should appear steady green. An orange LED may indicate a problem; a red LED may indicate a failure.

Controlling Recurring Paths with Spanning Tree

Although there are differences, switches share many common positives and negatives with bridges. For example, bridges frequently hide larger network problems and are invisible to the administrator. This differs significantly from routers, which are visible through increments in hop counters and MAC address changes in each frame. Bridges do not modify the frame in any way, so a frame may traverse multiple bridges with no changes to the frame. A changing frame provides indications that facilitate troubleshooting.

One of the more common problems in bridged networks involves loops, or a situation in which a single frame can continuously traverse the network. Note again that a bridge does not increment a counter—specifically, a time-to-live (TTL) value—in the packet to differentiate frame A from frame A the seventh time crossing the bridge. Such recurring paths can and should be controlled. The most common method of control is referred to as *spanning tree*.

The spanning-tree algorithm is defined in 802.1d and is used to control recurring paths among multiple switches, thus avoiding loops in the network.

If switches failed to prevent multiple forwardings of the same packet, and an administrator interconnects multiple switches (or bridges) between two segments, a loop can occur. This loop could theoretically take a single broadcast packet, which a bridge would automatically forward, and then resend it hundreds of times. Refer to Figure 11.1. Station A sends a broadcast, Switch One forwards the packet to the yellow cable, and Switch Two sends the broadcast back to the blue cable. Switch One then receives a forwarded broadcast packet that is in turn forwarded to the yellow cable. This continues infinitely without some type of intervention or control built into the software on the switch.

FIGURE 11.1 A simple bridge/switch loop configuration

Note that although Figure 11.1 denotes a single flow of packets that move counterclockwise, in a real loop, the initial broadcast is also forwarded clockwise. Although different cable colors have been used in this example, both cables are within the same VLAN.

Although Figure 11.1 reflects shared media connected to switches, a switch/bridge loop can occur in an all-switched network. This diagram simplifies the physical connections involved by moving them "outside the box."

Logically, an administrator could avoid the entire loop issue by removing one of the two bridges/switches. Because only one path would exist, no loop is created. However, there are advantages to installing multiple switches or bridges. With multiple switches/bridges, the network can incorporate some degree of fault tolerance.

Troubleshooting Spanning Tree Problems

There are several troubleshooting targets for isolating and resolving spanning tree protocol problems in a switched network. The most essential aspect of troubleshooting spanning tree problems is to understand the Spanning-Tree Protocol. It is also important to pay attention to indicators that there may be loops in the network. A simple indicator is the LED on the Supervisor engine: If the LED shows around 80% load, this may be a signal that loops are occurring.

Proper spanning tree functionality requires that there is only one unique bridge ID for each VLAN. You must also be aware that trunk ports on the Catalyst 5000 may belong to multiple spanning trees. This can cause the problem that if loops occur on one, the other spanning trees may be adversely affected. The `show spantree` command will display this information.

When the Cisco port-fast and uplink-fast modes are enabled on ports, some of the transitions of the spanning tree protocol are skipped. This could add to the potential of loops in the network. The `show spantree` command also shows whether the fast-start option has been enabled on a port-by-port basis.

 Real World Scenario

Eliminating Boot-Up Errors in a Switched Environment

Though the controls put in place to prevent spanning tree loops are necessary in order to ensure a stable network, they can have other unintended side effects. If an operating system manufacturer has optimized their operating system to immediately start using the network connection, the delay caused by the spanning tree loop-detection process, usually around 35 seconds, can be long enough to generate an error. These errors can manifest themselves as "No Domain Controller Found" messages in an NT environment, or even a "No DHCP Server Available."

In order to avoid these problems, I have found it best to set up user and server ports on the switch differently than ports that connect to other routers, switches, and hubs. Specifically, on user and server ports, I enable spantree portfast, and disable EtherChannel negotiation and trunk negotiation. In addition, I also hard-code the speed and duplex settings on the port. In this manner, the switch port starts forwarding packets from this port immediately after a link is detected. This effectively eliminates the errors caused by detection delays.

There are a couple of drawbacks to the above. The first and most obvious is that more manual configuration is required any time there is a move, add, or change in the environment. The second drawback is that ports are not checked when they come up to see if there is a spanning tree loop. However, it should be noted that spanning tree is still running on the port even with spantree portfast enabled. Therefore, if there is a loop it will be detected and the appropriate port put into blocking mode. However, this loop will not be detected before traffic from the port is allowed through. Therefore, there is a potential for a broadcast storm after the port is brought up but before the spanning tree protocol detects and eliminates the loop. Even with these drawbacks, I have found that the overall benefit to configuring user and server ports in this manner outweighs the risks.

The Catalyst 5000 Internal Structure

There are four significant components of the Catalyst 5000 system that manage the switching functions: *SAMBA*, *SAINT*, *SAGE*, and *EARL*. Each of these components is described in detail below. A clear understanding of these components is useful for overall troubleshooting of the Catalyst system in switched networks. This is especially true when evaluating different switches and options, such as the different Supervisor engines, and the RSM and Netflow features. This is also beneficial when isolating hardware-caused problems.

The Catalyst system uses a management bus to direct the switching process, whereas the actual data packets use a separate 1.2Gb backplane. The management bus operates at 761Kbps. These buses interconnect various cards within the chassis for Ethernet, Token Ring, FDDI, and, in some cases, ATM.

SAMBA

The *SAMBA ASIC* is located on line modules and on the Supervisor modules. On the line cards, this chip is responsible for broadcast suppression, based on thresholds established by the administrator. This ASIC also maintains statistics on packets.

From a troubleshooting perspective, the SAMBA ASIC proves to be most useful for obtaining various metrics to evaluate packet flow through the switch. In addition, there may be instances when administrators wish to suppress broadcast traffic on a threshold basis. Note that filtering broadcasts on a port basis may cause problems for upper-layer protocols.

Cisco's SAMBA should not be confused with the SAMBA utility for providing SMB (Windows NT) services on Unix platforms.

SAINT

The *SAINT (Synergy Advanced Interface and Network Termination)* handles Ethernet switching on the Catalyst 5000 platform, and it also handles ISL encapsulation. Each Ethernet port has an independent 192KB buffer for inbound and outbound packets, which is divided to provide 168KB to outbound traffic and 24KB for inbound frames.

The ISL functionality is covered in another section of this chapter. Although the buffer arrangement controlled by the SAINT has proven itself in hundreds of networks and rarely presents a troubleshooting issue, administrators must always consider buffer overflows and underruns as a factor. Again, capturing the appropriate counters with the show commands provides the administrator with troubleshooting tools.

SAGE

Although the *SAGE (Synergy Advanced Gate-Array Engine)* is similar to the SAINT, it is used for non-Ethernet applications—including FDDI, ATM LANE, Token Ring, and the Network Management Processor on the Supervisor engine.

From a troubleshooting perspective, there is little direct control that an administrator has over this ASIC. The `show test` command can verify problems indicated by various symptoms, including errors in Token Ring switching.

EARL

No kingdom is complete without an EARL, and, building on Cisco's apparent pun, the Catalyst 5000 is no different. In switching, however, *EARL* refers to the *Encoded Address Recognition Logic ASIC*. This chip works with the bus arbitration system to control access to the data-switching bus. EARL also controls the destination ports of packet transfers.

More specifically, the EARL monitors frame flow and compiles the list of MAC addresses, as related to port numbers and VLAN ID. In addition, the ASIC determines the destination port of frames and maintains the timer for aging entries out of the forwarding table. By default, entries are discarded after 300 seconds, although the administrator can change this value. Valid parameters are limited to between 1 and 20 minutes. The EARL can maintain a table of up to 128,000 addresses. As such, the EARL handles forwarding and filtering decisions within the switch.

Administrators do not troubleshoot the EARL, per se. Rather, issues with MAC address and port mappings controlled by EARL are more a part of the diagnostic process. Understanding the significant function of the EARL in the Catalyst line and its role in all switching can assist in hardware-related debugging.

Virtual LANs

In their simplest forms, *virtual LANs* (or *VLANs*) are no different from traditional LANs. The virtual component comes from the capability to define memberships based on individual ports, as administered by either a physical port or a dynamic relationship to the MAC address.

VLANs can potentially reduce the costs associated with moves, adds, and changes, in addition to reducing the costs for unused ports on non-VLAN hubs and switches. However, VLAN technology adds to the initial costs and may require additional training.

It is not uncommon to find a single switch serving more than one subnetwork. This logical segmentation of ports can create its own set of troubleshooting issues. However, the increased port utilization and other cost savings will more than offset these issues.

Administrators unaccustomed to segmented switches may find VLANs confusing. With hubs, all ports are part of the same network, and most networks are configured with a separate hub for each subnet—even if that subnet contains as few as two devices. Switches with VLAN capabilities, with their higher port cost and management systems, may have three or four subnets connected into the same chassis. In troubleshooting, it is important to have an accurate understanding of the current switch configuration and VLAN definitions, and—more importantly—verification that the end nodes match those definitions. It is not uncommon for a port to be defined to VLAN 1, where the workstation is configured with an IP address and default gateway matching VLAN 5. Under such circumstances, the workstation support staff will believe that the configuration is correct, and the network administrator will document that the port is correct. In addition to the `show port` command, it is important to have valid documentation of all VLANs and the associated network configurations for each VLAN.

Inter-Switch Link (ISL)

It is not possible for a switch to forward datagrams from one VLAN to another without a router or routing function. Recall that switches operate at Layer 2 of the OSI model, and although switches are available with routing engines and even Layer 4 processors, this section will retain a definition limited to Layer 2.

Inter-Switch Link (ISL) is a Cisco proprietary method of interconnecting two devices that support VLANs. These connections provide the administrator with a cost-effective option in deploying switches and VLANs in the network. For example, a normal switch installation requires a single port in each VLAN to be connected to the corresponding router interface, assuming a typical installation in which each VLAN is a logical extension of a subnet. This requires N ports on the router, in addition to the same number of ports on the switch.

Although this solution is easy to install and provides each VLAN with a dedicated 10 or 100Mbit port on the router, it also greatly increases the costs and fails to account for differences in local and remote traffic. Recall that networks were historically designed with 80 percent of the traffic remaining on the local subnet. Although the percentage of local traffic is significantly lower today, you would still be unlikely to find all traffic leaving the subnet.

What would happen if N VLANs on the switch could share a single 100Mbit connection to the router? The number of ports used for connectivity would equal two, as opposed to $(N*2)$, and the available number of ports for servers and workstations would increase substantially.

In this section, the use of ISL was defined with a switch-to-router connection. ISL should also be considered when the administrator wishes to connect multiple switches that are members of the same VLAN.

Administrators must keep the following issues in mind when considering ISL:

- ISL is available only on products that support ISL. Although a number of other vendors have licensed ISL technology (including Intel), the standard is proprietary to Cisco, and fewer vendors support the ISL standard compared to 802.1q. In addition, with the release of 802.1q and gigabit interfaces, Cisco has altered the default trunk encapsulation in favor of 802.1q. Gigabit EtherChannel trunk links default to 802.1q, whereas non-EtherChannel gigabit ports negotiate ISL or 802.1q. Fast Ethernet ports, as of this writing, continue to default to ISL.

- ISL links must be point-to-point.

- ISL should only be used on 100Mbit full-duplex or greater connections. Although it is possible to use ISL on 10Mbit links, the limited bandwidth and other considerations make such a plan impractical.

- ISL may require an upgrade of the IOS or memory on the router.

- ISL can encapsulate Token Ring. This is referred to as ISL+.

- ISL adds 30 octets to the original frame, which is encapsulated without modification.

- ISL includes a CRC value at the end of the frame.

Because ISL is an encapsulation of the original frame, an administrator must consider the overhead generated to support the encapsulation. Frequently, the available bandwidth is more than sufficient to cover this additional load. ISL adds 30 octets to the length of the original frame. In the case of Ethernet, this results in a frame 1548 octets long.

The ISL frame is shown in Figure 11.2.

FIGURE 11.2 The ISL encapsulation

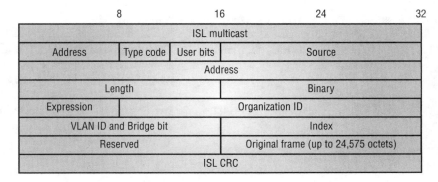

Figure 11.2 is indexed in Table 11.4.

TABLE 11.4 Key for Figure 11.2

Figure Symbol	Definition
ISL multicast address	The ISL multicast address of 01:00:0C:00:00. **Note that this is a 40-bit value**.
Type code	The encapsulated frame's type code. For Ethernet, this is 0000. Token Ring frames are defined with 0001 and FDDI is marked with 0010. ATM has been reserved for 0011 as a type code.
User bits	The user-defined bits are used to mark the encapsulated frame's priority. Frames marked 0000 are processed as normal priority, whereas 0011 marks the frame as high priority.
Source address	This is the 48-bit MAC address of the source port.
Length	The length field defines the length of the ISL frame minus the multicast address, the type and user-defined bits, and the source address of the ISL packet. The length field also omits its own length and the CRC from the 16-bit value. Thus, the length is always equal to the length of the ISL frame minus 18 octets.

Figure Symbol	Definition
Binary expression	ISL frames use SNAP LLC, and the binary expression noted in the table above decodes to AA:AA:03, which is the same as the SNAP header.
Organization ID	The Organization ID bits provide the unique organization identifier of the source address. This is equal to the first three octets of the MAC address.
VLAN ID, Bridge bit	The VLAN identifier is a 15-bit value that identifies the VLAN membership of the frame. Cisco uses only 10 bits in this header to support up to 1024 virtual LANs. The bridge bit is set for all encapsulated bridge protocol frames, including spanning tree updates, in addition to Cisco's CDP and VTP (VLAN Trunking Protocol) packets.
Index	The index field may be useful for troubleshooting and contains the source port value of the frame.
Reserved	The reserved bits are set to zero for Ethernet frames. However, when ISL encapsulates Token Ring, the access control (AC) and frame information (FC) octets are duplicated here. When encapsulating FDDI, the frame control octet is prefixed with 0x00 and copied in this field.
Original frame	The original frame field may be 24,575 octets long and includes Ethernet, Token Ring, or FDDI frames—along with the original CRC value for the encapsulated frame.
ISL CRC	The ISL CRC field is a new 32-bit CRC that is calculated for the entire ISL frame. It is calculated using the entire ISL frame, including the original frame.

802.1q Trunking

Although the *IEEE 802.1q* standard is similar to the Cisco proprietary ISL protocol in terms of function, as a standard it may be used to connect non-Cisco trunks to Cisco equipment. Note that the 802.1q encapsulation is accessed with the command `encapsulation dot1Q`, which is available in IOS versions 12.0.1(t) and higher on routers and CatOS 4.1 on the Catalyst 5000 switches.

ISL provides additional functions, when compared with 802.1q. For example, spanning trees are handled somewhat better in ISL. However, 802.1q should be recommended in any network that does not adhere to a strict Cisco-only policy, given the proprietary concerns.

From a troubleshooting perspective, 802.1q requires the same understanding of the VLAN's relationships to the subnets that are beneficial in all switching diagnostics. The 802.1q header differs from the ISL header, in that only 4 octets are added to the frame, as compared to the 30 added in ISL. Also, the 802.1q information is not wrapped around the original packet—the VLAN information is inserted into the frame, following the destination and source addresses in the original packet. This lack of overhead is another benefit of 802.1q.

Although most protocol analyzers provide decode filters for 802.1q in their current releases, administrators should check with their vendor. It is rare that the problem is directly related to the tag information itself, although administrators should consider this in researching trunk problems. Rather, most trunking problems, along with 802.1q, result from misconfiguration of the VLANs or mismatches between two sides of the trunk. Although they serve similar functions, ISL cannot connect to 802.1q on the same link.

VLAN Trunking Protocol (VTP)

VLAN Trunking Protocol (VTP) is a protocol that uses multicast messages to inform all other switches in the VTP domain about the VLANs within the domain. This domain is a management domain that allows control of the VTP multicast updates. A switch may be configured with three different VTP settings.

VTP Server   The server maintains the VLAN information for the VTP domain. If you are operating with a VTP server and clients connecting to it, all VLAN modifications, additions, and deletions must be done on the VTP server. These changes will then be propagated down to all the VTP clients in the domain. Trunk ports are then reconfigured to allow traffic from the new VLAN.

VTP Client   The client also maintains a copy of the VLAN information for the domain. It will transmit any changes it receives from the VTP server to other VTP clients in the same domain that are connected to it. When a change is detected, the trunk ports are then reconfigured to allow traffic from the new VLAN.

VTP Transparent When a switch is in transparent mode, changes made on the VTP server do not affect VLANs on this switch. It does, however, continue to forward VTP advertisements if you are running VTP version 2. If you need to modify, add, or delete VLAN from a switch in transparent mode, it must be done on the switch itself.

Cabling Issues

Today's networks operate at higher speeds than ever before. Bandwidth is measured in gigabits, with individual workstations accessing 100Mb connections or faster. Only recently it was still common to find a hundred stations sharing a 10Mbit segment.

Higher speeds bring added complexity at the Physical layer of the network. Installations must adhere to strict tolerances regarding distance, cable type, and installation to permit proper operation. This creates new troubleshooting issues for the administrator.

Frequently, an administrator will convert a workstation to 100Mbit (Fast) Ethernet, and will find an excessive number of errors that degrade performance so much that the link becomes unusable. The type of cable or the distance between the switch and workstation may cause this. For example, perhaps the original installation used Category 3 cable. Although satisfactory for 10Mbit Ethernet, 100Mbit Ethernet requires the higher-capacity Category 5. Also, although the distance for both 10 and 100Mbit Ethernet on copper media is 100 meters, it is possible to use longer lengths for 10Mbit without degradation. When converting to 100Mbit, problems may become evident. Consideration of the Physical layer is imperative when troubleshooting switched networks. Table 11.5 presents the Physical layer limitations.

TABLE 11.5 Physical Layer Standards

Cable	10Mbit	100Mbit
Distance with Category 3 copper	100 meters	Not available per 100BaseTX standard
Distance with Category 5 copper	100 meters	100 meters

TABLE 11.5   Physical Layer Standards *(continued)*

Cable	10Mbit	100Mbit
Distance with Multi Mode fiber	2000 meters	2000 meters
Distance with Single Mode fiber	10,000 meters	10,000 meters

Half-duplex Fast Ethernet implementations limit the Multi Mode fiber distance to 400 meters to allow for the round-trip time of the packet transmission.

Cable Problems

Cable problems may appear as intermittent issues or as a single failure. Clearly, the intermittent issues provide greater challenges, especially if the duration of the problem is very short. An intermittent cable problem may appear as slow performance or failure of the workstation, which requires a reboot.

An analyzer may be the best method for finding cable problems, and administrators should be familiar with the operation of an available cable tester, time domain reflectometer (TDR), or handheld analyzer. Even when certified by the cable installer, cables may break or develop problems during subsequent activity in the conduit or at the jack.

In addition to a tester, it is a good idea to have spare cables and a crimp set to quickly re-terminate circuits when troubleshooting.

Crossover Cables

A surprising number of network administrators have not used crossover cables, particularly when their previous experience is from the workstation installation and configuration segments of Information Services or other Information Technology departments. In other companies, such cables are used only when absolutely necessary and with a great deal of documentation, including highly recommended color-coding.

Normally, a workstation is connected to a hub that does not require the crossover of the transmit and receive pairs in the wire. However, there are times when a connection is needed and the pairs must be crossed. This occurs when connecting two 10BaseT workstations together without a hub or when connecting two network devices. Note that some devices provide a button or other administrator-selectable setting to enable or disable the function. Small hubs frequently provide this with an "uplink" port.

Connectivity problems may result when the wrong type of cable is installed or when a selectable port is set incorrectly. This may be masked by link lights and other indications that the connection is correct. The only way to isolate this problem is to look at the colors in the cube (the RJ-45 connector) and verify that they are correct. Figure 11.3 shows the appropriate pinout for an Ethernet crossover cable. It may be appropriate when troubleshooting to swap the original cable for another of the opposite type. This provides a quick check of the cable, and substituting a straight-through cable for a crossover cable may lead to evidence of equipment that is mislabeled or misconfigured. Note that Ethernet uses wires 1, 2, 3, and 6 while T1 circuits on RJ-45 use wires 1, 2, 4, and 5. Swapping different crossover cables will also lead to problems—for example, if a T1 crossover is used for an Ethernet connection.

FIGURE 11.3   Ethernet crossover pinout

Troubleshooting Switched Connections

Switched networks incorporate a number of unique problems for administrators, including the use of port mirroring for protocol analysis, and routing and trunking. Routing and trunking within the Catalyst system may include an RSM, or Route Switch Module, which is a 400Mbit 7500 series router on a card that operates within the Catalyst chassis. Trunking may incorporate one of many protocols, including ISL, 802.10, 802.1q, and ATM LANE. The effect of trunking is the same, however. A single physical medium may be used to connect multiple VLANs (or ELANs) between switches and routers.

The Switched Port Analyzer

This chapter previously noted that one of the difficulties in troubleshooting switched networks is the port isolation inherent in switches. Such isolation prevents the use of a protocol analyzer in a switched environment, without connecting directly to the wire between the switch and workstation, and such a connection cannot be full-duplex, as a general rule.

Cisco addresses this problem with SPAN, or the Switched Port Analyzer. Other vendors may refer to this function as *port mirroring*. Effectively, the switch is commanded to copy all packets that would be sent to the workstation interface to another port as well. This port is not assigned a VLAN—it takes on the identity of the original port. A detailed review of the SPAN command was provided in Chapter 3, but for completeness it is summarized below.

To configure the switch for SPAN, use the following commands:

```
set span enable|disable
set span <src_module/src_port> <dest_module/dest_port>
  [rx|tx|both]
set span <src_VLAN> <dest_module/dest_port> [rx|tx|both]
```

Note that traffic may be monitored on the receive or transmit channels, or both. The administrator may select to mirror a single port within the VLAN or have all traffic within the VLAN copied onto the mirroring port. It is important for the administrator to understand the problem's scope and the network topology before attempting to troubleshoot problems with the SPAN function.

The Route Switch Module and Catalyst Routing

The Route Switch Module, or RSM, is a Cisco router on a card within the Catalyst chassis. This card may be configured to provide routing between VLANs. With an external router, companies often incur additional expense and complexity—the RSM virtually attaches to VLANs, and as such does not occupy a port as an ISL or 802.1q-linked external router would. Of course, there are times when an external router is required. The performance of the 7513 is faster and a greater number of interface types are supported. However, when combined with the Netflow Feature Card (NFFC or NFFC II), the RSM and Catalyst can provide powerful Layer 2 and 3 switching.

The configuration of the RSM is very similar to the Cisco router platform. As shown in the following output, the router module supports IOS features, including password encryption and HSRP. Note that the interfaces are defined as VLAN1 and VLAN2. Unlike the router, the RSM is virtually connected to the VLANs via the backplane. This connection is 400Mbit half-duplex.

To connect to the RSM, administrators typically connect to the Supervisor engine CLI and use the `session` command to attach to the RSM. For example, if the RSM card were in slot 4, the command would read `session 4`. The following is the output from a `show running-config` command executed on the RSM.

```
Building configuration...



Current configuration:

!

version 11.3
service timestamps debug uptime
service timestamps log uptime
no service password-encryption

!

hostname RSM_A
!
interface Vlan1
 description Admin VLAN
 ip address 10.1.1.3 255.255.255.0
 no ip redirects
 standby 1 timers 5 15
 standby 1 priority 10
 standby 1 preempt
 standby 1 ip 10.1.1.1
 !
interface Vlan2
 description User VLAN
 ip address 10.1.2.1 255.255.255.0
 !
```

The show port command provides the following information regarding the RSM:

```
4/1  RSM_A       connected   trunk       normal   half   400
     Route Switch
```

As noted previously, an external router may be used to connect VLANs on the Catalyst switch. This usually occurs through a single connection configured for ISL or another trunking protocol. Fast Ethernet and Gigabit Ethernet connections are common for this configuration.

When configuring the router for this type of connection, each VLAN must be defined to a subinterface, and the main interface must be configured without a configuration. This usually appears as follows:

```
interface fastethernet 0/0
no ip address
full-duplex
interface fastethernet 0/0.1
description vlan1
ip address 10.1.1.1 255.255.255.0
encapsulation isl 1
```

The encapsulation isl 1 command defines that VLAN1 is using this physical interface and is trunked via ISL. This command is placed on each subinterface. Use the set trunk and clear trunk commands on the switch to configure the switch side of the connection.

VLANs across Routers and Switches

VLAN implementation has been described on Catalyst switches and Catalyst switches with Route Switch Modules. One VLAN implementation is left, using a router and a switch.

The router plays many important roles in the implementation of VLANs throughout a network. The overall role of a router is to provide communication among VLANs. Also, routers are able to perform many functions that add to the flexibility and scalability of VLAN deployment. Some of these major functions are broadcast management, routing, policy control, VLAN switching, and VLAN translation. Others include QoS management, redundancy, hierarchical design, and traffic shaping and management.

Broadcast Management

Simply put, routers will not forward broadcasts. Switches also control broadcasts by forwarding only to ports that are members of the source

VLAN. This property allows routers to lower broadcast traffic on the network backbone.

Policy Control

Switches do not have the capability to apply policy control to individual ports or VLANs on the switch. Use of a router provides the means to implement security and policy control to and from connected VLANs. Access lists may be written and applied to the VLAN subinterface on the router to provide this capability.

VLAN Switching

VLAN switching occurs when a packet destined for the same VLAN on a different interface crosses the router. The header remains intact and the frame is switched at Layer 2 to the destination interface where the VLAN resides.

VLAN Translation

Translation must occur in two scenarios. The first scenario occurs when VLAN A uses a different VLAN protocol than VLAN B. For example, VLAN A uses ISL for its VLAN protocol, whereas VLAN B uses 802.1q. In order for these two VLANs to communicate, the router must perform protocol translation. This occurs at Layer 2 and the frame headers are changed to accommodate the change in protocol.

The second scenario is when a VLAN protocol must be translated into a non-VLAN Layer 2 protocol. An example of this is when VLAN A (using ISL or 802.1q) needs to communicate with a Layer 2 destination that does not use any VLAN protocol. The router then translates the VLAN header into a header such as 802.10 so the two can communicate.

Routing

To enable communication between different VLANs or non-VLAN networks (Layer 3), routing must occur. The router maintains routes for the subnets/networks that belong to each VLAN. When VLAN A needs to reach VLAN B, a route lookup is performed and the packets are routed on Layer 3.

When a machine on a VLAN wants to communicate to a host on any other destination not on a local VLAN, routing is performed as well. It is important to realize that translation is not occurring because routing is a Layer 3 function, whereas translation occurs at Layer 2.

Troubleshooting VLANs on Routers

Some commands are similar across the IOS for the routers and the software running on the switches. It is important, however, to know which commands provide unique output and should be executed on a router rather than on a switch.

The following commands provide additional information regarding the VLANs from the router:

- show vlans
- show spanning-tree
- show arp
- show interface
- show cdp neighbor
- debug vlan packet
- debug spantree

Some of these commands have been covered in previous chapters and will not be repeated here. The commands that have not been discussed are covered below. The **debug** commands provide debug information with respect to VLAN packets and the spanning tree protocol.

show vlans

This command is executed from the router and it displays the details about the VLANs configured on the router. The detail includes the VLAN name, the interface, and the IP address used. It also includes the VLAN protocol (encapsulation) and interface protocol such as IP or IPX. Here is a sample:

```
Router_A#show vlans

Virtual LAN ID:  1 (Inter Switch Link Encapsulation)

   vLAN Trunk Interface:    FastEthernet1/0.1

   Protocols Configured:   Address:        Received:    Transmitted:
          IP              172.16.1.1      4236441842   854332923
```

```
Virtual LAN ID:   2 (Inter Switch Link Encapsulation)

  vLAN Trunk Interface:    FastEthernet1/0.2

  Protocols Configured:   Address:        Received:       Transmitted:
          IP              172.16.2.1      3002644583      2325942305


Router_A#
```

show spanning-tree

For IOS revisions prior to 12.0T, this command was known as show span (not to be confused with the similar command for switches). In the 12.0T IOS release the command was changed to show spanning-tree. This command displays spanning tree information for the router.

debug vlan packet

This debug command can be useful in determining which VLANs are being sent over a trunk to a router. When debug vlan packet is enabled and a packet comes in for a VLAN that is not defined on the router, the router will note the VLAN and interface that the packet was seen on. As with all debug commands, be careful when using this command, as it can place a load on the router if there are a lot of packets coming in the interface for an unknown VLAN.

```
Router_A#debug vlan packet

Virtual LAN packet information debugging is on

Router_A #
vLAN: ISL packet received bearing colour ID 10 on
   FastEthernet1/0 which has no subinterface configured
   to route or bridge ID 10.
vLAN: ISL packet received bearing colour ID 102 on
   FastEthernet1/0 which has no subinterface configured
   to route or bridge ID 102.
vLAN: ISL packet received bearing colour ID 23 on
   FastEthernet1/0 which has no subinterface configured
   to route or bridge ID 23.
```

```
vLAN: ISL packet received bearing colour ID 10 on
    FastEthernet1/0 which has no subinterface configured
    to route or bridge ID 10.
```

VLAN Design Issues and Troubleshooting

Although VLANs must adhere to most of the basic network design rules, there are a number of new issues for administrators to consider with Catalyst switches.

First, the network diameter should be less than eight switches. This limitation is mostly related to spanning tree concerns; however, it is also a good rule of thumb for manageability.

Second, VLANs must be numbered within certain limitations, and each VLAN needs to adhere to MTU considerations. Although a large MTU is desirable for FDDI and Token Ring, the Ethernet MTU limitation of 1500 is recommended for all interfaces. This is partly due to the Catalyst backplane and the conversions that are needed between different Physical layers.

The default configuration of the switch includes the following VLANs, as shown in Table 11.6.

TABLE 11.6 The Default Switch VLAN Configuration

VLAN Name	Type of VLAN	MTU	ISL VLAN ID	802.10 VLAN ID (SAID)
Default	ethernet	1500	0001	100001
Fddi-default	fddi	1500	1002	101002
Token Ring default	token-ring	4472	1003	101003
Fddinet-default	fddi-net	1500	1004	101004
Trnet-default	tr-net	4472	1005	101005

When troubleshooting switches and routers, administrators should consider each element in the network by using a layered approach. For example, configuring a bridge to link two ISL trunks could cause spanning-tree problems. In addition, there are two spanning-tree protocols available on the switch: IEEE and DEC. Failure to use the same protocol will again cause spanning-tree issues.

In addition, general routing rules apply to VLANs and the RSM module. For instance, a default router is still required on all devices, and all VLANs must have a router to go from one VLAN to another.

As an example, to display the physical interfaces, the administrator would use `show port` on the switch, as opposed to `show interface`, which is used on the router. The `show interface` command on the switch is used to check the SL0 and SC0 interfaces.

Remember that most troubleshooting is actually isolation. View the network from each layer and work through the system. For example, is there a link light denoting Layer 1 connectivity? Is the port configured for the same speed and duplex on each end? These basic questions, along with the Cisco debug and show commands, frequently provide the proper clues to isolate problems.

Although available, the use of automatic speed and duplex configuration settings is not recommended. Most administrators prefer the control and manageability that is available from manually configuring these settings. Administrators should familiarize themselves with the proper commands on various platforms. For example, NT usually permits the modification of this setting from the network control panel, but some installations may require registry modification. On Solaris, the `/kernel/drv/hme.conf` file is modified when using that type of NIC.

Summary

In today's network environment, switching has become an integral component. It allows for greater throughput and it better utilizes existing hardware. In the Cisco switching offering, one of the main switches used is the Catalyst 5000 series. Thanks to the number of different modules that are available for this series of switch, they are versatile enough to be used in almost any network.

Like the Cisco routers that were examined earlier, the Cisco switches also come with a fully featured command line interface (CLI) that allows for configuration as well as verification of the current functionality of the switch. Also like the routers, central to this CLI is the show command. This command, along with the keywords that can be used with it, allows for the display of nearly all of the switch's characteristics.

Another important aspect of a switched environment is loop detection and elimination. This is done through the spanning tree protocol. Spanning tree sends probing packets to all neighboring devices and uses these packets to determine whether there is a loop in the network. If a loop is detected, all except one of the paths that made the loop is put in blocking mode. Once a port is placed in blocking mode, it will not forward user data. By doing this, the spanning tree protocol ensures that there is only one path to a destination at a time. If that path were to go down, or if it was removed, then one of the "blocked" paths would be unblocked, or changed to a forwarding state, and used for user data.

The Application-Specific Integrated Circuit (ASIC) is one of the key components in the Catalyst 5000 series switch. Though there are many ASICs in the 5000 series switches, there are four that manage a significant portion of the switching functions. These are the SAMBA, SAINT, SAGE, and EARL ASICs. The SAMBA ASIC is responsible for broadcast suppression as well as maintaining packet statistics. The SAINT ASIC handles Ethernet switching as well as ISL encapsulation. The SAGE ASIC is used for all non-Ethernet switching. Finally, the EARL ASIC works with the bus arbitration system to control access to the bus.

One of the largest advantages of switches over the typical hub is the ability of the switch to create Virtual LANs, or VLANs. A switch can have multiple VLANs defined and each port can be put in a separate VLAN. Because of this capability, there is no longer a need for separate hardware to separate subnets. All of the subnets can be created on a single device and logically separated into VLANs.

Any new software feature needs a method for controlling and configuring it. For VLANs this is VTP, or Virtual Trunking Protocol. VTP allows VLAN configuration information to be changed in one location, a VTP server, and for this information to propagate automatically to all of the VTP clients in the VTP domain, thus easing the administrative overhead of a switched environment. If there is a concern about one change taking down the entire switched area, different VTP domains can be set up, or switches can be set to transparent mode. In transparent mode, each switch must be manually configured any time there is a change in the VLAN structure.

To better take advantage of the ability of the switches to use VLANs, Cisco has manufactured a routing card for the 5000 series switches. Called the Route Switch Module (RSM), this card provides full routing functionality to the switch. Because this card is connected to the switch's backplane, it has immediate access to any of the VLANs created on the switch. Alternatively, you can also uplink to an external router to get this functionality. This uplink can be done for a specific VLAN or for a range of VLANs if trunking is used.

One of the items that can be easily overlooked in the network is the cabling. As 100Mbit Ethernet is now the standard for most new Ethernet installations, many of the Cat 3 cable plants that were installed for 10Mbit Ethernet need to be replaced with Cat 5—or better, cabling. In addition, as switching allows for larger Layer 2 domains, and Layer 3 functionality is added to the switches, the use of the crossover cable is becoming more common to connect two switches together directly.

Exam Essentials

Know the differences between switches, bridges, and hubs. A hub can only run in half-duplex mode and has a broadcast and collision domain that includes all ports. Bridges do not generally have hardware ASICs and have a lower port density. Switches can operate in full- or half-duplex mode and have a collision domain of a single port and a broadcast domain of a single VLAN.

Know the show commands available for a switch. This includes but is not limited to show cdp, show config, show flash, show log, show mac, show port, show span, show system, show test, and show version.

Know how spanning tree is used in a switch. Spanning tree controls loops in a Layer 2 environment. The switch does this automatically.

Know the main ASICs used by a switch and what they are used for. These are SAMBA, SAINT, SAGE, and EARL. Each of these ASICs has a specific purpose on the switch, as explained in the text.

Understand the function of a VLAN.   A VLAN is used to logically separate traffic on a switch. This allows a switch to have multiple different subnets terminating on it.

Understand trunking and how it works.   Trunking on a Cisco switch can be done by using either ISL or 802.1q. It allows for multiple VLANs to share the same uplink.

Understand how VTP works.   Virtual Trunking Protocol allows for easy administration of VLANs in a large switched environment. VLAN changes performed on a VTP server are automatically updated on all the VTP clients in the VTP domain. If a switch is in transparent mode, it will pass along any VTP changes sent by the server but will not make any modifications to its own VLANs.

Know how to troubleshoot cabling problems and when to use a crossover cable.   A crossover cable is used any time that like network devices are directly connected together (e.g., router to router, switch to switch, or workstation to workstation). A straight-through cable is used to connect workstations or routers to switches.

Commands Used in This Chapter

The following list contains a summary of all the commands used in this chapter.

Commands	Descriptions
debug span	Debugs spanning tree.
debug vlan packet	On a router connected to a trunk port on a switch, will show errors in encapsulation and packets destined for an unknown VLAN. Debugs VLAN packets.
show arp	Displays the ARP information for the router.
show bridge {vlan number}	Shows which bridging encapsulations are enabled.
show cam	Reports the MAC address associated with the ports of the switch. These addresses are stored in the CAM table; this command accesses that table.

Commands	Descriptions
show cdp	Displays the Cisco neighbors.
show config	Similar to the show running-config command on Cisco routers. Provides all configuration settings on the switch for all modules, with a few exceptions for certain modules such as the RSM (Route Switch Module).
show flash	Reports the space required for the installed software and the version of code.
show interface	Reports the IP configuration of the supervisor module.
show log	Reports significant events, including reboots of all modules, traps, and power-supply failures.
show logging buffer	Shows logging information on a switch.
show mac	Maintains numerous counters in normal operation, including the frame traffic per port; the total number of incoming frames, including discards; and the total number of transmits and aborts due to excessive deferral or MTU violations. Broadcast counters are also maintained in addition to discards due to EARL page-full errors.
show port	Provides information about specific ports or all ports on a module. VLAN membership, port speed and configuration, and error statistics are available.
show span	Shows spanning tree information from the router. Very different from a show span on a switch.
show spantree	Reports the status of the spanning tree process for each VLAN, when spanning tree has been enabled on the switch.
show system	Provides high-level summary information regarding the switch, including the status of power supplies, uptime, and administrative settings, as well as the percentage of traffic on the backplane.

Commands	Descriptions
show test	The status of the switch, including interface cards, power supplies, and available memory.
show version	Provides hardware and software version numbers, in addition to memory and system uptime statistics.
show vlans	Provides VLAN information and status from the router.
show vtp domain	Provides status information for the VTP domain configured on the switch. Note that VTP updates are sent over VLAN 1 when troubleshooting.

Key Terms

Before you take the exam, be certain you are familiar with the following terms:

802.1q	spanning tree
broadcast domain	Spanning-Tree Protocol
Cisco Discovery Protocol	Synergy Advanced Gate-Array Engine (SAGE)
collision domain	Synergy Advanced Interface and Network Termination (SAINT)
Encoded Address Recognition Logic (EARL) ASIC	virtual LANs (VLANs)
Inter-Switch Link (ISL)	VLAN
Remote Monitoring (RMON)	VLAN Trunking Protocol (VTP)
SAMBA ASIC	

Laboratory Exercise

This lab exercise does not necessarily require access to a Catalyst switch.

The administrator finds that devices on at least one VLAN cannot communicate with devices on other VLANs. In addition, some devices within the VLAN cannot reach other intra-VLAN devices. Name at least five areas to examine and the commands needed to isolate these issues.

Review Questions

1. Catalyst 5000 switches are which one of the following?

   A. Devices that operate at Layer 2 of the OSI model

   B. Limited to 16 ports

   C. Limited to only one physical media

   D. Available for Ethernet only

   E. Available for ATM only

2. 100BaseTX requires which of the following?

   A. Category 1 cables

   B. Category 3 cables

   C. Category 5 cables

   D. Fiber cables

3. Which of the following does the SAINT handle? (Choose all that apply.)

   A. Token Ring

   B. Ethernet

   C. ISL

   D. ATM

   E. FDDI

4. Which of the following is true about VLANs?

   A. They define the broadcast domain.

   B. They define the collision domain.

   C. They are unique to each workstation.

   D. They are available only on Ethernet.

   E. They require the use of ISL or 802.1q.

   F. They require the use of 802.1d or spanning tree.

5. ISL is useful for which one of the following?

   A. Trunking between non-Cisco switches

   B. Trunking between Cisco switches

   C. Configuring VLANs

   D. Quadrupling the bandwidth between switches

6. Which of the following are the same encapsulation type? (Choose all that apply.)

   A. 802.1Q

   B. ISL

   C. 802.3

   D. 802.1D

   E. None of the above

7. The Catalyst command to display information on neighboring Cisco devices is which of the following?

   A. `show neighbors cdp`

   B. `display cisco neighbors`

   C. `show cdp neighbors all`

   D. `show cdp neighbors detail`

   E. `show neighboring cdp details`

8. Spanning tree provides which one of the following?

   A. A single path through multiple subnets

   B. Redundant paths while preventing loops

   C. Trunking multiple VLANs onto FDDI interfaces

   D. MAC layer address translation

9. In order to connect the Marketing VLAN to the Payroll VLAN, which one of the following must be true about a packet?

    A. It must use ISL.

    B. It must be forwarded at least once by a router.

    C. It must be greater than 1024 octets long.

    D. The packet cannot go from the Marketing VLAN to the Payroll VLAN.

    E. It must be converted into ATM cells.

10. Which of the following commands provides system uptime?

    A. `show version`

    B. `show config`

    C. `uptime`

    D. `show flash`

11. Switch utilization is available from which of the following?

    A. LEDs on the supervisor module

    B. Cisco WAN Manager

    C. CLI

    D. `show snmp utilization`

12. VLANs control the scope of which one of the following?

    A. The collision domain

    B. The broadcast domain

    C. Conversion from half to full duplex

    D. Port mirroring for troubleshooting with SPANs

13. Which of the following applications provides a graphical method for assigning virtual LAN ports?

A. VLANWorks

B. LANDesigner

C. TrafficDirector

D. PortMapper

E. VLANDirector

14. Cisco Discovery Protocol provides which of the following?

A. Ping services for Cisco devices

B. Automatic VLAN configuration services

C. VLAN security by controlling the ARP discovery process

D. Network management information regarding Cisco products

E. Automatic ISL and 802.1q services

15. Token Ring frames are handled by which of the following? (Choose all that apply.)

A. SAINT

B. SAGE

C. EARL

D. SAMBA

16. Which of the following commands provides information regarding individual ports on the switch?

A. show all ports

B. show port *<mod/port>*

C. show port detail *<mod/port>*

D. show switch port *<port/mod>*

17. An administrator adds a VLAN to Switch_A, a VTP server. Which of the following will be true about the VLAN?

   A. It will need to be added manually to each switch in the network.

   B. It will need to be added manually to each switch in the network that participates in the VLAN, but no others.

   C. It will automatically be added to each switch in the subnet.

   D. It will automatically be added to each switch in the VTP domain.

   E. It will automatically be added via the TrafficDirector tool.

18. How many VLANs can be active on a single non-trunk port?

   A. Two

   B. One

   C. Multiple

   D. None

19. How many VLANs can be present on an ISL port?

   A. Multiple

   B. Only one

   C. None

   D. Two

20. Collisions are possible on which of the following connections?

   A. FDDI

   B. Token Ring

   C. Fast Ethernet

   D. Full-duplex Ethernet

Answers to Review Questions

1. A. Switches operate at Layer 2 of the OSI model. The Catalyst 5000 has a variety of interfaces and media configurations.

2. C. Category 5 cables are required to ensure sufficient pairs of copper for the transmit and receive signals as well as to provide the electrical characteristics needed. 100BaseFX would use fiber cables.

3. B, C. The SAINT handles Ethernet protocol as well as ISL VLAN encapsulation.

4. A. The collision domain is controlled by the switch port. A VLAN can exist on multiple machines. ISL and 8021.q are both trunking protocols that can be used but are not required. 802.1d extends the concept of MAC bridging, and spanning tree ensures a loop-free Layer 2 environment, but neither is required to make a VLAN function.

5. B. Because ISL is a Cisco proprietary encapsulation, it does not work with non-Cisco switches.

6. E. None of these encapsulations are the same, and 802.1D is not a real frame encapsulation type.

7. D. The correct syntax is given by the answer D.

8. B. The main function of spanning tree is to prevent loops in a switched network.

9. B. In order for different VLANs to communicate, the packets must be routed.

10. A. The `show version` command displays the system's uptime.

11. A, C. Both of these, along with CWSI, allow the user to check the switch utilization.

12. B. VLANs control broadcast domains. Collisions, duplex, and mirroring are all done by the switch.

13. E. This is the proper software for VLAN configuration and management.

14. D. CDP discovers and retains information regarding directly connected Cisco devices.

15. B, C, D.   The SAGE handles non-Ethernet frames, but all frames are handled by the EARL and SAMBA ASICs.

16. B.   The correct syntax for the command that provides port information is given in B.

17. D.   VLAN information is automatically propagated via the VTP protocol within the domain. Each switch can belong to only one domain.

18. B.   One VLAN per non-trunking port. When a port is a trunk port, it handles all VLANs.

19. A.   An ISL port has the same function as a trunking port.

20. C.   Collisions are possible if there are multiple workstations on a switched port or the port is configured to half-duplex instead of full-duplex.

Chapter 12

Cisco Support Functions

TOPICS COVERED IN THIS CHAPTER INCLUDE:

✓ Describe and use the Cisco information resources (especially those in the CCO World Wide Web site) that can assist with troubleshooting processes.

✓ List the preferred methods for escalation of troubleshooting issues to Cisco's service and support programs.

With the vast number of products and technologies that Cisco must support, Cisco provides several means of access to technical documentation, product summaries, and support functions. Some of the major methods, found through Cisco's web page, are known as Cisco Connection Online, the Technical Assistance Center, and the Cisco Documentation CD.

Cisco Connection Family

Cisco Connection Family is a collection of interactive electronic media that is intended to provide technical assistance and support for Cisco products and networking technologies. There are five members of the Cisco Connection family:

- Cisco Connection Online (CCO)
- Cisco Technical Assistance and Software Center
- Cisco Connection Consultant Tools CD-ROM
- Cisco Commerce Agents
- Cisco MarketPlace

Cisco Connection Online (CCO)

The *Cisco website*, known as *CCO (Cisco Connection Online)*, is the repository for information regarding Cisco products, networking technology, configuration examples, troubleshooting tools, and network planning.

CCO has two access levels. The first is guest privilege, which does not require a login account. This level provides general product and company information. The second level is for registered Cisco users who purchased a Cisco support contract or are sponsored by a Cisco Authorized Partner. This level provides all information available to the guest level, in-depth detailed technical documentation, access to download Cisco IOS images, trouble ticket queries, and so on.

There are a few subtle differences between the guest page and the user page. The significant changes are under the Service and Support category. The guest has access only to see the Online Technical Support benefits, whereas the user actually has access to the Online Technical Support.

If you follow the Software Center link under guest access, you notice that it does not allow Cisco IOS image downloads. You have to be a registered user to have access to download Cisco IOS.

Online Information

The front page of CCO offers links to many different types of information. Network solutions, product and network technologies, corporate news, product ordering, and information about Cisco-related events are all available from CCO.

The network solutions section provides explanations about technology and how it can be used in many scenarios. Its examples range from customers interested in Cisco equipment to companies looking for enterprise-wide network solutions. Case studies are provided for businesses ranging from home offices to large enterprises.

Cisco customers are also able to access documentation on all of Cisco's products as well as other industry technologies. This information can be used to choose the correct Cisco equipment for the technologies that the website visitor has planned for implementation.

Ordering information can be found at the website, and product purchases can be made through the site as well. Purchasing is handled by the Networking Products MarketPlace.

Information for Cisco Partners and Resellers is also accessible through CCO. Finally, recent and historical corporate news and company press releases are available through the Corporate News and Information Menu, which covers Cisco acquisitions, information for investors, and methods of contacting Cisco Systems.

Features and Electronic Services

Cisco provides several electronic services and features within the menus of CCO. Many of the features can be considered to be services, as well. Some of the most prominent features and services along with their descriptions are as follows:

Software Center   The Software Center is an interactive site that allows the user to go directly to the software image that is needed. Alternatively, it has several categories that help the user select the IOS image that is best suited for the network resources and requirements. The subcategories are broken down by product type. The Software Center also provides an IOS upgrade planner. Patches to IOS bugs and the latest feature set are available through the Software Center.

Online Technical Support   This menu provides links to several electronic services and features. Here is a list of some of the services and features accessible from the Online Technical Support site:

- Networking Professionals Connection (replaces Open Q&A Forum)
- Software Bug Toolkit
- Bug Watcher
- Technical Tips
- IP Subnet Calculator
- Memory Calculator
- TAC Case Management

As of June 30th, 2002, the Networking Professionals Connection replaces the Open Q&A Forum. As you may see either one referred to on the test, we will explain both in this section. The Open Q&A Forum allowed a user to browse through previous technical questions and answers or post a new question. A search engine was available for locating specific topics or technologies. Questions were answered by anyone holding a CCIE certification. This was a good place to get "how to" or detailed questions answered.

The Networking Professionals Connection has all of these features as well as additional content. In fact, the most recent Open Q&A Forum questions were migrated over to the Networking Professionals Connection before the

Open Q&A Forum was shut down. The Networking Professionals Connection is divided into three main sections: Discussion Forums, Tech Talks, and Ask the Expert. The discussion forums are then further broken down into subtopics: Emerging Technologies, Network Infrastructure, Voice & Video, Wireless, Virtual Private Network (VPN), Security, and Certifications. The Tech Talks are live online presentations. Finally, Ask the Expert is a place where experts in specific networking technologies answer questions in a format similar to that of a news server.

If you have questions about an IOS bug or a problem you think may be a bug, you can use the Software Bug Toolkit. This allows the registered user to provide IOS revision information and search for bugs that are associated with a specified release of IOS.

The Bug Watcher is part of the Bug Toolkit. The Bug Watcher allows a user to identify the different bugs that are present in current IOS releases, track them, and update the user about the current status of the bug.

Technical Tips hosts information regarding different IOS versions, hardware platforms, and configuration guides. When new technologies are implemented, the Cisco Technical Tips page will have information to walk you through the configuration.

Special features include the IP Subnet and Memory Calculators. The IP Subnet Calculator is an interactive page that asks for user input, and then returns subnet information based on that input.

TAC Case Management involves querying, opening, updating, and closing Cisco TAC cases. All of these processes may be accomplished by using CCO. This is explained in more detail in the "Cisco's Technical Assistance Center (TAC)" section later in this chapter.

Analyze Command Output

In addition to the above, there is also a section on the website dedicated to analyzing command output. This allows you to enter the output of a command, a stack trace, or an error message and instantly see the results. These results can be sent to the screen or e-mailed to you for future reference. The three tools that allow you to do this are:

- Error Message Decoder

- Stack Decoder for IOS

- Output Interpreter

With the Error Message Decoder you can copy and paste any error message that you have received on a router, switch, or PIX firewall into the input field of the tool and have it report back to you the meaning of the error. In addition to the meaning of the error, you also receive a list of web pages on CCO that are relevant to the error that you are seeing. This tool can be useful when trying to determine the relative severity of an unknown error, or when looking for a place to start when researching a new problem.

Unlike the Error Message Decoder, the Stack Decoder tool only works with IOS traces. The Stack Decoder is a tool specifically designed to assist in the diagnosis of the root cause of a router crash. Specifically, when a router crashes, information from a `show stack` command will show the processes running at the time of the reload. Stack Decoder will then take this information and compare it to known bugs that could have been the cause of the crash. In addition to listing the bugs, the Stack Decoder also ranks the bugs based on which one most closely matches the information that you input.

Finally, the Output Interpreter tool allows you to paste in the output from many of the `show` commands available on the router and to receive an explanation of what this output means. For example, if you executed a `show interface` command and saw an interface in an up/down state, you could copy this output into the output interpreter and it would suggest what the problem could be. In addition, it will also give you suggested changes and links to web pages on the Cisco website discussing the potential issue.

Troubleshooting Assistant

The *Troubleshooting Assistant* is part of the Online Technical Support menu. This tool can be used to help isolate and diagnose many networking problems, based on user input and the Cisco database.

This interactive tool starts by asking the user to have a hard copy of the configuration in question, in addition to an accurate network topology. With these items in hand, the page lists a number of technology categories. Here are the categories currently available with troubleshooting assistant support:

IP   Support for RIP, IGRP, EIGRP, OSPF, BGP, IP addressing, and IP performance issues.

Security   Support for PIX products as well as VPN.

LAN   Support for password recovery, software management, LAN hardware, and LAN-switching issues.

Voice   Provides support for PSTN/PBX telephone signaling and CallManager IP phones.

Access Services   Provides support for access dial-up, AAA, cable technologies, DSL, and PPP.

Specific Hardware   Provides support for many of the hardware platforms, including 800, 1600, 2500, 3600, 4000, 7000, 7200, 7304, 7400, MSFC or MSFC2, and Access Servers (AS5200/5300, AS5800).

WAN   Provides support for ATM, WAN switching, Voice over WAN switching, and Frame Relay.

Network Management   Provides support for Cisco Network Registrar (CNR).

Here's an IP example to work through. You select the IP routing protocols link and proceed further into the Troubleshooting Assistant, which allows you to specify a particular problem or area of concern. Specifically, the options that are presented to you are as follows:

- BGP
- Configuring IP addressing
- Connections fail with certain applications
- EIGRP
- Forwarding BootP and other UDP broadcasts
- Local host cannot access remote host
- Local userstation/server cannot access local router
- Multicast
- OSPF
- Performance issues or error message meanings
- Routing Information Protocol (RIP)/Interior Gateway Routing Protocol (IGRP)

For this example, assume that we have a problem configuring an IP address. From the above menu, we would choose "Configuring IP addressing" then hit the next button. At this point, the Troubleshooting Assistant asks, "Are you trying to configure a subnet of all zeros?" We are not, so we select No and hit the next button. The Troubleshooting Assistant then outputs warning information regarding configuring IP addresses in reserved address space and provides a link to a website detailing IP addressing and subnetting. In addition to this information, there is also a survey that you can fill out about how helpful the information and the tool was, as well as suggest any improvements to the tool.

If you cannot remember which questions were asked or how you answered them, you can review the Q&A session by clicking the session log button on the left side of the screen.

If the information suggested by the Troubleshooting Assistant doesn't solve your problem, you can also open a TAC case from the troubleshooting engine's screen by selecting the Open A Case button on the left side of the page.

Additional problems can be analyzed by selecting the Start Over button.

Cisco Connection Documentation

Cisco's *Cisco Connection Documentation CD-ROM* is the collection of technical documentation, available on CCO as well as on the Documentation CD that accompanies new Cisco equipment purchases. Both forms of the technical documentation are very helpful for providing critical information regarding Cisco products, networking technologies, and configuration examples.

CCO

The CCO version of Cisco Connection Documentation CD-ROM may be accessed through the front page of CCO by using the Technical Documents link. The Documentation home page has links discussing the CD-ROM, Cisco product documentation, router configuration tools, technology information, and other information.

Documentation available on the CCO website covers Cisco products and technology including:

- Cisco IOS software configuration

- Routers

- Catalyst switches

- Optical networking

- Network security

- Voice/telephony
- 10BaseT hubs
- 10/100 hubs
- Aggregation
- Broadband/cable
- CDDI/FDDI adapters and concentrators
- ATM adapters and switching
- Access servers and routers
- Content delivery products
- FastHub repeaters
- Network management
- Customer contact software
- Integrated access devices
- IP/VC
- Layer 3 switches
- Layer 4 switches
- Long reach Ethernet
- Router configuration tools
- Storage networking products
- Virtual Private Networks
- WAN switches
- Wireless (LAN)

Cisco Connection Documentation CD-ROM

The Cisco Connection Documentation CD-ROM accompanies new Cisco equipment purchases. The information on the CD-ROM is updated as changes are made to IOS features and configuration options.

The CD-ROM contains all of the same information as the website, except for the documentation on telephony. The CD-ROM also includes technology information and router configuration tools.

The CD-ROM has the following technology information:

- Internetworking technology overview

- Troubleshooting internetwork systems

- Internetworking terms and acronyms

- Internetworking case studies

- Internetworking design guide

- Cisco site preparation guide

- Internetwork troubleshooting guide

- Remote configuration guide

These same topics are covered on the CCO website. Additional information shared by the CCO website and the Cisco Connection Documentation CD-ROM is in the Cisco product catalog. The product quick reference guide is available only from the CCO website.

CD-ROM navigation is best done by using existing menus. The search function on the Documentation CD-ROM is not as effective as navigating the menus provided.

For example, if you need to know how to configure ISDN BRI, the quickest way to get to it is to select the Cisco IOS Software Configuration link on the home page for the Documentation information. Next, you select the correct version of IOS—use 11.3 for this example. After selecting 11.3, the CD-ROM gives a summary of all the topics covered under IOS version 11.3. Select the first line, "Cisco IOS 11.3 Configuration Guides Command References." Upon selecting the configuration guide, you see a list of configuration topics.

To successfully navigate through the topics, you need to spend time investigating which technologies belong to which topic. In this scenario, you need to select the Dial Solutions Configuration Guide. Next, because you want information on how to configure a port, choose the Dial-in Port Setup. In this menu, you find the topic Setting Up ISDN Basic Rate Services. By selecting that link, you get the file that details how to configure ISDN BRI services.

If you enter a search on the keywords **ISDN BRI** from the home page, you get thousands of responses, with none of the top 10 being relevant to what you are trying to do.

The CD-ROM is an invaluable tool because it is mobile and does not require a network connection. This is important if you are installing a router at a remote site and don't yet have a network connection.

Cisco's Technical Assistance Center (TAC)

When you need additional resources to solve network failures, you can contact the *Cisco Technical Assistance Center*, or *TAC*. The TAC is accessible by phone, the CCO website, or e-mail.

The TAC provides support for Cisco contract holders, gives warranty service, and can even bill you directly if you do not have a Cisco maintenance contract.

If you can solve the network problem yourself, you can avoid the time that it takes to contact and receive assistance from the TAC. However, the TAC has access to information that the end user does not have. Often, this information proves invaluable for solving the problem. You also need to contact them if the problem is faulty hardware—the TAC can send you replacement equipment, if needed.

You need to give some basic information when contacting the TAC to open a case. First, the Customer Response Center operator asks you for a serial number or a contract number. (The Customer Response Center is the central point for incoming calls.) In addition to your contract or serial number, they ask you for your name and company name. They verify your address, phone number, and e-mail address. They take preliminary information and prioritize the case, assign a ticket number, and then forward the case to the proper engineering group. You should make sure to record the ticket number for future reference.

When you open your ticket, you can specify the priority of your case. There are *four priorities* to choose from:

Priority 1   Production network down

Priority 2   Production network performance seriously degraded

Priority 3   Network performance degraded

Priority 4   Information needed on Cisco products

If you choose to categorize your ticket as a Priority 1, the engineer is required to stay on the phone with you until the problem is resolved or the case priority is downgraded.

The TAC is divided into several engineering groups, so that the engineers that handle the case can specialize in a given area. For example, there is an ATM group, a routing protocols group, an NMS group, and so on. Once an engineer gets the case, they need more information from you.

You should be able to provide the engineer with a `show tech-support` output from all affected equipment. In addition to the `show tech-support` information, you should be able to provide information regarding recent configuration changes, any `debug` output you have, or third-party protocol analyzer information.

After you open a ticket, you receive automated updates on the status of your case. If you need to add information to your ticket, you can send e-mail to the engineer working on the case, or you can go to the website and add it to the case by using the CCO Case Management Toolkit.

The TAC engineer works with you on your case to implement necessary changes and then observe the results. This process is followed until the problem is resolved.

Here's a summary of the steps involved in opening a case with the Cisco TAC.

1. Gather relevant information about your problem. This includes the output of a `show tech-support` from all affected devices, recent configuration changes, any `debug` output you have, and protocol analyzer information.

2. Once you have this information, you can open a case one of three ways: by sending an e-mail to `tac@cisco.com`, using the TAC Case Management tools, or calling the TAC. No matter which option you choose to open your case, be sure to include the necessary contract or serial number. In addition, provide your name and company name, and verify the address, phone number, and e-mail. If you are using e-mail or the TAC Management Tools to open your case, you can also include the output from a `show tech-support` and other information that you gathered earlier.

3. If you are opening a case via e-mail or the website, most likely it will be assigned as a Priority 3. If you have a Priority 1 or 2 issue, it is best to call TAC directly. You will then be given a case number. Record it.

4. Your case will be forwarded to the appropriate TAC engineering group. Depending on priority and your stated preference for contact, the assigned engineer will either call you or e-mail you with

information pertaining to the case as well as with any requests for more information.

5. With the case number from above, you can use the Case Management Toolkit to add more information, change contact information, or update or close the case. This can be done in addition to opening a new case as described above.

6. Work with the engineer to make the necessary changes to resolve the problem, and then observe results to verify that the problem is solved. At any time during this process, you can request that the case priority be changed to reflect the current impact to the network. Such a change in priority will need to be done via the phone.

 Real World Scenario

Getting the Most out of TAC

In most cases, when you need to contact TAC it is a stressful time. Either there has been a network problem that is affecting your users or an unexplained error has shown up in the logs. Over the years, I have found that there are three ways to make this experience less stressful.

The first is to have a clear understanding of the Cisco support model. Cisco employs a "follow the sun" model for support. They have TAC centers around the world, and in general, the TAC centers that are open at any given time are the ones where it is currently daytime. Cisco takes care of routing calls and other requests to the appropriate center, so there is no need for you to change how you open a case. Therefore, if you are in the United States doing a late-night change and have a problem, when you call TAC you could very likely be assisted by the TAC in Australia. While it is extremely useful to have someone always available to help you diagnose and correct the immediate issue, a complication might arise if, for whatever reason, your problem can't be solved immediately. The engineer who was assigned your case works opposite your normal business hours. Therefore, if you update the case, these updates may not be seen by anyone until long after you have gone home for the day. If your issue does run into multiple days, then, it is usually best to get the case "requeued" to an engineer in the TAC who shares your general business hours. This can be accomplished over the phone, through the Case Management tools, or via e-mail.

The second way to make the process easier was already stated in the chapter but bears repeating. Be prepared to give the TAC as much information as possible about the problem when the case is opened. The show `tech-support` output as well any other relevant show commands are a minimum. Also include relevant diagrams and drawings of the network layout, a summary of recent changes, and a report of what has already been tried in an attempt to fix the problem. The more information that you can provide up front, the better the chances are that the TAC engineer will be able to quickly diagnose the issue correctly.

Finally, use an appropriate method for opening cases. For Priority 1 and 2 cases, be sure to call in the problem. You will be connected to an engineer who will assist you with the case immediately. Once the case is opened, you can use the Case Management tools or e-mail to add relevant documentation and show command output to the case. If you are opening a Priority 3 or 4 case, I have found it best to use either the Case Management tools or e-mail to open the case. In this manner, I can immediately upload/attach the documentation and show command output. Whichever method you choose, by understanding how TAC works, you can greatly improve your overall experience using TAC.

Other Cisco Documentation

Cisco has other methods of providing information to Cisco users. It provides seminars and presentations regarding new products and new network solutions.

Cisco also publishes Cisco books in a collection called Cisco Press. The books are written by Cisco to provide more information on products, technologies, case studies, and implementation. These books can be found on CCO at `http://www.cisco.com/cpress/home/home.htm`.

Summary

Cisco provides several means of getting important information. The Cisco Connection Family is designed to perform two functions: prevent problems from occurring, and resolve them when they do occur. The primary way that these services are delivered is via the Cisco website. The website has numerous different tools and sections that assist the user in every aspect of dealing with Cisco, from ordering new equipment to finding out how to install and configure this equipment to fixing this equipment when there is a problem.

The first of these tools is the Cisco MarketPlace. Through this utility, users can price tools and check lead times as well as order products from Cisco. Cisco MarketPlace can be used in conjunction with other tools on the site, such as the Memory Calculator and product documentation, to help find the most appropriate device for your needs.

In addition to these tools, the Cisco website also has tools such as the Software Center, where appropriate IOS images can be determined and downloaded, and the Troubleshooting Assistant, which will interactively help you diagnose the problem that you are having. You also can use tools such as the Stack Decoder, Output Interpreter, and Error Message Decoder to help determine the cause of a problem. If your problem turns out to be a bug, you can then use the Bug Toolkit to get more information on this bug and to track down a remedy or workaround for it. You can also get answers to many real-life questions through the use of the Networking Professionals Connection (formerly the Open Q&A Forum) section.

You can open, update, or close a case on the website as well. Cisco's Technical Assistance Center, or TAC, handles these cases. In addition to the website, you can also open, close, or update a case by e-mail or phone. All cases that are opened will need the same core amount of information in order for the TAC to properly assist you. This information includes your name, company name, contract number, serial number, address, phone number, e-mail address, and the best way to contact you. In addition, you should be ready to provide any relevant information about the problem you are having, including but not limited to `show tech-support` output, information about recent configuration changes, output from any other relevant `show` or `debug` commands that you have performed, and diagrams of the affected network.

Exam Essentials

Know what information the Cisco Marketplace can provide.   The Cisco Marketplace allows you to check lead times and pricing information as well as order Cisco product online.

Know the purpose of and how to use the Troubleshooting Assistant. The Troubleshooting Assistant is an interactive tool that can assist you in determining the root cause of a problem.

Know the purpose of the other online features. These include but are not limited to the Software Center to get current IOS, the Networking Professionals Connection (formerly the Open Q&A Forum) to get answers to real-world questions, the Bug Toolkit to get information on IOS bugs, as well as specialty tools such as the Technical Tips, Subnet Calculator, and Memory Calculator.

Know the different output interpretation tools that are available as well as what they are used for. The Stack Decoder assists in determining the reason for a router crash. The Output Interpreter helps you determine the meaning of the output from various show commands. Finally, the Error Message Decoder helps to determine the meaning of an error message.

Know the information that the TAC needs in order to open a case. This information includes your name, company name, contract number, serial number, address, phone number, and e-mail address. In addition, be able to provide them with a description of the problem and the output from a show tech-support command, any other show or debug command output, packet captures, diagrams, information about recent changes, and any other relevant information.

Know all of the ways to open, update, and close a case with TAC. A TAC case can be opened, updated, or closed via the phone, Web, or e-mail. The TAC Case Management tool provides this functionality on the Web.

Commands Used in This Chapter

The following list contains a summary of all the commands used in this chapter.

Command	Description
show tech-support	A comprehensive command that includes show running-config, show version, show stacks, show processes cpu, and show processes memory, along with many other commands relevant to troubleshooting.

Key Terms

Before you take the exam, be certain you are familiar with the following terms:

CCO (Cisco Connection Online)	Priority 1
Cisco Connection Documentation CD-ROM	Priority 2
Cisco Connection Family	Priority 3
Cisco Technical Assistance Center (TAC)	Priority 4
Cisco website	Troubleshooting Assistant
four priorities	

Review Questions

1. Which of the following are members of the Cisco Connection Family? (Choose all that apply.)

   A. Cisco Connection Online (CCO)

   B. CiscoWorks

   C. Cisco Technical Assistance and Software Center

   D. Cisco Connection Consultant Tools CD-ROM

2. Which of the following are valid access levels for CCO? (Choose all that apply.)

   A. Account holder

   B. Guest

   C. VIP

   D. User

3. Which of the following allow a guest to register for user access? (Choose all that apply.)

   A. Service contract number

   B. Purchasing Cisco equipment

   C. Referral of a Cisco employee

   D. Proof of Cisco equipment on the premises.

4. Which of the following features does the Software Center provide? (Choose all that apply.)

   A. Direct access to IOS images

   B. Automated upgrade service

   C. IOS upgrade planner

   D. Free upgrades for existing IOS

5. Which of the following are part of the Online Technical Support? (Choose all that apply.)

   A. Technical Tips

   B. IP Subnet Calculator

   C. Decimal to Hex address converter

   D. Memory Calculator

   E. All of the above

6. What resources are available through the Networking Professionals Connection (formerly Open Q&A Forum)?

   A. Posting technical answers

   B. Searching for technical documentation

   C. Searching the forum for past questions

   D. Searching for software bugs

7. Which of the following are components of the Software Bug Toolkit?

   A. Latest IOS revisions

   B. Bug Watcher

   C. Free upgrades

   D. IOS Planner

8. Which of the following categories can be found in the LAN category of the Troubleshooting Assistant?

   A. ATM

   B. IP

   C. LAN switching

   D. Network Management

9. What topics are supported in the WAN and Access category? (Choose all that apply.)

A. PPP

B. IP routing protocols

C. VoIP

D. Low-end router platforms

E. High-end router support

F. WAN switching

10. Which of the following is the correct method for displaying the question-and-answer dialog box from the Troubleshooting Assistant?

A. Select the Session Log button.

B. Select the Feedback button.

C. Select the Open a Case button.

D. None of the above.

11. Which forms of electronic media are used to provide access to Cisco's Documentation CD-ROM? (Choose all that apply.)

A. CCO

B. Fax

C. E-mail

D. Cisco Connection Documentation CD-ROM

12. What is the easiest way to navigate the Cisco Connection Documentation CD-ROM?

A. Use the search engine provided.

B. Use the existing menu structure.

C. Use Netscape as your browser.

D. Use the CCO search engine.

13. What tool would be most effective in diagnosing the cause of a router crash?

A. Subnet Calculator

B. Error Message Decoder

C. Output Interpreter

D. Stack Decoder

14. How many priority levels exist for a Cisco TAC case?

   A. 2

   B. 3

   C. 4

   D. 5

15. What information do you need to provide when opening a TAC case? (Choose all that apply.)

   A. Contract number

   B. Unit serial number

   C. show proc cpu information

   D. IANA handle

   E. Company name

16. Which of the following are valid descriptions for the four priority levels? If you are able to, you can also associate a description with the priority level. (Choose all that apply.)

   A. Production network performance severely degraded

   B. Information on products or configuration issues

   C. Production network down

   D. Network performance degraded

17. What is the online tool available for Cisco Case Management?

   A. Case Management Toolkit

   B. CCO Case Manager

   C. CCO TAC Manager

   D. None of the above

18. Via which means is the Cisco TAC accessible? (Choose all that apply.)

   A. Phone

   B. E-mail

   C. CCO

   D. Online chat

   E. AOL

19. Which of the following are methods Cisco uses to notify users of problems with new technologies? (Choose all that apply.)

   A. Phone calls

   B. CD distribution

   C. Mailing lists

   D. Website

20. Which of the following are valid points when working on a case with Cisco TAC? (Choose all that apply.)

   A. Work with the engineer to make the necessary changes to resolve the problem, and then observe results to verify that the problem is solved. If the problem gets worse, you can upgrade the case priority.

   B. Use the Case Management Toolkit to add more information, close the case, or open a new case.

   C. Give a brief description of the problem and assign the case the correct priority. You will be given a case number. Record it.

   D. Give the Customer Response Center the necessary contract or serial number. In addition, provide your name and company name, and verify the address, phone number, and e-mail.

   E. Gather relevant information about your problem. This includes the output from a `show tech-support` from all affected devices, recent configuration changes, any `debug` output you have, and protocol analyzer information.

Answers to Review Questions

1. A, C, D. There are five members of the Cisco Connection Family; not all were listed here. CiscoWorks is a software package.

2. B, D. These are the two valid access levels for non-Cisco employees.

3. A, B. Purchasing either Cisco equipment or a service contract will allow a guest the ability to apply for user status. There are other valid methods that were not listed.

4. A, C. Cisco doesn't provide automated upgrade service. You must have a maintenance contract to get "free" IOS upgrades. There are other features to the Software Center, as covered in this chapter.

5. A, B, D. There are many Online Technical Support features; only a portion were listed. There is no Decimal to Hex converter.

6. C. Users are not allowed to post answers. Technical documentation is provided through other resources.

7. B. The Bug Watcher and interim patches are available via the toolkit.

8. C. LAN switching is a topic within the LAN category. There are also three others: password recovery, software management, and LAN hardware.

9. A, F. There are several others that were not listed. Here is a complete list: Dial-up services, Authentication, Cable technologies, DSL, Frame Relay, PPP, TACACS, WAN, WAN switching.

10. A. This will display the questions asked and your responses to those questions.

11. A, D. These are the two methods Cisco uses to provide the documentation from Cisco Connection Documentation CD-ROM.

12. B. Because of the vast amount of data on the CD and discrepancies with the search engine, the most efficient way to access the information is via the menu structure.

13. D. The Stack Decoder is specifically designed to help determine the cause of a router crash.

14. C.   There are only four priorities at this point.

15. A, B, E.   The complete list of what needs to be given consists of the following: contract number, serial number, `show tech-support` output, name, phone number, e-mail, company name.

16. A, B, C, D.   These are all valid descriptions. They are listed as Priority 2, 4, 1, and 3, respectively.

17. A.   The Case Management Toolkit is the tool designed to provide online case management.

18. A, B, C.   These are valid methods of contacting and working with the TAC.

19. C, D.   These methods are used to notify customers of any major recent problems or bugs that have surfaced.

20. A, B, C, D, E.   All of these are valid points when working with TAC.

Chapter

13

Applying Cisco's Diagnostic Tools

TOPICS COVERED IN THIS CHAPTER INCLUDE:

- ✓ Describe an efficient problem-solving method when troubleshooting and documenting internetwork problems.
- ✓ Identify and use Cisco IOS software commands and debug utilities to filter, capture, and display protocol traffic flows.
- ✓ Use proven problem isolation techniques to list the symptoms of common TCP/IP problems.
- ✓ Use troubleshooting tools and minimize their impact on a Cisco router's switching type and data flow.
- ✓ Use Cisco IOS commands and problem isolation techniques to identify the symptoms of common WAN and Frame Relay problems.

In the previous chapters, you learned a great deal about Layer 2 and Layer 3 technologies and protocols. Additionally, you learned very useful information regarding router architecture and very detailed low-level information for understanding routing technology. With this knowledge, you will be able to better interpret the information provided by the troubleshooting tools and commands.

The time has come to implement all that you have learned, including applying the methodology from Chapter 1. Once you have the technical knowledge base, you must apply it by using a troubleshooting template if you are to efficiently and successfully troubleshoot network problems.

This chapter's format will be different from what you have seen up to now. Three different types of network problems will be outlined in detail, and each type will have two scenarios. The intent is for you to take the provided information and do the troubleshooting. You will see a great deal of router output and packet decodes from a protocol analyzer. The information is there for your reference and at times may not have a great deal of explanation. You must look at the output carefully in order to enable yourself to determine what is happening on the router or network.

For each scenario, you follow the steps outlined in Chapter 1 by listing observations, gathering facts, and proposing solutions. Because the book cannot be interactive, the scenarios are intended to accustom you to using the methodology, but you will not go so far as to actually verify that the proposed solution solved the network problem. Let's begin.

Identifying and Resolving Generic Router Problems

This section deals with Cisco routers and some simple generic problems that can be remedied easily, once they are identified. Each scenario will be accompanied by outputs from relevant diagnostic tools. The focus will be placed on the router itself, because many other scenarios involve additional network equipment.

Scenario #1

You are installing a Cisco 2600 series router that was sent to you after headquarters entered the preliminary configuration. You are connected to the console port. You power on the router, and this is what you see as the router boots:

List Observations

```
System Bootstrap, Version 11.3(2)XA3, PLATFORM SPECIFIC
   RELEASE SOFTWARE (fc1)
Copyright (c) 1998 by cisco Systems, Inc.
TAC:Home:SW:IOS:Specials for info
C2600 platform with 24576 Kbytes of main memory
program load complete, entry point: 0x80008000, size:
   0x37b090
Self decompressing the image :
   #######################################################
   #######################################################
   #######################################################
   #######################################################
   #######################################################
   ########################################### [OK]
Restricted Rights Legend
Use, duplication, or disclosure by the Government is
subject to restrictions as set forth in subparagraph
(c) of the Commercial Computer Software - Restricted
Rights clause at FAR sec. 52.227-19 and subparagraph
(c) (1) (ii) of the Rights in Technical Data and Computer
Software clause at DFARS sec. 252.227-7013.

           cisco Systems, Inc.
           170 West Tasman Drive
           San Jose, California 95134-1706
Cisco Internetwork Operating System Software
IOS (tm) C2600 Software (C2600-D-M), Version 11.3(4)T1,
   RELEASE SOFTWARE (fc1)
```

```
Copyright (c) 1986-1998 by cisco Systems, Inc.
Compiled Wed 01-Jul-98 11:42 by phanguye
Image text-base: 0x80008084, data-base: 0x8066A278

Cisco 2611 (MPC860) processor (revision 0x202) with
   18432K/6144K bytes of memory
 .
Processor board ID JAB023601NE (1537311773)
M860 processor: part number 0, mask 32
Bridging software.
X.25 software, Version 3.0.0.
2 Ethernet/IEEE 802.3 interface(s)
1 Serial network interface(s)
32K bytes of non-volatile configuration memory.
8192K bytes of processor board System flash (Read/Write)



Press RETURN to get started!



%LINK-3-UPDOWN: Interface Ethernet0/0, changed state to up
%LINK-3-UPDOWN: Interface Ethernet0/1, changed state to up
%LINK-3-UPDOWN: Interface Serial0/0, changed state to down
Cisco Internetwork Operating System Software
IOS (tm) C2600 Software (C2600-D-M), Version 11.3(4)T1,
   RELEASE SOFTWARE (fc1)
Copyright (c) 1986-1998 by cisco Systems, Inc.
Compiled Wed 01-Jul-98 11:42 by phanguye
%LINEPROTO-5-UPDOWN: Line protocol on Interface
   Ethernet0/0, changed state to down
%LINK-5-CHANGED: Interface Serial0/0, changed state to
   administratively down
%FR-5-DLCICHANGE: Interface Serial0/0 - DLCI 324 state
   changed to DELETED
```

Well, it looks like two interfaces on the router are down—so much for the preconfigured router. You change to the privileged level by entering the enable password. Here is where you need to start listing observations. The first one is that two of the interfaces on the router are down.

Before you look at the configuration or show commands, you check the cabling. Assuming that the cabling checks out, you should check the lights in the back of the router. Figure 13.1 shows the back of a 2611 router. The router comes with two Ethernet ports, a console port, an aux port, and a serial port. Each of the network interface ports (both Ethernet ports and the serial port) has a light next to it that indicates whether there is a physical connection. If any of these lights is not lit, there is a connectivity problem. In this example, assume that all three lights are lit.

FIGURE 13.1 Rear view of a Cisco 2611

Now that you've observed the connectivity, you need to gather more information about the router's configuration. Go back to the console. You know that the problem deals with two interfaces: Ethernet 0/0 and Serial 0/0. For this example, don't use show running-config or show startup-config. Instead, use the interface-specific show commands.

The first command issued is show interface ethernet 0/0. Here are the results:

```
Router_A#show interface ethernet 0/0
Ethernet0/0 is up, line protocol is down
  Hardware is AmdP2, address is 0010.7bd9.2880      (bia
    0010.7bd9.2880)
  MTU 1500 bytes, BW 10000 Kbit, DLY 1000 usec,      rely
    128/255, load 1/255
  Encapsulation ARPA, loopback not set, keepalive set
    (10 sec)
  ARP type: ARPA, ARP Timeout 04:00:00
```

```
Last input never, output 00:00:05, output hang never
Last clearing of "show interface" counters never
Queueing strategy: fifo
Output queue 0/40, 0 drops; input queue 0/75, 0 drops
5 minute input rate 0 bits/sec, 0 packets/sec
5 minute output rate 0 bits/sec, 0 packets/sec
    0 packets input, 0 bytes, 0 no buffer
    Received 0 broadcasts, 0 runts, 0 giants, 0 throttles
    0 input errors, 0 CRC, 0 frame, 0 overrun, 0 ignored,
       0 abort
    0 input packets with dribble condition detected
    250 packets output, 15309 bytes, 0 underruns
    250 output errors, 0 collisions, 1 interface resets
    0 babbles, 0 late collision, 0 deferred
    250 lost carrier, 0 no carrier
    0 output buffer failures, 0 output buffers swapped out
Router_A#
```

The following outputs are from the show interface Ethernet 0/1 and show interface Serial 0/0 commands, respectively:

```
Ethernet0/1 is up, line protocol is up
  Hardware is AmdP2, address is 0010.7bd9.2881 (bia
    0010.7bd9.2881)
  Internet address is 172.16.20.5/24
  MTU 1500 bytes, BW 10000 Kbit, DLY 1000 usec, rely
    128/255, load 1/255
  Encapsulation ARPA, loopback not set, keepalive set
    (10 sec)
  ARP type: ARPA, ARP Timeout 04:00:00
  Last input never, output 00:00:02, output hang never
  Last clearing of "show interface" counters never
  Queueing strategy: fifo
  Output queue 0/40, 0 drops; input queue 0/75, 0 drops
  5 minute input rate 983450 bits/sec, 875 packets/sec
  5 minute output rate 435097 bits/sec, 357 packets/sec
    0 packets input, 0 bytes, 0 no buffer
      Received 0 broadcasts, 0 runts, 0 giants, 0 throttles
```

```
              0 input errors, 0 CRC, 0 frame, 0 overrun, 0 ignored,
                 0 abort
              0 input packets with dribble condition detected
              274 packets output, 17062 bytes, 0 underruns
              0 output errors, 0 collisions, 11 interface resets
              0 babbles, 0 late collision, 0 deferred
              0 lost carrier, 0 no carrier
              0 output buffer failures, 0 output buffers swapped out
Router_A# show interface serial 0/0
Serial0/0 is administratively down, line protocol is down
    Hardware is PowerQUICC Serial
    Internet address is 172.16.20.5/30
    MTU 1500 bytes, BW 1544 Kbit, DLY 20000 usec, rely
    255/255, load 1/255
    Encapsulation FRAME-RELAY, loopback not set, keepalive
    set (10 sec)
    LMI enq sent  0, LMI stat recvd 0, LMI upd recvd 0, DTE
    LMI down
    LMI enq recvd 0, LMI stat sent  0, LMI upd sent  0
    LMI DLCI 1023  LMI type is CISCO  frame relay DTE
    FR SVC disabled, LAPF state down
    Broadcast queue 0/64, broadcasts sent/dropped 0/0,
    interface broadcasts 0
    Last input never, output never, output hang never
    Last clearing of "show interface" counters never
    Input queue: 0/75/0 (size/max/drops); Total output
    drops: 0
    Queueing strategy: weighted fair
    Output queue: 0/1000/64/0 (size/max total/threshold/drops)
        Conversations  0/1/256 (active/max active/max total)
        Reserved Conversations 0/0 (allocated/max allocated)
    5 minute input rate 0 bits/sec, 0 packets/sec
    5 minute output rate 0 bits/sec, 0 packets/sec
        0 packets input, 0 bytes, 0 no buffer
        Received 0 broadcasts, 0 runts, 0 giants, 0 throttles
        0 input errors, 0 CRC, 0 frame, 0 overrun, 0 ignored,
           0 abort
```

```
      0 packets output, 0 bytes, 0 underruns
      0 output errors, 0 collisions, 0 interface resets
      0 output buffer failures, 0 output buffers swapped out
      0 carrier transitions
      DCD=up  DSR=up  DTR=down  RTS=down  CTS=up
Router_A#
```

What are your observations? Check your list with the following:

- No IP address is configured on Ethernet 0/0.

- The output packets generated on Ethernet 0/0 are equal to the number of output errors.

- There are the same number of lost carrier errors as output errors.

- Serial 0/0 is administratively shut down.

- DLCI 324 on Serial 0/0 is in a deleted state.

- Serial 0/0 is a Frame Relay link.

- Ethernet 0/1 is up and up.

This list can contain more information regarding the interfaces, such as encapsulation types and so on. For clarity and simplicity, only the observations that are relevant to this scenario are listed.

After observations and fact-gathering are completed, it is time to formulate a problem description. Initially, from what you saw while the router booted, the problem description was vague. It could have been written something like this: "Interfaces Ethernet 0/0 and Serial 0/0 are down."

This is a good start, but it lacks detail. If this were a complicated problem, you could be troubleshooting for a long time because the description lacks focus.

Based on listed observations, you know exactly what the problem description is. Here is a sample of a focused and detailed problem statement or description: "Ethernet 0/0 is down because it doesn't have a carrier, and Serial 0/0 is down because it was administratively shut down. Since Serial 0/0 is shut down, the DLCI is in a deleted state."

With this problem statement, it should be obvious what needs to be done to fix the problems.

Propose Solutions

How did you do? Now that you've observed these problems, what are the solutions? This step relates to the "creating an action plan" part of the troubleshooting method. The more specific the problem statement, the more easily the solutions can be defined.

In the first scenario, there appear to be a few problems that need resolution. They are all simple solutions in this case:

- Check the cable and transceiver for the Ethernet port for a possible physical problem with the interface.

- Configure an IP address on Ethernet 0/0.

- Turn up interface Serial 0/0.

With the proposed solutions, the only thing left is to implement them and see if they work, as follows:

```
Router_A#conf t
Enter configuration commands, one per line. End with CNTL/Z.
Router_A(config)#interface ethernet 0/0
Router_A(config-if)#ip address 172.16.10.1 255.255.255.0
Router_A(config-if)#interface serial 0/0
Router_A(config-if)#no shut
172.16.20.5 overlaps with Ethernet0/1
Serial0/0: incorrect IP address assignment
Router_A(config-if)#^Z
Router_A#
```

List Observations—Take 2

It looks as if the Ethernet 0/0 interface is still not functional. We still need to check the cable and transceiver to try to isolate a physical problem. You test the cable and it is working properly so you swap the transceiver. Now let's check the interface status:

```
Ethernet0/0 is up, line protocol is up
Hardware is AmdP2, address is 0010.7bd9.2880 (bia
   0010.7bd9.2880)
  MTU 1500 bytes, BW 10000 Kbit, DLY 1000 usec, rely
     128/255, load 1/255
  Encapsulation ARPA, loopback not set, keepalive set
     (10 sec)
  ARP type: ARPA, ARP Timeout 04:00:00
  Last input never, output 00:00:05, output hang never
  Last clearing of "show interface" counters never
  Queueing strategy: fifo
```

```
Output queue 0/40, 0 drops; input queue 0/75, 0 drops
5 minute input rate 509000 bits/sec, 215 packets/sec
5 minute output rate 1167000 bits/sec, 315 packets/sec
   12900 packets input, 10324500 bytes, 0 no buffer
   Received 235 broadcasts, 0 runts, 0 giants,
    0 throttles
    0 input errors, 0 CRC, 0 frame, 0 overrun, 0 ignored,
     0 abort
   0 input packets with dribble condition detected
   18903 packets output, 15198309 bytes, 0 underruns
   283 output errors, 0 collisions, 2 interface resets
   0 babbles, 0 late collision, 0 deferred
   283 lost carrier, 0 no carrier
   0 output buffer failures, 0 output buffers swapped out
```

What happened to Serial 0/0? The console message stated that there was an address overlap with interface Ethernet 0/1, which means a duplicate IP address. The IP address on Ethernet 0/1 overlaps with the IP address on Serial 0/0. Let's look at the interface settings once more.

```
Router_A#show interface serial 0/0
Serial0/0 is administratively down, line protocol is down
  Hardware is PowerQUICC Serial
  Internet address is 172.16.20.5/30
  MTU 1500 bytes, BW 1544 Kbit, DLY 20000 usec, rely
  255/255, load 1/255
  Encapsulation FRAME-RELAY, loopback not set, keepalive
  set (10 sec)
  LMI enq sent  0, LMI stat recvd 0, LMI upd recvd 0, DTE
  LMI down
  LMI enq recvd 0, LMI stat sent  0, LMI upd sent  0
  LMI DLCI 1023  LMI type is CISCO  frame relay DTE
  FR SVC disabled, LAPF state down
  Broadcast queue 0/64, broadcasts sent/dropped 0/0,
   interface broadcasts 0
  Last input never, output never, output hang never
  Last clearing of "show interface" counters never
  Input queue: 0/75/0 (size/max/drops); Total output
   drops: 0
  Queueing strategy: weighted fair
  Output queue: 0/1000/64/0 (size/max total/threshold/
   drops)
```

```
    Conversations   0/1/256 (active/max active/max total)
    Reserved Conversations 0/0 (allocated/max allocated)
  5 minute input rate 0 bits/sec, 0 packets/sec
  5 minute output rate 0 bits/sec, 0 packets/sec
    0 packets input, 0 bytes, 0 no buffer
    Received 0 broadcasts, 0 runts, 0 giants, 0 throttles
    0 input errors, 0 CRC, 0 frame, 0 overrun, 0 ignored,
      0 abort
    0 packets output, 0 bytes, 0 underruns
    0 output errors, 0 collisions, 0 interface resets
    0 output buffer failures, 0 output buffers swapped out
    0 carrier transitions
    DCD=up  DSR=up  DTR=down  RTS=down  CTS=up
Router_A#
```

This output indicates that the interface is still administratively down. You saw the no shut command issued in the previous screen capture, so why is it still in shutdown? Here is the answer: If an interface has a configuration conflict with another interface, it will not initialize. Because the serial interface was configured with a duplicate IP address, it wouldn't initialize. It remains in its previous state, shutdown. In order to activate the serial link we must do some more analysis.

Referring to the show interface results for Ethernet 0/1, you see that it does have the same address as Serial 0/0. This problem can easily be resolved, as long as you know which interface should have the 172.16.20.5 address. In this scenario, we will assume that Ethernet 0/1 has the incorrect IP address.

In essence, you have made additional observations.

- Serial 0/0 is configured with IP address 172.16.20.5/30.

- Ethernet 0/1 is configured with IP address 172.16.20.5/24.

- You cannot change administrative state for Serial 0/0 because of the IP address overlap with Ethernet 0/1.

Propose Solutions—Take 2

Now, with these additional observations, new solutions must be proposed. Once the decision is made as to which IP address should be assigned to each interface, the problem should be resolved. The action plan is as follows:

- Leave IP address 172.16.20.5/30 to interface Serial 0/0.

- Assign IP address 172.16.30.1/24 to interface Ethernet 0/1.

- Remove the administrative shutdown from interface Serial 0/0.

Here is the configuration. Following the configuration, you see the show interface output for each interface. This is done to verify that all the changes that were made to the router fixed the problems that were observed.

```
Router_A#conf t
Enter configuration commands, one per line. End with CNTL/Z.
Router_A(config-if)#interface ethernet 0/1
Router_A(config-if)#ip address 172.16.30.1 255.255.255.0
Router_A(config)#interface serial 0/0
Router_A(config-if)#no shutdown
Router_A(config-if)#^Z
%LINK-3-UPDOWN: Interface Serial0/0, changed state to up
%FR-5-DLCICHANGE: Interface Serial0/0 - DLCI 324 state
     changed to ACTIVE
%FR-5-DLCICHANGE: Interface Serial0/0 - DLCI 368 state
     changed to ACTIVE
%FR-5-DLCICHANGE: Interface Serial0/0 - DLCI 324 state
     changed to DELETED
%LINEPROTO-5-UPDOWN: Line protocol on Interface Serial0/0,
     changed state to up
Router_A#
Router_A#show interface ethernet 0/0
Ethernet0/0 is up, line protocol is up
  Hardware is AmdP2, address is 0010.7bd9.2880    (bia
    0010.7bd9.2880)
  Internet address is 172.16.10.1/24
  MTU 1500 bytes, BW 10000 Kbit, DLY 1000 usec, rely
    255/255, load 29/255
  Encapsulation ARPA, loopback not set, keepalive set
    (10  sec)
  ARP type: ARPA, ARP Timeout 04:00:00
  Last input 00:00:00, output 00:00:00, output hang never
  Last clearing of "show interface" counters never
  Queueing strategy: fifo
  Output queue 0/40, 0 drops; input queue 1/75, 0    drops
  5 minute input rate 509000 bits/sec, 215 packets/sec
```

5 minute output rate 1167000 bits/sec, 315 packets/sec

   25800 packets input, 20685400 bytes, 0 no buffer

   Received 3235 broadcasts, 0 runts, 0 giants

   6 input errors, 1 CRC, 5 frame, 0 overrun,
     640 ignored,   0 abort

   0 input packets with dribble condition detected

   37800 packets output, 30249800 bytes, 0 underruns

   283 output errors, 4 collisions, 2 interface
     resets

   0 babbles, 0 late collision, 0 deferred

   283 lost carrier, 0 no carrier

   0 output buffers copied, 0 interrupts, 0 failures

Router_A#**show interface serial 0/0**

Serial0/0 is up, line protocol is up

  Hardware is PowerQUICC Serial

  Internet address is 172.16.20.5/30

  MTU 1500 bytes, BW 1544 Kbit, DLY 20000 usec, rely
  255/ 255, load 1/255

  Encapsulation FRAME-RELAY, loopback not set, keepalive
  set (10 sec)

  LMI enq sent 5, LMI stat recvd 6, LMI upd recvd 0, DTE
  LMI up

  LMI enq recvd 0, LMI stat sent 0, LMI upd sent 0

  LMI DLCI 1023 LMI type is CISCO frame relay DTE

  FR SVC disabled, LAPF state down

  Broadcast queue 0/64, broadcasts sent/dropped 0/0,
  interface broadcasts 1

  Last input 00:00:03, output 00:00:03, output hang never

  Last clearing of "show interface" counters never

  Input queue: 0/75/0 (size/max/drops); Total output
  drops: 0

  Queueing strategy: weighted fair

  Output queue: 0/1000/64/0 (size/max total/threshold/
  drops)

    Conversations 0/1/256 (active/max active/max total)

    Reserved Conversations 0/0 (allocated/max allocated)

  5 minute input rate 0 bits/sec, 0 packets/sec

  5 minute output rate 0 bits/sec, 0 packets/sec

```
        6 packets input, 94 bytes, 0 no buffer
        Received 0 broadcasts, 0 runts, 0 giants, 0 throttles
        0 input errors, 0 CRC, 0 frame, 0 overrun, 0 ignored,
          0 abort
        9 packets output, 129 bytes, 0 underruns
        0 output errors, 0 collisions, 3 interface resets
        0 output buffer failures, 0 output buffers swapped out
        0 carrier transitions
        DCD=up  DSR=up  DTR=up  RTS=up  CTS=up
Router_A#show interface ethernet 0/1
Ethernet0/1 is up, line protocol is up
    Hardware is AmdP2, address is 0010.7bd9.2881      (bia
      0010.7bd9.2881)
    Internet address is 172.16.30.1/24
    MTU 1500 bytes, BW 10000 Kbit, DLY 1000 usec, rely
      128/255,        load 1/255
    Encapsulation ARPA, loopback not set, keepalive set
      (10 sec)
    ARP type: ARPA, ARP Timeout 04:00:00
    Last input never, output 00:00:07, output hang never
    Last clearing of "show interface" counters never
    Queueing strategy: fifo
    Output queue 0/40, 0 drops; input queue 0/75, 0 drops
5 minute input rate 488000 bits/sec, 164 packets/sec
5 minute output rate 1473000 bits/sec, 297 packets/sec
        9840 packets input, 7815720 bytes, 0 no buffer
        Received 0 broadcasts, 0 runts, 0 giants, 0 throttles
        0 input errors, 0 CRC, 0 frame, 0 overrun, 0 ignored,
          0 abort
        0 input packets with dribble condition detected
        17820 packets output, 14352560 bytes, 0 underruns
        0 output errors, 0 collisions, 0 interface resets
        0 babbles, 0 late collision, 0 deferred
        0 lost carrier, 0 no carrier
        0 output buffer failures, 0 output buffers swapped
          out
Router_A#
```

List Observations—Take 3

From what you can see from the interface outputs, all interfaces are working properly. However, there are three messages regarding the DLCI information in messages that were displayed after the Serial 0/0 interface was brought up that are of concern. To be on the safe side, let's try to ping the router at the headquarters location.

Router_A#**ping 172.16.20.6**

```
Type escape sequence to abort.
Sending 5, 100-byte ICMP Echos to 172.16.20.6, timeout is
   2 seconds:
.....
Success rate is 0 percent (0/5)
Router_A#
```

As suspected, there is still another issue that needs to be resolved. From the show interface command we can see that the router is receiving LMI messages and that the circuit itself appears fine. Let's take a look at the PVCs and the Frame Relay mappings that are on the router.

```
Router_A#show frame-relay pvc

PVC Statistics for interface Serial0/0 (Frame Relay DTE)

DLCI = 324, DLCI USAGE = LOCAL, PVC STATUS = DELETED,
   INTERFACE = Serial0/0

  input pkts 0          output pkts 0          in bytes 0
  out bytes 0           dropped pkts 0         in FECN pkts 0
  in BECN pkts 0        out FECN pkts 0        out BECN pkts 0
  in DE pkts 0          out DE pkts 0
  out bcast pkts 0      out bcast bytes 0
  pvc create time 00:31:25, last time pvc status changed 00:31:25

DLCI = 368, DLCI USAGE = UNUSED, PVC STATUS = ACTIVE, INTERFACE = Serial0/0

  input pkts 0          output pkts 0          in bytes 0
  out bytes 0           dropped pkts 0         in FECN pkts 0
  in BECN pkts 0        out FECN pkts 0        out BECN pkts 0
```

```
  in DE pkts 0              out DE pkts 0
  out bcast pkts 0          out bcast bytes 0              Num Pkts Switched 0
  pvc create time 00:31:25, last time pvc status changed 00:31:25
Router_A#show frame-relay map
Serial0/0 (up): ip 172.16.20.6 dlci 324(0x144,0x5040), static,broadcast,
  CISCO, status deleted
Router_A#
```

Based on this output, there are two PVCs that are known to the router. One, 324, is in a deleted state and the other, 368, is in an active state. In addition, according to the `show frame-relay map` command, the IP address of the headquarters router is statically mapped to the deleted DLCI 324.

With this information in hand, let's restate our observations of conditions at this point.

- Ethernet 0/0 and Ethernet 0/1 are working fine at this point.

- Serial 0/0 is up and running without errors.

- You cannot ping the headquarters router.

- LMI is being sent and received successfully on Serial 0/0.

- There are 2 PVCs known by the router: 324 and 368.

- There is only one PVC that will be used at this location.

- The IP address of the headquarters router is statically mapped to DLCI 324.

Propose Solutions—Take 3

Based on these new observations, the most likely scenario is that when the router was preconfigured, the IP address was mapped to the incorrect DLCI. When a static IP-to-DLCI mapping is made, an entry for that DLCI is put in the router's PVC table. If the router does not receive an LMI message indicating that the frame switch knows about that DLCI, or if the interface on which this DLCI is assigned is down, the DLCI will go into a deleted state. In addition, when a router actively receives updates for a DLCI via LMI, it will add this DLCI to its table in an active state. This appears to be what has occurred with DLCI 368. Therefore, we are assuming that DLCI 368 is the correct DLCI for this location.

Based on this information, our plan is to change the DLCI-to-IP mappings to map 172.16.20.6 to DLCI 368. This change is shown below:

```
Router_A#conf t
Enter configuration commands, one per line. End with CNTL/Z.
Router_A(config)#interface serial 0/0
Router_A(config-if)#no frame-relay map ip 172.16.20.6 324
    broadcast
Router_A(config-if)#frame-relay map ip 172.16.20.6 368
    broadcast
Router_A(config-if)#^Z
Router_A#
Router_A#show frame-relay map
Serial0/0 (up): ip 172.16.20.6 dlci 368(0x170,0x5C00),
    static, broadcast, CISCO, status defined, active
Router_A#
Router_A#ping 172.16.20.6

Type escape sequence to abort.
Sending 5, 100-byte ICMP Echos to 172.16.20.6, timeout is
    2 seconds:
!!!!!
Success rate is 100 percent (5/5), round-trip min/avg/max
    = 28/30/32 ms
Router_A#
```

The changes made were effective, and they did not cause other network problems.

The final step is to document what was done:

- We added 172.16.10.1/24 to Ethernet 0/0.

- We left 172.16.20.5/30 on Serial 0/0.

- We changed administrative status for interface Serial 0/0 with the no shutdown command.

- We changed the DLCI used for the Frame Relay connection.

- We changed the IP address for interface Ethernet 0/1 from 172.16.20.5/30 to 172.16.30.1/24.

All of the necessary steps were taken to solve the observed problems. The first step was to record observations. Once the observations were made, a problem statement was written. Based on the problem statement, an action plan was devised to resolve the problems. After the first changes were made, interface Ethernet 0/0 came up. You saw that the router would not allow Serial 0/0 to be removed from administrative shutdown due to a duplicate IP address. The address conflicted with an IP address assigned to Ethernet 0/1. A new address was assigned to Ethernet 0/1, and Serial 0/0 was changed to an active state. After this, the DLCI used for the Frame Relay connection was changed and complete connectivity was achieved.

 Real World Scenario

Frame Relay and Subinterfaces

In the previous example, the entire Frame Relay configuration was done on the main interface and Frame Relay inverse ARP was turned off. This was done in order to make the example more interesting to troubleshoot. By configuring the interface in this manner, as long as the interface received LMI messages from the Frame Relay switch it would stay in an up/up state.

Though there are reasons to configure an interface in this manner (e.g., point-to-multipoint, multipoint-to-multipoint, consistency of configuration), using subinterfaces and the `frame-relay interface-dlci` command may have been more appropriate in this instance. If in our example, a subinterface (use Serial 0/0.1 for example) had been configured specifically for the connection back to headquarters, it would have made troubleshooting the DLCI problem easier. In this case, the main interface, Serial 0/0, would have still been in an up/up state, but the subinterface, Serial 0/0.1, would have been down/down until the DLCI issue was corrected. This correction would involve changing the `frame-relay interface-dlci` command to refer to DLCI 368 instead of the originally configured value of 324. Using subinterfaces would have made it easier to spot the DLCI issue as well as to verify when the problem had been corrected.

Scenario #2

This next scenario is a little more difficult. Look at Figure 13.2 to get a picture of the network that you will troubleshoot. Host Z is trying to FTP a file to Host A, but Host Z is unable to do so.

FIGURE 13.2 Network diagram for scenario #2

Let's move through the troubleshooting method to solve this problem. Start by listing your observations.

List Observations

As discussed in Chapter 1, you should define the boundary of dysfunctionality, which can be done in several ways. In this scenario, you test by attempting to FTP to Host A while observing the results.

The first test is an actual FTP attempt. Figure 13.3 shows the results of the FTP attempt. The software gives you a `host unreachable` error message, which is an ICMP response. EtherPeek was used to capture packets in this exchange. The first packet decode is Host Z sending an FTP connection request.

FIGURE 13.3 FTP attempt failure

```
connecting to 172.16.10.2:21
! Connection failed 172.16.10.2 - host unreachable
! Connection failed 172.16.10.2
```

```
Flags:          0x00
Status:         0x00
Packet Length:66
Timestamp:      22:11:39.486000 04/18/2002
Ethernet Header
Destination:  00:10:7b:d9:28:81   [0-5]
Source:       00:a0:24:a5:06:57   [6-11]
Protocol Type:08-00  IP  [12-13]
IP Header - Internet Protocol Datagram
```

```
Version:               4  [14 Mask 0xf0]
Header Length:         5  [14 Mask 0xf]
Precedence:            0  [15 Mask 0xe0]
Type of Service:       %000  [15 Mask 0x1c]
Unused:                %00  [15 Mask 0x3]
Total Length:          48  [16-17]
Identifier:            17152  [18-19]
Fragmentation Flags:   %010  Do Not Fragment
  [20  Mask 0xe0]
Fragment Offset:       0  [20-22 Mask 0x1fffff]
Time To Live:          128
IP Type:               0x06  TCP  [23]
Header Checksum:       0x1923  [24-25]
Source IP Address:     172.16.60.130  [26-29]
Dest. IP Address:      172.16.10.2  [30-33]
No Internet Datagram Options
TCP - Transport Control Protocol
Source Port:           1038  [34-35]
Destination Port: 21   FTP Control - File Transfer
  Protocol  [36-37]
Sequence Number:       6198340  [38-41]
Ack Number:            0  [42-45]
Offset:                7  [46 Mask 0xf0]
Reserved:              %000000  [46 Mask 0xfc0]
Code:                  %000010  [47 Mask 0x3f]
          Synch Sequence
Window:                8192  [48-49]
Checksum:              0x2bb5  [50-51]
Urgent Pointer:        0  [52-53]
TCP Options:  [54]
   Option Type:        2  Maximum Segment Size  [55]
      Length:          4
      MSS:             1460  [56-58]
   Option Type:        1  No Operation  [59]
   Option Type:        1  No Operation  [60]
   Option Type:        4  [61]
      Length:          2
```

```
                No More FTP Command or Reply Data
```
Frame Check Sequence: 0x00000000

Everything looks fine with this packet. Now, look at the ICMP message received. Notice that the source IP address in the ICMP packet is from 172.16.60.1. That is the gateway address for Host Z.

```
Flags:          0x00
    Status:        0x00
    Packet Length:74
    Timestamp:     22:11:39.489000 04/18/2002
Ethernet Header
```
Destination: 00:a0:24:a5:06:57 [0-5]
Source: 00:10:7b:d9:28:81 [6-11]
Protocol Type:08-00 IP [12-13]
```
IP Header - Internet Protocol Datagram
```
Version: 4 [14 Mask 0xf0]
Header Length: 5 [14 Mask 0xf]
Precedence: 0 [15 Mask 0xe0]
Type of Service: %000 [15 Mask 0x1c]
Unused: %00 [15 Mask 0x3]
Total Length: 56 [16-17]
Identifier: 2815 [18-19]
Fragmentation Flags: %000 [20 Mask 0xe0]
Fragment Offset: 0 [20-22 Mask 0x1fffff]
Time To Live: 255
IP Type: 0x01 *ICMP* [23]
Header Checksum: 0xe021 [24-25]
Source IP Address: 172.16.60.1 [26-29]
Dest. IP Address: 172.16.60.130 [30-33]
```
    No Internet Datagram Options
```
ICMP - Internet Control Messages Protocol [34]
ICMP Type: 3 *Destination Unreachable* [35]
Code: 1 *Host Unreachable*
Checksum: 0x6439 [36-37]
Unused (must be zero):0x00000000 [38-41]

```
Header of packet that caused error follows.
```

```
IP Header - Internet Protocol Datagram
  Version:               4   [42 Mask 0xf0]
  Header Length:         5   [42 Mask 0xf]
  Precedence:            0   [43 Mask 0xe0]
  Type of Service:       %000  [43 Mask 0x1c]
  Unused:                %00  [43 Mask 0x3]
  Total Length:          48  [44-45]
  Identifier:            17152  [46-47]
  Fragmentation Flags:   %010  Do Not Fragment    [48 Mask
    0xe0]
  Fragment Offset:       0   [48-50 Mask 0x1fffff]
  Time To Live:          127
  IP Type:               0x06  TCP  [51]
  Header Checksum:       0x1a23  [52-53]
  Source IP Address:     172.16.60.130  [54-57]
  Dest. IP Address:      172.16.10.2  [58-61]
  No Internet Datagram Options
TCP - Transport Control Protocol
  Source Port:           1038  [62-63]
  Destination Port: 21  FTP Control - File Transfer
    Protocol     [64-65]
  Sequence Number:  6198340  [66-69]
  Ack Number:            0
```

The key information is provided under the ICMP header section. Notice the ICMP type of 3, which is equivalent to an unreachable destination—the code specifies that the host is not reachable. The ping command may be issued, but it will render the same information—host unreachable.

What other tool might be used to aid in defining the border of dysfunctionality? There are a couple of different directions that may be taken. One method is to try to FTP a file to hosts that do not reside on the 172.16.10.0/24 network. Another consists of running a traceroute to see where the path to Host A is failing.

Let's try the latter. Following are the results of a traceroute to Host A:

```
C:\WINDOWS>tracert 172.16.10.2
Tracing route to 172.16.10.2 over a maximum of 30 hops
1     5 ms     2 ms     4 ms   172.16.60.1
2  172.16.60.1  reports: Destination host unreachable.
Trace complete.
```

These results indicate that Router C does not have a route to Host A. This allows you to draw the line of dysfunctionality to the boundary between Router C and Router B.

To further troubleshoot this problem, diagnostics must be executed from Router C. Let's bring up a console on Router C. The first command that should be issued is a show ip route. The results are as follows:

```
Router_C#show ip route
Codes: C - connected, S - static, I - IGRP, R - RIP, M -
   mobile, B - BGP D - EIGRP, EX - EIGRP external, O -
   OSPF, IA - OSPF inter area N1 - OSPF NSSA external type
   1, N2 - OSPF NSSA external type 2 E1 - OSPF external
   type 1, E2 - OSPF external type 2, E - EGPi - IS-IS,
   L1 - IS-IS level-1, L2 - IS-IS level-2, * - candidate
   default U - per-user static route, o - ODR
Gateway of last resort is not set
172.16.0.0/24 is subnetted, 2 subnets
C       172.16.60.0 is directly connected, Ethernet0/1
C       172.16.50.0 is directly connected, Ethernet0/0
Router_C#
```

Router C knows only routes for networks that are directly connected. This points to problems with routing updates or routing protocols between Routers B and C. Let's take a look at the configuration on both routers:

```
Router_C#show running-config
Building configuration...
Current configuration:
!
version 11.3
no service password-encryption
!
hostname Router_C
!
enable password aloha
!
interface Ethernet0/0
 ip address 172.16.50.2 255.255.255.0
!
interface Serial0/0
```

```
 no ip address
 shutdown
!
interface Ethernet0/1
 ip address 172.16.60.1 255.255.255.0
!
router eigrp 100
 network 172.16.0.0
 no auto-summary
!
ip classless
!
line con 0
line aux 0
line vty 0 4
 password aloha
 login
!
end
Router_C#
```

The show interface results should be reviewed before the configuration of Router B is displayed. The only interface that is of concern is the one that connects the two routers—interface Ethernet 0/0. The results are shown as follows. As depicted, interface Ethernet 0/0 is up and functioning. This is proved by using the ping command.

```
Router_C>show interface ethernet0/0
Ethernet0/0 is up, line protocol is up
  Hardware is AmdP2, address is 0010.7bd9.2880 (bia
    0010.7bd9.2880)
  Internet address is 172.16.50.2/24
  MTU 1500 bytes, BW 10000 Kbit, DLY 1000 usec, rely
    255/255,    load 1/255
  Encapsulation ARPA, loopback not set, keepalive set
    (10 sec)
  ARP type: ARPA, ARP Timeout 04:00:00
  Last input 02:54:40, output 00:00:00, output hang never
  Last clearing of "show interface" counters never
```

```
Queueing strategy: fifo
Output queue 0/40, 0 drops; input queue 0/75, 0 drops
5 minute input rate 0 bits/sec, 0 packets/sec
5 minute output rate 0 bits/sec, 0 packets/sec
    1006 packets input, 90611 bytes, 0 no buffer
    Received 990 broadcasts, 0 runts, 0 giants, 0 throttles
    0 input errors, 0 CRC, 0 frame, 0 overrun, 0 ignored,
      0 abort
    0 input packets with dribble condition detected
    4935 packets output, 402703 bytes, 0 underruns
    0 output errors, 0 collisions, 2 interface resets
    0 babbles, 0 late collision, 0 deferred
    0 lost carrier, 0 no carrier
    0 output buffer failures, 0 output buffers swapped out
Router_C>ping 172.16.50.1
Type escape sequence to abort.
Sending 5, 100-byte ICMP Echos to 172.16.50.1, timeout is
  2  seconds:
.!!!!
Success rate is 80 percent (4/5), round-trip min/avg/max =
  1/3/4 ms
Router_C>ping 172.16.50.1
Type escape sequence to abort.
Sending 5, 100-byte ICMP Echos to 172.16.50.1, timeout is
  2  seconds:
!!!!!
Success rate is 100 percent (5/5), round-trip min/avg/max
  =   4/4/4 ms
Router_C>
```

This output means that the routers are not sharing routing information. Something is causing the routing protocol to fail, but it is not because the interface is down. Before moving on, let's review our observations and make sure that the correct path is being followed.

- Host Z cannot FTP to Host A.

- Host Z cannot ping to Host A.

- Host Z cannot traceroute to Host A.

- ICMP "destination unreachable" responses were returned from the FTP request.

- Router C does not have a route to the destination network.

- Ethernet 0/0 is up and functioning.

- There is capability to ping Router B.

Before a problem definition statement can be devised, more information must be gathered from Router B. Let's telnet to Router B. Something looks wrong:

```
Router_C>172.16.50.1
Trying 172.16.50.1 ... Open
User Access Verification
Password:
Router_B(boot)>
```

Instead of coming up with the normal prompt, the router is in boot mode, which explains why no routing is taking place. When a router is in boot mode, routing protocols do not work. This is the last key observation needed, and it allows you to define the problem.

Here is the problem statement: Router B is in boot mode, it does not route in this state, so Host Z cannot FTP to Host A. This statement lists the actual problem as well as the reported problem.

Propose Solutions

With the observations made, and a detailed and focused problem statement, you can now move on to provide possible solutions to the problem. It is still important to consider the observations when determining the next action.

You know that the router is in boot mode, but what causes a router to be in boot mode? There are two simple reasons that a router may be in boot mode: there is a lack of IOS on the system flash or the router is not looking for the IOS in the right location.

Let's look at the contents of Router B's flash. Then look at the router's version information.

```
Router_B(boot)#show flash
System flash directory:
File  Length   Name/status
   1  4287696  c2500-i-1.112-15.bin
```

```
[4287760 bytes used, 4100848 available, 8388608 total]
8192K bytes of processor board System flash (Read/Write)
Router_B(boot)#
```

This shows one IOS image on the system flash. Now, you need to determine which version of IOS is running on the router:

```
Router_B(boot)#show version
Cisco Internetwork Operating System Software
IOS (tm) 3000 Bootstrap Software (IGS-BOOT-R), Version
    11.0(10c)XB1, PLATFORM SPECIFIC RELEASE SOFTWARE (fc1)
Copyright (c) 1986-1996 by cisco Systems, Inc.
Compiled Wed 10-Sep-97 13:06 by phester
Image text-base: 0x01010000, data-base: 0x00001000
ROM: System Bootstrap, Version 11.0(10c)XB1, PLATFORM
    SPECIFIC RELEASE SOFTWARE
(fc1)
Router_B uptime is 3 hours, 11 minutes
System restarted by reload
Running default software
cisco 2500 (68030) processor (revision A) with 4096K/2048K
    bytes of memory.
Processor board ID 01229726, with hardware revision 00000000
X.25 software, Version 2.0, NET2, BFE and GOSIP compliant.
Cisco-ET Extended Temperature platform.
1 Ethernet/IEEE 802.3 interface.
2 Serial network interfaces.
32K bytes of non-volatile configuration memory.
8192K bytes of processor board System flash (Read/Write)
Configuration register is 0x2101
Router_B(boot)#
```

The response is that it is running a bootstrap version of IOS, which displays in the first few fields. From these two outputs, it can be deduced that the IOS contained in flash memory was not used to boot the router.

As previously mentioned, the IOS image could be corrupt, or the router is looking for the IOS in the wrong place. The router uses a configuration register to point to the location of the IOS image that it should load during the boot process.

For a full description of config-register settings, refer to CCO. To briefly explain, the config-register is a 16-bit number that controls the router's boot sequence. The lowest four bits indicate from where the system image, or IOS, will be loaded. If the value is 0000, then the router enters into ROM monitor mode. If the register is set to 0001, then the IOS will be loaded from the boot ROM.

In this case, the configuration register was set to the hex value of 0x2101, which tells the router to look for the system image on the boot ROM. Remember that only the first four bits indicate the system image location.

The action plan for this scenario is to change the configuration register on Router B to load the image from system flash. The configuration changes follow. After the router reloads, a quick check can be made by issuing a show version command.

```
Router_B(boot)#conf t
Enter configuration commands, one per line. End with CNTL/Z.
Router_B(boot)(config)#config
Router_B(boot)(config)#config-register 0x2102
Router_B(boot)(config)#^Z
Router_B(boot)#
Router_B(boot)#reload
Proceed with reload? [confirm]
 [Connection to 172.16.50.1 closed by foreign host]
Router_C>172.16.50.1
Trying 172.16.50.1 ... Open
User Access Verification
Password:
Router_B>enable
Password:
Router_B#show version
Cisco Internetwork Operating System Software
IOS (tm) 2500 Software (C2500-I-L), Version 11.2(15),
   RELEASE SOFTWARE (fc1)
Copyright (c) 1986-1998 by cisco Systems, Inc.
Compiled Tue 07-Jul-98 21:51 by tmullins
Image text-base: 0x03022F80, data-base: 0x00001000
ROM: System Bootstrap, Version 11.0(10c)XB1, PLATFORM
   SPECIFIC RELEASE SOFTWARE(fc1)
```

```
BOOTFLASH: 3000 Bootstrap Software (IGS-BOOT-R), Version
    11.0(10c)XB1, PLATFORM
SPECIFIC RELEASE SOFTWARE (fc1)
Router_B uptime is 2 minutes
System restarted by reload
System image file is "flash:c2500-i-l.112-15.bin", booted
    via flash
cisco 2500 (68030) processor (revision A) with 4096K/2048K
    bytes of memory.
Processor board ID 01229726, with hardware revision 00000000
Bridging software.
X.25 software, Version 2.0, NET2, BFE and GOSIP compliant.
Cisco-ET Extended Temperature platform.
1 Ethernet/IEEE 802.3 interface(s)
2 Serial network interface(s)
32K bytes of non-volatile configuration memory.
8192K bytes of processor board System flash (Read ONLY)
Configuration register is 0x2102
Router_B#
```

This time, the system image file is `"flash:c2500-i-l.112-15.bin"` booted from flash. This means that it is running the proper IOS. Now look at the route table:

```
Router_B#show ip route
Codes: C - connected, S - static, I - IGRP, R - RIP, M -
    mobile, B – BGP, D - EIGRP, EX - EIGRP external, O -
    OSPF, IA - OSPF inter area N1 - OSPF NSSA external type
    1, N2 - OSPF NSSA external type 2 E1 - OSPF external
    type 1, E2 - OSPF external type 2, E - EGPi - IS-IS,
    L1 - IS-IS level-1, L2 - IS-IS level-2, * - candidate
    default
U - per-user static route, o - ODR
Gateway of last resort is not set
172.16.0.0/16 is variably subnetted, 2 subnets, 2 masks
D       172.16.60.0/24 [90/307200] via 172.16.50.2,
    00:00:16, Ethernet0
D   172.16.10.0/24 [90/300200] via 172.16.30.5, 00:00:19,
    Serial0
```

```
C        172.16.50.0/24 is directly connected, Ethernet0
C        172.16.30.4/30 is directly connected, Serial0
Router_B#
```

Now the route to 172.16.10.0/24 is present in the route table. The next step is to look at the route table on Router C.

```
Router_C>show ip route
Codes: C - connected, S - static, I - IGRP, R - RIP, M -
    mobile, B - BGP, D - EIGRP, EX - EIGRP external, O -
    OSPF, IA - OSPF inter area N1 - OSPF NSSA external type 1,
    N2 - OSPF NSSA external type 2 E1 - OSPF external type
    1, E2 - OSPF external type 2, E - EGPi - IS-IS,
    L1 - IS-IS level-1, L2 - IS-IS level-2, * - candidate
    defaultU - per-user static route, o - ODR
Gateway of last resort is not set
172.16.0.0/16 is variably subnetted, 3 subnets, 2 masks
C        172.16.60.0/24 is directly connected, Ethernet0/1
C        172.16.50.0/24 is directly connected, Ethernet0/0
D        172.16.30.4/30 [90/2195456] via 172.16.50.1,
    00:02:59, Ethernet0/0
D        172.16.10.0/24 [90/3295676] via 172.16.50.1,
    00:02:59, Ethernet0/0
Router_C>
```

Everything looks as if it is in place, but the ultimate test is to FTP from Host Z to Host A. The connection is successful.

```
C:\WINDOWS>ftp 172.16.10.2
> ftp: connect :10061
ftp>
```

Let's review the steps taken. The observation was that Host Z could not FTP to Host A. The problem was isolated by using the ping and traceroute commands. After the problem was isolated, the correct observations were made that enabled a problem statement to be made. The problem was that Router B was in boot mode. This happened because the IOS image was loaded from the ROM instead of flash. The problem was remedied by changing the configuration register to indicate that the image should be loaded from the system flash.

The effect of the configuration changes was validated by showing the routes present on each router, as well as establishing an FTP session with Host A.

Troubleshooting Ethernet Problems

As the heading indicates, this section includes troubleshooting Ethernet-related problems. The examples are simple, and you need to use only Ethernet-related commands to effectively troubleshoot these problems.

Scenario #1

The problem here is that Host A cannot telnet to Host Z. Figure 13.4 depicts the network that is used for this scenario. Troubleshooting will begin after the establishment of the boundary of dysfunctionality. You know that the problem exists between Router C and Host Z. Because this is a troubleshooting scenario for Ethernet, you know what to look for.

FIGURE 13.4 Network diagram for Ethernet scenario #1

List Observations

The first thing to do is verify that Host Z is still unreachable. Let's look at the results of a ping test:

```
Router_C#ping 172.16.60.130
Type escape sequence to abort.
Sending 5, 100-byte ICMP Echos to 172.16.60.130, timeout
   is 2 seconds:
```

```
.....
Success rate is 0 percent (0/5)
Router_C#
```

Because the ping test failed, the cause needs to be isolated. Let's look at the interface:

```
Router_C#show interface ethernet0/1
Ethernet0/1 is up, line protocol is up
  Hardware is AmdP2, address is 0010.7bd9.2881 (bia
    0010.7bd9.2881)
  Internet address is 172.16.60.1/24
  MTU 1500 bytes, BW 10000 Kbit, DLY 1000 usec, rely
    255/255,    load 1/255
  Encapsulation ARPA, loopback not set, keepalive set
    (10 sec)
  ARP type: ARPA, ARP Timeout 04:00:00
  Last input 00:41:42, output 00:00:00, output hang never
  Last clearing of "show interface" counters never
  Queueing strategy: fifo
  Output queue 0/40, 0 drops; input queue 0/75, 0 drops
  5 minute input rate 0 bits/sec, 0 packets/sec
  5 minute output rate 0 bits/sec, 0 packets/sec
     147 packets input, 9568 bytes, 0 no buffer
     Received 5 broadcasts, 0 runts, 0 giants, 0 throttles
     0 input errors, 0 CRC, 0 frame, 0 overrun, 0
       ignored, 0 abort
     0 input packets with dribble condition detected
     2009 packets output, 162455 bytes, 0 underruns
     0 output errors, 0 collisions, 2 interface resets
     0 babbles, 0 late collision, 0 deferred
     0 lost carrier, 0 no carrier
     0 output buffer failures, 0 output buffers swapped out
Router_C#
```

Everything looks good, except for the fact that no traffic is being sent across the interface. That can be another indication that there is a problem between the router and Host Z. Now, look at the ARP table:

```
Router_C>show arp
Protocol  Address    Age (min) Hardware Addr Type Interface
```

```
Internet  172.16.60.1  -     0010.7bd9.2881 ARPA  Ethernet0/1
Internet  172.16.50.2  -     0010.7bd9.2880 ARPA  Ethernet0/0
Internet  172.16.50.1  0     0000.0c09.99cc ARPA  Ethernet0/0
Router_C>
```

The address of interest is not listed in the ARP table, which means that Router C does not know where to send the Layer 2 PDU. A trace using Ether-Peek shows the router sending out an ARP broadcast:

```
Flags:         0x00
  Status:        0x00
  Packet Length:64
  Timestamp:     11:30:42.713000 04/19/2002
Ethernet Header
  Destination:  ff:ff:ff:ff:ff:ff Ethernet Brdcast  [0-5]
  Source:        00:10:7b:d9:28:81  [6-11]
  Protocol Type:08-06  IP ARP  [12-13]
ARP - Address Resolution Protocol
  Hardware:               1  Ethernet (10Mb)  [14-15]
  Protocol:               08-00  IP  [16-18]
  Hardware Address Length:  6  [19]
  Protocol Address Length:  4
  Operation:              1  ARP Request  [20-21]
  Sender Hardware Address:  00:10:7b:d9:28:81  [22-27]
  Sender Internet Address:  172.16.60.1  [28-31]
  Target Hardware Address:  00:00:00:00:00:00  (ignored)
    [32-37]
  Target Internet Address:  172.16.60.130  [38-41]
Extra bytes (Padding):
  ...............  00 00 00 00 00 00 00 00 00 00 00 00 00
    00 00 00  [42-57]
  ..                       00 00  [58-59]
Frame Check Sequence:  0x00000000
```

No response was received from this broadcast. Let's list the facts that you have gathered:

- Router C cannot ping Host Z.

- Interface Ethernet 0/1 is up and line protocol is up.

- There are no collisions on the Ethernet interface.

- No traffic is transiting the Ethernet 0/1 interface.

- There is no listing for Host Z in the ARP table.

- An ARP broadcast was sent out Ethernet 0/1, but no response was received from Host Z.

The problem statement is that Ethernet 0/1 is functioning properly, but it cannot communicate with Host Z. There is no listing for Host Z in the ARP table.

It is simpler to decide the possible causes and create an action plan by focusing on the ARP table. What possible reasons are there for Host Z not to be listed in the ARP table? Some reasons are as follows:

- Failed host

- Cabling failures

- Bad Ethernet NIC on Host Z

- Mismatching frame encapsulation type

Propose Solutions

You verified that the host is not down. No traffic is transiting the Ethernet interface on the router. This indicates that the Ethernet card is not starting to fail, but could have completely failed. Cabling is probably not the issue because you would see interface resets or carrier transitions. None of those symptoms are indicated on the interface. This leaves us with mismatching encapsulation type as the probable problem.

The easiest way to test it is to ping Router C from Host Z. The results follow:

```
C:\WINDOWS>ping 172.16.60.1
Pinging 172.16.60.1 with 32 bytes of data:
Reply from 172.16.60.1: bytes=32 time=7ms TTL=255
Reply from 172.16.60.1: bytes=32 time=1ms TTL=255
Reply from 172.16.60.1: bytes=32 time=2ms TTL=255
Reply from 172.16.60.1: bytes=32 time=4ms TTL=255
Ping statistics for 172.16.60.1:
    Packets: Sent = 4, Received = 4, Lost = 0 (0% loss),
Approximate round trip times in milli-seconds:
    Minimum = 1ms, Maximum =  7ms, Average =  3ms
C:\WINDOWS>
```

The ping was successful. Why is it that Router C can ping Host Z, but Host Z cannot ping Router C? Let's go back to the router. Look at the ARP table now.

```
Router_C>show arp
Protocol  Address       Age (min) Hardware Addr  Type  Interface
Internet  172.16.60.130 1         00a0.24a5.0657 SNAP  Ethernet0/1
Internet  172.16.60.1   -         0010.7bd9.2881 ARPA  Ethernet0/1
Internet  172.16.50.2   -         0010.7bd9.2880 ARPA  Ethernet0/0
Internet  172.16.50.1   111       0000.0c09.99cc ARPA  Ethernet0/0
Router_C>
```

Wait a minute! Host Z is listed in the table now. How did that happen? You must remember that although Cisco understands several different encapsulation types, its default is ARPA. When the router sent the ARP request, it was sent using ARPA. Host Z does not understand ARPA, and so it did not respond to the ARP request.

The process works differently on a Cisco router. When Host Z sent an ARP broadcast, it was sent with SNAP encapsulation. The difference is that the router understood the broadcast, recorded the encapsulation type, and entered it into the router's ARP table, as seen previously. The type allows the router to override the default encapsulation. Now, when the router needs to send a frame to Host Z, it uses SNAP encapsulation. Let's test it:

```
Router_C#ping 172.16.60.130
Type escape sequence to abort.
Sending 5, 100-byte ICMP Echos to 172.16.60.130, timeout
   is 2 seconds:
!!!!!
Success rate is 100 percent (5/5), round-trip min/avg/max
   = 4/4/8 ms
Router_C#
```

It worked great because the router now knows which encapsulation type must be used when communicating with Host Z. This problem has been resolved temporarily. To solve it permanently, you must manually change the encapsulation type used for the interface that Host Z connects to. Now let's move on to the next one.

Scenario #2

This is another simple Ethernet problem. Using the example network depicted in Figure 13.5, you will attempt to solve a less tangible network problem. The user at Host A complains of very slow throughput to Host Z.

He is able to ping and traceroute to the destination, but file transfers experience very slow transfer times.

FIGURE 13.5 Network diagram for Ethernet scenario #2

List Observations

List the observations given you by the user, and then move on to other fact-gathering procedures:

- Large transfer times
- Slow throughput
- Can ping and traceroute to host

The fact that ping and traceroute work indicates that the routing between Host A and Host Z is intact. There must be something that causes latency somewhere along the line. Again, start at the far end of the problem.

The following outputs are several show interface outputs of the same interface over an extended period of time. Look at them all and see if you can spot the problem.

```
Router_C#show int ethernet 0/1
Ethernet0/1 is up, line protocol is up
  Hardware is Lance, address is 0000.0c47.abea (bia
    0000.0c47.abea)
  Internet address is 172.16.60.1/24
  MTU 1500 bytes, BW 10000 Kbit, DLY 1000 usec, rely
    255/255,    load 46/255
  Encapsulation ARPA, loopback not set, keepalive set
    (10 sec)
  ARP type: ARPA, ARP Timeout 04:00:00
```

```
Last input 00:00:00, output 00:00:00, output hang never
Last clearing of "show interface" counters 00:00:05
Queueing strategy: fifo
Output queue 0/40, 0 drops; input queue 0/75, 0 drops
5 minute input rate 1259000 bits/sec, 629 packets/sec
5 minute output rate 1822000 bits/sec, 486 packets/sec
    3476 packets input, 455808 bytes, 0 no buffer
    Received 2 broadcasts, 0 runts, 0 giants
    0 input errors, 0 CRC, 0 frame, 0 overrun, 0 ignored,
      0 abort
    0 input packets with dribble condition detected
    1165 packets output, 1667097 bytes, 0 underruns
    0 output errors, 175 collisions, 0 interface resets
    0 babbles, 0 late collision, 182 deferred
    0 lost carrier, 0 no carrier
    0 output buffer failures, 0 output buffers swapped out
Router_C#show int ethernet 0/1
Ethernet0/1 is up, line protocol is up
  Hardware is Lance, address is 0000.0c47.abea (bia
  0000.0c47.abea)
  Internet address is 172.16.60.1/24
  MTU 1500 bytes, BW 10000 Kbit, DLY 1000 usec, rely
  255/255,    load 46/255
  Encapsulation ARPA, loopback not set, keepalive set
  (10 sec)
  ARP type: ARPA, ARP Timeout 04:00:00
  Last input 00:00:00, output 00:00:00, output hang never
  Last clearing of "show interface" counters 00:00:16
  Queueing strategy: fifo
  Output queue 0/40, 0 drops; input queue 0/75, 0 drops
  5 minute input rate 1243000 bits/sec, 627 packets/sec
  5 minute output rate 1826000 bits/sec, 484 packets/sec
      9872 packets input, 1760499 bytes, 0 no buffer
      Received 4 broadcasts, 0 runts, 0 giants
      0 input errors, 0 CRC, 0 frame, 0 overrun, 0 ignored,
        0 abort
      0 input packets with dribble condition detected
```

```
            2858 packets output, 3943213 bytes, 0 underruns
            0 output errors, 443 collisions, 0 interface resets
            0 babbles, 0 late collision, 471 deferred
            0 lost carrier, 0 no carrier
            0 output buffer failures, 0 output buffers swapped out
Router_C#show int ethernet 0/1
Ethernet0/1 is up, line protocol is up
  Hardware is Lance, address is 0000.0c47.abea
    (bia 0000.0c47.abea)
  Internet address is 172.16.60.1/24
  MTU 1500 bytes, BW 10000 Kbit, DLY 1000 usec, rely
    255/255,    load 46/255
  Encapsulation ARPA, loopback not set, keepalive set
    (10 sec)
  ARP type: ARPA, ARP Timeout 04:00:00
  Last input 00:00:00, output 00:00:00, output hang never
  Last clearing of "show interface" counters 00:00:37
  Queueing strategy: fifo
  Output queue 0/40, 0 drops; input queue 0/75, 0 drops
  5 minute input rate 1209000 bits/sec, 620 packets/sec
  5 minute output rate 1819000 bits/sec, 477 packets/sec
      21386 packets input, 3979009 bytes, 0 no buffer
      Received 9 broadcasts, 0 runts, 0 giants
      0 input errors, 0 CRC, 0 frame, 0 overrun, 0
        ignored, 0 abort
      0 input packets with dribble condition detected
      5590 packets output, 8237684 bytes, 0 underruns
      0 output errors, 889 collisions, 0 interface resets
      0 babbles, 0 late collision, 1006 deferred
      0 lost carrier, 0 no carrier
      0 output buffer failures, 0 output buffers swapped out
Router_C#show int ethernet 0/1
Ethernet0/1 is up, line protocol is up
  Hardware is Lance, address is 0000.0c47.abea (bia
    0000.0c47.abea)
  Internet address is 172.16.60.1/24
  MTU 1500 bytes, BW 10000 Kbit, DLY 1000 usec, rely
    255/255,    load 46/255
```

```
Encapsulation ARPA, loopback not set, keepalive set
 (10 sec)
ARP type: ARPA, ARP Timeout 04:00:00
Last input 00:00:00, output 00:00:00, output hang never
Last clearing of "show interface" counters 00:00:50
Queueing strategy: fifo
Output queue 0/40, 0 drops; input queue 0/75, 0 drops
5 minute input rate 1209000 bits/sec, 620 packets/sec
5 minute output rate 1819000 bits/sec, 477 packets/sec
    21386 packets input, 3979009 bytes, 0 no buffer
    Received 9 broadcasts, 0 runts, 0 giants
    0 input errors, 0 CRC, 0 frame, 0 overrun, 0
     ignored, 0 abort
    0 input packets with dribble condition detected
    6000 packets output, 8237684 bytes, 0 underruns
    0 output errors, 1020 collisions, 0 interface resets
    0 babbles, 0 late collision, 1006 deferred
    0 lost carrier, 0 no carrier
    0 output buffer failures, 0 output buffers swapped out
```

So, what do you think? What are your observations? This exercise was designed specifically to educate you about Ethernet capabilities. The principal observation that you should have made was the increasing number of collisions on the interface.

Collisions are a normal occurrence for CSMA/CD protocols. The fact that a connection is not full-duplex creates the opportunity for collisions. Although collisions are normal, excessive collisions can be detrimental to a network. Once collisions exceed five to eight percent of the output packets, the interface becomes very ineffective. The higher the collision rate, the more packets have to be retransmitted.

The output queue for the Ethernet interface doesn't stop filling up just because of collisions on the line. Therefore, not only does the interface have to transmit the normal queue of packets, it has to retransmit all of the frames that were lost due to collisions. The number of packets that need to be transmitted can grow exponentially. Let's calculate the collision percentage for the four show interface outputs:

- 175 collisions/1165 output packets = 15.02% collisions

- 443 collisions/2858 output packets = 15.5% collisions

- 889 collisions/5590 output packets = 15.9% collisions
- 1020 collisions/6000 output packets = 17.0% collisions

All of these values are well in excess of five to eight percent. It looks like a key observation has been made, and now the problem statement can be written. The collision percentage on Ethernet 0/1 exceeds healthy values and can be blamed for causing slow network throughput.

Propose Solutions

The hard part is to determine what is causing the collisions. In this scenario, solutions will be tried from Layer 1 up to Layer 2. Following are possible solutions:

- Replace a faulty cable.
- Replace a faulty transceiver.
- Replace a faulty interface by changing the router.

The proposed solutions are to test the cable—if the cable passes, then change the transceiver. If that doesn't help, assume that the interface on the router has gone bad. If the latter is the problem, the problem may be solved by moving the connection to another interface on the same router or to a different interface on a different router.

Figure 13.6 depicts the physical hardware involved in this scenario. The cable connects to the hub and to a transceiver that is connected to the router's AUI interface.

FIGURE 13.6 Ethernet physical hardware

You tested the cable and it passed, so you then change transceivers, execute a `clear counters` command to reset the interface counters, and look at the interface status again.

```
Router_C#show interface ethernet 0/1
Ethernet0/1 is up, line protocol is up
  Hardware is Lance, address is 0000.0c47.abea (bia
    0000.0c47.abea)
  Internet address is 172.16.60.1/24
  MTU 1500 bytes, BW 10000 Kbit, DLY 1000 usec, rely
    255/255,    load 28/255
  Encapsulation ARPA, loopback not set, keepalive set
    (10 sec)
  ARP type: ARPA, ARP Timeout 04:00:00
  Last input 00:00:00, output 00:00:00, output hang never
  Last clearing of "show interface" counters 00:00:11
  Queueing strategy: fifo
  Output queue 0/40, 0 drops; input queue 0/75, 0 drops
  5 minute input rate 1381000 bits/sec, 723 packets/sec
  5 minute output rate 1126000 bits/sec, 418 packets/sec
     8291 packets input, 1933415 bytes, 0 no buffer
     Received 3 broadcasts, 0 runts, 0 giants
     0 input errors, 0 CRC, 0 frame, 0 overrun, 0 ignored,
       0 abort
     0 input packets with dribble condition detected
     7172 packets output, 1446188 bytes, 0 underruns
     0 output errors, 251 collisions, 0 interface resets
     0 babbles, 0 late collision, 265 deferred
     0 lost carrier, 0 no carrier
     0 output buffer failures, 0 output buffers swapped out
Router_C#
Router_C#show interface ethernet 0/1
Ethernet0/1 is up, line protocol is up
  Hardware is Lance, address is 0000.0c47.abea (bia
    0000.0c47.abea)
  Internet address is 172.16.60.1/24
  MTU 1500 bytes, BW 10000 Kbit, DLY 1000 usec, rely
    255/255,    load 28/255
```

```
Encapsulation ARPA, loopback not set, keepalive set
  (10 sec)
ARP type: ARPA, ARP Timeout 04:00:00
Last input 00:00:00, output 00:00:00, output hang never
Last clearing of "show interface" counters 00:00:49
Queueing strategy: fifo
Output queue 0/40, 0 drops; input queue 0/75, 0 drops
5 minute input rate 1392000 bits/sec, 735 packets/sec
5 minute output rate 1114000 bits/sec, 425 packets/sec
    39411 packets input, 8957876 bytes, 0 no buffer
    Received 14 broadcasts, 0 runts, 0 giants
    0 input errors, 0 CRC, 0 frame, 0 overrun, 0 ignored,
      0 abort
    0 input packets with dribble condition detected
    38944 packets output, 6409017 bytes, 0 underruns
    0 output errors, 1556 collisions, 0 interface resets
    0 babbles, 0 late collision, 1368 deferred
    0 lost carrier, 0 no carrier
    0 output buffer failures, 0 output buffers swapped out
Router_C#
Router_C#show interface ethernet 0/1
Ethernet0/1 is up, line protocol is up
  Hardware is Lance, address is 0000.0c47.abea (bia
    0000.0c47.abea)
  Internet address is 172.16.60.1/24
  MTU 1500 bytes, BW 10000 Kbit, DLY 1000 usec, rely
    255/255,    load 28/255
  Encapsulation ARPA, loopback not set, keepalive set
    (10  sec)
  ARP type: ARPA, ARP Timeout 04:00:00
  Last input 00:00:00, output 00:00:00, output hang never
  Last clearing of "show interface" counters 00:01:16
  Queueing strategy: fifo
  Output queue 0/40, 0 drops; input queue 0/75, 0 drops
  5 minute input rate 1396000 bits/sec, 742 packets/sec
  5 minute output rate 1110000 bits/sec, 434 packets/sec
    60752 packets input, 13691996 bytes, 0 no buffer
```

```
    Received 22 broadcasts, 0 runts, 0 giants
    0 input errors, 0 CRC, 0 frame, 0 overrun, 0 ignored,
      0 abort
    0 input packets with dribble condition detected
    65212 packets output, 10035669 bytes, 0 underruns
    0 output errors, 2466 collisions, 0 interface resets
    0 babbles, 0 late collision, 2163 deferred
    0 lost carrier, 0 no carrier
    0 output buffer failures, 0 output buffers swapped out
Router_C#
Router_C#show interface ethernet 0/1
Ethernet0/1 is up, line protocol is up
  Hardware is Lance, address is 0000.0c47.abea (bia
  0000.0c47.abea)
  Description: 10BaseT to Core3
  Internet address is 172.16.60.1/24
  MTU 1500 bytes, BW 10000 Kbit, DLY 1000 usec, rely
  255/255, load 28/255
  Encapsulation ARPA, loopback not set, keepalive set
  (10 sec)
  ARP type: ARPA, ARP Timeout 04:00:00
  Last input 00:00:00, output 00:00:00, output hang never
  Last clearing of "show interface" counters 00:01:42
  Queueing strategy: fifo
  Output queue 0/40, 0 drops; input queue 0/75, 0 drops
  5 minute input rate 1415000 bits/sec, 753 packets/sec
  5 minute output rate 1135000 bits/sec, 442 packets/sec
    81784 packets input, 18845458 bytes, 0 no buffer
    Received 29 broadcasts, 0 runts, 0 giants
    0 input errors, 0 CRC, 0 frame, 0 overrun, 0 ignored,
      0 abort
    0 input packets with dribble condition detected
    97408 packets output, 14297058 bytes, 0 underruns
    0 output errors, 3498 collisions, 0 interface resets
    0 babbles, 0 late collision, 2986 deferred
    0 lost carrier, 0 no carrier
    0 output buffer failures, 0 output buffers swapped out
Router_C#
```

Collision percentage calculations result in an average of 3.72 percent collisions. This is much better than the 15 percent you saw previously. In this scenario, a bad transceiver was to blame for the excessive collisions.

Troubleshooting Token Ring Problems

The Token Ring scenarios in this section focus on troubleshooting Token Ring problems. Both scenarios may be effectively solved by using generic Cisco troubleshooting commands.

Scenario #1

Figure 13.7 displays the Token Ring network that is used for this scenario. You can see Routers A and B connected via Token Ring interfaces.

FIGURE 13.7 Network diagram for Token Ring scenario #1 and #2

You are connecting Router A to Router B via the Token Ring interfaces, and you cannot get the interfaces to come up. You have console access to both routers.

List Observations

You must now gather information from both routers that will allow you to create a problem statement. You start by gathering information from Router A.

```
Router_A#show interface tokenring 0
TokenRing0 is up, line protocol is down
```

```
Hardware is TMS380, address is 0007.787c.e14b (bia
  0007.787c.e14b)
Internet address is 172.16.30.1, subnet mask is
  255.255.255.0
MTU 4464 bytes, BW 4000 Kbit, DLY 630 usec, rely
  255/255,    load 1/255
Encapsulation SNAP, loopback not set, keepalive set
  (10 sec)
ARP type: SNAP, ARP Timeout 04:00:00
Ring speed: 4 Mbps
Single ring node, Source Route Transparent Bridge capable
Ethernet Transit OUI: 0x000000
Last input never, output never, output hang never
Last clearing of "show interface" counters never
Queueing strategy: fifo
Output queue 0/40, 0 drops; input queue 0/75, 0 drops
5 minute input rate 0 bits/sec, 0 packets/sec
5 minute output rate 0 bits/sec, 0 packets/sec
    0 packets input, 0 bytes, 0 no buffer
    Received 0 broadcasts, 0 runts, 0 giants
    0 input errors, 0 CRC, 0 frame, 0 overrun, 0 ignored,
      0 abort
    0 packets output, 0 bytes, 0 underruns
    0 output errors, 0 collisions, 0 interface resets
    0 output buffer failures, 0 output buffers swapped out
    1 transition
```

Nothing looks wrong, so get a copy of the configuration.

```
Router_A#show running-config
Building configuration...
Current configuration:
!
version 11.2
no service password-encryption
no service udp-small-servers
service tcp-small-servers
!
hostname Router_A
```

```
!
enable password aloha
!
interface Ethernet0
 no ip address
 shutdown
!
interface Serial0
 ip address 172.16.20.6 255.255.255.252
 shutdown
 clockrate 4000000
 dce-terminal-timing-enable
!
interface Serial1
 no ip address
 shutdown
!
interface TokenRing0
 ip address 172.16.30.1 255.255.255.0
 ring-speed 4
!
router eigrp 100
 network 172.16.0.0
!
ip classless
!
line con 0
line aux 0
 transport input all
line vty 0 4
 password aloha
 login
!
end
Router_A#
```

Everything seems to be configured properly. Now, move on to the console of Router B. First, issue a show interface command:

```
Router_B#show interface tokenring 0
TokenRing0 is up, line protocol is down
  Hardware is TMS380, address is 0007.787c.e1cb (bia
    0007.787c.e1cb)
  Internet address is 172.16.30.2, subnet mask is
    255.255.255.0
  MTU 4464 bytes, BW 16000 Kbit, DLY 630 usec, rely
    255/255,    load 1/255
  Encapsulation SNAP, loopback not set, keepalive set
    (10  sec)
  ARP type: SNAP, ARP Timeout 04:00:00
  Ring speed: 16 Mbps
  Single ring node, Source Route Transparent Bridge capable
  Ethernet Transit OUI: 0x000000
  Last input never, output never, output hang never
  Last clearing of "show interface" counters never
  Queueing strategy: fifo
  Output queue 0/40, 0 drops; input queue 0/75, 0 drops
  5 minute input rate 0 bits/sec, 0 packets/sec
  5 minute output rate 0 bits/sec, 0 packets/sec
     0 packets input, 0 bytes, 0 no buffer
     Received 0 broadcasts, 0 runts, 0 giants
     0 input errors, 0 CRC, 0 frame, 0 overrun, 0 ignored,
       0 abort
     0 packets output, 0 bytes, 0 underruns
     0 output errors, 0 collisions, 0 interface resets
     0 output buffer failures, 0 output buffers swapped out
     2 transitions
```

Now you should be able to distinguish some differences and pinpoint the problem. There are two fields within this output that differ from the output from Router A. The first hint is to look at the interface metrics. The second hint is to look at the ring speed.

Now, list the observations:

- The Token Ring interfaces on Routers A and B are in an up/down state.

- Router A ring speed is set to 4Mbps.

- Router B ring speed is set to 16Mbps.

The problem statement is "The ring speeds for Routers A and B are different."

Propose Solutions

The solution for this case is straightforward. Change the ring speed on Router A to match the ring speed on Router B. The configuration follows:

```
Router_A(config)#interface tokenring 0
Router_A(config-if)#ring-speed 16
Router_A(config-if)#^Z
Router_A#
```

Now, verify the interface status. The interface should be in an up and up state:

```
Router_A#show interface tokenring 0
TokenRing0 is up, line protocol is up
  Hardware is TMS380, address is 0007.787c.e14b (bia
    0007.787c.e14b)
  Internet address is 172.16.30.1, subnet mask is
    255.255.255.0
  MTU 4464 bytes, BW 16000 Kbit, DLY 630 usec, rely
    255/255,    load 1/255
  Encapsulation SNAP, loopback not set, keepalive set
    (10 sec)
  ARP type: SNAP, ARP Timeout 04:00:00
  Ring speed: 16 Mbps
  Single ring node, Source Route Transparent Bridge capable
  Ethernet Transit OUI: 0x000000
  Last input never, output never, output hang never
  Last clearing of "show interface" counters never
  Queueing strategy: fifo
  Output queue 0/40, 0 drops; input queue 0/75, 0 drops
  5 minute input rate 0 bits/sec, 0 packets/sec
  5 minute output rate 0 bits/sec, 0 packets/sec
     0 packets input, 0 bytes, 0 no buffer
```

```
Received 0 broadcasts, 0 runts, 0 giants
0 input errors, 0 CRC, 0 frame, 0 overrun, 0 ignored,
   0 abort
0 packets output, 0 bytes, 0 underruns
0 output errors, 0 collisions, 0 interface resets
0 output buffer failures, 0 output buffers swapped out
3 transitions
```

The interface is now up, and you can ping the interface on Router B:

```
Router_A#ping 172.16.30.2
Type escape sequence to abort.
Sending 5, 100-byte ICMP Echos to 172.16.30.2, timeout is
  2   seconds:
!!!!!
Success rate is 100 percent (5/5)
```

Scenario #2

Use the same network diagram found in Figure 13.7. The scenario is the same in that you cannot get the interface on Router A or B to initialize. The problem is different, so use Token Ring commands to find and solve the problem.

List Observations

The first command you issue on Router A is a show interface to0. The results follow:

```
Router_A#show interface tokenring 0
TokenRing0 is down, line protocol is down
  Hardware is TMS380, address is 0007.787c.e14b (bia
  0007.787c.e14b)
  Internet address is 172.16.30.1, subnet mask is
  255.255.255.0
  MTU 4464 bytes, BW 16000 Kbit, DLY 630 usec, rely
  255/255,    load 1/255
  Encapsulation SNAP, loopback not set, keepalive set
  (10 sec)
  ARP type: SNAP, ARP Timeout 04:00:00
  Ring speed: 16 Mbps
```

```
Single ring node, Source Route Transparent Bridge capable
Ethernet Transit OUI: 0x000000
Last input never, output never, output hang never
Last clearing of "show interface" counters never
Queueing strategy: fifo
Output queue 0/40, 0 drops; input queue 0/75, 0 drops
5 minute input rate 0 bits/sec, 0 packets/sec
5 minute output rate 0 bits/sec, 0 packets/sec
   0 packets input, 0 bytes, 0 no buffer
   Received 0 broadcasts, 0 runts, 0 giants
   0 input errors, 0 CRC, 0 frame, 0 overrun, 0 ignored,
      0 abort
   0 packets output, 0 bytes, 0 underruns
   0 output errors, 0 collisions, 0 interface resets
   0 output buffer failures, 0 output buffers swapped out
   5 transitions
```

The fact that the physical interface is down indicates a Layer 1 or Layer 2 problem. The line protocol indicates a Layer 2 or Layer 3 problem. In this case, if there is a Physical layer problem, the upper layers do not work. Troubleshooting the upper layers is a waste of time until the lower layer problems are resolved.

Propose Solutions

The principal observation is that there is a physical problem with the interface. Review the Token Ring architecture so you can create an action plan. Figure 13.8 depicts the manner in which a station connects via Token Ring.

FIGURE 13.8 Token Ring topology

You can see that from the Token Ring NIC on the station, the lobe wire connects to a multistation access unit, or MAU. The MAU is similar to an Ethernet hub. Therefore, there are three physical pieces to look at: NIC, cable, and MAU.

The action plan is to inspect each of these elements. Start with the easiest part—inspect the cable, inspect the MAU, and then inspect the NIC.

Assume that the NIC is functioning properly, and the cable tested clean. That leaves the MAU. There can be two problems: the cable connection between the NIC and MAU was not connected properly, or there is something wrong with the MAU itself. The MAU can have a variety of problems—it can have a bad port or it may not have been initialized.

The action plan is to reconnect the cable, change ports on the MAU, and verify that the MAU has been initialized.

Once the physical problem is resolved, the interface should change to interface up. The line protocol status depends on whether there are existing problems with the configuration.

Summary

Y ou will encounter several common problems with routers in general as well as Ethernet and Token Ring protocols when you are troubleshooting network issues. Most of these common problems are found to be on Layer 2 and Layer 1; however, occasionally some are Layer 3 problems. And many have simple solutions. For instance, problems may be solved by verifying that the correct IP address is assigned, that the correct DLCI is used, or that the Frame Relay DLCI-to-IP address mapping is correct, or by removing the administrative shutdown on an interface.

The boot mode on a router contains no routing functionality. Therefore, when a router comes up in boot mode, either by error or due to a problem, you need to take steps to return it to normal operation. Specifically, make sure you have the correct image in flash, change the configuration register to indicate that the system image should be loaded from flash, and then reload the router.

A couple of problems are common in the Ethernet environment. An encapsulation mismatch on a segment will preclude the mismatched devices from communicating with each other. When there is an Ethernet frame encapsulation mismatch, an easy way to determine the encapsulation type the host is using is to allow the host machine to ARP for the router. The router then records the frame type in the ARP table. Another issue in Ethernet is a high number of collisions. When there are a high number of collisions on a segment that is not being heavily utilized, a hardware problem is usually the culprit. In many of these cases, replacing the transceiver will correct the issue. Note that collisions are not excessive until they are over five to eight percent.

As was the case with Ethernet, a couple of common issues occur with Token Ring, such as ring speed mismatches and faulty MAUs. You can easily correct ring speed mismatches in the configuration of the router or offending device. Faulty MAUs, however, require you to replace the malfunctioning equipment too, thus requiring you to be onsite.

Exam Essentials

Know the show commands and how to interpret the output. Specifically, in this chapter we focused on show arp, show flash, show frame-relay pvc, show frame-relay map, show interface, and show version.

Know the seven steps to the Cisco troubleshooting model as well as the function that each performs. These steps are: define the problem, gather detailed information, consider possible scenarios, create an action plan, implement the action plan, observe the results of the implementation, and repeat if necessary. These steps define an effective step-by-step methodology for troubleshooting any problem.

Be able to apply the Cisco troubleshooting methodology to example situations. You should know how to apply each step of the model in real-life scenarios. You should be able to determine what step in a troubleshooting scenario is next in the series or to correlate a task with the correct step in the process.

Know how to use the ping and traceroute commands. This includes IPX and AppleTalk ping as well as the extended ping and traceroute options available under privileged mode.

Know the general steps that are required to identify and rectify a Physical layer issue.   Using the output of show commands referenced above, know what symptoms are characteristic of a physical issue and what possible components can be causing the problem.

Commands Used in This Chapter

The following list contains a summary of all the commands used in this chapter.

Command	Description
clear counters	Clears the interface counters for easier viewing of new interface statistics.
frame-relay map	Statically maps DLCI information to a Layer 3 address.
ping	Executes the ICMP reachability test.
show arp	Displays the contents of the ARP table.
show ip arp	Displays only IP information in the ARP table.
show flash	Displays the contents of the system flash, such as the IOS and any other files that may be present.
show frame-relay pvc	Shows information about the Frame Relay PVC on a router.
show frame-relay map	Shows the DLCI to Layer 3 mappings, both static and dynamic, on a router.
show interface	Lists the configuration details, status, and statistics for the interface.
show ip route	Displays the contents of the IP route table as well as the default gateway for the router.
show running-config	Displays the contents of the running configuration of the router.
show version	Displays the current IOS, hardware configuration, reason for last reload, and system uptime.
tracert	The trace command used in the Windows operating system. Provides a step-by-step ICMP trace from source to destination.

Review Questions

1. What do the following lines mean?

   ```
   Router_A#show interface ethernet 0/0
   Ethernet0/0 is up, line protocol is down
   ```

   A. The physical interface is receiving keepalive packets from the transceiver.

   B. The interface is actually down because the line protocol is down.

   C. The interface will work on Layer 2.

   D. None of the above.

2. What command would check for a missing host when troubleshooting a TCP connection?

   A. `show user`

   B. `show ip route`

   C. `show ip arp`

   D. `show host <ip address>`

3. What command is used to display the ARP table? (Choose all that apply.)

   A. `show ip arp`

   B. `show Ethernet arp`

   C. `show interface arp`

   D. `show arp`

4. Which generic troubleshooting tool is used to test for reachability and connectivity?

   A. Traceroute

   B. Debug

   C. Ping

   D. None of the above

5. What does it mean when the router is in "boot" mode?

   A. The IOS system image was loaded from the boot ROM or from BootFLASH.

   B. The IOS system image was loaded from RAM.

   C. The IOS system image was loaded from flash.

   D. The IOS system image was loaded from a BootP server.

6. How can the router be removed from boot mode?

   A. Reboot it.

   B. Change the configuration register so the system image is loaded from a source other than the boot ROM.

   C. Change the configuration by adding the `no system boot` command.

   D. None of the above.

7. Which of the following statements is accurate about a router that is in boot mode?

   A. It will route traffic as usual.

   B. It will not route traffic.

   C. It will not allow you to change the configuration register.

   D. Only traffic with high priority and established flows will be routed.

8. Which ARP types does a Cisco router recognize? (Choose all that apply.)

   A. ARPA

   B. SNAP

   C. HP

   D. Probe

9. How can the ARP type be changed on a Cisco router?

    A. By using the global command `arp type <type>`

    B. By issuing the interface command `arp <type>`

    C. By issuing the interface command `arp type <type>`

    D. By issuing the global command `arp <type>`

10. How do you calculate the collision percentage for an Ethernet interface?

    A. (collisions/input packets) * 100

    B. (collisions/interface resets) * 100

    C. (collisions/output packets) * 100

    D. (collisions/output rate bps) * 100

11. What physical device can be responsible for excessive collisions? (Choose all that apply.)

    A. Transceiver

    B. CSU/DSU

    C. Ethernet interface

    D. None of the above

12. What are the two ring speeds allowed for Token Ring? (Choose two.)

    A. 2Mbps

    B. 4Mbps

    C. 8Mbps

    D. 16Mbps

13. How is the ring speed changed on the token ring interface?

    A. By issuing the global command `ring speed <4 or 16>`

    B. By issuing the interface command `ring speed <4 or 16>`

    C. By issuing the global command `ring-speed <4 or 16>`

    D. By issuing the interface command `ring-speed <4 or 16>`

14. You execute multiple `show interface` commands on a particular interface and see the number of overruns incrementing. What does this mean?

    A. There are packets larger than the MTU size arriving at the interface.

    B. The interface is receiving data faster than it can send it to the hardware buffer.

    C. The interface is transmitting packets faster than it receives them from the hardware buffer.

    D. The hardware buffers are full.

15. What troubleshooting tool is used to test for step-by-step path connectivity?

    A. Debug

    B. Ping

    C. Traceroute

    D. CDP

16. What is the purpose of listing observations? (Choose all that apply.)

    A. To define the problem

    B. To create an action plan

    C. To diagnose the problem

    D. To resolve the problem

17. What is the purpose of proposing solutions?

    A. It is equivalent to considering possibilities.

    B. It is equivalent to creating an action plan.

    C. It is equivalent to defining the problem.

    D. It is equivalent to the iteration process.

18. Why should you clear the counters on an interface you are trouble-shooting?

   A. By clearing the counters, you may clear the problem that you are investigating.

   B. Clearing the counters flushes any corrupt packets from the interface.

   C. Clearing the counters creates a reference point.

   D. The show interface command will not work if the interface isn't cleared first.

19. What command would be used to see the last time the counters on a router were cleared?

   A. show cdp neighbor

   B. show counters

   C. show interface

   D. show running-config

20. You are troubleshooting a memory problem on a router and execute the show memory command. What information from the output are you specifically looking for? (Choose two.)

   A. Total bytes

   B. Free bytes

   C. Used bytes

   D. Lowest bytes

   E. Largest bytes

Answers to Review Questions

1. B.   Even though the interface says that it is up, if the line protocol is down, the interface will not function and therefore is actually down.

2. C.   The `show ip arp` command will show if the Layer 2 to Layer 3 correlation has been made for a host. You could also use `show arp`.

3. A, D.   Both of these commands may be used to display the ARP table.

4. C.   Ping is the tool that is used specifically to test for reachability and connectivity.

5. A.   Boot mode is caused when the image has to be loaded from the boot ROM and no other images are available or the configuration register was set to read only from the boot ROM.

6. B.   Rebooting will not help if the configuration register is still set to tell the router to only boot from the boot ROM. Option C is invalid syntax and as such would result in an error message if entered.

7. B.   No routing protocols run on the boot image for a router; therefore, it is unable to route traffic.

8. A, B, D.   The valid ARP types are ARPA, SNAP, and Probe. HP is not a valid ARP type.

9. B.   The correct syntax is described by B.

10. C.   Collisions are based on output packets.

11. A, C.   Collisions are characteristics of the Ethernet protocol. Any devices involved in an Ethernet connection can contribute to collisions.

12. B, D.   The two valid ring speeds are 4Mbps and 16Mbps.

13. D.   D represents the correct syntax for changing the ring speed.

14. B.   Answer C is an underrun and D is an ignore.

15. C.   Traceroute, or trace, is the tool used to test for each hop in the path to the destination.

16. A.   Listing observations is similar to gathering facts. Fact gathering is done to aid in the formation of a problem statement, thereby defining the problem.

17. B.   Proposing solutions is the same as creating an action plan of possible solutions.

18. C.   It is easier to watch for incrementing counters when they have been reset to zero.

19. C.   There is a line in the `show interface` output that shows the last time the counters for that interface were cleared—specifically, `Last clearing of "show interface" counters 00:01:42`.

20. B, D.   When looking at a potential memory issue, the two most important fields to look at first are the lowest and free bytes. This information will tell you if the router is or has been running out of memory.

Glossary

10BaseT Part of the original IEEE 802.3 standard, 10BaseT is the Ethernet specification of 10Mbps baseband that uses two pairs of twisted-pair, Category 3, 4, or 5 cabling—using one pair to send data and the other to receive. 10BaseT has a distance limit of about 100 meters per segment. *See also*: *Ethernet* and *IEEE 802.3.*

100BaseT Based on the IEEE 802.3u standard, 100BaseT is the Fast Ethernet specification of 100Mbps baseband that uses UTP wiring. 100BaseT sends link pulses (containing more information than those used in 10BaseT) over the network when no traffic is present. *See also: 10BaseT, Fast Ethernet*, and *IEEE 802.3.*

100BaseTX Based on the IEEE 802.3u standard, 100BaseTX is the 100Mbps baseband Fast Ethernet specification that uses two pairs of UTP or STP wiring. The first pair of wires receives data; the second pair sends data. To ensure correct signal timing, a 100BaseTX segment cannot be longer than 100 meters.

802.1q *See: IEEE 802.1.*

A&B bit signaling Used in T1 transmission facilities and sometimes called "24th channel signaling." Each of the 24 T1 subchannels in this procedure uses one bit of every sixth frame to send supervisory signaling information.

AAL ATM Adaptation Layer: A service-dependent sublayer of the Data-Link layer which accepts data from other applications and brings it to the ATM layer in 48-byte ATM payload segments. CS and SAR are the two sublayers that form AALs. Currently, the four types of AAL recommended by the ITU-T are AAL1, AAL2, AAL3/4, and AAL5. AALs are differentiated by the source-destination timing they use, whether they are CBR or VBR, and whether they are used for connection-oriented or connectionless mode data transmission. *See also: AAL1, AAL2, AAL3/4, AAL5, ATM*, and *ATM layer.*

AAL1 ATM Adaptation Layer 1: One of four AALs recommended by the ITU-T, it is used for connection-oriented, time-sensitive services that need constant bit rates, such as isochronous traffic and uncompressed video. *See also: AAL.*

AAL2 ATM Adaptation Layer 2: One of four AALs recommended by the ITU-T, it is used for connection-oriented services that support a variable bit rate, such as voice traffic. *See also: AAL.*

AAL3/4 ATM Adaptation Layer 3/4: One of four AALs (a product of two initially distinct layers) recommended by the ITU-T, supporting both connectionless and connection-oriented links. Its primary use is in sending SMDS packets over ATM networks. *See also: AAL.*

AAL5 ATM Adaptation Layer 5: One of four AALs recommended by the ITU-T, it is used to support connection-oriented VBR services primarily to transfer classical IP over ATM and LANE traffic. This least complex of the AAL recommendations uses SEAL (Simple Efficient ATM Layer), offering lower bandwidth costs and simpler processing requirements but also providing reduced bandwidth and error-recovery capacities. *See also: AAL.*

AARP AppleTalk Address Resolution Protocol: The protocol in an Apple-Talk stack that maps data-link addresses to network addresses.

AARP probe packets Packets sent by the AARP to determine whether a given node ID is being used by another node in a nonextended AppleTalk network. If the node ID is not in use, the sending node appropriates that node's ID. If the node ID is in use, the sending node will select a different ID and then send out more AARP probe packets. *See also: AARP.*

ABM Asynchronous Balanced Mode: When two stations can initiate a transmission, ABM is an HDLC (or one of its derived protocols) communication technology that supports peer-oriented, point-to-point communications between both stations.

ABR Area Border Router: An OSPF router that is located on the border of one or more OSPF areas. ABRs are used to connect OSPF areas to the OSPF backbone area.

access layer One of the layers in Cisco's three-layer hierarchical model. The access layer provides users with access to the internetwork.

access link A link used with switches; it is only part of one Virtual LAN (VLAN). Trunk links carry information from multiple VLANs.

access list A set of test conditions kept by routers that determines "interesting traffic" to and from the router for various services on the network.

access method The manner in which network devices approach gaining access to the network itself.

access server   Also known as a network access server; a communications process connecting asynchronous devices to a LAN or WAN through network and terminal-emulation software, providing synchronous or asynchronous routing of supported protocols.

acknowledgment   Verification sent from one network device to another signifying that an event has occurred. May be abbreviated as ACK. *Contrast with: NAK.*

ACR   Allowed cell rate: A designation defined by the ATM Forum for managing ATM traffic. Dynamically controlled using congestion control measures, the ACR varies between the minimum cell rate (MCR) and the peak cell rate (PCR). *See also: MCR and PCR.*

action plan   A list of steps or procedures used to resolve a network problem. This plan should possess four characteristics: make one change at a time, make non-impacting changes, do not compromise security, and have a procedure to back out of any changes made.

active monitor   The mechanism used to manage a Token Ring. The network node with the highest MAC address on the ring becomes the active monitor and is responsible for management tasks such as preventing loops and ensuring tokens are not lost.

address learning   Used with transparent bridges to learn the hardware addresses of all devices on an internetwork. The switch then filters the network with the known hardware (MAC) addresses.

address mapping   By translating network addresses from one format to another, this methodology permits different protocols to operate interchangeably.

address mask   A bit combination descriptor identifying which portion of an address refers to the network or subnet and which part refers to the host. Sometimes simply called the mask. *See also: subnet mask.*

address resolution   The process used for resolving differences between computer addressing schemes. Address resolution typically defines a method for tracing Network layer (Layer 3) addresses to Data-Link layer (Layer 2) addresses. *See also: address mapping.*

adjacency   The relationship made between defined neighboring routers, using a common media segment, to exchange routing information.

adjacency table   A table that contains all active/existing adjacencies of neighboring routers.

administrative distance   A number between 0 and 255 that expresses the value of trustworthiness of a routing information source. The lower the number, the higher the integrity rating.

administrative weight   A value designated by a network administrator to rate the preference given to a network link. It is one of four link metrics exchanged by PTSPs to test ATM network resource availability.

ADSU   ATM Data Service Unit: The terminal adapter used to connect to an ATM network through an HSSI-compatible mechanism. *See also: DSU.*

advertising   The process whereby routing or service updates are transmitted at given intervals, allowing other routers on the network to maintain a record of viable routes.

AEP   AppleTalk Echo Protocol: A test for connectivity between two Apple-Talk nodes where one node sends a packet to another and receives an echo, or copy, in response.

AFI   Authority and Format Identifier: The part of an NSAP ATM address that delineates the type and format of the IDI section of an ATM address.

AFP   AppleTalk Filing Protocol: A Presentation-layer protocol, supporting AppleShare and Mac OS File Sharing, that permits users to share files and applications on a server.

AIP   ATM Interface Processor: Supporting AAL3/4 and AAL5, this interface for Cisco 7000 series routers minimizes performance bottlenecks at the UNI. *See also: AAL3/4 and AAL5.*

algorithm   A set of rules or a process used to solve a problem. In networking, algorithms are typically used for finding the best route for traffic from a source to its destination.

alignment error   An error occurring in Ethernet networks, in which a received frame has extra bits—that is, a number not divisible by eight. Alignment errors are generally the result of frame damage caused by collisions.

all-routes explorer packet   An explorer packet that can move across an entire SRB network, tracing all possible paths to a given destination. Also known as an all-rings explorer packet. *See also: explorer packet, local explorer packet*, and *spanning explorer packet.*

AM   Amplitude Modulation: A modulation method that represents information by varying the amplitude of the carrier signal. *See also: modulation.*

AMI   Alternate Mark Inversion: A line-code type on T1 and E1 circuits that shows zeros as "01" during each bit cell, and ones as "11" or "00," alternately, during each bit cell. The sending device must maintain ones density in AMI but not independently of the data stream. Also known as binary-coded, alternate mark inversion. *Contrast with: B8ZS. See also: ones density.*

amplitude   An analog or digital waveform's highest value.

analog transmission   Signal messaging whereby information is represented by various combinations of signal amplitude, frequency, and phase.

ANSI   American National Standards Institute: The organization of corporate, government, and other volunteer members that coordinates standards-related activities, approves U.S. national standards, and develops U.S. positions in international standards organizations. ANSI assists in the creation of international and U.S. standards in disciplines such as communications, networking, and a variety of technical fields. It publishes over 13,000 standards, for engineered products and technologies ranging from screw threads to networking protocols. ANSI is a member of the IEC and ISO.

anycast   An ATM address that can be shared by more than one end system, allowing requests to be routed to a node that provides a particular service.

API   Application Programming Interface: A standardized connection point for use by applications on a system. This connection point allows multiple different applications on a system to access data in a controlled manner that does not affect the overall functioning of the system.

AppleTalk   Currently in two versions, the group of communication protocols designed by Apple Computer for use in Macintosh environments. The earlier Phase 1 protocols support one physical network with only one network number that resides in one zone. The later Phase 2 protocols support more than one logical network on a single physical network, allowing networks to exist in more than one zone. *See also: zone, AARP (AppleTalk Address Resolution Protocol).*

Application layer   Layer 7 of the OSI reference network model, supplying services to application procedures (such as electronic mail or file transfer) that are outside the OSI model. This layer chooses and determines the availability of communicating partners along with the resources necessary to make the connection, coordinates partnering applications, and forms a consensus on procedures for controlling data integrity and error recovery.

ARA   AppleTalk Remote Access: A protocol for Macintosh users establishing their access to resources and data from a remote AppleTalk location.

area   A logical, rather than physical, set of segments (based on CLNS, DECnet, or OSPF) along with their attached devices. Areas are commonly connected to others using routers to create a single autonomous system. *See also: autonomous system.*

ARM   Asynchronous Response Mode: An HDLC communication mode using one primary station and at least one additional station, in which transmission can be initiated from either the primary unit or one of the secondary units.

ARP   Address Resolution Protocol: Defined in RFC 826, the protocol that traces IP addresses to MAC addresses. *See also: RARP.*

ASBR   Autonomous System Boundary Router: An area border router placed between an OSPF autonomous system and a non-OSPF network that operates both OSPF and an additional routing protocol, such as RIP. ASBRs must be located in a non-stub OSPF area. *See also: ABR, non-stub area,* and *OSPF.*

ASCII   American Standard Code for Information Interchange: An 8-bit code for representing characters, consisting of seven data bits plus one parity bit.

ASICs   Application-Specific Integrated Circuits: Used in Layer 2 switches to make filtering decisions. The ASIC looks in the filter table of MAC addresses and determines which port the destination hardware address of a received hardware address is destined for. The frame will be allowed to traverse only that one segment. If the hardware address is unknown, the frame is forwarded out all ports.

ASN.1   Abstract Syntax Notation One: An OSI language used to describe types of data that is independent of computer structures and depicting methods. Described by ISO International Standard 8824.

ASP   AppleTalk Session Protocol: A protocol employing ATP to establish, maintain, and tear down sessions, as well as sequence requests. *See also: ATP.*

AST   Automatic Spanning Tree: A function that supplies one path for spanning explorer frames traveling from one node in the network to another, supporting the automatic resolution of spanning trees in SRB networks. AST is based on the IEEE 802.1 standard. *See also: IEEE 802.1 and SRB.*

asynchronous transmission   Digital signals sent without precise timing, usually with different frequencies and phase relationships. Asynchronous transmissions generally enclose individual characters in control bits (called start and stop bits) that show the beginning and end of each character. *Contrast with: isochronous transmission* and *synchronous transmission.*

ATCP   AppleTalk Control Program: The protocol for establishing and configuring AppleTalk over PPP, defined in RFC 1378. *See also: PPP.*

ATDM   Asynchronous Time-Division Multiplexing: A technique for sending information, it differs from normal TDM in that the time slots are assigned when necessary rather than preassigned to certain transmitters. *Contrast with: FDM, statistical multiplexing,* and *TDM.*

ATG   Address Translation Gateway: The mechanism within Cisco DECnet routing software that enables routers to route multiple, independent DECnet networks and to establish a user-designated address translation for chosen nodes between networks.

ATM   Asynchronous Transfer Mode: The international standard, identified by fixed-length 53-byte cells, for transmitting cells in multiple service systems such as voice, video, or data. Transit delays are reduced because the fixed-length cells permit processing to occur in the hardware. ATM is designed to maximize the benefits of high-speed transmission media, such as SONET, E3, and T3.

ATM ARP server   A device that supplies logical subnets running classical IP over ATM with address-resolution services.

ATM endpoint   The initiating or terminating connection in an ATM network. ATM endpoints include servers, workstations, ATM-to-LAN switches, and ATM routers.

ATM Forum   The international organization founded jointly by Northern Telecom, Sprint, Cisco Systems, and NET/ADAPTIVE in 1991 to develop and promote standards-based implementation agreements for ATM technology. The ATM Forum broadens official standards developed by ANSI and ITU-T and creates implementation agreements before official standards are published.

ATM layer   A sublayer of the Data-Link layer in an ATM network that is service independent. To create standard 53-byte ATM cells, the ATM layer receives 48-byte segments from the AAL and attaches a 5-byte header to each. These cells are then sent to the Physical layer for transmission across the physical medium. *See also: AAL.*

ATM user-user connection   A connection made by the ATM layer to supply communication between at least two ATM service users, such as ATMM processes. These communications can be uni- or bidirectional, using one or two VCCs, respectively. *See also: ATM layer and ATMM.*

ATMM   ATM Management: A procedure that runs on ATM switches, managing rate enforcement and VCI translation. *See also: ATM.*

ATP   AppleTalk Transaction Protocol: A transport-level protocol that enables reliable transactions between two sockets, where one requests the other to perform a given task and to report the results. ATP fastens the request and response together, assuring a loss-free exchange of request-response pairs.

attenuation   In communication, weakening or loss of signal energy, typically caused by distance.

AURP   AppleTalk Update-based Routing Protocol: A technique for encapsulating AppleTalk traffic in the header of a foreign protocol that allows the connection of at least two noncontiguous AppleTalk internetworks through a foreign network (such as TCP/IP) to create an AppleTalk WAN. The connection made is called an AURP tunnel. By exchanging routing information between exterior routers, the AURP maintains routing tables for the complete AppleTalk WAN. *See also: AURP tunnel.*

AURP tunnel   A connection made in an AURP WAN that acts as a single, virtual link between AppleTalk internetworks separated physically by a foreign network such as a TCP/IP network. *See also: AURP.*

authority zone   A portion of the domain-name tree associated with DNS for which one name server is the authority. *See also: DNS.*

auto duplex   A setting on Layer-1 and -2 devices that sets the duplex of a switch port automatically.

automatic call reconnect   A function that enables automatic call rerouting away from a failed trunk line.

autonomous confederation   A collection of self-governed systems that depend more on their own network accessibility and routing information than on information received from other systems or groups.

autonomous switching   The ability of Cisco routers to process packets more quickly by using the ciscoBus to switch packets independently of the system processor.

autonomous system (AS)   A group of networks under mutual administration that share the same routing methodology. Autonomous systems are subdivided by areas and must be assigned an individual 16-bit number by the IANA. *See also: area.*

autoreconfiguration   A procedure executed by nodes within the failure domain of a Token Ring, wherein nodes automatically perform diagnostics, trying to reconfigure the network around failed areas.

auxiliary port   The console port on the back of Cisco routers that allows you to dial the router and make console configuration settings.

B8ZS   Binary 8-Zero Substitution: A line-code type, interpreted at the remote end of the connection, that uses a special code substitution whenever eight consecutive zeros are transmitted over the link on T1 and E1 circuits. This technique assures ones density independent of the data stream. Also known as bipolar 8-zero substitution. *Contrast with: AMI. See also: ones density.*

B channel   Bearer channel: A full-duplex, 64Kbps channel in ISDN that transmits user data. *Compare with: D channel, E channel,* and *H channel.*

back end A node or software program supplying services to a front end. *See also: server.*

backbone The basic portion of the network that provides the primary path for traffic sent to and initiated from other networks.

bandwidth The gap between the highest and lowest frequencies employed by network signals. More commonly, it refers to the rated throughput capacity of a network protocol or medium.

baseband A feature of a network technology that uses only one carrier frequency—for example, Ethernet. Also named "narrowband." *Compare with: broadband.*

baseline Baseline information includes historical data about the network and routine utilization information. This information can be used to determine whether there were recent changes made to the network that may contribute to the problem at hand.

Basic Management Setup Used with Cisco routers when in setup mode. Only provides enough management and configuration to get the router working so someone can telnet into the router and configure it.

baud Synonymous with bits per second (bps), if each signal element represents one bit. It is a unit of signaling speed equivalent to the number of separate signal elements transmitted per second.

beacon An FDDI device or Token Ring frame that points to a serious problem with the ring, such as a broken cable. The beacon frame carries the address of the station thought to be down. *See also: failure domain.*

BECN Backward Explicit Congestion Notification: BECN is the bit set by a Frame Relay network in frames moving away from frames headed into a congested path. A DTE that receives frames with the BECN may ask higher-level protocols to take necessary flow-control measures. *Compare with: FECN.*

BGP4 Border Gateway Protocol Version 4: Version 4 of the interdomain routing protocol most commonly used on the Internet. BGP4 supports CIDR and uses route-counting mechanisms to decrease the size of routing tables. *See also: CIDR.*

binary A two-character numbering method that uses ones and zeros. The binary numbering system underlies all digital representation of information.

BIP Bit Interleaved Parity: A method used in ATM to monitor errors on a link, sending a check bit or word in the link overhead for the previous block or frame. This allows bit errors in transmissions to be found and delivered as maintenance information.

BISDN Broadband ISDN: ITU-T standards created to manage high-bandwidth technologies such as video. BISDN presently employs ATM technology along SONET-based transmission circuits, supplying data rates between 155Mbps and 622Mbps and beyond. Contrast with N-ISDN. *See also: BRI, ISDN*, and *PRI.*

bit-oriented protocol Regardless of frame content, the class of Data-Link layer communication protocols that transmits frames. Bit-oriented protocols, as compared with byte-oriented, supply more efficient and trustworthy, full-duplex operation. *Compare with: byte-oriented protocol.*

blue alarm A blue alarm on a T1 or E1 indicates a total absence of signal. The signal keeps the circuit synchronized by sending all ones.

Boot ROM Used in routers to put the router into bootstrap mode. Bootstrap mode then boots the device with an operating system. The ROM can also hold a small Cisco IOS.

bootstrap protocol A protocol used to dynamically assign IP address and gateway to requesting clients.

border gateway A router that facilitates communication with routers in different autonomous systems.

boundary of dysfunctionality The limit or scope of the network problem. This boundary lies between areas where the network is functioning properly and where it ceases to function.

BPDU Bridge Protocol Data Unit: A Spanning-Tree Protocol initializing packet that is sent at definable intervals for the purpose of exchanging information among bridges in networks.

breakout boxes These items are used to verify pin-outs (e.g., TD—transmit data, RD—receive data, CTS—clear to send) for all types of serial and parallel connections.

BRI   ISDN Basic Rate Interface: ISDN BRI was designed to provide digital services over existing pairs of copper. The service is used for videoconferencing, voice services, data, and out-of-band management. In addition, the D-channel function of BRI is used for replacement of legacy X.25 networks. *ISDN BRI* is a 192Kbps circuit that is divided into three distinct channels. The two primary data channels are the B channels. Each B channel provides 64Kbps. The third channel provides 16Kbps of bandwidth for commands and signaling, and is referred to as the D channel. *Compare with: PRI. See also: BISDN.*

bridge   A device for connecting two segments of a network and transmitting packets between them. Both segments must use identical protocols to communicate. Bridges function at the Data-Link layer, Layer 2 of the OSI reference model. The purpose of a bridge is to filter, send, or flood any incoming frame, based on the MAC address of that particular frame.

broadband   A transmission methodology for multiplexing several independent signals onto one cable. In telecommunications, broadband is classified as any channel with bandwidth greater than 4kHz (typical voice grade). In LAN terminology, it is classified as a coaxial cable on which analog signaling is employed. Also known as wideband. *Contrast with: baseband.*

broadcast   A data frame or packet that is transmitted to every node on the local network segment (as defined by the broadcast domain). Broadcasts are known by their broadcast address, which is a destination network and host address with all the bits turned on. Also called "local broadcast." *Compare with: directed broadcast.*

broadcast domain   A group of devices receiving broadcast frames initiating from any device within the group. Because they do not forward broadcast frames, broadcast domains are generally surrounded by routers.

broadcast storm   An undesired event on the network caused by the simultaneous transmission of a large number of broadcasts across the network segment. Such an occurrence can overwhelm network bandwidth, resulting in time-outs.

browsing   In a Windows 95/98/NT environment, available resources are shown in the Network Neighborhood through the use of browsing. The browser structure is hierarchical in nature, with one device per segment, called a master browser, that serves as an authoritative resource for that segment. In addition, there can also be a domain master browser configured for a domain that collects all information for the NT domain and distributes this as necessary to the master browsers. Browsing is designed to be automatic and not require administrative support. *See also: domain master browser, master browser, and Network Neighborhood.*

buffer   A storage area dedicated to handling data while in transit. Buffers are used to receive/store sporadic deliveries of data bursts, usually received from faster devices, compensating for the variations in processing speed. Incoming information is stored until everything is received prior to sending data on. Also known as an information buffer.

bus topology   A linear LAN architecture in which transmissions from various stations on the network are reproduced over the length of the medium and are accepted by all other stations. *Compare with: ring topology* and *star topology.*

bus   Any physical path, typically wires or copper, through which a digital signal can be used to send data from one part of a computer to another.

BUS   Broadcast and unknown servers: In LAN emulation, the hardware or software responsible for resolving all broadcasts and packets with unknown (unregistered) addresses into the point-to-point virtual circuits required by ATM. *See also: LANE, LEC, LECS,* and *LES.*

BX.25   AT&T's use of X.25. *See also: X.25.*

bypass mode   An FDDI and Token Ring network operation that deletes an interface.

bypass relay   A device that enables a particular interface in the Token Ring to be closed down and effectively taken off the ring.

byte-oriented protocol   Any type of data-link communication protocol that, in order to mark the boundaries of frames, uses a specific character from the user character set. These protocols have generally been superseded by bit-oriented protocols. *Compare with: bit-oriented protocol.*

cable range   In an extended AppleTalk network, the range of numbers allotted for use by existing nodes on the network. The value of the cable range can be anywhere from a single to a sequence of several touching network numbers. Node addresses are determined by their cable range value.

cable testers   A family of apparatus that are used to verify media integrity and connectivity. Several different devices can be considered cable testers

CAC   Connection Admission Control: The sequence of actions executed by every ATM switch while connection setup is performed in order to determine if a request for connection is violating the guarantees of QoS for established connections. Also, CAC is used to route a connection request through an ATM network.

call admission control   A device for managing traffic in ATM networks, determining the possibility of a path containing adequate bandwidth for a requested VCC.

call priority   In circuit-switched systems, the defining priority given to each originating port; it specifies in which order calls will be reconnected. Additionally, call priority identifies which calls are allowed during a bandwidth reservation.

call set-up time   The length of time necessary to effect a switched call between DTE devices.

CBR   Constant Bit Rate: An ATM Forum QoS class created for use in ATM networks. CBR is used for connections that rely on precision clocking to guarantee trustworthy delivery. *Compare with: ABR* and *VBR*.

CCO   Cisco Connection Online: The Cisco website, CCO, is the repository for information regarding Cisco products, networking technology, configuration examples, troubleshooting tools, and network planning. CCO has two access levels. The first is guest privilege, which does not require a login account. This level provides general product and company information. The second level is for registered Cisco users who have purchased a Cisco support contract, or are sponsored by a Cisco Authorized Partner. This level provides all information available to the guest level, in-depth detailed technical documentation, access to download Cisco IOS images, trouble-ticket queries, and so on.

CD   Carrier Detect: A signal indicating that an interface is active or that a connection generated by a modem has been established.

CDP   Cisco Discovery Protocol: Cisco's proprietary protocol that is used to tell a neighbor Cisco device about the type of hardware, software version, and active interfaces that the Cisco device is using. It uses a SNAP frame between devices and is not routable.

CDVT   Cell Delay Variation Tolerance: A QoS parameter for traffic management in ATM networks specified when a connection is established. The allowable fluctuation levels for data samples taken by the PCR in CBR transmissions are determined by the CDVT. *See also: CBR and PCR.*

cell   In ATM networking, the basic unit of data for switching and multiplexing. Cells have a defined length of 53 bytes, including a 5-byte header that identifies the cell's data stream and 48 bytes of payload. *See also: cell relay.*

cell payload scrambling   The method by which an ATM switch maintains framing on some medium-speed edge and trunk interfaces (T3 or E3 circuits). Cell payload scrambling rearranges the data portion of a cell to maintain the line synchronization with certain common bit patterns.

cell relay   A technology that uses small packets of fixed size, known as cells. Their fixed length enables cells to be processed and switched in hardware at high speeds, making this technology the foundation for ATM and other high-speed network protocols. *See also: cell.*

Centrex   A local exchange carrier service, providing local switching that resembles that of an onsite PBX. Centrex has no onsite switching capability. Therefore, all customer connections return to the CO. *See also: CO.*

CER   Cell Error Ratio: The ratio in ATM of transmitted cells having errors to the total number of cells sent in a transmission within a certain span of time.

channelized E1   Operating at 2.048Mpbs, an access link that is sectioned into 29 B-channels and one D-channel, supporting DDR, Frame Relay, and X.25. *Compare with: channelized T1.*

channelized T1   Operating at 1.544Mbps, an access link that is sectioned into 23 B-channels and 1 D-channel of 64Kbps each, where individual channels or groups of channels connect to various destinations, supporting DDR, Frame Relay, and X.25. *Compare with: channelized E1.*

CHAP   Challenge Handshake Authentication Protocol: Supported on lines using PPP encapsulation, it is a security feature that identifies the remote end, helping keep out unauthorized users. After CHAP is performed, the router or access server determines whether a given user is permitted access. It is a newer, more secure protocol than PAP. *Compare with: PAP.*

checksum A test for ensuring the integrity of sent data. It is a number calculated from a series of values taken through a sequence of mathematical functions, typically placed at the end of the data from which it is calculated, and then recalculated at the receiving end for verification. *Compare with: CRC.*

choke packet When congestion exists, it is a packet sent to inform a transmitter that it should decrease its sending rate.

CIDR Classless Interdomain Routing: A method supported by classless routing protocols, such as OSPF and BGP4, based on the concept of ignoring the IP class of address. This permits route aggregation and VLSM, enabling routers to combine routes in order to minimize the routing information that needs to be conveyed by the primary routers. It allows a group of IP networks to appear to other networks as a unified, larger entity. In CIDR, IP addresses and their subnet masks are written as four dotted octets, followed by a forward slash and the numbering of masking bits (a form of subnet notation shorthand). *See also: BGP4.*

CIP Channel Interface Processor: A channel attachment interface for use in Cisco 7000-series routers that connects a host mainframe to a control unit. This device eliminates the need for a front-end processor (FEP) to attach channels.

CIR Committed Information Rate: Averaged over a minimum span of time and measured in bps, a Frame Relay network's agreed-upon minimum rate of transferring information.

circuit switching Used with dial-up networks such as PPP and ISDN. Passes data, but needs to set up the connection first—just like making a phone call.

Cisco Connection Documentation CD-ROM The CD is the collection of technical documentation, available on CCO as well as the Documentation CD, which accompanies new Cisco equipment purchases. Both forms of the technical documentation are very helpful for providing critical information regarding Cisco products, networking technologies, and configuration examples.

Cisco Connection Family The Cisco Connection Family is a collection of interactive electronic media that is intended to provide technical assistance and support for Cisco products and networking technologies. There are five members of the Cisco Connection family: Cisco Connection Online (CCO), Cisco Technical Assistance and Software Center, Cisco Connection Consultant Tools CD-ROM, Cisco Commerce Agents, and Cisco MarketPlace.

Cisco Express Forwarding   Cisco Express Forwarding (CEF) is a switching function, designed for high-end backbone routers. It functions on Layer 3 of the OSI model, and its biggest asset is the capability to remain stable in a large network. However, it's also more efficient than both the fast and optimum default switching paths.

Cisco FRAD   Cisco Frame-Relay Access Device: A Cisco product that supports Cisco IPS Frame Relay SNA services, connecting SDLC devices to Frame Relay without requiring an existing LAN. May be upgraded to a fully functioning multiprotocol router. Can activate conversion from SDLC to Ethernet and Token Ring, but does not support attached LANs. *See also: FRAD.*

CiscoFusion   Cisco's name for the internetworking architecture under which its Cisco IOS operates. It is designed to "fuse" together the capabilities of its disparate collection of acquired routers and switches.

Cisco IOS software   Cisco Internet Operating System software: The kernel of the Cisco line of routers and switches that supplies shared functionality, scalability, and security for all products under its CiscoFusion architecture. *See also: CiscoFusion.*

CiscoSecure   Cisco's AAA tool. It works with both RADIUS and TACACS clients and can authenticate using an authentication database, NT credentials, or token passthrough.

Cisco Technical Assistance Center   The TAC provides support for Cisco contract holders, gives warranty service, and can even bill you directly if you do not have a Cisco maintenance contract.

CiscoView   GUI-based management software for Cisco networking devices, enabling dynamic status, statistics, and comprehensive configuration information. Displays a physical view of the Cisco device chassis and provides device-monitoring functions and fundamental troubleshooting capabilities. May be integrated with a number of SNMP-based network management platforms.

CiscoWorks   CiscoWorks combines several different Cisco management tools into one consolidated package. It can be used for monitoring, managing, and troubleshooting in a Cisco internetwork.

Class A network   Part of the Internet Protocol hierarchical addressing scheme. Class A networks have only 8 bits for defining networks and 24 bits for defining hosts on each network.

Class B network   Part of the Internet Protocol hierarchical addressing scheme. Class B networks have 16 bits for defining networks and 16 bits for defining hosts on each network.

Class C network   Part of the Internet Protocol hierarchical addressing scheme. Class C networks have 24 bits for defining networks and only 8 bits for defining hosts on each network.

classical IP over ATM   Defined in RFC 1577, the specification for running IP over ATM that maximizes ATM features. Also known as CIA.

classless routing   Routing that sends subnet mask information in the routing updates. Classless routing allows Variable-Length Subnet Mask (VLSM) and supernetting. Routing protocols that support classless routing are RIP version 2, EIGRP, and OSPF.

CLI   Command-line interface: Allows you to configure Cisco routers and switches with maximum flexibility.

CLP   Cell Loss Priority: The area in the ATM cell header that determines the likelihood of a cell being dropped during network congestion. Cells with CLP = 0 are considered insured traffic and are not apt to be dropped. Cells with CLP = 1 are considered best-effort traffic that may be dropped during congested episodes, delivering more resources to handle insured traffic.

CLR   Cell Loss Ratio: The ratio of discarded cells to successfully delivered cells in ATM. CLR can be designated a QoS parameter when establishing a connection.

CO   Central Office: The local telephone company office where all loops in a certain area connect and where circuit switching of subscriber lines occurs.

collapsed backbone   A nondistributed backbone where all network segments are connected to each other through an internetworking device. A collapsed backbone can be a virtual network segment at work in a device such as a router, hub, or switch.

collision The effect of two nodes sending transmissions simultaneously in Ethernet. When they meet on the physical media, the frames from each node collide and are damaged. *See also: collision domain.*

collision domain The network area in Ethernet over which frames that have collided will spread. Collisions are propagated by hubs and repeaters, but not by LAN switches, routers, or bridges. *See also: collision.*

composite metric Used with routing protocols, such as IGRP and EIGRP, that use more than one metric to find the best path to a remote network. IGRP and EIGRP both use bandwidth and delay of the line by default. However, Maximum Transmission Unit (MTU), load, and reliability of a link can be used as well.

configuration register A 16-bit configurable value stored in hardware or software that determines how Cisco routers function during initialization. In hardware, the bit position is set using a jumper. In software, it is set by specifying specific bit patterns used to set start-up options, configured using a hexadecimal value with configuration commands.

congestion Traffic that exceeds the network's ability to handle it.

congestion avoidance To minimize delays, the method an ATM network uses to control traffic entering the system. Lower-priority traffic is discarded at the edge of the network when indicators signal it cannot be delivered, thus using resources efficiently.

congestion collapse The situation that results from the retransmission of packets in ATM networks where little or no traffic successfully arrives at destination points. It usually happens in networks made of switches with ineffective or inadequate buffering capabilities combined with poor packet discard or ABR congestion feedback mechanisms.

connection ID Identifications given to each Telnet session into a router. The show sessions command will give you the connections that a local router will have to a remote router. The show users command will show the connection IDs of users telnetted into your local router.

connectionless   Data transfer that occurs without the creating of a virtual circuit. No overhead, best-effort delivery, not reliable. *Contrast with: connection-oriented. See also: virtual circuit.*

connection-oriented   Data transfer method that sets up a virtual circuit before any data is transferred. Uses flow and error control for reliable data transfer. *Contrast with: connectionless. See also: virtual circuit.*

console port   Typically an RJ-45 port on a Cisco router and switch that allows command-line interface capability.

control direct VCC   One of three control connections defined by Phase 1 LAN emulation; a bidirectional virtual control connection (VCC) established in ATM by an LEC to an LES. *See also: control distribute VCC.*

control distribute VCC   One of three control connections defined by Phase 1 LAN emulation; a unidirectional virtual control connection (VCC) set up in ATM from an LES to an LEC. Usually, the VCC is a point-to-multipoint connection. *See also: control direct VCC.*

convergence   The process required for all routers in an internetwork to update their routing tables and create a consistent view of the network, using the best possible paths. No user data is passed during a convergence time.

core layer   Top layer in the Cisco three-layer hierarchical model, which helps you design, build, and maintain Cisco hierarchical networks. The core layer passes packets quickly to distribution-layer devices only. No packet filtering should take place at this layer.

cost   An arbitrary value, based on hop count, bandwidth, or other calculation, that is typically assigned by a network administrator and used by the routing protocol to compare different routes through an internetwork. Routing protocols use cost values to select the best path to a certain destination: the lowest cost identifies the best path. Also known as path cost. *See also: routing metric.*

count to infinity   A problem occurring in routing algorithms that are slow to converge where routers keep increasing the hop count to particular networks. To avoid this problem, various solutions have been implemented into each of the different routing protocols. Some of those solutions include defining a maximum hop count (defining infinity), route poisoning, poison reverse, and split horizon.

CPCS   Common Part Convergence Sublayer: One of two AAL sublayers that is service-dependent, it is further segmented into the CS and SAR sublayers. The CPCS prepares data for transmission across the ATM network; it creates the 48-byte payload cells that are sent to the ATM layer. *See also: AAL* and *ATM layer.*

CPE   Customer Premises Equipment: Items such as telephones, modems, and terminals installed at customer locations and connected to the telephone company network.

crankback   In ATM, a correction technique used when a node somewhere on a chosen path cannot accept a connection setup request, blocking the request. The path is rolled back to an intermediate node, which then uses GCAC to attempt to find an alternate path to the final destination.

CRC   Cyclic redundancy check: A methodology that detects errors, whereby the frame recipient makes a calculation by dividing frame contents with a prime binary divisor and compares the remainder to a value stored in the frame by the sending node. *Contrast with: checksum.*

CSMA/CD   Carrier Sense Multiple Access with Collision Detection. A technology defined by the Ethernet IEEE 802.3 committee. Each device senses the cable for a digital signal before transmitting. Also, CSMA/CD allows all devices on the network to share the same cable, but one at a time. If two devices transmit at the same time, a frame collision will occur and a jamming pattern will be sent; the devices will stop transmitting, wait a predetermined amount of time, and then try to transmit again.

CSU   Channel Service Unit: A digital mechanism that connects end-user equipment to the local digital telephone loop. Frequently referred to along with the data service unit as CSU/DSU. *See also: DSU.*

CTD   Cell Transfer Delay: For a given connection in ATM, the time period between a cell exit event at the source user-network interface (UNI) and the corresponding cell entry event at the destination. The CTD between these points is the sum of the total inter-ATM transmission delay and the total ATM processing delay.

cut-through frame switching   A frame-switching technique that flows data through a switch so that the leading edge exits the switch at the output port before the packet finishes entering the input port. Frames will be read, processed, and forwarded by devices that use cut-through switching as soon as the destination address of the frame is confirmed and the outgoing port is identified.

D channel   (1) Data channel: A full-duplex, 16Kbps (BRI) or 64Kbps (PRI) ISDN channel. *Compare with: B channel, E channel*, and *H channel*. (2) In SNA, anything that provides a connection between the processor and main storage with any peripherals.

data direct VCC   A bidirectional point-to-point virtual control connection (VCC) set up between two LECs in ATM and one of three data connections defined by Phase 1 LAN emulation. Because data direct VCCs do not guarantee QoS, they are generally reserved for UBR and ABR connections. *Compare with: control distribute VCC* and *control direct VCC*.

data frame   Protocol Data Unit encapsulation at the Data-Link layer of the OSI reference model. Encapsulates packets from the Network layer and prepares the data for transmission on a network medium.

datagram   A logical collection of information transmitted as a Network layer unit over a medium without a previously established virtual circuit. IP datagrams have become the primary information unit of the Internet. At various layers of the OSI reference model, the terms *cell, frame, message, packet*, and *segment* also define these logical information groupings.

data link control layer   Layer 2 of the SNA architectural model, it is responsible for the transmission of data over a given physical link and compares somewhat to the Data-Link layer of the OSI model.

Data-Link layer   Layer 2 of the OSI reference model, it ensures the trustworthy transmission of data across a physical link and is primarily concerned with physical addressing, line discipline, network topology, error notification, ordered delivery of frames, and flow control. The IEEE has further segmented this layer into the MAC sublayer and the LLC sublayer. Also known as the Link layer. Can be compared somewhat to the data link control layer of the SNA model. *See also: Application layer, LLC, MAC, Network layer, Physical layer, Presentation layer, Session layer*, and *Transport layer*.

DCC   Data Country Code: Developed by the ATM Forum, one of two ATM address formats designed for use by private networks. *Compare with: ICD*.

DCE Data communications equipment (as defined by the EIA) or data circuit-terminating equipment (as defined by the ITU-T): The mechanisms and links of a communications network that make up the network portion of the user-to-network interface, such as modems. The DCE supplies the physical connection to the network, forwards traffic, and provides a clocking signal to synchronize data transmission between DTE and DCE devices. *Compare with: DTE.*

DDP Datagram Delivery Protocol: Used in the AppleTalk suite of protocols as a connectionless protocol that is responsible for sending datagrams through an internetwork.

DDR Dial-on-demand routing: A technique that allows a router to automatically initiate and end a circuit-switched session per the requirements of the sending station. By mimicking keepalives, the router fools the end station into treating the session as active. DDR permits routing over ISDN or telephone lines via a modem or external ISDN terminal adapter.

DE Discard Eligibility: Used in Frame Relay networks to tell a switch that a frame can be discarded if the switch is too busy. The DE is a field in the frame that is turned on by transmitting routers if the Committed Information Rate (CIR) is oversubscribed or set to 0.

debug The Cisco IOS command that provides the administrator with low-level, detailed information about processes that run on the router.

default route The static routing table entry used to direct frames whose next hop is not spelled out in the dynamic routing table.

delay The time elapsed between a sender's initiation of a transaction and the first response they receive. Also, the time needed to move a packet from its source to its destination over a path. *See also: latency.*

demarc The demarcation point between the customer premises equipment (CPE) and the telco's carrier equipment.

demodulation A series of steps that return a modulated signal to its original form. When receiving, a modem demodulates an analog signal to its original digital form (and, conversely, modulates the digital data it sends into an analog signal). *See also: modulation.*

demultiplexing The process of converting a single multiplex signal, comprising more than one input stream, back into separate output streams. *See also: multiplexing.*

designated bridge In the process of forwarding a frame from a segment to the route bridge, the bridge with the lowest path cost.

designated port Used with the Spanning-Tree Protocol (STP) to designate forwarding ports. If there are multiple links to the same network, STP will shut a port down to stop network loops.

designated router An OSPF router that creates LSAs for a multi-access network and is required to perform other special tasks in OSPF operations. Multi-access OSPF networks that maintain a minimum of two attached routers identify one router that is chosen by the OSPF Hello protocol, which makes possible a decrease in the number of adjacencies necessary on a multi-access network. This in turn reduces the quantity of routing protocol traffic and the physical size of the database.

destination address The address for the network devices that will receive a packet.

DHCP Dynamic Host Configuration Protocol; DHCP is a superset of the BootP protocol. This means that it uses the same protocol structure as BootP, but it has enhancements added. Both of these protocols use servers that dynamically configure clients when requested. The two major enhancements are address pools and lease times.

dialer map statements Configuration statements that link network addresses to ISDN numbers.

directed broadcast A data frame or packet that is transmitted to a specific group of nodes on a remote network segment. Directed broadcasts are known by their broadcast address, which is a destination subnet address with all the bits turned on.

discovery mode Also known as dynamic configuration, this technique is used by an AppleTalk interface to gain information from a working node about an attached network. The information is subsequently used by the interface for self-configuration.

distance-vector routing algorithm In order to find the shortest path, this group of routing algorithms repeats on the number of hops in a given route, requiring each router to send its complete routing table with each update, but only to its neighbors. Routing algorithms of this type tend to generate loops, but they are fundamentally simpler than their link-state counterparts. *See also: link-state routing algorithm* and *SPF.*

distribute lists   These lists are references to access-lists and are applied to interfaces via a routing protocol.

distributed switching   Distributed switching happens on the VIP (Versatile Interface Processor) cards (which have a switching processor onboard), so it's very efficient. All required processing is done right on the VIP processor, which maintains a copy of the router's routing cache.

distribution layer   Middle layer of the Cisco three-layer hierarchical model, which helps you design, install, and maintain Cisco hierarchical networks. The distribution layer is the point where access layer devices connect. Routing is performed at this layer.

divide-by-half troubleshooting   Troubleshooting method in which a point between two ends of a network problem is used as a troubleshooting reference point. Either half may be investigated first, thus narrowing down the trouble location.

DLCI   Data-Link Connection Identifier: Used to identify virtual circuits in a Frame Relay network.

DNS   Domain Name System: Used to resolve host names to IP addresses.

domain master browser   Browser that collects and disseminates information from the master browsers in the domain. This information is used to identify resources in the domain and can be used with Windows 95/98/NT networks. *See also: browsing, master browser, and Network Neighborhood.*

DSAP   Destination Service Access Point: The service access point of a network node, specified in the destination field of a packet. *See also: SSAP* and *SAP.*

DSR   Data Set Ready: When a DCE is powered up and ready to run, this EIA/TIA-232 interface circuit is also engaged.

DSU   Data Service Unit: This device is used to adapt the physical interface on a data terminal equipment (DTE) mechanism to a transmission facility such as T1 or E1 and is also responsible for signal timing. It is commonly grouped with the channel service unit and referred to as the CSU/DSU. *See also: CSU.*

DTE   Data terminal equipment: Any device located at the user end of a user-network interface serving as a destination, a source, or both. DTE includes devices such as multiplexers, protocol translators, and computers. The connection to a data network is made through data channel equipment (DCE) such as a modem, using the clocking signals generated by that device. *See also: DCE.*

DTR   Data terminal ready: An activated EIA/TIA-232 circuit communicating to the DCE the state of preparedness of the DTE to transmit or receive data.

DUAL   Diffusing Update Algorithm: Used in Enhanced IGRP, this convergence algorithm provides loop-free operation throughout an entire route's computation. DUAL grants routers involved in a topology revision the ability to synchronize simultaneously, while routers unaffected by this change are not involved. *See also: Enhanced IGRP.*

DVMRP   Distance Vector Multicast Routing Protocol: Based primarily on the Routing Information Protocol (RIP), this Internet gateway protocol implements a common, condensed-mode IP multicast scheme, using IGMP to transfer routing datagrams between its neighbors. *See also: IGMP.*

DXI   Data Exchange Interface: Described in RFC 1482, DXI defines the effectiveness of a network device such as a router, bridge, or hub to act as an FEP to an ATM network by using a special DSU that accomplishes packet encapsulation.

dynamic entries   Used in Layer-2 and -3 devices to create a table of either hardware addresses or logical addresses dynamically.

dynamic routing   Also known as adaptive routing, this technique automatically adapts to traffic or physical network revisions.

dynamic VLAN   An administrator will create an entry in a special server with the hardware addresses of all devices on the internetwork. The server will then assign dynamically used VLANs.

E1   Generally used in Europe, a wide-area digital transmission scheme carrying data at 2.048Mbps. E1 transmission lines are available for lease from common carriers for private use.

E.164   (1) Evolved from standard telephone numbering system, the standard recommended by ITU-T for international telecommunication numbering, particularly in ISDN, SMDS, and BISDN. (2) Label of field in an ATM address containing numbers in E.164 format.

E channel   Echo channel: A 64Kbps ISDN control channel used for circuit switching. Specific description of this channel can be found in the 1984 ITU-T ISDN specification, but was dropped from the 1988 version. *See also: B, D, and H channels.*

EARL   Encoded Address Recognition Logic ASIC: This chip works with the bus arbitration system to control access to the data-switching bus. EARL also controls the destination ports of packet transfers.

edge device   A device that enables packets to be forwarded between legacy interfaces (such as Ethernet and Token Ring) and ATM interfaces based on information in the Data-Link and Network layers. An edge device does not take part in the running of any Network layer routing protocol; it merely uses the route description protocol in order to get the forwarding information required.

EEPROM   Electronically Erasable Programmable Read-Only Memory: Programmed after their manufacture, these nonvolatile memory chips can be erased if necessary using electric power and reprogrammed. *See also: EPROM, flash, flash memory, PROM.*

EFCI   Explicit Forward Congestion Indication: A congestion feedback mode permitted by ABR service in an ATM network. The EFCI may be set by any network element that is in a state of immediate or certain congestion. The destination end-system is able to carry out a protocol that adjusts and lowers the cell rate of the connection based on value of the EFCI. *See also: ABR.*

EIGRP   *See: Enhanced IGRP.*

EIP   Ethernet Interface Processor: A Cisco 7000 series router interface processor card, supplying 10Mbps AUI ports to support Ethernet Version 1 and Ethernet Version 2 or IEEE 802.3 interfaces with a high-speed data path to other interface processors.

ELAN   Emulated LAN: An ATM network configured using a client/server model in order to emulate either an Ethernet or Token Ring LAN. Multiple

ELANs can exist at the same time on a single ATM network and are made up of a LAN emulation client (LEC), a LAN Emulation Server (LES), a Broadcast and Unknown Server (BUS), and a LAN Emulation Configuration Server (LECS). ELANs are defined by the LANE specification. *See also: LANE, LEC, LECS, and LES.*

ELAP   EtherTalk Link Access Protocol: In an EtherTalk network, the link-access protocol constructed above the standard Ethernet Data-Link layer.

encapsulation   The technique used by layered protocols in which a layer adds header information to the protocol data unit (PDU) from the layer above. As an example, in Internet terminology, a packet would contain a header from the Physical layer, followed by a header from the Network layer (IP), followed by a header from the Transport layer (TCP), followed by the application protocol data.

encryption   The conversion of information into a scrambled form that effectively disguises it to prevent unauthorized access. Every encryption scheme uses some well-defined algorithm, which is reversed at the receiving end by an opposite algorithm in a process known as decryption.

Enhanced IGRP   Enhanced Interior Gateway Routing Protocol: An advanced routing protocol created by Cisco, combining the advantages of link-state and distance-vector protocols. Enhanced IGRP has superior convergence attributes, including high operating efficiency. *See also: IGP, IGRP, OSPF, and RIP.*

enterprise network   A privately owned and operated network that joins most major locations in a large company or organization.

EPROM   Erasable Programmable Read-Only Memory: Programmed after their manufacture, these nonvolatile memory chips can be erased if necessary using high-power light and reprogrammed. *See also: EEPROM, flash, flash memory, PROM.*

error control   The control mechanism for verification of contiguous and non-erroneous packets.

ESF   Extended Superframe: Made up of 24 frames with 192 bits each, with the 193rd bit providing other functions including timing. An enhanced version of SF. *See also: SF.*

Ethernet   A baseband LAN specification created by the Xerox Corporation and then improved through joint efforts of Xerox, Digital Equipment Corporation, and Intel. Ethernet is similar to the IEEE 802.3 series standard and, using CSMA/CD, operates over various types of cables at 10Mbps. *Also called: DIX (Digital/Intel/Xerox) Ethernet. See also: 10BaseT, Fast Ethernet*, and *IEEE*.

EtherTalk   A data-link product from Apple Computer that permits Apple-Talk networks to be connected by Ethernet.

excess rate   In ATM networking, traffic exceeding a connection's insured rate. The excess rate is the maximum rate less the insured rate. Depending on the availability of network resources, excess traffic can be discarded during congestion episodes. *Compare with: maximum rate.*

expansion   The procedure of directing compressed data through an algorithm, restoring information to its original size.

expedited delivery   An option that can be specified by one protocol layer, communicating either with other layers or with the identical protocol layer in a different network device, requiring that identified data be processed faster.

explorer packet   An SNA packet transmitted by a source Token Ring device to find the path through a source-route-bridged network.

extended addressing   The technique used by AppleTalk Phase 2 to assign multiple network addresses to a single segment.

extended IP access list   IP access list that filters the network by logical address, protocol field in the Network layer header, and even the port field in the Transport layer header.

extended IPX access list   IPX access list that filters the network by logical IPX address, protocol field in the Network layer header, and even the socket number in the Transport layer header.

Extended Setup   Used in setup mode to configure the router with more detail than Basic Setup mode. Allows multiple-protocol support and interface configuration.

extended ping   The enhanced version of ping that allows user interaction to choose options when executing the ping command. This resource requires enable access to the router.

fact gathering   The process of using diagnostic tools to collect information specific to the network and network devices involved in a problem. Additional information should include data that excludes other possibilities and helps pinpoint the actual problem.

failure domain   The region in which a failure has occurred in a Token Ring network. When a station gains information that a serious problem, such as a cable break, has occurred with the network, it sends a beacon frame that includes the station reporting the failure, its Nearest Active Upstream Neighbor (NAUN), and everything between. This defines the failure domain. Beaconing then initiates the procedure known as autoreconfiguration. *See also: autoreconfiguration* and *beacon.*

fallback   In ATM networks, this mechanism is used for scouting a path if it isn't possible to locate one using customary methods. The device relaxes requirements for certain characteristics, such as delay, in an attempt to find a path that meets a certain set of the most important requirements.

Fast Ethernet   Any Ethernet specification with a speed of 100Mbps. Fast Ethernet is ten times faster than 10BaseT, while retaining qualities like MAC mechanisms, MTU, and frame format. These similarities make it possible for existing 10BaseT applications and management tools to be used on Fast Ethernet networks. Fast Ethernet is based on an extension of IEEE 802.3 specification (IEEE 802.3u). *Compare with: Ethernet. See also: 100BaseT, 100BaseTX,* and *IEEE.*

fast switching   A Cisco feature that uses a route cache to speed packet switching through a router. *Contrast with: process switching.*

FDM   Frequency-Division Multiplexing: A technique that permits information from several channels to be assigned bandwidth on one wire based on frequency. *See also: TDM, ATDM,* and *statistical multiplexing.*

FDDI   Fiber Distributed Data Interface: A LAN standard, defined by ANSI X3T9.5, that can run at speeds up to 200Mbps and uses token-passing media access on fiber-optic cable. For redundancy, FDDI can use a dual-ring architecture.

FECN   Forward Explicit Congestion Notification: A bit set by a Frame Relay network that informs the DTE receptor that congestion was encountered along the path from source to destination. A device receiving frames with the FECN bit set can ask higher-priority protocols to take flow-control action as needed. *See also: BECN.*

FEIP   Fast Ethernet Interface Processor: An interface processor employed on Cisco 7000 series routers, supporting up to two 100Mbps 100BaseT ports.

FIB   Forwarding Information Base: The FIB consists of information duplicated from the IP route table. Every time the routing information changes, the changes are propagated to the FIB.

firewall   A barrier purposely erected between any connected public networks and a private network, made up of a router or access server or several routers or access servers, that uses access lists and other methods to ensure the security of the private network.

flash   Electronically Erasable Programmable Read-Only Memory (EEPROM). Used to hold the Cisco IOS in a router by default. *See also: EPROM, EEPROM, flash memory.*

flash memory   Developed by Intel and licensed to other semiconductor manufacturers, it is nonvolatile storage that can be erased electronically and reprogrammed, physically located on an EEPROM chip. Flash memory permits software images to be stored, booted, and rewritten as needed. Cisco routers and switches use flash memory to hold the IOS by default. *See also: EPROM, EEPROM, flash.*

flat network   Network that is one large collision domain and one large broadcast domain.

flooding   Occurs when traffic is received on an interface and is then transmitted to every interface connected to that device with the exception of the interface from which the traffic originated. This technique is often used for traffic transfer by bridges, hubs, and switches throughout the network.

flow control   A methodology used to ensure that receiving units are not overwhelmed with data from sending devices. Pacing, as it is called in IBM networks, means that when buffers at a receiving unit are full, a message is transmitted to the sending unit to temporarily halt transmissions until all the data in the receiving buffer has been processed and the buffer is again ready for action.

FRAD   Frame Relay Access Device: Any device affording a connection between a LAN and a Frame Relay WAN. *See also: Cisco FRAD, FRAS.*

fragment   Any portion of a larger packet that has been segmented into smaller pieces. A packet fragment does not necessarily indicate an error and can be intentional. *See also: fragmentation.*

fragmentation   The process of intentionally segmenting a packet into smaller pieces when sending data over an intermediate network medium that cannot support the larger packet size.

FragmentFree   LAN switch type that reads into the data section of a frame to make sure fragmentation did not occur. Sometimes called modified cut-through.

frame   A logical unit of information sent by the Data-Link layer over a transmission medium. The term often refers to the header and trailer, employed for synchronization and error control, that surround the data contained in the unit.

Frame Relay   A more efficient replacement of the X.25 protocol (an unrelated packet-relay technology that guarantees data delivery). Frame Relay is an industry-standard, shared-access, best-effort, switched Data-Link layer encapsulation that services multiple virtual circuits and protocols between connected mechanisms.

Frame Relay bridging   Defined in RFC 1490, this bridging method uses the identical spanning-tree algorithm as other bridging operations but permits packets to be encapsulated for transmission across a Frame Relay network.

framing   Encapsulation at the Data-Link layer of the OSI model. It is called framing because the packet is encapsulated with both a header and a trailer.

FRAS   Frame Relay Access Support: A feature of Cisco IOS software that enables SDLC, Ethernet, Token Ring, and Frame Relay–attached IBM devices to be linked with other IBM mechanisms on a Frame Relay network. *See also: FRAD.*

frequency   The number of cycles of an alternating current signal per time unit, measured in hertz (cycles per second).

FSIP   Fast Serial Interface Processor: The Cisco 7000 routers' default serial interface processor, it provides four or eight high-speed serial ports.

FTP File Transfer Protocol: The TCP/IP protocol used for transmitting files between network nodes, it supports a broad range of file types and is defined in RFC 959. *See also: TFTP.*

full-duplex The capacity to simultaneously send and receive data between two network devices. *See also: half-duplex.*

full mesh A type of network topology where every node has either a physical or a virtual circuit linking it to every other network node. A full mesh supplies a great deal of redundancy but is typically reserved for network backbones because of its expense. *See also: partial mesh.*

GNS Get Nearest Server: On an IPX network, a request packet sent by a client for determining the location of the nearest active server of a given type. An IPX network client launches a GNS request to get either a direct answer from a connected server or a response from a router disclosing the location of the service on the internetwork. GNS is part of IPX and SAP. *See also: IPX and SAP.*

GRE Generic Routing Encapsulation: A tunneling protocol created by Cisco with the capacity for encapsulating a wide variety of protocol packet types inside IP tunnels, thereby generating a virtual point-to-point connection to Cisco routers across an IP network at remote points. IP tunneling using GRE permits network expansion across a single-protocol-backbone environment by linking multiprotocol subnetworks in a single-protocol-backbone environment.

guard band The unused frequency area found between two communications channels, furnishing the space necessary to avoid interference between the two.

H channel High-speed channel: A full-duplex, ISDN primary rate channel operating at a speed of 384Kbps. *See also: B, D*, and *E channels.*

half-duplex The capacity to transfer data in only one direction at a time between a sending unit and receiving unit. *See also: full-duplex.*

handshake Any series of transmissions exchanged between two or more devices on a network to ensure synchronized operations.

HDLC   High-level Data Link Control: Using frame characters, including checksums, HDLC designates a method for data encapsulation on synchronous serial links and is the default encapsulation for Cisco routers. HDLC is a bit-oriented synchronous Data-Link layer protocol created by ISO and derived from SDLC. However, most HDLC vendor implementations (including Cisco's) are proprietary. *See also: SDLC.*

helper address   The unicast address specified, which instructs the Cisco router to change the client's local broadcast request for a service into a directed unicast to the server.

hierarchical addressing   Any addressing plan employing a logical chain of commands to determine location. IP addresses are made up of a hierarchy of network numbers, subnet numbers, and host numbers to direct packets to the appropriate destination.

HIP   HSSI Interface Processor: An interface processor used on Cisco 7000 series routers, providing one HSSI port that supports connections to ATM, SMDS, Frame Relay, or private lines at speeds up to T3 or E3.

holddown   The state a route is placed in so that routers can neither advertise the route nor accept advertisements about it for a defined time period. Holddown is used to surface bad information about a route from all routers in the network. A route is generally placed in holddown when one of its links fails.

hop   The movement of a packet between any two network nodes. *See also: hop count.*

hop count   A routing metric that calculates the distance between a source and a destination. RIP employs hop count as its sole metric. *See also: hop and RIP.*

host address   Logical address configured by an administrator or server on a device. Logically identifies this device on an internetwork.

HSCI   High-Speed Communication Interface: Developed by Cisco, a single-port interface that provides full-duplex synchronous serial communications capability at speeds up to 52Mbps.

HSRP Hot Standby Router Protocol: A protocol that provides high network availability and provides nearly instantaneous hardware failover without administrator intervention. It generates a Hot Standby router group, including a lead router that lends its services to any packet being transferred to the Hot Standby address. If the lead router fails, it will be replaced by any of the other routers—the standby routers—that monitor it.

HSSI High-Speed Serial Interface: A network standard physical connector for high-speed serial linking over a WAN at speeds of up to 52Mbps.

hub A Physical layer device that is really just a multi-port repeater. When an electronic digital signal is received on a hub port, the signal is reamplified or regenerated and forwarded out all segments except the segment from which the signal was received.

ICD International Code Designator: Adapted from the subnetwork model of addressing, this assigns the mapping of Network layer addresses to ATM addresses. HSSI is one of two ATM formats for addressing created by the ATM Forum to be utilized with private networks. *See also: DCC.*

ICMP Internet Control Message Protocol: Documented in RFC 792, it is a Network layer Internet protocol for the purpose of reporting errors and providing information pertinent to IP packet procedures.

IEEE Institute of Electrical and Electronics Engineers: A professional organization that, among other activities, defines standards in a number of fields within computing and electronics, including networking and communications. IEEE standards are the predominant LAN standards used today throughout the industry. Many protocols are commonly known by the reference number of the corresponding IEEE standard.

IEEE 802.1 The IEEE committee specification that defines the bridging group. The specification for STP (Spanning-Tree Protocol) is IEEE 802.1d. The STP uses SPA (spanning-tree algorithm) to find and prevent network loops in bridged networks. The specification for VLAN trunking is IEEE 802.1q.

IEEE 802.3 The IEEE committee specification that defines the Ethernet group, specifically the original 10Mbps standard. Ethernet is a LAN protocol that specifies Physical layer and MAC sublayer media access. IEEE 802.3 uses CSMA/CD to provide access for many devices on the same network. FastEthernet is defined as 802.3u, and Gigabit Ethernet is defined as 802.3q. *See also: CSMA/CD.*

IEEE 802.5 The IEEE committee specification that defines Token Ring media access.

IGMP Internet Group Management Protocol: Employed by IP hosts, the protocol that reports their multicast group memberships to an adjacent multicast router.

ignore A Cisco IOS error, which can be caused in three ways: the hardware buffer fills up and it signals to the transmitting interface to throttle down; the interface is receiving frames faster than the SP can pull them off; the CxBus is so busy that the interface processor is unable to copy the packet from the hardware buffer to the SP buffers.

IGP Interior Gateway Protocol: Any protocol used by the Internet to exchange routing data within an independent system. Examples include RIP, IGRP, and OSPF.

IGRP Interior Gateway Routing Protocol: A Cisco proprietary routing protocol that uses a distance-vector algorithm. It uses a vector (a one-dimensional array) of information to calculate the best path. This vector consists of four elements: bandwidth, delay, load, reliability.

ILMI Integrated (or Interim) Local Management Interface: A specification created by the ATM Forum, designated for the incorporation of network-management capability into the ATM UNI. Integrated Local Management Interface cells provide for automatic configuration between ATM systems. In LAN emulation, ILMI can provide sufficient information for the ATM end station to find an LECS. In addition, ILMI provides the ATM NSAP (Network Service Access Point) prefix information to the end station.

in-band management In-band management is the management of a network device "through" the network. Examples include using Simple Network Management Protocol (SNMP) or Telnet directly via the local LAN. *Compare with: out-of-band management.*

input queues These queues reside on the RP, and they are used to link the SP buffers to the RP buffers. The queue reserves RP buffer space for a packet that was forwarded from the SP/SSP. If the Router Processor doesn't process the queued packets at the same rate, the queue fills up and the incoming packets are dropped.

inside-out troubleshooting   This method of troubleshooting directs the troubleshooter to start near the user and work their way toward the far end of the area of dysfunctionality.

insured burst   In an ATM network, it is the largest temporarily permitted data burst exceeding the insured rate on a PVC and not tagged by the traffic policing function for being dropped if network congestion occurs. This insured burst is designated in bytes or cells.

inter-area routing   Routing between two or more logical areas. *Contrast with: intra-area routing. See also: area.*

interface buffer   A buffer used for intermediate storage. Packets from all of the hardware buffers are copied to the interface buffers. The switch processor houses the intermediate buffers by using 512KB for the SP board memory. This memory is also shared with the autonomous switching cache.

interface processor   Any of several processor modules used with Cisco 7000 series routers. *See also: AIP, CIP, EIP, FEIP, HIP, MIP, and TRIP.*

Internet   The global "network of networks," whose popularity has exploded in the last few years. Originally a tool for collaborative academic research, it has become a medium for exchanging and distributing information of all kinds. The Internet's need to link disparate computer platforms and technologies has led to the development of uniform protocols and standards that have also found widespread use within corporate LANs. *See also: TCP/IP and MBONE.*

internet   Before the rise of the Internet, this lowercase form was shorthand for "internetwork" in the generic sense. Now rarely used. *See also: internetwork.*

Internet protocol   Any protocol belonging to the TCP/IP protocol stack. *See also: TCP/IP.*

internetwork   Any group of private networks interconnected by routers and other mechanisms, typically operating as a single entity.

internetworking   Broadly, anything associated with the general task of linking networks to each other. The term encompasses technologies, procedures, and products. When you connect networks to a router, you are creating an internetwork.

intra-area routing   Routing that occurs within a logical area. *Contrast with: inter-area routing.*

Inverse ARP   Inverse Address Resolution Protocol: A technique by which dynamic mappings are constructed in a network, allowing a device such as a router to locate the logical network address and associate it with a permanent virtual circuit (PVC). Commonly used in Frame Relay to determine the far-end node's TCP/IP address by sending the Inverse ARP request to the local DLCI.

IP   Internet Protocol: Defined in RFC 791, it is a Network layer protocol that is part of the TCP/IP stack and allows connectionless service. IP furnishes an array of features for addressing, type-of-service specification, fragmentation and reassembly, and security.

IP address   Often called an Internet address; an address uniquely identifying any device (host) on the Internet (or any TCP/IP network). Each address consists of four octets (32 bits), represented as decimal numbers separated by periods (a format known as "dotted-decimal"). Every address is made up of a network number, an optional subnetwork number, and a host number. The network and subnetwork numbers together are used for routing, while the host number addresses an individual host within the network or subnetwork. The network and subnetwork information is extracted from the IP address using the subnet mask. There are five classes of IP addresses (A–E), which allocate different numbers of bits to the network, subnetwork, and host portions of the address. *See also: CIDR, IP, and subnet mask.*

IPCP   IP Control Program: The protocol used to establish and configure IP over PPP. *See also: IP and PPP.*

IP multicast   A technique for routing that enables IP traffic to be reproduced from one source to several endpoints or from multiple sources to many destinations. Instead of transmitting only one packet to each individual point of destination, one packet is sent to a multicast group specified by only one IP endpoint address for the group.

IPX   Internetwork Packet Exchange: Network layer protocol (Layer 3) used in Novell NetWare networks for transferring information from servers to workstations. Similar to IP and XNS.

IPXCP   IPX Control Program: The protocol used to establish and configure IPX over PPP. *See also: IPX and PPP.*

IPXWAN   Protocol used for new WAN links to provide and negotiate line options on the link using IPX. After the link is up and the options have been agreed upon by the two end-to-end links, normal IPX transmission begins.

ISDN   Integrated Services Digital Network: Offered as a service by telephone companies, a communication protocol that allows telephone networks to carry data, voice, and other digital traffic. *See also: BISDN, BRI*, and *PRI.*

ISL routing   Inter-Switch Link routing is a Cisco proprietary method of frame tagging in a switched internetwork. Frame tagging is a way to identify the VLAN membership of a frame as it traverses a switched internetwork.

isochronous transmission   Asynchronous data transfer over a synchronous data link, requiring a constant bit rate for reliable transport. *Compare with: asynchronous transmission* and *synchronous transmission.*

iteration   The repetition of certain steps within the troubleshooting model. Certain steps may need to be repeated in order to solve the problem at hand.

ITU-T   International Telecommunication Union Telecommunication Standardization Sector: A group of engineers that develops worldwide standards for telecommunications technologies.

LAN   Local Area Network: Broadly, any network linking two or more computers and related devices within a limited geographical area (up to a few kilometers). LANs are typically high-speed, low-error networks within a company. Cabling and signaling at the Physical and Data-Link layers of the OSI are dictated by LAN standards. Ethernet, FDDI, and Token Ring are among the most popular LAN technologies. *Compare with: MAN.*

LAN switch   A high-speed, multiple-interface transparent bridging mechanism, transmitting packets between segments of data links, usually referred to specifically as an Ethernet switch. LAN switches transfer traffic based on MAC addresses. Multilayer switches are a type of high-speed, special-purpose, hardware-based router. *See also: multilayer switch*, and *store-and-forward packet switching.*

LANE   LAN emulation: The technology that allows an ATM network to operate as a LAN backbone. To do so, the ATM network is required to provide multicast and broadcast support, address mapping (MAC-to-ATM), SVC management, in addition to an operable packet format. Additionally, LANE defines Ethernet and Token Ring ELANs. *See also: ELAN.*

LAPB   Link Accessed Procedure, Balanced: A bit-oriented Data-Link layer protocol that is part of the X.25 stack and has its origin in SDLC. *See also: SDLC and X.25.*

LAPD   Link Access Procedure on the D channel. The ISDN Data-Link layer protocol used specifically for the D channel and defined by ITU-T Recommendations Q.920 and Q.921. LAPD evolved from LAPB and is created to comply with the signaling requirements of ISDN basic access.

latency   Broadly, the time it takes a data packet to get from one location to another. In specific networking contexts, it can mean either (1) the time elapsed (delay) between the execution of a request for access to a network by a device and the time the mechanism actually is permitted transmission, or (2) the time elapsed between when a mechanism receives a frame and the time that frame is forwarded out of the destination port.

Layer 1 S/T Interface   This connection uses a physical connector of RJ-45, as defined in ISO 8877. A straight-through pin configuration connects the terminal end point (TE) to the network termination (NT).

Layer-3 switch   *See: multilayer switch.*

layered architecture   Industry standard way of creating applications to work on a network. Layered architecture allows the application developer to make changes in only one layer instead of the whole program.

LCP   Link Control Protocol: The protocol designed to establish, configure, and test data-link connections for use by PPP. *See also: PPP.*

leaky bucket   An analogy for the basic cell rate algorithm (GCRA) used in ATM networks for checking the conformance of cell flows from a user or network. The bucket's "hole" is understood to be the prolonged rate at which cells can be accommodated, and the "depth" is the tolerance for cell bursts over a certain time period.

learning bridge   A bridge that transparently builds a dynamic database of MAC addresses and the interfaces associated with each address. Transparent bridges help to reduce traffic congestion on the network.

LE ARP   LAN Emulation Address Resolution Protocol: The protocol providing the ATM address that corresponds to a MAC address.

leased lines   Permanent connections between two points leased from the telephone companies.

LEC   LAN Emulation Client: Software providing the emulation of the link layer interface that allows the operation and communication of all higher-level protocols and applications to continue. The LEC client runs in all ATM devices, which include hosts, servers, bridges, and routers. The LANE client is responsible for address resolution, data transfer, address caching, interfacing to the emulated LAN, and driver support for higher-level services. *See also: ELAN and LES.*

LECS   LAN Emulation Configuration Server: An important part of emulated LAN services, providing the configuration data that is furnished upon request from the LES. These services include address registration for Integrated Local Management Interface (ILMI) support, configuration support for the LES addresses and their corresponding emulated LAN identifiers, and an interface to the emulated LAN. *See also: LES and ELAN.*

LES   LAN Emulation Server: The central LANE component that provides the initial configuration data for each connecting LEC. The LES typically is located on either an ATM-integrated router or a switch. Responsibilities of the LES include configuration and support for the LEC, address registration for the LEC, database storage and response concerning ATM addresses, and interfacing to the emulated LAN. *See also: ELAN, LEC, and LECS.*

link-state routing algorithm   A routing algorithm that allows each router to broadcast or multicast information regarding the cost of reaching all its neighbors to every node in the internetwork. Link-state algorithms provide a consistent view of the network and are therefore not vulnerable to routing loops. In general the link-state algorithm provides for faster convergence than the distance-vector algorithm. However, this is achieved at the cost of somewhat greater difficulty in computation and greater complexity (compared with distance-vector routing algorithms). *See also: distance-vector routing algorithm.*

LLAP   LocalTalk Link Access Protocol: In a LocalTalk environment, the Data-Link layer protocol that manages node-to-node delivery of data. This protocol provides node addressing and management of bus access, and it also controls data sending and receiving to assure packet length and integrity.

LLC   Logical Link Control: Defined by the IEEE, the higher of two Data-Link layer sublayers. LLC is responsible for error detection (but not correction), flow control, framing, and software-sublayer addressing. The predominant LLC protocol, IEEE 802.2, defines both connectionless and connection-oriented operations. *See also: Data-Link layer* and *MAC.*

LMI   Local Management Interface: An enhancement to the original Frame Relay specification. Among the features it provides are a keepalive mechanism, a multicast mechanism, global addressing, and a status mechanism.

LNNI   LAN Emulation Network-to-Network Interface: In the Phase 2 LANE specification, an interface that supports communication between the server components within one ELAN.

local explorer packet   In a Token Ring SRB network, a packet generated by an end system to find a host linked to the local ring. If no local host can be found, the end system will produce one of two solutions: a spanning explorer packet or an all-routes explorer packet.

local loop   Connection from a demarcation point to the closest switching office.

LocalTalk   Utilizing CSMA/CD, in addition to supporting data transmission at speeds of 230.4Kbps, LocalTalk is Apple Computer's proprietary baseband protocol, operating at the Data-Link and Physical layers of the OSI reference model.

loopback tests   These tests aid in physically isolating serial line and Frame Relay problems. Four different loopback tests can be performed to troubleshoot the circuit: local loopback on the local CSU/DSU, local loopback on the remote CSU/DSU, remote loopback from the local NIU to the remote CSU/DSU, and remote loopback from the remote NIU to the local CSU/DSU.

LSA   Link-state advertisement: Contained inside of link-state packets (LSPs), these advertisements are usually multicast packets, containing information about neighbors and path costs, that are employed by link-state protocols.

Receiving routers use LSAs to maintain their link-state databases and, ultimately, routing tables.

LT/ET The line termination and exchange termination points are called LT and ET, respectively. They handle the termination of the local loop and switching functions.

LUNI LAN Emulation User-to-Network Interface: Defining the interface between the LAN Emulation Client (LEC) and the LAN Emulation Server, LUNI is the ATM Forum's standard for LAN emulation on ATM networks. *See also: LES and LECS.*

MAC Media Access Control: The lower sublayer in the Data-Link layer, it is responsible for hardware addressing, media access, and error detection of frames. *See also: Data-Link layer and LLC.*

MAC address A Data-Link layer hardware address that every port or device needs in order to connect to a LAN segment. These addresses are used by various devices in the network for accurate location of logical addresses. MAC addresses are defined by the IEEE standard and their length is six characters, typically using the burned-in address (BIA) of the local LAN interface. Variously called hardware address, physical address, burned-in address, or MAC-layer address.

MacIP In AppleTalk, the Network layer protocol encapsulating IP packets in Datagram Delivery Protocol (DDP) packets. MacIP also supplies substitute ARP services.

MAN Metropolitan-Area Network: Any network that encompasses a metropolitan area—that is, an area typically larger than a LAN but smaller than a WAN. *See also: LAN.*

Manchester encoding A method for digital coding in which a mid-bit-time transition is employed for clocking, and a 1 (one) is denoted by a high voltage level during the first half of the bit time. This scheme is used by Ethernet and IEEE 802.3.

master browser Browser that collects and disseminates resource information in Windows 95/98/NT networks. There is one master browser per segment. This browser is automatically elected when the stations on a segment come online. *See also: browsing, domain master browser, and Network Neighborhood.*

maximum burst   Specified in bytes or cells, the largest burst of information exceeding the insured rate that will be permitted on an ATM permanent virtual connection for a short time and will not be dropped even if it goes over the specified maximum rate. *Compare with: insured burst. See also: maximum rate.*

maximum rate   The maximum permitted data throughput on a particular virtual circuit, equal to the total of insured and uninsured traffic from the traffic source. Should traffic congestion occur, uninsured information may be deleted from the path. Measured in bits or cells per second, the maximum rate represents the highest throughput of data the virtual circuit is ever able to deliver and cannot exceed the media rate. *Compare with: excess rate. See also: maximum burst.*

MBS   Maximum Burst Size: In an ATM signaling message, this metric, coded as a number of cells, is used to convey the burst tolerance.

MBONE   Multicast backbone: The multicast backbone of the Internet, it is a virtual multicast network made up of multicast LANs, including point-to-point tunnels interconnecting them.

MCDV   Maximum Cell Delay Variation: The maximum two-point CDV objective across a link or node for the identified service category in an ATM network. The MCDV is one of four link metrics that are exchanged using PTSPs to verify the available resources of an ATM network. Only one MCDV value is assigned to each traffic class.

MCLR   Maximum Cell Loss Ratio: The maximum ratio of cells in an ATM network that fail to transit a link or node compared with the total number of cells that arrive at the link or node. MCDV is one of four link metrics that are exchanged using PTSPs to verify the available resources of an ATM network. The MCLR applies to cells in VBR and CBR traffic classes whose CLP bit is set to zero. *See also: CBR, CLP,* and *VBR.*

MCR   Minimum Cell Rate: A parameter determined by the ATM Forum for traffic management of the ATM networks. MCR is specifically defined for ABR transmissions and specifies the minimum value for the allowed cell rate (ACR). *See also: ACR and PCR.*

MCTD   Maximum Cell Transfer Delay: In an ATM network, the total of the maximum cell delay variation and the fixed delay across the link or node.

MCTD is one of four link metrics that are exchanged using PNNI topology state packets to verify the available resources of an ATM network. There is one MCTD value assigned to each traffic class. *See also: MCDV.*

metrics These measurements are associated with each route that is present in the route table. Metrics are calculated by the routing protocol to define a cost of getting to the destination address. Some algorithms use hop count (the number of routers between it and the destination address), whereas others use a vector of values.

MIB Management Information Base: Used with SNMP management software to gather information from remote devices. The management station can poll the remote device for information, or the MIB running on the remote station can be programmed to send information on a regular basis.

MIP Multichannel Interface Processor: The resident interface processor on Cisco 7000 series routers, providing up to two channelized T1 or E1 connections by serial cables connected to a CSU. The two controllers are capable of providing 24 T1 or 30 E1 channel groups, with each group being introduced to the system as a serial interface that can be configured individually.

mips Millions of instructions per second: A measure of processor speed.

MLP Multilink PPP: A technique used to split, recombine, and sequence datagrams across numerous logical data links.

MMP Multichassis Multilink PPP: A protocol that supplies MLP support across multiple routers and access servers. MMP enables several routers and access servers to work as a single large dial-up pool with one network address and ISDN access number. MMP successfully supports packet fragmenting and reassembly when the user connection is split between two physical access devices.

modem Modulator-demodulator: A device that converts digital signals to analog and vice versa so that digital information can be transmitted over analog communication facilities, such as voice-grade telephone lines. This is achieved by converting digital signals at the source to analog for transmission, and reconverting the analog signals back into digital form at the destination. *See also: modulation* and *demodulation.*

modem eliminator A mechanism that makes possible a connection between two DTE devices without modems by simulating the commands and physical signaling required.

modulation   The process of modifying some characteristic of an electrical signal, such as amplitude (AM) or frequency (FM), in order to represent digital or analog information. *See also: AM.*

MOSPF   Multicast OSPF: An extension of the OSPF unicast protocol that enables IP multicast routing within the domain. *See also: OSPF.*

MPOA   Multiprotocol over ATM: An effort by the ATM Forum to standardize how existing and future Network-layer protocols such as IP, IPv6, AppleTalk, and IPX run over an ATM network with directly attached hosts, routers, and multilayer LAN switches.

MTU   Maximum transmission unit: The largest packet size, measured in bytes, that an interface can handle.

multicast   Broadly, any communication between a single sender and multiple receivers. Unlike broadcast messages, which are sent to all addresses on a network, multicast messages are sent to a defined subset of the network addresses; this subset has a group multicast address, which is specified in the packet's destination address field. *See also: broadcast, directed broadcast.*

multicast address   An IP address whose binary representation of its first octet begins with the pattern 1110. In decimal notation, this range is defined as any address between 224.0.0.0 and 239.255.255.255. Multicast addresses are used for the purpose of identifying recipients of multicast transmissions. Identical to group address. *See also: multicast.*

multicast send VCC   A two-directional point-to-point virtual control connection (VCC) arranged by an LEC to a BUS; one of the three types of informational link specified by Phase 1 LANE. *See also: control distribute VCC and control direct VCC.*

multilayer switch   A highly specialized, high-speed, hardware-based type of LAN router, it filters and forwards packets based on their Layer 2 MAC addresses and Layer 3 network addresses. It's possible that even Layer 4 can be read. Sometimes called a Layer 3 switch. *See also: LAN switch.*

multimeter   Hardware used to measure voltage, resistance, and current. It works with electrical-based cabling and can be used to test for physical connectivity.

multiplexing   The process of converting several logical signals into a single physical signal for transmission across one physical channel. *Contrast with: demultiplexing.*

NAK Negative acknowledgment: A response sent from a receiver, telling the sender that the information was not received or contained errors. *Compare with: acknowledgment.*

NAT Network Address Translation: An algorithm instrumental in minimizing the requirement for globally unique IP addresses, permitting an organization whose addresses are not all globally unique to connect to the Internet regardless, by translating those addresses into globally routable address space.

NBP Name Binding Protocol: In AppleTalk, the transport-level protocol that interprets a socket client's name, entered as a character string, into the corresponding DDP address. NBP gives AppleTalk protocols the capacity to discern user-defined zones and names of mechanisms by showing and keeping translation tables that map names to their corresponding socket addresses.

neighboring routers Two routers in OSPF that have interfaces to a common network. On networks with multi-access, these neighboring routers are dynamically discovered using the Hello protocol of OSPF.

NetBEUI NetBIOS Extended User Interface: An improved version of the NetBIOS protocol used in a number of network operating systems including LAN Manager, Windows NT, LAN Server, and Windows for Workgroups, implementing the OSI LLC2 protocol. NetBEUI formalizes the transport frame not standardized in NetBIOS and adds more functions. *See also: OSI.*

NetBIOS Network Basic Input/Output System: The API employed by applications residing on an IBM LAN to ask for services, such as session termination or information transfer, from lower-level network processes. *See also: API.*

Netflow switching Collects detailed data for use with circuit accounting and application-utilization information. Because of all the additional data that Netflow collects (and may export), expect an increase in router overhead—possibly as much as a five-percent increase in CPU utilization.

NetView A mainframe network product from IBM, used for monitoring SNA (Systems Network Architecture) networks. It runs as a VTAM (Virtual Telecommunications Access Method) application.

NetWare   A widely used NOS created by Novell, providing a number of distributed network services and remote file access.

network address   Used with the logical network addresses to identify the network segment in an internetwork. Logical addresses are hierarchical in nature and have at least two parts: network and host. An example of a hierarchical address is 172.16.10.5, where 172.16 is the network and 10.5 is the host address.

network analyzer   Also known as protocol analyzer. A device that collects and analyzes data on a connected broadcast domain. The information provided is a packet decode of data transiting the network. This data is used to troubleshoot network problems.

Network layer   In the OSI reference model, it is Layer 3—the layer in which routing is implemented, enabling connections and path selection between two end systems. *See also: Application layer, Data-Link layer, Physical layer, Presentation layer, Session layer,* and *Transport layer.*

Network Monitor   This software-based tool simply monitors the network. It can do this in several ways, including the Simple Network Management Protocol (SNMP) and the Internet Control Message Protocol (ICMP).

Network Neighborhood   A Windows tool that allows users to see the resources that are available in the network. The information is displayed by domain to allow for easier viewing and is populated through the use of browsing. *See also: Browsing, Domain Master Browser and Master Browser.*

NFS   Network File System: One of the protocols in Sun Microsystems' widely used file-system protocol suite, allowing remote file access across a network. The name is loosely used to refer to the entire Sun protocol suite, which also includes RPC, XDR (External Data Representation), and other protocols.

NHRP   Next Hop Resolution Protocol: In a nonbroadcast multi-access (NBMA) network, the protocol employed by routers in order to dynamically locate MAC addresses of various hosts and routers. It enables systems to communicate directly without requiring an intermediate hop, thus facilitating increased performance in ATM, Frame Relay, X.25, and SMDS systems.

NHS Next Hop Server: Defined by the NHRP protocol, this server maintains the next-hop resolution cache tables, listing IP-to-ATM address maps of related nodes and nodes that can be reached through routers served by the NHS.

NIC Network interface card: An electronic circuit board placed in a computer. The NIC provides network communication to a LAN.

NLSP NetWare Link Services Protocol: Novell's link-state routing protocol, based on the IS-IS model.

NMP Network Management Processor: A Catalyst 5000 switch processor module used to control and monitor the switch.

NMS Network Management Systems: A software/hardware package that is used to monitor availability, network performance, security, services, and policies.

node address Used to identify a specific device in an internetwork. Can be a hardware address, which is burned into the network interface card, or a logical network address, which an administrator or server assigns to the node.

nondesignated port The Spanning-Tree Protocol tells a port on a Layer-2 switch to stop transmitting and creating a network loop. Only designated ports can send frames.

non-stub area In OSPF, a resource-consuming area carrying a default route, intra-area routes, inter-area routes, static routes, and external routes. Non-stub areas are the only areas that can have virtual links configured across them and exclusively contain an autonomous system boundary router (ASBR). *Compare with: stub area. See also: ASBR and OSPF.*

NRZ Nonreturn to Zero: One of several encoding schemes for transmitting digital data. NRZ signals sustain constant levels of voltage with no signal shifting (no return to zero-voltage level) during a bit interval. If there is a series of bits with the same value (1 or 0), there will be no state change. The signal is not self-clocking. *See also: NRZI.*

NRZI Nonreturn to Zero Inverted: One of several encoding schemes for transmitting digital data. A transition in voltage level (either from high to low or vice versa) at the beginning of a bit interval is interpreted as a value of 1; the absence of a transition is interpreted as a 0. Thus, the voltage assigned to each value is continually inverted. NRZI signals are not self-clocking. *See also: NRZ.*

NT1 Network termination 1: Is an ISDN designation to devices that understand ISDN standards.

NT2 Network termination 2: Is an ISDN designation to devices that do not understand ISDN standards. To use an NT2, you must use a terminal adapter (TA).

NVRAM Non-Volatile RAM: Random-access memory that keeps its contents intact while power is turned off.

observing results Using the exact same methods and commands that were used to obtain information in order to define the problem and see whether the changes implemented were effective.

OC Optical carrier: A series of physical protocols, designated as OC-1, OC-2, OC-3, and so on, for SONET optical signal transmissions. OC signal levels place STS frames on a multimode fiber optic line at various speeds, of which 51.84Mbps is the lowest (OC-1). Each subsequent protocol runs at a speed divisible by 51.84. *See also: SONET.*

octet Base-8 numbering system used to identify a section of a dotted decimal IP address. Also referred to as a byte.

ones density Also known as pulse density; a method of signal clocking. The CSU/DSU retrieves the clocking information from data that passes through it. For this scheme to work, the data needs to be encoded to contain at least one binary 1 for each eight bits transmitted. *See also: CSU and DSU.*

optimum switching Switching method that replaced fast switching on higher-end Cisco routers. Switching is done by comparing incoming packets against the optimum switching cache.

OSI Open System Interconnection: International standardization program designed by ISO and ITU-T for the development of data networking standards that make multivendor equipment interoperability a reality.

OSI reference model Open System Interconnection reference model: A conceptual model defined by the International Organization for Standardization (ISO), describing how any combination of devices can be connected for the purpose of communication. The OSI model divides the task into seven functional layers, forming a hierarchy with the applications at the top and the physical medium at the bottom, and it defines the functions each layer must provide. *See also: Application layer, Data-Link layer, Network layer, Physical layer, Presentation layer, Session layer,* and *Transport layer.*

OSPF Open Shortest Path First: A link-state, hierarchical IGP routing algorithm derived from an earlier version of the IS-IS protocol, whose features include multipath routing, load balancing, and least-cost routing. OSPF is the suggested successor to RIP in the Internet environment. *See also: Enhanced IGRP, IGP,* and *IP.*

OTDR Optical Time Domain Reflectors: An optical cable tester used to locate physical problems in the cable. *See also: TDR*

OUI Organizationally Unique Identifier: Is assigned by the IEEE to an organization that makes network interface cards. The organization then puts this OUI on each and every card they manufacture. The OUI is 3 bytes (24 bits) long. The manufacturer then adds a 3-byte identifier to uniquely identify the host on an internetwork. The total length of the address is 48 bits (6 bytes) and is called a hardware address or MAC address.

out-of-band management Management "outside" of the network's physical channels—for example, using a console connection not directly interfaced through the local LAN or WAN or a dial-in modem. *Compare with: in-band management.*

out-of-band signaling Within a network, any transmission that uses physical channels or frequencies separate from those ordinarily used for data transfer. For example, the initial configuration of a Cisco Catalyst switch requires an out-of-band connection via a console port.

output queue This queue resides on the RP and is used to hold the packet until the packet can be copied to the buffers on the SP/SSP. From there, it is forwarded to the specified interface processor.

outside-in troubleshooting Troubleshooting method that consists of choosing the opposite end of the connection and working back toward you or the user that reported the problem.

overrun Phenomenon that occurs when the receiver receives packets faster than it can transfer them to the hardware buffer.

packet   In data communications, the basic logical unit of information transferred. A packet consists of a certain number of data bytes, wrapped or encapsulated in headers and/or trailers that contain information about where the packet came from, where it's going, and so on. The various protocols involved in sending a transmission add their own layers of header information, which the corresponding protocols in receiving devices then interpret.

packet switch   A physical device that makes it possible for a communication channel to share several connections. Its functions include finding the most efficient transmission path for packets.

packet switching   A networking technology based on the transmission of data in packets. Dividing a continuous stream of data into small units—packets—enables data from multiple devices on a network to share the same communication channel simultaneously but also requires the use of precise routing information.

PAP   Password Authentication Protocol: In Point-to-Point Protocol (PPP) networks, a method of validating connection requests. The requesting (remote) device must send an authentication request, containing a password and ID, to the local router when attempting to connect. Unlike the more secure CHAP (Challenge Handshake Authentication Protocol), PAP sends the password unencrypted and does not attempt to verify whether the user is authorized to access the requested resource; it merely identifies the remote end. *See also: CHAP.*

parity checking   A method of error-checking in data transmissions. An extra bit (the parity bit) is added to each character or data word so that the sum of the bits will be either an odd number (in odd parity) or an even number (even parity).

partial mesh   A type of network topology in which some network nodes form a full mesh (where every node has either a physical or a virtual circuit linking it to every other network node), but others are attached to only one or two nodes in the network. A typical use of partial-mesh topology is in peripheral networks linked to a fully meshed backbone. *See also: full mesh.*

path cost   *See: cost.*

path determination   Condition where the router is aware of a route that leads to the desired destination address.

PCR   Peak Cell Rate: As defined by the ATM Forum, the parameter specifying, in cells per second, the maximum rate at which a source may transmit.

PDN   Public Data Network: Generally for a fee, a PDN offers the public access to computer communication network operated by private concerns or government agencies. Small organizations can take advantage of PDNs, to aid them in creating WANs without having to invest in long-distance equipment and circuitry.

PGP   Pretty Good Privacy: A popular public-key/private-key encryption application offering protected transfer of files and messages.

Physical layer   The lowest layer—Layer 1—in the OSI reference model, it is responsible for converting data packets from the Data-Link layer (Layer 2) into electrical signals. Physical-layer protocols and standards define, for example, the type of cable and connectors to be used, including their pin assignments and the encoding scheme for signaling 0 and 1 values. *See also: Application layer, Data-Link layer, Network layer, Presentation layer, Session layer,* and *Transport layer.*

physical test equipment   A genre of testing equipment including multimeters, cable testers, TDRs, and OTDRs. Used for testing cable integrity and end-to-end physical connectivity.

ping   Packet Internet groper: A Unix-based Internet diagnostic tool, consisting of a message sent to test the accessibility of a particular device on the IP network. The acronym (from which the "full name" was formed) reflects the underlying metaphor of submarine sonar. Just as the sonar operator sends out a signal and waits to hear it echo ("ping") back from a submerged object, the network user can ping another node on the network and wait to see if it responds.

pleisochronous   Nearly synchronous, except that clocking comes from an outside source instead of being embedded within the signal as in synchronous transmissions.

PLP   Packet Level Protocol: Occasionally called X.25 Level 3 or X.25 Protocol, a Network-layer protocol that is part of the X.25 stack.

PNNI Private Network-Network Interface: An ATM Forum specification for offering topology data used for the calculation of paths through the network, among switches and groups of switches. It is based on well-known link-state routing procedures and allows for automatic configuration in networks whose addressing scheme is determined by the topology.

point-to-multipoint connection In ATM, a communication path going only one way, connecting a single system at the starting point, called the "root node," to systems at multiple points of destination, called "leaves." *See also: point-to-point connection.*

point-to-point connection In ATM, a channel of communication that can be directed either one way or two ways between two ATM end systems. *See also: point-to-multipoint connection.*

poison reverse updates These update messages are transmitted by a router back to the originator (thus ignoring the split-horizon rule) after route poisoning has occurred. Typically used with DV routing protocols in order to overcome large routing loops and offer explicit information when a subnet or network is not accessible (instead of merely suggesting that the network is unreachable by not including it in updates). *See also: route poisoning.*

polling The procedure of orderly inquiry, used by a primary network mechanism, to determine whether secondary devices have data to transmit. A message is sent to each secondary, granting the secondary the right to transmit.

POP (1) Point Of Presence: The physical location where an interexchange carrier has placed equipment to interconnect with a local exchange carrier. (2) Post Office Protocol (currently at version 3): A protocol used by client e-mail applications for recovery of mail from a mail server.

port security Used with Layer-2 switches to provide some security. Not typically used in production because it is difficult to manage. Allows only certain frames to traverse administrator-assigned segments.

PDU Protocol Data Unit: The name of the processes at each layer of the OSI model. PDUs at the Transport layer are called segments; PDUs at the Network layer are called packets or datagrams; and PDUs at the Data-Link layer are called frames. The Physical layer uses bits.

PPP   Point-to-Point Protocol: The protocol most commonly used for dial-up Internet access, superseding the earlier SLIP. Its features include address notification, authentication via CHAP or PAP, support for multiple protocols, and link monitoring. PPP has two layers: the Link Control Protocol (LCP) establishes, configures, and tests a link, and then any of various Network Control Programs (NCPs) transport traffic for a specific protocol suite, such as IPX. *See also: CHAP, PAP,* and *SLIP.*

Presentation layer   Layer 6 of the OSI reference model, it defines how data is formatted, presented, encoded, and converted for use by software at the Application layer. *See also: Application layer, Data-Link layer, Network layer, Physical layer, Session layer,* and *Transport layer.*

PRI   Primary Rate Interface: A type of ISDN connection between a PBX and a long-distance carrier, made up of a single 64Kbps D channel in addition to 23 (T1) or 30 (E1) B channels. *See also: ISDN.*

primary nodes   SDLC protocol nodes that are responsible for the control of secondary stations and for link management, such as link setup and teardown.

priority 1   Production network down situation. The highest priority when opening a ticket with the Cisco TAC.

priority 2   Production network performance seriously degraded. The second highest priority when opening a ticket with the Cisco TAC.

priority 3   Network performance degraded. The third highest priority when opening a ticket with the Cisco TAC.

priority 4   Information needed on Cisco products. Priority associated with cases that do not require immediate troubleshooting support.

priority queueing   A routing function in which frames temporarily placed in an interface output queue are assigned priorities based on traits such as packet size or type of interface.

problem definition   The step in the troubleshooting model where details are used to define the most likely cause of a problem. This should be a concise yet accurate description of the problem at hand.

process switching   The procedure that occurs when a packet arrives on a router to be forwarded, is copied to the router's process buffer, and the router performs a lookup on the Layer 3 address. Using the route table, an exit interface is associated with the destination address. The processor forwards the packet with the added new information to the exit interface, while the router initializes the fast-switching cache. Subsequent packets bound for the same destination address follow the same path as the first packet.

PROM   Programmable read-only memory: ROM that is programmable only once, using special equipment. *Compare with: EPROM.*

propagation delay   The time it takes data to traverse a network from its source to its destination.

protocol   In networking, the specification of a set of rules for a particular type of communication. The term is also used to refer to the software that implements a protocol.

protocol analyzer   Also known as network analyzer. A device that collects and analyzes data on a connected broadcast domain. The information provided is a packet decode of data transiting the network. This also includes a protocol analysis of the traffic that is captured from the network. This data is used to troubleshoot network problems.

protocol parameters   The options that are passed with connection setup within many connection-oriented protocols. An example would be the TCP window size.

protocol stack   A collection of related protocols.

PSE   Packet Switch Exchange: The X.25 term for a switch.

PSN   Packet-switched network: Any network that uses packet-switching technology. Also known as packet-switched data network (PSDN). *See also: packet switching.*

PSTN   Public Switched Telephone Network: Colloquially referred to as "plain old telephone service" (POTS). A term that describes the assortment of telephone networks and services available globally.

PVC   Permanent virtual circuit: In a Frame-Relay network, a logical connection, defined in software, that is maintained permanently. *Compare with: SVC. See also: VC.*

PVP   Permanent virtual path: A virtual path made up of PVCs. *See also: PVC.*

PVP tunneling   Permanent virtual path tunneling: A technique that links two private ATM networks across a public network using a virtual path, wherein the public network transparently trunks the complete collection of virtual channels in the virtual path between the two private networks.

q.921   The q.921 is the Layer 2 protocol used by ISDN, on the D channel. It establishes a connection between the central office switch and the router.

q.931   The third layer of ISDN is addressed in the ITU-T I.451 specification, which is also called q.931. This protocol includes several message commands, which are viewed with the `debug isdn q931` command. These commands include call setup, connect, release, cancel, status, disconnect, and user information.

QoS   Quality of Service: A set of metrics used to measure the quality of transmission and service availability of any given transmission system.

queue   Broadly, any list of elements arranged in an orderly fashion and ready for processing, such as a line of people waiting to enter a movie theater. In routing, it refers to a backlog of information packets waiting in line to be transmitted over a router interface.

R reference point   Used with ISDN networks to identify the connection between an NT1 and an S/T device. The S/T device converts the 4-wire network to the two-wire ISDN standard network.

RAM   Random access memory: Used by all computers to store information. Cisco routers use RAM to store packet buffers and routing tables, along with the hardware addresses cache.

RARP   Reverse Address Resolution Protocol: The protocol within the TCP/IP stack that maps MAC addresses to IP addresses. *See also: ARP.*

rate queue   A value, assigned to one or more virtual circuits, that specifies the speed at which an individual virtual circuit will transmit data to the remote end. Every rate queue identifies a segment of the total bandwidth available on an ATM link. The sum of all rate queues should not exceed the total available bandwidth.

RCP   Remote Copy Protocol: A protocol for copying files to or from a file system that resides on a remote server on a network, using TCP to guarantee reliable data delivery.

red alarm   A red alarm on a T1 or E1 indicates that the incoming signal is corrupted. The equipment in red alarm will be sending out a yellow alarm on its outbound signal. *See also: yellow alarm.*

redistribution   Command used in Cisco routers to inject the paths found from one type of routing protocol into another type of routing protocol. For example, networks found by RIP can be inserted into an IGRP network.

redundancy   In internetworking, the duplication of connections, devices, or services that can be used as a backup in the event that the primary connections, devices, or services fail.

reload   An event or command that causes Cisco routers to reboot.

RIF   Routing Information Field: In source-route bridging, a header field that defines the path direction of the frame or token. If the Route Information Indicator (RII) bit is not set, the RIF is read from source to destination (left to right). If the RII bit is set, the RIF is read from the destination back to the source (right to left). It is defined as part of the Token Ring frame header for source-routed frames, which contains path information.

ring   Two or more stations connected in a logical circular topology. In this topology, which is the basis for Token Ring, FDDI, and CDDI, information is transferred from station to station in sequence.

ring topology   A network logical topology comprising a series of repeaters that form one closed loop by connecting unidirectional transmission links. Individual stations on the network are connected to the network at a repeater. Physically, ring topologies are generally organized in a closed-loop star. *Compare with: bus topology* and *star topology.*

RIP   Routing Information Protocol: One of the most commonly used interior gateway protocols in the Internet. RIP employs hop count as a routing metric. *See also: Enhanced IGRP, IGP, OSPF,* and *hop count.*

RJ connector   Registered jack connector: Used with twisted-pair wiring to connect the copper wire to network interface cards, switches, and hubs.

RMON   Remote Monitoring: Another method for obtaining environmental and statistical information from devices. Much of the RMON technology implementation is based on the deployment of RMON probes that gather the information from the circuit (physical media) because the router or switch may not support all levels of RMON information.

ROM Read-only memory: Chip used in computers to help boot the device. Cisco routers use a ROM chip to load the bootstrap, which runs a power-on self test, and then find and load the IOS in flash memory by default.

root bridge Used with the Spanning-Tree Protocol to stop network loops from occurring. The root bridge is elected by having the lowest bridge ID. The bridge ID is determined by the priority (32,768 by default on all bridges and switches) and the main hardware address of the device. The root bridge determines which of the neighboring Layer-2 devices' interfaces become the designated and nondesignated ports.

routed protocol Routed protocols (such as IP and IPX) are used to transmit user data through an internetwork. By contrast, routing protocols (such as RIP, IGRP, and OSPF) are used to update routing tables between routers.

route maps Small scripts used to manipulate routing that can contain multiple instances and multiple conditions for each instance. Route maps are somewhat like access lists if you specify that the packet must match an access list. In addition to having the capability of permitting or denying the packet, you can define what is done before the packet is forwarded. Route maps can be used to set metrics for route updates, set a command to its default value, and so on.

route poisoning Used by various DV routing protocols in order to overcome large routing loops and offer explicit information about when a subnet or network is not accessible (instead of merely suggesting that the network is unreachable by not including it in updates). Typically, this is accomplished by setting the hop count to one more than maximum. *See also: poison reverse updates.*

route summarization In various routing protocols, such as OSPF, EIGRP, and IS-IS, the consolidation of publicized subnetwork addresses so that a single summary route is advertised to other areas by an area border router.

router A Network-layer mechanism, either software or hardware, using one or more metrics to decide on the best path to use for transmission of network traffic. Sending packets between networks by routers is based on the information provided on Network layers. Historically, this device has sometimes been called a gateway.

routing   The process of forwarding logically addressed packets from their local subnetwork toward their ultimate destination. In large networks, the numerous intermediary destinations a packet might travel before reaching its destination can make routing very complex.

routing domain   Any collection of end systems and intermediate systems that operate under an identical set of administrative rules. Every routing domain contains one or several areas, each individually given a certain area address.

routing metric   Any value that is used by routing algorithms to determine whether one route is superior to another. Metrics include such information as bandwidth, delay, hop count, path cost, load, MTU, reliability, and communication cost. Only the best possible routes are stored in the routing table, while all other information may be stored in link-state or topological databases. *See also: cost.*

routing protocol   Any protocol that defines algorithms to be used for updating routing tables between routers. Examples include IGRP, RIP, and OSPF.

routing table   A table kept in a router that maintains a record of only the best possible routes to certain network destinations and the metrics associated with those routes.

RP   Route Processor: Also known as a supervisory processor; a module on Cisco 7000 series routers that holds the CPU, system software, and most of the memory components used in the router.

RSP   Route/Switch Processor: A processor module combining the functions of RP and SP used in Cisco 7500 series routers. *See also: RP and SP.*

RTMP   Routing Table Maintenance Protocol: Protocol responsible for AppleTalk routing tables and their information. AppleTalk's proprietary method of maintaining route tables on AppleTalk-enabled machines.

RTS   Request To Send: An EIA/TIA-232 control signal requesting permission to transmit data on a communication line.

S reference point   ISDN reference point that works with a T reference point to convert a 4-wire ISDN network to the 2-wire ISDN network needed to communicate with the ISDN switches at the network provider.

S/T reference point   If no NT2 is installed, the connection between the NT1 and either the TA or the TE1, depending on which is installed, is the S/T reference point. As the installation of NT2 devices is rare, most ISDN installations will have an S/T reference point.

SAGE   Synergy Advanced Gate-Array Engine: A chip used for non-Ethernet applications—including FDDI, ATM LANE, Token Ring, and the Network Management Processor on the supervisor engine. *See also: supervisor module.*

SAINT   Synergy Advanced Interface and Network Termination: The SAINT handles Ethernet switching on the Catalyst 5000 platform, and it also handles ISL encapsulation.

SAMBA ASIC   ASIC located on line modules and the supervisor modules. On the line cards, this chip is responsible for broadcast suppression, based on thresholds established by the administrator. This ASIC also maintains statistics on packets. *See also: supervisor module.*

sampling rate   The rate at which samples of a specific waveform amplitude are collected within a specified period of time.

SAP   (1) Service Access Point: A field specified by IEEE 802.2 that is part of an address specification. (2) Service Advertising Protocol: The Novell NetWare protocol that supplies a way to inform network clients of resource and service availability on the network, using routers and servers. *See also: IPX.*

SCR   Sustainable Cell Rate: An ATM Forum parameter used for traffic management, it is the long-term average cell rate for VBR connections that can be transmitted.

SDLC   Synchronous Data Link Control: A protocol used in SNA Data-Link layer communications. SDLC is a bit-oriented, full-duplex serial protocol that is the basis for several similar protocols, including HDLC and LAPB. *See also: HDLC and LAPB.*

secondary nodes   Nodes as designated by the SDLC protocol. Secondary nodes talk only to the primary node when they fulfill two requirements: first, they have permission from the primary node; second, they have data to transmit.

seed device   A root device specified in an NMS configuration. From this device the network discovery begins. The seed device's neighbors are discovered and the continuing process spreads out starting at the seed device.

seed router   In an AppleTalk network, the router that is equipped with the network number or cable range in its port descriptor. The seed router specifies the network number or cable range for other routers in that network section and answers to configuration requests from nonseed routers on its connected AppleTalk network, permitting those routers to affirm or modify their configurations accordingly. Every AppleTalk network needs at least one seed router physically connected to each network segment.

sequenced data transfer   The process of assigning sequence numbers to every PDU that leaves a host so that it may be resequenced once all of the PDUs in a transmission reach the destination host.

server   Hardware and software that provide network services to clients.

set-based   Set-based routers and switches use the `set` command to configure devices. Cisco is moving away from set-based commands and is using the command-line interface (CLI) on all new devices.

Session layer   Layer 5 of the OSI reference model, responsible for creating, managing, and terminating sessions between applications and overseeing data exchange between Presentation layer entities. *See also: Application layer, Data-Link layer, Network layer, Physical layer, Presentation layer,* and *Transport layer.*

setup mode   Mode that a router will enter if no configuration is found in nonvolatile RAM when the router boots. Allows the administrator to configure a router step-by-step. Not as robust or flexible as the command-line interface.

SF   Super frame: A super frame (also called a D4 frame) consists of 12 frames with 192 bits each, with the 193rd bit providing other functions including error checking. SF is frequently used on T1 circuits. A newer version of the technology is Extended Super Frame (ESF), which uses 24 frames. *See also: ESF.*

signaling packet   An informational packet created by an ATM-connected mechanism that wants to establish connection with another such mechanism. The packet contains the QoS parameters needed for connection and the ATM NSAP address of the endpoint. The endpoint responds with a message of acceptance if it is able to support the desired QoS, and the connection is established. *See also: QoS.*

silicon switching   A type of high-speed switching used in Cisco 7000 series routers, based on the use of a separate processor (the Silicon Switch Processor, or SSP). *See also: SSE.*

simplex   The mode at which data or a digital signal is transmitted. Simplex is a way of transmitting in only one direction. Half-duplex transmits in two directions but only one direction at a time. Full-duplex transmits both directions simultaneously.

sliding window   The method of flow control used by TCP, as well as several Data-Link layer protocols. This method places a buffer between the receiving application and the network data flow. The "window" available for accepting data is the size of the buffer minus the amount of data already there. This window increases in size as the application reads data from it and decreases as new data is sent. The receiver sends the transmitter announcements of the current window size, and it may stop accepting data until the window increases above a certain threshold.

SLIP   Serial Line Internet Protocol: An industry standard serial encapsulation for point-to-point connections that supports only a single routed protocol, TCP/IP. SLIP is the predecessor to PPP. *See also: PPP.*

SMDS   Switched Multimegabit Data Service: A packet-switched, datagram-based WAN networking technology offered by telephone companies that provides high speed.

SMTP   Simple Mail Transfer Protocol: A protocol used on the Internet to provide electronic mail services.

SNA   System Network Architecture: A complex, feature-rich, network architecture similar to the OSI reference model but with several variations; created by IBM in the 1970s and essentially composed of seven layers.

SNAP   Subnetwork Access Protocol: SNAP is a frame used in Ethernet, Token Ring, and FDDI LANs. Data transfer, connection management, and QoS selection are three primary functions executed by the SNAP frame.

SNMP   Simple Network Management Protocol: This protocol polls SNMP agents or devices for statistical and environmental data. This data can include device temperature, name, performance statistics, and much more. SNMP works with MIB objects that are present on the SNMP agent. This information is queried then sent to the SNMP server.

socket   (1) A software structure that operates within a network device as a destination point for communications. (2) In AppleTalk networks, an entity at a specific location within a node; AppleTalk sockets are conceptually similar to TCP/IP ports.

software test equipment   *See: Network Monitor.*

SONET   Synchronous Optical Network: The ANSI standard for synchronous transmission on fiber optic media, developed at Bell Labs. It specifies a base signal rate of 51.84Mbps and a set of multiples of that rate, known as Optical Carrier levels, up to 2.5Gbps.

SP   Switch Processor: Also known as a ciscoBus controller, it is a Cisco 7000 series processor module acting as governing agent for all CxBus activities.

span   A full-duplex digital transmission line connecting two facilities.

SPAN   Switched Port Analyzer: A feature of the Catalyst 5000 switch, offering freedom to manipulate within a switched Ethernet environment by extending the monitoring ability of the existing network analyzers into the environment. At one switched segment, the SPAN mirrors traffic onto a predetermined SPAN port, while a network analyzer connected to the SPAN port is able to monitor traffic from any other Catalyst switched port.

spanning explorer packet   Sometimes called limited-route or single-route explorer packet, it pursues a statically configured spanning tree when searching for paths in a source-route bridging network. *See also: all-routes explorer packet, explorer packet,* and *local explorer packet.*

spanning tree   A subset of a network topology, within which no loops exist. When bridges are interconnected into a loop, the bridge, or switch, cannot identify a frame that has been forwarded previously, so there is no mechanism for removing a frame as it passes the interface numerous times. Without a method of removing these frames, the bridges continuously forward them—consuming bandwidth and adding overhead to the network. Spanning trees prune the network to provide only one path for any packet. *See also: Spanning-Tree Protocol and spanning-tree algorithm.*

spanning-tree algorithm (STA)   An algorithm that creates a spanning tree using the Spanning-Tree Protocol (STP). *See also: spanning tree* and *Spanning-Tree Protocol.*

Spanning-Tree Protocol (STP)   The bridge protocol (IEEE 802.1d) that enables a learning bridge to dynamically avoid loops in the network topology by creating a spanning tree using the spanning-tree algorithm. Spanning-tree frames called bridge protocol data units (BPDUs) are sent and received by all switches in the network at regular intervals. The switches participating in the spanning tree don't forward the frames; instead, they're processed to determine the spanning-tree topology itself. Cisco Catalyst series switches use STP 802.1d to perform this function. *See also: BPDU, learning bridge, MAC address, spanning tree,* and *spanning-tree algorithm.*

SPF   Shortest Path First algorithm: A routing algorithm used to decide on the shortest-path spanning tree. Sometimes called Dijkstra's algorithm and frequently used in link-state routing algorithms. *See also: link-state routing algorithm.*

SPID   Service Profile Identifier: A number assigned by service providers or local telephone companies and assigned by administrators to a BRI port. SPIDs are used to determine subscription services of a device connected via ISDN. ISDN devices use SPID when accessing the telephone company switch that initializes the link to a service provider.

split horizon   Useful for preventing routing loops, a type of distance-vector routing rule where information about routes is prevented from leaving the router interface through which that information was received.

spoofing   (1) In dial-on-demand routing (DDR), where a circuit-switched link is taken down to save toll charges when there is no traffic to be sent, spoofing is a scheme used by routers that causes a host to treat an interface as if it were functioning and supporting a session. The router sends "spoof" replies to keepalive messages from the host in an effort to convince the host that the session is up and running. *See also: DDR. (2)* The illegal act of sending a packet labeled with a false address, in order to deceive network security mechanisms such as filters and access lists.

spooler A management application that processes requests submitted to it for execution in a sequential fashion from a queue. A good example is a print spooler.

SPX Sequenced Packet Exchange: A Novell NetWare transport protocol that augments the datagram service provided by Network layer (Layer 3) protocols; derived from the Switch-to-Switch Protocol of the XNS protocol suite.

SQE Signal Quality Error: In an Ethernet network, a message sent from a transceiver to an attached machine indicating that the collision-detection circuitry is working.

SRB Source-Route Bridging: Created by IBM, the bridging method used in Token Ring networks. The source determines the entire route to a destination before sending the data and includes that information in route information fields (RIFs) within each packet. *Contrast with: transparent bridging.*

SRT bridging Source-Route Transparent bridging: A bridging scheme developed by IBM, merging source-route and transparent bridging. SRT takes advantage of both technologies in one device, fulfilling the needs of all end nodes. Translation between bridging protocols is not necessary. *Compare with: SR/TLB.*

SR/TLB Source-Route Translational Bridging: A bridging method that allows source-route stations to communicate with transparent bridge stations aided by an intermediate bridge that translates between the two bridge protocols. Used for bridging between Token Ring and Ethernet. *Compare with: SRT.*

SSAP Source Service Access Point: The SAP of the network node identified in the Source field of the packet. *See also: DSAP and SAP.*

SSE Silicon Switching Engine: The software component of Cisco's silicon switching technology, hard-coded into the Silicon Switch Processor (SSP). Silicon switching is available only on the Cisco 7000 with an SSP. Silicon-switched packets are compared to the silicon-switching cache on the

SSE. The SSP is a dedicated switch processor that offloads the switching process from the route processor, providing a fast-switching solution, but packets must still traverse the backplane of the router to get to the SSP and then back to the exit interface.

standard IP access list   IP access list that uses only the source IP addresses to filter a network.

standard IPX access list   IPX access list that uses only the source and destination IPX address to filter a network.

star topology   A LAN physical topology with endpoints on the network converging at a common central switch (known as a hub) using point-to-point links. A logical ring topology can be configured as a physical star topology using a unidirectional closed-loop star rather than point-to-point links. That is, connections within the hub are arranged in an internal ring. *See also: bus topology* and *ring topology.*

startup range   If an AppleTalk node does not have a number saved from the last time it was booted, then the node selects from the range of values from 65280 to 65534.

state transitions   Digital signaling scheme that reads the "state" of the digital signal in the middle of the bit cell. If it is five volts, the cell is read as a one. If the state of the digital signal is zero volts, the bit cell is read as a zero.

static route   A route whose information is purposely entered into the routing table and that takes priority over those chosen by dynamic routing protocols.

static VLANs   VLANs on a switch that were manually configured as opposed to dynamically learned. In most cases, static VLANs are used in environments where there are few VLANs defined on a switch and/or these VLANs do not change often.

statistical multiplexing   Multiplexing in general is a technique that allows data from multiple logical channels to be sent across a single physical channel. Statistical multiplexing dynamically assigns bandwidth only to input channels that are active, optimizing available bandwidth so that more devices can be connected than with other multiplexing techniques. Also known as statistical time-division multiplexing or stat mux.

STM-1   Synchronous Transport Module Level 1. In the European SDH standard, one of many formats identifying the frame structure for the 155.52Mbps lines that are used to carry ATM cells.

store-and-forward packet switching   A technique in which the switch first copies each packet into its buffer and performs a cyclic redundancy check (CRC). If the packet is error-free, the switch then looks up the destination address in its filter table, determines the appropriate exit port, and sends the packet.

STP   (1) Shielded Twisted Pair: A two-pair wiring scheme, used in many network implementations, that has a layer of shielded insulation to reduce EMI. (2) Spanning-Tree Protocol.

stub area   An OSPF area carrying a default route, intra-area routes, and inter-area routes, but no external routes. Configuration of virtual links cannot be achieved across a stub area, and stub areas are not allowed to contain an ASBR. *See also: non-stub area, ASBR,* and *OSPF.*

stub network   A network having only one connection to a router.

STUN   Serial Tunnel: A technology used to connect an HDLC link to an SDLC link over a serial link.

subarea   A portion of an SNA network made up of a subarea node and its attached links and peripheral nodes.

subarea node   An SNA communications host or controller that handles entire network addresses.

subchannel   A frequency-based subdivision that creates a separate broadband communications channel.

subinterface   One of many virtual interfaces available on a single physical interface.

subnet   *See: subnetwork.*

subnet address   The portion of an IP address that is specifically identified by the subnet mask as the subnetwork. *See also: IP address, subnetwork,* and *subnet mask.*

subnet mask   Also simply known as mask, a 32-bit address mask used in IP to identify the bits of an IP address that are used for the subnet address. Using a mask, the router does not need to examine all 32 bits, only those selected by the mask. *See also: address mask* and *IP address.*

subnetwork   (1) Any network that is part of a larger IP network and is identified by a subnet address. A network administrator segments a network into subnetworks in order to provide a hierarchical, multilevel routing structure, and at the same time protect the subnetwork from the addressing complexity of networks that are attached. Also known as a subnet. *See also: IP address, subnet mask,* and *subnet address.* (2) In OSI networks, the term specifically refers to a collection of ESs and ISs controlled by only one administrative domain, using a solitary network connection protocol.

supervisor module   A module on Cisco switches that holds the CPU, system software, and most of the memory components used in the switch.

SVC   Switched virtual circuit: A dynamically established virtual circuit, created on demand and dissolved as soon as transmission is over and the circuit is no longer needed. In ATM terminology, it is referred to as a switched virtual connection. *Compare with: PVC. See also: VC.*

switch   (1) In networking, a device responsible for multiple functions such as filtering, flooding, and sending frames. It works using the destination address of individual frames. Switches operate at the Data-Link layer of the OSI model. (2) Broadly, any electronic/mechanical device allowing connections to be established as needed and terminated if no longer necessary.

switch fabric   Term used to identify a Layer-2 switched internetwork with many switches.

switched LAN   Any LAN implemented using LAN switches. *See also: LAN switch.*

switching path   The logical path that a packet follows when it's switched through a router. Some examples are process switching, fast switching, optimum switching, CEF, dCEF, and distributed switching.

synchronous transmission   Signals transmitted digitally with precision clocking. These signals have identical frequencies and contain individual characters encapsulated in control bits (called start/stop bits) that designate the beginning and ending of each character. *See also: asynchronous transmission* and *isochronous transmission.*

T reference point   Used with an S reference point to change a 4-wire ISDN network to a 2-wire ISDN network.

T1   Digital WAN that uses 24 DS0s at 64K each to create a bandwidth of 1.536Mbps, minus clocking overhead, providing 1.544Mbps of usable bandwidth.

T3   Digital WAN that can provide bandwidth of 44.763Mbps. A T3 is composed of 28 T1s.

tag switching   Based on the concept of label swapping, where packets or cells are designated to defined-length labels that control the manner in which data is to be sent, tag switching is a high-performance technology used for forwarding packets. It incorporates Data-Link layer (Layer 2) switching and Network layer (Layer 3) routing and supplies scalable, high-speed switching in the network core.

tagged traffic   ATM cells with their cell loss priority (CLP) bit set to 1. Also referred to as discard-eligible (DE) traffic. Tagged traffic can be eliminated in order to ensure trouble-free delivery of higher priority traffic, if the network is congested. *See also: CLP.*

TCP   Transmission Control Protocol: A connection-oriented protocol that is defined at the Transport layer of the OSI reference model. Provides reliable delivery of data.

TCP/IP   Transmission Control Protocol/Internet Protocol. The suite of protocols underlying the Internet. TCP and IP are the most widely known protocols in that suite. *See also: IP* and *TCP.*

TDM   Time division multiplexing: A technique for assigning bandwidth on a single wire, based on preassigned time slots, to data from several channels. Bandwidth is allotted to each channel regardless of a station's ability to send data. *See also: ATDM, FDM,* and *multiplexing.*

TDR   Time domain reflectors: Complex cable testers, used to locate physical problems in a cable. They can detect where an open circuit, short circuit, crimped wire, or other abnormality is located in a cable. *See also: OTDR.*

TE   Terminal equipment: Any peripheral device that is ISDN-compatible and attached to a network, such as a telephone or computer. TE1s are devices that are ISDN-ready and understand ISDN signaling techniques. TE2s are devices that are not ISDN-ready and do not understand ISDN signaling techniques. A terminal adapter must be used with a TE2.

TE1   Terminal equipment type 1: A device with a four-wire, twisted-pair digital interface. Most modern ISDN devices are of this type.

TE2   Terminal equipment type 2: A device with no native ISDN capabilities. In order for TE2 devices to use ISDN, a terminal adapter must be used to convert the ISDN signaling into a format understood by the device.

telco   A common abbreviation for the telephone company.

Telnet   The standard terminal emulation protocol within the TCP/IP protocol stack. Method of remote terminal connection, enabling users to log in on remote networks and use those resources as if they were locally connected. Telnet is defined in RFC 854.

terminal adapter   A hardware interface between a computer without a native ISDN interface and an ISDN line. In effect, a device to connect a standard async interface to a non-native ISDN device, emulating a modem.

terminal emulation   The use of software, installed on a PC or LAN server, that allows the PC to function as if it were a "dumb" terminal directly attached to a particular type of mainframe.

TFTP   Conceptually a stripped-down version of FTP, it's the protocol of choice if you know exactly what you want and where it's to be found. TFTP doesn't provide the abundance of functions that FTP does. In particular, it has no directory-browsing abilities; it can do nothing but send and receive files.

Thicknet   Also called 10Base5. Bus network that uses a thick cable and runs Ethernet up to 500 meters.

Thinnet   Also called 10Base2. Bus network that uses a thin coax cable and runs Ethernet media access up to 185 meters.

token   A frame containing only control information. Possessing this control information gives a network device permission to transmit data onto the network. *See also: token passing.*

token bus   LAN architecture that is the basis for the IEEE 802.4 LAN specification and employs token passing access over a bus topology. *See also: IEEE.*

token passing   A method used by network devices to access the physical medium in a systematic way based on possession of a small frame called a token. *See also: token.*

Token Ring   IBM's token-passing LAN technology. It runs at 4Mbps or 16Mbps over a ring topology. Defined formally by IEEE 802.5. *See also: ring topology* and *token passing.*

toll network   WAN network that uses the Public Switched Telephone Network (PSTN) to send packets.

trace   IP command used to trace the path a packet takes through an internetwork.

transparent bridging   The bridging scheme used in Ethernet and IEEE 802.3 networks; it passes frames along one hop at a time, using bridging information stored in tables that associate end-node MAC addresses within bridge ports. This type of bridging is considered transparent because the source node does not know it has been bridged, because the destination frames are sent directly to the end node. *Contrast with: SRB.*

Transport layer   Layer 4 of the OSI reference model, used for reliable communication between end nodes over the network. The Transport layer provides mechanisms used for establishing, maintaining, and terminating virtual circuits, transport fault detection and recovery, and controlling the flow of information. *See also: Application layer, Data-Link layer, Network layer, Physical layer, Presentation layer,* and *Session layer.*

TRIP   Token Ring Interface Processor: A high-speed interface processor used on Cisco 7000 series routers. The TRIP provides two or four ports for interconnection with IEEE 802.5 and IBM media with ports set to speeds of either 4Mbps or 16Mbps set independently of each other.

Troubleshooting Assistant   Part of the Online Technical Support menu. This tool can be used to help isolate and diagnose many networking problems, based on user input and the Cisco database.

troubleshooting model   A series of steps or procedures that can be methodically executed or followed to effectively troubleshoot and resolve network failures or outages.

trunk link   Link used between switches and from some servers to the switches. Trunk links carry information about many VLANs. Access links are used to connect host devices to a switch and carry only VLAN information that the device is a member of.

TTL   Time To Live: A field in an IP header, indicating the length of time a packet is valid.

TUD   Trunk Up-Down: A protocol used in ATM networks for the monitoring of trunks. Should a trunk miss a given number of test messages being sent by ATM switches to ensure trunk line quality, TUD declares the trunk down. When a trunk reverses direction and comes back up, TUD recognizes that the trunk is up and returns the trunk to service.

tunneling   A method of avoiding protocol restrictions by wrapping packets from one protocol in another protocol's packet and transmitting this encapsulated packet over a network that supports the wrapper protocol. *See also: encapsulation.*

U reference point   Reference point between a TE1 and an ISDN network. The U reference point understands ISDN signaling techniques and uses a 2-wire connection.

UDP   User Datagram Protocol: A connectionless Transport layer protocol in the TCP/IP protocol stack that simply allows datagrams to be exchanged without acknowledgments or delivery guarantees, requiring other protocols to handle error processing and retransmission. UDP is defined in RFC 768.

underrun   Occurs when the transmitter runs at a higher rate than the packets sent from the hardware buffer.

unnumbered frames   HDLC frames used for control-management purposes, such as link start-up and shutdown or mode specification.

UTP   Unshielded twisted-pair: Copper wiring used in small-to-large networks to connect host devices to hubs and switches. Also used to connect switch to switch or hub to hub.

VBR   Variable Bit Rate: A QoS class, as defined by the ATM Forum, for use in ATM networks that is subdivided into real time (RT) class and non-real time (NRT) class. RT is employed when connections have a fixed-time relationship between samples. Conversely, NRT is employed when connections do not have a fixed-time relationship between samples, but still need an assured QoS.

VC   Virtual circuit: A logical circuit devised to assure reliable communication between two devices on a network. Defined by a virtual path connection (VPC)/virtual path identifier (VCI) pair, a virtual circuit can be permanent (PVC) or switched (SVC). Virtual circuits are used in Frame Relay and X.25. Known as virtual channel in ATM. *See also: PVC and SVC.*

VCC   Virtual Channel Connection: A logical circuit that is created by Virtual Channel Links (VCL). VCCs carry data between two endpoints in an ATM network. Sometimes called a virtual circuit connection.

VIP   (1) Versatile Interface Processor: An interface card for Cisco 7000 and 7500 series routers, providing multilayer switching and running the Cisco IOS software. The most recent version of VIP is VIP2. (2) Virtual IP: A function making it possible for logically separated switched IP workgroups to run Virtual Networking Services across the switch ports of a Catalyst 5000.

virtual circuit   *See: VC.*

virtual ring   In an SRB network, a logical connection between physical rings, either local or remote.

VLAN   Virtual LAN: A group of devices on one or more logically segmented LANs (configured by use of management software), enabling devices to communicate as if attached to the same physical medium, when they are actually located on numerous different LAN segments. VLANs are based on logical instead of physical connections and thus are tremendously flexible.

VLSM   Variable-length subnet mask: Helps optimize available address space and specify a different subnet mask for the same network number on various subnets. Also commonly referred to as "subnetting a subnet."

VTP   VLAN Trunk Protocol: Used to update switches in a switch fabric about VLANs configured on a VTP server. VTP devices can be a VTP server, client, or transparent device. Servers update clients. Transparent devices are only local devices and do not share information with VTP clients. VTPs send VLAN information down trunked links only.

WAN   Wide area network: The network components and infrastructure that are used to connect LANs together across a DCE (data communications equipment) network. Typically, a WAN is a leased line or dial-up connection across a PSTN network. Examples of WAN protocols include Frame Relay, PPP, ISDN, and HDLC.

wildcard Used with access-list, supernetting, and OSPF configurations. Wildcards are designations used to identify a range of subnets.

window size The amount of data that a station can transmit before needing an acknowledgment from the destination system. The acknowledgment confirms that all the data was received without error, or that errors existed and part of the data will need to be retransmitted.

windowing Flow-control method used with TCP at the Transport layer of the OSI model.

WinSock Windows Socket Interface: A software interface that makes it possible for an assortment of applications to use and share an Internet connection. The WinSock software consists of a Dynamic Link Library (DLL) with supporting programs such as a dialer program that initiates the connection.

workgroup switching A switching method that supplies high-speed (100Mbps) transparent bridging between Ethernet networks as well as high-speed translational bridging between Ethernet and CDDI or FDDI.

X.25 An ITU-T packet-relay standard that defines communication between DTE and DCE network devices. X.25 uses a reliable Data-Link layer protocol called LAPB. X.25 also uses PLP at the Network layer. X.25 has mostly been replaced by Frame Relay.

yellow alarm A yellow alarm on a T1 or E1 indicates that the far end of the circuit is has a corrupted incoming signal. *See also: red alarm.*

ZIP Zone Information Protocol: A Session-layer protocol used by AppleTalk to map network numbers to zone names. NBP uses ZIP in the determination of networks containing nodes that belong to a zone. *See also: ZIP storm* and *zone*.

ZIP storm A broadcast storm occurring when a router running AppleTalk reproduces or transmits a route for which there is no corresponding zone name at the time of execution. The route is then forwarded by other routers downstream, thus causing a ZIP storm. *See also: broadcast storm* and *ZIP*.

zone A logical grouping of network devices in AppleTalk. *See also: ZIP.*

Index

Note to the Reader: Throughout this index **boldfaced** page numbers indicate primary discussions of a topic. *Italicized* page numbers indicate illustrations.

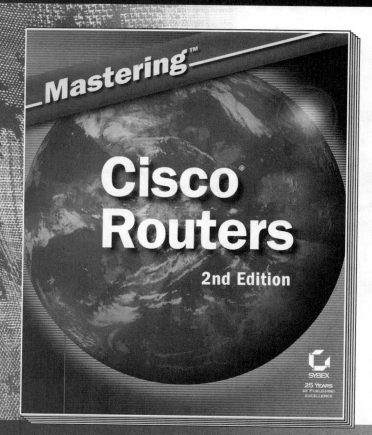

Mastering™ Cisco® Routers

2nd Edition

FROM SYBEX™

Mastering™ Cisco® Routers
Chris Brenton
ISBN 0-7821-4107-2
708pp • $49.99

*Designed for administrators and students
who need to get up to speed quickly
with Cisco routers*

- Learn how to administer, configure, and
manage Cisco routers

- Install, configure, and manage the Cisco
Internetworking Operating System

- Implement secure and reliable virtual
private networking

SYBEX®

www.sybex.com

Now More Than Ever...

... you need respected certifications to secure a job in the midst of the IT shakeout.

... you need an economical approach to getting hands-on experience with Cisco routers and switches.

... you need best-selling Virtual Labs from Sybex.

0-7821-2728-2 • US $99.99

0-7821-3018-5 • US $149.99

0-7821-5014-4 • US $199.99

CCNA Virtual Lab

- Basic network simulation of three routers, one switch, and one host

- Allows you to create custom labs

CCNA Virtual Lab Gold Edition

- **Enhanced, real-world network simulation** of four routers, two switches, and four hosts

- Includes more instructional labs and supports more IOS commands

CCNP Virtual Lab

- Includes multiple simulated network configurations

- Covers all four CCNP exams—Routing, Switching, Support, and Remote Access

To find out more about
Sybex certification products, visit **www.sybex.com**.

Sybex—The Leader in Certification

Take Your
Cisco® Expertise
to the
Next Level!

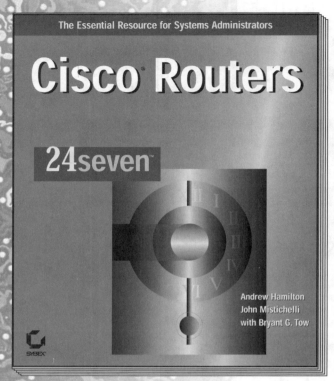

The Essential Resource for Systems Administrators

Cisco® Routers

24seven™

Andrew Hamilton
John Mistichelli
with Bryant G. Tow

SYBEX®

Cisco® Routers 24seven™
Andrew Hamilton and John Mistichelli
with Bryant Tow
ISBN 0-7821-2646-4
624pp • $34.99

- Integrate Cisco routers into your existing network environment

- Plan and build new environments around an infrastructure of Cisco routers

- Configure TCP/IP, IPX, and AppleTalk for routing

- Troubleshoot problems at the physical layer and the network layer

SYBEX®

www.sybex.com

CABLING:
The Complete Guide to Network Wiring

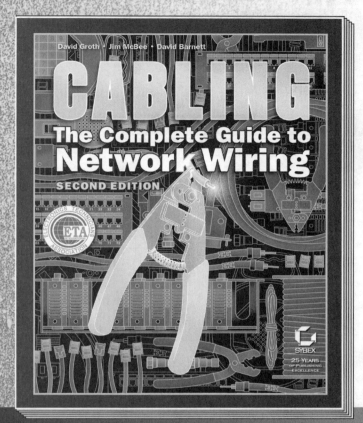

*Cabling: The Complete Guide
to Network Wiring*
David Groth, Jim McBee, and David Barnett
ISBN 0-7821-2958-7
808pp • $49.99

The most comprehensive guide to network cabling available!

■ Coverage spans cabling system design and
installation, electrical and security issues,
cabling components, and documenting and
troubleshooting your system.

■ Provides all the information you need to know
to work safely and effectively with cables in the
workplace.

■ Includes a full-color section for quick
identification of connectors and cables, as well
as vendor information and recommendations.

SYBEX®
www.sybex.com

TELL US WHAT YOU THINK!

Your feedback is critical to our efforts to provide you with the best books and software on the market. Tell us what you think about the products you've purchased. It's simple:

1. Go to the Sybex website.
2. Find your book by typing the ISBN number or title into the Search field.
3. Click on the book title when it appears.
4. Click **Submit a Review.**
5. Fill out the questionnaire and comments.
6. Click **Submit.**

With your feedback, we can continue to publish the highest quality computer books and software products that today's busy IT professionals deserve.

www.sybex.com

SYBEX Inc. • 1151 Marina Village Parkway, Alameda, CA 94501 • 510-523-8233

The Complete Cisco Certification Solution

CCNA: Cisco Certified Networking Associate

For the CCNA Exam, #640-607

CCNA: Cisco Certified Network Associate Study Guide, 3rd Edition
ISBN: 0-7821-4167-6 · $49.99

CCNA: Cisco Certified Network Associate Study Guide, Deluxe Edition,
2nd Edition · ISBN: 0-7821-4169-2 · $89.99

CCNA : Cisco Certified Network Associate Exam Notes
ISBN: 0-7821-4168-4 · $29.99

CCNA Certification Kit, 2nd Edition · ISBN: 0-7821-4170-6 · $159.99

CCNA Virtual Lab, Gold Edition · ISBN: 0-7821-3018-6 · $149.99

CCNA Virtual Training Certification Kit · ISBN: 0-7821-3033-X · $139.99

CCNP: Cisco Certified Networking Professional*

*Prerequisite: Valid CCNA certification

CCNP: Routing Study Guide, 2nd Edition · ISBN: 0-7821-4154-4 · $49.99
Routing, Exam #640-603

CCNP: Switching Study Guide, 2nd Edition · ISBN: 0-7821-4153-6 · $49.99
Switching, Exam #640-604

CCNP: Remote Access Study Guide, 2nd Edition · ISBN: 0-7821-4151-X
$49.99
Remote Access, Exam #640-605

CCNP: Support Study Guide, 2nd Edition · ISBN: 0-7821-4152-8 · $49.99
Support, Exam #640-606

CCNP: Virtual Lab · ISBN: 0-7821-5014-4 · $199.99
Support, Exam #640-606

Also available:
CCNP Study Guide Kit, 2nd Edition · ISBN: 078212718-5 · $159.96
Covers all four exams

CCDA: Cisco Certified Design Associate

For the Designing Cisco Networks Exam, #640-441

CCDA: Cisco Certified Design Associate Study Guide
SBN: 0-7821-2534-4 · $49.99

CCDA: Cisco Certified Design Associate Exam Notes
SBN: 0-7821-2776-2 · $24.99

Visit www.sybex.com or www.sybexetrainer.com for all of your Cisco certification needs.